D1595739

Warfare and History

General Editor
Jeremy Black
Professor of History, University of Exeter

Warfare, State and Society in the
Byzantine World, 565–1204

Warfare, State and Society in the Byzantine World, 565–1204

John Haldon

University of Birmingham

First published 1999 in the UK and the USA
by UCL Press
11 New Fetter Lane
London EC4P 4EE

The name of University College London (UCL) is a registered
trade mark used by UCL Press with the consent of the owner.

UCL Press is an imprint of the Taylor & Francis Group

Typeset in Bembo by Graphicraft Limited, Hong Kong
Printed and bound in Great Britain by T.J. International

British Library Cataloguing in Publication Data
A catalogue record for this book is available from the British Library.

Library of Congress Cataloging in Publication Data
A catalogue record for this book has been requested

ISBN: 1-85728-494-1 HB
      1-85728-495-X PB

Contents

Preface and acknowledgements

Many friends and colleagues have contributed, directly or indirectly, to the present volume. Through discussion, advice, bibliographical assistance, reading sections of the draft manuscript and countless other ways they have enriched my own perspective on the history of the Byzantine world and on how warfare fits into the pattern of human social and cultural life. It would be invidious to name one or two and to omit others, and so I shall name no names at all. But I hope that those who have the patience, or the interest, or both, to read what follows might recognize the traces of their own contribution, and derive some benefit from what I have written.

I do want to thank explicitly the members of staff and postgraduate students in my own university department, however, not only for their intellectual input, which was usually far greater than they imagined – given that most of them have only a limited interest in the subject of this book – but also for their patience. Their support and their expertise have been invaluable.

A note on transliterations

All technical terms and titles (e.g. *strategos*, *tourmarches*, *thema* etc.) have been transliterated directly from their Greek or Latin forms with as few changes as possible: thus *drouggarios* rather than *droungarios*, which is neither Latin nor Greek. To avoid overly complicating the text, however, macrons on Greek long vowels are omitted (thus not *tourmarchēs* or *stratēgos*).

Names of people and places are slightly more problematic. For those which have well-known and standardised English equivalents, such as Constantine or Constantinople, I have retained them. Otherwise I have tended for the most part to use Greek forms where they would normally so appear in the sources: thus Kaisareia rather than Caesarea (although this rule does not work so well for the Balkans, where both Latin and Greek forms are commonly found and used). I likewise use the Byzantine Greek forms for the names of administrative districts or provinces, the latinized or anglicized version for regions in general e.g. Kappadokia for the Byzantine *kleisourachia* or *thema*; but Cappadocia for the area as a whole.

John Haldon
Birmingham
September 1998

Abbreviations of journals and collections

AB	*Analecta Bollandiana* (Brussels, 1882ff.)
AS	*Acta Sanctorum* (Antwerp, 1643ff.)
BAR	*British Archaeological Reports*
B	*Byzantion* (Brussels, 1924ff.)
BbA	*Berliner byzantinistische Arbeiten* (Berlin, 1955ff.)
BBP	*Byzantinon Bios kai Politismos*, Ph. Koukoules, I–IV (Athens, 1948–51)
BCH	*Bulletin de correspondance Hellénique* (Paris, 1877ff.)
BF	*Byzantinische Forschungen* (Amsterdam, 1966ff.)
BGA	*Bibliotheca Geographorum Araborum*, eds M.-J. de Goeje (1870ff.) and R. Blachère (1938ff.) (Leyden, 1870ff.)
BMGS	*Byzantine and Modern Greek Studies* (Oxford, 1975–83; Birmingham, 1984ff.)
BS	*Byzantinoslavica* (Prague, 1929ff.)
BZ	*Byzantinische Zeitschrift* (Leipzig/Munich/Cologne, 1892ff.)
CFHB	*Corpus Fontium Historiae Byzantinae* (Series Washingtoniensis, Washington, DC, 1967–; Series Berolinensis, Berlin/New York, 1967–; Series Vindobonensis, Vienna, 1975–; Series Italica, Rome, 1975–; Series Bruxellensis, Brussels, 1975–)
CSHB	*Corpus Scriptorum Historiae Byzantinae* (Bonn, 1828–97)
DOP	*Dumbarton Oaks Papers* (Washington, D.C., 1941ff.)
DOT	*Dumbarton Oaks Texts*
EEBS	*Epeteris etaireias Byzantinon spoudon* (Athens, 1924ff.)
EHR	*English Historical Review* (London, 1885ff.)
EI	*Encyclopaedia of Islam*, new edn (Leyden/London, 1960ff.)
EO	*Échos d'Orient*, 1–39 (Paris,1897–1941/2)
FHG	*Fragmenta Historicorum Graecorum*, eds C. and Th. Müller, 5 vols (Paris, 1874–85)
GRBS	*Greek, Roman and Byzantine Studies* (1: *Greek and Byzantine Studies*) (Durham,1958ff.)

Hell.	*Hellenika* (Athens, 1928ff.)
JGR	*Jus Graecoromanum*, eds I. and P. Zepos, 8 vols (Athens, 1931/Aalen, 1962)
JHS	*Journal of Hellenic Studies* (London,1880ff.)
JöB	*Jahrbuch der österreichischen Byzantinistik*, 18ff. (Vienna, 1969ff.)
JöBG	*Jahrbuch der österreichischen byzantinischen Gesellschaft*, 1–17 (Vienna, 1951–68)
JRS	*Journal of Roman Studies* (London, 1911ff.)
JThS	*Journal of Theological Studies*
OCP	*Orientalia Christiana Periodica* (Rome, 1935ff.)
ODB	*The Oxford Dictionary of Byzantium*, eds A.P. Kazhdan et al. (Oxford/New York, 1991)
PG	*Patrologiae Cursus completus*, series Graeco-Latina, ed. J.-P. Migne (Paris, 1857–66, 1880–1903)
RE	*Paulys Realencyclopädie der classischen Altertums-Wissenschaft*, neue Bearbeitung, ed. G. Wissowa (Stuttgart, 1893ff.: vol. I, no. 1 – vol. XXIII, no. 2, 1893–1959, with index of additions; vols. XXIV, 1963; vol. I/A1–vol. X/A, 1914–72; Suppl. I–XIV, 1903–74)
REA	*Revue des Études Arméniennes*, n.s. (Paris, 1964ff.)
REB	*Revue des Études Byzantines* (vols 1–3: *Études Byzantines*) (Paris, 1944f.)
REG	*Revue des Études Grecques* (Paris, 1888ff.)
RESEE	*Revue des Études Sud-Est Européennes* (Bucarest, 1913ff.)
RH	*Revue Historique* (Paris, 1876ff.)
ROC	*Revue de l'Orient Chrétien*, ser. 1, vols 1–10 (Paris, 1896–1905); ser. 2, vols 1–10 (Paris, 1906–15/17); ser. 3, vols 1–10 (Paris, 1918/19–35/6): vols 1–30.
RSBN	*Rivista di Studi Bizantini e Neoellenici*, n.s. (Rome, 1964ff.)
TM	*Travaux et Mémoires* (Paris, 1965ff.)
VV	*Vizantiiskii Vremmenik*, vols 1–25 (St Petersburg/Leningrad, 1894–1927); n.s. (Moscow, 1947ff.)
WBS	*Wiener Byzantinistische Studien* (Vienna, 1964ff.)
ZRVI	*Zbornik Radova Vizantoloshkog Instituta* (Belgrade, 1952ff.)

Maps

Introduction

The term "Byzantine empire" refers to the eastern Roman empire from the end of the "late Roman" period in the eastern and central Mediterranean/ Balkan region (from the sixth century, therefore) to the fifteenth century, that is to say, from the time when a distinctively East Roman political formation began to evolve with the recognition of the cultural divisions between "Greek East" and "Latin West" in the empire's political structure, to the fall of Constantinople on 29 May 1453 at the hands of the Ottoman sultan Mehmet II "Fatih", "the Conqueror". And although within this long period there were many substantial transformations, the elements of structural continuity are marked enough to permit such a broad chronological definition. "Byzantine" should be understood as the convenient label which it is – a shorthand for "medieval East Roman", for the Byzantines referred to themselves as *Romaioi* or Romans, a term which subsumed at once their identity as Orthodox Christians, the Chosen People who, in the eyes of God, had succeeded to the place of the Jews from the time of Christ; and as Romans, the inheritors of a world empire protected and guided by God. From the point of view of the medieval observer, the artificial chronological divisions imposed by modern historians, sometimes for perfectly valid reasons, upon Byzantine history are quite meaningless; and even from the perspective of the modern specialist historian, the divide between late Roman (i.e. up to the later sixth century) and Byzantine (from the early seventh century) serves, as often as not, to obscure the fact that continuity in every respect – socio-economic, political, institutional and ideological – was the norm.[1]

Interest in the history and culture of Byzantium can be traced back to the fifteenth and sixteenth centuries, as the expanding power of the Ottoman empire encouraged closer familiarity with the history of the regions which it had swallowed up, the better to understand how to oppose what appeared to central and western European political and religious leaders to be an apparently irresistible advance. "Modern" Byzantine studies, informed by new and

1

more rigorous methods of source criticism and analysis than had been employed by previous commentators, can be said to have begun in western Europe in the second half of the nineteenth century, partly an offshoot of classical and late ancient history and philology, partly the result of a renewed interest in the history of Europe and the Near East after the "decline and fall" of the Roman empire and the subsequent fate of the eastern churches and the Hellenic peoples.[2]

Yet the history of Byzantine military organization and warfare is in many respects still a relatively underdeveloped field. This reflects to a degree the complexity, and also the sparseness, of relevant source material (although there are plenty of narrative accounts of battles and campaigns); but it is also the result of a certain romanticism, typified in the otherwise valuable early analysis of Sir Charles Oman's *The Art of War in the Middle Ages*, whereby the Byzantines are portrayed as noble victims of an impossible strategic situation, forced constantly to defend their beleaguered empire – a bastion of Christendom and classical culture – against wave after wave of barbarian or infidel. This is perhaps to caricature the words and ideas of these historians to a degree, and in the pioneering *Geschichte der Kriegskunst im Rahmen der politischen Geschichte* of the German military historian Hans Delbrück, the empire's longevity was ascribed predominantly not to purely military but rather geopolitical factors. But even Delbrück devoted only 12 pages to Byzantine warfare and military organization. Nevertheless, the notion of Byzantium as a beleaguered bulwark, which still informs some popular writing on the history of that empire, is in fact an attitude which takes its inspiration from the ideas of the Byzantines themselves.

There are few modern treatments of the relationship between Byzantine society, its armies and warfare, and fewer still in English. We have already mentioned the works of Oman and Delbrück (the latter available in a modern English translation based upon the second edition published in Berlin in 1923[3]), which deal primarily with military organization and tactics. In French, Ferdinand Lot's *L'Art militaire et les armées au moyen age en Europe et dans le Proche Orient* (Paris, 1946) has a still useful, but very old-fashioned, chapter on the Byzantine armies. A number of other writers, both in the field of Byzantine and medieval history, and in that of military history more particularly, have devoted sections or chapters to the armies of the Byzantine period. Many of these are factually inaccurate, however, and present a highly idealized, if not romanticized, picture founded on somewhat simplistic views of Byzantine society and state organization.[4] Modern works are more reliable and based on up-to-date research, but still treat the army *en passant*, and in relation to society and the state as a whole hardly at all.[5]

Works devoted entirely to the army are rare. Many articles have been written in the last twenty years or so dealing with various aspects of Byzantine military administration, weaponry and military technology, strategy, and the interface between armies and politics. Numerous articles on these and related topics by contemporary scholars will be found in the bibliography of this volume. But no one has yet undertaken a general survey either of the history of east Roman military development from the beginning – the later

2

sixth century in this case – or of the relationship between army, society and warfare in general.[6]

Two recent monographs have appeared on the subject. Mark Bartusis produced in 1992 a survey and analysis of the history of the late Byzantine army from the thirteenth to mid-fifteenth centuries, a subject which has been more or less entirely neglected in the literature referred to above. In 1995 Warren Treadgold also published a book, covering the period from the third to the eleventh centuries, dealing with late Roman and Byzantine military organization, especially tactical structure, pay and numbers.[7] Between them, these two books should have filled the gap in the material available to both the general as well as the more specialist reader. Treadgold's book deals only with the technical issues mentioned and ignores the issue of how the army fits into society in general, while Bartusis' study necessarily assumes a great deal about the situation prior to its starting point so that the developments which pre-ceded those discussed are – understandably – barely mentioned.

Only one scholar has made even the slightest attempt, in monograph form, to relate the army over the longer term to the day-to-day politics of Byzantine state and society. In his study of Byzantine military unrest pub-lished in 1981, Walter E. Kaegi essayed a survey of the history of Byzantine military intervention in "politics" in the broadest sense, relating the rebellions and mutinies of the armies at different times over the period from the fifth to the ninth centuries to their conditions of service, the wider political and social situation within the empire, and to the relations pertaining between the East Roman state and its neighbours. Although there are criticisms to be made, this was, and remains, a pioneering work which has contributed a great deal to raising the profile of the study of the Byzantine army in its social and political context.[8]

There thus remains a great deal to be done, most particularly in respect of the study of the effects of warfare and military demands upon the state and society of the Byzantine empire, particularly in relation to the experiences of the vast mass of the ordinary population of the empire.[9] A short monograph such as this, which attempts to set these various aspects of a series of very complex problems in their context, cannot hope to arrive at all the answers, still less to convince every reader that the answers which are suggested, or the overall interpretation which does eventually emerge, is necessarily the best or the only one which the evidence can bear. But the hope is that, by the end of the volume, those problems will at the least have been clearly stated and a plausible sketch of the relations between Byzantine society, its military organiza-tion and the effects upon them of warfare will have been developed.

The relationship between soldiers as individuals and the wider society of which they are a part, as well as that between armies, which represent the coercive arm of an organized state, and both "civil society" and the rest of the state apparatus itself, is rarely straightforward. Tensions always exist between the army in its purely military role (however that may be defined in each specific culture), for example, and the army as a focus of social opinions and people of different regional loyalties and traditions. The approach we adopt to such issues depends on what structural significance we attach to the army in the state and society: which elements of the army played what roles in politics, and where in the pattern of relationships of social power are they to be situated at different times? How did the state organize such things as the recruitment and payment, the equipping and supplying of its soldiers, and in which social strata or regional groups were they located? Indeed, should we define what sort of state we are talking about before we can begin such a discussion? How was the term "soldier" understood in a society in which there were quite clearly both technical and everyday usages, reflected in the employment of the word for soldier to mean different things in different contexts?

Closely associated with such questions are issues of normative roles and behaviour. How did people in East Roman or Byzantine society regard soldiers of differing status and function? How did they respond to them under different sorts of conditions – were there different responses during periods of warfare and fighting in contrast to periods of peace, and if so, is this picture also affected by location in respect of such fighting – do those far from the areas affected have different responses and views to those more directly involved (as we might, perhaps, expect)? What legal status did soldiers of all types have in respect of their position in regard to the state and in respect of civil society at large, and how did this affect attitudes to soldiers and warfare? Then again, how did the political ideology of the state in question fit soldiers into its scheme of things, and in particular to what extent did early Christian views on violence affect later Byzantine attitudes? And how did soldiers use this ideological system at different times, to whose advantage did they act and with what intention? What was the self-perception of soldiers, and to what extent was there a difference, for example, between the views of officers and those of their men (and if there was a real difference between the two groups), between fighters and logistics staff, or across time, as the social origins of soldiers changed?

These are difficult questions under the best of conditions, and the documentary and other evidence for them in the Byzantine world, in which the majority of the "ordinary" population were illiterate or almost so, renders them even more difficult, so that we must exploit a vast range of materials which have no obvious connection with the themes of our examination for relevant information and insights.

I will also be looking at the technical aspects of warfare – questions of siege techniques, the management of strategy and tactical issues, the problems of logistics which face all armies, and issues of supplying mounts, pack-animals, transportation of provisions and materials and so forth. These are not separate matters – on the contrary, they are integrally connected with the first set of concerns, for the extraction of surplus wealth in one form or another directly impacted, materially and ideologically, upon the producing population, the state administrative apparatus and the political structure of the empire.

4

Apart from the chronicle literature and historiography of the period, which contains a great deal of relevant information – narrative accounts of battles and campaigns, occasionally by eyewitnesses or those who had spoken with or had access to eyewitnesses and their reports – there are several classes of evidence for military administration and organization. Lead seals provide a particularly rich source of information for the administrative structures of the Byzantine state, since from the seventh until the eleventh centuries especially most officials, even quite humble ones, had a seal bearing their name and/or their title(s) and rank which they attached to official documents or correspondence. Equally important are the semi-official lists of precedence of the ninth and tenth centuries, drawn up by palace officers to determine who sat where at imperial receptions, and including fairly elaborate descriptions of the various administrative departments of central and provincial administration. In addition, we possess important information regarding the army from Arab geographers' descriptions of the Byzantine empire, and in particular from a series of Byzantine treatises, from the sixth to the eleventh centuries, dealing with warfare on land and at sea, and military and naval organization. Problems of reliability, sources of information and related issues in connection with the former group of sources (in particular the Arab geographers) affect all these types of evidence, of course, and these will be dealt with as appropriate in the discussion which follows. Among the more important texts from the latter tradition are two from the middle and later sixth century: an anonymous treatise on strategy and the *Strategikon* ascribed to the emperor Maurice (582–602) although probably written by one of his generals; and a cluster of texts from the late ninth and tenth centuries: the so-called *Tactica* ascribed to the emperor Leo VI (886–912); a mid-tenth-century treatise known as the *Sylloge taktikon* ("collection of tacticians"); the treatise on skirmishing or guerrilla tactics, written in the 950s or 960s by a close associate of the Phocas clan and the emperor Nikephros II (963–9); an anonymous treatise on campaign organization dating probably from the reign of John I Tzimiskes (969–76) or Basil II (976–1025); the so-called *Praecepta militaria* ("military precepts") ascribed to Nikephros II; the *Tactica* of one of Basil II's most eminent officers, the general Nikephros Ouranos. In addition, there are a series of treatises dealing with siege warfare or artillery, in particular the treatise on artillery ascribed to Hero of Byzantium (mid-tenth century), and an anonymous mid-tenth-century text on siege warfare. In addition, specialist texts deal with naval warfare, although these are especially suspect in respect of the technical information they purvey. There are also a number of minor treatises dealing with military expeditions.

The relationship between these texts, and several others not mentioned here, is complex and is still the subject of discussion. In particular, the tendency to copy or borrow material from ancient, Hellenistic and Roman writers such as Aeneas, Arrian, Polybius and many others; together with the frequent misunderstanding and garbled rendering of technical details which the original texts contained, makes the Byzantine treatises particularly treacherous sources at times.[10] Such specialist texts are not extant after the eleventh century, although there is evidence that some may have been compiled. An exception is the treatise written by Theodore Palaiologos, Marquis of Montferrat (he was the second son of the emperor Andronikos II and Yolante-Irene of Montferrat), originally in Greek but translated into Latin in the 1320s and then into French under the title *Enseignemens et ordenances pour un seigneur qui a des guerres et grans gouvernemens a faire* ("instructions and ordinances for a Lord who has wars to fight and government to exercise"). But this deals primarily with the western tradition and rarely offers specific insights into eastern warfare as such.

There are many other types of written source material, of course. Theological writings, the letters of churchmen or monks, even the acts of church councils provide valuable insights into attitudes towards warfare, fighting, the role and status of soldiers and so on. And although such sources have little to say about the attitudes of most Byzantines in town and country, hagiography – the writing of saints' lives – provides some help in redressing the balance. Hagiographical and related writings for the sixth to the tenth centuries – the period during which a relatively high degree of originality can be found – represent a particularly important source, since they can reflect popular and unofficial views and attitudes in a way less open to works which are conceived as belonging to the genre of historiography and chronography. Saints' lives and related collections of miracles have regularly been used by historians to shed light on Byzantine society and institutions as well as beliefs and everyday life. But they are also a dangerous source, since they are always informed by a clear ideological programme – representing the saint or chief character in the best possible light, encouraging the reader or listener to imitate the piety and spiritual purity of the protagonists as far as they were able, and imbued in consequence with sets of values, implicit and explicit, which invariably meant the introduction of a strongly interpretative element by the writer or compiler. Hagiographies were a widely used type of literature, read by both individuals and groups as well as listened to by even larger numbers of people – in churches or monasteries, for example. Nevertheless, used with caution, they can be of great value in helping to answer some of the questions in which we are interested in this volume.[11]

The evidence of archaeology has been crucial, of course, in respect of our knowledge of Byzantine fortifications and defensive technology;[12] but – in contrast to its role in the history of western military technology – it has played thus far only a minimal role in helping us to trace the history and evolution of Byzantine weaponry and defensive military equipment. This is in great contrast, of course, to the situation with regard to the Roman armies before the fourth and fifth centuries, although enough late Roman material from the western, Balkan and eastern frontier regions has been recovered to give some idea of the situation at the beginning of the period with which this volume is concerned.[13]

The reasons for this unfortunate situation with respect to the period after the sixth century in particular are many, not the least of which is the probable misrecognition of artefacts found on excavated sites as belonging to other cultures, or their accidental destruction. In addition, no battlefield excavations have been carried out and few warriors' graves or interments have been located which are clearly Byzantine. Remarkably few military artefacts – swords or blades of any sort, arrowheads, shield bosses, buckles, pieces of armour or helmets – can be firmly identified as "Byzantine" for the period after the sixth century in Asia Minor or the southern Balkans. The result is that Byzantine weapons technology has to be reconstructed almost entirely on the basis of literary accounts of often dubious, or at least problematic, reliability, illustrations in manuscripts, frescoes or mosaics, or relief carving in stone, all of which media again bring problems of stylization and archetype with them. Only recently, indeed, has a monograph dealing with the subject of personal arms and armour been published, and this manages with only minimal reference to archaeological documentation.[14]

It should be apparent from the foregoing that students of Byzantine military equipment, as well as those of the relationship between Byzantine society and warfare in general, face a difficult task in respect of the sources at their disposal. The latter issues are further complicated, however, by the Byzantines' own attitudes to warfare and fighting, for there existed a substantial difference between the various "official" views sanctioned by church and imperial ideology, and those of soldiers as well as of ordinary people – peasant farmers, merchants or townsfolk. Equally, and perhaps more importantly, the grounds on which the Byzantines based their views of warfare are somewhat more complex than those commonly ascribed to them, and this very complexity has sometimes led to the most crude misunderstanding of Byzantine attitudes. Even quite recently, a commentator on the Crusades could write "In the Greek Orthodox Church of the Byzantine empire war was always regarded as unchristian . . . The Byzantines preferred to use mercenaries in their wars rather than allow Greek Christians themselves to fight." The absurdity of such views will become apparent in Chapter 1.[15]

For the Byzantines themselves had their notions of their position in the order of things, a political morality which was expressed in the writings of emperors and members of the social and cultural elite, and which gave expression to two facets of the Byzantine worldview: on the one hand, the way they wanted to see themselves; and on the other, the way they wanted others to see them and, through seeing them, to be persuaded of the "correctness" of Byzantine political claims to be the true heirs of imperial Rome. Military handbooks compiled by literati or by active or retired generals or field-officers, contributed to, and indeed are partly responsible for, the formation of such notions in which the Byzantines – the true heirs of imperial Rome in their eyes (and at first, at any rate, in the eyes of most others in western Europe, at least until the later eighth century) – stood for Christendom against the chaos and disorder of barbarian or non-believer. There has thus evolved a consensus to the effect that the Byzantines (or at least, the political and governing elite) appear to have disliked fighting wars. If they could possibly avoid warfare, even at the cost of paying subsidies to foes who might (and usually did) claim such subsidies as "tribute" from an inferior power, they tended to do so. Byzantine rulers preferred to use craft, intelligence, wiles, bribery, ideological blackmail and countless other devices rather than commit themselves to set battles or even warlike confrontations of any sort. Even in warfare, the predominant tendency is for armies to proceed with the utmost caution.

Now although there is a substantial element of truth to this view so expressed, the reasons for the Byzantine attitude were not merely a reflection of Christian beliefs and an innate dislike of warfare and violence – Byzantine soldiers, officers and governments could be as bloodthirsty, aggressive and merciless as any of their various enemies at different times, and there is plenty of evidence to demonstrate the point. While religious convictions and motives certainly account for the mode through which this pacific ideology was expressed, what really determined its centrality in the Byzantine perspective was the strategic situation of the empire, a situation noted and commented upon, and not envied, by outside observers such as the papal legate Liudprand of Cremona in the tenth century.[16] The nature of the relationship between Byzantine theoretical expressions of their views of warfare and the realities of strategical and logistical demands is one element which can help us understand more precisely what role warfare played in the Byzantine mind, and how it affected attitudes and practice, from the simple soldier in the field to the general or the emperor himself.

The Christian Roman state – from the fourth and fifth centuries and on through the period of transformation in the seventh and eighth centuries – was structured as a hierarchy of administrative levels: at the top was the emperor, understood to be God's representative, surrounded by a palatine and household apparatus, the centre of imperial government and administration. Civil and fiscal government was delegated until the middle of the seventh century from the emperor to the praetorian prefects, whose prefectures were the largest territorial circumscriptions in the state; each prefecture was further divided into *dioecesae* or dioceses, which had a predominantly fiscal aspect; and each diocese was divided into *provinciae* or provinces, territorial units of fiscal and judicial administration. These were further divided into self-governing *poleis* or *civitates*, the cities, each with its *territorium* or hinterland (which might be more or less extensive, according to geographical, demographic and other factors).[17]

The church and the theological system it represented (from the late fourth century the official religion of the Roman state and, probably by the mid-sixth century, the majority religion within the empire) played a central role in the economy of the Roman world – it was a major landowner – as well as in imperial politics, in influencing the moral and ethical system of the Roman world, and in directing imperial religious policy. Emperors were inextricably involved in the conflicts generated by theological disagreements, given the prevailing view that the emperor was chosen by God, that he had to be Orthodox (the definition of which was, however, debated at times), and that his role was to defend the interests of Orthodoxy and the Roman, i.e. Christian, *oikoumene* (the inhabited, civilized – Roman – world). The political implications were such that heresy was treated in effect as treason, and opposition to the (orthodox) emperor could effectively be treated as heresy. The late Roman state was thus a complex bureaucracy, rooted in and imposed upon a series of overlapping social formations or regional "societies": it is important to stress this since, although the state and the church and their complex administrative structures acted as a unifying force, local society and culture in the Balkans was rather different from that of central and southern Asia Minor, which was in turn very different from that of the eastern Anatolian regions. But all these local subsystems were structured by essentially the same social relations of production – the ways in which wealth was produced, distributed and consumed – across the whole central and east Mediterranean and Balkan world. Social and political tensions were exacerbated by religious divisions, local economic conditions, imperial politics and the burden placed upon the taxpaying population as a result of the state's needs in respect of its administrative apparatus and, in particular, its armies.

This was not a static society, nor even at times was it particularly stable. From the seventh century until the eleventh the rise of a new social-administrative elite, closely connected with the state and the army, can be traced, which evolves eventually into a real aristocracy of birth. This development is accompanied by changes in the relationship between different types of peasant producer and the state, and in the social and economic status of the former, as well as between the state as represented by the "power elite" at Constantinople and the various elements of the social elite upon which it depended for its position. Byzantine social relations are thus very dynamic, and the army, the state's military administrative structures, soldiers and warfare are crucial to their development.

War and the need to wage it, the organizational constraints it imposes, its effects on society and economy as well as its ideological justification and the debates it engenders, are always a radical force for social and political transformation. However unpleasant the effects of war, it is an undeniable fact of human history that war has been on many occasions and in many different historical contexts a powerful stimulus both to technological innovation and social and political change.[18] This is not necessarily to argue that, because war has been a necessary element in human social evolution, it must continue to be so – although that point of view has been defended; and it is certainly not to suggest that violence and aggression are, by themselves, a fundamental element in the human biogenetic inheritance.[19] On the other hand, it does suggest that the crucial role of war and its concomitants cannot be ignored in the history of any culture. Byzantium is no exception. Indeed, in many respects the history of the Byzantine state (as of most states, perhaps) is also the history of its ability successfully to defend itself and to organize for war, for its military organization was central both to the inflection of its social relations in general as well as to the ways in which the central government extracted and redistributed the resources available to it, whether in the form of agricultural produce or money taxes on agriculture and trade. This is obvious already from the later third and early fourth centuries, when the administrative and military reorganizations undertaken by the emperors Diocletian (284–305) and Constantine I (312–37) produced a militarization of even civil elements of the state apparatus, insofar as military grades and titles came to be awarded to officials within fiscal and related departments of the central government, and a military vocabulary permeated day-to-day governmental practice and language.[20] But it is just as obvious, if not more so, from the seventh century, when the much-reduced eastern Roman empire had to fight for its existence against an array of external foes who were able to extract a fearful price for survival in terms of economic dislocation and political-ideological disarray.

Military organization and the ability to wage war are intimately connected with the question of the extent and nature of state power. The degree to which the government is able to monopolize coercive force is crucial to the extent of the control exercised by the central political power over the resources necessary to its continued existence. Thus armies and those who comprise them – both leaders and rank-and-file – necessarily play a crucial role in the functioning of states, and an understanding of their workings can provide essential information about the way in which a particular state, within the constraints of the social relations in which it is rooted, evolves. At the same time, the nature and structure of the relations between the centre and its bureaucracy and administrative apparatus, and that between the latter and the social-economic elites of the society as a whole, play an important part in determining both how soldiers and the military are situated in the social order of things, and how the state actually maintains them. Although itself a focus of debate and controversy, I will employ the term "state" to refer simply to a more-or-less territorially unified political entity, with a "centre" from which a ruler or ruling group exercises political authority, and which has generated administrative structures and power relationships which facilitate its maintenance over more than a single generation.[21] States evolve institutional structures (fiscal and military, for example) which establish their own sets of roles and discourses, divorced from the practices of "ordinary" society. States thus generate specialist sets of institutions and generally create their own civil, judicial and military administrative castes or groups, which can survive only by maintaining control over the appropriation and distribution of surplus wealth and by promoting the continued existence of the political, social and economic relations which are perceived as necessary to their own continued existence.

From the point of view of maintaining armies, the means by which the state is able to appropriate, allocate and distribute or redistribute resources ultimately determine both the internal limits and the reach of state power on the one hand, and the effectiveness of the central authority in respect of its foreign policies on the other. But the ways in which states exercise power and authority vary enormously along a scale which alternates between two extremes: at one end, power can be concentrated at and exercised from the centre, through the ruler and an administration which remains under close and effective central supervision even in the provinces; at the other, state power may be diffused through an economically and sometimes politically independent elite (usually in the form of a nobility or magnate group), with a consequent parcelling out of surplus distribution, and the attendant danger that the state or rulers lose effective power over the resources necessary to their own continued existence. Most of these features are evident, at one stage of its history or another, in the structure and evolution of the East Roman state.

In the late Roman and Byzantine empire, while the state always succeeded in maintaining at least a nominal control over its fiscal resources, there is a gradual movement from one pole to the other across the period from the seventh to the fifteenth century. During the seventh and eighth centuries, the state seems able to have exercised a fairly powerful grip over its fiscal base and the resources of the empire in general. As a new social-political elite evolved, to become politically active as well as socially self-aware during the ninth–eleventh centuries, however, so the state – as represented by the abstract concept of a political entity on the one hand, and by the power-elite which actually controls government on the other – was obliged to recognize the reality of the power of elements in society which constituted in effect an alternative focus of political and economic authority and a demand for resources. What is significant from a structural perspective is thus the contradiction between the interests of the state, whose leading personnel had come by the early tenth century to be almost entirely recruited from this dominant social elite, and the interests of the members of this same elite as representatives of their clans and families and as landlords in their own right. The problem was resolved temporarily through the seizure of state power by one of the magnate families, whose first representative, the emperor Alexios I, was able through an astute use of inter-clan marriage alliances and the parcelling out of key state positions to members of the aristocracy to stabilize the state, maximize resource extraction to the advantage of the central government and the emperor's long-term internal and foreign political strategies, and reassert central authority and control.

But this dynastic politics – which also involved the empire in similar political alliances with members of the western aristocracy – eventually broke down and, following the Fourth Crusade, resulted in the establishment on what turned out to be a permanent basis of a single imperial family at Constantinople – the Palaiologos family – the victory of a purely hereditary and dynastic succession, and the progressive fragmentation and decentralization of political authority as the emperors handed out imperial positions and resources on a permanent basis to members of other aristocratic clans. An imperial administration continued to exist and to function and the efficient bureaucracy of former centuries continued to lead a shadowy existence. The government was increasingly unable to pay its way; and since the maintenance of military forces was expensive, it was increasingly less able to defend its territory or its internal policies. Private retinues played a significant role in all this, of course, so that the power of the Byzantine state was eventually effectively overshadowed, not simply by the strength of its political neighbours, but by that of some of the magnates within its territory, a point illustrated by the history of the civil conflicts which engulfed the empire in the fourteenth century in particular. Under such conditions, of course, the state could not hope to survive long, and it was primarily by virtue of the near-impregnable walls of Constantinople itself that it survived the first 50 years of the fifteenth century.

It is the opening phase of this process which provides the context for the later evolution of military organization as well as attitudes to warfare in the East Roman world, and which explains at least partially the ability of this beleaguered remnant of the Roman state to survive into the late medieval world. In the chapters which follow I will examine in succession each of the key areas raised in this introduction: the physical, social and economic context in which Byzantine military organization and warfare are to be understood, the army and soldiers in society, the administrative and logistical structures which supported it, the interaction between military and non-military aspects of the state, as well as the technology of warfare in the Byzantine world. I have not been able to devote space to the organization of the armies of the empire's enemies which, since weapons and tactics in particular are always directly influenced by one's foes, will perhaps be found to be a disadvantage at certain points. But this was in order to avoid expanding the book even further, and perhaps also overburdening the reader, while the military structures and warfare of the empire's Arab and Frankish enemies and allies has been dealt with by other scholars, some in the present series. This book does not represent, strictly speaking, a "polemological" analysis of Byzantine social and state forms: that remains a task, of much greater breadth, for the future.[22] But I hope nevertheless to have shed some light, and from a slightly different angle than that normally adopted, on the history of the Byzantine state and society as a whole.

CHAPTER ONE

Fighting for peace: attitudes to warfare in Byzantium

Warfare and the Christian Roman empire: the problem

Since God has put in our hands the imperial authority . . . we believe
that there is nothing higher or greater that we can do than to govern
in judgement and justice . . . and that thus we may be crowned by
His almighty hand with victory over our enemies (which is a thing
more precious and honourable than the diadem which we wear) and
thus there may be peace . . .[1]

This passage, taken from the introduction to the *Ecloga* of the emperors Leo
III and Constantine V, issued in 741, admirably sums up the key elements in
the East Roman attitude to warfare, which was seen as undesirable but at the
same time justified in order to maintain order and achieve peace. But the
evidence for eastern Roman or Byzantine attitudes to warfare and fighting contains a number of ambiguities and paradoxes. Such ambiguities have existed
throughout the history of cultures dominated by Christianity. Some of these
societies have developed a reputation for being more warlike or more peace-
loving than others, however – both in the eyes of their contemporaries as well
as in those of the modern commentator. Western medieval society gave the
former impression to others when it was involved in warlike confrontation
with them (as during the Crusading period, for example), and Byzantium is
placed usually in the second category. In this chapter, we will look at the
ways in which early Christian ideas about warfare evolved in the later Roman
and the medieval East Roman world, to produce the peculiarly Byzantine
attitude to war which permitted western Crusaders and others, as well as
some modern commentators, to caricature them as cowardly and effete.

Christianity has never developed formally an ideological obligation to
wage war against "infidels" presented in the terms of Christian theology, even
if, at times and on an *ad hoc* basis, individuals have spoken and acted as though

such a justification could be made. Indeed, the thirteenth canon of St Basil expressly advised those who engaged in warfare to abstain from communion. So how did medieval East Roman Christians confront the issue of warfare and killing?

Early Christian thinkers had evolved a number of objections to warfare in general, and more especially to serving in the armies of the pagan Roman emperors. Humane considerations obviously played a crucial role in this respect, but the Christians' attitude to the state was the key issue. Although there were some notable exceptions, Christians did not, on the whole, believe that the Roman state represented the rule of the Antichrist; on the contrary, it was felt that the existence of the state was a necessary element for the expansion of Christian belief – St Luke had himself noted the coincidence between the *Pax Augusti* and the consolidation of imperial power on the one hand, and the birth of Christ on the other. This coincidence came to play a key role in later medieval, especially eastern Christian, apocalyptic writings, and lay at the heart of the Christian belief that, once the state had become a Christian empire (after the late fourth century), it was the Roman people, representing Orthodoxy and the rule of order against the rule of chaos and barbarism, which had achieved the status of the Chosen People, replacing the Jews who had murdered the Saviour. But Christians in the era before the "conversion" of Constantine could not serve two masters – Christ and the Roman state – especially when the latter was on occasion actively hostile to their beliefs or their very existence. Indeed, the liturgy of the period before the Peace of the Church and the Edict of Toleration issued by Constantine I in 313 forbade soldiers who wished to become Christians to take life, whether under orders or not.[2]

Such views were well summarized by the Christian apologist Origen, writing in the third century, who argued that Christians formed another sort of army which, rather than fighting in wars for the emperor, prayed for the success of the state which made possible their continued existence and the expansion of their community. This was, of course, a compromise, particularly in view of the fact that Origen's ideas were developed in response to the criticisms of Christian communities and pacifism made by the pagan Celsus, who suggested that Christians needed to support the earthly empire against its barbarian foes if only in order to ensure their own continued survival (arguments not dissimilar to those directed against Protestant pacifist sects in North America during the eighteenth and nineteenth centuries). And, although a hard-line position did continue to have adherents throughout the medieval period, especially among ascetics and in monastic circles, such a compromise nevertheless signalled the end of a serious mass opposition or hostility to either the state or its military undertakings.[3]

Origen's views in this respect echoed the attitudes of many Christians, who had to carry on their ordinary lives in what was potentially a hostile political or cultural environment. Pragmatic considerations carried the day. One of Origen's key ideas was that conversion of barbarians outside the empire would end the need for war altogether; until that happened, of course, fighting and warfare, and therefore the need to maintain armies, were a necessary evil. While this did not mean that Christians could fight for the empire with a clear conscience, the evidence does suggest that by the end of the third century AD there was a substantial number of Christians in the ranks of the imperial armies. The existence of a small Christian church in the Roman military base at Doura Europos on the eastern frontier, dated to the period AD 193–235 approximately, has been invoked as good support for this, and the fact that Christian worship was tolerated, possibly even encouraged, by the military command.[4] Such pragmatism could not banish conflicts of interest, of course: service in the army involved acceptance of the emperor cult – the emperor as a god – and a whole range of pagan traditions and rituals, so that the annals of early Christianity, especially in the third century, are littered with tales of persecution and martyrdom as individual recruits refused to carry out the appropriate ceremonial and ritual observances.[5]

The adoption of Christianity by the emperor Constantine I, however, and the reformulation of imperial political ideology which followed, radically altered this situation. To begin with, the Christianization of the ruler cult resolved one of the most intractable problems: an earthly emperor chosen by God to lead the (Christian) Roman people was clearly acceptable where an emperor credited with divine power and authority had not been. And from this time two distinct perspectives in respect of Christian attitudes to warfare and military service evolve. An officially promulgated and supported view on the one hand encouraged support for the state, as personified by the orthodox emperor, and all its undertakings. The council of Arles, convened in 314 – immediately after Constantine I's victory over his last (pagan) opponent in 312 and the Edict of Milan of 313 – clearly permitted Christians to join the army, although there is some doubt as to the interpretation of the passage dealing with conscientious objectors (that they should be excommunicated as deserters). Leading churchmen in the fourth century, such as Athanasius, archbishop of Alexandria, and Ambrosius, bishop of Milan, announced that it was praiseworthy for a Christian to take up arms against the enemies of the state; St Augustine defended a similar position, although all expressed the hope that violent conflict could be avoided and that bloodshed would not be necessary.[6] As the central government became increasingly, and eventually exclusively, Christian, such a point of view culminated during the last years of the century in the prohibition on non-Christians serving in the imperial armies at all![7]

This line of reasoning left military service up to individual choice. But there remained a strong minority opposition to Christian involvement in bloodshed of any kind, which developed the argument outlined a century earlier by Origen. Many churchmen expressed their doubts about participation in military activities involving the taking of life – Paulinus of Nola and Basil of Caesarea both repeated and strengthened reservations expressed by others – and at the end of the fourth century, Pope Siricius could condemn those who served in the army and prohibit them from later taking up holy orders. But

Basil's reservations allowed for a defensive war and the taking of life when threatened by robbers or hostile invasion, while in his thirteenth canon his penalty was restricted to a three-year period of exclusion from the church:

> Our Fathers did not consider killing in war as murder because, in my view, they forgave those who defended wisdom and piety. Nevertheless, it is perhaps good to advise them [i.e. those who kill in war] to abstain from communion for three years, since their hands are unclean.

And in spite of the intellectual commitment and rhetorical vigour with which such views were often expressed, they do not appear to have reflected mass opinion, either among the ordinary population or among the state elite. While condemning murder, for example, Athanasius of Alexandria accepted not only that those who killed in war had acted lawfully, but that their actions brought honour and distinction upon them. Indeed, it can be said that the accommodation reached during and after the reign of Constantine I between the old, pagan emperor cult, and its newly Christianized form rendered the discussion for the most part academic. This is especially clear in later discussions of Basil's thirteenth canon for, as canonists of the twelfth century noted, its rigorous application would mean that most active soldiers would be permanently excluded from communion. That this was clearly not the case is admitted both by the canonists in their commentaries, and is also evident in the presence in Byzantine armies of clergy, the holding of services before battle and to bless the insignia, and indeed the presence of religious symbols and images of great potency.[8]

Soldiers now became, not servants of an oppressive pagan empire, but fighters for the faith and defenders of Orthodoxy, at least in theory. Soldiers were fully accepted members of the Christian community who had a recognized and indeed worthy role to play. Liturgical prayers evolved from the fourth and fifth centuries in which the military role of the emperors and the need for soldiers to defend the faith were specifically recognized: "Shelter their [the emperors'] heads on the day of battle, strengthen their arm, . . . subjugate to them all the barbarian peoples who desire war, confer upon them deep and lasting peace" is an illustrative example from a fifth-century liturgical text. But this did not, of course, mean that warfare and the killing of enemies were in themselves intrinsically to be praised or regarded as in some way deserving of a particular spiritual reward. Quite the reverse, for however much Christians were able to justify warfare, whether from a defensive need (to preserve Orthodoxy, for example) or in what we would see as an offensive context (to recover "lost" Roman territory from non-Christian or barbarian or heretic, still judged as defensive action) killing remained (and continues to remain) a necessary evil from the Christian standpoint. This is such a strong tradition within Christian culture, indeed, that even in the modern highly secularized world of advanced technological warfare, western strategists, military theorists and anthropologists or sociologists of war point to the need still felt to justify warmaking in terms established by this pre-medieval moral-ethical context.[9]

Warfare and the question of "Holy War"

One of the questions which has intrigued scholars in this respect has been that of the supposed absence of a theory of "holy war" in Byzantium. No concept of holy war comparable to that familiar from Islam nor again of the just war similar to that enunciated before, during and after the Crusades in western Europe, ever evolved in Byzantium. The waging of war against unbelievers is, of course, only one – and in Islamic theory not the most important – of four ways to fulfil the duty of *jihād*, which signifies the struggle to propagate Islam by the heart (i.e. inner struggle), the tongue, the hand (i.e. by upholding good against evil) and the sword: the latter is waged in order to gain effective control over societies so that they may be administered in accordance with the principles of Islam. Those who died in the course of this struggle for the faith were understood immediately to be brought to paradise.[10] Nothing approaching this complex and multi-faceted notion was generated by Christianity.

The answer to the question, "did the Byzantines have a concept of holy war?" depends, of course, on the way in which the question is framed and what is understood by the term "holy war". As we will see, reducing the terms of the debate to a crude opposition between the western Crusade and Islamic *jihād* hardly assists in the appreciation of the much more complex reality of Byzantine attitudes and practice.[11]

In spite of the reservations expressed by a number of Christian thinkers, the view that warfare – however regrettable – in a just cause was acceptable became widespread, partly, of course, because from a pragmatic standpoint the Roman state, whatever faith it professed, had to defend its territorial integrity against aggression. So some rationalization of the need to fight was inevitable. Eusabius of Caesarea, the Christian apologist for Constantine I whose intellectual influence in this respect played a key role in the compromise between pagan and Christian attitudes to the empire, the emperor and the imperial cult, expressed a view which can indeed be understood to represent warfare with the aim of promoting the new imperial faith as a type of holy war.[12] The symbol of the Cross appeared both in imperial propaganda and, more significantly, among the insignia of the imperial armies; the Christian *labarum* and the *chi-rho* symbol – seen in a vision by Constantine himself before his victory over Galerius in 312 – was carried by the standard-bearers of the legions, as well as appearing on imperial coins and in association with images or busts of the emperors. Warfare waged against the enemies of the empire was now warfare to defend or extend the religion favoured by the emperor and, from the time of Theodosius I, the official religion of the state as such. Enemies of the empire could be portrayed as enemies of Christianity, against whom warfare was entirely justified, indeed necessary if the True Faith were to fulfil the destiny inhering in divine providence. To a degree, therefore, warfare of the Christian

Roman empire against its enemies and those who threatened it, and therefore God's empire on earth, was holy war. That this was a paradox within Christian attitudes to warfare is clear, but pragmatic considerations made a solution essential.

Throughout its history and the many wars it had to fight – given the strategic and geopolitical situation it occupied discussed in Chapters 2 and 3 below – religious motifs played a key role in the ideological struggles waged by the empire. During the later sixth century, and on numerous occasions thereafter, religious images were taken with the armies on their campaigns, designed to ensure divine support for the expedition and to encourage the soldiers against their non-Christian foe. Most famous was the image of Christ "not made by human hand", the so-called Camuliana image, used by imperial commanders in the eastern wars in the 570s and after.[13] Other such palladia were placed above city gates as a symbol of the protection afforded by the figure depicted – at Alexandria, Kaisareia in Palestine, Antioch and Constantinople, for example.[14]

This religious element was especially the case when the rulers of neighbouring hostile peoples or states actively persecuted the Christian communities within their territories, and the wars with the Persians were frequently presented both to the soldiers of the Roman armies and to the wider populace in the light of a struggle between Christianity and the forces of evil.[15] The war that broke out between the Romans and Persians in 421 was directly associated with Zoroastrian persecution of Christians in Persia (although the hostility of some Christian leaders in Persia to Zoroastrian worship had certainly inflamed the situation), and was presented by contemporary and later Roman commentators as a just war to defend Christians from pagan attack. Christian refugees from Persian oppression inflamed opinion in the eastern provinces and at Constantinople; at the same time as the expedition was under preparation, the emperor despatched a bejewelled gold cross to the patriarch of Jerusalem as a token of imperial devotion to the Christian cause, while a new iconography on imperial coinage, showing the figure of Victory raising aloft a cross, betokened divine support for the Christian empire. The Roman military victory which followed the brief conflict and the ensuing treaty (which included clauses designed to protect the Christians of Persia from persecution) were ascribed to divine support for the imperial cause and, of course, legitimated the act of war which had involved the loss of life on both sides.[16]

Mostly the conflicts between Persia and East Rome revolved around issues of strategic control along the eastern frontier, yet there was always a religious-ideological element present. In the peace treaty signed by both powers in 562, for example, while the chief concern on both sides was their respective strategic situations in the Caucasus (especially the region of Lazica), other clauses specified that the Christians should be free of persecution and able to worship without harassment, and in addition that neither of the two main religious groups in Persia – both Christians and Zoroastrians – should attempt to proselytise in each other's communities.[17] Although it is difficult to find any explicitly religious motivation in the wars of the later sixth century, which involved primarily political and strategic concerns, it is nevertheless important to note that Roman writers regularly refer to their own side as "the Christians", as well as "the Romans", and that this awareness of difference is especially pronounced when dealing with enemies of a distinctly different faith. Given that the mid-sixth century was marked by efforts on the part of the Persian king Khusru I to promote a Zoroastrian religious organization similar to that evident in the Christian church, this consciousness, and the greater profile given to religious-ideological differences, is perhaps not surprising. But although it played a role, it does not predominate in the contemporary accounts of the reasons and motives for warfare between Byzantium and Persia.[18]

Awareness of difference in religion as at least one element among many in the accounts of war between the Christian Roman state and its enemies is hardly surprising, of course, and that is not an issue here. Throughout the seventh century Byzantine theologians as well as writers of miracle collections and saints' lives raise the issue of Jewish or heretical hostility to orthodoxy; religious debate and theological argument became, indeed, the language through which politics and theories of power and authority were expressed. This is a development which can be seen increasingly from the later sixth century, but was given huge impetus after the defeats suffered by the Romans at the hands of Islam and the Arabs in the 630s and 640s.[19] Yet the wars which were fought against the Persians by the emperor Heraclius, culminating in the complete defeat of the Sassanid forces in 626–7, had an ideological quality which, as has several times been pointed out, differentiates them from earlier conflicts.

The emperor Maurice had been killed in 602, following a mutiny among the Danube forces and the seizure of power by the centurion Phocas who ruled until 610. It was Maurice, however, who had intervened to help the young Khusru II recover his throne during the Persian civil war of 590–1, and upon news of Maurice's death reaching him, the Persian king declared war on the tyrant, claiming to act on behalf of one of Maurice's sons who had ostensibly escaped the massacre of the imperial family.

Fighting began in 603, and until 611–12 consisted for the most part of regular Persian attacks and raids across the frontier, pillaging and amassing booty from the Roman provinces. There seems to have been little meaningful opposition from Roman armies, which were at the same time divided between factions supporting Phocas and those under commanders who opposed the new emperor. In 610 a coup was mounted under Heraclius, the son of the exarch of Africa (military governor), also named Heraclius, the latter formerly a general under Maurice, together with the cousin of Heraclius the younger, Nicetas. While the latter marched overland via Egypt and Syria against the loyalist forces, Heraclius sailed with a fleet to Constantinople where, in collaboration with elements within the city, Phocas was deposed and executed. But the Persians refused to halt the war, and indeed what had begun as a war of raiding and extortion of booty began from 611/12 to be transformed into a war of conquest.

By 614 Persian troops had occupied much of Syria and Palestine; from 618 the occupation of Egypt began. The relic of the True Cross was taken from Jerusalem to Persia, and in 626 Persian and Avar forces attempted to mount a combined attack on Constantinople. But in the early 620s the emperor had set about reorganizing and reconstituting his field forces, and in 622 inaugurated a long-term campaign which involved ignoring the direct threat from Persian armies in Anatolia, attacking instead through eastern Asia Minor behind the main Persian lines and threatening both their supply lines and communications with their home bases as well as posing a major challenge to the Persian heartlands. With consummate strategic skill, greatly increased morale and improved discipline, and the aid of Turkic allies from beyond the Caucasus, the emperor's policy paid off, with the result that Persian forces were defeated piecemeal both in Persia, as well as Asia Minor. The failure of the siege of 626, the withdrawal of the Avars and of the besieging Persian troops meant the end of effective Persian strategy, and the deposition and assassination of Khusru II brought also a reversal of Persian policy with regard to the Romans. A peace was negotiated, Persian forces were eventually withdrawn peacefully from Egypt and Palestine/Syria, and the status quo of the 590s was restored.[20]

One of the hallmarks of the contemporary and later accounts of these wars is the pre-eminence of the Cross as a symbol of imperial victory, and of the strongly religious element in imperial propaganda: this was a war fought by Christians under the victorious sign of the Cross, with the aid of the Theotokos, the mother of God, against pagans who had not only impugned the integrity of the Roman empire, protected by God, but that of the True Cross, the symbol of the faith itself. The emperor himself cast the Persian king Khusru as the enemy of God, and the court panegyrist, George of Pisidia, represented Heraclius as the chosen instrument of God's divine wrath as well as the pious and orthodox ruler leading the Chosen People – the Romans – to victory, safeguarding the faith and – of crucial symbolic significance – recovering the True Cross and restoring it to Jerusalem. This attitude did not arise without good reason: for as well as the longer-term context we have already discussed, Khusru is reported to have himself set out on his war to crush the Christian Roman empire and even to restore the realm of his distant forebears Cyrus, Xerxes and Darius.[21] Already at the outset of the campaign Heraclius adopted a strongly religious tone, using the Easter celebrations of 622 as his starting point; the symbolism of imperial coinage, especially the introduction of the so-called "cross on steps" motif, emphasized this message. And George of Pisidia, the emperor's propagandist, hammered the point home in each of his compositions.[22] During the siege of 626 the patriarch Sergios and the Master of Offices, the emperor's deputy during his absence, had lead the defence. But the key figure for the Byzantines themselves had been the Virgin Mary, who had been seen by both Byzantines and Avars during the fighting. It was her image which had been paraded around the walls of the city, and it was to her intervention that the city owed its salvation. And it was her image which

accompanied Heraclius on his campaigns against the Persians as well as –
importantly – in his coup against Phocas in 610.[23] The churchman Theodore
the *syncellus*, a member of the patriarchal clergy, had composed and delivered
a sermon on the defeat of the Avars, and his tone was similarly one of religious
war, a war to defend the faith of an empire chosen by God to lead humankind
to Orthodoxy and salvation.[24]

As the East Roman empire became increasingly threatened and beleaguered during the second half of the seventh century and afterwards, so its
religious identity came ever more to the fore; and logically enough, its struggle
for survival took the form of a struggle between good and evil, between Christianity and its enemies. This affected internal politics and social attitudes as
much as it affected attitudes to warfare, of course.[25] But it meant that, in one
sense, all wars were now holy wars, for the very survival of the God-protected
realm of the Chosen People was under threat.

The wars fought by Heraclius against the Persians, and the very explicitly
religious profile they were given by the emperor in the way he planned and
timed his departures from the city, as well as by contemporary imperial and
ecclesiastical propaganda, are nevertheless unusual in degree and frequency.[26]
It seems certainly to have been the case that contemporaries perceived something special and exceptional in the nature of the struggle and its aims. Yet,
as we will see, it is equally clear that no specific doctrine of holy war ever
evolved out of these experiences.

"By the grace of Christ . . . you will . . . annihilate them": the political justification of warfare

It is precisely because the Byzantine, or East Roman, self-image was one of a
beleaguered Christian state, fighting the forces of darkness, that this was the
case. Against its foes it had constantly to be on its guard and evolve a whole
panoply of defensive techniques, among which warfare was only one element
and by no means necessarily the most useful. In the middle of the tenth
century the Italian diplomat Liudprand of Cremona described the position of
the empire accurately enough when he described it as being surrounded by the
fiercest of barbarians – Hungarians, Pechenegs, Khazars, Rus' and so forth.
For him, this was a truly frightening situation, quite unlike anything faced by
the Lombard princes or the papacy in Italy.[27]

Symbols of the faith reflecting this awareness of difference (and also a felt
superiority) were ever present in Byzantine military contexts as we have noted,
but the association of the faith with the struggle against the outsider was constantly reinforced also in day-to-day religious observance. At one level – that
of public petitions for peace or success in war, as enunciated in the Orthodox
liturgy – this had a formal, almost ritualistic quality which may have impacted
only superficially on the awareness of most listeners. But at another level, that
of occasional sermons or homilies praising imperial victories or warning of

the dangers of barbarian attack, or that of the cult of saints, especially the various military saints whose exploits in saving soldiers and armies as well as ordinary people from enemies or intervening to bring about Christian victories, the association must have been very apparent.[28] And while it can hardly have encouraged a simple pacifism among the mass of the population, neither can warfare in the name of the Orthodox faith have seemed a particularly exceptional state of affairs. Indeed, the church and the emperors actively employed religious symbols – as we have seen in the case of Heraclius – as palladia in the wars with enemies of the state: quite apart from the sacred images carried with armies or placed as protective devices on the walls or gates of cities, emperors endowed their armies with ceremonial crosses richly adorned with precious stones. These were important enough to act both as standards and talismans for the Byzantine soldiers and as worthwhile objects for capture by their opponents: the capture of richly decorated crosses of gold and silver is frequently mentioned in Arab historical accounts of campaigns against the *Rum*, the Byzantines, just as their recovery is praised in Byzantine texts. Nikephros II recaptured a number of crosses during his campaigns in Syria, and they are mentioned specifically as "military crosses" (*stavroi strategikoi*) in some documents.[29] Relics of saints or other figures in the Christian symbolic world were similarly deployed: in the ninth–twelfth centuries, for example, and almost certainly beforehand, emperors on campaign took along with them as a talisman an elaborate cross, including at its centre reliquaries containing a number of relics of saints and other sacred items, including a part of the Virgin's girdle and residue of her milk. Special imperial crosses, richly bejewelled and decorated, were kept in the precincts of the palace for ceremonial processions. They also accompanied the emperors when they went on campaign.[30] Such a cross was lost at the battle of Myriokephalon in 1180, for example, and again in battle under Isaac II in 1190.[31] This tradition, legitimating warfare directed against those who threatened the Christian Roman state, is expressed in many contexts, not least the Byzantine war cry "The Cross has conquered".[32] A sixth-century anonymous writer expresses this point of view thus:

> I know well that war is a great evil and the worst of all evils. But since our enemies clearly look upon the shedding of our blood as one of their basic duties and the height of virtue, . . . we have decided to write about strategy. By putting it into practice we shall be able not only to resist our enemies but even to conquer them.[33]

The author of the tenth-century treatise on skirmishing warfare notes that it is Christ "who has greatly cut back the power and strength of the offspring of Ismael". A brief tenth-century account of imperial military expeditions claims that it is itself following the practices of the great Constantine, the first Christian ruler of the Romans.[34] In non-military contexts, too, it has been shown that imperial and other donations to monasteries made reference to the military role of the emperor, divine support for the empire's military enterprise and prayers spoken for the success of the armies,[35] while throughout the military handbooks the authors refer constantly to the help given to the Romans by God under whose protection (and that of the Virgin) the soldiers fight. The sentiment expressed at the beginning of this section is not untypical.[36] The tenth-century treatise on the administration of the empire, attributed to the emperor Constantine VII, ascribes fundamental features of Byzantine custom and practice to Constantine the Great, and, importantly, those who encountered these features tended to believe the tradition, even if they were less happy with the results.[37] Liudprand of Cremona's report on his two visits to the imperial court in the middle years of the tenth century illustrates the point clearly.[38] In every aspect of its public and private existence, what Byzantines did was explained in terms of divine providence and justified by recourse to God's will and design. In military contexts, this becomes especially apparent on the occasion of imperial triumphs, staged entries into the capital city involving the whole senior bureaucracy and court, the clergy of several churches, set acclamations orchestrated by imperial officials at key points along the processional route, frequent stops for prayer at churches along the route, the distribution of largesse, the display of prisoners and booty, and the close association of Christian spiritual with secular concerns.[39]

Thus the connection between warfare and Christianity, the struggle for survival of the Chosen People led by the emperor chosen by God at the head of his armies (frequently also described as *theophylaktoi* – protected by God) was quite explicit. All warfare was, in this sense, about Christianity and the Christian empire, so that to isolate a particular war or type of war as "holy" was unnecessary and would indeed have seemed absurd. This is reinforced by the fact that a desire for peace and a regret that war should be necessary were constant motifs in imperial and church ideology. It is also reinforced by the constant reminder of the Heavenly support which Byzantine armies received. Successful warfare without God's help is impossible, as the writer of the late sixth-century *Strategikon* emphasizes:

> we urge upon the general that his most important concern be the love
> of God and justice; building on these, he should strive to win the
> favour of God, without which it is impossible to carry out any plan,
> however well devised it may seem, or to overcome any enemy, how-
> ever weak he may be thought.[40]

Seventh-century texts dealing in particular with the events of the Arab conquests explain the defeats of the Romans as a result of God's anger with the Romans, the Chosen People, who are thus being punished for their sins. And like all the military treatises, the outcomes of battles were seen as reflecting God's will. The eleventh-century writer Michael Attaleiates similarly thus saw the military defeats and barbarian inroads of his own time as a reflection of God's anger with the Romans – only when they returned to the path of righteousness and corrected their sins would success once again attend Roman arms.[41]

23

Liturgies for the troops were often held before battle; supplicatory prayer before and prayers of thanksgiving after battle were recommended; priests accompanied the army, at least on major expeditions, and played an important role in maintaining the soldiers' morale; and whether the enemy was pagan or Christian (for example, the Bulgars) these tokens of Byzantine Orthodoxy and God's support against those who threatened the Chosen People were regularly employed.[42] When the soldiers went into battle, they were instructed to remain as silent as possible until the command was given to shout the battle-cry. But they should also cry out, in unison, on leaving camp, either "*nobiscum deus*" (God is with us) or "*Kyrie eleison*" (Lord have mercy) and invoke Christ as the Lord of Battles before advancing in formation upon the enemy.[43]

These values are constants throughout the existence of the empire. In the thirteenth century the courtier Nikephros Blemmydes composed a short treatise belonging to the genre generally known as *Mirror of Princes*, a book of advice but also in praise of the emperor of the day, a genre which reached back into Roman times.[44] In this, Blemmydes, writing for Theodore II Laskaris (1254–8), the son of the emperor John III Vatatzes (1222–54), offers advice on, among other aspects of the imperial office, military discipline and training, strategy and tactics. He stresses the need for ruthless action in dealing with enemies (the empire at the time was engaged in conflicts with the Seljuk Turks in Asia Minor, the Latin empire and princes who had partitioned the Byzantine empire after the Fourth Crusade in 1203–4 and the Bulgars), and warfare is clearly taken for granted as a normal activity for an emperor. Yet at the same time, fighting and the need to wage war are understood as regrettable, something forced upon an emperor by the circumstances in which his beleaguered state finds itself.[45] This is especially obvious in the letters of the patriarch Nikolaos I in the early tenth century where, in his correspondence with the Bulgar tsar Symeon, he notes both his regret that Christians should have to fight each other and at the same time stresses the fact that there can be only one Roman empire protected by God, and that efforts to destroy it, however successful they may temporarily appear to be, are ultimately doomed. Michael Psellos makes no bones about praising the emperor Michael VII for his distaste for war and fighting.[46] Anna Comnena condemns as bad generalship purposefully provoking an enemy to battle or armed conflict when peace is supposedly the ultimate aim of all warfare.[47] And while privileged members of a relatively small cultural elite such as these were quite capable of expressing very different views where appropriate to the dramatic purpose of their narrative, there is equally no reason to doubt the force of such statements for the readers or listeners who could identify with this set of values. By the same token, they varied the vocabulary they used according to the context, deploying now a fiercer, warlike rhetoric and language, now a more pacific, peace-loving discourse. Byzantine military and diplomatic priorities evolved in a specific historical context in order to ensure the survival of a beleaguered state and were seen as both universally better and morally superior.[48]

Similarly, the writer Theognostos, writing in the first half of the thirteenth century, penned a *Mirror of Princes* in which military activity is a taken-
for-granted part of a ruler's life, and in which warfare to defend the empire of
the Romans, the Orthodox empire of the Chosen People, was a day-to-day
matter. When victories are achieved, God should be thanked; when defeats
are suffered, these are to be accepted as God's punishment for the sins of
the Romans. Warfare was, on this account, by definition a religious matter;
but it was a regular, everyday affair, unexceptionable in this respect. Whatever
the achievements of individual emperors or the Christian Roman people as a
whole, therefore, there was no reason in this context to treat warfare against
the enemies of the empire as a special event. All fighting was for Orthodoxy
and the empire; all warfare was, thus, holy war; and while it was to be
regretted, and avoided wherever possible, it was also part of daily life for
the empire and many of its inhabitants. Crucially, and in contrast to the
west, fighting and warfare was ultimately the responsibility of the emperor,
appointed by God to lead the faithful in defence of the Chosen People. Such
views were particularly clearly enshrined in the preambles to imperial grants
of revenue to soldiers in the twelfth century and after, texts which neatly sum
up these values:

> But we must welcome with the best we can the soldiers and warriors
> who show courage against blood-thirsty barbarians, since they give up
> body and soul for the people called after Christ, and expose themselves
> to the greatest of dangers, and dance upon swords and almost engage
> with Ares himself and death, in goodwill to their ruler and facing
> perils for their kinsmen. Should not we too welcome them, repaying
> this purpose of theirs as best we can and consoling them for their
> dangers and calling them to greater efforts against the barbarians . . . ?[49]

In respect of official secular as well as religious belief, therefore, warfare was endemic, unavoidable, but nevertheless a bad thing. This is clear
from the texts we have mentioned so far, as well as from a range of official or
semi-official pronouncements throughout the Byzantine period. The opening
statement of the emperor Leo VI, "the Wise" (886–912), in the preface to his
treatise on military tactics and strategy, provides an excellent example of this
attitude. In Leo's view, humans are essentially peaceful by nature, valuing their
own security and embracing peace as the best means of maintaining a tranquil
life. But the devil, by tempting people to sin, causes conflict and violence,
stimulating men to wage war in spite of themselves and contrary to their own
real interests and desires. The Orthodox Christian empire was – as the earthly
version of the Kingdom of Heaven – quite justified in fighting to defend itself
against external aggression. Defensive warfare was, in this view, God's struggle,
and was perfectly acceptable. And even though the interpretation of "defensive" could vary so that warfare to recover formerly imperial lands might
also thus be justified, yet Leo insists that aggressive warfare and the needless

shedding of the blood of even barbarians should be condemned.[50] Similar sentiments are attributed to the emperor Justin II on the occasion of the elevation of Tiberius Constantine, his eventual successor, to the rank of *Kaisar*, for the emperor exhorts Tiberius to eschew acts of bloodshed and yet to look after the soldiers.[51] And although the sentiments of the fourth-century patriarch Athanasius of Alexandria in this respect were taken up and given the status of a canon of the church in the Quinisext Council held in 691 in Constantinople, it is worth noting that the ambiguity was explicit even in the words of a father of the church: for while condemning murder, Athanasius emphasizes that killing one's enemies in battle is both just and praiseworthy, bringing honour on those who distinguish themselves in battle.[52] In the tenth-century treatise on tactical organization and battle dispositions, the emperor Nikephros II recommends that the whole army, officers and men, should fast for three days before battle, banishing all evil thoughts, repenting their sins and promising God not to take up their bad habits should they survive the fighting. The need to go into battle with a pure spirit was essential to victory, of course; yet the desire to purify the souls of the soldiers was also intimately connected with the anxieties associated with the taking of life which all Christians were supposed to feel. Whether or not it was made explicit, the effects of such views, summed up in Basil's thirteenth canon, are apparent.[53]

Byzantine political theory thus incorporated a theory of imperial and Christian Roman *philanthropia*, a theory, reflected in individual practice and beliefs and promulgated by church and state ceremonial and ritual, which was fundamental to the ways in which the Byzantines thought of warfare and the related issue of the value of human life and the relationship between human action and divine will.[54] Yet in other ways they were in practical respects – particularly when the political and military context allowed (as in the tenth century) – no more nor less "peace-loving" than their enemies. And suspicion of the foe was always a factor: "do not be deceived by humane acts of the enemy . . .", warns the sixth-century *Strategikon*.[55]

Peace was thus the ideal, and philanthropy was a quality highly valued in diplomatic discourse. But on what terms was peace to be welcomed? Writing in the early twelfth century of the fierce wars fought between Byzantines and Pechenegs, Turks and Normans, Anna Comnena, daughter of the emperor Alexios I, supplies one answer: it was the terms and conditions set by her father the emperor which counted, terms which reflected both the practical needs of a hard-pressed ruler and his army and the ideological demands of the Roman state. And this was not a personal view: in the official ideology – reflected, for example, in tenth-century Constantinopolitan acclamations – peace was the rule of the Roman emperors and the Christian *oikoumene*, the civilized world.[56] While acclaiming emperors as victorious over their enemies, warfare was acknowledged as a necessarily unpleasant means to a worthwhile end.[57] Yet Anna also relished a detailed account of military action, especially where her side wins, a fact indicative of the two-sided nature of the Byzantine attitude. The same can be said of the account by Leo the Deacon of the wars of the middle and later tenth century, which makes no effort to conceal the pride felt by the writer in the victories of those years; the same can be said of the official Michael Attaleiates' account of the campaigns of Romanos IV in the late 1060s which, although culminating disastrously for the empire in the Manzikert campaign of 1071, nevertheless permitted a Constantinopolitan writer to express a certain pleasure in the imperial victories.[58] More explicitly, the boastful threats of Nikephros II – reflecting also the values of a provincial and militarized elite – place great emphasis on the glories of warfare, whatever the ideological-religious justification and legitimization offered.[59] But this illustrates the point. Imperial ideology had constantly to balance two extremes: to maintain a sufficient element of threat together with confidence in the military strength of the empire on the one hand, and to represent the Romans and their rulers as peace-loving and war-avoiding, because that is what their beliefs and their view of themselves actively demanded, and because God was, of course, ultimately on their side.[60] The latter is expressed most vividly by the patriarch Nikolaos I, for example, in the early tenth century in a letter to the Bulgar tsar Symeon. Nikolaos stressed the awful fate awaiting those who dared challenge the legitimate, God-protected empire. The fact that temporary gains might be won by its enemies was unimportant – in the end, the foes of the Roman world order were merely elements in God's divine plan or tools of the Antichrist, doomed to extinction. Similar notions appear in Leo's *Tactica*, as the following words illustrate:

> For we have always welcomed peace, both for our subjects and for the barbarians, through Christ, God and ruler of all, if the foreigners enclosed within their own bounds are content, professing no injustice, while you yourself (the general) withhold your hand from them, sprinkling the earth neither with foreign nor with our own blood . . .
> . . . But if the foe is not sensible, and himself commences the injustice, then indeed there is a just cause present – an unjust war having been begun by the enemy – to undertake war against them with good courage and with eagerness, since they furnish the causes, raising unjust hands against our subjects. So take courage, for you have the God of righteousness as a help, and taking up the fight on behalf of your brethren you will achieve complete victory.[61]

The rejection of "Holy War"

> Lord Jesus Christ, our God, have mercy on us. Come to the aid of us Christians and make us worthy to fight to the death for our faith and our brothers, strengthen our souls and our hearts and our whole body, the mighty Lord of battles, through the intercession of the immaculate Mother of God, Thy Mother, and of all the saints. Amen.[62]

It is such a background that explains the reluctance of the church to accept the proposal of the emperor Nikephros II Phocas (963–9) that soldiers who fell fighting for the empire should be counted among the martyrs. Certainly, there was a hidden agenda on the part of the patriarch Polyeuctos, in view of the emperor's measures to restrict the growth of monastic landholding, which played a role in the refusal of the synod which met to discuss the issue to endorse the emperor's request.[63] And although Basil's canon 13 was cited as the overt reason for the rejection, it is also clear from the remarks of the later canonists that this canon was not strictly observed, as noted already. The attitude of the church at this time, and as was frequently the case, seems in fact to have been determined largely by the relations pertaining between emperor and patriarch (with the senior clergy). For as has also been pointed out, there are many examples where the church willingly offered substantial amounts of gold and silver plate to be converted into coin or otherwise employed by the state to avert a crisis (during the reigns of Heraclius, for example, or of Romanos I in the year 920, when church plate was turned into coin for paying the army and for buying barbarian military assistance), and other cases where, when relations between church and emperors were less friendly, the church refused such assistance.[64] The request of the emperor Nikephros was, in any case, an exceptional one, the acceptance of which would have involved recognizing the warfare of the tenth century as of a somehow different (more holy) quality than other wars, or admitting that the martyrs of the early church showed no greater courage than the common soldiers of the day who would have been henceforth their equals. This was certainly a major objection raised by both contemporary and later commentators, and the idea was rejected and never again revived.[65]

Yet this notion does not appear for the first time in the time of Nikephros II. For already in the military treatise compiled by Leo VI, the *Tactica*, the reward of the soldier who fights for the faith is expressed in terms not simply of doing his duty as the companion in arms of the emperor, but also in spiritual terms: fighting the enemies of Christendom brings immediate spiritual benefit, and for those who die in battle perpetual contentment. It has been pointed out that in the same treatise, Leo describes his understanding of the Islamic notion of *jihād*, and that his own remarks suggest a remarkable parallel between the spiritual rewards reaped by the Christian soldier who falls in battle and Muslim attitudes.[66] On the other hand, the idea that soldiers who fall in the fight for the true faith will receive the appropriate spiritual reward and that the Christian Romans are the Chosen People and are clearly to be distinguished from all others is by no means new – a sixth-century writer expresses similar sentiments,[67] they are implicit in the views of Athanasius of Alexandria, as we have seen, and they can be found throughout the middle and later Byzantine periods.[68] And, as we have seen, the material rewards were also admitted (quite apart from the official recompense for military service, all the military treatises along with the historical narratives recognize the significance of booty for the ordinary soldier). True, the model for Leo's views may well be the Islam with which he and other Byzantines of the time were familiar. But this seems to have simply generated a slightly more nuanced version of already current Christian ideas, a product of a particular political and ideological moment in which the Roman empire was at last seeing the possibility of going over to the offensive and making good the losses – both territorial as well as political and ideological – of the preceding centuries.

By the tenth century, a distinct elite of magnate clans had come to dominate the military leadership and administration of the empire, expressed most clearly in the persons of those who led the armies which reconquered such large areas from Islam in the tenth century.[69] A warrior culture had evolved in the Anatolian context where this elite originated, not unlike that of the nobility of western Europe in its attitude towards warfare, at least superficially, and involving an ideology of personal honour, bravery and skill in fighting. The Christian warrior attitude of this culture is reflected in the preference among its members for the military saints as both images on their lead seals and as patrons.[70] And it is no accident that the very period when the idea that fighting the unbelievers should be rewarded more explicitly by the church makes an appearance was also the time of greatest imperial expansion and conquest or reconquest, and at the same time a period in which the magnate aristocracy of the provinces both led and set the tone for the armies of the state. The attempt of Nikephros II to redefine the morality of warfare represents an attempt to bring into the mainstream the ideology of the warrior and the frontier, and therefore of the magnate clans, as opposed to that of the metropolitan political elite and the church.

There is no doubt that the enthusiasm displayed by Nikephros II in particular for the war in the east had a powerful religious element. Traditionally, no difference was observed between dying in battle against the Christian Bulgars and the unbelieving Arabs. Phocas, and his immediate successor John I Tzimiskes, implied or suggested outright that there was indeed such a difference, and that the war was for the glory of the Christians, the rescue of the Holy Places and the destruction of Islam. This was proclaimed not only within the empire but formed part of the message communicated to Muslim rulers themselves.[71] Nikephros is reported in his letter to the Caliph al-Muti' to have declared that he would soon march on Baghdad, Jerusalem and Egypt, and that he would establish the throne of Christ in Mecca itself. John I Tzimiskes, in a letter to the Armenian king Ashot, stated that his desire "was to free the Holy Sepulchre from the outrages of Muslims".[72] In other words, a real "crusading" zeal was being promoted with the intention of transforming the Byzantine offensive into a holy war. But the effort made by Nikephros threatened the very Christian and typically Byzantine notion of philanthropy. For as noted already, it was that characteristic more than any other which encapsulated Byzantine diplomatic and strategic theory and practice.

What the attempt of Nikephros II does highlight is the difference between the official and theologically respectable views of various elements of what we might loosely call the "establishment" in both secular and religious terms, and those of the ordinary population of the empire, especially of the soldiers who did the fighting and the rural or urban populations who experienced warfare on a regular basis. And here we can find a rather different set of values in operation. Of course, all accepted the fundamental ethics of Christianity, and along with them the officially maintained political-ideological values of the Christian Roman empire. There was considerable room for variation between Constantinople and the provinces, and especially between those groups most directly involved with warfare and fighting the enemies of the empire, and the rest of society. The polarity between Constantinopolitan and provincial culture and attitudes has frequently been noted and analysed from a variety of standpoints, and need not detain us here.[73] But it is clear that there was indeed a gulf between the common sense of everyday life on the frontier or in the provincial armies and that of Constantinople and the metropolitan provinces. These differences are only rarely given expression in literary form, but when they are they are very clear.

The treatise on guerrilla strategy written for the general, later emperor, Nikephros Phocas in the 950s or 960s reflects a frontier society very different from that of the inner provinces of the empire. The strategy it describes is, however, no longer in use, since the Romans are now everywhere victorious. But, the writer states, it will be useful for future generations to have a record of the methods of the generals and soldiers who employed it, should it ever be needed again. The values in respect of the position of soldiers in society and the way they are treated by the tax-collectors, for example, make it very clear that warfare and soldiering occupied an esteemed position in the views of the writer, and that these views were widespread among provincial military officers and, presumably, soldiers. There is equally a much more obviously pragmatic approach to killing: in a difficult situation, writes the author of the treatise on skirmishing, "prisoners should either be killed or sent on ahead", sentiments which fit badly with notions of *philanthropia* and mercy.[74]

In the later eleventh century, the writer Kekaumenos (probably himself a military officer) compiled a book of advice addressed to his son, in which the life and values of a provincial soldier and magnate are described. Although by no means glorifying warfare, nor representing Byzantine warfare against enemies as in any way special, it is nevertheless very clear that the values – honour, integrity, justice – expected of a provincial noble and soldier are contrasted favourably with the (purportedly) dubious behaviour of city officials and bureaucrats, pen-pushers and sycophants at court: "don't wish to be a Constantinopolitan official, for you can't be a general and a clown at the same time" warns the writer.[75] His world is one in which right belief and actions guided by God, through prayer and the scriptures, predominate, but in which cunning and intelligence should be applied to extract every advantage from a situation in which one deals with enemies, actual or potential. This is also a world of frontier warfare, in which pitched battles may not be the norm, in which shadowing and ambushing the enemy are still recommended, and in which no shame is attached to avoiding battle if one is at a disadvantage.[76]

Most indicative of all is the epic *Digenis Akritas*, a border romance re-counting the life and deeds of a frontier lord and his retinue. It may first have been written down in the eleventh century, and reflects a timeless frontier world in which honour, shame, family and God are the dominant motifs. Single combat, heroic feats of arms, and the merciless slaughter of the dishonourable enemy are the key features (as well as the love story around which the tale, or tales, are built). Once again, God and the key values of Orthodoxy inform the moral universe of the Christian characters, but the leading Muslim protagonists also possess honour and bravery in equal measure, so that here we have an insight into a society which was accustomed to warfare and in which a somewhat different day-to-day code had evolved. The emperor and the court, indeed the whole apparatus of the East Roman state, are remote and figure barely at all. What counts are the martial achievements and the honour of the hero of the stories.[77]

All these sources reflect the main elements of "official" political ideology, of course; yet they all, in slightly variant ways, represent a more "grassroots" aspect of military or provincial life, which allows us to realize that there were – as we should, of course, expect – several different levels at which official ideas were interpreted and put into practice. This becomes clear through accounts in chronicles, saints' lives and other texts of the attitudes and responses of soldiers to various events at different times during the history of the empire. In 812/13 soldiers cried out at the tomb of the emperor Constantine V (741–75) for him to return to lead them to victory instead of the ruling emperors who had allowed the empire to be humiliated by the Bulgars and the Arabs.[78] Indeed, the reintroduction of an imperial policy of iconoclasm (image-breaking) was partly a response to this feeling in the army and in military circles.[79] Soldiers throughout the late Roman period took action on occasion – whether through mutinies, involvement in *coups d'état* or similar demonstrations against their generals or the central government because of defeats or slights against them.[80] And soldiers actively invoked the saints to help them with their illnesses or in their battles – the cult of military saints, such as George, Theodore the Recruit, Demetrios, Anastasios the Persian and Merkourios was a widespread and popular form of devotion among soldiers. Soldiers in the ninth century had images of the saints painted on their shields, while – as we have already noted – armies as well as individual emperors carried sacred images with them into battle. The eleventh-century chronicler Michael Psellos notes that the Roman emperors traditionally carried an image of the Virgin Mary with them on their campaigns, and the emperor Basil II held it on his arm when he went into battle against the rebel general Bardas Phocas. Warfare and fighting were quite comfortably housed in the ideological universe of Christian East Rome.[81]

Yet the differences between metropolitan and provincial culture should not be exaggerated. Both shared a common Christian and Hellenized tradition; both shared also similar structures of family relationships and the loyalties that accompanied them; and both shared, at base, similar notions about public and private expressions of honour and shame.[82] The court actively emphasized the divine support granted to imperial military undertakings. Both central and provincial forces were accompanied from the fourth century by crosses of varying patterns and sizes from simple wooden constructions to much larger and more elaborate bejewelled examples. That their religious and ideological significance was recognized is clear in the ninth century and after from the efforts made by Muslim forces to capture them and from the attempts made by the Byzantines to recover them, the latter an event greeted with great jubilation.[83] Equally important were other symbols of this support – as when, for example, the emperor Constantine VII sent holy water blessed by relics of the Passion to a campaign force which he was himself unable to accompany. And on leaving the city for campaign, the emperors prayed for the success of the expedition and for the safety of Constantinople, while in the event of a victorious outcome both church and people were actively engaged in the triumphal reception of the returning victors in which both public and private prayers played a significant role.[84]

It is indeed partly because of this set of fundamental common motifs that, in spite of its dynamism in a provincial setting, the "warrior" ideology (if we can, somewhat crudely, so describe it) was, in the context of the metropolitan society of the ruling elite fairly rapidly toned down and accommodated to the framework of Constantinopolitan administrative culture. To survive, it had to adopt metropolitan values in order to attain ideological legitimization and respect. Indeed, the population of Constantinople found the presence of large numbers of soldiers there during the reign of Nikephros II especially objectionable. But the result was, in the eleventh century and after, an interesting blend and merging of two potentially exclusive and possibly antagonistic cultural traditions. The ruling elite of the Comnene period could happily accommodate aspects of both, as a result of a blend of aristocratic clan alliances and theories of imperial political service which Alexios I achieved during his efforts to consolidate and to stabilize his rule. Their use of soldier saints on imperial coinage illustrates the point.[85]

Thus it is precisely because the Byzantines fought under the symbol of the Cross, and because they saw themselves as soldiers of Christ fighting to preserve God's kingdom on earth, that no theory or doctrine of "holy war" evolved. Warfare was almost by definition of a religious character, since the East Roman empire was the sole orthodox polity fighting to preserve and extend the Christian faith. Together with the doubts expressed by the Fathers of the Church in respect of killing and the unbroken cultural tradition which bound medieval East Rome to its late Roman and early Christian origins, it is not difficult to understand this. Indeed, the elements of discontinuity in the medieval west and in the nascent Islamic civilization in the east have been singled out as major factors which contributed in both cases to the evolution on the one hand of the notion of *jihād*, and on the other of a warrior caste, the theory of the "three orders" (or its practical realization in the period from the ninth to the twelfth centuries) and the notion of the Crusade.[86]

From the fifth century to the end of the empire, therefore, there is a mass of evidence both for the formal and official acceptance by both Church and court, as well as by the ordinary population, of the need to wage war, the fact of divine support for such warfare, and the need to maintain and to rely upon heavenly aid in waging war. And although the notion of "holy war" in the sense understood by the Crusaders or by non-Muslims as typical of Islam had thus a very brief life in the Byzantine world, this does not mean that the ways in which warfare on behalf of the Christian Roman state were understood did not experience a certain evolution. On the contrary, it is very clear that Byzantines were constantly aware of the need to justify their wars, and this need became the more pressing in a time of political and military expansionism such as the tenth century. Constantine V is reported to have characterized as "noble" his campaign into Bulgaria in 772/73 because no Roman soldiers died, and by the time of the compilation of the *Tactica* of Leo VI the notion that a war had to be justified in accordance with orthodoxy and the existence of the Roman state was clearly set out: as long as the defence of Roman interests, however broadly defined, was at stake, then warfare was acceptable and just. From this time on, the notion of the just war in defence of the God-granted mission and purpose of the East Roman emperors and the Chosen People was a standard aspect of imperial political propaganda, directed both externally to the empire's neighbours, whether hostile or not, and internally as an element in the practice of political-ideological legitimization of state, society and their institutional structures.[87] War with other orthodox Christians was, of course, to be avoided, yet it could also be justified if the one true empire, that of the Romans, were to be attacked by the misguided rulers of such lands, a position perfectly exemplified in the letters of the patriarch Nikolaos I in the early tenth century to the Bulgar tsar Symeon.[88]

Given that this was the situation, we may ask how these values actually affected Byzantine theories of warfare – strategy – and how they were realized in practice.

CHAPTER TWO

Warfare and the East Roman state: geography and strategy

The person who wants to wage war against an enemy must first make sure that his own lands are secure. By secure I mean not only the security of the army but of the cities and the entire country, so that the people who live there might suffer no harm at all from the enemy.[1]

Strategy and diplomacy: theories and practice

Strategy teaches us how to defend what is our own and to threaten what belongs to the enemy. The defensive is the means by which one acts to guard his own people and their property, the offensive is the means by which one retaliates against his opponents.[2]

Strategy, *strategia*, associated with or derived from *stratos*, army, and *strategos*, leader of an army, "general", means "the art of generalship". In contrast to the modern sense of the word – the art and technique of deploying all available resources to gain the objects of war, a meaning which developed only from the nineteenth century – strategy for East Roman and Byzantine generals and governments was not always easily distinguished from tactics, so that the medieval military treatises which provide us with so much of our information on military matters treat the two as part of a continuum, normally using the word strategy to refer to the structure and organization of warfare, and the art of planning and directing specific campaigns, bearing in mind geographical and climatic factors, communications and the dispositions and movements of the military forces available to the general. In the opening section of the *Tactica* of the emperor Leo VI, compiled in the first years of the tenth century, we read the following:

Tactics is the science of movements in warfare: there are two types of such movement – by land, and by sea. Tactics is the strategical art of formations, weaponry and military movements. Strategy is the discipline, which is to say the study and exercise, of the virtues of commanders together with strategems, or indeed the achievement of victories. The aim of tactics is to defeat the enemy by all possible plans and actions.[3]

Late Roman and Byzantine military writers, particularly as expressed in the texts of the fifth, sixth and tenth centuries, thus had a well-developed set of theories and practical guidance which could be applied to generalship in war, intimately coupled with the notion that it was also only with divine support and approval that battles could be won.[4] Although we shall discuss in detail the evolution and structure of Byzantine strategic dispositions in a later chapter, a word is in order at this stage to set the developments which follow in context.

For while there was no consistent concept of "strategy" in the wider sense, this does not mean that there was an absence of planning and of thinking in broader strategic terms. The major elements of the imperial political ideology – in particular defence of the Christian Roman *oikoumene* and the recovery of formerly imperial lands – assumed implicitly a concept of a world-order which it was the destiny of the Roman empire to realize. Such general expressions of political-ideological intent were an integral part of any emperor's self-presentation and of the duties attendant upon the imperial position itself, and they clearly had an effect upon the disposition of imperial forces. Similar assumptions were embodied in the tradition of apocalyptic writings which, although quite unconnected with that of military handbooks and "strategy", nevertheless purported to foretell the future and assumed that, with divine assistance and guidance and led by pious rulers, the Christian Roman empire would eventually triumph over its adversaries and, in particular, Islam.

That long-term military planning, and military dispositions in general, were ever organized with any of these grander political intentions in mind must be doubted, however. Even Justinian's efforts at reconquest were based on short-term reactions to changes in the immediate political environment rather than a serious attempt at strategic planning over the long term, although there can be no doubt that they were informed by some of the elements of imperial ideology noted above. The same considerations are valid for other rulers: no longer term fiscal or strategic policy was evolved which could actually lead, in a consistent and logistically rational way, to the implementation, still less the realization of, the policy of reconquest. There was, nevertheless, awareness of the relationship between the allocation and redistribution of resources – in manpower, supplies, equipment, livestock and so forth – and the ability of the empire to ward off hostile military action or to strike back at its enemies. The treatises make it quite apparent that the Byzantines recognized the imbalance in resources between themselves and their enemies. Byzantine military handbooks, both those which represent the archaising and learned tradition of the Roman and classical past as well as those which reflect contemporary, up-to-date conditions and views, invariably touch upon this issue. Generals are exhorted not to give battle in unfavourable conditions because this might lead to waste of life and resources; indeed the dominant motif in these works is that it was the Byzantines who were compelled to manoeuvre, to use delaying tactics, to employ ambushes and other strategems to even the odds stacked against them, but that it was quite clearly a main war aim to win without having to fight a decisive battle: in other words, actual fighting, and consequent loss of life, was, in theory as well as often in practice (as we will see), to be avoided wherever possible. Victory could be achieved through a combination of delaying tactics, intelligent exploitation of enemy weaknesses, the landscape, seasonal factors and diplomacy.[5]

This awareness was expressed very clearly not only in the military treatises, but also in the occasional remarks of historians and other commentators on the relationship between Byzantium and its neighbours. Byzantine rulers and their generals usually preferred to use craft, intelligence, wiles, bribery, ideological blackmail and a range of other means rather than commit themselves to warlike confrontations. Where warfare was unavoidable, the predominant tendency was for armies to be instructed to proceed with the utmost caution. This passage from the sixth-century *Strategikon* admirably sums up these attitudes:

> Wild animals are taken by scouting, by nets, by laying in wait, by stalking, by circling around, and by other such strategems rather than by sheer force. In waging war we should proceed in the same way, whether the enemy be many or few. To try simply to overpower the enemy in the open, hand to hand and face to face, even though you might appear to win, is an enterprise which is very risky, and can result in serious harm. Apart from extreme emergency, it is ridiculous to try to gain a victory which is so costly and brings only empty glory.[6]

An obvious reason for this reluctance to fight wars can be found in the strategic-geographical position of the state and in its economic situation. Wars were costly, and for a state whose basic income derived from agricultural production, and which remained relatively stable as well as being vulnerable to both natural and man-made disasters, they were to be avoided if at all possible.[7] This was certainly recognized by the Romans and Byzantines: in the mid-sixth century an anonymous writer remarks that "The financial system . . . is principally concerned with paying the soldiers. Each year most of the public revenues are spent for this purpose."[8] For the fact that the empire was strategically surrounded had major implications for the state's fiscal system, the history of which is also a history of crisis management on a grand scale. The same writer comments:

when we are in absolutely no condition to continue fighting, we then choose to make peace, even though it may cause us some disadvantage. When faced with two evils, the lesser is to be chosen. Negotiating for peace may be chosen before other means, since it might very well offer the best prospect for protecting our own interests.[9]

This neatly sums up one aspect of the relationship between warfare and diplomatic activity, and was a leitmotif of the diplomatic and strategic policy of Byzantine rulers and ruling elites.[10]

Another, closely related, factor in imperial strategic thinking was manpower: from a Byzantine perspective, they were always outnumbered, and strategy as well as diplomacy needed to take this factor into account in dealing with enemies. One way of evening the balance was to reduce enemy numbers: delay the enemy forces until they could no longer stay in the field, destroying or removing any possible sources of provisions and supplies, for example, misleading them with false information about Byzantine intentions – these are all methods which the military treatises recommend. Avoiding battle, which was a keystone of Byzantine strategy, would also increase the possibility that the enemy host might be struck by illness, run out of water and supplies, and so forth.[11]

But quite apart from these material considerations, and the Christian tradition and attitude to war, Byzantine strategic thinking was deeply influenced by its cultural antecedents. The concern to minimize loss of life, to act as cautiously as possible when on campaign, to avoid pitched battles wherever possible, and to employ cunning, intelligence and trickery to outwit and outmanoeuvre the enemy, both in actual military conflicts and in diplomatic terms, this was part and parcel of a long established tradition going back to the early imperial period and beyond. The fundamental principles embodied in the works of several Greek writers of tactical and strategic manuals – Aeneas Tacticus, Onosander, Arrian and Aelian, for example, who wrote in the first and second centuries AD (but who were, in their turn, following an even older Hellenistic tradition) – reappear in only slightly altered form in the late Roman and Byzantine treatises. Byzantine generals and military thinkers derived not only the fundamentals of disciplined military-tactical organization from such writings, therefore – and the importance of the older tacticians in this respect cannot be overemphasized – but a whole tradition of how best to conduct war. The emphasis in this pre-Christian Greco-Roman tradition was, however, no different from that of the Christian East Roman world in its somewhat different strategic context, and the principles of this tradition were entirely compatible with those of a Christian culture. Key precepts, such as avoidance of battle, passive resistance to, complemented by harassment of, the enemy, leading the enemy to overextend his lines of communication, attrition of enemy forces by scorched earth tactics, depriving his forces and animals of water and forage, using deserters (without their knowledge) and spies to plant false rumours, both in the enemy camp and among one's own troops (where enemy spies, or traitors, might be active), these appear regularly in the Hellenistic and Roman treatises and are integral to the later Byzantine tracts.[12]

The description of such methods in military treatises, and their application in actual practice, should not be seen, in consequence, as somehow the reflection of a peculiarly Byzantine or East Roman approach (which has generally been the case). On the contrary, they were an essential part of the classical Roman military theoretical tradition, a tradition which had as much relevance in the medieval East Roman context, at the level of strategic thinking, as it had possessed at the time of its composition.

All these factors were fundamental features affecting Byzantine strategic thinking in both the short and the long term, of which both military writers and governments were clearly aware, and which directly affected the possibilities for action at the level of broad strategy as well as its more localized application. For the Roman empire in the East always had to face enemies on at least two fronts and occasionally, if we include the "western" theatre – Italy – three. From the middle of the seventh century, in addition, the formerly safe East Mediterranean became a field of conflict between Byzantine and Arab fleets – in effect, a fourth front – so that the empire again had to devote considerable resources to coastal defences and the maintenance of fleets.[13] By the same token, the consequent economic dislocation and reduction of resources further affected the ability of the government to do more than react to the short-term situation. The success of the Bulgars in establishing themselves in the Balkans can be to a large degree attributed to this factor: the empire had only limited resources with which to oppose them, and the weight of those resources was not in the Balkans. On the contrary, they were almost permanently tied up in the east during the later seventh and first half of the eighth century. It is noticeable that, when an emperor was able to secure the eastern front, as in the case of Constantine V, John I Tzimiskes and Basil II, they turned their attention to the Balkans – just as Justinian I had been compelled to bargain for peace on the eastern front when contemplating aggressive military undertakings elsewhere. But it was rarely the case that the East remained quiet for long, and only in the later tenth and early eleventh centuries that conditions actually permitted a serious investment of resources sufficient to overwhelm the Bulgars.

In the light of this strategic situation, defence was the primary concern of Byzantine rulers and generals. Byzantine military dispositions were organized and administered upon a consistent and logistically well-considered basis, and their main purpose was to secure the survival of the empire by deploying the limited resources available to the best effect. That they were, necessarily, defensive in orientation is a point noted quite clearly by the mid-tenth-century visitor from Italy, the ambassador Liudprand of Cremona, with regard to the precautions taken to secure Constantinople at night in case of an unexpected enemy attack.[14] The emphasis placed by Byzantine writers and governments on effective and intelligent diplomacy is not just a question of cultural preference informed by a Christian distaste for the shedding of blood: to the contrary, the continued existence of the state depended upon the deployment of a sophisticated diplomatic arsenal. The whole history of Byzantine foreign relations reflects this, as well as in the few explicit statements of political theory which survive, most obviously in the tenth-century *De administrando imperio* ("On governing the empire"), as well as in the theory and practice of Byzantine diplomacy. As the emperor Constantine VII states in the introduction to this treatise, a ruler must study what is known of the nearer and more distant peoples around the Roman state, so that he can understand "the difference between each of these nations, and how either to treat with and conciliate them, or to make war upon and oppose". Diplomacy had its military edge, of course: good relations with the various peoples of the steppe were essential to Byzantine interests in the Balkans and Caucasus, because a weapon might thereby be created which could be turned on the enemies of the empire – such as the Bulgars, for example – when necessary, as frequently counselled in the *De administrando imperio*.[15] Such contacts were also an essential source of information, of course, and much effort was expended – through diplomatic contacts and embassies, as well as through spies, the use of merchants and other travellers including churchmen – in gathering information which might be relevant to the empire's defence. Military treatises devote considerable attention to information-gathering, which became even more important from the later seventh century when, following 50 years of warfare, both sides began in Asia Minor to establish a sort of "no man's land", across which information travelled only with difficulty through the usual channels of social and commercial intercourse.[16]

Being at war was, in consequence, rarely the result of a planned choice made by emperors or their advisers, for the empire was perpetually threatened from one quarter or another and was thus in a constant state of military preparedness. In such conditions, it is clear that the potential for the reconquest and restoration of lost territories was severely limited. While recovery of former territories was permanently on the political-ideological agenda, efforts actually to implement it always reflected an *ad hoc* reaction to a usually unforeseen advantage gained through victories in battle and the exploitation of favourable circumstances. True, Justinian clearly had a notion of a "grand strategy" in the sense of the realization of a political-ideological programme to restore the Roman empire, expressed both through the wars he fought and in statements of ideological intent as in the proemium to the *Codex Iustinianus*. Yet the minimalist resources he devoted to the realization of his project illustrates the problem. Occasionally, it is clear that the particular circumstances of a war had – or at least, evolved – the aim of destroying the enemy completely: Heraclius' war against the Persians would appear to be such an example, if one reads the literary sources, especially the panegyrical poems of Heraclius' court poet George of Pisidia. Yet having utterly defeated it militarily, it was Heraclius who, thinking pragmatically, helped to stabilize the Persian kingdom after its defeat, merely restoring older frontiers favourable to the Romans and attempting to ensure its status thereafter as a client of Constantinople. There is no reason to think that Heraclius would have evolved such an all-out strategy of annihilation at the military level had he been left any alternative. But the Persian occupation of the eastern provinces and the two major attacks on Constantinople made the traditional cross-frontier counterstroke impossible. In this respect, it is a reasonable conclusion that Heraclius was in fact compelled by strategic circumstances to adopt a strategy of annihilation as the only means to "restore" the previous arrangement. Menander the Guardsman reports Justin II to have desired the destruction of the Persian kingdom altogether, but notes that contemporaries clearly found this entirely unrealistic.[17]

Whether Constantine V's policy of attrition against the Bulgar power in the east Balkan region had the longer-term aim of eradicating the Bulgar khanate and re-establishing imperial power up to the Danube is impossible to say. It could, of course, be argued that imperial policy in respect of Bulgaria always reflected imperial territorial claims in the Balkans and traditions about the "shameful" treaty that Constantine IV had been compelled to make with the Bulgar khan Asparuch (see Chapter 3). But while this may have been an ever-present element in imperial awareness, the response of a succession of emperors from Constantine V onward suggests that warfare on this front was never more than a holding action in which imperial attacks, far from representing the opening of a serious war of reconquest, were merely the Roman side of the continuous war of attrition, broken only by occasional periods of peace. During the later ninth century, indeed, there is every reason to believe that the imperial government was thoroughly resigned to the existence of the Bulgar state, and the effort to convert the khan and his court was as much a response to the need to find alternative ways of taming a potentially dangerous neighbour as it was to the growing influence of the papacy in the area. The conquest of Bulgaria in the later tenth century was, in this light, the result of an unexpectedly favourable strategic situation: having discovered the advantage he had inherited from the wars fought by his predecessor John I Tzimiskes, Basil's destruction of Bulgaria and recovery of the Balkan provinces was very clearly the intelligent reaction to a situation which had only recently developed and which he was compelled to confront on what was at first quite clearly a purely defensive basis.[18]

The imperial defeat of the Russians under Svyatoslav in the 970s on the Danube, and of Bulgaria between c. 991 and 1018 was possible chiefly because the emperors could divert resources from the eastern to the northern front. It was this which made it possible for the emperor Maurice in the 590s, and after securing the eastern frontier, to mount a series of successful campaigns in the Balkans to subordinate Slav immigrants and drive out the Avars. It was precisely the same transfer of resources and logistical support from east to west which enabled Basil II to concentrate his efforts on the Balkans (although he had at times to devote extraordinary energy to dealing with sudden crises in the east). And in the crisis of the mid-630s and the sweeping and entirely unexpected successes of the Arabs, the armies of the Balkans were removed to the east to help the hard-pressed armies in Palestine, Syria and Egypt, leaving the Balkans, as far as we can tell, more or less denuded of troops. Indeed, a tenth-century account of a mid-ninth-century campaign in the east makes it quite clear that major offensives could only be undertaken when troops on one front could be moved to support those on the other.[19]

In the east, both Nikephros II Phocas and John I Tzimiskes announced, at various stages, plans for the subjection of the Muslims, and in particular the recovery of the holy places in Palestine, although there is no reliable evidence that these were successful. But the sentiments accorded with the religious enthusiasm for war against the infidel with which Nikephros II in particular was associated.[20]

It is nevertheless clear from the contemporary account of Leo the Deacon, prone to glorify the exploits of these emperors as he was, that even the most penetrating and damaging raids into Syria, Palestine and Jazīra (Mesopotamia) remained raids, and that the extension of their lines of communication beyond a certain point made further advances or the attempt to maintain occupying forces deep within hostile territory for any length of time extremely dangerous. The nearer regions could indeed be garrisoned and permanently absorbed – the districts around and to the south of Antioch provide a good example, regions which could be supplied by sea, the borders of which were delineated by the Orontes river and partly covered by the natural barrier of the Amanus range. Yet Basil II preferred to maintain Aleppo and similar centres in Syria as client, or at least neutral, emirates, chiefly because the occupation of the north Syrian coastline beyond the region of Antioch was directly exposed to Fatimid sea-power. The same can be said of his refusal to exploit the opportunities presented in Jazīra in the 980s and 990s, where he permitted the fragmented and squabbling local tribes around Mosul, Amida and Edessa to maintain a precarious independence, hence serving to a degree as a screen before the Byzantine territories proper.[21] The resources necessary to extend permanently beyond north Syria were simply not available, however much the propaganda of the military magnate elite of Asia Minor, as personified by John Tzimiskes and Nikephros Phocas, hoped for a process of continued expansion leading to the recovery of the lost provinces of the east and the incorporation of all the Christian populations still under Islam into a revived Orthodox empire.[22] And in the case of both emperors, committed warfare on one front was contingent upon a peaceful situation on the others. Defensive potential was the key, and even offensive wars were fought from a defensive standpoint: the acquisition of new territory served to create a deeper barrier zone to protect the heartlands of the empire.[23] The creation of the new commands, grouped into ducates, which covered the eastern and northern frontiers from the 960s and 970s on (see Chapter 3 below) illustrates the existence of a coherent overall and quite pragmatic (and practical) strategy in this respect, and shows that Byzantine governments certainly possessed the geographical and strategic understanding to defend what had been recovered and to plan further expansion.

Strategy was thus determined by the interplay between resources and political beliefs, tempered by ideological pragmatism: most of the warfare we will consider was fought not on the basis of delivering a knock-out blow to the enemy but on that of attempting to reach or maintain a state of parity or equilibrium though attrition, raid and counter-raid, and destruction of the enemy's short-term potential.[24] Members of the government and imperial court may have shared common ideals in respect of their relations with the outside world, but the strategic dispositions of the armies of the later Roman and Byzantine empire were not necessarily arranged with these concerns as a priority.

The loss of prestige which successful enemy inroads and conquests generated was an important consideration in the formation of the government's – the emperor's – response. Warfare was thus not necessarily conducted with a purely material advantage in mind, since ideological superiority played an important role in Byzantine notions of their own identity and role in the order of things; nor was it conducted with any longer-term strategic objective in mind. Any damage to the enemy was a good thing, but some ways of hitting the enemy also carried an ideological value: Heraclius' destruction of the Zoroastrian temples, the sack by Nikephros I of the Bulgar khan's capital at Pliska, Theophilos' attack on Melitene and Sozopetra in 837, the grandiose claims of Nikephros Phocas and John Tzimiskes about their impending recovery of the Christian Holy Places or destruction of Islamic cult centres, all carried a particular nuance for contemporaries (so that the disasters which befell the second and third of these thereafter appeared the more catastrophic in terms of divine providence). In turn, some theatres were ideologically more important than others. Fighting the barbarians in the Balkans and north of the Danube was regarded as much less prestigious and glorious than combating the religious foe, the Muslims, in the east: as the eleventh-century intellectual and courtier Michael Psellos remarks: "There seemed nothing grand [in fighting] the barbarians in the West . . . , but were he [the emperor Romanos III] to turn to those living in the East, he thought that he could perform nobly . . ."[25]

Indeed, there is little evidence to support the view that warfare was conducted specifically to gain resources which could then be deployed in a coherent way to further a given strategy, except in the sense that more territory and the wealth that usually accompanied it were desirable in themselves. For the most part, warfare was conducted on the basis of inflicting maximum damage to the enemy's economy and material infrastructure – enslavement or killing of populations, destruction of fortifications and urban installations, devastation of the countryside. By the same token, measures to protect one's own side had to be taken, and the Byzantines had developed both aspects of such warfare to a fine art by the middle of the tenth century, as we shall see. Both in the war against the Arabs in the east from the seventh to the tenth centuries, and against Slavs and Bulgars in the west, Byzantine warfare can be described under Delbrück's rubric of *Ermattungskrieg*, war of attrition. Only in the case of the accelerated eastward expansion under Nikephros Phocas and John Tzimiskes, and in the slightly later but closely related conquest of Bulgaria under Basil II, is it possible to suggest that there was an ulterior motive involved: in the first case, through an aggressive imperialism towards the minor Muslim powers in Syria and Jazīra, the extension and consolidation of the empire's territorial strength in the area (as well as the extension of the power of the Anatolian magnate clans); in the second case, and as a reaction to the first development, the creation of a new resource-base for the emperors and Constantinopolitan government independent of the power and influence of these magnates, but in the context of an equally practical decision to eradicate the threat from an independent Bulgaria and reassert imperial dominance throughout the Balkan regions. Both facets of these processes mirror very particular structural tensions within Byzantine state and society, and at the same time they also demonstrate particularly clearly the extent to which the foreign policies and military strategy of a state can reflect power relations within the society as a whole.

A Byzantine grand strategy?

Byzantine rulers and generals clearly could pursue coherent and consistent strategic plans where the resources and the political will were present: the progress of the late tenth-century conquests and the coherence of the strategic arrangements which followed provide adequate illustration of this point.

But did Byzantine governments pursue a "grand strategy"? Insofar as the defence of its borders and the maintenance of its territorial integrity were guarantees of the empire's survival, to which end its wide-ranging international diplomacy, the disposition of its armies and the administration of its logistical and fiscal system were consistently directed, the answer could be affirmative. But this is to tell us very little, and "grand strategy" implies a good deal more than this, particularly in respect of long-term political-military aims and methods which, while certainly implicit in imperial ideology, were only occasionally voiced in terms of specific projects, as we have seen. The dominant element in Byzantine military thinking throughout the long history of the empire was defensive, and necessarily so in view of its strategic situation. Different means were employed in different theatres to achieve the same ends, as we shall also see. Byzantium survived as long as it did because it was able to defend itself and intelligently exploit natural frontiers or boundaries in the crisis years of the seventh and eighth centuries and diplomatic and political relationships thereafter. Whatever the specific details of the process of its political-historical withering away after 1204, the gradual demise of the Byzantine empire went hand in hand with its declining ability to muster the resources necessary to maintain itself against powers which, either cumulatively or individually, far surpassed it in these respects. Strategy was thus a matter of pragmatic reaction to events in the world around the empire, only loosely informed by the political-ideological imperatives of the Christian Roman empire as expressed by the emperor Justinian in the sixth century, and repeated by later rulers throughout the following centuries. The political and strategic conditions of existence of the East Roman or Byzantine state rendered "grand strategy" in the narrower sense irrelevant.

In spite of the common elements which can be traced in Byzantine attitudes towards warfare throughout the period, the focus of the imperial government, and of society at large, shifted from time to time according to the dominant trends in the situation of the empire with regard to its enemies and neighbours. Thus in the tenth century, as noted a period of great military success, territorial expansion and reassertiveness on the international political scene, warfare and fighting for the faith evolved new facets, or at least brought to the fore elements of Byzantine political ideology which had not hitherto been greatly stressed (except during the wars of Heraclius with the Persians), but which laid emphasis on conquest, the subordination of the enemy to Byzantine (i.e. God's) rule or hegemony and a relatively hard-line attitude towards foreign relations. When Bulgarian envoys arrived at the court of Nikephros II in 965/6, for example, to request the usual annual tribute (paid since 927 from the imperial point of view as part of a marriage agreement – the tsar Peter married the emperor Romanos I's grand-daughter Maria – but seen by the Bulgars in a somewhat different light), the emperor refused, made a brief warning expedition to the Bulgarian border and called in the empire's northern allies, the Kiev Rus' under their leader Svyatoslav.[26]

This changed during the eleventh century, when the confidence and wealth, international respect and military pre-eminence generated by the wars of the later tenth century were taken for granted. Peace – established by the success of arms – appeared to be secure, and thus the need for large and expensive armies, it was argued by some, was diminished. In terms of imperial ideology, this was a welcome state of affairs, for the emperor's epithet as *eirenopoios*, "peacemaker", reflected important Byzantine values and stressed the positive, philanthropic concerns which the Christian Roman emperors should seek to implement in their governance of the Chosen people. "Many years to the peace-making emperors", and ". . . peace has taken hold . . . Rejoice, . . . army of the Romans!" – these were entirely standard acclamations on formal ceremonial occasions at Constantinople in the tenth century and well beforehand. The Byzantine preference for peace was to be presented to foreigners, particularly those who could be looked down upon as barbarians, as a mark of their strength of purpose and of divine support rather than as weakness: this was certainly the way in which Byzantines presented these values to themselves, as Anna Comnena stresses in portraying her father, the emperor Alexios I: ". . . Alexius . . . cultivated peace to an unusual degree; its presence was always and by every means cherished and its absence worried him . . . By nature, then, he was a man of peace, but when circumstances forced him he would become most warlike." Such sentiments occur time and again in rhetorical texts, of course, but they are constant elements in historians' accounts of the reigns and characters of various emperors.[27]

In fact, the arguments for reductions in military expenditure were also put forward in the context of dissension and factionalism within the political elite of the empire, with contemporaries crudely, but not entirely inaccurately, describing the struggle in terms of the opposition between a "military" and a "civil" (i.e. Constantinopolitan and bureaucratic) faction. One of the results was the demobilization of numbers of frontier troops in the east, the commutation of military service in other provinces and on the frontier for cash taxes (which were more easily controlled and redistributed according to the wishes of the governing circle at court), and the alienation of the "military" element of the social and political elite from the imperial government. Although the government realized that an alternative to a purely military strategy was necessary and appears to have tried to disarm potential threats along the Danube frontier through economic means, the result was the inability to respond adequately to new and hitherto underestimated or unsuspected external enemies (in the first case the Pechenegs in the Balkans, in the second the Seljuk Turks in Asia Minor) and the collapse of the whole system in the last quarter of the eleventh century in civil strife and external invasion.

What appears, therefore, as the complacency and arrogance supposedly characteristic of the policy of emperors during the middle years of the eleventh century was in fact merely the reflection of a different aspect of imperial ideology. Peace – a fundamental aim of imperial foreign policy, as we have seen – had been achieved, and the Roman empire could glory in that achievement. Its other aspect was, of course, the aggressive confidence which typified attitudes in the second half of the tenth century. Both were replaced during the twelfth century and after by attitudes closer to those of the period from the seventh to early tenth centuries: warfare was still something which, when successful, could bring glory to the name of the Romans, who were still the Chosen People fighting God's cause on earth. But pragmatic concerns increasingly dominated. Grand schemes – although revived during the reign of Manuel I (1143–80) in particular – played a less important role and a more fatalistic realism prevailed. Indeed, with the visible territorial reduction of the empire and the corresponding decline in resources and political influence which was perceptible to all during the last two centuries of the empire's existence, recourse to the notion that barbarian and infidel success was God's punishment for the sins of the Chosen People became ever more frequent, and the notion that the empire would one day be overwhelmed – hitherto almost unthinkable – became commonplace. Victories might still be won, but they, too, were due to God's goodwill. The early fourteenth-century chronicler Pachymeres attributes a speech to the emperor Michael VIII, given before the people of Constantinople shortly after its recovery from the Latins in 1261. It contains all the classic *topoi* of the imperial ideology, with warfare serving both as a chastisement from God and Roman victory as a reward for righteousness.

God had "made use of the Italians"; the recovery of the City is due to God's divine support; its retention is dependent upon the orthodoxy and piety of the Romans; and further victories will be forthcoming as God avenges the harm done to the Romans, crushing the pride of their enemies, just as in the Old Testament God avenges the injury done to the Israelites, His Chosen People.[28]

In practical terms, leading statesmen and emperors in the late Byzantine world recognized that they no longer possessed the resources to achieve a reassertion of Christian Roman rule in either the Balkans or – and more especially – Anatolia; and they were compelled seriously to consider ecclesiastical and theological compromise in order to attract western support: as Theodore Metochites put it at the Council of Florence in 1275, in order to promote the "extermination" of the infidel and the victory of the true faith.[29] These efforts at compromise foundered on the rocks of both western inability to compromise and Byzantine popular rejection of "Latin" heresy. As offensive warfare became increasingly impractical for lack of resources, and as the empire became the victim of the powers arrayed along its fragmented frontiers, so diplomatic means came to play an even greater role, and the gap between the ideological theory of the East Roman state and its God-protected empire, and the realities of an ever-shrinking territorial base forced more frequent compromises.[30] This situation encouraged a retreat into alternative theories of the resolution to the problem of the future of God's kingdom on earth, permitting eventually the compromise between the Orthodox Church within the Ottoman empire and the Sultans. Meanwhile, the fatalism with which the empire struggled through its last two centuries – riven by civil strife and economic dislocation – was only encouraged by Byzantine interpretations of the duration of the seven ages of the world. For according to these beliefs, the Christian Roman empire was the last empire before the rule of Antichrist and the Second Coming. More pertinently, several of these computations suggested that the seventh age would end in the fourteenth or fifteenth century. For many Byzantines, the fate of the empire was already sealed, and efforts to alter this foreordained pattern were pointless.[31]

Physical context

The prerequisites for any discussion of Byzantine society and warfare are twofold: a knowledge of the geopolitical context of the empire and the factors which both constrained and promoted warmaking on the one hand, and a knowledge of the institutional and logistical arrangements, and the nature of the resources available to its rulers, on the other. Byzantine rulers were themselves enjoined to familiarize themselves with the capacity and condition of their provinces, for without such knowledge they would be unable to assess the potential of the empire they ruled to defend itself and to resist foreign invasion:

. . . go out into the countries which are in your obedience and among
your provinces . . . you will know the capacity of each province and
fortress and country; you will know how each is situated, what injuries
it suffers, and what benefits it receives . . .[32]

For most of the period during which the Byzantine empire was in existence its territories were restricted to the Balkans and Asia Minor, including
the Aegean islands and Crete and Cyprus. The exceptions after the early
eighth century were vestigial imperial possessions in northern and southern
Italy, a tenuous presence in the Balearics and Sardinia during the eighth century and, briefly during the tenth and eleventh centuries, parts of northern
and western Syria and the Lebanon region. Before the Islamic conquests, the
empire had been considerably greater in extent: Italy, southeastern Spain, the
North African coastal plain and its extensions inland east of modern Algeciras
as far as Egypt (recovered from the Ostrogoths, the Visigoths and the Vandals
respectively during the reign of the emperor Justinian I (527–65)), Egypt,
Syria, Palestine and Transjordan (the Roman province of Arabia), and western
and northwestern Iraq. The losses in respect of tax-income and manpower
incurred during the seventh century were among the key factors leading to
the radical transformation of late Roman institutions; the remaining territories
and their potential were the prime elements in determining the logistical and
strategic possibilities henceforth available to Byzantine rulers. The accompanying maps (IA/B, II) illustrate the extent of the changes.

The regions which remained in imperial hands were among the least
wealthy of its former provinces, among which Egypt had contributed as the
most productive, the main source of grain for Constantinople and a major
source of the state's tax income. From figures given by a range of late Roman
sources for the eastern half of the empire (thus excluding Italy and Africa,
which anyway contributed only one eighth or so of the total),[33] it has been
calculated that Egypt contributed something like one-third of the state income
(both gold and grain) derived from the prefectures of Oriens and Illyricum
together; that the dioceses of Asiana, Pontica, Macedonia and Oriens together
contributed about four-fifths of the gold revenue, with Pontica and Oriens
(which included the frontier regions and their hinterlands) providing a further
proportion – over 50 per cent – of the grain levied for the army.[34] Comparing
these figures with more detailed budgetary details from the sixteenth-century
Ottoman records, it can be suggested that the income of the Balkan region up
to the Danube and that of Ottoman Anatolia were very approximately equal.[35]
While there are some disparities in coverage between these regions in their late
Roman and Ottoman forms, this gives a crude idea of the relative economic
value of the two regions. In the late Roman period, however, the bulk of the
state's income outside of Egypt had been derived from the rich provinces of
Syria, Mesopotamia, Euphratensis, Osrhoene, Phoenicia, Palestine and Cilicia,
all lost after the 640s and only partially, in their northern perimeter, recovered
in the tenth century. With the loss of Egypt and these eastern provinces,

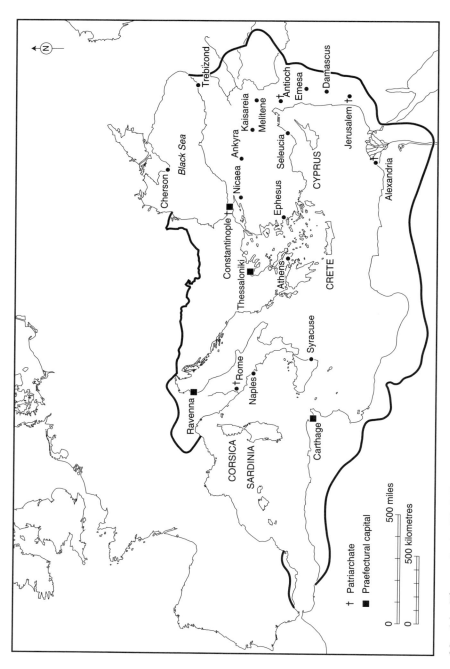

Map 1A   The empire in AD 565: approximate extent

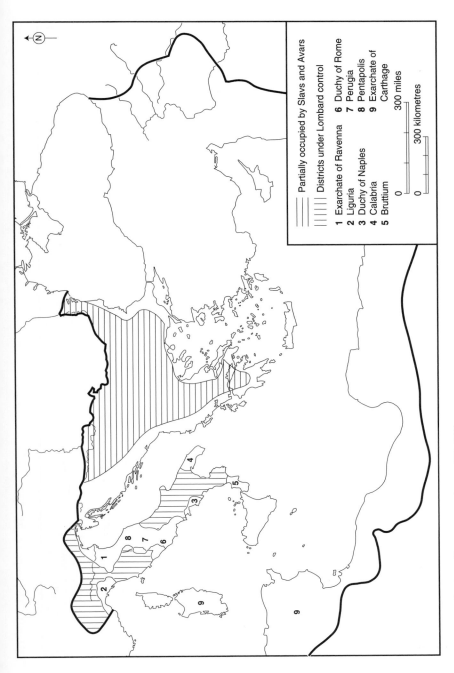

Map IB The East Roman empire *c.* AD 600

Partially occupied by Slavs and Avars

Districts under Lombard control

1 Exarchate of Ravenna
2 Liguria
3 Duchy of Naples
4 Calabria
5 Bruttium
6 Duchy of Rome
7 Perugia
8 Pentapolis
9 Exarchate of Carthage

300 miles

300 kilometres

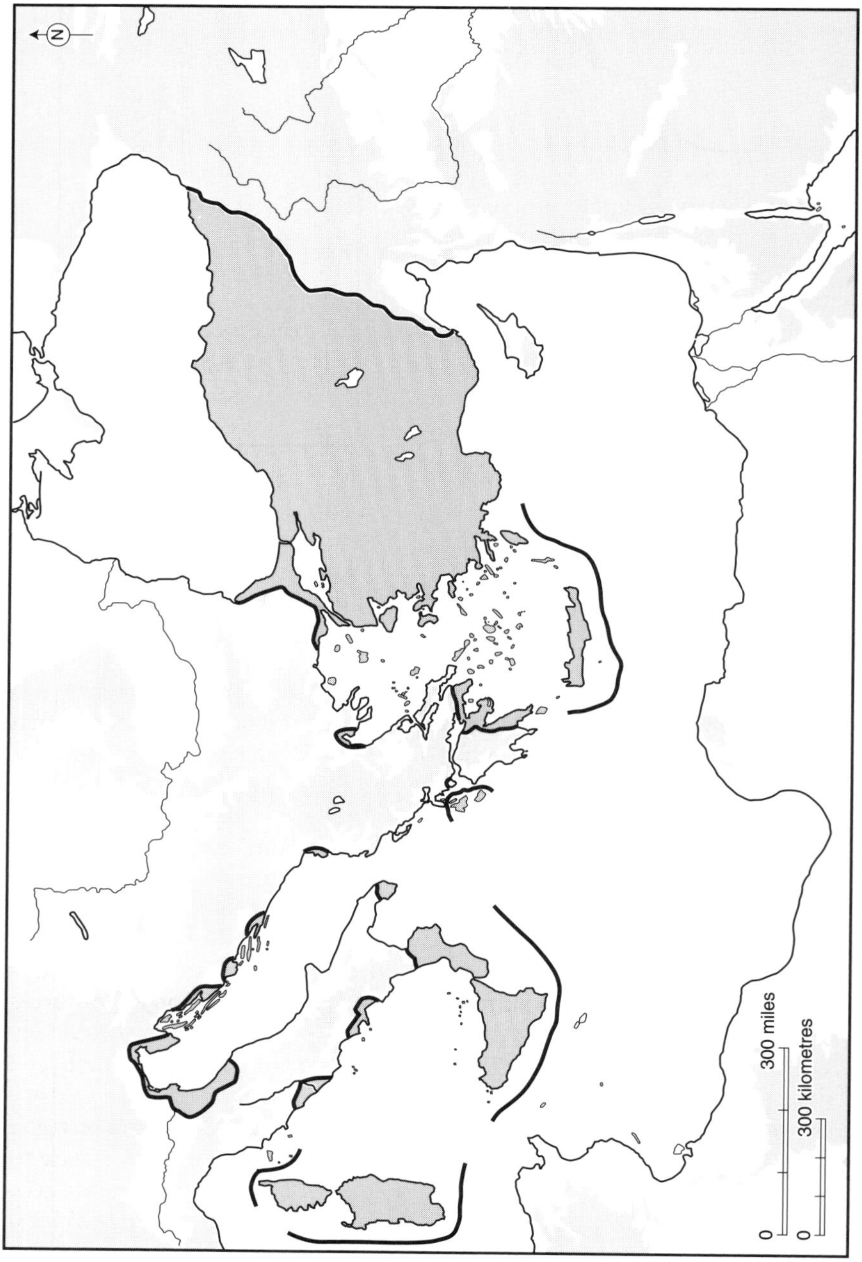

Map II The empire *c.* AD 700

300 miles

300 kilometres

0

0

therefore, and with effective control over all but the coastal periphery of much of the southern Balkans lost during the later sixth and first half of the seventh centuries, the overall income of the state collapsed to a fraction of the sixth-century figure: one figure plausibly suggested is that it was reduced to a quarter.[36]

Communications: the strategic infrastructure

> When he was intending to go on an expedition . . . [the emperor found out] how long the route was . . . and of what sort; and whether one road or many led to the objective, and of what sort; and whether the regions along the route were waterless or not. And then he enquired as to which road was narrow, precipitous and dangerous, and which the broad and traversible; also whether there was any great river along the way which could not be crossed.[37]

One of the recognized achievements of the Roman armies during the first century BC and up to the late second century AD was the construction of a network of major arterial roads suitable for the rapid movement of men and materials from the inner provinces to the frontiers, and connecting these provinces "laterally", as it were, to one another and to major political centres. It was in large part this system of roads which made the Roman army so efficient in its response to external threat and in its use of resources. During the later third century this system was further expanded in certain frontier districts, linking military bases and forts to their sources of supply, for example, and facilitating the movement of small and larger bodies of troops to meet external threats. The network associated with the *strata Diocletiana* in Arabia, for example, has received a great deal of attention from historians.

The passage quoted above, from a tenth-century account of imperial expeditions (actually drawing largely on material from the time of Basil I (867–86)), nicely sums up the dramatic change that occurred in these arrangements over the period from the later fourth to seventh centuries. For there set in a gradual decline in the standard of many – if not most – major public roads. The reasons for this remain unclear: in terms of maintenance and up-keep, it seems in part to reflect a shift in priorities in the allocation of resources and an unwillingness on the part of provincial cities to devote the necessary resources. Already in the *Codex Theodosianus*, laws of the later fourth and early fifth centuries regret the poor state of many roads.[38] A fifth-century historian notes that the western sections of the Via Egnatia – the major route westwards from Constantinople to the Adriatic coast – was in such a state of disrepair that travellers could barely pass along it, while in the last years of the sixth century the general Comentiolus supposedly had to rely on an aged local man to find the military road leading south from the Danube plain through the "Gates of Trajan". But the route was known and regularly used throughout the Byzantine period, and Constantine VII in the tenth century notes that it took an individual eight days to travel from Thessaloniki to Belgrade (Singidunum) along it (including pauses).[39] Even if the story of Comentiolus has been exaggerated, it is indicative of what contemporaries thought about the road system in the region. In addition, the transformation in the role of urban centres during the late Roman period must have had equally dramatic consequences for the upkeep of the provincial road systems. Longer-term changes, exacerbated by constant devastation and raiding in the Balkans from the later sixth century and in Anatolia from the middle of the seventh century, led to the near total collapse of the late Roman urban network, and it had been local municipalities which had borne the chief responsibility for maintaining the roads in their administrative territories.[40]

The change in the fortunes of the Roman road network seems also in part to reflect the availability, or non-availability, of the requisite engineering skills in the army. Evidence about other aspects of late Roman engineering and technical know-how would support the notion of a decline in high-level technical skills applied to military engineering, for example: the move during the fifth–sixth centuries from torsion-powered artillery, which requires fairly complex construction techniques as well as highly trained artificers, to tension-powered machines is one example, although there are others. But "decline" is probably the wrong term: for it is quite clear from the evidence for fortification and defensive construction, as well as in ecclesiastical architecture, that a sufficient knowledge in engineering was available to maintain often very elaborate and sophisticated military building. Rather, late Roman and Byzantine culture seems – as in other fields – to have invested its knowledge and intellectual wealth differently than during the previous period, relying upon, but not further developing, the inheritance of the Romano-Hellenistic past.

Only in the area of a few major cities – chiefly, in fact, around Constantinople – is there evidence for road maintenance or repair work undertaken by the state, and much of this comes from the middle of the sixth century, associated with the emperor Justinian's building schemes. Thus Procopius reports that efforts were made to resurface short stretches of road along the Via Egnatia between Constantinople and Rhegion, for example, along the main highway from Bithynia to Phrygia, as well as on the road from Antioch in Syria northwards across the mountains into Cilicia (a dangerous route at the best of times, as Procopius notes). Justinian is also credited by Procopius with repairing or building several bridges – across the Sangarios and Drakon rivers in Bithynia, or the Siberis in Galatia.[41] An inscription from Serdica (Sofia) dated to 580 records repairs to an aqueduct under a certain Julianus bearing the rank of *candidatus*, and a number of such local inscriptions for the fifth and sixth centuries from across the empire shows that work of this sort was carried out fairly regularly. This is particularly the case for Constantinople, of course, where the emperors frequently committed substantial resources to the upkeep of defensive structures, cisterns, aqueducts and so forth.[42] After this time there is no evidence for any central direction of road-building or maintenance in the provinces, except on a purely *ad hoc* basis, even in the laudatory accounts of the building programmes of emperors such as Basil I in the second half of the ninth century.

Roads were, however, certainly maintained and, in the case of some bridges, newly constructed. Some bridges survived well into the middle Byzantine period in this way – several historians report the existence of a bridge at Zompos (or Zompe) over the Sangarios for the eleventh and early twelfth centuries.[43] Late Roman and Byzantine sources make it clear that road and bridge maintenance was achieved through the compulsory duties imposed upon local communities by local military or provincial authorities and sanctioned by the central government. Obligations in the fourth–sixth centuries such as *viarum et pontium sollicitudo*, known certainly from the ninth century and probably before by a variety of terms such as *odostrosia* or *gephyrosis*, occur in various sources from the late Roman period up to the twelfth century and beyond.[44] But the results were patchy in the extreme. And while military treatises regularly include sections on bridging rivers, for example through the construction of pontoons, a tactic also referred to in the histories and chronicles, such constructions were, of course, of a very temporary nature.[45]

Not all roads were of the same standard, nor were they constructed for the same purpose. Byzantine sources often differentiate between wide roads and narrow roads or paths, between paved and unpaved roads, and between roads that were suitable for wagons or wheeled vehicles and other roads. A tenth-century treatise on guerrilla strategy distinguishes clearly between "public roads", maintained at least irregularly by the local administration through compulsory services imposed on local communities, and paths and tracks of a humbler nature.[46] Procopius notes with pride the fact that the repaved sections of road between the capital and Rhegion were wide enough to permit two wagons to pass each other.[47] Roads that were strategically important to the state may in general have been maintained more regularly and by the means noted already. Yet the majority of these routes, even the major arterial roads, were often mere tracks, and even where formerly well-paved they had generally decayed substantially by the eighth and ninth centuries. Basil I had to lay branches and logs along the road leading out of Koukousos in 877 to make it passable, and he led his army shortly afterwards through the mountain passes on foot, so narrow and inaccessible was the track he followed. The coastal road taken by most of the French army during the Second Crusade from Lopadion to Adramyttion was so decayed and overgrown that many troops wandered off it and became lost. In contrast, a smaller contingent followed the shorter, broader and more accessible but less well-supplied route over the Mysion hill-country to Adramyttion, illustrating the variations between routes.

Seasonal variations clearly affected unpaved or deteriorated roads and tracks more dramatically than properly paved routes, so that the flexibility and mobility of large Byzantine forces must necessarily have been adversely affected, at least in comparison with earlier Roman armies which had a much better strategic road network at their disposal. During the summer it was possible to move wheeled vehicles relatively easily, if not very rapidly, along the broader tracks, even in fairly hilly regions, as the evidence of Manuel I's expedition which ended at Myriokephalon in 1176 demonstrates. In winter and during periods of rainfall the reverse was the case, and indeed it was precisely this feature which made winter campaigns both less viable but (potentially) more effective, since they were so unusual. Michael Psellos remarks on the emperor Basil II's refusal to be bound by the seasons, to which his military success is partly attributed, and the military treatises generally include some words of advice on the campaigning seasons and what precautions to take at particular times of the year.[48] The need for good, reliable scouts with local knowledge of roads, passes and river crossings is constantly emphasized in both the military treatises and the historians' accounts, and highlights the uncertainty and difficulty attendant upon any military undertaking in a context in which both major routes and local tracks were generally of such poor quality.[49]

One result of the changes described above was an increasing reliance upon beasts of burden for the movement of goods and people rather than on wheeled vehicles drawn by draught animals.[50] The late Roman government laid down strict regulations on the size, loads and use of different types of wheeled vehicle employed by the public transport system, which was divided into two branches, the slow (ox-carts and similar heavy vehicles) and the fast (faster-moving pack animals, light carts and horses or ponies). Some of these regulations were retained in Byzantine times. While the fast branch of the service certainly continues to operate through the Byzantine period, the slow service either disappears or lost its independent status and was merged with the fast service. The evidence is ambiguous, and we will return to the question of transport in a later chapter.[51]

What does evolve from the middle of the seventh century is a clearly defined system of predominantly military routes along which imperial and provincial marching camps were established. A similar pattern emerges also in the Balkans, although without the marching camps, and in both cases, while based on the pre-existing Roman network, the new emphasis reflects a specifically Byzantine strategic response to invasion in both regions. Although there is little direct evidence for it, the situation of many settlements and the continued occupation of most late Roman urban sites, even if much reduced, suggests that the roads of the late Roman period continued in use, in spite of their gradual dilapidation, at least until – as was the case with the stretch of the Via Egnatia in the sixth century, noted above – they became so pot-holed and irregular that even pack animals and soldiers could not pass. Since, as also noted, their maintenance was a localized and infrequent matter, many must have become little more than paths or tracks unsuitable for any wheeled vehicles at all by the sixth and seventh centuries.[52]

In the Balkans, four arterial routes dominate in accounts of Byzantine campaigning, as well as that of their opponents (see Map III).[53] The best known is the Via Egnatia, a major route running from Constantinople across to Herakleia in Thrace, passing along the coastal plain south of the Rhodope mountains on to Thessalonike, thence via Edessa, Bitola, Achrida (Ohrid) and

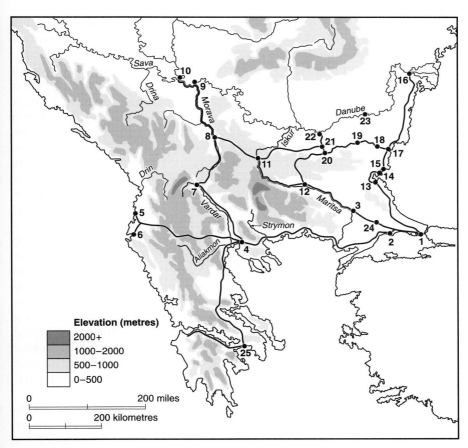

Towns/fortresses

1	Constantinople	2	Heracleia	3	Adrianople
4	Thessaloniki	5	Dyrrhachium	6	Avlona
7	Skopje	8	Naissus (Niš)	9	Viminacium
10	Singidunum (Belgrade)	11	Serdica (Sofia)	12	Philippoupolis
13	Develtus	14	Anchialus	15	Mesembria
16	Noviodunum	17	Varna	18	Marcianoupolis
19	Pliska	20	Trnovo	21	Nicopolis
22	Novae	23	Dorostolum	24	Arcadioupolis
25	Corinth				

Map III Balkans: geography and communications

Elbasan across the mountains to Dyrrachium (*Durreš*) on the Adriatic coast.
The second route runs north from Thessaloniki, through the Rhodope range
along the Axios (Vardar) valley and the pass of Demir Kapija (with an alternative easterly loop avoiding this defile and leading through another pass, known
to the Byzantines as Kleidion – the key), then via Stoboi (Stobi*)* and Skopia

(Skopje) up to Naissos (Niš), a key crossroads along the routes southwards to the Aegean and Macedonia, westwards to the Adriatic, southeastwards to Thrace and Constantinople, and northwards to the Danube. The third route begins at Constantinople and runs northwards across Thrace to Adrianople (Edirne), and thence along the Maritsa via Philippoupolis (Plovdiv). North of Philippoupolis the route led through the pass of Succi guarded at its northern exit by the so-called "gates of Trajan", barred by a wall and two forts, before proceeding over the pass of Vakarel to Serdica (Sofia), and then over the mountains via a further series of passes, before meeting the Nisava valley and following it up to Naissos. From Naissos it continued up the valley of the Morava to Viminacium (nr. mod. Kostolac) and then along the Danube to Singidunum (Belgrade). This was a key military route, and it was complemented by a number of spurs to east and west, giving access to the south Danube plain, the Haimos mountains and Black Sea coastal plain, as well as, in the west, the valleys of the West Morava, Ibar and Drin rivers. Particularly important were the roads north from Constantinople parallel with the coast to Anchialos (Pomorie), Mesembria (Nesebar) and Odessos (Varna), and then along the coast up to the mouth of the Danube; and a parallel inland route up through Adrianople, across the Sredna Gora range and then over the Shipka pass through the Balkan range itself to Nikopolis (Veliko Trnovo) and on to Novae (Svistov) on the Danube. All these routes pass in several places through relatively narrow and often quite high passes, easily blocked both by human agency – ideal, for example, for ambushing an enemy army – and the weather: winter snows frequently drift to considerable depths, and make even modern transit difficult in severe conditions.

Communications in Anatolia are subject to similar geophysical and climatic constraints. The pre-medieval communications network was complex, and while much of it continued in use locally, maintenance, if there was any at all, was certainly very irregular from before the seventh century. But there evolved a series of major military routes, the upkeep of which was in the state's interest, and along which developed also a string of fortified posts and military bases as the same routes became corridors of access to Arab raiders (Map IV).[54]

Several major routes belong in this category. The first, starting from Chrysoupolis opposite Constantinople, went via Nikomedeia and Nikaia to the major imperial military base at Malagina, thence to Dorylaion. Here the road forks: a westerly route goes via Kotyaion, and an easterly via Amorion, down to Akroinon and from there either southeast to Ikonion or south and southwest via Synnada to Kolossai/Chonai. Along this latter route there are two options to turn off to the south, down to Kibyra and eventually across the mountains to the coast at Attaleia or, farther west, at Myra. Alternatively, the road from Chonai can be followed westwards via Laodikeia and Tralles to Ephesos on the coast.

From Ikonion again the route can be followed east to Archelais and then south to Tyana; or onwards to Kaisareia; or again from Ikonion south via

Savatra to Thebasa, Kybistra/Herakleia, Loulon, Podandos and the Çakit gorge. The route south from Kaisareia eventually joins the same road, via Tyana, at Loulon. These then converge, via two passes south of Podandos, called Maurianon and Karydion by the Byzantines, and lead by different ways over the Tekir plateau down to the "Cilician Gates" (Külek Boğazı) in the Yeşiloluk defile and thence into the plain, to continue to either Tarsos or Adana.[55] A variety of roads can then be taken from Kaisareia northwest up to Ankara; north to Basilika Therma and on up to Tabion and thence to Euchaita; or northeast up to Sebasteia, then west and north to Dazimon and Amaseia. Alternatively, a series of easterly routes leads from Sebasteia across to either Kamacha, or to Koloneia and Satala.

The second major military route branches off to the east at Dorylaion, running along the valley of the Tembris river (mod. Porsuk Su) via Trikomia, Gorbeous, Saniana and then on to Timios Stavros, Basilika Therma, on to the north of Charsianon Kastron and across to Bathys Ryax and Sebasteia. Thence it can be taken southwest to Kaisareia, north to Dazimon, east to Koloneia and Satala, or southeast to Melitene. A second branch turns off to the southeast at Saniana, proceeding via Mokissos and Ioustinianoupolis to Kaisareia. Significantly, these routes do not always follow the major paved Roman roads, but lesser (and in some cases much older) routes which provided better opportunities for watering and pasturing animals and provisioning armies. Their use probably also reflects the difficulties of trying to move along the older but greatly dilapidated paved roads.[56] In many cases, there were a number of parallel alternatives, some of which were suitable for wheeled vehicles and had been paved in Roman times, others of which remained tracks, sometimes accessible only to men in single file and sure-footed beasts of burden. Local knowledge of such tracks was vital to successful military operations, and there are several tales of Roman armies outflanking their enemy by using such tracks.

It is the second of these major arterial systems that was most used by imperial armies marching against the Arabs up to the eleventh century, for it follows a slightly better terrain and along it were established a number of permanent marching camps, disposed to support forces campaigning either on the southerly branch via Kaisareia, or the northeasterly branch via Sebasteia. These were located at Malagina, Dorylaion, Kaborkin (between Trikomia and Midaion), Koloneia (there is some disagreement about the identity and location of this camp),[57] Kaisareia and Dazimon. Major difficulties facing armies, both large and small, when marching across Asia Minor, included the long stretches of road through relatively waterless and exposed terrain on the one hand, and the rough mountainous land separating the coastal regions from the central plateau on the other. But these features were also fundamental influences on the ways in which hostile forces moved and, once taken into account, could be used with great effect against an invader. The strategy of middle Byzantine armies was largely dictated by these features.

There were several major routes of access from the Cilician and north Syrian regions into Asia Minor. North of Tarsos in the gorge of the Yeşiloluk

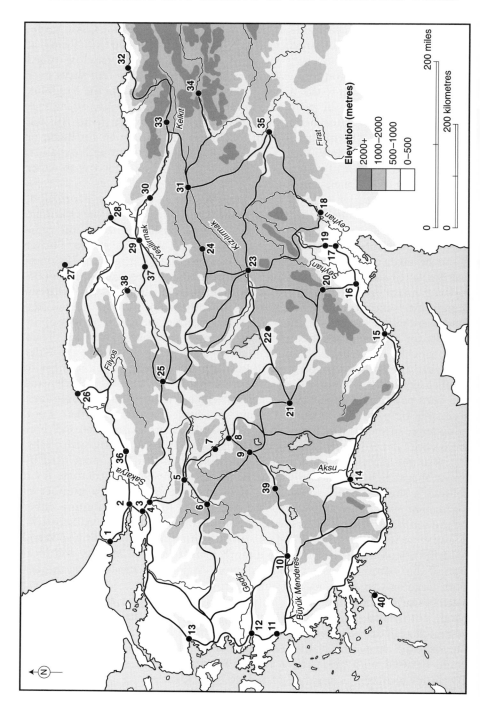

the defile of the Cilician Gates led through the Taurus to Podandos and either westwards to Loulon, Herakleia and eventually, turning off to the north, Ikonion; or northwards, either directly or via Tyana to Caesarea. A second route led northwards from Germanikeia (Mar'aş) to Koukousos and then westwards via the Kuru Çay pass to Kaisareia; while another led from Adata, to the north east of Germanikeia, across the Anti-Taurus past Zapetra to Melitene; while a third started at Melitene and similarly passed a series of defiles and passes either to Kaisareia via the pass of Gödilli Dağ, the Byzantine *kleisoura* or frontier pass of Lykandos, or to Sebasteia via the valley of the Kuru Çay. There were also a number of minor routes through defensible defiles, some farther to the west, some along the eastern stretch of the frontier, which were covered by Arab and Byzantine forts, and were the scene of frequent clashes, such as that from Mopsouestia (al-Massisa) up to Anazarba ('Ain Zarba) and through the defile to Sision, thence north to Kaisareia. Farther to the east other routes led from Melitene eastwards to Arsamosata (Simsat) and on to Chliat on Lake Van, as well as northwards. A tenth-century guide on frontier warfare lists several regions possessing defiles through the mountains through which enemy forces might pass and which were to be guarded. Arab sources similarly describe in some detail the routes which an invader could follow across the Taurus and Anti-Taurus mountains.[58]

Towns/fortresses

1	Chalkedon	2	Nikomedeia	3	Nikaia
4	Malagina	5	Dorylaion	6	Kotyaion
7	Kaborkion	8	Amorion	9	Akroinon
10	Chonai	11	Ephesos	12	Smyrna
13	Adramyttion	14	Attaleia	15	Seleukeia
16	Tarsos	17	Anazarbos	18	Germanikeia
19	Sision	20	Podandos	21	Ikonion
22	Koron	23	Kaisareia	24	Charsianon
25	Ankyra	26	Amastris	27	Sinope
28	Amisos	29	Amaseia	30	Dazimon
31	Sebasteia	32	Trapezous	33	Koloneia
34	Kamacha	35	Melitene	36	Kaludioupolis
37	Euchaita	38	Gangra	39	Sozopolis
40	Rhodos				

Ancient/medieval river names

Sakarya	*Sangarios*	Filyos	*Billaios*
Yeşilirmak	*Iris*	Kelkit	*Lykos*
Kizilirmak	*Halys*	Gediz	*Hermos*
Büyük Menderes	*Maeander*	Aksu	*Eurymedon*
Seyhan	*Saros*	Ceyhan	*Pyramos*
Firat	*Euphrates*		

Map IV Anatolia: geography and communications

From the last years of the eleventh century the focus of imperial strategy in Anatolia shifted radically as a consequence of the Seljuk occupation of much of the central plateau, so that between the early years of the twelfth century and the 1160s a new frontier zone evolved along the belt of marginal lands separating lowlands and coastal plain from highland and plateau. Around the western edge of this zone fortress towns such as Chonai, Choma (Soublaion), Philomelion, Kotyaion, Dorylaion, Ankyra and Kastamon represented by the 1160s and 1170s the most advanced frontier posts covering the territories recovered from the Turks, with a network of smaller outposts and fortresses controlling the key routes from the interior into the coastal regions. Although most of them, and others such as Neokaisareia or Gangra, were held only briefly, they give a good indication of the relative success of Manuel I's incremental advance from lowlands onto the edge of the central plateau, and the advantages this brought with it for the less troubled lowland regions. A similar role was fulfilled by centres such as Tarsos and Adana in Cilicia, and Trebizond in the north. The basic geography was unchanged, of course, but the strategic implications of the change, both for the financing of the army and the methods employed to maintain the frontier and the districts behind it, were considerable.

The evolution of strategy: principles and techniques

In general terms, it seems that the East Roman or Byzantine state up to the end of the twelfth century evolved a number of variants on a system of defence in depth. But all the variations were the result of the interplay between three fundamental features of the political and social-economic situation of the Byzantine world: first, the resources that were available to the government for the training, equipping and maintenance of armies, and the ways through which those resources could be appropriated and redistributed; second, the international political context, and especially the level of political organization and ideological sophistication – "statehood" – attained by the empire's neighbours; third, the technological/organizational sophistication of its enemies.

The late Roman system, grounded in a division between mobile field forces and less mobile (but not entirely static) defensive garrisons both along and well behind the frontier regions, was orientated entirely towards defence, although the field forces could be mobilized for occasional counterstrikes into enemy territory. Longer-term offensive operations normally involved taking considerable bodies of troops away from other regions, thus weakening their defences and making attacks on those areas more attractive, as Justinian's offensives in the west demonstrate. This system had evolved from the third century, through several permutations, primarily to withstand the pressures of large numbers of small attacks along the frontiers with occasionally much larger invading armies pushing deeper into Roman territory. The Romans – and their medieval successors – certainly had a clear notion of a linear frontier or border, both in respect of political demarcation and in terms of cultural differentiation. But such linear distinctions had little or no military relevance and were of only limited strategic value. On the contrary, frontier zones were established in which local garrisons based in fortified centres could respond to local attacks either by meeting them in the field and driving them off, or retiring into their bases and sallying out to harass and hinder enemy movement, deprive them of supplies and generally make the raid unviable and unprofitable as quickly as possible. The same system was intended to deal with challenges of a more serious nature, whether better organized or simply larger in numbers. Defensive strategy permitted the invaders to penetrate the frontier, but then ensured that they had to confront a series of "hard points", major fortified centres or military garrisons. If these were attacked, the enemy's resources and lines of communication became vulnerable as time and energy were expended in trying to capture them; if they were avoided, the soldiers based there could sally out to harass the enemy column or columns, preventing them from collecting forage and supplies, limiting their freedom of movement and so forth. At the same time, this allowed time for other mobile forces to concentrate and march to meet the enemy in battle. Warfare then became a war of manoeuvre and attrition, as the enemy force attempted to avoid contact and escape with its booty, and as Roman commanders attempted either to surround the enemy and overwhelm his forces numerically before attacking, or alternatively, and in order to avoid a full-scale battle, to persuade him to withdraw quickly due to lack of resources.

The technological-organizational advantage held by the Romans in the Balkans generally meant that this strategy worked reasonably well at the first level until the later sixth century: barbarian forces were generally after short-term gains in booty and slaves. In fact, archaeological evidence suggests that this system never worked quite like this, and that from the beginning defence in depth involved a much more differentiated pattern of settlement and distribution of military resources than the written record might suggest. Against the Persians, technologically the equals of the Roman forces and able to conduct successful long-term siege warfare, Roman defences generally operated at the second level: small-scale raids did occur (from both Persians and from Arab raiders), but major attacks deep into Roman territory were well planned and had a specific purpose (to extract tribute and booty) as well as a longer-term political-strategic aim. Occasionally the "hard points" were taken, but for the most part the Roman defensive system worked reasonably well, certainly if judged by the continued political and territorial integrity of the empire.[59]

In the late sixth and early seventh centuries, however, the system was seriously compromised on both fronts, as we have seen. Maurice's aggressive offensive against the Avars in the Balkans appear to have been remarkably successful, but its longer-term implications remain unknown, since the *coup d'état* in which he perished meant the return to a more passive defensive strategy and the continued infiltration of Roman territory by Slav immigrants. By the middle of the seventh century the Romans could control some of the Danube and the Danube delta, the Aegean coastlands to a point, but hardly any of the interior away from major fortified settlements and arterial routes. In the east, initial Persian successes were facilitated by the disaffection of substantial elements of the eastern field armies, allowing the Sassanian commanders to deal with each army group on a piecemeal basis and roll up the defensive system in Syria and then Palestine before turning their attention to Egypt and Anatolia. Heraclius' defeat of the Persians enabled him to start rebuilding the old system with a certain degree of success, but the Arab invasions effectively put an end to this process and totally altered the strategic geography of the Middle and Near East in the process.

The new strategic system which evolved out of this situation was even more clearly defensively orientated, although from an institutional perspective it grew organically out of the late Roman arrangements. Three defensive zones gradually evolved – an outer band of territories subject to regular raiding and devastation based around a series of hard points, fortresses and forts which frequently changed hands but which always had to be dealt with before any longer-term penetration of Byzantine territory could be contemplated; an inner belt of territories in which the forces most regularly employed to respond to enemy attacks were based, again focused on a series of more heavily defended foci which served also as fiscal and military administrative centres; and a third core zone which was the object of enemy attacks on occasion, which was also organized along the same lines as the second zone, but which also provided the resources for the maintenance of the imperial capital and government and its field armies, a last line of defence before the walls of the city itself. This was a highly flexible system which could tolerate extreme pressure in terms of economic damage and demographic dislocation – as in the invasion and occupation of some of the core zone in the years 674–8 and 717–18, for example – but which, by adopting a strategy of avoidance and harassment for its armies, reliance upon the survival of major fortified centres and dispersal of resources, made a knock-out blow extremely difficult, and rendered a full-scale occupation and pacification of the provinces simply too costly a proposition.

Yet such a defensive option was clearly often – indeed, frequently – exercised to the detriment of the population of regions most exposed to hostile activity. In Asia Minor the empire relied heavily upon a network of frontier outposts and forts covering major routes and passes and other strategic locations, well fortified or well concealed refuges to which the local populace could flee when warned of an impending attack, and provincial armies which were organized at a local level to harass and hinder enemy movements rather than to confront and defeat their armies. Although large Arab armies sometimes did successfully invest and capture major fortified centres, this was – in proportion to the much larger number of simple booty-collecting raids or attacks intended to seek out and destroy Byzantine armies – comparatively infrequent. The Byzantine policy of simply avoiding confrontation and holding out until the enemy forces were compelled to retire, in spite of the considerable costs borne by the provincials in the most exposed areas, seems to have been effective enough to discourage successful permanent penetration of the frontier regions and ensure the state's continued ability to extract resources sufficient to maintain its apparatus.[60] In the Balkans, a less defensive system was operated. Given the less sophisticated logistical arrangements of its enemies and greater Byzantine efficiency and flexibility in tactical organization, the empire could rely upon a military stand-off, moderated by diplomatic activity, to maintain a degree of equilibrium, although frequent raids deep into imperial territory, and vice versa, raids intended to reinforce political demands rather than ideological claims, gave warfare in this theatre some of the characteristics of warfare in Asia Minor.

Two aspects may be worth highlighting at this point. The first is that there is virtually no evidence for the Byzantine government or individual military commanders ever having attempted to establish a "hard" frontier, in the sense represented by, for example, the artificial linear defensive structures typified by Hadrian's wall in North Britain. There are some minor and short-lived exceptions, but the generalization appears valid throughout the period in question. The corollary of this is that, in the second place, the alternative "soft" or permeable defensive arrangements were not simply a response to lack of resources, or the appropriate technology, or the overwhelming advantage which the enemies of the empire sometimes possessed in respect of manpower and related logistical matters. A "soft" defence was not merely a reflection of circumstances.

In the Balkans the late Roman state – in the form of the provincial and military administration – appears to have recognized the development of a greater diversity of fortified settlement types, as a direct response to the nature of hostile activity and its effects on the economies of the provinces concerned, reflecting the need to protect the provincial populations from the implications of a permeable frontier. Even this arrangement succumbed to the pressure on resources and the nature of the trans-Danubian immigration from the later sixth century. Yet there is some evidence to suggest that the methods which had been evolved in the Balkans may then have been pursued somewhat more deliberately and even systematically in the Anatolian context during the second half of the seventh century, so that the system which evolved there was directly related to imperial experience in the Balkans.[61] The rate at which this occurred remains to be established; neither is it clear to what extent the evidence from inscriptions in the fortifications of a number of fortified sites in Asia Minor demonstrates the activity of the central government in this respect. A defensive strategy very similar to that which had evolved in the Balkans from the third century emerges in Anatolia from the middle and later seventh century, in an area where such a strategic infrastructure had been entirely unnecessary until the Persian invasions of the early seventh century.

The chief characteristic of the Byzantine system was thus the permeable frontier. Not only are raiders or invading armies not halted at the "frontier", they are not even brought to battle, except under the most favourable circumstances (or where a foolhardy commander risks a battle). Instead, conflict is avoided wherever possible (conserving limited manpower), and the populations of the countryside and their moveable possessions and livestock brought into places of security (conserving limited resources). Ensconced in their fortresses and strongholds or mountain refuges, the army and the civil population wait until the enemy have had enough and go away. This usually occurred after a relatively short time, since larger forces were subject to the dangers of disease as well as problems of water supply and fodder, while substantial amounts of booty made withdrawal slower and more subject to ambush and counter-attack. Such a strategy was only one side of an imperial response to its defensive needs, of course. For the role of diplomacy was absolutely crucial in complementing this military activity: fomenting discontent among enemy troops or leaders, delaying negotiations until the enemy armies ran out of supplies or were assailed by disease, persuading the enemy that relief forces were about to fall upon them or that their homeland had been attacked by imperial allies, these and a host of other methods were employed in a sophisticated armoury of non-military weapons at the disposal of an imperial government, and there can be little doubt that it was this combination which enabled the imperial government to survive so many apparently fatal onslaughts.[62]

During the period of military expansion and reconquest in the late tenth and early eleventh centuries, this system began to change. Instead of a defence in depth, a system of frontier districts based on one or more major fortified positions and their mobile garrisons was established. Outside this were in turn arranged a number of client emirates or states in the east, kept in check by occasional displays of imperial military force and by diplomatic efforts. In the west, a linear frontier with neighbouring states could be maintained by diplomatic means and through mutual economic arrangements. From the last quarter of the tenth century, the eastern end of the Danube was re-established as a semi-permeable frontier, a frontier that was extended westwards after Basil II's destruction of the second Bulgarian empire. Archaeological evidence for the systematic reoccupation or reconstruction of a number of late Roman installations in this region and the dating of this work suggests that this was associated with the perceived threat from the Rus' after their defeat at imperial hands in the early 970s. There is little evidence that this policy was maintained under Basil II, however, and its abandonment is probably to be connected with the assumed disappearance of the threat after the alliance made between Byzantium and Kiev in the late 980s. Nevertheless, the Danube and its associated river systems in the northwest Balkan region did function as a frontier between the empire and its northern neighbours, especially the kingdom of Hungary, during the twelfth century, although the sources suggest that it was guarded by a skeleton force of watchposts and forts at key crossing places, as well as a frontier hinterland zone which was deliberately kept depopulated to discourage raiding. Indeed, the evidence demonstrates that the disposition of imperial forces from the early eleventh to the end of the twelfth century in the Balkans was directed as much at internal security as at external pressures, which were contained by a combination of diplomatic activity and occasional demonstrations of imperial military power.[63]

The international context had changed sufficiently by this period to negate some of the advantages held by the East Roman state in the sixth and seventh centuries. If we exclude the nomadic peoples of the steppe, most of the peoples neighbouring the empire – whether potential enemies or friends – had evolved more complex state forms, including the administrative and logistical arrangements necessary to put substantial and well-armed forces into the field, even if only on a short-term seasonal basis. This had always been the case in the east, of course, even in the time of the early caliphate, but not in the west. In addition, the tactical advantage held by well-disciplined imperial armies over barbarian forces had been in most cases equalized by developments in heavy cavalry warfare and siege technology by the eleventh and certainly by the twelfth centuries. If the emperors of the seventh and eighth centuries could treat most of their enemies as barbarians, those of the tenth and eleventh, and more particularly the emperors of the twelfth century, had to recognize that they were, for the most part, dealing with peoples or states who were no longer their organizational and logistical inferiors. Strategy had to respond to this changed context.

The system of the later tenth and early eleventh centuries evolved as a preclusive defence – reflecting a political-military context in which incursions into imperial territory were rare, while permitting imperial field forces to reinforce diplomacy on the territory of the empire's neighbours or enemies. As long as enemies appeared infrequently, or singly, on one front at a time, and in an international political context where the empire's military standing would generally discourage territorial incursions, this was sufficient; and these appear to have been the assumptions made by emperors and their advisors in the period c. 1025–59. But it was inflexible when confronted by a multiplicity of threats, because the underlying lack of resources did not permit any sudden expansion of armed forces necessary adequately to combat such challenges. The sudden increase in military pressure on the empire in the middle and later eleventh century, combined with internal factionalism and diversion of military resources away from the external threat, was too much for this revised system, and it began to break down, with the results that will be discussed in Chapter 3. In addition, and especially significant from the overall strategic perspective, the failure of the empire to maintain an effective warfleet through the later eleventh and especially the later twelfth centuries meant that terrestrial strategic dispositions could always be – and sometimes were – outflanked by maritime forces. The events of 1203–4 made the point disastrously clearly.

Paradoxically, the principles, although not the form, of the defensive system in Anatolia after the recovery under Alexios I Komnenos were at base the same as those which had prevailed in the eighth and early ninth centuries. In the Balkans, in contrast, the Komnenoi made an effort to re-establish and maintain the principle of a linear frontier, although a defence-in-depth element was also recognized and taken into account. But the fiscal costs to the population, and the political dangers inherent in extracting the necessary resources in regions which were already culturally disaffected, were enormous. The structural tensions within this system, in the Balkans in particular, become obvious when, following the Fourth Crusade, the territories of the empire dissolved into a series of regional powers, to a greater or lesser degree reflecting ethnic, cultural and religious lines of difference.

CHAPTER THREE

Protect and survive: a brief history of East Roman strategic arrangements

Strategy is the means by which a commander may defend his own lands and defeat his enemies. The general is the one who practices strategy.[1]

The later sixth century

At the end of the sixth century, and following Justinian's reconquests in Italy and North Africa, East Roman forces were disposed in seven field armies and a large number of smaller regional divisions along and behind the frontier regions of the empire.[2] The former were known as *comitatenses*, were each commanded by a *magister militum*, "Master of the Soldiers", and were organized into divisions for the East, Armenia Thrace, Illyricum, Africa, and Italy, with two further "praesental" divisions (i.e. they were "in the presence" of the emperor) based in northwest Asia Minor and in Thrace to defend Constantinople. The troops making up the frontier divisions and permanent garrisons were known as *limitanei*, mostly composed of older legionary units, together with their attached auxiliaries, augmented by auxiliary and legionary cavalry forces brigaded together to provide local static and mobile reserves.[3] By the end of Justinian's reign there were over 25 such commands based in both the frontier provinces of the empire and inland, from Scythia in the northwest Balkans through the Middle East and Egypt to Mauretania in northwest Africa.[4] Although the titles of units often reflected the category to which they were originally allocated, cross-postings between divisions complicated matters considerably, and the practical differences in military terms between field troops and *limitanei* were not always very clear. Civil and military authority had been combined in several regions, the better to deal with internal security matters: in Egypt, for example, where the post of *dux* of the Thebaid was given civil authority, and the position of *praefectus Augustalis* (civil governor) was combined with that of the military commander, the *dux Aegypti*; or in southern Asia Minor, where civil and military authority was combined in Pisidia, Lycaonia and Isauria.

An important new field command, the *quaestura exercitus*, had been introduced during the reign of Justinian. It was equivalent to that of a *magister militum*, placed under the authority of an officer entitled *quaestor*, with authority over troops based in the Danube frontier zone (the provinces of Scythia and Moesia II), but including also the Asia Minor coastal province of Caria and the Aegean islands. The purpose appears to have been to supply the Danube frontier forces by sea from a secure hinterland, thus sparing the hard-pressed population and ravaged countryside of the frontier districts where the armies were based.[5]

As well as the regular field armies and the frontier divisions, the empire also employed substantial numbers of federate or allied forces, especially in the east: Arab clans and tribes formed a key element in the empire's defences, and were heavily subsidized in food, cash, vestments, regalia (generally signifying an honorary position in the Roman hierarchy) and weaponry to maintain their loyalty. Different tribal alliances competed among themselves for supremacy in this respect, so that the dominant group changed from time to time; although corresponding to the districts under each *dux* there was a *phylarchos*, a paramount tribal leader. By Justinian's time it was the Christianized Ghassanids who represented imperial interests in this respect, and they were faced by a similar tribal confederacy, subsidized by the Sasanian Persian kings, the Lakhmids.[6]

Lastly, the emperors had a number of guards units based in their proximity, the most important of which were the Scholae palatinae and the Excubitores. The former, organized into seven divisions (or *scholae*) each of 500 soldiers, were cavalry, and had originally been elite cavalry shock units, recruited chiefly, but not exclusively, from Germanic peoples neighbouring or inside the empire. By the middle of the fifth century, however, they had become little more than parade units, the German element disappearing entirely, suitable only for quite limited military duties, although technically still classed as fighting troops. By Justinian's time they were billeted in the provinces of Thrace and northwest Asia Minor, with one or two divisions serving in the palace on a rotational basis.[7] To replace them as a proper imperial guard the emperor Leo I had recruited a new, much smaller elite unit of only 300 men, originally Isaurians, it would seem, although by the early sixth century they were recruited more widely. They remained active throughout the sixth century, and indeed both ranking soldiers and officers of the Excubitores were often given special imperial tasks of a diplomatic or otherwise delicate nature. They remained based in the palace at Constantinople.[8]

The empire's naval forces were relatively limited in the late sixth century. A series of small flotillas was maintained along the Danube, another fleet was based at Ravenna and there was a squadron at Constantinople. For the expedition to Africa in 533 the state was able to assemble some 500 vessels of varying capacity as transports, together with 92 single-decked warships or *dromones* with crews of marines totalling 2,000. The latter probably represented the squadrons of Constantinople, the Danube and Italy, although this is a guess. Most of the transports will have been requisitioned, possibly from the grain fleets which normally supplied Constantinople. With the establishment of the *quaestura* a further fleet of transports was also established.[9]

The strategic disposition of these forces reflects the pressures placed on the imperial frontier from external sources, and the various threats to the empire's territory as perceived by the high command and the government at Constantinople. The principles upon which strategy was based were those of the fourth century: a first line of defence consisting of a linear frontier screened by fortified posts, major fortresses and a connecting network of minor fortified positions, and a second line made up of a reserve of mobile field units grouped into a number of subdivisions scattered in garrison towns and fortresses across the provinces behind the frontier. But by the end of Justinian's reign the gap between the different functions of the "frontier" and "field" armies had been narrowed, as field army units became permanently garrisoned in or near provincial towns and cities, serving in many cases as reinforcement to the frontier garrisons rather than as a mobile reserve. Indeed, it seems to have been the case that up to three-quarters of each field army was actually distributed through the provinces behind the frontier zone, or along the frontier itself, and under the immediate command of the local *duces* of the *limitanei*, leaving the commanders-in-chief – the *magistri militum* – with inadequate reserves to meet any serious hostile breakthrough. *Ad hoc* recruitment of warlike groups within the empire, or barbarians, on a short-term mercenary basis was the means used to make up numbers. The result was a relatively expensive force of very variable quality, depending upon field service experience, recent postings and similar factors, which consumed a large proportion of the state's fiscal revenue each year, both in respect of cash payments as well as in terms of equipment and maintenance in kind for troops on campaign.

It is also clear from the dispositions we know of from the sources, in particular epigraphic and papyrological material, that units of the "frontier" were in fact based well behind the border regions, especially in the eastern provinces, where they functioned also as an internal police, so that the concept of a frontier as a line along a clearly marked political divide does not adequately account for the situation along most Roman frontiers. Indeed, while there were recognized points at which two political entities met – for commercial as well as other purposes – the frontier as a whole needs to be understood as a deep band or zone stretching between, for example, the Persian and Roman states, narrower in some parts than others (for example, very broad along the desert "frontier" in Syria and the Roman province of Arabia, in modern east Syria and central/eastern Jordan).[10]

While it displayed certain weaknesses, this arrangement nonetheless seems to have functioned reasonably effectively, in view of the pressures placed upon it both in respect of internal resourcing (especially problems of manpower during the fifth century, and of pay and emoluments during the later sixth century) and external threats. It has been argued that as a result of these conditions morale and discipline were problems in the middle and later sixth century, and the evidence seems to bear this out.

Nevertheless, while Slav and other barbarian raids across the Danube and deep into imperial territory harmed the provinces in the Balkans, and major successes were occasionally registered by the Persians in the east, the latter were exceptional rather than usual, and the war in the east was a war of small raids against strongholds, booty-collecting expeditions on the part of the Persian kings and counter-raids by the Romans.[11] Conquest of Roman territory may have been a seriously considered objective of Persian attacks in the later sixth century (this is certainly an assumption underlying Roman hostility towards the Persians), but there is little direct evidence for it until the wars which began after the deposition of Maurice (582–602). The emperor Justin II was presented by contemporary historians as desirous of the annihilation of the Persian state, an idea which, it is implied, was shared by Romans in general. But the rhetorical and ideological element in this played an important role, and it is difficult to say how far it actually reflected genuine strategic intentions. In spite of problems of morale and discipline, it is apparent that, under the vigorous regime applied by Maurice, the armies in the Persian theatre and on the Danube front fought remarkably well and registered a number of successes, regardless of occasional mutinies, poor supply lines and inadequate pay.[12]

In view of the relatively thin spread of active troops across the empire at the end of Justinian's reign, who had to defend a vast frontier, respond to sudden incursions and deal with internal unrest in many areas, it is surprising that the imperial armies managed to maintain the integrity of the imperial frontiers for so long and to restore them when they were breached. On the Roman side, a reasonably efficient logistical structure, competent leadership and the continued ability of the Romans to field well-motivated and tactically cohesive and disciplined armies partly accounts for this. In contrast, the lack of strategic co-ordination, as well as the relatively limited numbers of the enemy forces, must also be taken into account. Roman campaign strategy placed heavy emphasis on delaying tactics to wear down the enemy, deprive him of supplies and fodder for horses, foment anxiety and discontent among his troops, and so on – traditional methods which became especially important in a period of overstretched resources and a strained economy.[13] Roman arms were complemented by Roman diplomatic skills, which frequently invoked also the use of generous "subsidies" to potential enemy leaders.

For those areas most frequently affected by the army's presence – and by enemy activity – this meant devastation and the disruption of economic activity on a constant basis, leading in turn to depopulation and abandonment of agricultural land, to the extent that the army could barely supply itself adequately. This applied especially to Thrace in the later fifth century, for example, when the emperor Anastasius had to enact special measures to cater for the forces based there, [14] and to Moesia and Scythia in Justinian's reign when the establishment of the *quaestura* was intended to alleviate the problem.

With two exceptions in command structure, the strategic basis of the armies remained more or less unaltered until the middle years of the reign of Heraclius, that is until the 620s. Those two exceptions concern the establishment in Italy (with its headquarters at Ravenna) and Africa (headquarters at Carthage) of new commands entitled exarchates. The creation of these new commands, which united military and civil authority in the hands of a single official, was a response respectively to the threat posed by the Lombards from the time of their invasion in 568 and subsequent establishment in the Po valley and in the central regions of the peninsula, and to that presented by the constant raids of Berber tribes into the coastal plain of the North African provinces (see Map V).

During Heraclius' wars with the Persians further important changes took place: the two praesental armies, in Thrace and in Bithynia, seem to have been amalgamated. In the east, the armies of the *magistri militum per Orientem* and *per Armeniam* continued to exist (although during the Persian wars they may have partially dissolved), and in the Balkans the army of the *magister militum per Thracias* was certainly restored – all three were later involved in fighting the Arabs in the 630s.[15] Of the armies under the *magister militum per Illyricum* there is no trace. Given the occupation in the period 610–30 of much of the central and north Balkan region by Slav settlers under Avar hegemony, it is entirely possible that this army had broken up, the surviving elements absorbed into the other field armies.

At the beginning of the 630s, after the end of the Persian wars, the traditional strategic arrangements were re-established, except for the single praesental army and the disappearance of the army of Illyricum already noted. This involved also the restoration of the system of Arab allies along the eastern frontier, and the restoration of at least some *limitanei* posts and garrisons. The traditional regional command structure re-emerges in the 630s and continues to appear in the sources well into the 640s.[16] Some local changes were probably introduced by Heraclius into the administration of the provinces of Palestine and Syria (for internal security reasons), perhaps reflecting also the absence of a Roman administration in these areas during the Persian occupation from 614 until 627. There is no evidence in support of any major administrative reforms or changes.[17]

The transformation of the seventh century

The Arab conquest of the empire's Middle East regions promoted considerable changes. After attempts to meet and drive back the invaders in open battle were defeated, a major shift in strategy was introduced whereby open confrontations with the Muslim armies were avoided. After the defeat at the Yarmuk in 636, the field armies withdrew first to North Syria and Mesopotamia, and shortly after the loss of the latter and the severing of communications with the remaining non-Muslim Arabs and the Persians (with whom a military alliance may have been considered), back to the Taurus–Anti-Taurus line. The net result was the withdrawal of those field armies which had operated in Syria,

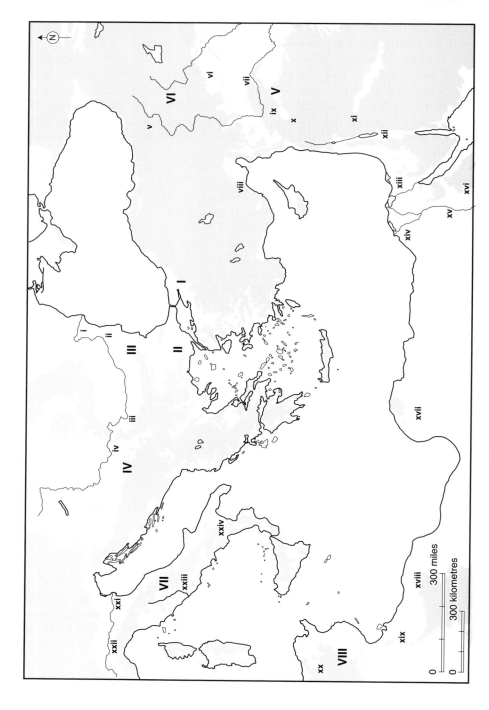

Palestine and Mesopotamia, as well as in Egypt, into Anatolia, and their re-establishment in a radically different strategic and economic context.[18]

Evidence for the process of withdrawal itself is virtually non-existent, and so the situation has perforce to be reconstructed from later sources. All the field armies in the eastern campaigns in the late 630s were withdrawn into the inner provincial regions behind their original geographical location, and the regions across which they were based were determined by the ability of these districts to provide for the soldiers in terms of supplies and other requirements. The imperial praesental forces were withdrawn into northwest Asia Minor and Thrace; the army of the *magister militum per Orientem*, henceforth known under its Greek name, the Anatolikon division, occupied southern central Asia Minor; while that of the *magister militum per Armeniam*, now known as the Armeniakon (Lat. Armeniacum), occupied the remaining eastern and northern districts of Asia Minor. The exception to this was the army of the *magister militum per Thracias*, which had apparently been transferred to the eastern theatre in the mid-630s and had been employed unsuccessfully to defend Egypt, which was allocated the rich provinces of central western Anatolia and known thenceforth as the Thrakesion army. By the later seventh century, the provinces across which these different divisions were established had come to be known collectively by the name of the army based there. It seems probable that this distribution of armies occurred primarily for logistical reasons: the districts nearest the new "frontier" were simply too poor to support this massive influx of military manpower and livestock. But the implications of the distribution for defensive strategy were considerable, for this dispersal

---

Magistri militum

I	*Magister militum praesentalis I*
II	*Magister militum praesentalis II*
III	*Magister militum per Thracias*
IV	*Magister militum per Illyricum*
V	*Magister militum per Orientem*
VI	*Magister militum per Armeniam*
VII	*Magister militum per Italiam (Exarchus Italiae)*
VIII	*Magister militum per Africam (Exarchus Africae)*

Duces

i	Scythia	ix	Syria	xvii	Libya
ii	Moesia II	x	Phoenice	xviii	Tripolitania
iii	Dacia	xi	Arabia	xix	Byzacena
iv	Mocsia I	xii	Palaestina	xx	Numidia
v	Armenia	xiii	Augustamnica	xxi	Ravenna
vi	Mesopotamia	xiv	Aegyptus	xxii	Liguria
vii	Osrhoene	xv	Arcadia	xxiii	Roma
viii	Isauria	xvi	Thebais	xxiv	Neapolis

Not shown (in west):	xxv	Mauretania
	xxvi	Hispania

Map V Strategic dispositions *c.* 565

henceforth meant that imperial counter-attacks were relatively slowly organized, while defence was fragmented and responded on a piecemeal and not particularly effective basis, at least at first.

The districts ascribed to the old *quaestura exercitus* established by Justinian did not survive the Slav and Avar invasions of the Balkan provinces (although isolated fortresses on the Danube delta and along the coast of the Black Sea were maintained and supplied by sea); but its Aegean regions remained, as before, the source of men, ships and resources for a maritime corps known in the later seventh century as the "ship troops", or Karabisianoi, probably based at first on Rhodes, although also drawing its soldiers from the mainland. Given the dramatically increased threat posed to the coastal regions of the empire, especially the Aegean basin, by Arab seapower from the 660s, this unit was to develop into the core of the middle Byzantine state's provincial naval power. In the late 690s there appears also a fleet attached to the region of Hellas, which may have evolved in connection with the *quaestura* after its establishment under Justinian. At the same time, the imperial fleet based at Constantinople was probably expanded, and was involved in a series of actions with the nascent Muslim sea power from the 650s on, being instrumental in the defeat of the sieges of the period 674–8 and 717–18. In the remainder of the empire the armies of the *magistri militum* or exarchs of Italy and Africa with Sardinia (referred to as the army of Septensis) continued in existence, although the latter was finally extinguished with the completion of the Arab conquest of North Africa in the 690s.[19] The army of Italy survived, on an increasingly fragmented, regionalized and localized basis, until the demise of the Exarchate of Ravenna in the middle of the eighth century; that of Africa was still in existence in the late 680s, but must have ceased to exist as a significant military force during the 690s, once Carthage and the last imperial possessions on the north African mainland had been conquered by Islamic forces.[20]

Consolidation of the "theme system"

Within a period of some 20 years, therefore, a strategic organization which had been established in the early fourth century, in turn based upon principles of linear defence which dated back to the second century, had been overturned and then abandoned, along with much of the territory it was evolved to protect. Instead, the rump of the East Roman empire was left with a core territory in central and northern Asia Minor, the southern Balkan littoral, the Aegean islands including Crete (Cyprus was attacked several times until, in the 680s, the emperor Justinian II reached an agreement with the Caliphate to establish a joint administration on the henceforth demilitarized island) and, in the west, parts of Italy, Sardinia and the central and western North African provinces. But by the year 700 North Africa had been lost to Islam, and the situation in Italy was steadily deteriorating, so that the empire, in spite of the existence of an important fleet, was increasingly confined to the eastern Mediterranean basin (see Maps VIA and B).[21]

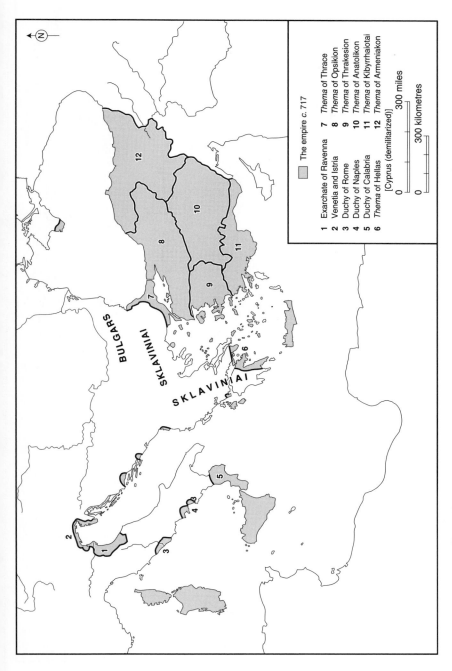

Map VIA Strategic dispositions *c.* 750

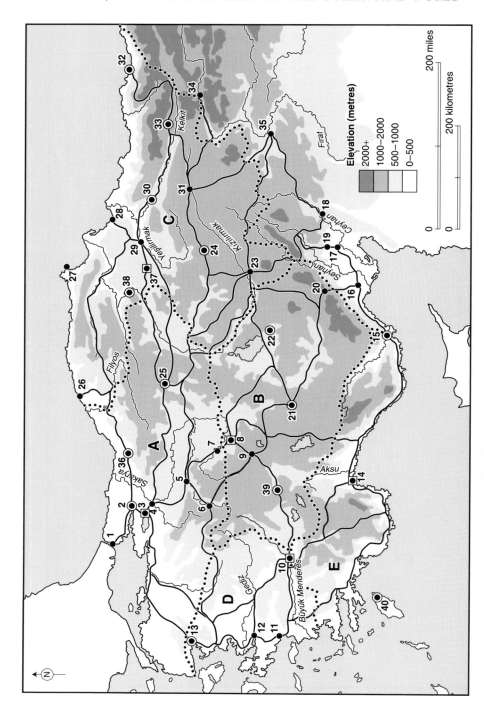

The military and naval organization which evolved out of this situation in the east has traditionally been called the "theme system", after the new Greek term *thema* applied to the armies and the districts across which they were based. There were many continuities with the older arrangements out of which it had grown, but one major change in East Roman perceptions is marked by the abandonment of a linear concept of defence. Initially, from the end of the reign of Heraclius, the army attempted to control the major passes through the mountain barrier; yet the abandonment of Cilicia at the end of the seventh century and the failure to establish any sort of artificial barrier illustrates the lack of resources as well as of any notion of constructing a fortified *limes*. Instead, field armies pursued a double strategy, of meeting major invading forces in pitched battles and throwing them back – a policy which met with more or less unmitigated defeat – and, more usually from the later part of the seventh century, of pursuing and ambushing invaders once they had entered imperial territory and completed their attack.

This approach meant that substantial areas behind the imperial frontiers were subject to regular raids and devastation, and the economic results of this for the empire were considerable, resulting eventually, during the first half of the eighth century, in the creation of what was in effect a "no-man's land" between the regions on both sides which remained settled and economically productive. East Roman strategy did, however, prevent Arab attempts to establish permanent bases to the north or west of the Taurus and Anti-Taurus ranges – combined with the Anatolian climate, unsuitable, for the most part, for the pastoralism of the Beduin, Byzantine harassment of raiding parties, large and small, and the insecurity of lines of communication, made anything other than short-term and seasonal occupation virtually impossible. Arab forces did winter on the Anatolian plateau or in captured towns and fortresses on occasion, but this had no longer-term results. From the 690s, and possibly a little earlier, the naval command of the Kibyrrhaiotai (named after the coastal town of Kibyrrha in Caria) had come into existence, separated from the older Karabisianoi and with additional territories taken, probably, from the districts initially attributed to the Anatolikon or eastern army, as a defensive shield for southwestern Anatolia.[22] In addition to the warfleet maintained at Constantinople, therefore, the empire was also evolving a screen of naval forces around its most exposed coastal regions.

One of the results of the establishment of the field armies across Asia Minor, and the ways in which the state was able to support them, was an increasing localization of the imperial forces, and the growth of a distinction

---

Town and fortress sites numbered as in Map IV

A	Opsikion	B	Anatolikon	C	Armeniakon
D	Thrakesion	E	Kibyrrhaiotai		

▣ thematic HQ   ◉ *tourma* HQ

Map VIB The early *themata* in Asia Minor *c.* 717

between the standing elements – full-time, professional soldiers – and the seasonal "militia"-like elements in each *thema*. During the reign of Constantine V a small elite force, known as the *tagmata* ("the regiments") was established, and this rapidly grew to become the elite field division of the emperors themselves. It was never very large, but it had better pay and discipline and served as a valuable nucleus of picked troops on campaign. This was, in fact, the first step in a rapidly-growing tendency to recruit mercenary forces, both foreign and indigenous, to form special units and to serve for the duration of a particular campaign or group of campaigns. When the empire went fully on to the offensive in the second half of the tenth century, it was such *tagmata*, now referring to all such units rather than simply the original "imperial" units, who spearheaded the campaigns, although the thematic contingents remained important. And it was such units which formed the garrisons of the extensive territories, divided up into small military-administrative districts, which were (re-)conquered from the Muslim emirs of northern Syria, Armenia and northwest Iraq between 940 and 1030 (Maps VII and VIII).[23]

The fundamental principles of Byzantine strategy in the east, as it evolved out of the disasters of the early Arab conquests and raids into Asia Minor, were threefold: where possible, raiding forces should be held and turned back at the passes before they could do any harm. Occasionally, when a unified command over the field armies was established, this policy worked quite well. At the end of the seventh century, for example, Herakleios, the brother of the emperor Tiberios Apsimar, was made *monostrategos* of the frontier cavalry forces, and was able to achieve a series of spectacular successes before his career was brought to a premature end by the seizure of the throne by Justinian II in 705. In 697/8 Herakleios was sent to Cappadocia, from which he was able to launch successful attacks into Syria in 699/700, and heavily defeat a series of major raids in 700/1, 702–3 and 703–4.[24] But where this policy of meeting and repulsing hostile attacks at the frontier did not work (which seems generally to have been the case), then the local forces were to harass and dog the invading forces, making sure to follow their every movement so that the location of each party or group was known. A key aspect of this strategy was the garrisoning of numerous small forts and fortresses along the major routes, on crossroads and locations where supplies might be stored, and above and behind the frontier passes through which enemy forces had to pass to gain access to the Byzantine hinterland. As long as these were held, they served to hinder any longer-term Arab presence on Byzantine soil, since they posed a constant threat to the invaders' communications, to the smaller raiding or foraging parties they might send out and to their logistical arrangements in general. Small and feebly occupied though many of them were, they were usually sited on good sources of water, and as long as they had advance notice of the raiders, they could store supplies adequate for most eventualities. They were a constant threat to any invading force, yet to stop and lay siege to them was more trouble than it was worth for most raiding parties. Except when a major military effort under caliphal or some other central authority was intended, in which case siege equipment and appropriate supplies and manpower would be present, time was precious and the soldiers and warriors themselves were interested in collecting as much booty as they could and getting out again. Although both small and large fortified places frequently changed hands, the Byzantines clearly understood the importance of maintaining their control as a means of preventing efforts at permanent settlement and of minimizing the extent and effect of the raids.[25]

From the later eighth and early ninth centuries the *themata* were complemented by a series of special frontier districts which constituted independent commands. These were known as kleisourarchies (*kleisourarchiai*), created from subdivisions of the *themata* from which they were detached, which seem to represent the crystallization out of the previous strategy of a new policy: a locally focused defence, involving a "guerrilla" strategy of harassing, ambushing and dogging invading raiders, designed to stymie all but the largest forces and to prevent both the pillaging of the countryside and the economic dislocation which followed, as well as to make raiding expeditions riskier and less certain, in terms of easy booty, than before. The change is signalled, possibly, by the report in the chronicle of Theophanes that, in the year 779, the emperor Leo IV ordered each *strategos* to select 3,000 elite troops to harass the Arab army which had reached Dorylaion, rather than attempt a direct confrontation. Theophanes states that this was specifically to prevent them sending out pillaging raids, and he also reports the emperor's order to destroy pasture and other supplies, with the result that the Arab force had to retire after 15 days.[26] The creation of the *kleisourai* appears to mark the development of a strategy specifically aimed at frontier provinces and the conditions there prevailing, and suggests an awareness in Constantinople of the need for greater autonomy at local level. As well as these administrative *kleisourai*, however, the individual passes and defiles through the mountains continued to be referred to by the same term, so that we read, for example, of the *kleisoura* of Podandos, north of the Cilician Gates, as well as those of Seleukia or Kappadokia.[27]

Over the same period, the naval arrangements of the empire were expanded, so that by about 830 there were three main naval *themata* – of the Aegean, of Samos and the Kibyrrhaiotai – in addition to the imperial fleet and the much smaller provincial fleets of Hellas and the Peloponnese. The maritime front was thus covered in the east, and while continued raiding and piracy was not stopped, it was at least checked and occasionally thrown back. The situation in the west was somewhat different. The loss of Carthage in the 690s and of the North African coast had deprived the empire of its naval bases there. Sicily probably continued to function in this way, and there is some slight evidence for imperial naval activity in the Balearics. Sardinia remained an imperial possession throughout. From the late 840s, however, the Balearics too were providing shelter for Muslim pirates and raiders, and by the early ninth century the empire seems to have lost interest in the western Mediterranean; the failure to provide adequate naval support when Sicily and then Crete were invaded in the 820s proved costly, since the latter in particular rapidly became the source of constant maritime raids on the empire's coastal lands.[28]

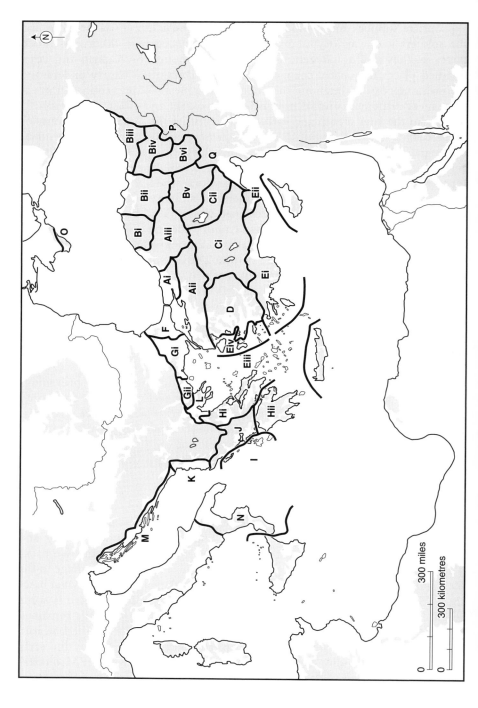

The Balkan front presents a somewhat different aspect, and for two basic reasons. First, the absence of any concept such as *jihād* on either side meant that war for purely ideological purposes was also absent: ideological differences focused on territory and resources, although warmaking to avenge defeats, maintain honour or respond to internal political pressures certainly was a factor. Second, Bulgar khans and Byzantine emperors recognized, through a series of agreements beginning with that between Constantine IV and Asparuch in 680, that a territorial boundary could be drawn. In organizational terms, however, the same pattern of defensive arrangements was applied, with *themata* or armies established to defend imperial territory evolving gradually a territorial identity, before this military-administrative system was employed by the government to win back lost territories.

Warfare involved both sides crossing this frontier and marching to meet and defeat the enemy host, or devastating the countryside, but neither side was able to deliver a knock-out blow, so that campaigns generally represented a war of attrition, with the advantage swinging back and forth according to the extent to which one side or the other was preoccupied elsewhere. There is no

New *themata*		Original *Themata*	New *themata*	
Ai	Optimaton	Opsikion	I	Kephallenia
Aii	Opsikion			
Aiii	Boukellarion		J	Nikopolis
Bi	Paphlagonia	Armeniakon	K	Dyrrhachion
Bii	Armeniakon			
Biii	Chaldia		L	Thessaloniki
Biv	Koloneia			
Bv	Charsianon		M	Dalmatia
Bvi	Sebasteia		N	Laggobardia
Ci	Anatolikon	Anatolikon	O	Cherson
Cii	Kappadokia			
D	Thrakesion	Thrakesion	P	Mesopotamia
Ei	Kibyrrhaiotai	Karabisianoi/Kibyrrhaiotai	Q	Lykandos
Eii	Seleukeia			
Eiii	Aegaios Pelagos (Aegean Sea)			
Eiv	Samos			
F	Thrake	Thrake		
Gi	Makedonia	Makedonia		
Gii	Strymon			
Hi	Hellas	Hellas		
Hii	Peloponnesos			

See Table 3.1. Not shown here are short-lived commands such as Leontokome, created in the region around Tephrike after Basil I's armies destroyed the town *c.* 879, originally a *kleisoura*, then renamed and established as a *thema* by Leo VI.

Map VII   The *themata c.* 920

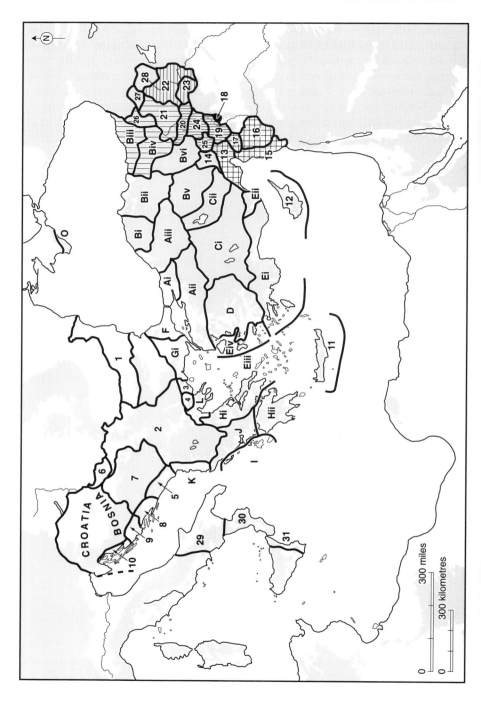

evidence for a "frontier" society such as evolved in the east, although banditry in the hills and forests meant that "peace" was a relative affair for the rural and urban populations of both sides, while the isolated Byzantine fortress-settlements were dependent for much of the time on their own resources and initiative for their survival, until they were, eventually, incorporated into the expanding territory of the empire from the early ninth century. And both Bulgars and Byzantines were active in moving population groups to occupy border districts and to serve as frontier soldiers – the latter involving generally the immigration of populations from central and eastern Asia Minor to Thrace, the former the movement of Slav tribes or confederacies to the regions behind the frontier.[29]

Defensive equilibrium: the short life of the "theme system"

The development of imperial strategy is marked by the incremental evolution of the "theme system", both in respect of the distribution of troops and their command structure, as well as in respect of its administrative importance. For the latter, the *themata* were at first merely groupings of provinces across which different armies were based. By about 700–30 they had acquired a clear geographical identity (reference is made to "the provinces of such and such a

1	Paristrion	2	Boulgaria
3	Strymon	4	Neos Strymon
5	Diokleia	6	Sirmion
7	Serbia	8	Terbounia
9	Zachloumoi (autonomous)	10	Arentanoi (autonomous)
11	Crete	12	Cyprus
13	Kilikia	14	Lykandos
15	Antiocheia	16	Aleppo (autonomous)
17	Doliche (Teloukh)	18	Edessa
19	Trans-Euphrates cities	20	Keltzine-Chortzine
21	Derzene/Phasiane (Basean)	22	Vaspurakan
23	Taron	24	Mesopotamia
25	Melitene	26	Iberia
27	Kars	28	Shirak/Ani
29	Laggobardia	30	Kalabria
31	Sikelia (1038–42)		

Croatia and Bosnia were only briefly under imperial control, and remained autonomous.

Regions under the *doux* of Antioch: ⊞   Regions under the *doux* of Edessa: ■

Regions under the *doux* of Chaldia: ‖‖   Regions under the *doux* of Mesopotamia: ‖‖‖

Regions under the *doux* of Vaspurakan: ☰

See Table 3.2 for detailed list and bibliography.

Map VIII   Strategic dispositions *c.* 1050: *themata* and ducates

thema", for example); and by the later eighth century some elements of fiscal administration as well as military organization were constituted on a thematic basis, although the late Roman provinces continued to subsist (see Maps VIA and B).

But by the middle of the ninth century, it is clear that *themata* had both an administrative and military-administrative structure, which was rapidly replacing the vestiges of the late Roman arrangements, and that the *strategos* acted effectively as generalissimo in his province, with at the very least a supervisory authority over fiscal and judicial officials. Table 3.1 illustrates the process of expansion of this system from its beginnings up to the middle of the tenth century (see Map VII).[30]

From the point of view of troop dispositions, the number of *themata* expands with the stabilization of the empire's political situation (during the reigns of Leo III and Constantine V), initially in terms of internal subdivisions to create politically and logistically more manageable units; then – from the later eighth century – with the reimposition of imperial authority over former imperial lands in the south Balkans. As the empire reasserted its military strength in the east during the ninth century, so the role and the proportion of full-time "tagmatic" units becomes ever more important. As a reflection of this, there emerged, first, a centralized overall command of the active field forces, the *tagmata* and similar units, under the *domestikos* of the Scholai, and then the subdivision of this command into two spheres, the West and the East.

The final stage begins in the first half of the tenth century when, following a series of successful campaigns on both the eastern and Balkan frontiers, a whole range of new military districts under independent commanders had to be established. Initially, this involved the upgrading of former *kleisourai* to the status of *themata* as well as the incorporation of new regions as *themata*, with the difference that they were generally quite small in extent, centred on a particular fortress and a clearly delineated geopolitical entity, and placed under officers often referred to as "lesser" *strategoi*. Along the eastern frontier they were called "frontier" or "Armenian" themes, because Armenians made up a substantial portion of the populations who were indigenous to the regions in question or who had migrated there. This nomenclature also served to differentiate them organizationally and culturally from the older "great" or "Roman" *themata*.[31] But this system was further modified with the stationing of ever larger and militarily more effective detachments of the imperial *tagmata* and similarly recruited professional units in a broad band of fortified centres, most the headquarters of newly established small *themata*. From the late 960s, these were grouped into a series of larger commands, each under a *doux* or *katepano*, independent of the local thematic administration, and who were given a general authority over the lesser generals across whose regions their military authority was granted.

These new commands generally encompassed a group of new small *themata*, together with major fortified centres in the *themata* in their rear. Strategically, these new commands formed a screen of buffer provinces protecting what had now become the hinterland of the old *themata*, each covering a segment of the expanded frontier, strategically orientated for offensive operations, and independent of one another in terms of their available manpower. Similar arrangements were established in the west. One of the results of this development was, inevitably, the increasing irrelevance of the older thematic militias, which gradually lost most of their military potential and capacity. Instead, the field armies both along the frontiers of the empire and within the provinces were composed increasingly of either mercenary, professional troops or forces sent by subordinate and vassal princes and rulers of the various smaller states bordering the empire.

The appearance and rank of the new ducates testifies to the imperial strategy of expansion and conquest on both the eastern and western frontiers. By the 970s a new array of such commands – the ducates of Chaldia, Mesopotamia and Antioch – covered the eastern frontier, and were expanded to include the ducates of Iberia, Vaspurakan, Edessa and Ani in the period from 1000–45. In the west, similarly, the progress of the frontier and the function of these ducates or katepanates can be seen very clearly in the establishment in the 970s and 980s of a ducate of "Mesopotamia in the West", of Adrianople and of Thessaloniki, and after the destruction of the Bulgar empire by Basil II (by 1015), the commands of Sirmion, Paristrion and Bulgaria. Similar commands appear a little later in Byzantine southern Italy – partly associated with the aggressive activities of the Normans in that region – and in the southern Balkans (see Map VIII).[32] Table 3.2 illustrates the evolution of this system from the middle of the tenth up to the later eleventh century.

From strategy to crisis management, 1025–c. 90

The successes of Basil II in destroying the Bulgarian empire and incorporating it into the Roman state, and of Basil and his predecessors in recovering large swathes of territory in northern Syria and northwest Iraq, produced a situation in which, paradoxically, the empire was less protected than hitherto from any serious external attack, for several of the buffer states and districts which had covered it previously had now been absorbed under direct imperial rule. It also substantially eroded the thematic structures which had evolved in the period from the later seventh to ninth centuries. While the new command structure of ducates and katepanates created a protective curtain of buffer districts between the inner regions of the empire and the frontier zones, military organization in the newly established ducates was fragmented and designed to address local threats or respond to the need to mobilize for larger expeditionary offensives. While this was not a linear defensive structure but rather an active defence in depth, the fragmentation of command around the periphery did have certain disadvantages. When a major threat appeared, it was still up to the emperor, or one of the two commanders-in-chief, rather than a local commander to assemble

Table 3.1 Transformations in strategic administration *c.* 660–920 (dates in parentheses are first clear references to the commands)

Sixth century	Seventh century	Eighth century	Ninth century	Tenth century
Mag. mil. *Praes. I and II*	Opsikion (680)	Opsikion Optimaton (by 775) Boukellarion (768)	Opsikion Optimaton Boukellarion	Opsikion Optimaton Boukellarion
Mag. mil. *per Orientem*	Anatolikon (669/70)	Anatolikon	Anatolikon Kappadokia (830)	Anatolikon Kappadokia
Mag. mil. *per Armeniam*	Armeniakon (667/68)	Armeniakon	Armeniakon Charsianon (863) [Lykandos] (by 916) Paphlagonia (by 826) Chaldia (prob. by 824) Koloneia (863) Leontokome/ Tephrike (c. 879)	Armeniakon Charsianon Paphlagonia Chaldia Koloneia [Mesopotamia] (by 911) [Sebasteia] (by 911)
Mag. mil. *per Thracias*	Thrakesion (741/2)	Thrakesion	Thrakesion	Thrakesion
Quaestura *exercitus*	Karabisianoi (670s)	Karabisianoi Kibyrrhaiotai (697/98) Aigaion Pelagos/ Dodecanese (mid-eighth century?)	Kibyrrhaiotai Seleukeia (by 934) Aigaion Pelagos (842) Samos (late eighth century) (899)	Kibyrrhaiotai Seleukeia Aigaion Pelagos Samos
(Hellas)	Hellas (698)	Hellas	Hellas [Kephallenia] (809) [Peloponnesos] (811)	Hellas Kephallenia [Nikopolis] (899) Peloponnesos

(Thrace)	Thrake (by 680)	Thrake (Makedonia) (by 802)	Thrake Makedonia Thessaloniki (by 824) [Dyrrhachion] (by 856)	Thrake Makedonia Strymon (by 899) Thessaloniki Dyrrhachion Dalmatia (by 899)
(Sicily)	(Sicily)	Sikelia (c. 700)	Sikelia	Sikelia
Mag. mil. per Italiam and exarchate	Exarchate and *duces*	Exarchate and *duces*	Lagobardia (by 892)	Lagobardia
Bosphorus (Crimea)	Cherson (mid-seventh century)	Cherson/ Klimata (by 833)	Cherson (by 892)	Cherson
Crete	Crete (*tourma*)	Crete (*thema c.* 760)	(Lost to Arabs 824–8)	[Crete] (from 961)
Cyprus (in *quaestura*)	Cyprus (condominium with caliphate)	Cyprus (condominium with caliphate, except for short period under Basil I)	[Cyprus] (965)	Cyprus

Notes: 1. The division of the original *themata* did not necessarily involve merely the separation of a *tourma* and its elevation to the position of a *kleisourarchia* or *thema*. Many independent new districts incorporated regions from adjacent *themata*, as well as newly incorporated territory.

2. Names of *themata* in brackets represent those created from newly conquered districts.

3. For more detailed analysis and sources, see Pertusi (ed.), *De Thematibus*, and Oikonomides, *Listes*, with extensive further literature.

4. Thematic and *tourma* headquarters are marked, where known or hypothesized, on Map VIB.

Table 3.2 Transformations in strategic administration on the eastern and western frontiers c. 920–1118 (dates in parentheses are first clear references to the commands)

c. 920–49	950s	960s	970s	1000–70	Ducates and katepanates
			Taron (from c. 966–75)		Antioch (969–1084/5)*
Abara (orig. tourma of Sebasteia; kleisoura by 920; thema from c. 951)†	Derzênê (by 952)**		Chortzinê (by 975)†		
			Koptos (by 975)†		Mesopotamia† (969/71–1071/75)
			Taranta (by 975)†		
Larissa (tourma of Sebasteia; kleisoura c. 900; tourma of Sebasteia from 911–?; thema by 975)†	Samosata (or Asmosaton) (either 938 or 958)†	Anabarza (from 964)*	Hexakômia (by 975)†	Abydos (by 1001)	
	Tziliapert (from c. 948–52)**	Germanikeia (from 962)*	Podandos (by 975)*	Iberia (Tayk') (by 1022)	Chaldia** (969–1071/75)
			Kama (by 975)†	Telouch (1030)	
Melitênê (from 934)†	Chasanara (from 956)†	Eirênoupolis (from 965)*	Kymbaleos (tourma of Charsianon; thema by 975)		Iberia (1000–71/75)
Chozanon (from c. 938)†		Tarsos (from 965)*		Trans-Euphrates cities (1032)	
	Tzamandos (from 957)†	Artach (from 966)*	Limnia (by 975)†	Perkri (c. 1034)	
Rômanoupolis (from 942, thema by 969)†	Adata (from 957–69)*	Palatza (c. 966)*	Mouzariou (by 975)†	Shirak/Ani (from 1045)	Vaspurakan (1022–59/75)
Charpezikion (by 949)†	Zermiou (after 956)†	Kaloudia (by 969)†	Sôtêroupolis (Bourtzô) (by 975)**	Artzike and Arkeravon (from c. 1050)	
Chavzizin (after 940)†	Erknê (after 956)†		Chouit (by 975)	Vaspurakan (from 1022)	Edessa (1031–87)
			Meltê (by 975)**	Kogovit (c. 1050)	
Theodosioupolis (c. 949; ceded to Iberia 979; returned to Byz. in 1000)**			Artzê (by 975)**	Mantzikert (by 1054)	Ani (1045–64)
			Chantiartê (by 975)†	Hierapolis (1069)	
			Hagios Elias (by 990)*		
			Pagrach (by 990)*		

88

				Mesopotamia/ Presthlavitza (971–86)
Kalabria (from c. 940s)	Kyklades (from c. 950s–975)	Mauron Oros (by 990)*		Adrianoupolis (969/71–1204)
		Balaneas (by 990)*		Thessaloniki (969/71–1204)
		Marakeos (by 990)*		Paristrion/ Paradounavon (1000/20–1185)
		Strymôn/Chrysava (by 975)	Philippoupolis (by 1001)	Boulgaria (1018–1185)
		Neos Strymôn (by 975)	Serbia (1000–1)	Sirmion (1019–1183)
		Drougoubiteia (before 975)	Achrida (1014)	Italy (katepanate) (969–1071)
		Jericho (before 975)	Kastoria (1014)	Dyrrhachion (1042–1204)
		Edessa (before 975 until 980s)	Koloneia (1018)	Sardikê (1059/67–1170)
		Euxinos (by 975)	Dryinoupolis (1018)	Hellas & Peloponnesos (1051/67–1204)
		Beroê (c. 971–86)	Raousion (1040)	
		Dristra (from 971)	Loukania (1042)	
		Mesopotamia/ Presthlavitza (by 975)	Brindision (1059–67)	
			Serrai (1062)	
			Diabolis (1073)	
			Mosynopolis (1078)	
			Smolena (1079)	

† Territories under *doux* of Mesopotamia.

* Territories under *doux* of Antioch.

** Territories under *doux* of Chaldia.

Note: For detailed analysis, sources and further literature, see Oikonomidès, *Listes*; Oikonomidès, "L'organisation de la frontière orientale de Byzance aux Xe–XIe siècles et le taktikon de l'Escorial", *Rapports du XIVe Congrès Internat. des Études Byzantines*, II (Bucarest, 1971), pp. 73–90 (repr. in Oikonomidès, *Documents et études sur les institutions de Byzance [VIIe–XVe s.]* [London, 1976], no. XXIV); and Kühn, *Die byzantinische Armee*.

an appropriate force and march to deal with it. Typical is the expedition of Basil II in 995, who had to march from Constantinople to relieve Aleppo: the emperor completed the march, which normally took up to 60 days, in a quarter of the time, but under half of his original force actually arrived with him. Similarly the campaigns of John I against the Bulgars and the Rus' in the 970s relied heavily upon the emperor's presence with his elite units for any coherent response to the threat; those of Romanos III – less successful – in Syria in the early 1030s illustrate the same point.[33]

Strategy was thus localized and well capable of dealing with threats of an equivalent status. It was not designed to deal with major invading armies, except insofar as the principles of guerrilla warfare and harassment were kept alive. And this was a fundamental weakness, since in the event of an attack or threat on more than one front the emperor or commander-in-chief and the main army could rarely get from one to the other in time without extraordinary efforts. Success in the tenth and early eleventh centuries, under a series of vigorous military emperors who possessed both the tactical and military know-how to deploy their armies and their resources intelligently, thus produced a system which relied almost entirely on the ability of an individual commander-in-chief and his subordinates. On the whole, the system of ducates acted as an effective deterrent to most attacks or threats of attack. But the shock-absorbing strength of the old thematic system, focused on defence and on harassment of the enemy, was transformed into the aggressive field armies of the later tenth and eleventh centuries, while the defensive capacities of the older establishment were neglected or allowed to wither away in order to cater for the increased expense of the predominantly full-time mercenary armies.

The nature of the problem is illustrated by several events from the 1040s on. When Maniakes rebelled and marched against Constantinople, no local or provincial troops were available near the capital, so that Constantine IX was compelled hastily to recruit levies and mercenaries with which to oppose him. During the rebellion of Leo Tornikes in 1047 Michael Psellos, who was an eyewitness to the events, makes it quite clear that, with the eastern field army engaged in Armenia and the western armies having rallied to Tornikes, there were simply no forces to defend the capital. He states explicitly that there were no local, provincial troops at all, nor were there any allied or auxiliary forces available apart from a few mercenaries in the palace guard. The emperor was compelled to recruit a scratch force from soldiers held on various charges in the prisons of the capital and from the streets. When, in 1057, the general Isaac Komnenos marched with the eastern field army against Constantinople, only the western army, scattered in the Balkans, and a small mercenary force in the capital was available to the emperor (Michael VI).[34]

Combined with an effective diplomacy and the establishment of a series of buffer-states or regions around the empire's borders, one of the main policies of both Basil II as well as Constantine IX (1042–55), the effects of this situation on the old thematic forces was ignored. The extent to which these developments affected the naval *themata* and their military potential remains obscure.

The commutation of naval service in the coastal *themata* necessarily meant a reduction in provincial naval resources. At the same time, it appears that the emperors – from Basil II on – clearly found it less expensive to call upon allied or dependent states (such as Venice) to provide naval power than to maintain a high-cost standing fleet at Constantinople, with the result that the imperial fleet seems to have been considerably reduced in numbers during the eleventh century. The increasing dependence of the empire on non-Byzantine powers, whose interests were eventually hostile to those of the Roman state, has correctly been seen as a major cause of the political-military difficulties the empire experienced throughout the later eleventh and twelfth centuries, in spite of the attempt of Alexios I and then Manuel to re-establish an effective home fleet.[35]

Whereas Basil II had appreciated both the need for, as well as the dangers of, substantial standing armies in the frontier regions, by the 1040s it seems to have been thought that the political-diplomatic system of alliances or buffer states had rendered many of the expensive standing forces in the provinces inessential. This is perhaps particularly clear along the northern frontier, at the eastern end of the Danube, where Byzantine defensive arrangements confronted potentially hostile peoples without any intermediary buffer zone, and where the government encouraged the economic colonization and integration of the steppe peoples to the north through trade and commerce, reducing the costs of maintaining the complex system of advance posts and fortresses established at the end of the reign of Basil II (and, possibly, increasing the need for cash which was reflected in the policy of commuting taxes in kind applied in the western Balkans at about the same time).[36] There was more than simply a military-strategic aspect to this process, of course: the anxieties of the Constantinopolitan power elite in respect of the growth of provincial retinues and patronage between commanders who were also local lords and the thematic soldiery also played a key role, and determined the nature of the fiscal and strategic response.[37] But even the soldier-emperor Isaac I Komnenos recognized that the expense of constant standing forces and constant warfare was too much for the state in the long term, and actively pursued a foreign policy which would enable him to call on vassals and neighbouring rulers for troops rather than maintain a full standing army within the empire.[38]

Yet the alienation of the "military" aristocracy through the reduction in resources for the thematic armies and the reduction or disbandment of frontier provincial forces, whatever the short-term gains might appear to be, placed undue pressure on this arrangement. The breakdown of imperial defences during the middle years of the eleventh century, chiefly a result of the fact that the balance between diplomacy and military strength was destroyed by civil war and provincial or military rebellion (the former a result of poorly judged fiscal policies) and the complete disintegration of the bulk of the indigenous army after 1071, illustrate this very clearly.[39] Reliance on mercenaries was such that when Frankish troops under their most successful leader Russel de Bailleul, rebelled and seized Amaseia and the old Armeniakon region in north eastern

Anatolia, the government had the greatest difficulty in assembling an army with which to oppose him. Not only did it have no substantial resources with which to pay such a force, it had few means at its disposal to actually recruit the soldiers in the first place.[40]

The traditional thematic militias, that is the seasonally recruited troops of the provinces, had all but disappeared as a result of the government's fiscal policies in the period *c.* 1030–60. The bulk of the effective units in the imperial army had in any case consisted even before this time of numerous *tagmata*, salaried units of full-time soldiers recruited from the provinces of the empire, and this continued to be the case under Alexios, although there may not have been a great deal of continuity from the period before the defeat at Manzikert in 1071 and the civil wars which followed. Foreign mercenary troops, especially of western knights – Franks, Germans and Normans – also played a prominent role, usually under their own leaders.[41]

This massive increase in the employment by and reliance of the central government upon mercenary forces has often been seen as a bad thing, the assumption being that the older thematic forces were both more loyal to the empire and their homelands and hence more reliable, as well as cheaper, than mercenaries. But several studies suggest that this is a misleading view. First, the growth in the employment of such forces was an incremental response to a changing strategic context, closely paralleling the stages by which the empire moved between the later ninth and later tenth centuries from a more-or-less entirely defensive strategy to one of aggressive offence. This was a context in which the full-time "professional" mercenaries hired by the empire were both more effective tactically and provided (usually) greater value for money than the cheap but largely ineffective thematic militias, the militarily useful core elements of which were too small to be able to prosecute a long-term strategy of expansion with all its implications (permanent frontier garrisons, rapid mobilization, constant military readiness and so forth). And it should be borne in mind that many of the empire's core units, including all the imperial *tagmata* in and around Constantinople between the later eighth and early tenth centuries, as well as the small standing elements in each *thema*, were in effect indigenous mercenary units anyway. Second, it should be remembered that since professional full-time soldiers are usually better trained than the majority of the thematic, provincial militia troops, fewer of them are required to do the same task. The overall quality of men recruited was better, and a much better selection and balance of specialists in particular arms could be made – archers, heavy or light cavalry and so forth. As we will see below, total numbers of foreign mercenaries were never large, yet they fulfilled extremely effective service for the empire in whatever theatres they were engaged. In addition, as long as they were regularly paid, they were at least as reliable and often more so than provincial levies, if only because they were less closely involved with local or imperial politics – whether they were Byzantine or not played no significant role. And indigenous provincial levies were just as likely as mercenaries to rebel if they were not properly paid or treated, as has also been demonstrated.

Third, the use of mercenary troops gave the central government a greater degree of control over its armies, since it controlled the pay-chest and the rate of recruitment as well as the dispositions of such units. Mercenary soldiers were more dependent on their paymasters than provincial levies and less prone to involvement in local politics. This was an advantage to rulers such as Basil II, for example, who wished to challenge the pre-eminence of the provincial military magnates of the eastern *themata*, or to rulers such as Constantine IX who wished to lessen their reliance upon this provincial elite in military matters as well as political affairs. Of course, things could go wrong, but the mercenaries hired by the empire were generally a loyal and effective fighting force. And when they rebelled or betrayed their commanding general or the emperor, it was usually in a political context where native Byzantine troops were also equally implicated (as in the rebellion of George Maniakes in the 1030s, for example, or before, during and after the battle at Mantzikert), and where their strategic situation was advantageous: in the rebellion of Bailleul, for example, the greater proportion of the Frankish mercenaries serving the emperor appears to have been quartered in the Armeniakon region, which gave de Bailleul both an adequate military force and the logistical and resource-base to maintain his position. As has been noted, when Alexios I had established his authority, he avoided the establishment of large concentrations of foreign troops in the provinces as well as placing Byzantine officers in command of his mercenary units wherever possible. [42]

The system of defence as re-established ultimately under Alexios I Komnenos (1081–1118) was a continuation of these developments and the methods he had found to be most successful in his wars to repel the Pechenegs, Normans and Seljuk Turks. Strategy in the broader sense in the opening years of his rule did not exist: the emperor had to respond to a series of emergencies in different parts of the empire on an entirely reactive basis, although it is apparent that the Balkan theatre preoccupied him in the opening years of his rule. In his first year he had a small but effective central army that had been raised during the reigns of the preceding emperors Michael VII (1071–8) and Nikephros III (1078–81), consisting of foreign mercenary units (the Varangians) and some elite corps – the Exkoubitoi, the Athanatoi (immortals) and the Vestiaritai – alongside some indigenous *tagmata* from Thrace and Macedonia as well as from particular ethnic groups – Paulicians in the Balkans, Turks from the Vardar region – and the usual foreign mercenaries, chiefly Turks and Franks. But this force was destroyed in Alexios' first years, as he was defeated first by the Normans (at Dyrrachion in 1081) and then by the Pechenegs in 1089/90. Indeed, the army which was assembled in 1089 consisted of the emperor's guards, a contingent of Flemish knights, 500 strong, supplied by count Robert of Flanders, a hastily recruited levy of conscripted peasants from the region and a new unit of 2,000 men called the *archontopouloi*, i.e. the sons of former soldiers and those who had died in battle. This army, too, was defeated and scattered, and by the winter of 1090 the emperor could muster a mere 500 soldiers. For the following decade he relied on a combination of mercenary units and units formed from retainers or hired soldiers in the retinues of his extended family and the members of the landed class, and after his defeat of the Pechenegs at the battle of Lebounion in 1091, the surviving Pechenegs themselves, who formed a core element in his armies thereafter. But his resources were always stretched thinly, and it is clear that virtually no provincial defensive units existed under local command. Apart from motley town militias and the retinues of local landlords and imperial officials in the provinces, the imperial army was the only effective force available to deal with attacks on three different fronts.[43]

A precarious balance: strategy under the Komnenoi and Angeloi (c. 1090–1203)

After the situation had been stabilized – immediately before the passage of the First Crusade (1097–8) – Alexios was able to turn to re-establishing a coherent defensive strategy. The imperial armies now consisted of three main types of unit: mercenaries, both foreign and under their own leaders, and indigenous, drawn from a particular region (Thrace, Macedonia, etc.); the Pechenegs; and Byzantine troops formed from the retinues of his nearer and more distant relatives and their clients. These now acted as an extension of the imperial family throughout the empire and were gradually given a near-monopoly of high military positions. In addition, Alexios attempted to re-establish a connection between landholding and military service, insofar as foreign populations settled within the empire were required to provide soldiers in return for the continued possession of their lands.

Under his successors John II (1118–43) and more particularly Manuel I (1143–80) this link may have been slightly strengthened by a more widespread use of the system of *pronoia*, by which state revenues from a given district or estate were awarded to an individual or group in return for the provision of soldiers and their equipment. But it has been argued that the generalized use of this method really dates from the period of the Latin conquest of Constantinople and after, in both the territories ruled by westerners and those which continued under Byzantine rule.[44]

The re-establishment of imperial political control in the Balkans was achieved by 1094. The Normans were hemmed into a small enclave on the Illyrian coast; a little before this, the Pechenegs were crushed in battle and placed under treaty or incorporated into the imperial armies. The stabilization of the situation in this theatre brought a return to the administrative arrangements of the middle of the eleventh century, and it was now the Balkan provinces which provided the resources with which the emperor could begin to reassert imperial authority in the east. The emphasis placed by Manuel I on defending imperial interests in the Balkans, on protecting the hinterland behind the frontier zone and on maintaining a firm control of the Danube frontier with its constituent fortresses demonstrates the recognition by the imperial government that the resources of the area were essential to the empire's financial and political survival. Western commentators note that the areas to the south of the Danube were kept more or less depopulated in order to discourage raids from either the Hungarians or the Galician Russians to the north.[45]

The network of diplomatic relations built up by John II and by Manuel I in particular was essential to the empire's overall strategic stability, although relations with the Hungarians in particular were volatile. The Serbs were able to play off Byzantine and Hungarian interests to their own advantage, and Byzantine efforts to maintain a political hegemony over the region involved frequent displays of military strength. These were mostly successful, but when they were unsuccessful they encouraged increased Hungarian aggression along the Danube, the temporary loss of tribute and manpower from the Serbs and potentially the aggression of other trans-Danubian neighbours. Balkan separatism, fostered by local dynasts and princes in both the eastern and western areas demanded constant watchfulness on the part of the government at Constantinople, and the investment of considerable resources in the maintenance of local garrisons and centres of local imperial military-political authority. The threat from the Normans of Sicily required a constant diplomatic effort (with considerable financial consequences) in the west in order to maintain a network of alliances between the empire and a disparate anti-Sicilian group, the interests of whose members varied over time so that both military action as well as the regular reconfiguration of the alliance were necessary. Manuel especially promoted the western alliance and the interests of westerners in Byzantium, since this was the only way to maintain the western margins of the empire secure. Since the permanent defence and garrisoning of the western Balkan littoral was financially out of the question, such a system was the only practical way to maintain imperial hegemony over the region. As soon as the emperors neglected this system, or alienated its erstwhile allies – especially the Italian maritime cities and the Papacy – the weaknesses of this strategic system revealed themselves with disastrous results.[46]

In Asia Minor the strategic situation was no less complex because so much territory had been lost to the Turks, who had been able to establish a solid military control over substantial regions. Imperial control in western Asia Minor had more or less entirely lapsed when Alexios I seized the throne in 1081, and was only restored through the efforts of Alexios jointly with the armies of the First Crusade, described in detail by his daughter Anna. It was imperative to create a new frontier, not simply in order to demarcate the points which imperial forces were to defend, but to establish a safe area from which resources could be extracted and within which economic life could safely be carried on. The results of imperial efforts under Alexios can be seen in the numerous new commands established to deal with hostile threats and to consolidate imperial progress in the recovery of territorial control, especially in Asia Minor: in the west, Abydos (1086), Anchialos (1087), Crete (1088–9), Philippoupolis (1094–6), Belgrade (1096) and Karpathos (c. 1090–1100) mark imperial successes; in the east, Trebizond (1091), Nicaea, Ephesos, Smyrna (all in 1097), Cyprus (1099),

Kourikos and Seleukeia (1103), Korypho (1104/5) and Samosata (1100) similarly illustrate Alexios' progress. John and Manuel built upon this beginning, and were as a result radically to restructure the military and civil administrative landscape (see Map IX).

Military dispositions continued to be dominated by the pattern set during the eleventh century: the existence of a single imperial field army, with additional divisions involved on specific fronts for specific campaigns when they could be afforded, and in the interior – in the Balkans particularly – for the maintenance of state control and the extraction of fiscal resources. The tradition of dividing the command into an eastern and a western section (with units referred to appropriately) similarly was maintained. Frontier defence and protection of local communities was placed in the hands of local lords and their retinues, or specific groups of landholders with military obligations of one sort or another attached to their tenure. The empire continued to settle foreigners on its soil under the obligation to provide military service of one sort or another, usually of a local defensive nature – defeated Pechenegs were given lands in Macedonia by Alexios I, and Serbs and Pechenegs were given lands in Anatolia during the reign of John II, for example, in return providing soldiers for the imperial army and the local defences. In the same way Cuman soldiers were given military estates in Macedonia during the reign of Manuel. This was a tradition which continued until the end of the empire.[47]

The imperial navy – called by Kekaumenos "the glory of the Romans" – experienced a minor recovery under Alexios. Initially entirely dependent upon Venice for help against Robert Guiscard, Alexios established the post of *megas doux* as commander-in-chief of the imperial fleets, bringing together what remained of the provincial fleets and the imperial flotilla at Constantinople and devoting some resources to re-establishing a respectable imperial naval presence in the Aegean and Adriatic. John II re-established (or maintained) the maritime service, imposed on the Aegean islands, for the provision of a certain number of warships and sailors or provisions and supplies in money or in kind for the imperial fleet, although Manuel seems to have allowed these obligations to be commuted. Nevertheless, during his reign substantial fleets of warships and transports could be assembled for major combined operations, crewed according to one contemporary panegyrist by native Roman citizens. Mercenary sailors and ships as well as allied forces continued to play a key role, but after Manuel his successors allowed the fleet once more to decay. By the end of the century the empire was helpless against the overwhelming naval force that could be assembled by Venice or the other major maritime republics of Italy.[48]

In the first stage of the process of re-establishing imperial power in Asia Minor, strongholds and key towns and fortresses along the coast and coastal plain were to be garrisoned to serve as bases for the expansion of imperial authority; from here, imperial forces were to push into marginal or enemy-occupied lands and seize key centres, which were in turn to be garrisoned and became the focus of further moves outward. This was a slow and incremental

96

process, but it was successful insofar as substantial lost areas were recovered in the period from the death of Alexios I in 1118 and the 1160s. Indeed, by the reign of Manuel, it was possible to push onto the plateau itself and establish forward outposts, although the empire held most for only short periods before they were retaken. A second stage involved the establishment of new *themata*, military and civil administrative regions which replaced the older, defunct *themata* of the pre-Seljuk years. John II re-established a *thema* of Thrakesion, although geographically smaller than its predecessor; he also established a new *thema*, of Mylasa and Melanoudion, from the northernmost districts of the old Kibyrrhaiot theme and the southern sections of the old Thrakesion. Under Manuel I, the *thema* of Neokastra was established to the north, based around Atramyttion, Pergamon and Khliara, while a large number of small forts covering the major routes of access to the region from the Anatolian plateau were constructed, garrisoned with militias from the local rural population who in return received land and fiscal privileges.

By the end of Manuel's reign, the Byzantine *themata* – a word which now meant simply a province and had no military implications – stretched from Chaldia and Trebizond on the Pontic coast westwards through the districts of Paphlagonia/Boukellarion, Optimaton, Nikomedeia, Opsikion, Neokastra, Thrakesion, Mylasa/Melanoudion, Kibyrrhaioton and Cilicia. The commanders of the forces – *tagmata* – that were based in each of these regions and their strongholds were *doukes*, and they were usually also the governors of these regions, for their commands were for the most part coterminous with the province – *thema* – in which they were based.[49]

While the length of the land frontier in Asia Minor meant constant exposure to hostile raiders, the construction and garrisoning of expensive forts and fortresses and the maintenance of costly mercenary forces, this was a considerable achievement. Indeed, in his last years Manuel was able to consider the recovery of Cappadocia, an achievement which would have made possible the encirclement of the Seljuk Sultanate of Rum based at Konya, as well as the Danishmendid chieftains to their north. But this was not to be – not, in the last resort, because of the defeat in 1176 of Manuel's field army at the battle of Myriokephalon at the hands of the Rum sultan Kilic Aslan II, but because such an expansive strategy was too much for the imperial exchequer and for the resources at the emperor's disposal. And the structural weaknesses within what has been called "the Comnenian system", reflected partly in the internecine conflicts which followed Manuel's death in 1180, the intervention of the Normans of Sicily in the Balkans and the Fourth Crusade, ended forever any hope of a Byzantine recovery in Asia Minor. The empire of Nicaea, established in western Asia Minor after the seizure and sack of Constantinople by the Crusaders in 1204, owed much of its success to the work of the emperors John II and Manuel I in the region. It is ironic that the recovery of Constantinople in 1261 led the emperors thereafter increasingly to turn their attention away from this region, so that within a century of the re-establishment of the empire its Anatolian lands had been lost forever.[50]

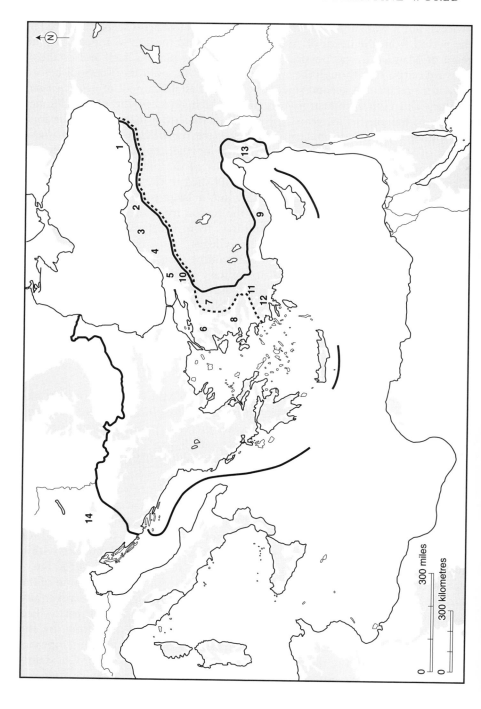

Numbers

The sixth and seventh centuries

The numbers involved in military activities at any given time, whether as soldiers or in one of the many other capacities attendant upon an army's movement, varied enormously both across time and according to the context. But all needed to be supplied, clothed and fed, and were thus a substantial burden on the ordinary population of town and countryside. It will be useful to give some general indications of the magnitudes in question in the period with which we have dealt in this volume.

Estimating numbers for armies at any period before reliable figures are available is fraught with difficulties, especially when the different types of source give such varying figures for armies involved in battles or other events. Eyewitness accounts based simply on observation are notoriously unreliable, as the Byzantines themselves recognized:

If we want to keep the enemy from finding out the strength of our forces, we should order them to march on foot and in close formation. This can be deceptive and prevent the enemy from forming a clear estimate of our numbers.[51]

The fact that there do exist some official documents from which some figures for the total of the later Roman army can be deduced does not, unfortunately, make things much easier, because the value, reliability and status of those documents has been subject to as much debate and disagreement among historians as the figures they are supposed to provide. Nevertheless, some consensus has been reached, although with a fairly wide margin for disagreement, on approximate numbers for different classes of troops in the sixth and early seventh centuries.

The only overall figure for the sixth-century armies is given by the historian Agathias, who states that Justinian's army numbered a mere 150,000,

Note: The Balkans remain as on Map VIII, with the addition of Rascia/Serbia

1	Trapezous/Chaldia	2	Oinaion/Sinope
3	Paphlagonia	4	Boukellarion
5	Optimaton/Mesothynia	6	Opsikion
7	Achyraous/Neokastra	8	Thrakesion
9	Attaleia/Seleukeia	10	Malagina
11	Laodikeia/Maeander	12	Mylasa/Melanoudion
13	Principality of Antioch	14	Rascia/Serbia (vassal status)

Approximate line of frontier c. 1118 ················

Maximum extent of imperial territory under Manuel I ─────

Map IX The evolution of ducates in the tenth–twelfth centuries

reduced by that emperor and his predecessors from an original 645,000. But Agathias almost certainly omits the *limitanei* from his first figure (perhaps because, according to Procopius, writing a little earlier, Justinian had deprived the *limitanei* of their military status, an assertion which was in reality not true, as we have seen), and his second fits – more or less – with what we might deduce from the size of field armies described or assumed in the *Strategikon* of Maurice. Here, an average force of between 5,000 and 15,000, and a large force of from 15,000 to 20,000 is discussed, figures which coincide with those which can be deduced from an earlier "official" document, the *Notitia dignitatum* of the early fifth century.[52] This includes a statement of the units, and the category to which they belong, attributed to the various commanders of the field armies and the *limitanei*. Although any deductions as to unit strengths are also subject to discussion (for example, were the newly formed legions of Diocletian 1,000 or 3,000–4,000 strong? – such variations make a substantial difference to the final sums arrived at),[53] the following tabulation is probably a reasonable approximation for the various *magistri militum*:

Magister militum per Orientem	20,000
Magister militum per Thracias	23,500
Magister militum per Illyricum	17,500
Magister militum praesentalis I	20,500
Magister militum praesentalis II	22,500

This gives a hypothetical total of some 104,000; if we then include also the armies based at this time in Africa and Italy we obtain a total of some 170,000, not much larger than the figure cited by Agathias. The fifth-century military writer Vegetius recommends similar figures to those described in the *Strategikon*: for lesser campaigns a field force of some 12,000; for larger undertakings, up to 24,000 men.[54] Figures for specific campaigns in Procopius and Agathias, as well as occasional references in other sources of the period, reveal quite small field armies for the later fifth and sixth centuries: forces of anything from 7,500 to 30,000 are recorded, varying obviously according to the context, with several campaign armies under single *magistri* numbering around 16,000–20,000 at the most.

In the 550s there were perhaps 15,000 troops in Africa and 18,000 in Italy, based on totals offered by Procopius for the regular units in Belisarius' field force in 533, and on figures for Italy in Agathias. The number of troops in Illyricum may have declined, although this is not certain.[55] Using this information, it is possible to suggest figures which coincide with those given by Agathias, and suggest a total for all the *comitatenses* of the empire, including the western divisions in Africa and Italy, of between 150,00 and 160,000. *Limitanei* would number as many again, possibly twice as many, producing a grand total of some 300,000–350,000, although it is important to stress the hypothetical nature of this conclusion given the variations between units on active service or in garrisons, as well as the unknown factor, the strength of the various categories of unit. Whether this many soldiers could actually be mobilized is, of course, an entirely different matter: the paper strength of all armies is modified, sometimes quite dramatically, by the results of illness, slowness of replacements to arrive and related effects. In addition, units which had been based in one garrison town for a long time might well have failed to maintain their correct strength as some at least of their members became more intimately involved in local life.[56] But these figures provide an approximate basis for calculations of the size of the Byzantine army thereafter.

From the seventh to the tenth centuries

As with the army of the late Roman period, so with that of the early and middle Byzantine period, the question of numbers remains one of the most debated issues. Starting from the raw figures noted above for the late Roman field divisions under the *magistri militum*, and including the armies of Italy and Africa[57] but not that of Illyricum, the Byzantine field armies in the last quarter of the seventh century could technically have numbered as many as 140,000. But this assumes (a) that both the armies of the *magistri militum praesentales* remained intact, which seems in fact not to have been the case, and (b) that the armies in question remained at (what we have assumed to be) full strength across the period of the wars with the Persians and the first phase of the Arab conquests, an assumption which is, to say the least, questionable. In particular, it assumes that (c) the armies in Italy remained at the same strength as before, which – given the appeals for soldiers to be sent which were made already during the reign of Tiberius Constantine – seems unlikely.[58]

In fact, it is agreed that all the armies suffered considerable losses during the Persian wars, and that, even if such losses could have been partially made up before the effects of the Arab wars were felt, the latter will have produced an even clearer reduction in numbers through loss in battle and other forms of attrition. The form of the redistribution of the field armies in Asia Minor already discussed suggests that numbers in the two imperial ("praesental") field armies – amalgamated at some point during the early seventh century in the army later known as the Opsikion – and those in the other remaining armies were about equal, while the figures from the narrative histories, official and semi-official, and non-Byzantine sources for the period up to and including the tenth century would all suggest that in fact the size of these field armies must have been very considerably reduced, perhaps by as much as half in most cases. There are, however, no convincingly reliable figures for either unit strengths or for expeditionary forces, although narrative histories offer various figures. But these must be treated with caution. Indeed, the figures given in the Byzantine chroniclers' accounts range from the fantastic to the entirely plausible. Thus in 778 the general Michael Lachanodrakon is reported to have marched against Germanikeia with an army of 100,000 from the themes of Thrakesion, Boukellarion, Armeniakon, Anatolikon and Opsikion.[59] Yet the same chronicle records that shortly thereafter the emperor raised a force of

12,000 cavalry and a fleet for a combined offensive into Bulgar territory. The first figure is without a doubt grossly exaggerated; the accuracy of the second remains doubtful, even though more realistic, but can perhaps be taken as indicative of the order of magnitude of regular campaign armies at the time.[60] Similarly inflated is the figure of 80,000 men supposedly in the army of Thomas the Slav in 821, which seems doubtful.[61] More reasonable is the figure of 20,000 men raised by Constantine VI to oppose the Arabs in 797 (although the fact that it seems "reasonable" is no guarantee that it is accurate).[62] For an expedition in 773, the chronicler Theophanes records that the emperor Constantine V marched with a force of 80,000 men made up of all the *themata* and the *tagmata*. While this is an implausibly large figure for an expeditionary force, it has been suggested that this figure actually reflected the nominal total of the provincial and Constantinopolitan units at the time.[63]

There are some grounds for accepting this last figure as a total; and if we do, it would imply that by the later eighth century, and taking into account the longer-term consequences of the wars with the Arabs, the loss of the armies of Africa (after the 690s) and of Italy (after the 740s, although they must have been reduced to a minimum long before this), the changed mode of recruiting and remunerating troops, as well as the changed strategic situation, the field armies of the later sixth century which remained in Asia Minor had been reduced by some 35 per cent of their original strength.[64] It would also support the assumption generally, and reasonably, made that the *limitanei* disappear from the scene with the frontiers along which they were originally based.[65]

These conclusions are partially borne out by the figures offered for the army during the first half of the ninth century by some Arab sources, notably the account of a certain al-Jarmi, whose report may include information from before the 840s and even earlier.[66] Other Arab writers, mostly derivative of this first report, also provide figures, and it has been calculated that the total number of soldiers theoretically available in the middle of the ninth century may have been 120,000. This depends in part, however, on quite high round figures for some of the *themata*, on the assumption of a total of some 24,000 soldiers (of the *tagmata* and related units) based in or near Constantinople, and on the assumption of an entirely regular internal tactical organization with equivalent numbers in like units, which, as noted above, cannot be safely taken for granted. Nevertheless, taking the figures given by these writers for individual *themata*, and aggregating those *themata* which were originally part of the same field command before the reforms and changes of the eighth or first half of the ninth centuries, does produce some plausible totals for the overall nominal strengths of the armies in question.[67]

But there can be little doubt that, in practice, the figure of 120,000 probably represents the nominal roll of the army, i.e. its paper strength, rather than a total of active troops. The figures from other sources – contemporary or near-contemporary accounts of battles and campaigns, some semi-official and official documents and the like – suggest very much smaller numbers for the *tagmata* (a total of some 4,000 for all four imperial *tagmata*) and relatively small field armies, and that the active soldiers on the military registers numbered considerably less than this.[68] One Arabic source gives a total of 40,000 for all the cavalry forces of the empire in the second half of the ninth century. Leo's *Tactica*, as well as narrative accounts of the wars of the later tenth century, suggest that field armies of from 3,000 to 4,000 were more usual than anything bigger. Such magnitudes are corroborated by a ninth-century Arabic military treatise, the *Brief Policy of War* by Harthama b. A'yan, which notes that armies may consist of anything from 800 men to 12,000. A force of up to 4,000 men counts as a good-sized force, while more than 12,000 is regarded as huge. Recommended numbers are 4,000 or, for major expeditions, 12,000, but that the active elements selected for battle could be much smaller is clear – in the attack on the Paulician position at Bathys Ryax in 878, for example, the forces of the Armeniakon and Charsianon *themata* were divided into two: a selected force of 600 from both armies, under the two *strategoi*, would make the attack. The rest of the "numerous Roman force" would take up position on the ridges around the enemy camp, and at a given signal would make a great din to shock and terrify the enemy while the 600 and the generals went in to the attack.[69] The totals for Byzantine provincial armies in the Arabic sources leave out of account the imperial fleet, of course (although they include the soldier-sailors of the so-called "maritime" *themata* in western Asia Minor), which may at times have been considerable. In the expedition to Syria and Crete in 910–11 the imperial fleet included some 13,500 sailors, and the thematic fleets some 17,540 soldiers and sailors altogether, so that in any consideration of overall military manpower the maintenance of several thousand more sailors/soldiers should be borne in mind.[70]

Reconquest and retrenchment, c. 950–1204

The evidence for the indigenous provincial *tagmata* varies: the Armeniakon *tagma* in the 1020s and 1030s probably numbered about 1,000; in contrast, the Antolikon *thema* raised several such *tagmata*, so that its overall effective strength was several times greater. On the basis of assuming some 4,000 effective soldiers for each of the 20 or so larger *themata*, and some 500 from each of the 60 newer, smaller *themata* established by the 970s (although both figures undoubtedly varied from theme to theme), an overall estimate of approximately 110,000 men, distributed across the whole empire, plus the imperial *tagmata* at Constantinople, has been suggested for the late tenth century. Many of these will have been infantry, of course, and even this figure is probably far too high when compared with the mid-sixth-century paper total of 150,000–160,000 for the field armies, and for an empire more than twice as extensive. But it may well be not too far from the manpower theoretically available on paper to the emperors at that time.[71]

The size of the various contingents about which the sources provide information suggests that there was no standard unit size: numbers depended upon the source and organization of the foreign troops themselves. The Varangian contingent employed by Basil II in the 990s, and which became a permanent mercenary force thereafter, numbered from less than 4,000 to 6,000; the Archontopouloi, a unit raised by Alexios I, numbered some 2,000. Foreign princes on several occasions sent substantial bodies of troops to serve the Byzantine emperors for particular campaigns: Ashot of Armenia thus despatched some 10,000 cavalry to assist John I Tzimiskes in the 970s, while in 979 the prince of Tayk or Tao in the far northeastern corner of Asia Minor (between northwest Armenia and Georgia) is reported to have sent 12,000 cavalry to Basil II.[72] In contrast, the individual *tagmata* of Frankish knights employed as mercenaries under their own leaders in the middle of the eleventh century numbered some 400–500, with a total of perhaps 3,000 such soldiers in units scattered across the empire. Individual units of 400–500 men are frequently mentioned; regional armies in the various ducates of the eastern frontier numbered variously from a few hundred to a standard force of from 4,000 to 5,000 infantry and cavalry. Indicative of the sort of force with which a competent commander could operate effectively is the figure given for the army of Russel de Bailleul during his rebellion in the 1070s, numbering some 2,700. While this was also seen by contemporary commentators as on the small side, they do not suggest that it was impossibly so, and there is no reason to think that most Byzantine campaign armies were greatly superior.[73] Field armies of anything from 8,000 to 25,000 men appear (as well as the more fantastic figures which occur regularly in the chronicles – armies of 300,000, for example, are simply implausible, although that the army in question was "large" need not be doubted).

After 1071, and well into the reign of Alexios I, the manpower and resources available for warfare seem to have been considerably reduced for a while (which, given the territorial losses and political situation he faced before the late 1090s, is hardly surprising), but increased once more after the partial political recovery of the empire: by the reign of John II and Manuel I forces comparable in size to those mentioned in the tenth- and early eleventh-century sources reappear. But field armies of fewer than 10,000 seem quite usual in many campaigns, and it is unlikely that Manuel raised as many as 30,000 for his grand expedition against Ikonion in 1176. This involved most of the mobile professional and mercenary forces the empire could muster, leaving mainly static garrison and militia-like forces in major towns and fortresses, so that the maximum of all the soldiers, of all the different grades and of very different quality, is unlikely to have been as much as 50,000 across both western and eastern provinces. Of these, we may probably dismiss as many as 50 per cent as effective soldiers.[74] During the reigns of Manuel's successors – Andronikos Komnenos and Isaac II Angelos – the account of Choniates suggests that forces appear to be standard: three or four divisions of 2,000 or so make up most armies that are described in the sources, and are sometimes much smaller; the battle fought outside the walls of Constantinople in 1186 between the forces of the emperor Isaac II and those of Alexios Branas was typical. Niketas

Choniates, who was an eyewitness, recorded that on the imperial side there fought some 250 Latin cavalry and 500 heavily armed foot, an equivalent number of Georgian and Turkish mercenaries, and some 1,000 or so Byzantine mercenaries and palace guardsmen. An unspecified number of mercenary soldiers manned the walls of the city, but the total appears not to have been much larger than this. This imperial army, put together hastily and at the last minute, was able to defeat the rebel force which represented most of the Byzantine field army that had been fighting the Bulgar rebels of John and Peter Asen and their Cuman allies: a field force, therefore, which cannot have numbered much over 3,000–4,000 at the outside. Apart from this army, there seems also to have been a force based at Serres, possibly of about the same strength, but it is clear from Choniates' account that the imperial forces were spread very thinly indeed, and that once the field forces had retired to the region around Constantinople, Vlachs, Cumans and Bulgars could ravage Thrace more or less at will. Broadly similar considerations apply to the Anatolian provinces. In both cases, Roman control of the major strategic fortresses and towns enabled them to maintain a precarious hold over imperial territory, although occasional victories, particularly in the Balkans against the less well equipped Vlachs and Bulgars especially, reinforced their position.[75]

These relatively small numbers should not surprise us. The costs of maintaining a heavy cavalryman, his mount (and spare horses) and his servants – usually at least two, in some cases more – were considerable. Figures from the sources describing the Crusading armies during the last years of the eleventh and the twelfth centuries, often corroborated by both Latin and Arabic sources, show that major expeditions were undertaken with forces of fewer than 1,500 heavy cavalry, together with supporting light cavalry and infantry, who might number in total three or four times more than the heavy cavalry troops. Armies of well under 10,000, often considerably smaller, were entirely usual. The much poorer evidence from the Byzantine sources, where it can be corroborated from Latin or Arabic accounts, would tend to support this general picture. Western medieval armies in the period up to the eleventh century were similarly quite small.[76]

These figures should be borne in mind when attempting to interpret those from the middle Byzantine period, and it is probably wise to assume much lower overall estimates for armies even than those suggested above. A number of other factors should also be borne in mind. First, the resources and the logistical arrangements which were available at any given time and context played a crucial role in determining how long, and in what regions, particular numbers and categories of troops could be maintained on active service. Second, political considerations should not be ignored: the maintenance of large numbers of soldiers near sensitive political centres was always risky, for example. Third, the logistical implications of a given number and category of troops needs to be borne in mind, an important issue that will be taken up in detail in Chapter 5 below. The numbers of ancillary personnel accompanying a small infantry force, for example, will have been far inferior to those required to support a cavalry force of the same size. Expeditionary armies in which the emperor participated may have required even greater numbers of support personnel, depending upon the size of the imperial baggage train, for example. Remounts and pack-animals will normally have trebled or quadrupled the demand for fodder and water in an army of cavalry soldiers, an issue that will be discussed in Chapters 5 and 6 below. Thus an army reported to have consisted of 12,000 cavalrymen can be assumed to have entailed double that number of animals, if not more, although of course there were exceptions. Unfortunately, the medieval sources are hardly ever explicit on such matters. But this is all the more reason to err on the cautious side. Fourth, the purpose of an expedition, the season in which it operated and the terrain on which it operated were also important factors. As we have seen, Byzantine armies and those of their enemies did not have a well-paved and maintained network of roads at their disposal. Commanders must have been very aware of the nature of the terrain in which they had to campaign and – as the treatise on guerrilla warfare of the 960s notes – adjusted the size of their forces accordingly. By the same token, the density of the population of a region also played a role, for where armies were compelled to transport the greater part of their supplies, numbers were by force of circumstances drastically limited.

Indeed, it is worth bearing in mind that the constant and repetitious references in the military treatises to the possible disparity between imperial forces and their enemies hardly supports the notion that the empire's armies usually numbered in the tens of thousands. There is no reason to doubt that at times, and in special circumstances, forces of as many as 20,000 soldiers might have been raised. The evidence for such numbers is, on the whole, scarce but would suggest that the large numbers given for the Byzantine armies by the mid-ninth-century Arab geographers can only represent theoretical paper strengths, derived quite possibly, as has been suggested, from Byzantine written sources but reflecting in no way any realistic active numbers. It is reasonable to conclude that the armies fielded by the late Roman and Byzantine state, as well as by most of their enemies, were relatively small throughout the period concerned here.

CHAPTER FOUR

Organizing for war: the administration of military structures

From late Roman to "thematic" tactical structures

Tactics is a science which enables one to organise and manoeuvre a body of armed men in an orderly manner. Tactics may be divided into four parts: proper organisation of men for combat; distribution of weapons according to the needs of each man; movement of an armed body of troops in a manner appropriate to the occasion; the management of war, of personnel and materials, . . .[1]

As this quotation illustrates, the concept of "tactics" for the East Romans encompassed all those aspects of warmaking associated with fighting in the field: order of battle, unit structure and organization, field discipline and man-oeuvre, the realization of the different potential of various types of soldier (light and heavy, cavalry and infantry, missile weapons, shock weapons and so forth), as well as the psychology and morale of the soldiers, their officers and the enemy. It also included to a degree what Leo's *Tactica* refers to as "logistics", that is to say the structure and organization of the field army into divisions, brigades, units and sub-units.[2]

The evolution of middle Byzantine military units

The tactical organization of the late Roman army presents a bewildering array of different types of unit, reflecting the complex development of the army up to that time. From before the third century, the older legions (which may have been kept up to the established strength of 6,000 men) and associated auxiliary units – cavalry *alae*, infantry *cohortes (peditatae)* and mixed units (*cohortes equitatae*), organized in units of 1,000 or 500 – continued to function, although there is some question as to their numerical strength, which was probably much lower in the sixth century than in the fourth. Alongside them were brigaded newer legions which probably numbered only 1,000 to 1,500, although the issue is debated. In addition, there were so-called *vexillationes*, originally *ad hoc* detachments from various units (*alae, cohortes, legiones*), put together for particular purposes during the later second and first half of the third century, and in some cases kept together thereafter and turned into permanent, independent units. Then came detached legionary cavalry units, *equites*, some of which formed the basis of the later Diocletianic and Constantinian *comitatus*, and newly formed units, not associatd with the legions, recruited during the fourth century on the same basis: these all came to be referred to as *vexillationes* (or sometimes, according to regional variations, *cunei equitum*) by the end of the fourth century.

Under Constantine, new infantry units, *auxilia*, were established, often replacing the older *cohortes*. New units, modelled on the *vexillationes* and *equites* in the case of cavalry, and on the *auxilia* in the case of infantry, continued to be recruited into the seventh century. In all these cases, the evolution of the internal command of the units is hazy after the end of the fourth century for want of clear evidence. But enough information survives to suggest that, in its fundamentals, the tactical administration of such units was not radically altered until the later sixth century.

As we have seen, these forces were grouped generally under two main heads, field armies, including those based around Constantinople, generally called *comitatenses*, and units established more or less permanently along and behind the frontier zones as well as inland for security and police purposes, usually, although not exclusively, referred to as *limitanei*. But cross-postings between categories were by no means unusual, and there is some evidence to suggest that "static" garrison forces associated with divisions of the *limitanei* could be brigaded with field armies at times. By the late sixth and early seventh centuries there is a tendency for the tactical administration of most units formed from the fourth century and afterwards to conform to a basic pattern, although among the older units a wide variation in the titles and functions of senior and subordinate officers seems to survive.

All units had an administrative structure, consisting of a number of officials and clerical assistants, responsible for the logistical management of the unit's needs, the issue of pay and emoluments, and so forth. Each unit was also divided for tactical purposes into a number of sub-sections, so that at the end of the sixth century the chain of command ran from the senior officer commanding and his second-in-command, through the section or troop commanders, via officers in charge of variously 200, 100, 50 and 10 men. Officers bearing such numerically determined titles only rarely commanded numbers of men which matched their title, however, and this is a structural peculiarity which exists in many formations throughout the Byzantine period also.

During the late sixth and early seventh centuries a standardization of ranks and titles appears to have been established for some units, at least those in the two imperial field armies based near Constantinople; and although it is impossible to say whether, and at what rate, this process affected other field armies, it does appear that by the later seventh and eighth centuries it had indeed been established within most field army units across the empire. In the late sixth and early seventh century, and drawing on evidence from papyri (Egyptian and Palestinian), the legislation of Justinian and his immediate successors and the *Strategikon* of Maurice, a late-sixth or early-seventh-century military handbook dealing with the structure of the imperial field armies, the grades and ranks within cavalry units appeared as follows:[3]

6th–early-7th-century grades	Grades in *Strategikon c.* 590–610
comes/tribunus	*komes/tribounos*
vicarius	*bikarios*
primicerius	
senator	
ducenarius	*ilarches*
centenarius	*hekatontarches*
campiductor	*kampidouktor*
draconarii, signiferi	*drakonarioi, bandophoroi, ornithoborai* (inf. only)
primus (inf.)	*lochagos* (inf. only)
circitor (secundus, inf.)	*dekarches*
tubatores	*boukinator, toubator*
biarcus	*pentarches*
semissalis	*tetrarches*
miles (i.e. soldier)	*stratiotes*

At the same time as these grades were becoming standard, titles for senior ranks which had hitherto been confined to a specific military context or a particular linguistic area became generalized and applied more widely. Thus the position of *drouggarios*, originally applied to a temporary commander of an *ad hoc* brigade of cavalry, becomes firmly established as the commander of a group of cavalry *banda* under their *komites*, while that of *tourmarches*, originally equivalent probably to the title of *dux* and likewise associated with cavalry units, appears as the divisional commander of a field army, below the *magister militum*, or master of soldiers, generally referred to from the later seventh century as the *strategos*. While coexisting with the older titles, these appear to have become firmly established within the field armies by the time they were withdrawn into Asia Minor in the late 630s and 640s.

Incidental references in a variety of sources – including letters, hagiographical and related writings, and Arab geographers' descriptions of Byzantine military organization – show that this basic structure survived well into the middle Byzantine period as the standard pattern of both the thematic and the centrally paid and maintained *tagmata* or elite units at Constantinople. The *Tactica* of Leo VI repeats in their essentials the details of unit command structures given in the *Strategikon* of Maurice, with a few minor substitutions of names. Thus the basic subdivisions of cavalry and infantry into groups of 10 or 16, respectively, with junior officers called tetrarchs, pentarchs and dekarchs (the leading men in groups of 4, 5 and 10), in turn organized in detachments under pentekontarchs and hekatontarchs (groups of 50 and 100) and forming units of variable strength under *komites*, is repeated; and as we have seen, in purely tactical terms this seems to reflect the late Roman Latin terminology for such officers in a Greek form. This structure is borne out by other types of source.[4]

The Arab geographers provide some interesting information about the command structure of the Byzantine forces, as far as they understood or heard about it, for the period from the middle of the ninth century. The geographer Ibn Khurradādhbīh describes the command structure as follows:

> The patrikios commands 10,000 men; he has two turmarchs under his command, commanding 5,000 men each; each turmarch has under his orders 5 drungars in charge of 1,000 men each; under the command of each drungar are 5 komites in charge of 200 men each; each *komes* commands 5 kentarchs with 40 men each, and each kentarch has under his command 4 dekarchs with 10 men each.

The same description is repeated by the writer Kudāma in the 930s. These figures vary somewhat from those given in the *Tactica* of Leo VI, in which the chain of command for a *thema* of 4,000 cavalry is described: this was divided into two *tourmai* of 2,000 men, each consisting of 2 *drouggoi* or chiliarchies of 1,000, subdivided into 5 units (*banda*) of 200 men under *komites*, each *bandon* consisting of 2 groups of 100 under *kentarchai*, further grouped into units of 50, 10 and 5.[5]

Apart from the size of the *tourmai*, however, and of the units under the *kentarchoi*, the two descriptions are close. The tactical structure described by these sources is not to be doubted – *thema, tourmai, drouggoi, banda* and their commanders are all attested in the sources, the last two names from the sixth century and before as popular expressions for different types of unit. The variations almost certainly represented differences of both time and place which could coexist within a common framework. It is quite clear from the late Roman material that substantial variations could exist in unit strengths due to a whole range of factors about which our sources tell us virtually nothing.[6] The abbot Theodore of Stoudios refers in a letter of the early ninth century to a deserving man promoted to the position of *komes*, even though that of a *tourmarches* would not have been too good for him. Similarly, in hagiographies and other documents of the ninth century provincial officers with titles such as dekarch, pentekontarch, hekatontarch or kentarch, as well as *komes* and *drouggarios*, appear, and there are many extant lead seals throughout the period *c.* 650–930 for provincial *komites*.[7]

One of the difficulties historians face in trying to trace the evolution of such structures is the great variation in terminology used by the writers of the period. Thus in the early ninth-century Life of Philaretos, a saintly landowner and philanthropist from Paphlagonia, we read of commanders of units of 1,000, 100 and 50 as the basic divisions of the thematic army (*chiliarchai, hekatontarchai* and *pentekontarchai*). Whether these were the official terms, or merely those used by the (non-military) biographer, is unknown. They may reflect a literary/rhetorical usage; they may equally reflect the fact that a rigid and fixed titulature clearly did not prevail. Thus the fact that older titles from the pre-Diocletianic establishment also appear should not necessarily be understood as a deliberately archaizing form used by the hagiographer: the continued existence of units whose origins lay both before and after the early fourth century is not to be doubted, and their different internal establishment and titulature is unlikely to have been made entirely uniform or consistent. This can be illustrated from a version of the Life of Theodore of Stoudios, written after 868 and therefore at the time that other sources assert the existence of the titles of *drouggarios* and *komes*, which refers to the hierarchy of ranks in drawing a parallel between military and monastic organization: chiliarchs, hekatontarchs, pentekontarchs and dekarchs are listed. And even in Leo's *Tactica*, he uses terms such as *chiliarchia* for *drouggos* on occasion, suggesting that the terms were often interchangeable.[8]

Only in the case of certain Constantinopolitan units do we have a little more detailed information. The so-called *Arithmos*, later referred to as the imperial Watch (*Vigla*), was a provincial brigade of several *banda* from the *themata* upgraded to a guards unit by the empress Eirene in the 780s. It was probably a cavalry vexillation before its posting to Asia Minor or Thrace after the first wave of Arab conquests in the 630s. If we can assume it was typical of provincial units of that type and at that time, its internal organization does give some idea of other ranks and functions which survived. Indeed, it shows that, for the most part, and although the titles were sometimes garbled and may even have changed function, there was a good deal of continuity. Thus the ranks of *komites, kentarchai, doukiniatores* (= *ducenarii*), *semeiophoroi* (= *semafori*) and *labouresioi* (= carrying the *labarum*) can all be traced back to the fifth and sixth centuries and before, and represent standard ranks within the internal administration of cavalry vexillations of the fourth century and later. If they survived in a provincial cavalry division as late as the later eighth century, there is no reason to doubt their survival in other similar units.[9] A similar element of continuity can be found in a number of other cases for units of the ninth and tenth centuries, in particular the imperial *tagmata*, elite forces established first by Constantine V and later expanded by his successors.[10] Given the often very clear degree of continuity in title and function from late Roman to middle Byzantine military administration which can be shown to have existed, it is highly likely that many other administrative/clerical functions about which we know nothing from the Byzantine sources also survived into the later period.

The armies of the themata

The *themata* or provincial armies of the Opsikion, Anatolikon, Armeniakon, Thrakesion, as well as the maritime and naval division of the Karabisianoi, represent in a Hellenized form the older armies of the *magistri militum* who had commanded the field armies of the period up to the Arab conquests.[11] The territorial extent of the later *themata* conformed more or less to the boundaries of groups of civil provinces or *eparchiai*, and it seems that the size of the districts in question was connected with the ability of the land to support the appropriate number of troops in each field army, as well as the strategic task allocated to each army upon its withdrawal in the late 630s/early 640s.[12] Recent work on the origins and etymology of the word *thema* would tend to bear this out, too, for the term evidently meant (among other things) a "designated area/region", so that an expression such as *thema (ton) Anatolikon* would mean something like "designated area of the *Orientales*", i.e. the area specifically allocated to the soldiers under the authority of the *mag. mil. per Orientem*.[13]

Many units retained their original late Roman identities: a tenth-century source refers to the two *tourmai* of the Theodosiaci and Victores, based in the Thrakesion region, units originally formed in the fourth and fifth centuries. Other units similarly survived as identifiable bodies, including the Optimates and Bucellarii in northwest Asia Minor and the division of *foederati* in the Anatolikon region, all associated with the establishment of the sixth century and the praesental field armies – although nothing is known of their internal structure.[14] But by the tenth century older regimental names and identities had for the most part been forgotten, first because of the long-term process of regionalization of the original field armies by which they came to be permanently established in certain districts, and second because of the coincidence between the garrison areas and the regions from which recruits were drawn to the extent that each unit or *bandon* came to be identified with a given area and its inhabitants. In addition, the late Roman tendency to refer to many units simply as the *arithmos* or *numerus* of the place in which they were based must also have played a role.

The tenth-century evidence makes it very clear that many, probably most, units had local, purely toponymical identities.[15] Differences which may have subsisted after the 640s between *limitanei* and *comitatenses* are no longer evident. The provincial armies are sometimes referred to simply as the *kaballarika themata*, the cavalry armies. Their major subdivisions were referred to as *tourmai* and *drouggoi*, traditionally both terms (especially the second) applying to cavalry units of varying size. This terminology strongly suggests that within the field armies it was the cavalry which were central in the defensive and offensive warfare along the frontiers and on Roman or Arab territory, although, as we shall see, infantry continued to play a significant role.[16] Parallel with these developments, there took place a generalized levelling down of the different arms into simply light cavalry and infantry, so that it was up to the local commanders to establish field units and determine how they should be made up and armed as each separate occasion or campaign demanded.

The *themata* were subdivided for tactical purposes into *tourmai*, *drouggoi* and *banda*. The first and last of these divisions came to be associated eventually with a territory, so that each *tourma* had a headquarters or base, a fortified town or fortress, and each *bandon* was identified with a specific district whose boundaries were clearly defined. As far as the evidence can tell us, the middle level of this structure, the *drouggos*, remained always a purely tactical unit and never acquired any territorial significance. In a compilation attributed to him known as the *De Thematibus* ("On the Themes"), the emperor Constantine VII (913–59) defines the extent of each theme as it was known in his own time and is clearly drawing on geographically precise descriptions, while a document included in another compilation attributed to the same emperor, known as the *De administrando imperio* ("On governing the empire"), names a number of *tourmai* and *banda* in different *themata*. In their territorial form the smaller units, or *banda*, were also referred to as *topoteresiai* (which might very approximately be translated as "lieutenancy" or "county").[17]

The sizes of individual units on the battlefield varied according to tactical need and was left to the discretion of the commander in the field.[18] Thus there was not necessarily any neat equation between *bandon* and *tourma* as territorial and administrative districts, on the one hand and the equivalent terms applied to units or divisions of soldiers on the other. Individual administrative *tourmai* could thus be brigaded together on campaign or in battle to make up a larger tactical *tourma* (and, conversely, large administrative *tourmai* might be broken up into smaller units), for example. Tactical units or divisions may therefore not have coincided with the districts in which the soldiers were recruited or based. Important confirmation of this comes from a statement in the *Tactica*, that the general should try to attain unit cohesion by keeping men from the same communities and districts together, thus retaining some local identities and solidarity.[19] Because a *thema* might have, say, three *tourmai*, in consequence, must not mean either that they consisted of an equal number of smaller units, nor that they were the same size as the *tourmai* in a different *thema*.[20] This has important implications for the numbers of soldiers available to the army of the period, since to assume that the number of administrative *banda* in a *thema* necessarily reflected a particular number of soldiers or the strength of the thematic forces from that province would be methodologically unsound. There may well have been some coincidence between the two in the early period of thematic development (although even this is supposition) but localization of recruitment, demographic changes, settlement pattern and so forth will have transformed the original situation. The number of infantry or cavalry soldiers needed for the tactical units – *banda* – could only rarely have matched the number of soldiers of the same type – infantry or cavalry – registered or available from each administrative *bandon* or *topoteresia*, particularly since this came to reflect social status and wealth rather than military training.

The subdivisions of the *themata* vary according to the sources, both within the Byzantine material and in the Arab or other evidence. Thus Leo's *Tactica*, repeating the formulation in the *Strategikon* of Maurice, describes each army corps (*thema*) as consisting of three *tourmai*, each under a *tourmarches*; each *tourma* was then divided into three *drouggoi*, and each *drouggos* into a number of *banda* or *tagmata*. The naval *themata* were organized on the same basis, with minor variations in the command structure which at the lowest level – the warship crew – was more or less equivalent to the *bandon*, the basic tactical unit in the land armies.[21] In practice, as we have said, thematic forces consisted at different times of varying numbers of *tourmai*, and the numbers in each *bandon* can clearly also vary – according to the *Tactica*, from 200 to 400, according to other sources, from 50 to 200: there was clearly a great deal of variation, and the actual figures which survive in documents of the tenth century confirm this.[22] There is some evidence for how many *tourmai* there were in certain *themata* at certain times. The districts across which they exercised authority, with the evidence for the known headquarters in each *thema* at different periods, is presented in Chapter 3, Table 3.1 and Map VIb.

Each *tourmarches* had a base, usually a fortress town, and these are sometimes named on the few surviving lead seals which such officers employed to validate official business. The *tourmarches* was an important figure in the military administrative structure. Like the overall commander of the *thema*, the *strategos*, he had formal jurisdiction over all those directly under his military command, was responsible for the key fortresses and strongpoints in his district, for the safety of the local population and their property, and for dealing with local raids and informing his own superior of enemy movements.[23] Not all the *tourmarchai* in a theme were necessarily of equal rank, however: the tourmarch attached to the theme *strategos* was also known as the *mer(i)arches*, the older term for tourmarch which had dropped out of use except in this case, and seems to have been slightly lower in status than the others, perhaps because he was directly subordinate to the theme commander.[24]

This system was complemented by a number of other features. Most significant were the so-called *kleisourai* or frontier passes, effectively districts including important routes of access to the empire and deserving an independent command and greater autonomy than the usual provincial subdivisions. Their origins are unclear, but it is possible that the emperor Heraclius established such a command to cover the Cilician Gates across the Taurus mountains as early as the late 630s. The first established *kleisourai* were formed from *tourmai* of the themes: lesser Cappadocia, originally a *tourma* of the Anatolikon region, was elevated to *kleisoura* status, under a *kleisourarches*, during the first half of the ninth century, as were the regions of Seleukia (also Anatolikon) and Charsianon (Armeniakon). Together, these covered the frontier passes and the territory most immediately threatened by hostile activity, and their commanders had similar authority to the tourmarchs.[25] Other military commands existed which may or may not have a territorial significance, such as the title of *katepano*, sometimes associated with naval commands,[26] or that of *doux*, an independent commander for a specific area, probably for a short-term purpose.[27] As with *katepano*, it is likely that the presence of a *doux* signalled either a naval or other special unit, independent of the command of the theme or other provincial commanders.[28]

From *c.* 930 to the Fourth Crusade (1204)

Unit administration

From the middle years of the reign of Constantine VII it is apparent that the organization described for the preceding period was evolving fairly rapidly, and by the end of the reign of John I Tzimiskes (969–76) presented a rather different appearance to that of the armies of the preceding period. The changes affected modes of recruitment and equipping armies as well as organizational matters, but the former will be dealt with in the appropriate chapter below. The latter are signalled in the written sources by a shift in terminology. As we have already noted, the titles of various ranks and positions in the provincial armies had been from the seventh century a mixture of both Hellenized Latin words and Greek terms – thus both *drouggarios* and *chiliarches* occur for the same position, the former being the everyday term, the latter occurring – albeit infrequently – in literary contexts.[29]

By the 960s, many of these Latin technical terms were supplemented by a range of newer, and purely Greek, words. The rank of *taxiarches* first appears in a military treatise attributed to the emperor Nikephros II Phocas (963–9), an infantry commander in charge of a *taxiarchia* or unit of 1,000 men: these two terms are used in parallel with the terms *chiliarchia* and *chiliarches*, equivalent in turn in a thematic context to *drouggos* and *drouggarios*. At the same time the titles *archegetes* and *hoplitarches* appear for commanders of larger infantry divisions in field army contexts. Other new commands which appear include the *stratopedarches* ("field marshal") of the west and of the east, and an officer called the *ethnarches* (ethnarch, "commander of foreigners"), these last two referring to commanders of both infantry and cavalry formations.

These new terms did not replace the older vocabulary entirely: on the contrary, they represent on the whole the desire to find terms suitable for describing larger standard units than were normally available from the thematic armies. The sources hint that the manpower available from the *themata* – that is, those registered in the muster-rolls for each regional army – was slowly decreasing, so that the government needed to find alternative ways to maintain the strength of its forces. Already in Leo's *Tactica* the need to brigade together elements from several *tourmai* or even *themata* to create a reasonable offensive army is apparent, and the same tendency is clear also in another military treatise, "On skirmishing warfare", written probably in the 960s. One result of the gradual decline in the size and numbers of thematic units was that, as the average size of the *bandon* shrank, so must that of the *drouggos* and *tourma.* One of the results was the appearance, beginning already in the later ninth century, of the amalgamation of the ranks and functions of the *komites* in charge of *banda* and the *douggarioi* in charge of *drouggoi*. The new title of *drouggarokomes* thus makes its appearance, suggesting that there was very little difference in size and tactical value between the older, large *bandon* of 200–400 men, and the reduced *drouggos*, which may have numbered only about the same. At the same time, the average *tourma* must also have been reduced in size, approximating in practice to the old *drouggos* of as many as 1,000 soldiers: there is some evidence to suggest that the *tourmai* in the *thema* of Thrakesion in the 940s, for example, numbered from 600 to 800 or slightly more, and since there appear to have been four *tourmarchai*, the total strength of the thematic army for that region would have been about 3,000, perhaps slightly more.[30]

Another result of the shortfall in thematic numbers seems to have been that the terminology of *drouggoi* and *tourmai* no longer accurately described these joint battlefield formations, so that new terms – for units of 500 and 1,000 – became current. Already in the 950s one text notes that the "imperial" units in the Charsianon and Thrakesion regions (i.e. those units raised as professional, mercenary *tagmata* but based in the provinces) number from 320 to 400, while the usual cavalry *bandon* was a mere 50–150 strong. The word *drouggos* fades from use during this period, having had a tactical significance only, whereas *tourma* continues in use to describe both a territorial district of a theme and a body of soldiers from that area. But in practical terms words such as *allagion* (meaning a "rotation", i.e. of duties), *taxiarchia* and *parataxis* occur with increasing frequency, eventually to the exclusion of the older terminology, during the later eleventh century. In contrast, the primary unit of both tactical and territorial administration, the *bandon*, survives through this period and into the late empire.[31]

It is important to emphasize that the increase in the employment and establishment of mercenary *tagmata* (on the model of the four imperial *tagmata*), during the tenth century reflects not just the demands of government expansion along the eastern front, but also the reduction in suitably registered manpower in the older *themata*. But as such recruitment of mercenary *tagmata* increased dramatically during the middle and later tenth century, so an ever greater proportion of the effective military strength of the state was represented by this source, and the officers who commanded such units, whether infantry or cavalry, received titles appropriate to the size of their unit. In the cavalry, in fact, very few new terms appear, except for the term *parataxis* to describe a cavalry unit of 10 *banda* of 50 men each, and below the level of the new larger taxiarchies of infantry, the traditional subdivisions into hundreds, fifties, tens and so on was maintained, with an appropriate level of junior or non-commissioned grades. The difference seems primarily to have lain in the fact that a commander of one hundred men – *kentarchos* or *hekatontarches* – actually commanded something like this number rather than a nominal century of far fewer men, as seems regularly to have been the case in the thematic forces up to and including the time of Leo VI.[32]

These arrangements seem to have continued in use as the basic framework of Byzantine infantry and cavalry units, whether indigenous or foreign (i.e full-time, "mercenary" units) right through the eleventh century, through the militarily disastrous years of the period from 1071 until well into the reign of Alexios I and up to the time of the Fourth Crusade. The sources frequently mention the hierarchy of middling and junior officers who commanded the units and sections of units making up the imperial infantry and cavalry forces.[33] Beyond that, and partly because such a large proportion of the imperial army consisted of foreign mercenaries under their own leaders, it is difficult to be precise, although the limited evidence suggests that many of the technical terms for ranks, even if their exact significance had changed, continued in use. The continued organization of infantry and cavalry into *parataxeis* and *taxiarchiai* is confirmed by the accounts of contemporary or near-contemporary historians such as Niketas Choniates, and this implies that the internal structures and grading of such formations likewise continued in use: certainly the junior ranks of *pentekontarches* and *dekarchos* continued in use, and since the twelfth-century historians refer on several occasions to the subordinate officers within the infantry and cavalry units, it is likely that the rest of the ranking system within indigenous Roman units remained much the same.[34]

Tactical structures

The changes which are known to have taken place in the middle years of the tenth century, as the empire went increasingly on to the offensive and as the need for a wider variety of different arms became apparent, had important consequences for the development of the army thereafter. Until that time, the heavy cavalry had (probably) been supplied by the imperial *tagmata* and other elite units based in and around the capital, although even here the evidence for these troops being substantially more heavily armed and better equipped than the regular contingents of the provincial theme armies is slim, to say the least.[35] Most of the theme cavalry was light-armed or regular horse, and the infantry were chiefly employed to man strongpoints, garrison fortresses and defend settlements. The armies of the *themata* in the period from the 660s to the early tenth century had needed to respond rapidly to attack, to harass enemy raiders or make rapid raids into enemy territory. The increased importance of heavy infantry, and the introduction of a special heavy cavalry brigade (the latter during the middle years of the tenth century), all signal the change to a more aggressive form of warfare.[36]

The full-time units, or *tagmata*, both infantry and cavalry, became increasingly preponderant in the overall composition of Byzantine armies from the 950s for the reasons outlined above. The thematic militias correspondingly fell into the background, especially as the frontier advanced and they were needed less and less frequently, although soldiers were still raised in considerable numbers when necessary, brigaded in taxiarchies if infantry or *parataxeis* if cavalry, when the need arose, and they were probably also posted to frontier garrisons for periods of duty. Several "named" units appear in the later tenth and eleventh centuries: the Athanatoi (Immortals), established by John Tzimiskes and re-established by Alexios I; the *tagma* of the Stratelatai, first mentioned during the reign of John I and again in 1069, after which it vanishes from the record; the unit of the Satrapai, which appears briefly in administrative sources for the 970s and then disappears; the Maniakalatoi, formed of Franks from Italy by the general George Maniakes, are recorded up to the 1070s; the unit of the Megathymoi, which appears in the 1040s, likewise only once; and the Archontopouloi, established by Alexios I but not mentioned thereafter. Alexios I recruited the defeated Pechenegs whom he settled in the district of Moglena (southeast Macedonia) into a *tagma* "of the Moglena Pechenegs", while during the wars he fought in the 1080s a unit of "Manichaeans" also fought – recruited from among the Paulicians settled around Philippoupolis by John I – although they were later disbanded.[37]

As we have seen, the newly conquered territories were organized into smaller units than the older *themata,* given regular garrisons of professional cavalry and infantry, and placed under new military officials, the *doukes.* And until the middle of the eleventh century, there existed a substantial technical difference between the position of the various *doukes* in their commands – *doukata* – and the older *strategoi* in their *themata.* In the first place, this was because the former had much more important military resources at their disposal, and in the second, because they came to rank above the thematic commanders in the imperial hierarchy, an illustration of the importance of the military at this time.

As the older thematic armies fade into obsolescence during the eleventh century, so the system of commands based on ducates expands. Under officers commanding substantial forces of full-time professional troops, both infantry and cavalry, and organized in the taxiarchies and parataxeis discussed above, this system replaces almost completely the *themata* as the standard tactical and strategic framework for the organization of both defensive and offensive operations. And even though the emperors of the Komnenos dynasty, especially John II, attempted to re-establish a provincialized system of military recruitment based to an extent on land, like the older system of the tenth century and before, it was essentially an imperial army organized in local commands with full-time mercenary units at their disposal which characterized the imperial forces throughout the twelfth century.[38]

Whereas the armies of the period from the seventh to the tenth centuries had been provincially based and primarily defensive in focus, those of the later tenth and eleventh centuries were organized for offensive operations, consisted of full-time mercenary forces and were concentrated in the ducates making up the deep frontier zone along the northern and particularly the eastern frontiers. The centralized command structure – the *domestikoi* of east and west; their associated high-ranking officers of both regions, the *stratopedarchai*; the *ethnarches* commanding larger divisions of non-Byzantine mercenaries; the commanders of the infantry divisions of the imperial field armies entitled *hoplitarchai* or *archegetai* – is in stark contrast to the dispersed command structure of the preceding period. As the eleventh century progressed, these titles were often qualified by a variety of epithets intended to signify their position in the overall hierarchy. Thus the *domestikos* of east or west was often ranked as the *megas domestikos* (grand domestic), for example, just as the commander of the imperial fleet, the *drouggarios tou ploimou*, becomes the *megas drouggarios* (the grand *drouggarios*, or high admiral), and eventually gives way to the *megas doux*, the grand duke, and so on.

In addition, other positions attached to the court or palace service rise in importance in the military context, so that the *protostrator*, from the middle of the eighth century head of the imperial esquires or mounted attendants of the emperor, rises by the later eleventh century to become second-in-command of the imperial armies after the grand domestic. The older *chartoularios tou stavlou* in charge of the imperial and provincial stud-farms, now known as the *megas chartoularios* or grand chartulary, had a series of districts or stations under his control in the south Balkans called *chartoularata*, and was responsible, as before, for the provision of the imperial baggage train as well as for pack-animals for the army.[39]

The major strategic division of the armies into eastern and western sections also survived until at least the 1180s.[40] With a few similar, incremental changes, and leaving to one side for the moment the question of the sources of recruitment and methods of remuneration, it was this tactical and administrative structure which remained in force, with modifications forced by the variable strategic and fiscal fortunes of the empire across the period, until the partition of the empire after 1204.

As in the period from the 1050s onward, so the sources for the Comnene period speak of a wide range of nationalities serving in the imperial forces under Alexios I, John II, Manuel and their immediate successors, and mention also the extensive recruiting campaigns to supply the forces for specific undertakings. Allied soldiers, and those supplied by treaty arrangement – Georgians, Alans, Cumans, Pechenegs, Serbs, Turks and Hungarians (from which nations mercenary soldiers were also hired) – fought alongside north Italian or Lombard, German and Norman mercenaries. For the most part, these troops fought under their own leaders, obeying the Roman divisional commander in whose section they were placed.[41] The native Byzantine forces were also identified chiefly by their province of origin: Macedonians, Paphlagonians, Armenians and so forth were brigaded in the "eastern" and "western" divisions, as we have seen, and continued to be organized by taxiarchies, at least as far as concerns the infantry. During the rebellion of Isaac Komnenos in 1057, the sources refer to the *tagmata* or regiments of various themes, including Koloneia, Chaldia, Charsianon, Anatolikon (specified as of Pisidia and Lykaonia), Armeniakon, Macedonia, as well as of Franks and Rus'.[42] Whether these are mixed units of infantry and cavalry, or of only cavalry (in the case of the Franks) or only infantry (as in the case of the Rus'), is rarely clear. In many cases, it is likely that they represent full-time or mercenary equivalents of the older thematic *tourmai*, since in one or two cases the eleventh-century sources suggest their equivalence. The palatine units continued to be recruited for the most part from foreigners. The Hetaireia survived, under its commander the *megas hetaireiarches*, as did the Vestiaritai, associated with the imperial treasuries, and the (after the 1060s mostly English) Varangians. The Vardariotai, who first appear in the later tenth century, associated with the region around Thessaloniki and the river Vardar, also continue to exist. Other groups, such as the Hikanatoi and Exkoubitoi disappear by *c.* 1100, replaced mostly by foreign mercenary units. By the time of the emperor Manuel I, still commanded by a *primmikerios*, but no longer recruited originally from Turks or Hungarians, they served as a purely palatine regiment.[43]

Recruitment and remuneration

The sixth–ninth centuries

As with any other aspect of its military organization, the ways in which soldiers were recruited and paid closely reflects both strategic needs and, perhaps even more closely, the political and economic situation in which the empire found itself at various times. The changes which took place during the seventh century radically affected both these aspects, as well as the means through which armies were maintained and supplied when in the field or otherwise on active service. Since these elements of military organization are closely associated, it will be convenient to treat them together in this section.

During the sixth century, soldiers were recruited partly through the attraction of volunteers, partly through the application of a conscription calculated on the basis of the relationship between taxable land and manpower, although the latter was increasingly replaced by the former as the sixth century drew on. Soldiers in the *limitanei* had the privilege of putting down their sons' names for recruitment to a more or less guaranteed place if they wished, a reflection of the relative security a soldier's career was seen to represent, at least in such garrison units, and this arrangement seems also to have applied to the *comitatenses* in certain contexts or for certain grades as well. Joining up brought a number of advantages, specially in respect of exemptions from certain fiscal demands of the state and in respect of the protected status of personal property in relation to the legal rights of relatives. In units which had been established in a particular area or garrison town for a long period, recruitment would certainly have seemed like a sensible career choice, except where the regiment was posted away on active service or campaign duties elsewhere.[44]

There had been two basic ways of supplying soldiers with their basic needs. Soldiers received cash grants, or donatives, at quinquennial intervals or at an imperial accession, and the regular salaries of the troops based in towns or garrisons were calculated as "rations", *annonae*, with for cavalry units in addition *capitus* for their fodder. By the later fifth century in the east, these supplies were usually commuted at locally fixed tariffs into gold, so that the regimental actuaries, commissariat officials, bought the necessary requirements at local markets or direct from the producers before issuing them to the soldiers. In the case of mobile units, actuaries and special officers were allowed to draw supplies from the regular revenues of the provinces affected in return for receipts. The whole system was operated by the administration of the praetorian prefecture at its various administrative levels (urban, provincial and diocesan), so that the supplies demanded for the army could be taken into account when making the regular land-tax assessment.[45]

Rates of pay are debated, and certainly varied over the empire according to the different local rates at which rations were commuted into cash. In the middle of the sixth century, it has been calculated that the standard rates for troops – following the pattern established by Justinian for the new military command in Africa – was as follows for each of the grades in units of the *comitatenses*. The sums below are given in gold *solidi* or *nomismata*: each unit of *annonae* was commuted at a rate of 4–5 *solidi* (variations according to province/fiscal region may have been greater even than this), and each unit of *capitus* (issued to cavalry troopers and mounted officers only) at a rate of 4 *solidi*.

Grade	*Annonae*	Commutation	*Capitus*	Commutation
primicerius	5	20–25 *sol.*	2	8 *sol.*
senator	4	16–20 *sol.*	2	8 *sol.*
ducenarius	3½	14–17½ *sol.*	1½	6 *sol.*
centenarius	2½	10–12½ *sol.*	1	4 *sol.*
biarcus	2	8–10 *sol.*	1	4 *sol.*
circitor	2	8–10 *sol.*	1	4 *sol.*
miles (i.e. soldier)	1	4–5 *sol.*	1	4 *sol.*

Some idea of the value of this income to the soldiers of the various grades can be seen from the fact that a hired worker or labourer received the equivalent of 6 *solidi* a year in late sixth-century Egypt.[46]

To complement this meagre pay, however, the soldier had access to a whole range of benefits: special donatives for imperial birthdays or accessions; a regular quinquennial donative (amounting to the equivalent of 5 *solidi* until the reign of Heraclius, although probably incorporated into the annual pay by Justinian); fiscal exemption for himself and his family from a series of state taxes and extra impositions; a special juridical status and the protection of the army in most legal disputes; and his equipment and weapons were provided by the state, either directly or through a cash grant. Many soldiers did nevertheless augment their pay by taking up other occupations, where conditions permitted – not only *limitanei*, but soldiers of the *comitatenses* also.[47]

The seventh and eighth centuries brought changes to this complex organization, although the evidence is almost all from the later ninth to the twelfth centuries. What seems to have occurred is that the state transferred much of the burden of supporting the armies away from the fisc directly onto local populations. Beginning with the reign of Heraclius, but possibly occurring during that of Constans II, there is some slight evidence that a general conscription was reintroduced, and that military service became, at some point during the seventh century, a hereditary obligation, perhaps a result of a shortage of manpower occasioned by the Persian wars or possibly by the results of the losses incurred in the first wave of Muslim conquests in the 630s and 640s. This type of conscription became a central element in the later system of registering soldiers in the provinces and of assessing the manpower of each thematic army.

The criteria and methods of recruitment altered with the changes of the seventh and eighth centuries. The details of the process are vague, but this is where the origins of the so-called military lands are to be sought: there is evidence to show that from the later seventh century, at least, some categories of provincial soldier were dependent on their households for their provisions, arms and other items of equipment, and by comparing the situation as it had evolved by the ninth century, it is probable that the state acknowledged and encouraged this. Since soldiers and their immediate dependents received certain fiscal privileges by virtue of their military status, it will not have been difficult to move in this direction. This will anyway have been encouraged by the fact that there was a reduction of cash salaries to a nominal and occasional sum from the 660s, as later Arabic sources, together with the available numismatic material, strongly suggest.[48]

The state seems to have contributed thus to the development of a category of provincial soldier who served, usually on a seasonal basis, at his own expense, thus leading to a division between the regular core of salaried and full-time troops in each provincial or thematic army and the "militia"-like bulk of the thematic forces. The relationship between the two types of soldier remains unclear, although it probably fluctuated according to local financial constraints and local military demands. What is known is that the thematic soldiers were entered on lists or registers, along with their military obligation (called in Greek their *strateia*), and were called up as and when required. Eventually, as it became increasingly relevant to the fiscal requirements of the state, the obligations to serve in the army became more closely associated with the property in land held by each soldier's family, so that during the tenth century the military obligation could be divided between several properties and shared out, was attached in law to the properties in question, and could not be alienated (sold, bequeathed, etc.) without the military obligation. There is no evidence to support the notion that the state issued the regular soldiers with land, the (rent) income from which would support their military service, although it is important to point out that granting land to foreign populations on a conditional basis was entirely within traditional Roman practice and certainly continued to occur in the Byzantine period.[49]

Lending further stimulus to these developments, other evidence suggests that in the period from the middle of the seventh to some time in the eighth centuries, the state reverted almost entirely to a system of supporting troops in kind, and this is in part at least the explanation for the distribution of the armies across the provinces of Anatolia. The system operated in the ninth and tenth centuries was remarkably similar to that which pertained in the later Roman period. There exists an excellent tenth-century description of this system which shows just how it worked (and which will be discussed below);[50] and there is no reason to think that the same system did not operate throughout the seventh and eighth centuries also, although some of the officials in charge of assessing and in particular of co-ordinating such operations will have changed over the period in question.[51]

The changes that occurred in the seventh century, therefore, and which established the basis for the administrative pattern until the later tenth century, involved chiefly what might be seen as the farming-out of the production of arms and other military equipment, the reversion to a system of levies of provisions in kind[52] and the increased dependance of the government on the support of private households for the maintenance of some of the provincial soldiery. Imperial authority was effected through centrally appointed fiscal and other clerical officials to the civil and military staff of each thematic commander. Assessments of military needs were measured against the ability of the population to support such demands; demands for provisions for moving forces were carefully recorded, so that they could be balanced against the total fiscal demand for taxes for the areas in question.[53]

The tenth–twelfth centuries: categories of soldier

The soldiers of the middle Byzantine world were drawn from a wide range of sources, and for the period from the early ninth until the later tenth centuries may briefly be classified as follows. First, there were the regular *thematikoi*, soldiers entered on the *kodikes* (registers), along with their *strateia*, their obligation to serve. These registers were held in each theme and in the central government department responsible for such matters, the military *logothesion*. Within this group were those who could afford to appear for duty properly equipped and provisioned; those who could pay for their service but preferred not to serve in a personal capacity, in which case they had to provide the equipment, provisions and the soldier (or an equivalent value in cash); and those who had to be maintained by the thematic administration. This was done through what was termed *syndosis*: a number of taxpayers were grouped together and made responsible for the cost of equipping and supplying the soldier. As an alternative, wealthy but unwilling registered soldiers were made responsible for their equipment and provisions. In addition, as a result of the subdivision of registered landed properties due to inheritance, the various parcels or subdivisions of holdings which resulted became proportionately responsible to the local military administration. This procedure overlaps with that described under the term *syndosis*. Most of the regular thematic troops served on a seasonal basis. By the tenth century, and probably already by the later eighth century, substantial differences in wealth and status seem to have developed between those who could support service as a cavalry soldier and those who served as infantry or, in the maritime provinces, as sailors in the provincial fleets.[54]

During the tenth century this system of raising and equipping soldiers became subject to increasing fiscalization, that is to say, military service was converted into a cash payment. The Arab chronicler Ibn Hawkal describes the methods of raising troops for expeditionary forces from an outsider's perspective during the reign of Nikephros II, which accords with much of what we can extract from contemporary or near-contemporary Byzantine documents, in particular a collection of important papers drawn from the military archives of the government for three expeditions mounted in 911, 935 and 949. In addition, fragments or excerpts from other state documents dealing with matters such as exemptions or substitution for military service in the provinces of the west and the Peloponnese in the time of Romanos I provide invaluable information. According to the latter material, for example, each household paid a certain rate according to the type of service it had to support, the resources thus extracted going to the maintenance of a soldier or sailor. Similar procedures were employed in some themes for the expedition of 949 against Crete. Ibn Hawkal records that from the wealthy, a mounted soldier with all his equipment was required.[55] But the central government could vary the demand: a particular cash sum from each registered household, or a contribution in livestock, cavalry mounts and equipment and so on, could also be required.[56]

Each *thema* also had a contingent of full-time core troops based in key fortresses and with the *strategos* or *doux* in his headquarters. These standing units, made up from registered holders of a *strateia* who were able to (or wished to) serve on a permanent basis and from non-registered volunteers, were supported by the state on a full-time basis from the income derived from the fiscalized *strateia* of others. A later source, relying on tenth-century information, remarks on the quadripartite division between the different categories of landed wealth required to support respectively a heavy cavalryman, a regular cavalryman, an infantry soldier and a sailor/marine. All these different categories of soldier enjoyed the same privileges of military status. How numerous such troops were in each *thema* in the eighth and ninth centuries, and how they were paid, remains unclear – they may always have been paid through the methods for fiscalizing military obligations referred to already, but there was probably always an element of their pay from central resources: the tariff of pay described by the Arab geographer Ibn Khurradādhbīh,[57] the fact that the state seems regularly to have despatched officers from Constantinople with the salaries of the thematic forces[58] and the fact that this was done in the later ninth century at least on a three- or four-yearly rotational basis makes this clear.[59] But it is apparent that as the tenth century progressed the state increasingly preferred to raise cash from the commutation of military service which it could then invest in the more professional and permanent units of the themes – units which will have included the heavy cavalry referred to in the legislation of the emperor Nikephros II.[60] It was these core elements of the thematic forces which became the *tagmata*, or permanent units, of the provinces and themes of the later tenth and eleventh centuries. The demand for such units from the government is directly associated with the generalized fiscalization of thematic military obligations, which seems to have been especially stimulated by the policies of Nikephros II.[61]

In addition, there were the "mercenary" forces, consisting of units made up of individuals of varying background (including already registered soldiers) to serve for a particular length of time or a particular campaign, at specific rates and equipped by the state: the four imperial *tagmata* may be seen in this light,[62] as well as the units occasionally recruited by emperors for special service, such as the special naval troops raised by Michael II, the Tessarakontarioi, or the Athanatoi established under John I Tzimiskes, as well as the numerous other special *tagmata* referred to for the later tenth and eleventh centuries. As well as these, there were units of non-Romans from a particular ethnic group or region – some sections of the *Hetaireia*, for example the Chazars and Pharganoi serving at court – which seem normally to have come under Roman command.[63]

Last of all, the various foreign units serving under their own leaders for a particular length of time or campaign become a standard element of the military establishment – the "Ethiopian" unit raised during the reign of Theophilos provides an early example, or the Rus' or Varangians with their boats in the campaigns of 935 to Italy, and 949 and 965 against Crete, for example.[64] During the tenth century a number of rulers of vassal or neighbouring states sent units of varying strength to support the campaigns of individual emperors, usually on imperial request – the rulers of Tao and Armenia, for example, already mentioned in Chapter 3 – while independent bands of mercenaries on occasion seem to have presented themselves in the hope that the empire would employ them.[65] The numbers of such units increased dramatically during the eleventh century as the provincial soldiery – less efficient and less effective in respect of the needs of the state – was neglected and the *strateia* fiscalized. Already from the reign of Nikephros II various commentators note the great range of nationalities present in the Byzantine armies.[66]

During the later eleventh and twelfth centuries, as the traditional mode of recruiting thematic troops was abandoned, the multiethnic, even motley, character of Byzantine forces continued to evolve. Recruitment of mercenaries, both Byzantine and foreign, was the means of supplying most of the imperial armies. The emperors of the Comnene dynasty also obtained substantial supplies of troops through treaty arrangements. The army besieging Brindisi in 1156 was composed of Norman allies, Italian mercenaries and "Byzantine" units made up chiefly of Cuman, Alan and Georgian forces serving through treaty arrangements or on the basis of cash bounties. In 1145 Manuel I concluded a marriage alliance with the emperor Conrad, as part of which 500 knights would be sent to bolster the emperor's army; and when Manuel defeated the Serbs in 1150, the Grand Zhupan became once more a client of the emperor, agreeing to provide 500 troops for campaigns in Anatolia and 2,000 soldiers for campaigns in Europe. Only fortress guard-duty and frontier patrols and lookout service retained a connection with the ownership of land and associated fiscal exemptions, a system evolved during the reigns of John II and Manuel, but relatively limited in its application.[67] More important was the use of grants of state revenue to individuals, through which cavalry soldiers and their equipment and other needs could be financed. Such grants were called *pronoia*, but on the whole their use even under Manuel, who is supposed to have extended the application of this system, appears to have been fairly restricted. Regular recruitment on the basis of bounties and salaries or annual payments remained the norm. The government always retained the right to revoke and reassess or redistribute such grants, and it is really only after 1261 and the recovery of Constantinople from the Latins that its use becomes both more widespread and, eventually, semi-permanent or even hereditary.[68]

Remuneration

The cash salaries paid to soldiers were delivered on a yearly basis, although there may have been exceptions to this rule. Elite units and some mercenary forces appear to have been paid on a monthly basis, certainly in respect of those elements of their income relevant to food, equipment and fodder for their animals, although their cash pay may have been issued imediately before a campaign and, along with that of other (thematic) units, on a less frequent basis.[69] The amount of pay and other income of these different categories of soldier in the middle Byzantine period remains unclear. For the ninth and tenth centuries, however, some estimates have been made and, with care, these can be used to attempt to establish rates of pay for soldiers in the preceding century and a half, from the time of the Islamic conquests. Several sources provide evidence of pay, but the figures they give are generally large sums for whole armies or bodies of soldiers, of different quality and status, and include also unspecified proportions for higher grades and officers of varying degree. Specific figures, in contrast, are offered by some Arab sources; but as with the information they offer on numbers of soldiers in the army, it is not easy to know how accurate they are, or whether they are simply an attempt to present an apparently more detailed knowledge of the situation than was really the case. One calculation suggests that the standard salary of an ordinary provincial soldier in the early ninth century was about 5 *nomismata*, whereas other figures suggest a sliding scale by length of service, ranging from a basic 1 *nomisma* up to a total of 12 *nomismata*, or that simple soldiers received between 12 and 18 *nomismata* per year. The pay issued to field units for campaigns also varied, so that the documents excerpted from the archives for the Syrian campaign of 910–11 and the Cretan campaign of 949 give a range of figures, differentiating tagmatic from thematic or mercenary from militia troops.[70]

126

The whole issue is complicated by the fact that it is not always clear how often the armies were paid: thus there is evidence that during the ninth century and before a four-yearly rotation of pay among the original *themata* had been usual, although by the tenth century such a system had been abandoned.[71] But when the statistics are looked at as a whole, then the real differences between the salaries received by regular and elite units in the ninth and tenth centuries, and those of the sixth century, are not great: given the stability of the relationship between staple goods and gold, which fluctuates a little over the period from the sixth to the middle of the eleventh century (excluding periods of crisis such as drought, large-scale crop failure and so forth), this is not surprising.[72]

On the basis of this sort of evidence, therefore, it has been possible to provide figures for different grades of officer during the ninth and tenth centuries. Thus, one mid-ninth-century Arab source gives an annual salary for senior officers of different ranks varying between 40 lb and 6 lb in gold coin according to the officers' positions in the hierarchy and their seniority; pay of from 3 to 1 lb for the various junior officers (from *tourmarchai* down to the *komites* of the thematic *banda*); and pay of from 18 *nomismata* down to 12 *nomismata* or less, depending upon length of service, for "non-commissioned" officers and soldiers. In its general form, this hierarchy is borne out by Byzantine accounts of the imperial system of precedence, and by a Byzantine list of pay for senior officers preserved in the so-called *Book of Ceremonies*, compiled in part at the behest of Constantine VII (913–59) but completed in the 960s. This lists the pay of the leading imperial military commanders, or *strategoi*, in the order of precedence of their posts and *themata*. Beginning with the generals of Anatolikon, Armeniakon and Thrakasion at 40 lb of gold, it proceeds through those of Opsikion, Boukellarion and Macedonia (30 lb), Kappadokia, Charsianon, Paphlagonia and Thrace (20 lb), down to the *strategoi* of Samos and the Aegean Sea who received 10 lb.[73] Although the salaries varied by rank and grade, they probably did not vary dramatically over time, given the relative price stability over the period in question, and an attempt has been made on the basis of these figures and several others which occur in the Byzantine sources for the period from the seventh through to the tenth centuries to arrive at some conclusions about the military budget of the empire as a whole, and to generalize about the pay scales of specific units or *themata*.[74] Additional information comes from some documents detailing the campaign pay for certain units involved in expeditions against Syria in 910–11 and against Crete in 949 which, while it does not help much in determining the regular salaries of thematic units, does give some notion of the differences in pay resulting from the origins and status of different types of soldier.

This material illustrates the great variability in the pay scales for different types of unit from different regions of the empire. Ordinary Mardaites in the naval *themata*, and the "Slavs" recruited from the Opsikion district, received 3 *nomismata* campaign pay each; the soldiers from the Charpezikion district on the eastern frontier (whose pay was drawn from the commuted service of part of the Thrakasion army), received only 2 *nomismata* each. In contrast, and predictably, the soldiers of the cavalry *tagmata* received a vastly greater salary: in both the 911 documents and in those for 949, the *scholarioi* of the *tagmata* of Thrace and Macedonia, as well as of the peratic Hikanatoi and Exkoubitoi, received much greater sums in addition to valuable silk garments.[75] The numbers of each grade of officer remains uncertain: but rates of two or three times higher than the best-paid thematic contingents result, reflecting the greatly superior position of these units.[76] There were also major differences between units of comparable type, however. The senior officers of the Charpezikion *thema*, for example, were paid at a lower rate than those of the *thema* of Sebasteia, and both were paid at a lower rate than the officers of the regular naval *themata*, whose *tourmarchai* and *drouggarioi* received three and two times as much as their Armenian counterparts.

Such variations probably reflected social as well as administrative and organizational differences between the regions concerned, in addition to the conditions under which the units in question were recruited: the naval *themata* represented a part of the old, well-established military administrative system of the empire. The newer *themata* of Sebasteia and of Charpezikion reflected a somewhat different social and cultural as well as geopolitical context. But these factors render it a risky undertaking to assume any uniformity across the empire's military-administrative organization, and especially of assuming standardization of unit sizes, budgets and internal establishment (ratios of different classes of officer to men, etc.). And although there is virtually no direct evidence relating to the rates of pay of soldiers in the later eleventh and twelfth centuries, we may reasonably assume that the same general principles governed the amounts paid to different types of soldier for different purposes, and that mercenary forces such as the small Frankish and Norman contingents, which had a high military value, were remunerated accordingly (and probably better than, for example, the empire's Turkish mercenaries, although this is entirely hypothetical).[77]

Arms, armour and technology

The soldiers: defensive and offensive equipment

Byzantine military technology was part of a much wider picture, and both shared in and contributed to the evolution of the defensive and offensive techniques common to the western Eurasian world: in the former, in respect of the adoption of techniques and products from the East; in the latter, in respect of transmitting the Byzantine version of these techniques to neighbouring cultures. Through the various peoples who inhabited or passed through the steppe regions north of the Danube and the Black Sea the empire maintained regular contacts with more distant societies, so that elements of central Asian and even more easterly military panoply or practices permeated into the Balkans,

Asia Minor and Middle East. In the late sixth century, the stirrup was adopted from the Avars, who had carried it across from the eastern steppe and China; the same people seem also to have stimulated the use of lamellar armour on a much greater scale than hitherto, while in the eighth or ninth century the single-edged cavalry sabre and the lamellar cuirass with associated splinted arm-guards was adopted from the steppe, probably through the Chazars and Magyars. A number of descriptions of Byzantine soldiers' panoply are included in the various military treatises we have exploited; in addition, some archaeological material – actual items of weaponry and armour – contribute to the picture, while pictorial representations of different types of arms and armour also add substantially to our knowledge, both from the Byzantine world and from those areas whence the major influences were derived.[78]

Cavalry during the sixth and early seventh century are described by Procopius and, in particular, in the *Strategikon*, whose precepts suggest that the influence of the Avars was at this time particularly powerful. According to Procopius, the best-armed horseman wore a mail coat reaching to the knee on top of a thick padded coat to absorb the shock of any blows; he wore a helmet,[79] a small circular shield strapped to the left shoulder (another feature found on the steppe), and was armed with a lance, sword (hung from a shoulder strap on the left side)[80] and bow with quiver (on the right side).[81] The horse was unarmoured, since the cavalry described by Procopius functioned both as shock troops and highly mobile mounted archers.[82] The sixth-century anonymous treatise specifies further that the front-rank cavalry mounts were to be armoured (for the neck, chest and flanks) and that their hooves were to be protected against caltrops by metal plates. This practice was clearly continuously observed, for an account of an eleventh-century battle between imperial cavalry and Arab forces in Sicily refers to the metal plates protecting the Roman cavalry's hooves.[83]

In the infantry it was primarily those who made up the first and second ranks who wore the full defensive panoply – breastplate, helmet, leg-armour (splinted greaves of iron, leather or felt), and wide round or oval shields of 1½ m (about 5 feet) in diameter to afford maximum protection. The shields of those in the front rank were also supposed to have spiked bosses. Spears and swords were the main offensive arms of such soldiers. There is a certain element of antiquarian detail in this information – the writer assumes that a solid breastplate will be worn, for example, which may have applied to some officers, and perhaps to soldiers in parade uniform, but for which there is no evidence from other contexts. The sources would indicate that, in reality, a mail shirt would be worn, with padded jerkin or coat beneath.[84]

It is clear, both from incidental references in accounts of battles and from these treatises, that such heavy armament was limited to relatively small numbers of men, destined primarily to serve in the foremost rank or ranks of the battle line. The majority of infantry and cavalry were less expensively equipped, with quilted or padded coats (*zabai*) reaching to the knee, and protection for the chest of leather, possibly in the form of scale armour. For the infantry, whether or not helmets were worn, shields spears and padded coats will have been the predominant form of armament. Light infantry wore quilted jerkins, may have carried small shields, and were armed with slings, bows or javelins. These descriptions match what is known of the standard panoply of Roman infantry in the third century from pictorial and archaeological evidence, and suggest a considerable degree of continuity in basic style and form of military garb.[85]

By the end of the sixth century, Avar influence was clearly expressed in the armament of the cavalry: troopers in the heavy cavalry were protected by long coats of mail (referred to as both *lorikia* and as *zabai*),[86] intended to cover them down to the ankle, of either quilting or mail-on-quilting, a mail hood and neck-guard, spiked helmet and small circular shield. Elite units also had arm-guards. The treatise states explicitly that much of this equipment was modelled on the Avar panoply, in particular the throat-guard or gorget, the thong attached to the middle of the lance and the loose-fitting and decorated clothing. Troopers also wore a wide, thick felt cloak to protect them from the weather and were equipped with two stirrups, an innovation copied from the Avars. The bow is not specified, but was probably of the Hunnic type as before, although the quiver and bowcase apparently followed the Persian style. The panoply was completed by a cavalry sword, and the horses were to be armoured in front with a skirt and neck-covering, either of iron (mail or scale – the text does not specify) or felt, or "in the Avar fashion", perhaps suggesting lamellar of iron or, more likely, leather.[87] Lamellar does not appear to have been used widely, although various types of lamellar construction for both horse- and body-armour were certainly known.[88]

Infantry were less well-armed. The best of the heavy infantry wore *zabai*, if they were available, and those in the front rank were also to wear greaves (of iron or wood, thus probably splinted), and helmets. All carried a spear, shield and "Herul" sword – the Herul infantry figure prominently in Procopius' accounts of the war in Italy and clearly influenced imperial fighting techniques to a degree. The light infantry carried a small shield, a sling, javelins and bow, together with an arrow-guide to enable them to fire short, heavy bolts as well as arrows of the normal length (a device common in the Islamic world, and perhaps also introduced via the Avars to the Byzantine and western world). Barbarian influence is clear here, too, as with the cavalry: the *Strategikon* notes that the infantry should wear "Gothic" boots, short cloaks rather than the large, cumbrous "Bulgar" (i.e. Hunnic) capes, and that some of the light infantry are equipped with Slav javelins.[89]

The basics of heavy and light infantry equipment seem to have changed little during the period from the fifth to the early seventh centuries, except for the admission in the *Strategikon* that the majority of the heavy infantry did not possess the more expensive mail armour of those who made up the front rank of the line of battle. In contrast, the heavy and medium cavalry panoply shows marked steppe influence, as well as the influence of Sassanian cavalry tactics and arms – an early seventh-century bas-relief in Persia at Taq-i-Bustan shows the king Khusru II in armour remarkably similar to that described for the heavy cavalryman of the *Strategikon*, with the horse protected by what appears to be a lamellar skirt of metal or leather plates, while there is a great deal of fragmentary archaeological and pictorial evidence to support the picture described in the same source.[90]

The imperial arms factories which were responsible for producing a large part of the defensive and offensive equipment will have assured a certain element of uniformity within and between units. On the other hand, many items such as helmets, shields or bows may also have been produced on the basis of government commissions to provincial craftsmen, and this will have encouraged a certain amount of variation. Archaeological evidence from the fourth through to the sixth centuries certainly suggests this, and that, independently of the imperial manufactories, there were a number of private production centres in many cities producing bows and arrows, helmets and items of field artillery. In particular, it seems that frontier fortresses and cities maintained a small-scale arms production tailored to the needs of the permanent garrison units of the region in question.[91] Although some imperially controlled arms production continued after the middle of the seventh century, most production appears to have been carried out through commissions or compulsory levy by the thematic or provincial administration.

By the tenth century, this basic panoply had altered very little, although the seventh, eighth and ninth centuries had seen a number of developments in both the forms and appearance of armour and weaponry, and in fighting technique.[92] The latter may be reflected for mounted troops in the appearance of the single-edged sabre (which seems to be the meaning of the term *paramerion* in tenth-century treatises, described as slung from the waist and of the same length as the regular cavalry sword, the *spathion*),[93] while the greater use of felt and quilted defences are the most obvious changes, the latter in particular a reflection of the general impoverishment in the levels of equipment of the thematic infantry and cavalry already discussed. Thematic cavalry were armed with mail, lamellar or quilted armour, according to individual wealth and status – the waist-length *klibanion* of lamellar appears to have been standard, but mail surcoats – *lorikia* – were also worn. The long coat described in the *Strategikon*, and copied by Leo, no longer appears in the mid-tenth-century sources, suggesting that it probably fell out of use during the seventh century, although knee-length coats of what may be lamellar appear in an eleventh-century Byzantine manuscript illumination.[94] Helmets were probably also, standard, although some soldiers may not have possessed them, using felt caps with neck-guards instead;[95] while the main weapons were the lance or spear and sword, complemented by the light cavalry shield. Bows and quivers (on the Iranian pattern) completed the armament. Light cavalry had less body-armour, and carried javelins or bows, or both.

Infantry wore quilted or lamellar body-armour or mail, although those that could afford the more expensive mail or lamellar equipment may also have possessed horses and been classed among the mounted troops: the evidence suggests that, on the whole, the foot soldiers were less well outfitted than in the late Roman period. The majority of infantry, even the heavy infantry, had felt caps rather than metal helmets, for example, and this must have been standard wear from the later seventh or eighth century on, and remained so until the eleventh century and after (although there were certainly exceptions, especially among infantry *tagmata* recruited from foreign mercenaries, for example, whose panoply reflected their own cultural and martial traditions). Shields for the infantry were round or four- or three-cornered and up to 137 cm (54") in diameter, or circular and about 81 cm (30") in diameter for light-armed troops; for the cavalry they were circular and about 86 cm (27") in diameter for the light cavalry and up to 101 cm (40") in diameter for the heavier troops.[96] Weapons included the heavy javelin, the *menavlion*, as well as various types of mace and axe (single-bladed, double-bladed, blade-and-spike, etc.), along with the traditional sword, although not all heavy infantrymen carried the latter. The standard infantry spear in the mid- and late-tenth-century treatises seems to have been longer than during the earlier period and probably reflects the enhanced status and battlefield role of heavy infantry at this time, troops who had to stand firm against heavy cavalry and present a "hedgehog" of spears to repel the enemy.

The elite units of the imperial *tagmata*, and later the heavy cavalry soldiers who made up the small cataphract corps recruited by Nikephros Phocas in particular were much more heavily armoured; indeed, it is likely that the *tagmata*, equipped and outfitted directly by the central government, had been from the beginning much more heavily armed than the thematic forces, and may have been issued with horse armour as well. The mid-tenth-century heavy cavalryman is described in several sources, and was protected by a lamellar *klibanion* with splinted arm-guards, sleeves and gauntlets, the latter from coarse silk or quilted cotton. From the waist to the knee they wore thick felt coverings reinforced with mail; over the *klibanion* was worn a sleeveless quilted or padded coat (the *epilorikon*); and to protect the head and neck an iron helmet with mail or quilting attached and wrapped around the face. The lower leg was protected by splinted greaves of bronze. Offensive weapons included iron maces with a three-, four- or six-flanged head, the *paramerion*, and the standard sword or *spathion*. The mace was a particularly favoured weapon for the heavy cavalry and heavy infantry, and indeed acquired such a degree of notoriety that enemy soldiers were reported to have fled at the sight of mace-bearing Byzantine troops. The horses were also armoured, with felt quilting, or boiled leather lamellar or scale armour, or hides – the head, neck and front, flanks and rear of the animal should be thus protected. Their hooves appear also to have been protected against caltrops by metal plates.[97] In addition to this information, the so-called *Sylloge tacticorum* gives some details on the bow used by Byzantine soldiers, which together with descriptions and illustrations of the curved Byzantine bows suggests that the basic model remained that of the Hunnic bow, adopted in the fifth and sixth centuries, measuring from 114 cm to 122 cm (45" to 48") in length, with arrows of 68 cm (27").[98]

Imperial troops strung their bows more or less tautly according to their role: cavalry were instructed to string them less tautly, for ease and speed of use while mounted, for example. In addition, infantry soldiers may also have employed an arrow-guide, a channelled tube used to shoot short bolts very rapidly. This was certainly in use in the Muslim world after the seventh century, it first appears in the *Strategikon* of Maurice in the late sixth century, and – according to the later Arab sources – was introduced from the steppe. If this is indeed the case (and there is no reason to doubt it), the arrow-guide will have been yet another example of military technology from the central Asian and Chinese sphere carried westward by the steppe peoples – probably the Avars again – and adopted by the East Romans. Whether Byzantine soldiers also used the hand-held crossbow, some evidence for which exists from the late Roman period (as opposed to the much larger frame- or swivel-mounted weapon used as field- or siege-artillery, which certainly did continue in use), seems doubtful. Why it was not used is unclear: the answer must be sought in the conditions and nature of the fighting carried on by infantry in the period from the later fifth century on. But it appears to have been quite alien to the Byzantines when it appeared in the hands of the western soldiers of the later eleventh century.[99]

One of the advantages of the heavy cavalry panoply of the tenth century was that it could be worn in sections according to the context – much of the body-armour could be left off, along with the horse armour if these troops had to act in a different role. Pictorial illustrations from the twelfth-century Skylitzes manuscript in the Escorial Library in Madrid show cavalry from the ninth century up to the middle of the eleventh century armed with mail or scale/lamellar (it is difficult to say from the often rather vague representations which is intended), round or kite-shaped shields, plain round helmets, helmets with crests or tufts, or with aventails, straight swords, spears and maces. There are no illustrations of heavily armoured cataphract cavalry – the horses throughout are shown unarmoured, and it is likely that this represented the norm throughout the period in question. On the other hand, the manuscript certainly reflects contemporary style and panoply, so that it should not be taken at face value: the ubiquity of Norman and Frankish styles of cavalry armament must have had a considerable influence, both on illuminators and on Byzantine cavalry panoply itself. What became the "western" style of heavy cavalry attack, with the spear or lance couched under the arm, seems already to have been used before the 1070s by some Frankish mercenaries in Byzantine service. In the 1070s the unit of the Athanatoi were trained in this technique, according to a contemporary Byzantine account, so that its development in east and west was parallel.[100]

Many elements of Byzantine weaponry and defensive equipment can be found in neighbouring as well as more distant cultural contexts, which illustrates the international milieu in which Byzantine military technology evolved. Evidence for splinted leg- and arm-guards is found in contemporary Scandinavian archaeological contexts as well as in both archaeological contexts and representational art from regions such as Turkestan and Iran, Hungary and the

South Russian steppe region. The use of knee-length lamellar or quilted coats, mail and scale defences, as well as neck- and face-guards for helmets similar to those described in the *Praecepta*, is also attested from similar sources. Byzantine military technology was part of a continuum, evincing some entirely indigenous particularities in style or technique, but sharing to a greater or lesser extent the production techniques and form of a broader Eurasian technology of fighting. I exclude from consideration issues of which we know next to nothing of course: it is entirely probable that in terms of, for example, types and styles of sword-hilt, scabbard, shield and helmet construction and related issues of decoration, Byzantine weaponry had its own individual traditions and specificities, and the descriptions in the military treatises of uniform unit colours for shields, pennons and so forth, for tufts or crests on helmets or other accoutrements, or for the length of spear- and lance-heads, arrows and arrow-heads, give some hint of this. But few specific examples have been firmly identified.[101]

As well as that of the Normans and Franks, the influence of the Seljuks or Pechenegs certainly affected Byzantine cavalry dress, as well as, in particular, the evolution of the *klibanion*. One variation on the *klibanion* may have been a purely Byzantine technical development, namely the use of a type of banded-lamellar construction which afforded both more protection and more flexibility than the traditional, relatively solid forms, and introduced probably from the later tenth or eleventh centuries.[102] The evidence suggests that the Byzantine armies continued to be equipped in their own style, while foreign mercenary forces – Normans, Pechenegs, Varangians, for example – arrived and fought in their own traditional garb. The long axes of the Rus' or Varangians, for example, thus contributed to the epithet by which they were frequently known, the "axe-bearers". As time went on, especially during the twelfth century, and as the field armies of the emperors were increasingly recruited from foreign mercenaries, so the indigenous, Byzantine panoply gave way to influences and styles from elsewhere, particularly western Europe (already by the 1150s and 1160s the court of Manuel I preferred the western joust to the traditional hippodrome horse- or chariot-racing) and the Seljuks of Anatolia. Byzantine heavy cavalry were armed more after the fashion of westerners where the panoply could be afforded; light cavalry and infantry continued to be armed – like their Seljuk or Saracen enemies – with the traditional combination of lamellar corselets or mail, quilted fabrics or boiled leather, felt and cotton head-gear, and the weapons described above.[103] Indeed, the almost total reliance of the government upon mercenaries had led by the end of the twelfth century to a situation where indigenous Roman units were not always able to match their enemies on equal terms, and a foreign warlord could plausibly assign imperial defeats to the inferiority of Byzantine weapons and artillery.[104]

Artillery

The question of the degree of continuity maintained across the period from the fourth and fifth centuries into the later Byzantine period has still not been adequately addressed, although several recent treatments have begun to take the issue seriously. Many of the older writers on the subject of Byzantine military matters simply take for granted that Roman torsion-powered artillery continued to be produced in Byzantium, although there is virtually no solid evidence for such a claim. The subject cannot be dealt with in any detail here, but some idea of the issues can be offered, and some notion of the nature of Byzantine artillery weapons sketched.

In fact, recent work strongly suggests that, although there is clear archaeological evidence of their continued use well into the second half of the fourth century, two-arm horizontally mounted torsion-powered weapons had dropped out of use by the end of the fifth century and certainly by the middle of the sixth century, although Procopius describes the much simpler single-armed vertically mounted torsion-powered *onager*, a stone-thrower, at the siege of Rome. While depicting a number of torsion-powered devices, the tenth-century illuminated manuscript of the treatises on artillery ascribed to Hero of Byzantium copies in many respects archaic exemplars, and it is unlikely that all the engines described existed in more than theory.[105] The bolt-projecting artillery described by Procopius, employed by the Romans at the siege of Rome by the Goths in 537/8, is tension-powered, and the vocabulary employed in the Byzantine military treatises, where it sheds any light on the matter at all, reinforces this probability: the term *cheirotoxobolistra*, with the use of the element *toxo-*, bow, for example, indicates the nature of the means of spanning the device: Roman torsion-powered machines were frequently differentiated from tension machines by the presence or absence of this term.[106] In a tenth-century list of artillery and their parts a clear distinction is also made between the terms *toxobolistra* and *cheirotoxobolistra* (i.e. bow-ballista and hand-bow-ballista). It has been argued that this was a reflection of the size of the weapon, and that the latter must be equivalent to the crossbow, that is to say it was a hand-held tension-spanned weapon. But there is no real evidence that the hand-held crossbow – which was certainly known to the Romans, although apparently fairly limited in its use – was actually employed in late Roman or Byzantine times.

The Byzantines appear rather to have used the larger, frame-mounted version of such weapons as field or siege artillery, the term *cheirotoxobolistra* signalling most probably a manually spanned weapon, the other term referring to such weapons in general and, where specified, weapons spanned by means of a windlass. One technical text notes a difference between *cheirotoxobolistrai* and *megalai toxobolistrai meta trochilion* (hand-bow-ballistae and large bow-ballistae with pulleys, i.e. a windlass) in the list of artillery equipment for the Cretan expedition of 949. Both types of weapon are referred to, sometimes indirectly (e.g. as *cheiromaggana*) in the technical military treatises, and *toxobolistrai* appear in some of the narrative chronicles also. [107]

Whether the wagon-mounted *carroballista* used in late Roman infantry field units continued in use is another problem, since there is little solid evidence. In the treatise *On administering the empire* commissioned by Constantine

Porphyrogenitus in the tenth century, a reference to artillery units equipped with *cheiroballistrai* in the time of Diocletian and Constantine I (284–305, 307–37) seems in fact to be a garbling of the Latin term and refers to such artillery, but this has no relevance for the middle Byzantine period. In contrast, however, the *Tactica* of Leo, in bringing the *Strategikon* of Maurice up to date in the section on field artillery that might accompany infantry units, refers to wagon-mounted artillery known as *alakatia* (he actually calls them *eilaktia*, presumably a variant, or garbling, for the term *elakatia* or *alakatia*). The term means literally distaff or pole, but could also be used in later Greek for a winch or windlass and was presumably its nickname (cf. the late Roman *onager*, or "mule", a torsion-powered vertically mounted stone-thrower). This machine is also referred to in the same contexts as the others, but is in addition described as mounted on carts and swivelling from side to side.[108] In the *De obsidione toleranda* the "so-called" *elakatai* are paired with *cheiromaggana* and listed after *tetrareai* and *magganika* (see below). At another point in the *Tactica* they are described as *ta magganika alakatia*, mounted on wagons, and also as "stone-throwing *magganika* called *alakatia*" which can also shoot fire-arrows. This suggests that they must have been weapons with a slider, a windlass or similar mechanical spanning device and a trigger release and associated parts, which could be used to project both bolts and stones, similar to the late Roman *carroballista*, a carriage-based, swivel-mounted tension- or torsion-powered weapon.[109] Other middle Byzantine texts also interpret *elakation* as windlass. Cumulatively, this evidence strongly suggests that the tenth-century Byzantine *alakation* was most probably (and in view of its name) a light, frame-mounted tension weapon on a swivel stand which could discharge both arrows and stones.[110]

While the simplest form of torsion-powered stone-thrower, the *onager*, appears to have survived in the Islamic, Byzantine and medieval western worlds, stone-throwing engines were also employed which were based on neither torsion nor tension.[111] During the late sixth century, the Avars introduced the traction-powered counterweight lever machine, originating in China but quickly adopted by the Byzantines.[112] In its simplest form this is described by a seventh century account of the Avar siege of Thessaloniki in the following terms: "These [*petroboloi*] were quadrangular, rising from broad bases to narrower tops, upon which were thick cylindrical [pieces] with the ends covered in iron, and onto these were affixed timbers like the beams of houses, having the slings suspended from the rear, and from the front sturdy ropes." By pulling on the ropes, the team could project heavy stones considerable distances.[113] The words used for such machines are not always clear: the generic term was often employed – *petrobolos* (stone-thrower) or *petrarea*, as in the Miracles of St Demetrios, but the technical terms *tetrarea* (for which *petrarea* may well be a commonsense confusion) and *labdarea* were also used.[114]

There appear to have been at least two classes of such engines, the second being called *labdareai*, presumably mounted on a lambda-shaped frame.[115] In the ninth-century *Scriptor incertus de Leone*, Bulgar siege engines are said to include both *triboloi* and *tetraboloi*, which may be the equivalent of *labdareai* and *tetrareai* respectively.[116] Their operation clearly involved some technical knowledge and skill: at one point the defenders of Thessaloniki received the assistance of sailors – described as *empeiromagganous* ("experienced in the use of mechanical devices") – from ships which had put into the port to operate their *petrareai*.[117] In the twelfth-century Madrid manuscript of the history of John Skylitzes, for example, there are two illustrations of a traction-powered (manually hauled) lever machine, one of which, depicting the siege of Mopsouestia in 965, shows the device based on a single central stanchion or post supported by a framework of three or four subsidiary posts attached laterally half-way down, with the catapult-arm affixed by a swivel or hinge at the top and a number of ropes descending from the shorter end; the second, showing the Byzantine attack and capture of Preslav in 971, shows two men preparing to haul on the ropes and a third loading the sling with stones.[118] There are clear differences in construction between the two devices, which may possibly reflect the differences between the four-post and three-post trebuchets reflected in the terms *tetrarea* and *labdaraia*. Similar devices appear in western medieval pictures also.[119]

As well as these technical terms, the general word *magganika* was also employed, but it is unclear whether it refers simply to "machines" or to something more specific. Since the word *magganon* could also mean any block or block-and-pulley mechanism,[120] it may refer simply to other machines employing a windlass and/or ratcheted bracing device, whether of the bow-ballista type or not. In the list of materials for the attack on Crete in 949 supplies and parts for four *tetrareai*, four *labdaraiai* and four *magganika* are mentioned, where *magganika* replaces the term *eilaktia* (i.e. *alakatia*) of a list in the previous section. The non-specific term *cheiromaggana* also occurs in a context where we would expect to read of the bow-ballista, so that *magganika* may be taken in all probability to refer to weapons of the large or small *toxobolistra* type already discussed rather than stone-throwers.[121]

The reasons for the disappearance of most torsion-powered artillery remain unclear, but it has been pointed out that tension-driven artillery is much cheaper and easier to produce and to maintain, and while being less powerful, was more reliable: maintaining the torsion at equivalent levels in both springs of a two-armed torsion catapult required mathematical and technical skills which appear not to have been maintained into the fifth and sixth centuries. The Byzantine army seems always to have included a number of specialist engineers responsible for the artillery: they are mentioned in most of the treatises as well as in other sources.[122] But Procopius's description of the single-armed *onager*, a vertically mounted torsion stone-thrower, shows that the simplest torsion engines continued to be used in the eastern empire well into the sixth century; and since they appear also to have been employed in all the neighbouring cultures thereafter, it is unlikely that they dropped entirely out of use in Byzantium and may be covered by the general catch-all term *magganika* along with the other devices mentioned above. Their main disadvantage was that, to be both effective and stable, they had to be constructed very solidly, which required considerable logistical support and planning. That this was generally available in the Byzantine world will be demonstrated in the following chapters. But the advent of traction-powered lever stone-throwers, which were potentially far more powerful and much easier to construct and to operate, must have affected the need and the desire to construct even this simple torsion-driven device.[123]

Perhaps the best-known Byzantine "artillery" device is the liquid fire projector, about which there is still no consensus among those who have studied the sources. It was available as a large-scale projector for use on board ship and in sieges, but during the later ninth and tenth centuries a smaller, hand-held version (which may not, however, have operated on exactly the same principles) was also employed, described in both Byzantine and Arab sources. The various scraps of evidence for the way in which liquid fire was projected suggest that the weapon consisted of a tube attached, via a leathern swivel joint, to a sealed canister containing crude petroleum (obtained from the Caucasus and the South Russian steppe region where the imperial government showed a particular interest in maintaining a diplomatic presence), which could be placed under slight pressure before being released and ignited. The Byzantine sources provide evidence of the various component parts and the general effects of the device, and a ninth- or tenth-century Latin account gives a fairly clear account of this arrangement. Whether the weapon was as effective as the Greek sources appear to suggest (and they make no reference to the dangers inherent in its use – for example, overheating of the petroleum in the enclosed container must on occasion have had literally explosive results) depends on the nature and reliability of the sources which describe it. The Byzantines themselves clearly regarded it as an effective weapon, if only because of its psychological effect.

The hurling of combustibles from catapults was universally practised, of course, and it is clear that the empire's enemies employed this means where relevant or practicable. Whether the Arabs also possessed the same type of projector as the Byzantines, as has been suggested, is still at issue, since the sources remain ambiguous (whether in respect of their date, their description or the precise meaning of the technical language employed). But it was the device itself, and the form of projection, which differentiates this "liquid fire" from incendiary weapons in general, although confusion was introduced by the indiscriminate use – from the time of the First Crusade – of the term "Greek fire" for any and all such weapons by western knights and chroniclers who had fought in the east.[124]

CHAPTER FIVE

The army at war: campaigns

Logistics and field support

The outcome of armed conflict is rarely, if ever, determined by the quality of the soldiers and their leaders alone – aspects we will examine in the next chapter – but, crucially, by the degree and nature of the logistical support which makes fighting between relatively complex social-political organizations possible in the first place. In this respect, the East Roman empire up to the twelfth century was well served by an efficient – indeed, ruthless – fiscal and logistical system which, by maximizing the often limited resources at the state's disposal, gave the imperial armies an advantage which on occasion meant the difference between success and failure, and certainly facilitated the survival of both the military and civil administration of the empire in times of adversity.

Arms, equipment and livestock: from the late Roman to the Byzantine system

Until the middle of the seventh century, clothing, mounts and weapons for the army were provided by a combination of taxation or levy in kind (for example, certain items of clothing and boots appear to have been raised in this way), and through state manufactories. Of the latter, the arms factories were among the most important. Weapons and clothing were, by the later sixth century, bought by the soldier, either directly or through the regimental actuary, with a cash allowance issued for the purpose. Maurice (582–602) tried to reform this by returning to the older system of issuing such materials in kind, but it is unclear if he was successful. Horses were provided partly by levy, partly through purchase at fixed prices. Imperial stud farms contributed a proportion of the mounts required, but again, cannot have provided for all mounted units. The so-called *Strategikon* of Maurice, composed at the end of the sixth century, advises generals to establish winter quarters in areas where such supplies will be readily available for purchase, or to make it possible for traders and others to reach the army in order to provide the required provisions and equipment. Iron ore, charcoal and wood were also provided by levy, sometimes remitted from the tax-burden of the area or community in question, sometimes raised through compulsory impositions upon certain categories of the population.[1]

The cost of moving all these supplies was considerable. Transportation was cheapest by sea, but this was rarely relevant to inland campaigns, either on the eastern front or in the Balkans. Usually, the public post – *cursus publicus* – was employed in either its "fast" or "slow" versions (the former using horses and mules, the latter oxen) to transport materials not directly connected with the army.[2] The army itself provided guards and transport for weapons, as laid down in Justinian's regulations of the middle of the sixth century, although it should be stressed that we have no way of knowing to what extent these prescriptions were actually followed.[3]

Field armies on campaign were provided with their supplies by a complicated process involving liaison between local and central fiscal departments. According to the sixth-century regulations preserved in the legislation of Justinian, the provincial officials are to be given advance notice of the army's requirements in foodstuffs and other goods, which are to be deposited at named sites along the route of march. The materials, food supplies and other requirements demanded by the provincial authorities on behalf of the central government were referred to as *embole*, a term which meant simply that part of the regular tax assessment owed by each taxpayer (whether an estate, an individual peasant freeholder or whatever) not paid in coin. Exact records of the produce supplied by the taxpayers as *embole* were to be kept and reckoned up against the annual tax owed in this form; if more supplies were required than were due in tax, then the extra was to be supplied by the taxpayers, but this was then to be paid for, at a fixed rate established by the appropriate state officials, out of the cash revenues collected in the regular yearly assessment from that particular province. This process was referred to as a *coemptio* in Latin, or *synone* in Greek, effectively a compulsory purchase. If the provincial treasuries in question had insufficient local cash revenues left over to pay for these extra supplies, then they were to be paid for instead *either* from the general bank of the praetorian prefecture, in other words the *coemptio* was still applied, or they were to be collected anyway and then their value (at the prices fixed by the state) deducted from the following year's assessment in kind.[4]

The provision of raw materials for weapons had been achieved in the late Roman period through the regular taxation (iron ore, for example, formed part of the tax burden – *synteleia* – of those who extracted ore in the Taurus mountain region) together with compulsory levies in wood and other materials. The tenth- and eleventh-century evidence suggests that a similar combination of levies (wood, charcoal, etc.) and purchases (or compulsory purchases) was operated, as noted above. But in contrast to the later Roman arrangements, the production of different types of weapon was commissioned and passed on to provincial craftsmen and manufacturers of items such as spears, arrows, bows, shields and so forth. After the period of the initial Arab conquests in the 630s and 640s, most of the late Roman workshops were outside the imperial frontier; of those that remained within the state – at Sardis, Nicomedia, Adrianople, Kaisareia, Thessaloniki – virtually nothing is known, although there is very slight evidence that production may have been resumed at Kaisareia.[5] Arms workshops continued to exist in Constantinople, but whether the official in charge of these – the *archon tou armamentou* – was in charge of the provincial establishments as well as these is unclear.[6] There is some evidence that state officials known as *kommerkiarioi*, originally responsible only for the import or redistribution of luxury goods, in particular silks, may have been given some responsibilities, on an interim basis, for the commissioning of weapons and related military requirements during the second half of the seventh century: there is a degree of coincidence between evidence for certain military expeditions, on the one hand, and the activities of these officials in areas from which logistical support might be drawn, either overland or by sea. But the exact nature of their role remains unresolved.[7]

Eighth-century evidence suggests that some provincial soldiers were responsible for obtaining and providing their own weapons and armour – signalling the abandonment of the state monopoly which had been introduced by Justinian. There is some evidence in inscriptions as well as texts for provincial armourers and weapon-makers. By the ninth century, the provincial military officers, through their own officials, were commissioned with raising the necessary extra weapons and equipment, which was done by applying compulsory levies on provincial craftsmen and artisans.[8] The government departments of the *eidikon* and the *vestiarion* appear as major repositories and suppliers of a whole range of requirements for the fleet and the army, alongside the armouries established in Constantinople itself.[9]

The supply of animals for the army was always a major expense as well as a central concern of the government. Cavalry mounts were provided in the later Roman period from imperial stud farms, as were pack-animals, although requisitions from private sources were also made. After the sixth century, imperial stud farms for cavalry horses as well as animals for the imperial post and for the army's supply train continued to be maintained – the best-known was that at Malagina in northwest Anatolia. The *metata*, or stock-raising ranches, of the provinces of Asia and Phrygia are the most prominent in the middle Byzantine period, but certainly existed long before this: the ranch in Phrygia was situated in the triangle formed by the small towns of Synnada, Dokimon and Polybotos. There were also *metata* in Lydia. As a result of territorial losses, these ranches had moved by the middle of the twelfth century, mostly to Europe. Malagina still served as an imperial base after the 1140s, when it was recovered by Manuel; but the main ranches and bases were in the Balkans, in the *themata* of Dyrrhachion, Berroia, Hellas-Peloponnesos and Nikopolis. They continued in the charge of the *chartoularios*, now entitled the *megas chartoularios* (originally a subordinate of the *logothetes ton agelon*, the logothete of the herds); and they were referred to no longer as *aplekta* or *metata*, but as *chartoularata*. Their function was unchanged.[10]

Close cooperation between the imperial official in charge of these establishments, the military logothete (responsible for military expenditures and accounts), the *komes tou stablou* (in charge of the imperial stables) and his representatives at Malagina, and other fiscal departments was essential. Although the titles of the officials involved, and the relationships between their various departments within the imperial administration, changed over time, particularly from the reign of Alexios I, the fundamentals of this system remained the same until the end of the twelfth century. In the sixth century there had also been military stock-raising estates in Thrace as well as eastern Asia Minor; imperial studfarms in Cappadocia had raised racehorses, and may have specialized in other types of animal also – the Villa Palmati near Tyana was well-known in this respect, as was the estate of Hermogenes in the Pontos. But a wide variety of different sources of animal was exploited. If the imperial household was involved, then all the main state departments, the leading civil and military officers, the metropolitanates and the monastic houses of the empire had to provide a certain number of mules or other pack-animals to transport the household and its requirements. For regular non-imperial campaigns the main sources for the army were the imperial stud farms referred to, requisitions from the estates of the church, from secular landholders and from the soldiers themselves. In the late Roman period, horses were provided, or at least made available for purchase using special grants issued for the purpose. During the middle Byzantine period in the provinces the thematic soldiers were often supposed to provide their own horses, although this sometimes caused problems. Tagmatic units seem generally to have had their mounts provided for them, or were required to purchase their requirements on the market using grants incorporated in their salaries and campaign payments.[11]

The supply of horses for the cavalry would also need to cater for remounts, of course. The ratio of remounts to soldiers in the late Roman and Byzantine army is difficult to assess. The rate of replacement of horses for the public post was set at 25 per cent per annum in the fourth century. It was probably much lower for a field army on the move, but a rate of replacement of 10 per cent would only barely cover average rates of loss. According to the late sixth- or early seventh-century *Strategikon*, the remounts which accompanied cavalry units into battle numbered only some 5–6 per cent of the total. But the same text also notes that remounts should be held back at the base camp with the rest of the baggage train, so that this was clearly a minimum provision for the battlefield only. Similar provisions are mentioned in an independent text, the *Praecepta* of Nikephros. The tenth-century treatise on imperial military expeditions suggests a remount stock of about 20 per cent

– 100 animals for 482. Two of the later tenth-century treatises imply a remount rate for advance units and the main lancer division (as opposed to mounted archer units) of 1 : 1. Yet the *Praecepta* of Nikephros II also specifies that not too many spare horses should be taken along with raiding parties lest they unnecessarily encumber the raid. Similarly, in the report sent by Heraclius to Constantinople of his campaign in 627–8, mention is made of the cavalry being ordered by the emperor to leave their spare horses in the houses of Kanzak, near which he had established his main base, and that each soldier should retain only one horse. The implication is that at least one spare animal per soldier was available.[12]

Supplying campaign forces after the seventh century

A very similar process operated in the ninth and tenth centuries and after, according to a treatise on military expeditions compiled by the *magistros* Leo Katakylas, describing very probably the campaign practice of the emperor Basil I. Here it is noted that the *protonotarios* of each *thema* through which the imperial force passes must provide certain supplies in kind from the *aerikon* (the cash resources of the province) and the *synone*, which by this time no longer meant a compulsory purchase but was an equivalent for the older *embole*, that portion of the state's revenues collected in kind rather than in cash. If this was not sufficient, then the *protonotarios* was to obtain the necessary produce from the *eidikon*, the central treasury at Constantinople which dealt with tax in kind and with imperial reserves.

The thematic *protonotarios* was to be informed in advance as to the army's requirements, which was to be provided from the land-tax in kind and the cash revenues of the *thema* and stored at appropriate points along the route of march. An exact account of the supplies was to be kept, so that (where the thematic taxpayers provided more than their yearly assessment demands) the amount could be deducted (from the assessment for the following year). Both passages note that, where supplies could not be paid for out of the local fiscal revenues, the cash (or the supplies – the text does not specify which, although the former would be far more likely) was to be taken from the bureau of the *eidikon*, just as in the sixth century the cash was taken from the general bank of the prefecture. The second text notes that the final accounts were worked out in the *eidikon* after the expedition had been stood down.[13]

It is clear from these texts that the basic mechanism in the sixth and in the ninth–tenth centuries was effectively the same. The *protonotarios* was now the link between the provincial thematic fiscal administration and the central government. He belonged to the department of the *sakellion*; but he worked with the *eidikon*, as well as with local officials of the department of the *genikon*, responsible for the general land-tax and related state demands.[14] The *protonotarios* replaced earlier officials, *eparchai* or prefects, who were the successors of the *ad hoc* praetorian prefects referred to already responsible for liaising between the army and its demands on the one hand, and the provincial fiscal officials in whose area the army was operating on the other.[15]

Fragments of several tenth-century archival collections dealing with expeditions in 910–11, 935 and 949, referred to above, can supplement this basic information. They list troops, vessels, supplies and armaments,[16] and provide a wealth of information about the organization of an expedition. It is clear that in addition to the regular supplies to be provided by the thematic *protonotarioi*, extra supplies in foodstuffs and in kind had to be raised. Large amounts of coined gold and silver were required, not only for the campaign pay and largesse issued to the soldiers, but also for the fitting out of the ships involved. This was supplied until the eleventh century through the *eidikon* and from other revenue-producing departments through the *sakellarios*, the chief treasury official in the empire, whose supervisory capacity permitted him to exercise a general control over expenditures. At Constantinople, several departments had associated with them warehouses or storehouses, workshops and the like: the evidence for the expedition of 949, for example, shows that the *eidikon* had a storehouse which maintained supplies of raw materials, including iron ore,[17] lead and a range of other items for the equipping of both land forces and warships; similarly the imperial *vestiarion* stored items of naval equipment, clothing and even cooking utensils. In addition, and continuing the practice established during the late Roman period, the public post was employed in the movement of supplies and material for the army. Although little is known in detail of its functioning in the period after the sixth century, it acted essentially as a state transportation system operating both a rapid courier as well as a (probably quite limited) slower transport service, supported by its own stock-breeding ranches and with a complex administration based at Constantinople and in the provinces.[18]

The theme *protonotarioi* were made responsible for raising additional supplies for the expedition, working with officials of the *genikon*, a point supported by evidence from the earlier ninth century. In certain circumstances, imperial officials were despatched to the *themata* to assist in collecting and transporting the supplies: an imperial officer – described simply as "a certain *basilikos*" – was sent to the Anatolikon region in 910/11 to raise barley, biscuit, corn and flour for the Kibyrrhaiotai forces. Specific directions were given for the route by which it was to be transported. After the changes introduced during the later eleventh century, especially by Alexios I, the provisioning of the fleet was placed under the supervision of the *megas doux* and the *megas domestikos*. As well as his purely military attributes, the former was also given a substantial administrative function, insofar as the coastal regions of certain provinces, in particular Hellas-Peloponnesos (of which the *megas doux* was the general governor anyway), were organized into districts or *oria*, serving probably to provide the resources, manpower and supplies for the fleet. A similar procedure to that of 949 was probably followed in most such cases, as in 1169, for example, when a naval expedition to Damietta in Egypt was provided with three months' supplies from the provinces.[19]

Armies were usually accompanied by a supply train, the *touldon*. The late tenth-century treatise on campaign organization stipulates a basic supply of 24 days' rations of barley for the horses, which according to other sources was similarly to be put aside by the thematic *protonotarios* for collection by the army en route;[20] historians' accounts of campaigns frequently mention the baggage train or the supplies and fodder it carried.[21] Not all these supplies were derived from the regular land-tax, however: depending on the local circumstances, much of it must also have been raised through compulsory exactions, as in the late Roman period. This was certainly the case when the emperor was present.[22] Similarly, the *protonotarioi* of the affected themes had to provide supplies that could be transported by wagon or mule to the army on enemy territory if the surrounding districts had been devastated. But smaller units clearly foraged for their own fodder and supplies, whether in enemy territory or on Roman soil, which must have caused some hardship to the communities affected, while once on hostile terrain the commander must either have arranged to keep his supply lines open by detaching small units to hold key passes and roads,[23] or let the army forage for all its requirements once the supplies had run out.[24] Some incidental evidence from the contemporary historians illustrates these methods in operation.

The burden of supporting soldiers passing through on campaign had always been onerous, as a number of sources from the later Roman period through to the tenth century testify. This was not just because of the demands made by the army on local productive capacity, but reflected also the fact that state intervention into local exchange relations on such a large scale could adversely affect the economic equilibrium of an area. In the fourth, fifth and sixth centuries there is very clear evidence of the distortion of prices by these means: either through the state's fixing artificially low prices for the sale of produce to the army, thus harming the producers, or by sudden heavy demand driving prices for non-state purchasers upwards. Even more telling is the evidence of the sixth-century legislation on the situation in Thrace and the combined effects of barbarian inroads and military supply demands on the economy of the region. The establishment of the *quaestura exercitus* was aimed at resolving one element of this problem, for through the administrative linkage between the Aegean islands and coastal regions concerned with the Danube zone the troops in that theatre could be supplied from relatively wealthy productive areas by sea and river transport.

But the problem remained acute enough for Maurice to attempt to have his armies winter on the non-Roman side of the river in 593 and 602.[25] Leo VI advised generals to carry sufficient supplies with the army and to forage on enemy territory.[26] Even where proper administrative arrangements were enforced, large numbers of soldiers, their animals and their followers will rarely have been welcome.[27] The provincial administrators do seem to have tried to minimize the effects of passing military forces, and one should not over-exaggerate the problem. But several letters of the ninth–tenth centuries appeal to state officials against the burden imposed upon them, or their clients, through the imposition of *mitaton* (the billeting of troops) and related expenses; these are on several occasions related explicitly to the effects of the presence of soldiers on campaign. In the early thirteenth century, Niketas Choniates writes that at times during the later years of Manuel I the Roman lands were "ravaged by our own soldiers". And while we must allow for some degree of hyperbole on the part of the more privileged and literate elements in society, some of the complaints are on behalf of those less fortunate than the writers themselves.[28]

The pattern of catering for expeditionary forces changed very little between the later tenth and later twelfth centuries. Provincial officials were, as before, told of the necessary requirements which had to be prepared in advance ready for the army to collect, and supplies provided were set against the annual tax demand for the region in question. But one important development does bring about some changes. For from the early eleventh century, if not already a little earlier, the majority of the soldiers were no longer stood down for much of the year and called up only when a major expedition was planned or when an attack threatened. This system, which had evolved from the middle of the seventh century, had the obvious advantage – from the standpoint of the management and distribution of resources – that soldiers thus supported themselves, at least to a substantial extent, and constituted only a limited burden on the taxpayers. With the change to an aggressive mercenary army soldiers must have been present all year round in many regions, needing to be fed, housed, their animals catered for and so on throughout the year.

We are fortunate to possess a number of imperial grants of exemption for the tenth century and beyond which give some idea of what sort of demands were made. The burdens were, in themselves, not new: the impositions of billeting and feeding soldiers and officers, of grinding corn and baking bread, of providing extra supplies for units passing through or based in a district, of providing craftsmen and artisans for public and military works, of burning charcoal, of providing labour for the maintenance or construction of roads and bridges – these had existed from Roman times and were still found in the eleventh and twelfth centuries.[29] By the tenth century, if not already long before, a group of new impositions had evolved, including the provision or fabrication of weapons and items of military equipment, as we have seen, a reflection of the breakdown of the late Roman system of *fabricae* or state arms factories. For other materials, cash could be issued from the central bureaux, especially the *eidikon*, with which to purchase iron or similar requirements from provincial sources for the production of specialized items, for example for naval construction.

During the eleventh century, a number of landlords, both lay and monastic, succeeded in obtaining exemptions for their estates from the levy of weapons and other supplies. Furthermore, since units of mercenary or tagmatic soldiers were often based permanently in a particular location through the winter season – *eis paracheimasian* as it is called in the sources – such demands seem to have occurred both more frequently and on a more arbitrary basis, according to the needs of individual units and their commanders, than hitherto.[30] Contemporaries were perfectly aware of these burdens: in the eleventh century the intellectual and courtier Michael Psellos writes a letter about the weight of the burden of state exactions in the form of demands for livestock, probably horses, which were needed when the army was present, and an anonymous author remarks on the burden imposed upon the taxpayers when the imperial cortège and troops pass through a region.[31]

In the period before the changes of the later tenth century, it is likely that the overall burden on the rural population of the provinces was fairly evenly distributed, and that, although the transit of imperial forces did involve unusually heavy demands on the communities closest to the routes used by military detachments, such demands were neither frequent nor regular, the more so since the emperors seem to have maximized their use of the system of base camps or *aplekta* as points for the concentration of smaller forces from a wide area. Thus very large armies marching across imperial territory will have been comparatively unusual – and hence also the much more devastating consequences when civil strife broke out (as in the civil war between Michael II and Thomas the Slav in the early 820s, for example).

The presence of many more full-time units, whether indigenous or foreign, needing supplies, fodder, housing and other necessities throughout the winter and possibly all year round, and who could not draw upon their families and their own resources, must have considerably increased the overall burden on the rural populations which provided these provisions. The result was, in effect, the extension of the traditional system for maintaining armies on campaign, which had been in operation from late Roman times but which had affected most provinces only occasionally,[32] into the standard or regular means of maintaining all the imperial forces. In contrast to the general situation in the ninth and earlier years of the tenth century, the bulk of the provincial soldiery could no longer be said to support itself over the greater part of the year. Furthermore, unlike the older thematic "militia", the full-time soldiers generally had no common interest with the provincials who supported them. Exemptions, particularly those granted to monastic foundations, are instructive and show that the number of groups of foreign mercenaries, for example, who were directly dependent upon the local population increases very sharply from the 1040s.[33] But the process was already under way from the middle of the tenth century. Thus the most costly units and a greater proportion of the armies came to be maintained at the direct expense of a rural or sometimes urban population. But there were probably substantial regional variations, evidence for which is lacking, so that some districts, especially those from which the imperial forces conducted operations over several seasons, will have been more drastically affected than others. The rapacity of imperial officials in extracting the resources needed to maintain the soldiers was notorious, and even though many landlords, particularly those with access to imperial patronage, attempted to free themselves from such impositions through obtaining grants of exemption, the needs and demands of the local military meant that such privileges were often ignored entirely.[34]

In spite of tactical organizational developments, however, and changes in the internal political context, the basic organization of military expeditions and campaigns in the eleventh century remained the same as in the preceding centuries. The information for the process of supplying and maintaining forces in the field to be found in the details of some eleventh-century campaigns, including the campaigns of Romanos IV in 1068 and that which led up to the battle of Mantzikert in 1071, and in the preparations made by Alexios I to deal with the passage through imperial territory in the Balkans of the Crusader armies, show that the same principles operated, and that the same pattern of collection, concentration and redistribution of military provisions was maintained. And although the administrative departments responsible had evolved or changed somewhat from the period before Alexios I, the same arrangements were still in place for the campaign mounted by Manuel I which ended in defeat at Myriokephalon in 1176. The imperial *armamenta* in Constantinople continued to function as weapons repositories. (Along with the imperial *vestiarion* and the bureau of the *eidikon*, they could clearly contain substantial stores, for when he was faced by the rebel army of Leo Tornikes at Constantinople in 1047, the emperor Constantine IX was able to equip and arm a considerable scratch force from this source.[35])

One important change which is worth noting involved an expansion of the authority of the thematic *kritai*, or "judges", civil officials seconded from Constantinople whose authority grew in the older *themata* in proportion to the decline in the importance of the thematic armies and their *strategoi*, and a corresponding reduction of the importance of the *protonotarioi*, a process which reflects the efforts made by the central government from the later tenth and into the eleventh century to extend the judicial authority of its fiscal departments in order to retain control over taxable resources.[36]

The enormous demands made upon the ordinary population of the empire when a military expedition was undertaken required an administrative structure which could deal with all facets of the armies' needs, whether in terms of raising and equipping new recruits or in respect of supplying the vast number of men, horses, mules and other animals which an army on the march needed. But it is evident that the basic structures which had evolved by the late Roman period retained their relevance even as they continued to evolve in response to the changed context, fiscal needs and political emphases of the period after the sixth century.

Armies on campaign

The Byzantine army mounted three types of campaign: large-scale offensives directed at specific targets in hostile territory with well-defined strategic objectives; small-scale raiding or skirmishing and counter-raiding operations confined for the most part to frontier regions and intended to disrupt the economic life of the regions in and behind the enemy frontier or to harass and destroy enemy raiding parties; and defensive expeditions directed from Constantinople or other major centres designed to challenge and defeat invading armies which had already penetrated, or were about to enter, deep into imperial territory. The second frequently served as a prelude to the last, of course, and might also merge with the first, depending on the strategic context and the numbers of men and resources committed to the action. In general, however, it can be said that the period from the later sixth through to the early tenth century was dominated by the second type of activity, with short periods in which especially active emperors undertook longer-term projects against particular enemies – Constantine V's campaigns against the Bulgars, for example, in the 750s to the 770s.

This representation is, perhaps, a simplification of the reality of any given campaign or military confrontation, but it provides the observer with a starting-point for analyzing the course of Byzantine military activites. There is no convincing evidence that Byzantine strategists differentiated in theory between what Delbrück characterized as wars of annihilation and wars of attrition, although it is clear that both, and gradations between the two, were certainly practised. In the circumstances of defeat at the hands of the Islamic armies in the late 630s and the loss of Syria and then Mesopotamia, for example, the emperor Heraclius appears to have deliberately withdrawn to a chosen defensive line and in the process devastated the abandoned regions. By the same token, and after the failure of the siege of 717–18, Umayyad generals appear to have set up a "no man's land" between the two frontiers, a policy to which the Byzantines also contributed.[37] Although the sources are often patchy, there is enough material to generate a fairly detailed picture of how the Byzantine army conducted its field operations. The military handbooks provide a great deal of information and, although there is no doubt that there was at times a wide gap between theory and practice, the evidence of contemporary historians shows that in many respects the handbooks give a fairly accurate picture of actual practice. In the following I will try to give some idea of these operations across the period in question.

The army on the march

The military treatises provide detailed instructions on how to conduct a campaign on enemy territory, prepare for a pitched battle or for skirmishing, undertake a siege, withdraw after a defeat or follow up a victory. Such prescriptions reflect a combination of "common sense" and tradition, tailored, in the case of the more "contemporary" manuals, to the developments and situation of their own day. Their testimony is largely borne out by the accounts of historians and chroniclers of the period, some of whom, such as the historians Leo the Deacon in the later tenth century, Michael Attaleiates in the 1060s and

1070s and Niketas Choniates in the later twelfth century, were eyewitnesses of much that they describe.

The symbolic preliminary to an offensive or defensive campaign involving the emperor was the hanging out of a mail surcoat, a sword and a shield on the Bronze Gate of the imperial palace, the Chalke: this was the signal that the emperor himself would participate. In the case of a response to enemy invasion, the message that an enemy force was on its way was often delivered by a series of fire-signals or beacons, situated on prominences stretching from the fortress of Loulon in the Taurus to the north of the Cilician Gates, across Asia Minor to the Bosphors and to the imperial palace itself, where a constant lookout was maintained. A similar arrangement appears to have been operational in the Peloponnese for a while, as a ninth- or tenth-century inscription on a signal-tower near Corinth attests. When these sytems of beacons were inaugurated is not known, neither is the duration of their existence: a tenth-century story (almost certainly spurious) maintains that they were closed down for economic reasons by the emperor Michael III. When the imperial high command received word of an attack, various officials of the imperial stables and central administration would set in train an established pattern of preparations for the despatch of an army to confront and, if possible, throw back the enemy attack.[38]

For large-scale offensives, preparations were begun well before the campaigning season. A fundamental aspect of Byzantine defensive and offensive warfare was intelligence-gathering. Advance scouting parties were a part of every campaign army, of course, and combined with lookouts and border guards were responsible for providing a great deal of essential information about enemy movements, size and quality of raiding or invading forces, and so on. Information was also gathered by diplomatic envoys, travellers and merchants (the military treatises recommend the employment of all these groups), and apart from the interrogation of deserters and sometimes the torture of prisoners for information, spies disguised as merchants or travellers were also employed to collect and pass on vital information. In addition, visitors to Byzantine prisoners held in Muslim prisons were also exploited for the information they might be able to obtain. No doubt the quality and reliability of the information varied considerably, but it was regarded as an essential element in warmaking and in the defence of the empire, and was organized on a relatively sophisticated basis.[39]

Once the decision to mount an operation had been taken, orders went to the various provincial authorities to supply or prepare to deliver the necessary provisions, fodder and other *matériel*, and to the provincial armies or other locally based units to assemble at key bases, ready to join the main column as it arrived. There evolved a chain of major strategic base camps which formed the main links along the routes into enemy territory. When these first appeared is difficult to say, although the period of the reign of Constantine V is most likely: Malagina, the major base nearest to Constantinople, is first mentioned when the *tagmata* were ordered to assemble there in 786/7 by Eirene; it was seized and sacked by an Arab force in 798/9 (there is some disagreement over the chronology), and appears as a base for the imperial baggage train and as a stock-raising centre. The other bases, strategically located for expeditions aimed against the eastern or southern frontier with the Arabs, were probably established as part of a systematic strategy under Constantine V, since there is no evidence for their existence before this time (although Caesarea in Cappadocia frequently appears as a major base much earlier).[40]

These base-camps became major asembly points for troops marching against the Arabs from the later eighth and early ninth centuries. Thus in a set of instructions derived from campaigning practice in the reign of Basil I (867–86), a tenth-century text notes that:

> The *strategoi* of the *Thrakesion* and the *strategos* of the *Anatolikoi* must join the emperor at Malagina. The *domestikos* of the *Scholai* and the *strategos* of the *Anatolikoi* and the *strategos* of Seleukia ought to meet the emperor at Kaborkin. If the expedition is to Tarsos, the remaining *themata* ought to assemble at Koloneia, but if it is to the eastern regions, the *strategos* of Kappadokia and those of Charsianon and of the *Boukellarioi* ought to meet the emperor at Koloneia, those of the *Armeniakoi* and of Paphlagonia and of Sebasteia at Kaisareia. The Armenian *themata* should assemble at Bathys Ryax if the expedition is to Tephrike.[41]

In fact, this list is less prescriptive than descriptive: the combination of armies and meeting places actually seems to derive from extracts or details from specific campaigns rather than describe any general plan, and the list itself is the product of a garbling of such information by redactors or editors in the tenth century. But it gives some idea of the way in which armies were to be brought together to make up a larger force before proceeding against the enemy. Several sources mention the musters and inspections of armies before campaigns or battles, and there were a number of major concentration points where this could take place. The various imperial *aplekta* already mentioned, of course, played a role in this. But in addition, assembly and mustering grounds existed at Kepoi (near the mouth of the Maeander) and at Phygela (mod. Kuşadası) on the coast of the Thrakesion *thema*, at Kaisareia in Cappadocia, and at Diabasis in Thrace. At all these places the emperor or commander-in-chief of the armies might review his troops before setting off on the campaign or before marching to battle. There was also a major parade ground immediately outside the Theodosian land-walls of Constantinople, another at the Hebdomon, a few miles west of the city and another outside Adrianople in Thrace. During the eleventh and twelfth centuries, new mustering grounds are mentioned – at Gounaria in Paphlagonia, for example, and at Chrysoupolis in Bithynia, while the emperors John II and Manuel I Komnenos also had major bases located at Pelagonia (west of Thessaloniki, strategically situated on the Via Egnatia), at Serdica (Sofia) and at Kypsella in Thrace (near the Maritsa), as well as at Lopadion in the plain of the Rhyndakos in western Asia Minor.[42]

Marching camps

Once in hostile territory, it was assumed that the army would encamp and entrench whenever it needed to stop, and the treatises refer, often in great detail, to the procedure for selecting, laying out and fortifying the encampment.[43] Scouts and guides responsible for locating suitable sites and for laying out the camp went ahead of the main force (see below). The chief requirements were a defensible situation, a good supply of water and forage for the horses and pack-animals, and adequate space for the different contingents which had to be accommodated. Details also survive of the order in which the tents of the different units were to be laid out, the distances between them, the system employed for establishing watches and picket lines, passwords and camp security, and associated matters. Great stress was laid on camp security: passwords were issued for each watch, and watch-commanders were enjoined to allow no one past without the correct password (usually the name of a saint or similar symbol of Orthodoxy). Elaborate instructions were also issued – and apparently followed – on the circuits and patrols made by the watch at regular intervals; and there was often more than one perimeter, an inner and an outer, particularly if the emperor was present. Camps were protected by ditches and palisades, sometimes cut locally, sometimes made from the spears of the infantry; entrances were placed so that they could be covered by archers and not easily rushed; and a well-drilled system of manoeuvres was practised to enable a force under attack to march out against the enemy, to retreat into the camp, or to set up and entrench a camp while under attack.[44]

The layout of the Byzantine marching camp derives from that of the late Roman pattern which seems by the fourth century, in the east at least, to have begun to evolve away from the earlier classical legionary marching camp. The basic plan was rectangular – usually square – divided internally into four quadrants separated by centrally crossing paths or roads leading to entrances in the middle of each side. This pattern is described in the mid-sixth-century anonymous treatise on *Strategy* and in the *Strategikon* of Maurice, repeated in the *Tactica* of Leo VI. By the time the *Praecepta* of Nikephros was compiled, two or even three sets of intersecting paths were ordained, further subdividing the internal space of the camp, possibly a reflection of the differences in status and function between the different units of the field army.[45] The normal arrangement was then to have the infantry around the outer perimeter, nearest the palisade and/or ditch, sometimes using their shields propped against their spears and lashed together to form a defensive wall. Within the infantry formation the cavalry and their horses were then stationed (to protect the horses from enemy misiles); and at the centre, the commander-in-chief and his guards or, if present, the emperor and the various imperial elite units encamped around him. In the latter case, a second, internal perimeter was also marked out. Both the main and the internal exits were guarded, of course; passwords were issued to enhance security; and a strict discipline was enforced – although the sources recount several examples of poor camp discipline, or even failure to establish a proper camp, resulting in defeat and disaster.[46]

To what extent these theories were put into practice clearly varied according to circumstances, but the evidence suggests that the standard precautions were observed when in enemy territory. Leo the Deacon, a chronicler of the wars of the emperors Nikephros II Phocas and John I Tzimiskes, notes that the Romans customarily fortified their camps with a ditch and bank surmounted by spears, a technique described exactly in contemporary military treatises. He often mentions Roman generals throwing up earthworks around besieged cities or fortresses, and his testimony together with that of other chroniclers of the period suggest that Roman forces were thoroughly accustomed to such undertakings. Other accounts report the establishment of marching camps along the advance, to which Roman forces were able to withdraw on their return march. The early seventh-century historian Theophylact Simocatta describes the distance covered by the army on certain occasions as representing a "march of so many camps", indicative of the standard practice.[47] Some of these encampments were obviously substantial and able to ward off major attacks by the enemy at times, while the army needed to be able to set up such an encampment under the most difficult of conditions. The sources refer to Roman forces establishing and entrenching their camp in good order while under attack, to the construction of deep ditches around the Roman marching camps, as well as to defeated Roman forces besieged inside their encampment, to camps in which the baggage and supernumeraries were left and to the capture of camps after Roman defeats. Indeed, Anna Comnena, writing of a campaign in the early twelfth century, feels the need to explain why on one occasion her father did not entrench and fortify his encampment, so that we may assume that the practice was generally followed. During his campaigns against the Turks in Asia Minor the emperor John II Komnenos habitually entrenched his camps, as did Manuel I: indeed, the latter appears to have followed the precepts of the tactical treatises in respect of both entrenched camps and the order which was to be observed in marching out of them. During the campaign of 1176 which led to Myriokephalon, the Roman vanguard established its own fortified encampment once it had pushed through the pass where the main army under Manuel was attacked, and Choniates notes specifically that the Turks were unable to do further serious damage to the latter once it had withdrawn from the pass and encamped. The general Alexios Branas bivouacked and entrenched his camp while on campaign against the Vlachs and Cumans in 1186. The principle was clearly a well-established tradition in Byzantine military circles.[48] Other peoples also entrenched or palisaded their encampments, of course: this was clearly the usual practice when in enemy territory for both Anatolian Turks and German soldiers of the Second Crusade. Whether this reflects military common sense or an East Roman influence is not clear. Michael Psellos notes that the Pechenegs did not entrench or fortify their camps with a ditch (implicitly contrasting them to the Romans), and seems to think this an indication of their barbarity.[49]

Byzantine writers also note occasions when careless or ignorant commanders failed either to establish a secure camp or, having done so, failed to ensure adequate supplies in the locality or to maintain adequate guards and piquets to warn of hostile attack: thus Niketas Choniates castigates the foolhardy commander John Kantakouzenos, who rarely established a properly defended camp, suffered the consequences and barely escaped with his life on one occasion. This was the more blameworthy in that success had already been partially achieved and the defeat which followed was thus clearly due to incompetent generalship or poor discipline. The same author notes with approval the encampment established by another commander in the late 1170s, serving both as a base to protect the army's baggage and animals and from which to launch a series of damaging light cavalry raids into Turkish territory.[50] In Roman territory, in contrast, the army could be housed either in marching camps of this sort or in the several military base camps, or *aplekta*, mentioned already, and situated at key points along various major military routes. Soldiers and officers could also take lodgings with the civilian population, and as noted already, the imposition of *mitaton* and *aplekton* – demands for board and lodging made upon local populations – were often particularly oppressive. One ninth-century hagiography, describing how a soldier was billeted in an inn, provides a good insight into the rights of soldiers in this respect.[51]

The order of march

The order of march varied according to the size of the army and the nature of the terrain and whether or not the emperor was present. Where the latter was the case, the instructions for camps and the order of march are very carefully set out. The imperial *tagmata* were allocated specific positions in camp and on the march, grouped in order of precedence around the emperor's tent or position in the column;[52] when they were not present, commanders were recommended to pay attention to the relative disposition of mounted and infantry units. And while the order of march for large forces was very different from that for smaller detachments or raiding parties, all the treatises agree that only the minimum of baggage should accompany the force into hostile regions; the greater part was to be left in home territory, and the *protonotarios*, or chief fiscal administrator, of the theme from which the army enters the lands of the enemy should take charge of it. This included extra tents, for example, and there is even the suggestion that lower-ranking officers should not be permitted to bring their own tents, since precious carrying-capacity for food would thus be squandered. What was taken was to include spare equipment and ammunition, tools for entrenching or other engineering work, and especially materials necessary for bridging rivers. Siege weapons and field artillery might also be taken, depending upon the context.[53]

Great emphasis was laid on using local guides or scouts to make sure that the route followed by the army was secure. Regardless of the terrain, the column should always be organized into a main body, baggage, flank, rear and vanguards, although the order of march varied according to whether an attack was expected, whether the army was in enemy territory, and whether the route taken passed through defiles where ambushes could be laid or was on open ground where it might be harassed by light cavalry. Specially assigned officers referred to by traditional Latin terms were responsible for planning the route and setting up the camps. The former, the *doukatores*, should be selected because of their familiarity with the roads and paths the army might take, the passes and their environs, and the distances and times between camps and watering places. The latter, known as *minsouratores*, were to locate suitable sites for encampments, measure out the ground for the various divisions and the perimeter, and lay out markers for the soldiers to use when encamping. Whether the *mensouratores* were selected from each individual unit, as in the pre-sixth-century army, or were made up of specialized soldiers permanently assigned to such duties, remains unclear. The late tenth-century treatise on campaign organization refers to the appointment of a senior *mensourator* and the *mensouratores* "of all the other officers", which suggests that there were *mensouratores* from each *bandon* or equivalent unit. These instructions are borne out by the treatise on imperial expeditions, which clearly recounts actual events, and by the historians' accounts of campaigns of the period.[54]

The order of march for different situations is set out by several of the treatises. The first rule was to be cautious: the commander must send out, a day's march in advance, an adequate force of scouts – light cavalry – as an advance party, among whom were the *doukatores* and *mensouratores* already noted. The rear and flanks of the column should similarly be covered by light-armed units marching parallel to or behind the main body of soldiers and baggage. If the army has to pass through a narrow defile or pass – where the soldiers might be able to march only two abreast or even in single file – cavalry should dismount and their horses, with the baggage, be placed in the centre. Such dangerous locations should be carefully scouted out in advance, and a detachment of troops left behind to hold it until the army returns, if that is the intention. Failure to do just this led to the defeat at Myriokephalon in 1176, for Manuel seems to have sent on the van division without attempting to scout the narrow pass of Tzibritze. The Turkish forces allowed the van and main division to pass through, but then blocked off the pass at both ends, trapping the right wing which was very badly mauled, and bringing the supply and siege train to a halt by shooting the draught-animals. The rest of the army seems to have been able to cut its way through, join up with the van and withdraw under terms, but the siege train was lost.[55] In dire straits, the column should use any prisoners it may have as human shields, on whichever side the enemy attacks, to protect itself.

The column as a whole was divided into brigade or divisional sections: each *drouggos* or *tourma* headed by its commander, his immediate bodyguard in front with their standards, then the general or commander, followed by his *spatharioi* or other elite troops and retinue, followed by their personal baggage. Behind them came the rest of the division, each unit followed by the soldiers' own pack-animals carrying their personal equipment, tents and so forth. The *touldon*, or supply train for the army as a whole, was placed in the middle. In one's own territory the main baggage train could follow behind the army, but in hostile terrain it should be brought up into the centre of the column, with units posted to protect it in the event of attack. Light infantry and light cavalry were to be posted in the rear and, terrain permitting, along the flanks of the army, and the whole force was to be able to redeploy into battle formation should the enemy attack from either the flank or the van or rear.[56]

These regulations derive from the treatises of the fifth, sixth and early seventh centuries, but the same basic format and procedures are outlined in those of the tenth century, and accounts of the Mantzikert and Myriokephalon campaigns in 1071 and 1176 show that the formal pattern was indeed adhered to. In the campaign of 1176, for example, Choniates describes the imperial column as made up of the van division (chiefly infantry), followed by the main division (made up of the eastern and western *tagmata*), the right wing under Baldwin of Jerusalem, the Roman left wing with the pack and baggage train and then the siege train between the two; then came the emperor's own division and picked troops, followed by the rearguard under a trusted senior commander. Changes in the technical names applied to the various elements of the column occurred, such as the introduction of the Arabic word *saqat*, Hellenized as *saka*, for the rearguard. During the first half of the tenth century there evolved a further marching formation which was employed as a defensive marching column when the army had to run the gauntlet of hostile attack. Where the terrain through which the army was passing permitted, the various divisions of the army – posted on the flanks, in the van and in the rear – formed in effect a loosely articulated square formation, so that in the event of an attack they could close up to form a solid bulwark from which to resist the enemy, while they were also thus enabled easily to protect the units constructing the encampment. This hollow column was generally drawn up with the infantry divisions forming its outer walls, shielding the cavalry, baggage and spare horses, and permitting the cavalry to move out to attack the enemy when appropriate. An account of one of Alexios I's campaigns, in 1116, particularly notes the strength of this marching arrangement, which Anna describes as like a moving city.[57]

The cavalry units which preceded and flanked the infantry were, as always, responsible for protecting stragglers, as well as preventing deserters from escaping; while when the emperor was present, he rode at the head of the column with the leading cavalry units protecting him, preceded by his own riding horses and followed by the courtiers and other attendants of the palace. Extra security measures were taken in this case, both on the march and in the camp, with double perimeters and security in the hands of the *drouggarios* of the Watch, the third in seniority of the four imperial guards units. With minor variations, noted in texts deriving from the time of Basil I, for example, as well as of the period from the

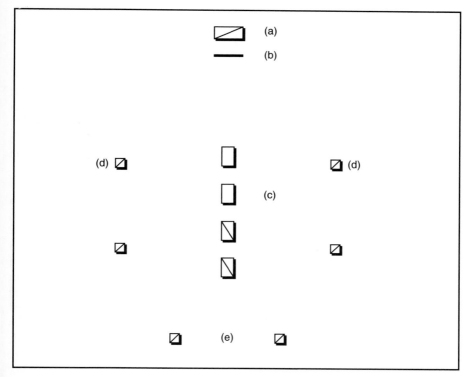

(a) advance guard   (b) *mensores*   (c) main column
(d) flank guards   (e) rearguard

Figure 5.1   Order of march c. 600.

later tenth to late twelfth centuries, this basic pattern was followed by all major expeditionary forces. An interesting snippet of information from Anna Comnena, writing of Alexios' campaigns in the early twelfth century, shows that fifes or pipes were used to maintain the tempo of the march.[58]

Interestingly, Anna claims that this marching order was an invention of her father's. This may reflect her own bias and the possibility that the decline in military efficiency and the use of indigenous troops which had set in especially after Mantzikert and the civil wars which followed had meant that this formation had been of little practical relevance. Yet the fact that the armies of the First Crusade clearly also employed a comparable arrangement when in hostile territory – described similarly by a later Muslim commentator as being "akin to a walking city" – may suggest some Byzantine influence (Alexios I certainly offered advice to the Crusader leaders while they remained in Constantinople on Seljuk tactics, on drawing up the line of battle, on ambushes and so forth), as well as the practical response of intelligent commanders such as Bohemond (see Figures 5.1 to 5.6).[59]

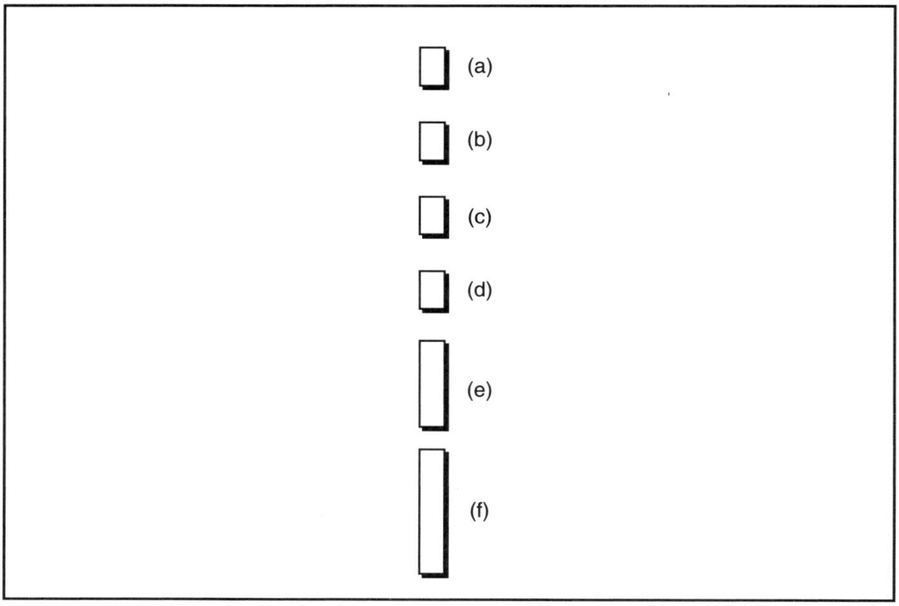

(i) If a commander-in-chief's column

(a) bodyguard/retinue	(b) spare mounts	(c) c-in-c + officers
(d) *spatharii*	(e) *bucellarii*	(f) baggage

(ii) If a regular column (line troops)

(a) retinue	(b) spare mounts	(c) commander + guards
(d) *spatharii*	(e) regular troops	(f) baggage

Sources: Maurice, *Strat.*, i, 9; v, 5; vii, 12; ix, 3–4; xii B, 19–20; *Strategy*, §§ 20, 26.

Figure 5.2   Detail of main column in Figure 5.1.

Baggage, supplies and the rate of march

The baggage train – *touldon* or *touldos* – was a crucial component of any field army, of course, and great care was devoted to ensuring that it was properly assembled. From the middle of the eighth century the formerly elite corps of Optimatoi had been downgraded, primarily for political reasons, to become a logistics and supply corps whose task it was to provide support for the imperial *tagmata*. Several accounts record their role as responsible for the pack-animals of the *touldon*, as well as the methods by which they were assigned a certain number of pack-animals and how far their responsibilties went.[60] But the imperial *tagmata* were especially privileged in this respect, and regular units had to provide for their own baggage: soldiers could band together to hire or support one or more retainers and the necessary animals or, if they were wealthy enough, bring their own personal pack-animals and attendants.

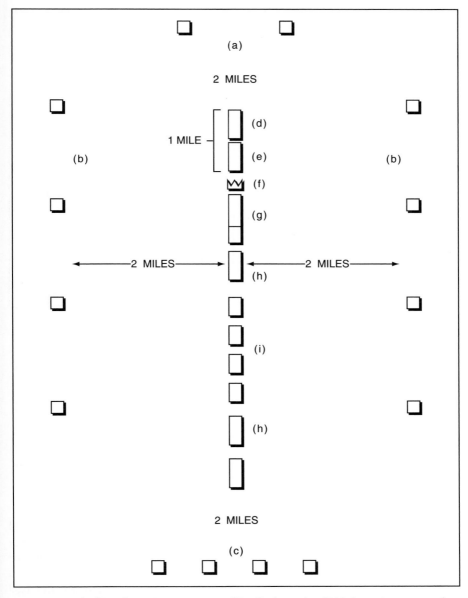

(a) vanguard of 500 thematic troops   (b) flankguards of 500 thematic troops each
(c) rearguard of 500 thematic troops   (d) imperial processional horses
(e) palatine officials, officers   (f) emperor with the Hetaireia
(g) palatine officials; baggage train   (h) thematic divisions
(i) *tagmata*

Source: *Const. Porph., Three Treatises*, (B) 107–21, 134–50; (C) 474–96, 561–69.

Figure 5.3 Order of march for imperial force *c.* 860–960.

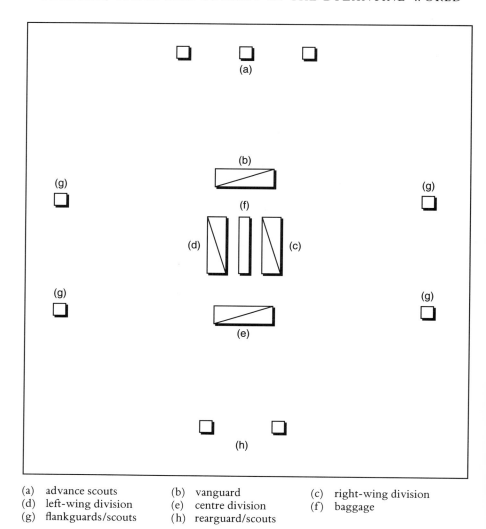

(a) advance scouts   (b) vanguard   (c) right-wing division
(d) left-wing division   (e) centre division   (f) baggage
(g) flankguards/scouts   (h) rearguard/scouts

Cf. Leo, *Tact.*, ix, 29–38.

Figure 5.4   Order of march in hostile territory *c.* 900.

    Although the baggage train was regulated to a degree, there seems to have been no permanent logistics bureau. Commanding officers were enjoined to set an officer in command of the train, with a detachment of soldiers to protect it (and to maintain order); these were to ensure that soldiers did not bring too many pack-animals, or too much extra or showy equipment, thus distracting from the primary task of making war effectively. Those who did so were to have their baggage controlled and, if necessary, superfluous items were to be confiscated and abandoned. While in imperial territory, it was permitted to

160

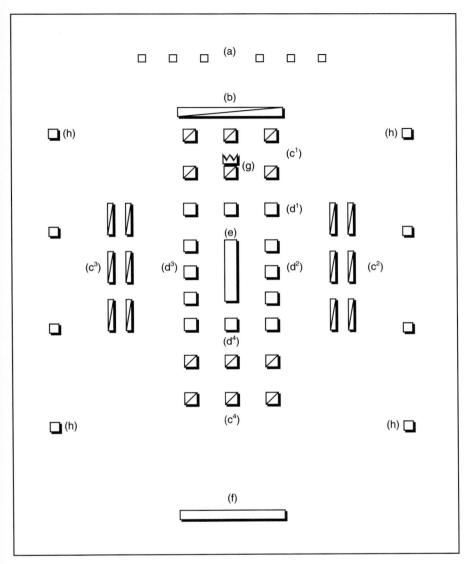

(a)   advance scouts   (b)   vanguard
(c^1) cavalry centre division   (c^2) cavalry right wing
(c^3) cavalry left wing   (c^4) cavalry centre/second line
(d^1) infantry centre   (d^2) infantry right wing
(d^3) infantry left wing   (d^4) infantry rearguard
(e)   baggage/siege train   (f)   rearguard
(g)   emperor & household troops   (h)   outriders/flank scouts

Sources: Leo, *Tact.*, ix, 29–38, 61; Nikeph. Ouranos, *Taktika*, § 64; *Campaign Organisation*, § 10.

Figure 5.5   Order of march in hostile territory *c.* 970.

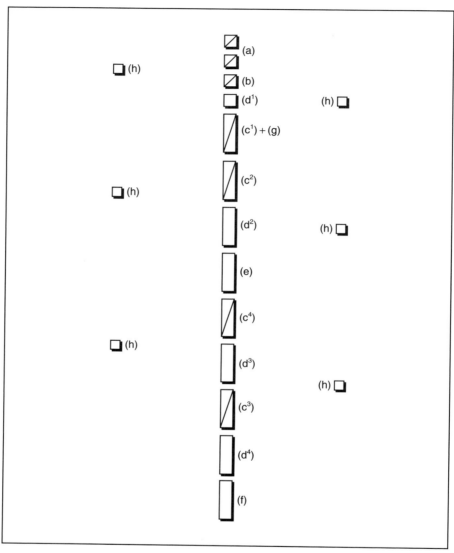

Key and sources as for Figure 5.5.

Figure 5.6 Order of march through defiles, narrow tracks and friendly territory *c.* 970.

take a relatively extensive train, but this had to be cut down to the minimum before entering hostile regions. Provincial officials of the local *protonotarios* were detailed to take care of excess baggage and to send it on to the expected point of egress from enemy lands, so that upon re-entry into imperial territory the army could replace lost animals and other equipment.[61]

The baggage train could consist of both pack-animals as well as ox-drawn carts, yet most of the evidence for the period suggests that pack-animals were more usual – the *Praecepta* of Nikephros specifies mules for carrying spare arrows, for example, and the treatises on imperial expeditions, referring to the practice of the later ninth and tenth centuries, make no mention of wagons or carts at all. Yet when a large siege train was needed, wagons did accompany the army, and the routes which were taken had to be selected accordingly.[62] Wagons slowed the army down, of course, so the *Tactica* of Leo notes that on occasion infantry units accompanied by baggage animals with provisions for 8–10 days should be sent on ahead.[63]

An obvious limit on both the size and duration of an expedition was the rate of march of the forces involved, the supplies that would be required, the capacity of the pack-animals in the baggage train, as well as the feed and fodder needed for the baggage train itself. The logistical calculations for major expeditionary forces were, in this respect, quite complex, and the degree of cooperation between the different fiscal and administrative departments at Constantinople and in the provinces affected must have had important consequences for the success or failure of an expedition. In hostile territory, light cavalry scouts were sent ahead to spy out the army's line of march, the position of enemy forces and fortifications and the availability of wood, water, fodder and food, and were responsible for providing the commanders of the Roman forces with sufficient information for them to plan their route and the marching camps.[64] In Roman territory, in contrast, the route of march for large forces was generally prepared in advance and supplies provided through the activities of the local *protonotarios* of each district affected. Large concentrations of provisions seem to have been deposited at a few key locations in granaries or storehouses, according to the ninth-century report of Ibn Khurradādhbīh, from which they were collected by the army and loaded onto pack-animals, carts and the soldiers themselves as they passed through. This is clearly the system described in one of the tenth-century treatises on imperial military expeditions. But Ibn Khurradādhbīh also notes that the provincial soldiers were expected to bring their own provisions for a limited period: "there is no market in the Roman camp. Each soldier is obliged to bring from his own resources the biscuit, oil, wine and cheese that he will need", a point confirmed by numerous references in Byzantine hagiographies from the eighth, ninth and tenth centuries. The thematic troops would thus provide for themselves for the first few days after their call-up, no doubt until they had marched and been assembled at the first major supply point en route to join the main column of the expedition.[65]

As far as rate of march itself is concerned, general factors of terrain and climate, as well as the quality of the roads, tracks or paths used by the army, all played a role, so that very considerable variations must have been usual. In general, bearing in mind the points about roads and tracks made in Chapter 2 above, and in marked contrast to the armies of the period up to the third and fourth centuries, the medieval East Roman army did not have a system of paved military roads at its disposal. The rapid strategic dispersal or concentration of troops was thus greatly hindered and, although small forces were able to move to intercept invading troops fairly quickly, the assembly and movement of larger armies was a slow and cumbersome process. The speed at which large forces can move varies considerably according to these limitations: anything from 7 or 8 miles per day to 18 or 20. Unaccompanied cavalry can achieve distances of up to 40 or 50 miles per day, provided the horses are regularly rested and well nourished and watered. Similarly, small units can move much faster than large divisions: distances of up to 30 miles per day for infantry have been recorded from different pre-modern historical contexts. But the average marching speeds for infantry are 3 miles per hour on even terrain, 2½ on uneven or broken/hilly ground. The distances at which supply dumps could be established or stops made to feed and water men and animals was also directly related to the distance covered in a day's march and how much provisions and water could be carried before resupply was necessary.[66] The emperor Nikephros II, for example, considered a march of 16 miles (approx. 24 km) to be both long and tiring for men and horses,[67] and although his account concerns specifically the mountainous and broken terrain of the Taurus and Anti-Taurus regions, there are a series of other factors which crucially affect the rate of march of a body of troops.

For the number of men, animals and carts involved in a column, and the space they occupy, also plays a fundamental role. The reason a large force moves more slowly than a small force is simple: the men and horses do not all start off at the same moment, but one after the other. Hence the longer the column, the longer it takes for the rearmost files to set off; correspondingly, the rearmost groups will arrive at the next camp later than the foremost groups; and the delay between the arrival of the first and the last men is proportional to the length and breadth of the column. Thus an army of 5,000 infantry, marching at the standard infantry rate of about 3 miles per hour (4.5 km/hr) over good ground, ordered five abreast and with each row occupying a (minimal) 2 metres would stretch over a distance of 2 km. Assuming a one-second delay between each row setting off, there would be a gap of some 17 minutes between foremost and rearmost ranks. This is, in fact, an exceedingly optimistic set of assumptions. In much of the campaigning against the Arabs, the terrain was broken and mountainous, so that marching rates were slower, and because of the narrowness of many of the tracks used, columns longer: a column of 1,000 cavalry in double file would stretch over 2 km, where each rank took up approximately 4 m space; an army of 10,000 infantry and 5,000 cavalry would, even with the infantry five abreast and the cavalry two abreast, stretch over 14 km, and the rearmost ranks would be some 75 minutes at the very least behind the first. The bigger the army and the narrower its front, therefore, the longer (and more exposed) the column, the more difficult the maintenance of regular marching time and discipline, and the greater the delay between the first and last ranks arriving at a given destination.

Wherever possible, therefore, an army would march with as broad a front as was feasible to minimize this delay and to maintain the cohesion and tactical flexibility of the units (and the military treatises regularly assume that this would be the case, except where the army has to pass through defiles and so forth). The reality was, of course, even more complex: armies must ford rivers, pass through defiles, and stop for rests from time to time. The changes in marching order which these movements entail (and for which the treatises provide detailed instructions) would further slow down the rate of march, and further exacerbate possible delays between starting off and arrival times. Bottlenecks – bridges, narrow passes and so forth – were especially problematic in this respect. When in 877 Basil I led his army on foot, probably in rows of two or three abreast at the most, through the defiles of the Anti-Taurus on his way from Koukousos to the siege of Germanikeia,[68] and assuming that he was accompanied by an army of 8,000 or so horse and foot (although it was probably larger than this), the column would have stretched at least 8 km along the track, and moved at the slower rate of 2 miles per hour (3 km/hr). With at least a two-second delay between each rank starting off, the van would have been some 1½–2 hours ahead of the rearmost ranks. This takes no account of baggage animals, of course. It should be stressed that these figures are entirely hypothetical, but they are based on established ratios of movement to space and provide some idea of the sorts of practical problems facing a commander on the march.[69]

In most conditions, the average length of a day's march for infantry or combined forces was probably rarely more than 12–14 miles, which has been an average for most infantry forces throughout recorded history, and this figure would more often than not be reduced where large numbers of troops, particularly including infantry, were involved. The average can be increased when no accompanying baggage train is present: thus Roman legionary troops of the first century AD, carrying most of their immediate requirements in equipment and provisions, were supposed to maintain a rate of 20 Roman miles in five hours (18.4 miles), on metalled roads or good tracks and in good weather. A faster pace, intended to cover 24 Roman miles in five hours, was also practised. These rates are repeated by Vegetius for the fifth century. Such rates could be increased even further by forced marches, although there is an inverse relationship between the length and speed of such marches and the loss of manpower and animals through exhaustion. The sources record a variety of rates of march, determined by the condition of the roads and the type of troops involved – Procopius refers to a march of some 6–7 miles per day over a seven-day period during the Vandal war (a figure which reflects the presence of infantry, a baggage train and a supply train).[70]

Although the sources disagree over details, an example of a Byzantine forced march is provided by the expedition of Basil II in 995 from Constantinople to relieve Aleppo. The emperor supposedly set out with a force estimated at 40,000; the journey, normally taking some 60 days, was completed in a quarter of the time, but only 17,000 men and their mounts or pack-animals arrived at Aleppo. Horses need regular rest and regular breaks for grazing (at least one day in six, or the equivalent), if they are not to develop sores and damage to their feet and backs, such that they are temporarily (and if not rested and cared for, permanently) useless. The drop-out rate in Basil's forces was probably due in large part to these factors. In 1159 the imperial army made a night-march, lighting its way through the winter snow by affixing cressets or portable torches onto the spears and lances of the cavalry. Manuel I made a forced march in 1179 to relieve Claudioupolis from a Seljuk attack, and Choniates notes that he did not take along the imperial pavilion or any other luxuries.[71]

One of the most influential features determining rate of march as well as size of armies was the availability of suitable transport. Most flexible were men and pack-animals, but for major undertakings requiring siege equipment, wheeled transport may sometimes have been essential. When accompanied by wagons, which was occasionally the case with major forces, rates of march will have been considerably reduced, unless the column was divided. Imperial expeditionary forces certainly had wagons or carts in their baggage train on occasion: in the campaign of 1176 against the Sultanate of Konya, Manuel I's army is reported to have been accompanied by some 3,000 wagons, conveying the imperial baggage and siege equipment. The *Strategikon* and the *Tactica* of Leo refer on numerous occasions to baggage carts accompanying the column carrying the soldiers' tents and other heavy equipment, while other wagons bearing artillery and related items are also mentioned. But Leo's text copies Maurice almost verbatim, so that it is difficult to know whether the use of wheeled transport on a large scale really was so usual. Most of the other texts and the chroniclers rarely mention carts: pack-horses, mules and the soldiers themselves were the main form of transport.[72]

Supplies and rations

In the fifth century, soldiers were trained to carry a load of up to 60 Roman pounds (about 19.6 kg). This included 17–20 days' worth of rations. Whether this amount was regularly carried by the troops, except when making rapid marches in hostile territory, has been doubted, however; although the evidence of the *Strategikon* suggests that it was. In Roman territory the greater part was probably transported by accompanying pack-animals, as noted in the *Strategikon*, which also recommended that cavalry soldiers carry three to four days' supply with them in their saddlebags. The same treatise asserts that troops camped between 6 and 10 days' march from the enemy should take 20–30 lb of hard tack each when they march to battle. The *Codex Theodosianus* includes regulations stipulating the 17–20 day ration to be carried, and Procopius corroborates this for the sixth century. There is no reason to doubt that it remained standard thereafter for the regular units.[73]

In the fifth and sixth centuries rations were consumed on a three-day rotation: bread for one day in three, *bucellatum* (hard tack) for two days in three, salt pork for one day in three, mutton for two days in three, wine and sour wine on alternate days. Other foods such as fish, cheese and oil, depending on context and availability, could also be eaten. The weight of such rations varied, but the figure of 1 Roman pound (327 g) of meat and/or 2–3 Roman pounds (654–981 g) of bread *per diem* per man given in one document for stationary troops seems to have been standard into the seventh century in Egypt, and the limited evidence suggests that this was more or less constant in the preceding and following periods. The tenth-century treatise on skirmishing warfare notes that basic rations for soldiers consisted of bread and either cheese or dried and salted meat.[74] We should bear in mind that even though the amount of meat proportional to the rest of the diet might frequently be reduced to a minimum or to nothing under some campaign conditions, this would still provide a reasonable amount of nutrition, since ancient strains of wheat and barley had considerably higher protein content than modern strains. The bread ration of soldiers in ancient and medieval times provided adequate nutrition for the duration of a campaign season even without meat.[75]

On this basis, the maximum 60 (Roman) pound load per man would indeed suffice for about 20 days. In normal marching conditions much of the individual's supplies would be transported by pack-animal or wagon, however.[76] A 15,000-man army would thus require a minimum of some 900,000 (Roman) lb (i.e. 288,400 kg) of provisions for a period of between two and, in exceptional cases, three weeks. This excludes drinking water/wine and necessary "extras", such as lard and/or oil, cheese or fish, and so on, as well as fodder for the horses and the pack-animals. The evidence suggests that, while the state provided the main elements of the soldiers' diet – grain and on occasion dried meat – the soldiers' households generally catered for items such as oil, cheese and so forth, at least for the provincial troops registered for service in the *themata*.[77] Assuming an average rate of march for infantry and cavalry together of between 12 and 14 miles per day in good conditions (an optimistic figure compared with the majority of known military marches from pre-industrial contexts),[78] such a force could thus travel some 240–80 miles in a three-week march, which provides a very crude guide to the distances at which supply dumps would have had to be established in advance. As we shall see below, however, in friendly territory, and when provisions could be garnered more readily from the districts through which the army passed, it will have replenished its supplies much more frequently to avoid the necessity of taking along a huge number of pack-animals until it became absolutely essential, a question which also raises a number of problems.

Soldiers were issued with two main varieties of bread: simple baked loaves and double-baked "hard tack", referred to in late Roman times as *bucellatum* and by the Byzantines as *paximadion* or *paximation*. In campaign conditions, it was normally the soldiers themselves who milled and baked this. The hard tack was more easily preserved over a longer period, was easy to produce and demanded fairly simple milling and baking skills.[79] Hard tack could be baked in field ovens – *klibanoi* – or simply laid in the ashes of camp-fires, an advantage when speed was essential. One tenth-century treatise notes that the best such bread was baked in thin oval loaves cooked in a field-oven, and then dried in the sun.[80] Hand-mills were a requirement of the Byzantine infantry-unit baggage train, at least in theory, and such mills are known from the later Roman period.[81]

The chief grains employed comprised wheat, barley and millet, although other grains were used depending upon both the region and the period.[82] Barley was regarded primarily as hard feed for livestock, although it, and millet, may have been regularly used for the hard-tack *paximadion*. The military treatises often refer to the soldiers' baggage train carrying both barley as well as millet, although wheat was the normal ingredient for bread. But it is not the case that meat – either fresh when in camp or garrison, or dried/salted when in the field – was not also a regular element, even if reduced to a minimum in campaigning contexts – a tenth-century treatise refers to dried fish as an element in the provisions to be taken on expeditions.[83]

The tenth-century treatise on campaign organization confirms the estimate of the provisions that could be carried for a three-week march, noting that "it is not feasible, in turn, for an army to transport more than a twenty-four days' supply of barley from its own country for its horses", which suggests the recognized maximum period for a cavalry force.[84] If this fodder were to be transported by mule-train, the amount of feed required by these pack-animals would itself add enormously to the supply problem. In fact, for the 8,200 cavalrymen envisaged by the treatise in question, assuming each animal carried between one and two days' supply of barley, and assuming at least 1,000 remounts accompanied the corps, each loaded with the 68 kg barley feed stipulated in the tenth-century treatise on imperial military expeditions (providing enough feed for 4–5 days), some 6,460 extra pack-animals would be required to enable this force to stay in the field for a further 18 or so days, without being resupplied with hard fodder.[85] If 2,000 remounts were taken, similarly encumbered, over 1,000 fewer pack-animals would be required (thus reducing proportionally at the same time the amount of pack-animal feed necessary). In practice, the context of this passage suggests that much of this fodder would be carried by a separate supply train, including carts as well as pack-animals, and that the cavalry itself would be less heavily burdened and accompanied by far fewer pack-animals as it moved along.

Horses and mules require considerably more in weight of provisions than soldiers, and are in economic terms relatively inefficient animals, needing a much greater weight of supplies proportional to their carrying capacity than men. Roman military mounts required something in the order of 20 lb (9 kg) of fodder per day in rest conditions: 5–6 lb (2.2–2.7 kg) barley and a further 10–15 lb (4.5–6.8 kg) hay or grazing.[86] The area required for grazing depended on several factors – quality of pasturage, seasonal variations and so forth. The basic requirements per horse amount to four–five hours' grazing per day, so that 20 horses would graze one acre of medium-quality pasture in that time. On campaign, they were probably fed less. But they need also an average of

22.75–36.4 l of water per day – the amount varies according to temperature, nature of work and so on.[87] The availability of grazing obviously depends upon regional and seasonal variations: where fodder had to be transported in addition to grain, mobility would be drastically limited and transport costs increased.

The mules and pack-horses of the expeditionary armies of the tenth century had to carry their own grain rations as well as the equipment or provisions for the soldiers, but the loads were strictly controlled.[88] One treatise specifies that ordinary pack-mules or ponies should carry up to 104 kg (85 kg load, plus pack-saddle and harness of 16–19 kg), riding horses carrying packs should be loaded up to a maximum of 68 kg (plus military saddle of c. 12 kg) and riding horses with a rider and some baggage (in this case their own barley ration of about 34 kg) up to 116 kg. The care shown over the loads reflects similar concerns evident in the later Roman legislation.[89]

These figures have interesting implications: the 34 kg barley feed carried by the higher-quality horses for their own consumption will have been sufficient for a march of no more than 15 days, for example. The treatises are clear that barley was carried, not hay or other fodder, which is to be supplied by the various protonotarioi of the different themata through which the army passes, deposited in advance according to the route planned by the commander.

The normal campaigning seasons were in the late spring/early summer or the early autumn, when pasturage would be available for the horses. A tenth-century Arab source notes that at these times there is abundant pasturage in the land of the Romans, from which the Arab raiders can maintain their mounts without difficulty. Special arrangements were made for the grazing of the animals of the baggage train and for the imperial riding horses. Although security was less important in imperial territory, grazing horses and pack-animals were carefully supervised, if only to prevent theft by the locals or by soldiers. In enemy territory, the perimeter of the camp was laid out to accommodate and protect all the animals. A special official, the epeiktes, on the staff of the imperial stables (a whole department, headed by a komes and chartoularios, which supervised the imperial horses and cortège), was responsible for the pasturage as well as for the feed of the animals.[90]

On the basis of this information, it is likely that major supply dumps were needed at stages of approximately 200–250 miles, although under good conditions fast-moving cavalry forces will have been less demanding, even though fodder and water will have been essential. Large state storehouses had been maintained in the late Roman period, and continued to be maintained during the Byzantine period, where supplies delivered from the local population for the army were kept. The thematic protonotarioi, as described in the Three Treatises on Imperial Military Expeditions, were responsible for these establishments, some at the sites of major marching camps or aplekta, others presumably located along major military routes.[91] The tenth-century treatise on imperial expeditions requires a total of 1,086 pack-animals of varying categories (mules and horses) to transport the requirements of the imperial household alone.

Taking these figures as a crude measure of needs, they will have consumed a basic 24,435 l of water, 280 ha of pasture, and 2,468 kg of barley feed per day.[92] Both green fodder – grazing – required as well as water consumption will have fluctuated fairly sharply acording to local conditions, the weight of the loads carried, the nature of the ground traversed and so forth. In addition, the amount of pasturage required increased considerably where barley feed was not available for short periods, while an expedition which set off in seasons when pasturage was not available will have needed to carry dry fodder with it, thus enormously increasing the overall demand for pack-animals exponentially. But the figures give some idea of the quantities of supplies involved. A cavalry force of similar strength will have required about the same for the horses of each soldier. In addition, however, supplies for remounts and pack-animals must be included, so that the total provisions necessary for the animals of a fast-moving cavalry force of 1,000 men will have amounted to at least half as much again (see Appendix 3, example A).

In principle, a simple application of the law of diminishing returns operates whenever troops need to carry their own provisions; and the more provisions needed to be carried, the lower the return on outlay on beasts of burden. Thus, if the average load of a pack-animal is taken as 96 kg, and the animal's own minimum requirements amount to 2.2 kg per day, it will carry 93.8 kg for others for the first day, but only 91.6 the second, 89.4 the third, 87.2 the fourth and so on, as it consumes the difference itself. A mule could thus supply 43 other animals for one day, 42 for two days, 40 for three days, 38 for five days, 33 for ten days, 29 for 15 days, and so on. The more supplies have to be carried, the greater the rate of diminution of supplies. If a mule had to carry a full green fodder ration as well as grain, the rate would be even quicker: 96 kg ÷ 9 kg feed × no. of days. Beginning with a full load, a pack-animal could thus feed 9 animals for one day, 8 for two days, 7 for three days, 6 for four days, 5 for five days and so on up to a maximum of nine days, when its entire load will have been consumed (see Appendix 3 for further illustrations).

The further the distance over which supplies had to be carried, the greater the amount of supplies to be transported, and the greater the number of pack-animals. The greater the number of pack-animals, the greater the total amount of fodder, since they will themselves consume a portion of their loads; the longer the journey, the greater the relative rate of consumption, until the expedition becomes a logistical impossibility. The establishment of regular supply dumps, as well as the availability of pasture, were thus crucial determinants of the route of march.[93] In order to maximize logistical resources, major armies were split up into a number of separate columns which were kept separate until as late as possible. This had always been understood by Roman commanders and is explicitly stated to be the case in the late sixth-century *Strategikon*: "The whole army should not be brought together in one place because the men might quickly find themselves starving, . . . and fodder might be hard to obtain. As they are drawing closer to the enemy, about six, seven or even ten days

away, the troops should be drawn closer together and at the same time set up camp . . ." The same advice is repeated in Leo's *Tactica*. But it was anyway facilitated by the distribution of the provincial forces across the *themata* from the middle of the seventh century on. The tenth-century *Three Treatises on Imperial Expeditions*, and the list of major base camps or *aplekta*, describe the process by which the different corps met up according to the direction and target of the campaign, while the historical accounts regularly note the gathering of the different columns in Cappadocia before they embarked upon their offensive.[94] The armies which were assembled for the counter-attack after the loss of Amida to the Persians in 503 were so numerous that, according to Procopius, they were compelled for logistical reasons to march separately to the theatre of war. Once arrived, special arrangements had to be made to supply and provision them.[95]

In Byzantine territory, and also when the army arrived in an "enemy" district which had not been warned of its approach (and depending also upon the attitude of the commander towards the local populace), troops could be sent out to purchase corn and other requirements from local sources, and accounts of the campaigns of Romanos IV in the late 1060s and early 1070s report the detachment of small units or troops of soldiers sent off to purchase corn, and of the rearguard lagging behind the main body of the army in order to protect those sent to purchase supplies. The depredations caused by one's "own" troops attests to the fact that, wherever possible, commanders did not take along a large supply train, relying instead wherever possible on the availability of local resources. But in spite of the general's best intentions, his soldiers might frequently cause as much damage to his own side as an enemy raid: Roman units caused considerable hardship and dislocation when they were quartered without advance warning for too long a period in Thrace in the campaign of 812/13; Roman and foreign mercenary units caused severe dislocation in the region of Krya Pege when they arrived there during a campaign of 1069 in the search for provisions and especially fodder for their horses.[96]

In hostile territory, the official advice in Leo's *Tactica* was to take enough supplies to last for the duration of the raid if it had limited objectives. But this will often have encumbered the army and slowed it down and, as we have seen, another treatise points out that it is not feasible to take along more than 24 days' supply of barley feed for the horses. This is directly corroborated by an Arab account, which remarks that should a winter raid (in February/March) into Byzantine territory be mounted, the raiders should not spend more than 20 days there and back, since that is the maximum time for which they can carry supplies with them (and the pack-animals whose loads had been consumed could then be used to carry the booty). This was in strong contrast to the spring raid, which lasted about 30 days, and the summer raid, lasting up to 60 days. In both cases, fodder and grain for the animals and provisions for the soldiers and camp attendants will have been extracted from the areas through which the army marched.[97] The military treatises make it clear that the route of march planned for an offensive campaign should take these logistical issues into account: the localities through which the army is to pass – especially those in enemy territory – should be preserved from plunder and devastation so that they can supply the armies on their return march. In particular, the supply of water should be adequate for the army's needs: several accounts note the results of a failure to secure the water supplies, as when in 594 the guides attached to the field army under Priscus campaigning against the Avars led the army to the wrong place, resulting in near disaster.[98]

More usually, the army in enemy territory foraged for its own supplies (as did the Arab armies when in East Roman districts), but in this case it was essential that commanders made sure that they took the army into districts where supplies could be found: there are several examples in the chronicles of commanders who failed to ensure this. Correctly informed (as the military treatises insist every commander should be, by sending out advance parties of scouts and by employing spies in enemy country), disaster could be avoided, as when Romanos IV discovered in time that the district of Melitene, to which he was marching, could not support his troops because of the ravages and devastation of the previous year. Where the enemy might destroy or carry off the supplies upon which the army, especially the horses, depended, the commander should make sure he brings adequate provisions along with him. But it was chronic shortage of provisions that forced Basil I to abandon the sieges of Tephrike in 871 and Melitene in 873, for example, and it was the arrival and subsequent defeat of a Byzantine relief army, with the supply train, at Tyana in 708/9 which enabled the Arab besiegers to continue the siege – which they had been about to abandon for want of provisions – to a success-ful conclusion.[99] Lack of water and scarcity of provisions cut short John I Tzimiskes' campaign into Ecbatana in 974. Shortage of supplies curtailed the expedition against the Hungarians in 1130, and the death of many pack-animals (through starvation, although the text is not explicit) meant the abandonment of part of the imperial baggage. Similar shortages beset the siege of Damietta by Manuel's army in 1169, and the expeditionary army of 1176 suffered from the fact that the Turks polluted the water supply along the route and destroyed any supplies that the Roman forces might have consumed. As a result, the army was struck by enteric infections (possibly dysentery, typhus or cholera, or all of these). The treatises note the dangers of poisoned water supplies or grain, and advise that all such resources be tested before use. By the same token, of course, denying supplies to enemy forces was a simple and often bloodless way of defeating an invading army, as in 778/9, for example, when Leo IV ordered Byzantine troops to burn the pastures along the Arab invaders' route to Dorylaion, which they were able to besiege for just two weeks before running out of provisions, losing many of their animals and being forced to withdraw (a procedure recommended in the military manuals), while in 782 one column from an otherwise successful Arab invading force was bottled up between the mountains and the Sangarios river in Bithynia. As a result of the seizure of the two Byzantine negotiators, the empress Eirene was forced to permit the Arab force to escape on favourable terms which, interestingly, included the provision by the imperial authorities of guides and access to markets where the Arab soldiers could buy provisions. The presence of large numbers of troops was always a logistical nightmare: in 717 the invading Arab column commanded by Masalmas was unable to stop en route to Ikonion because of the great numbers of the force, presumably because no area could support it for more than a day or so.[100]

The military treatises of the tenth century and the historians' accounts of many of the campaigns of this period show that foraging for supplies was one of the most risk-laden activities which the commander had to organize – failure to guard against surprise attack while foraging or dealing with the pack-train on the one hand, and the failure of the foragers to locate and secure adequate provisions on the other, could prove disastrous: it was by surprising the Paulician troops while they were attending to such matters that the *domestikos* John defeated the forces of the Paulician leader Chrysocheir at Bathys Ryax in 873. By the same token, the ill-disciplined Roman troops campaigning against the Bulgars in 707/8 were similarly caught while foraging and the army put to flight. Basil II's ill-fated first campaign against the Bulgars in 986 failed in part because the forage parties were inadequately protected and were consequently ambushed and cut to pieces by the enemy. Within a few days the imperial army was forced to retire in disorder, losing much of its baggage train in the process. Choniates notes that Manuel I defeated Turkish attempts to disrupt the work of his forage parties in the 1175 campaign to Dorylaion by establishing a regular system of picquets and counter-raids on the Turkish forces, something which the military treatises themselves advise.[101] Equally, of course, it was clearly understood that attacking the enemy while they were out foraging (or collecting booty) offered a good opportunity to break up an invading force; indeed, by depriving the enemy of fodder and other provisions, they might be encouraged to send out foraging parties farther and farther away from the main force, thus providing even better opportunities to destroy the invading forces piecemeal.[102]

In general, it appears that the campaigns of both Byzantine armies and those of their enemies were carried out over terrain and at times of the year when conditions were most favourable. Most of the expeditions about which we possess any detailed information make it clear that the armies usually foraged for their own supplies, for both men and animals, most of the time. Only in imperial territory was this not (usually) necessary, because the local authorities, even at fairly short notice, appear to have been able to get supplies to key depositories along the army's routes of march in time, and where this was not the case, detachments were sent off to local settlements to purchase (or otherwise obtain) what was needed – although as we have noted already both military officers and authors of military treatises, as well as other commentators, note the dangers inherent in this procedure for the local population.[103] Where campaigns in the winter were involved, commanders had to be particularly careful to locate adequate sources of provisions and fodder, and to operate with forces which could transport their own supplies on occasion, without turning the operation into a logistical nightmare. Heraclius' campaigns in 624–8, for example, frequently involved difficult marches through the rough terrain of the eastern Anatolian mountain country, where the importance of adequate supplies for the army is stressed and where the choice of routes to be followed in manoeuvring against the Persians was determined on several occasions by the availability of provisions.[104] Only when he was able to attack with a small picked force an area in which Persian troops were dispersed for the winter, for example, did he risk campaigning in that season, and having seized the districts in question established his own winter quarters.[105] Thus in 627 the emperor opened a campaign in September, as winter set in in the mountainous region of northwest Iran, which the historians themselves note was unusual and took the Persian forces by surprise. Theophanes also notes that the Chazar allies themselves gradually fell away because of the harsh campaigning conditions. Heraclius' field army at this point seems to have been quite small – Theophanes notes at one point that the emperor was anxious to join battle with the Persian commander Razates before the 3,000 reinforcements sent by the Persian king arrived, which suggests that they would have made a substantial difference to the Persian force, while he also notes that only 50 Roman soldiers died in the day-long battle that ensued. Whether this is a plausible or reliable figure can be debated, but it is indicative again of the relative sizes of the armies involved.[106] The importance of being able to end the year's campaigning within reach of a well-supplied district where the army could be rested for the winter is frequently mentioned in the accounts of these campaigns.[107]

As long as fodder for the animals in particular could be secured, most expeditions could afford to carry basic supplies for the soldiers and other personnel for periods sufficient to see them across difficult terrain. Choice of season and target was usually determined by this consideration above all others: "We should campaign against the enemy when the grain is ripe, so that our troops will not lack provisions and the expedition will cause the enemy more damage", as the anonymous author of the late sixth-century *Strategikon* puts it.[108] Fodder for the horses and a good water supply were the key in this respect, as noted above, but even when these were secure, movement across arid or uncultivated terrain was risky and had to be accomplished quickly. A tenth-century account of Basil I's expedition of 877/8 remarks that he passed through the deserted regions between imperial and enemy territory as quickly as he could; the treatises on imperial expeditions note that the emperor should be as unencumbered as possible, leaving all non-essential personnel and much of the imperial baggage behind once he enters this zone.[109]

The importance of logistics

What the great strength and the mighty force of the enemy were unable to bring about, the lack of necessities will achieve . . .[110]

It was thus logistics – the complex, expensive, but efficient system of marching camps, supply dumps and provincial collection and redistribution of material resources – which enabled the widely dispersed Byzantine provincial armies to call up their troops, combine their forces and march to meet enemy invaders at the appropriate place and in sufficient numbers. It was a system which took on a truly Byzantine aspect, in the sense that it evolved in Asia Minor after the withdrawal from the east in the late 630s and 640s and in direct response to the contingencies of the time: reduced fiscal resources, disrupted local economies, constant enemy raids and harassment, dispersal of armies and optimization of defensive possibilities. Moreover, it was a system which aimed to encircle the enemy by facilitating the concentration of several different columns from widely different locations, in the right place and at the right moment, so that the enemy would find his way blocked, whichever way he turned, by a force large enough to bring it to battle, and allow the remaining columns to attack his lines at a point of their choosing – on the flank, in the rear or frontally. Several ninth-century encounters illustrate this: the defeat of the Paulicians at Bathys Ryax in 878, for example, involved the convergence of the forces of Charsianon and Armeniakon, some of which had shadowed the enemy for several days beforehand, upon the Paulician camp, where the imperial forces occupied the heights surrounding the enemy position. In a much larger operation in 863 the commander Petronas encircled the forces of the emir of Malatya (Melitene) with a total of 13 different corps, which had marched by separate routes to meet near the point at which the action took place: the *themata* of Thrakesion, Thrace and Macedonia, along with the four imperial *tagmata* under Petronas' direct command, approached from the west; those of Anatolikon, Opsikion and Cappadocia, along with the smaller corps from the *kleisourai* of Charsianon and Seleukia from the south; and those of Koloneia, Paphlagonia, Armeniakon and Boukellarion from the north. In both cases the enemy forces were almost annihilated.[111] It was probably a similar strategy which was followed in 772/3 when Constantine V marched with the combined *themata* and *tagmata* into Bulgaria and defeated the Bulgar forces at the place called Lithosoria, and pre-emptively in 778 when – in order to forestall an Arab raid – Leo IV despatched the forces of five *themata* under a unified command to attack the region of Germanikeia (Mar'ash), where they were able to defeat the enemy army before it reached imperial territory.

In 781/2, when Harun ar-Rashid led a major incursion into imperial territory, it was again a number of Byzantine divisions operating in combination that marched to meet his columns. Moving rapidly through the frontier districts, one Arab force was left to besiege Nakoleia on the borders of the Opsikion and Anatolikon *themata*, a second diverged into the Thrakesion region, and the main force under Harun proceeded to Chrysoupolis on the Bosphorus. The first detachment was surprised and routed by a Byzantine division, while the attack on the Thrakesion *thema* was turned back after an apparently drawn battle. The *tagmata* and other unnamed corps (but including the Boukellarion division) were able to encircle the main raiding force in the Sangarios valley on their return march, and it was only the treachery of the Armenian commander of the Boukellarion division, Tatzates, which enabled the Arabs to strike a deal (more favourable to them than the empire) and escape with their booty.

The strategy did not always succeed: in 770/1 the emperor was informed of an Arab raiding force and ordered the cavalry *themata* of Anatolikon, Thrakesion and Boukellarion to occupy the pass through which the raiders would have to return, and at the same time he issued instructions to the Kibyrrhaiot troops and their ships to occupy the harbour of the fortress town of Syke, which the Arabs had attacked. Although demoralized by their failure to take the town, the raiders nevertheless were able to force their way back through the pass with most of their booty intact: the treatise on skirmishing warfare warns the general to be on the look-out for ambushes set by retreating Arab forces, and notes that apparently victorious pursuits of enemy forces have resulted in ignominy and failure through neglecting to take such matters into account.[112] Again, in 787/8 Roman forces marched separately to trap and destroy an Arab force at Podandos, but were themselves ambushed and defeated. Yet some 90 years later, in 878, five Roman corps were able to combine to destroy a large Arab force which had attacked the same region.[113]

In all these examples and in many others – regardless of the final result for the Byzantine forces – it was the ability of the empire to mobilize its provincial armies and organize a coherent strategy of defence from the centre which made imperial military reaction to Arab invasion so effective. In many ways, the fact that as many battles were lost as were won is not important. For in combination with the geographical conditions which provided the empire with a series of natural defences in Anatolia, the mere existence of a permanent opposition and the knowledge that no Arab presence beyond the Taurus and Anti-Taurus could survive unmolested acted as fundamental deterrents to the investment necessary to a permanent and effective occupation of Byzantine territory in this region. The logistical arrangements of the empire and the centrally coordinated defensive strategy that they facilitated were a crucial element in this.

Frontier warfare

As we have seen already in Chapter 3, it is difficult to know how soon an effective strategy for border warfare evolved in either the Anatolian or Balkan contexts. The extent to which border warfare had settled down into a regular raid and counter-raid pattern by the later seventh century is unclear. Certainly during the later seventh and eighth centuries strategy seems to have been relatively centralized and not especially flexible at local level (although the sources reveal no details of border warfare). The emperors themselves led a number of major expeditions against key enemy fortresses or to re-establish Byzantine fortified strongholds which had been taken and destroyed by the

Arabs or Bulgars. It may be that the establishment from the later eighth century of *kleisourai* as independent commands – Seleukeia, Kappadokia, Charsianon – coincides with the formal establishment of a more flexible strategy which had before been left at an *ad hoc* level determined by the skills and ability of local commanders and the initiative of the *tourmarchai* along the borders of the themes affected by regular raiders. It is significant in this context that from the mid-780s Byzantine efforts also succeeded in stabilizing a Balkan frontier between the empire and the Bulgars, represented by a line of fortified posts (Philippoupolis, Beroea, Markellai and Anchialos), from which local officers could respond to threats independent of their *strategos* or Constantinople. As noted in Chapter 3 above, the report in Theophanes that Leo IV ordered the implementation of a guerrilla strategy against a large invading force in 779 may support this contention. It may also have evolved as a response to changes in Arab strategy after the abandonment of serious efforts to push through Asia Minor to take Constantinople (i.e. after 718) and establish permanent bases north of the Taurus/Anti-Taurus line.[114] The *Tactica* of Leo VI implies that such frontier warfare follows an established pattern and some advice is given for the frontier commander on how best to deal with enemy raiders, advice which is very close, albeit less detailed, to that given in the anonymous treatise *On Skirmishing Warfare*.[115] The latter states in its introduction that, because of recent imperial successes in pushing forward the frontier, the traditional system of defensive warfare was no longer practised, and although the author ascribes its perfection to generals of the Phocas family – a major clan of the eastern provinces – it is likely that it was already practised long before this.

The arrangements for smaller raids and expeditions on the eastern front were very different from those established for large-scale campaigns.[116] In the first place, a chain of look-out posts and advance scouts had been established along the frontier, particularly covering the various points of ingress into imperial territory. Since the frontier was a broad band of territory rather than a linear border, the location of such watch-posts undoubtedly changed according to the situation, just as it is clear that raids and counter-raids intended to destroy fortifed outposts or more important local fortresses and bases frequently altered the pattern of local strategy.[117]

The principles of this type of warfare are carefully explained in the treatise in question. First, the local commanders should make sure that their network of watch-posts is functioning. Scouts should be locals with experience, with a good knowledge of local routes and the different qualities they possess; they should be sent out in small groups to watch the roads and routes that might be used by the enemy, and should work on a 15-day rota. In addition, the commander should make extensive use of spies, including merchants and others on genuine business in the enemy's land – a long tradition in Byzantine strategic thinking.[118] The call-up of registered soldiers should be strictly observed, and the scouting parties should be checked by an officer from time to time.

They should also change their location in order to avoid capture. Other officers were instructed to put into operation a pre-planned scheme for evacuating the non-military population of the regions through which an enemy raiding party would pass – once its route had been determined by the scouts – both to preserve the local population and to deprive the enemy of the chance to collect easy booty and, more importantly, provisions and supplies. Interestingly, the author of the treatise notes that in the so-called Armenian *themata* salaried scouts should be employed, since the usual Armenian thematic militia troops are especially unreliable and slack in their duties.

The bulk of the treatise describes the range of methods which a local commander has at his disposal for dealing with enemy raiding forces, large and small. Shadowing and harassing the enemy by utilizing one's own knowledge of the local terrain was one aspect; keeping a close watch on his column and especially his encampment in order to attempt ambushes on forage parties and other isolated groups was another. Crucial to all operations is the notion – already described for the larger-scale expeditions – of the combined operations of several small Byzantine divisions and the gradual build-up of forces, leading eventually to a full-scale confrontation with the imperial forces at a numerical advantage or a pincer movement designed to encourage the enemy force to give up and return home, but with imperial troops having occupied the passes or exit routes which he would follow. The subsequent surprise attack or ambush could result in the recovery of all or most of the booty, and certainly in the destruction and rout of the enemy army. But equal emphasis is placed on the commander being aware of the possibility that his own forces might themselves become the victims of shadowing and ambush, and he is urged to use scouts and outriders in order to prevent this from happening.

One of the hallmarks of the treatise on skirmishing is the importance placed upon the judgement and independence of the local commanders. Not only should they organize themselves regular, small-scale raids over the border, quite independently of the larger strategy (unless, of course, the empire had made a formal truce with the Arab emirs or the caliphate itself); they should be prepared to attack an invading force whenever an appropriate opportunity arose and not necessarily wait for the arrival of reinforcements or the local senior commander.[119]

The author of the treatise envisages three types of raid, differentiated either by size or by timing. First, small, rapid raiding parties of cavalry might invade Roman territory at any time. Their entry should be communicated to the local commanders as quickly as possible by the border scouts and watch-posts so that they might be met, ambushed or hemmed in, and turned back – where possible without any substantial gains in booty.[120] Second, major raids, usually in August and September, involving quite large forces made up of volunteers for the *jihād* as well as regular troops from the Arab borderlands – Aleppo, Tarsos, Antioch – fulfilled both an economic and an ideological function, the former in respect of the desire for booty and to inflict damage on the Romans, the latter in respect of the desire of many Muslims to participate in the *jihād*. The local commander was enjoined to use every means at his disposal to find out when such raids would begin, by which route and how numerous the enemy host would be.[121] The invading force should then be shadowed; smaller raiding parties which were sent out once it had reached Roman territory should likewise be shadowed and attacked or harassed, as appropriate. The landscape should be deprived of provisions where possible, to maximize the invaders' logistical difficulties, and the enemy force should be subject to constant harassment as it moved, foraged for supplies, set up camp or attempted to collect booty. The passes through which it would return should be occupied and ambushes laid, the water supplies should be held by Byzantine forces and the enemy should be attacked as they returned laden with captives and captured livestock or other booty.[122]

The third type of attack for which the local commander must be prepared was the surprise raid, launched before the local population had been evacuated or any sort of ambush or shadowing-party organized. In this case, a series of emergency measures are set out, particularly involving the general in preparing a feint attack to distract the enemy from pillaging the villages while they are being hastily evacuated. Thereafter, the strategy of harassment, ambush, feint attacks by day and by night and a whole range of other guerrilla tactics come into play. And the author cites some examples: on three different occasions, for example, the Hamdanid emir Ali was ambushed on his return from major raids by local forces, and suffered substantial defeats, barely escaping himself on one occasion.[123]

Warfare at this level was not simply defensive, however. Local commanders should also maintain small bands of raiders, specially selected for their physical prowess and bravery, whose task it was to raid deep into enemy territory in order to foment insecurity and uncertainty. These soldiers, referred to as *trapezitai* or *tasinarioi*, were also to take prisoners who could inform the Byzantine command of the movements of troops, the intentions of the Arab commanders and so forth. Similar soldiers were employed on the northern front in the Balkans, called *chonsarioi*, and although the eastern soldiers were registered as soldiers whereas those in the west appear to be more independent, both groups appear as mercenary troops and required regular payment, rewards, largesse and so forth to keep them loyal; they were also not to be trusted, but should be regularly checked by other agents of the commander who should on no account reveal his own plans to them. They represented more often than not semi-independent peoples whose marginal situation between the two cultures suited them ideally for this task; but they were also potential enemies and needed careful handling. In the tenth century, and with the large-scale migration of Armenians into the Taurus and North Syrian regions, and later into Cilicia as well, these irregulars were drawn from among these newly settled migrant populations. But there is every likelihood that they were drawn at an earlier period from similarly marginal groups – Isaurians, for example, a mountain people whom it had always been difficult to control or administer from Constantinople, or the Mardaites, for example, during the seventh century.[124]

It was from such sources that the regular light cavalry, especially those who formed the advance scouting parties of larger forces, were ideally to be recruited, for they had detailed knowledge not just of the regular routes, but also of the side-paths, hidden tracks, and watering- and camping-places in the mountains, as well as the habits and customs of the enemy.[125]

According to the later tenth-century military treatises – *On Skirmishing Warfare* and *Campaign Organisation and Tactics* – both the eastern as well as the Balkan frontier thus had an offensive aspect at the local level as well as a defensive one, involving a complex relationship between local border peoples, regular troops and imperial administrators, and regional traditions of banditry and raiding. But it is difficult to know whether these traditions had a long history in the middle of the tenth century, describing as they did a situation which no longer existed along the eastern frontier, and a situation along the Balkan frontier which had changed so rapidly within living memory that it can only recently have evolved in the areas to which it applied.

The type of warfare described in the anonymous treatise, and more briefly in the *Tactica* of Leo, was by the later tenth century, and as we are told by the author of the treatise on skirmishing, no longer relevant to the strategic needs of the day. As the empire advanced on all fronts, particularly in the east, the frontier moved away from the land of mountain passes, ambuscades and the guerrilla strategy which had evolved in it. Instead, Byzantine troops found themselves engaged in the role of an occupying army, garrisoning major fortresses, combining with neighbouring garrisons to strike at enemy strong-holds or to meet potential invaders in direct confrontation in the field. But the fundamental logistical requirements outlined above remained unchanged: the concerns of officers and soldiers, of strategists and officials involved in the supply and provisioning of the armies, were unchanged. It was the scale and context which had been transformed. By the twelfth century, the Byzantines found themselves once again on the defensive in Asia Minor, but this time defending the lowlands and foothills of western and southern Asia Minor against nomad warriors who occupied the central plateau, and the strategy of raiding and defending a countryside dotted with fortress towns and villages against determined raiders and booty once more became relevant. Whether the officers of the provinces or the imperial court were aware of the tradition of defensive skirmishing warfare is not known, although it is very probable, but the hit-and-run tactics of the Seljuks and Türkmen, involving large numbers of small raiding parties as well as a seasonal conflict over pasturelands in the no man's land between the two cultures, generated a defensive strategy during the reigns of John II and Manuel I not unlike that which had evolved on the eastern frontier two centuries earlier, with a chain of larger fortress towns connected by smaller forts and fortified settlements from which counter-raids and defensive operations could be mounted at a local level. Indeed, Manuel I himself frequently led mounted raids deep into the Turk-held regions of. Anatolia, and the seasonal pattern of raid and counter-raid in the years

1162–77 became so regular that Niketas Choniates expressly omits any details, as it is so well known and familiar to his readers.[126]

The geopolitical imperatives of a state perpetually facing two or more fronts had once again reasserted themselves, and with a vengeance. Once more, the empire found itself facing a situation in which it had only a very limited spare capacity for aggressive warfare. As long as the Balkans remained a source of manpower and taxable wealth, an offensive–defensive strategy was possible in Asia Minor, as the reigns of John and Manuel in particular demonstrated. But from the 1190s most of the Balkans was effectively independent once again as local autonomy was conceded by Alexios III Angelos (1195–1203); and after the restoration of imperial rule in Constantinople from 1261, the resources available to the central government were barely sufficient to maintain a coherent defensive strategy. Civil war and internecine strife in the fourteenth century only worsened the situation, and the government's inability to pay the mercenaries it hired to act as its central army serves to emphasize the nature of the problem. In this context, it is scarcely appropriate any more to speak of "Byzantine" armies or warfare, except insofar as the emperor paid the bills for his foreign troops. The Byzantine contribution was reduced to that of local militias serving in guardposts and minor defensive installations.

Offensive campaigns and siege warfare

Major offensives were mounted by the emperors throughout the period in question, with the possible exception of the years between c. 640 and 680. The strategic purpose of these campaigns varied according to the general political-military context, of course: the campaigns of Constantine V in both northern Syria and the Balkans, as well as their symbolic and ideological function of reasserting East Roman superiority, were aimed at re-establishing East Roman parity along the frontier regions. Their success illustrated the Romans' ability to push deep into enemy territory, defeat defensive forces assembled to oppose them, ravage the countryside, besiege and capture towns, carry off the population, and in general serve as a deterrent to further aggression on the part of the enemy. On a smaller and less successful basis the campaigns of Justinian II along the eastern frontier appear to have been similarly conceived. In contrast, the major offensives launched during the last years of the reign of Constantine VII and lasting into the early eleventh century in both eastern and western theatres were intended to bring about the reincorporation under imperial rule of "lost" East Roman lands. The sources provide us with little detail about the campaigns of Constantine V (or his father Leo III) in the eighth century, but we are quite well informed about some of the major tenth-century offensives led by generals such as John Kourkouas, Nikephros Phocas, John Tzimiskes and Basil II, as well as some of the campaigns waged in the eleventh and twelfth centuries.

In contrast to the defensive campaigns and the frontier warfare discussed already, such offensive warfare required considerable advance planning. Indeed, it appears usually to have been the case that the process was set in train the year before, the routes of march of the different columns being planned out in time for the local provincial officials to collect and lay up stores of grain and other provisions and supplies – arrows, spears, shields and so forth – which the forces would collect en route for enemy territory.[127] Mustering points for the troops from the provincial armies were nominated in advance, and at the commencement of the campaigning season the different corps would march to pre-arranged assembly points, at which their column would be formed up, or be summoned by mandates despatched from the commander's headquarters.[128] Advance planning for such campaigns was essential if the requisite numbers of pack-animals and carts or wagons for the siege train were to be assembled in time, although light siege equipment could certainly be carried in sections or, along with heavier items, where locally available wood was to be had constructed at the site of the siege (as, for example, during the Roman attempt to recover Amida in 503/4, or during the siege of the Muslim stronghold on Crete by Nikephros Phocas in 961).[129] Campaigns in the Balkans, especially against the Bulgars or Rus' in the eastern Balkan region, were greatly facilitated by using ships to ferry both troops and supplies. Key points at which the land forces could pause to replenish their supplies were at Anchialos, for example, or at the Danube delta. This had been a standard practice during the later sixth century, for example (and indeed the establishment of the *quaestura exercitus* under Justinian I was intended in part to support such a strategy). Constantine IV in 681 and Justinian II in 707/8 employed warships and transports in this way, while Constantine V mounted some seven such campaigns between 761/2 and 774/5, outflanking the Bulgars' defence and enabling large numbers of troops to be supplied without an impossibly cumbersome supply train. John I's campaign against the Rus' in 972 was similarly a combined operation.[130] Campaigns into Syria and northern Iraq were in this respect more complex, and commanders had to ensure that the baggage train they took with them did not overburden the available supplies or involve too many encumbrances such as excess personnel and baggage, a point repeatedly stressed in the military treatises.[131]

A large baggage train consisting of ox-drawn carts was both slow and cumbersome on the one hand, and on the other easily exposed to enemy attack. It had to be protected – all the treatises detail different marching formations, according to the terrain, by which this can be achieved – and hence took up the time of a substantial number of active troops. It consumed considerable amounts of supplies, both for the draught-animals as well as for the wagoneers and muleteers, and it required extra specialist personnel for its maintenance, such as carpenters, wheelwrights and so forth. In the normal run of events, an advance corps went ahead to secure the routes and to sweep any enemy opposition out of the way, so that the siege materials and other supplies could be guaranteed a safe passage and follow on more slowly.[132] But the potentially disruptive effects of the baggage train on an army's march were well recognized: the late tenth-century treatise on campaign organization advises on the measures to be taken if the army has a long march to accomplish before reaching the next camp site, and how to prevent the column from becoming strung out, leaving infantry units and the baggage train exposed to enemy raiders. The vulnerability of baggage trains, especially where they include wagons, was only too clearly demonstrated by the fate of the baggage train at Myriokephalon in 1176. But there are several other examples mentioned by contemporary historians which must have involved similar circumstances.[133] The author of the treatise on *Skirmishing* remarks on this vulnerability, and strongly recommends attacks on the enemy baggage and supply trains. For the Romans would thus gain a great deal in the way of booty, provisions, livestock and equipment, while the enemy expedition would be forced to abandon the campaign. But he is just as aware of the danger to the Romans themselves from the same quarter, remarking "That this has been done against the baggage train of the enemy, as well as by them against ours, we have witnessed, read about in history books, and have learned from our predecessors."[134]

Crucial to such campaigns was the process of gathering intelligence about enemy movements, and the treatises of the tenth century give clear accounts of this. But it was not simply enemy movements that concerned the planners: they needed to have exact information about the state of the roads or tracks to be followed by the army, about the availability of water and fodder for the animals, and about the crossing points of rivers or the various defiles through the mountains that the army would have to negotiate.[135] In both cases, commanders were advised to send small parties well ahead of the main force to secure these against enemy action.[136] Especial emphasis was placed on the work and skills of the scouts sent out to check that water supplies were adequate along the route and those who planned and laid out the marching camps, the sites of which had to be chosen with regard to water, cover, defensibility and forage.[137]

If intelligence was a key prerequisite for an effective offensive campaign, advance raiding and the softening up of the enemy were equally important aspects of a campaign involving a siege or sieges. The commander was to make sure not only that the enemy forces posed no serious threat to his own troops, but also, by sending out frequent parties of raiders to pillage and harass the target regions, to make sure that no relief forces were concealed in the area which might surprise the Byzantine troops.[138] Thus Basil I raided extensively the countryside around Tephrike before attempting his first siege of the Paulician stronghold in the early 870s, and conducted similar operations in the regions of Germanikeia and Adata later in his reign – although he did not succeed in taking the latter towns himself.[139] Once again, the question of supplies and fodder for the army is a major preoccupation in all the treatises which deal with this topic, and is frequently referred to in the historians' accounts, as we have seen.

Siege warfare, both offensive and defensive, was recognized by Byzantine historians, generals and writers of military handbooks as an essential element of the empire's military effort. Without adequate defences many major fortresses could not have survived hostile attack, and the territory they controlled and hence the empire as a whole would the more easily have succumbed to the invasions and attacks which it had to confront throughout its history. Detailed accounts of the preparations necessary to withstand a siege are given in the military handbooks, and especially in the tenth-century *De obsidione toleranda*, "On resisting a siege". By the same token, the treatises also include information on how to carry out aggressive siege warfare and reduce enemy strongholds. East Roman siege techniques during this period were not especially sophisticated. The sources rarely give exact details or information about sieges, being content usually to describe the strength of the enemy fortress or city and the Byzantine tactics employed against it: cutting off its supplies, bombarding the garrison from a distance with siege engines of various types, and attempting to mine the walls so that storming parties could exploit the breach and force a passage for the main army. But it becomes clear that the chief weapon was starvation – it was far preferable to minimize one's own losses and starve an enemy out than engage in attacks which cost lives and which might more often than not be repulsed:

> The first thing the besieger should do, if possible, is to keep the necessities, such as food and water, from getting to the people within the walls. If the besieged possess these supplies in abundance, then it is necessary to resort to siege engines and to fighting.

This passage, from the late sixth-century *Strategikon*, epitomizes Byzantine siege craft. In turn, advice in the military treatises stresses the importance of storing sufficient supplies to outlast a siege, and of having a good water supply.[140] Although the military treatises describe various stratagems for outwitting the enemy, the use of sophisticated siege artillery plays a relatively minor role, and is not gone into in any detail – siege engines are listed, but few details are given, even in the tenth-century treatise on resisting sieges specifically devoted to the subject. Most treatises simply note that the reader either knows what they are like or can find out about them by looking in the treatises of the ancients.[141] Far more attention is devoted to methods of luring the enemy out of his defences, demoralizing or terrifying the besieged population, and causing factional strife among the population of the fortress or town under attack – and, by the same token, how to counter each of these when they are practised on the Romans.[142] Luring the enemy out of the fortress was clearly perceived as a practical way to shorten the siege and to limit the cost in human and material terms, and a classic example is to be found in Leo the Deacon's account of the battle before and siege of Tarsos. Arriving in the region of the city – the richest and, militarily, the mightiest fortress in Cilicia – the emperor Nikephros II established first of all a strongly fortified camp for his troops. The rich and fertile districts around the city were then devastated and, outraged by this treatment and convinced of their military strength, the Tarsiot army ventured out from its fortifications (which the emperor recognized were virtually impregnable, as the chronicler notes), to be heavily defeated and driven back into the town. The emperor then encircled the town, cut it off from any hope of relief, and within a short time had starved it into submission – a textbook operation, in fact![143] The emperor Michael IV achieved an even more rapid, albeit less significant, victory in the Balkans, when he similarly encouraged the garrison of the fortress of Bojana (southwest of Serdica/Sofia) to sally out. The Roman forces quickly put the Bulgar troops to flight, and were able to chase them right into the fortress which they captured. But the Romans might also be victims of the same ruse and Kekaumenos, who recounts this tale, warns the commander of a castle not to be misled by the enemy's tricks.[144]

Should these stratagems fail, then the treatises recommend an outright attack, but only once the appropriate preparatory work has been undertaken. Most attention is paid to digging saps, or tunnels, under the walls which, once completed and supported by wooden beams, were filled with combustibles and, at the appropriate time, set on fire: once the props had burned away, the tunnel collapsed, and the section of wall or tower above it collapsed, opening a breach in the walls. Perhaps the best-known ancient mine is that uncovered during the excavations of the Roman fortreess at Doura Europos (mod. Salihiya) on the Euphrates, taken by the Sassanids in AD 256; counter-mining was intended to cut off the enemy sapping activity before it became a danger – a good example is provided by Procopius' account of the Roman counter-sapping activities at the siege of Dara, and an excavated example comes from Doura Europos.[145] Nearly all the treatises, from the sixth century to the tenth, devote attention to this aspect of warfare, and it is stressed by Nikephros Ouranos that sapping, rather than the use of elaborate or complex siege machines as described by the ancients, was the chief means of reducing an enemy fortress if it could not be starved out or otherwise induced to surrender.[146]

Evidence from the histories and chronicles which recount the deeds of the generals and emperors of the period generally supports the prescriptions set out in the treatises. Making sure that the enemy was cut off from their supplies of food and water was obviously a first priority and several accounts note this: Michael II had a trench dug around the city of Adrianople in 823, for example, in order to force the surrender of the remaining supporters of Thomas the Slav. And make sure that your own force has adequate supplies – as noted already, Basil I's sieges of both Tephrike and Melitene failed because the cities in question were well provisioned whereas the besieging force ran out of supplies.[147] In particular, make sure that the besieging army is encamped at a suitable distance so that it cannot be attacked by surprise by an enemy sortie, and that it is properly defended with a trench and/or a palisade. Several cases illustrate the dangers associated with failing to observe these precautions, as when in 883, intending to besiege Tarsos, the commander Kestas Styppeiotes failed properly to site, entrench and defend his camp or set up a proper watch. The Tarsiots attacked by night, and using a ruse were able to inflict a substantial defeat on the otherwise superior Roman forces. When the general of the

Kibyrrhaiot and other thematic forces landed on Crete in 828, he defeated the Berber raiders who had established themselves there, but failed to set adequate watches or defend the camp properly afterwards. Sallying out at night while the Byzantine troops were still celebrating their victory, the Muslim forces inflicted a crushing defeat on them. Similar accounts appear in the *History* of Leo the Deacon, both in the eastern and Balkan theatre, during the wars of Phocas and Tzimiskes.[148] The wise general should also lay ambushes and devise strategems to draw the enemy out, and above all he should make sure that his own force is adequately supplied with all necessities, that scouts are posted to ensure that relieving forces cannot take it by surprise, and that there is a clear exit should the army be forced to raise the siege and withdraw. Such advice is repeated from treatise to treatise, and even within the same treatise, or chapter. If the enemy could not be induced to surrender, then an attack might be necessary, in which case artillery should be brought to bear and sapping employed.

Good positioning of artillery was important: if necessary, generals could build earth and timber embankments upon which to place stone-throwers or other projectors. This was clearly a technique practised right through the Byzantine period, for it is recorded by Vegetius, by Procopius (as used by both Persians and Romans), and by Kekaumenos in his account of Basil II's siege of the Bulgar fortress of Moreia, between Philippoupolis and Triaditza: in the last case, the Bulgars were able to sally out and penetrate the timber framework of the mound, set it on fire from within (so that the Romans failed to see what had happened) and destroy it. Assault ramps of earth reinforced by timber, stone or brickwork might also be employed: again, an outstanding example survives at the site of Doura Europos, where the Sassanid assault ramp is angled sufficiently for a wheeled siege tower to be moved up its length and still stands higher than the main curtain wall it was intended to attack. It is constructed of stamped earth and sun-baked brick revetments.[149] The accounts of the siege of Amida by the forces of the Persian king Kavadh in 502/3 describe the construction of a ramp of this sort, which the Roman defenders tunnelled into from inside their walls, carrying away the earth until it eventually collapsed, killing a number of defenders in the process.[150] Sometimes cities or fortresses could be taken by the most obvious means, although lack of diligence on the part of the guards or watchmen often played a role: the Bulgar tsar Symeon seized one Byzantine fortress by sending five of his soldiers disguised as workers and with axes concealed beneath their cloaks into the stronghold, where they were quite simply able to cut the hempen hinge supports on the gates, with the result that the garrison could not close them and keep the main force of Bulgars from rushing into the town.[151]

Attacking defended positions and beginning the process of tunnelling involved the use of a variety of protective devices. The most important, mentioned in treatises and texts throughout the Byzantine period up to the tenth century, were penthouses or "tortoises" (*chelonai*), wooden-framed sheds of varying sizes, some wheeled, others light and portable, roofed in wood, wicker or straw, covered in goats' hair mats or other cloth soaked in water to resist fire, and designed to resist arrows and spears or slingstones, the sturdier versions sufficiently sturdy to resist heavy stones or other objects dropped from the battlements. Tortoises were equipped with battering-rams, the size, weight and capability again determined by the size of the tortoise in which it was enclosed, and were also used to protect men equipped with picks and sledgehammers whose job was to attack the structure of the walls. From the tenth century a new term appears, *laisa*, a Slav word describing a light, portable, house-shaped structure of woven branches with a steep roof and several entrances covered by matting or wicker screens, again varying in size or dimensions and designed to protect the men carrying them or working behind or beneath them. They appear to have been similar to the screens called *vineae* employed in late Roman times and described, under this or other terms, by Vegetius and later writers such as Procopius and Agathias. These "recently devised" *laisai* appear to have been especially light and manageable, hence their frequent appearance during the tenth century and after during tunnelling operations, and seem in fact to replace the older tortoise, since they could also be used to conceal and screen the actions of a ram.[152]

Although the treatises which do go into technical detail about siege machinery give often quite complex descriptions, with illustrations, of the workings of the devices in question, there is very little evidence that the majority were really used. In the period from the fourth to sixth centuries the Roman army appears to have still disposed of the full panoply of siege machinery, including large wooden towers with rams and torsion-powered *ballistae* of various types. But it is likely that many of the devices listed in the Byzantine treatises, as well as appearing occasionally by name in the chronicles, may actually be no more than archaic repetition or literary *topoi*: as noted already, Nikephros Ouranos states explicitly that besieging armies rely principally on mining to destroy enemy defences, and Leo the Deacon's account of the siege of Chandax on Crete by Nikephros Phocas is copied from a similar description of a siege in Agathias.[153] Nevertheless, artillery certainly played a role: the expedition against Crete in 949 was equipped with an unspecified number of frame-mounted bow-ballistae, four large bolt-projectors, and eight stone-throwers, almost certainly trebuchets. Leo's *Tactica* has the army's infantry units accompanied by wagon-mounted field artillery, for example, and while this is copied directly from Maurice, the vocabulary used of the artillery pieces themselves suggests a contemporary reality.[154] By the same token, technical expertise, however transmitted, certainly continued to be available. In the early ninth century, for example, a disaffected Byzantine artillery engineer deserted to the Bulgars, taking with him a number of specialist skills. The Byzantines were aware of technical differences between themselves and certain of their enemies. Michael II was reluctant to construct siege engines when he was besieging Thomas the Slav in Adrianople in case his Bulgar allies should learn their secret. But by Basil II's time in the late tenth century the Byzantines recognized that the Bulgars had become experts in siege warfare.[155]

The extent to which siege towers were employed remains unclear. They appear in several sixth-century accounts of siege machinery (for example, the Roman siege of Amida in 503, the Persian siege of Martyropolis in 530, and Belisarius' siege of Rome). Twelve such towers are reported to have been constructed by the Avar besiegers of Constantinople in 626, and they appear again at the Avaro–Slav siege of Thessaloniki in the period 616–18. The list of equipment for the Cretan expedition of 949 mentions the various iron components for a "wooden tower", probably a siege tower with wheels, while an eleventh-century MS illumination shows a siege tower from which liquid fire is projected. Alexios I uses siege towers against the forces under Bryennios during the siege of Kastoria.[156] They occur, in other words, throughout the period from the sixth to the twelfth centuries. Islamic armies certainly employed similar devices while Crusader accounts show that the western soldiers were familiar with a wide variety of such devices. It is unlikely that the Byzantine army did not also employ them, even if it is often difficult to tell from the historical narrative sources whether or not the term *helepolis*, used to mean any kind of large siege engine, actually refers to siege towers proper.[157]

It is probable, therefore, that the comments of Nikephros Ouranos relate specifically to rapid campaigns in which heavy siege equipment would not normally be part of the army's baggage (for it is also apparent from references to siege towers that they were time-consuming to construct, and that most besieging commanders had only one or two at their disposal): the reliance upon the light, easily constructed *laisa* rather than the heavier wheeled penthouse or "tortoise", for example, supports the idea that the usual imperial field army would have to depend on sapping if it attacked an enemy fortress or city, and that major expeditions in which particular towns were specifically targeted would involve the heavier sort of siege equipment. The planning and preparation that went into the Cretan expedition, and the corresponding nature of the material listed in the documents in question (including the presence of only one wooden siege tower with its fittings), would support this.[158]

There is some interesting pictorial evidence of Byzantine (and other) armies involved in siege warfare, to be found in a twelfth-century illustrated manuscript of the *History* of John Skylitzes who describes the reigns of the emperors from the time of Michael I (811–13) to that of Constantine IX Monomachos (1042–55). The scenes depicting sieges usually show ladders being placed against the walls, the arrows and spears hurled by attackers and defenders, and in two cases the use of a traction powered (i.e. manually hauled) trebuchet. This was introduced from China via the Avars in the later sixth century, and appears to have been used by the Byzantines, and later the Arabs, until the twelfth century when the counterweight trebuchet was developed.[159]

Scaling the walls by means of ladders, tunnelling beneath and undermining the walls or inducing the enemy to surrender by starvation or other less violent means seem thus to have dominated the Byzantine siege repertory. Missile-projecting artillery and stone-throwing artillery were also used, of course, although the former are rarely mentioned in the chronicles, in contrast to the latter. The texts are somewhat vague about these devices, but it is clear from a document of the mid-tenth century, detailing the equipment employed in the attack on Crete in 949, that large and small frame-mounted or hand-held "bow-ballistae" – tension-powered weapons similar to the crossbow and descended from the *arcuballistae* of the later Roman period – were used. There is no evidence for the continued use of torsion-powered weapons which seem not to have survived the sixth century.[160] Apart from such weapons, there was also the notorious "liquid fire", an early type of napalm consisting apparently of crude oil (collected in the Caucasus and South Russian steppe, to one or both of which the Byzantines had regular access until the later twelfth century). Introduced during the later seventh century, this was primarily employed at sea, projected from tubes mounted in the bows or amidships on the larger warships of the imperial navy. It seems to have been effective when it was employed and certainly served as a terror-weapon, and in the early tenth century, a hand-held siphon seems to have been developed for use on land. But it must have been as dangerous to the Byzantines as to their enemies, and its exact form remains a mystery. Incendiary projectiles had been a standard element of siege warfare for millenia, of course, involving both the hurling of pots filled with combustibles as well as fire-arrows and similar devices. The liquid fire projectors were rather different, however, and the limited evidence suggests that they were a type of simple flame-thrower.[161]

It must be clear that the impact of the logistical arrangements described above, and of the constant presence of soldiers and their needs upon Byzantine society and economy as a whole, was enormous. In Chapter 7 I will examine some aspects of this in greater detail. But there remains one facet of the army in action – on the battlefield itself – which deserves treatment first. That is the subject of the next chapter.

CHAPTER SIX

The army at war: combat

It has been remarked by several historians and commentators on warfare, whether of ancient, medieval or modern, that descriptions of battles can rarely afford any real idea of what actually occurred during the different phases of a violent confrontation. In the first place, those involved, whether in positions of authority or not, rarely if ever know what is happening away from their own particular field of vision throughout the battle – they receive reports (which may or may not be accurate), they respond to the reports, they hear or experience the results, but the connection between orders and effects is impossible to trace exactly. Equally, there is inevitably a tendency to dramatize, to present things, for whatever reason, in a worse or better light, to exaggerate the results of the actions of particular individuals, together with the inevitably different views of what happened, and why, of those involved in, or observing, the fighting from different vantage points. Finally, there is also a tendency for those who win the battle to see the results in terms of their original assumptions or intentions, so that their version of events, and the causal relationships they assume, will be artificially neat and tidy, in contrast with the reality.

These factors are as pertinent to Byzantine literary sources, whether officially sanctioned (or commissioned) or not, as they are to those of any other period, and it is for the most part impossible to extract from a chronicle account of a battle any idea of what actually went on apart from a crudely generalized picture: "The imperial troops advanced with the cavalry in the centre; the enemy line held firm at first, but eventually gave way; the imperial reserve cavalry were then brought up and the enemy retreat turned into a rout. Many were slain on both sides." Such accounts are scattered through all the Byzantine histories and chronicles, but tell us very little of what individual soldiers experienced, how the enemy forces appeared to them or the nature of the hand-to-hand combat which was involved. Assuming a certain degree of descriptive accuracy, they may give us an idea of the use by one side or another of a particular formation, which can in turn tell us whether certain sorts of tactics were employed. The Byzantine military treatises lay down certain prescriptions about how to conduct a battle, and also offer a great deal of advice to the general on how to approach a wide range of tactical problems. But while we can show with some degree of certainty, for some periods of Byzantine history, that real commanders of armies in real situations did put these prescriptions into practice, battles remain – as they in reality were, and are – a zone of uncertainty. In this respect, the historian's efforts to find out how a battle was actually fought, as opposed to how we imagine it may have been fought on the basis of what the military treatises tell us was the "official" pattern, are mostly destined to remain guesswork and supposition.[1]

In the present chapter, therefore, I will attempt to provide sufficient detail from both narrative sources and technical manuals to paint a picture of how the Byzantine army fought its battles across this long period. But it will necessarily concentrate largely on preparations for, methods of organizing for and means of controlling fighting. The battles themselves must remain vague and even insubstantial accounts of what is without doubt one of the most traumatic experiences a human being can undergo.

General perspectives: infantry and cavalry from the sixth to tenth centuries

Late Roman order of battle

Until the later fourth century there is a consensus that Roman armies still consisted predominantly of infantry units, with cavalry employed chiefly in the role of scouts, flank and rear guard, to attempt, or threaten, the enemy flank, and to exploit and then follow up any weakness or retreat of units in the enemy line. Roman tactics revolved around the heavy infantry, who formed both the main battle line, and whose auxiliaries – slingers, archers, javelin-men – functioned as light-armed troops. Cavalry remained ancillary to these functions. Even after the introduction of more, and more heavily armed, mounted units from the later third century, this basic pattern hardly changes.

The relative increase in the importance of cavalry seems in fact to have been fairly late, contrary to assumptions usually made. Most of the limited evidence for the later fourth and fifth centuries shows that the proportion of cavalry to infantry did not increase dramatically as a result of the defeat at Adrianople, but on the contrary, remained much the same – at Strasbourg, Julian had some 3,000 cavalry and 10,000 infantry, and over a century later in 478 a field army in the east is reported to have consisted of 30,000 infantry and 8,000 cavalry. The proportion of mounted to foot soldiers is certainly greater than in a legionary army of the first century, but cavalry are still by no means either the dominant or the key element in late Roman armies of this period.[2] Adrianople is usually named as the defining moment at which heavy cavalry decisively proved their superiority over infantry and ushered in the new age of mounted warfare.[3] Yet the Gothic victory resulted not from some dramatic superiority of cavalry over infantry, but rather from the simple facts that the emperor Valens received incorrect information about the numbers of the Gothic force, and that a substantial detachment of Gothic horsemen joined the battle after the main Roman line was committed, were able to take it by surprise in the flank and roll up the whole formation upon itself. This is not to minimize the impact of the defeat (which was clearly expressed by Ammianus); nor is it to ignore both the gradual adoption of a heavier panoply by Roman cavalry units, as well as the creation of some new heavy cavalry units, during the later third, fourth and fifth centuries.

But there is plenty of evidence throughout this period and well after Adrianople that Roman infantry were able to hold off and defeat barbarian cavalry, and that the proportion of cavalry to infantry units remained approximately the same for the next century: roughly 1 : 3 in numbers of units, but far fewer in absolute numbers of men, since the unit sizes in the cavalry were smaller.[4] Within the Roman cavalry there was an increase from the late third to the early fifth century in the numbers of very heavily armoured units, and it has been calculated that by the time of the *Notitia Dignitatum*, a late fourth/ early fifth century document giving the order of battle of the eastern and western armies, heavy armoured cavalry (*cataphracti* and *clibanarii*) made up some 15 per cent of the *comitatenses* cavalry, in comparison with lancers and other heavy cavalry (61 per cent) and light cavalry (24 per cent). Yet there were in turn more of these cavalry units assigned to the *limitanei* than to the field armies, which suggests strongly that cavalry were still regarded throughout the fourth and fifth centuries as most valuable in scouting and patrolling, or covering the wings and flanks of a mainly infantry army.[5]

But Roman infantry no longer differed substantively in their arms and armour from their barbarian counterparts. During the third century at the latest the adoption of a somewhat lighter panoply for regular infantry units (in comparison with the classic legionary equipment) seems to have been completed, corresponding to a change in infantry training and tactics. The combat engineering skills of the heavy infantry of the first centuries BC and AD are concentrated in a few specialist units, for example, while the emphasis moves away from the highly trained individual, fighting within a distinctive tactical sub-unit, to the infantryman as one of a mass, whose effectiveness depended not on individual skills so much as on unit coherence. The change corresponds in the archaeological picture to the adoption of the Germanic *spatha* and the greater diversity of weaponry within each tactical unit, as described, in fact, by Vegetius. The chief qualities which now distinguished Roman infantry from their foes were tactical discipline and training in close-order drill and battlefield manoeuvring, together with the heavier personal armour – mostly mail – of those soldiers selected to serve in the first ranks of the battle line. This certainly gave Roman infantry a continued advantage in most contexts over their barbarian enemies in the European and Balkan theatres. And there seems little doubt that the increasing significance of cavalry during the second half of the third century parallels and is causally related to these changes.[6]

The development of heavily armoured cavalry was a response to the use of similar mounted shock troops in the east, especially following the defeats suffered at the hands of Sassanid armies from the middle of the third century. But such armoured mounted units were not intended to replace, but rather to supplement the usual cavalry formations, generally on the flanks, and to stiffen the main battle line of the Roman army, still composed of disciplined and well-trained infantry, and thus served to neutralize the equivalent forces on the enemy side. They certainly neither replaced the basic infantry order of battle, nor did they function as the main battle arm. Indeed, the mass of both the Parthian and Sassanid armies were light horse archers or infantry, the heavy cavalry representing a noble elite which was relatively limited in numbers. And even against the Sassanid heavy cavalry (and once the lessons of the third-century defeats had been learned), disciplined Roman infantry formations, correctly handled, held their own, and could on occasion move out against cavalry which had not charged in order to reduce the effects of the enemy archery.[7]

The sixth century

That Roman battlefield tactics continued well into the sixth century to regard well-trained and disciplined infantry as essential – whether or not they were the majority of the troops involved – is clear from several sources. First, there was great concern voiced by a number of authorities precisely on the question of discipline in the ranks – this is a major issue raised in the introduction to the late sixth-century *Strategikon*; it recurs in comments of the slightly earlier chroniclers Menander Protector and John of Ephesus. Indiscipline seems to have become increasingly common from the 530s onwards, a reflection of irregular payments as well as alienation between officers and men. The sources provide many instances.[8] We read frequently of officers reintroducing strict order and discipline; and Roman commanders themselves referred to Roman discipline as the quality that set them apart from and gave them an advantage over their adversaries. Both Belisarius and Narses, in speeches attributed to them, referred to the traditional high standards of Roman discipline and efficiency.[9] Attention to drill and manoeuvres is also referred to in the narrative sources, whether on the eastern or western fronts, although a distinction between infantry and cavalry is rarely drawn.[10]

Second, the few detailed descriptions we have of major battles show infantry continuing to play an important role. At the Roman defeat at Kallinikon in 531, where infantry drawn up on the wing formed a less numerous element than the cavalry in the battle line, they defeated a frontal heavy cavalry assault. At Taginae (Busta Gallorum) in 551/2 infantry formed the centre of the main Roman line, and Procopius emphasizes the discipline and order of the Roman troops, drawn up in their ranks and columns by squadron or regiment, both in this battle and in the battle of Mons Lactarius the follow-ing year. At the battle on the Casilinus river, Agathias describes the classical Roman battle line of the late Roman period, as discussed also in Vegetius: the infantry formed the main battle line, drawn up in serried ranks, the front rank consisting of the most heavily armed and armoured soldiers with the lighter troops behind them. The discipline and training of the Roman formation is illustrated by the fact that, while the Frankish charge succeeds in pushing through the line, the troops do not break but fall back around the gap, allow-ing the reserve infantry – made up of allied Heruli – to counter-charge and the line to reform, while at the same time, the Roman mounted units on the flanks, equipped with both spears and bows, are able to outflank the enemy wedge and break it up with concentrated archery. A similar description occurs for the Roman infantry line in an engagement during the eastern wars in 556/7 (well-armoured Roman troops advancing with linked shields).[11]

Discipline and order were key components of the Roman infantry forma-tion frequently singled out by commentators. And while allowing for a degree of rhetoric and ideological bias, there are enough references to the contrast be-tween Roman orderliness and the disorder of their foes (and sometimes their allies) to suggest that there was indeed a real difference. In the fighting against both Moors and Vandals in North Africa, against the Goths in Italy, as well as against the formidable Sassanid armies, contemporaries refer on several occasions to the discipline and order of the Roman forces, both infantry and cavalry, in contrast with their opponents. Theophylact Simocatta compares the Roman and Persian forces cooperating in the Persian civil war in 591: the Romans were disciplined, ordered, calm; they displayed "ordered cohesion", and saved their foolhardy allies from a defeat when the latter, having been routed by the enemy, were compelled to withdraw behind the Roman line which protected them and threw the enemy back. Theophylact recounts a similar tale, in which the steady infantry line saves the retreating Roman cavalry during the wars against the Avars.[12] Procopius records an incident from the Gothic war in which Belisarius is taken to task by members of his own retinue for not trusting his infantry. Although too few in numbers to be drawn up in the main battle line, it is nevertheless pointed out that their poor fighting record immediately beforehand was due to their bad officers who, as the only mounted soldiers in their formation, tended to run away before battle was joined, thus quite naturally totally demoralizing the men who broke easily when attacked.[13] In terms of numbers, too, infantry remain a substantial element: in the invasion of Vandal Africa, for example, Belisarius' army was made up of 10,000 foot and 5,000 horse, even though the infantry played for the most part a secondary role in the two main battles.

Although there is no persuasive indication that infantry had declined in importance by the end of the fifth century, this evidence does suggest that infantry discipline and order was a frequent cause of concern in the middle of the sixth century and afterwards. Belisarius was clearly sceptical of the steadiness of his infantry on two occasions in different theatres, suggesting that there was more than just a local issue here, while the speeches put into the mouths of both Belisarius and the Persian leader Firuz at Daras in 530 allude to the usual weakness and lack of order among the Roman infantry. In addition, there is no doubt that the emphasis does swing towards cavalry by the later sixth century, and there appear to be several reasons for this.

In the first place, while the empire had relied on allied mounted troops for a number of specialized roles – especially horse archers – during the fifth and first half of the sixth centuries, it is clear from Procopius' account of the contemporary Roman cavalry soldier that Roman traditions and styles of mounted fighting were beginning to alter as a result of such contacts, and that the Romans were themselves training their mounted troops in such skills. That the numbers of such composite archer-lancer units was probably quite small is suggested by the fact that, while the advantage accruing to the Romans from their archery in respect of the Goths in Italy is emphasized, they do not seem to achieve parity with the Persians, even if Roman archery was, bow for bow, more effective than the Persian, as Procopius claims. Indeed, massed Persian archery remains a problem for Roman forces throughout.[14]

In the second place, the nature of much of the warfare of the middle years of the sixth century – the reign of Justinian – demanded armies that could move rapidly, confront equally mobile enemies, bring them to battle or harass them, and then move again to take up new dispositions elsewhere. This is especially true of the Italian and North African wars where, although infantry continued to play a key role – obviously in respect of garrison and related duties, but also in the line of battle – warfare assumed a guerrilla aspect to which rapidly moving cavalry were well suited. The accounts of battles in both Procopius and Agathias often give cavalry the main role (particularly in view of the versatility as both shock- and missile-troops ascribed to them by Procopius), and the reinforcements which arrive from time to time are frequently disproportionately of cavalry. This was also true of the later sixth-century warfare against the Avars in the Balkans, where again infantry continue to play a role, but where the account of Theophylact, the main narrator for these events, frequently implies that cavalry played the dominant role (as one might expect in a highly mobile war against a mounted nomadic people).[15] It seems often to have been the case that either cavalry forces fought with minimal or no infantry support, or that infantry acted merely as a reserve and a protective wall for retreating cavalry. This was certainly so at Ad Decimum and Tricamerum (535) in Africa and at battles in the Gothic war already noted. It seems to have been even more the case by the 570s and afterwards: at Melitene in 575, at the battle on the Nymphios in 583, at Solachon in 586, on the Araxes in 589, as well as in a series of victories won by the general Priscus along the Danube in 600 and in Heraclius' campaigns against the Persians in the years 622–6.[16]

In the third place, there is a good deal of evidence to suggest that the empire recruited substantial numbers of new cavalry units during the sixth century, thus altering the overall balance between the two arms. Evagrius reports, for example, that Tiberius Constantine recruited large numbers of cavalry from among various barbarian and indigenous peoples in 575/6 ("squadrons of excellent cavalry"), and it is probably at this point that the new formation of the Optimates (see above) was established. If so, this suggests a substantial increase in mounted units, and given the composition of the praesental armies which later made up most of the forces in the Opsikion region, cavalry now began to dominate the field armies of the empire: indeed, the latter division included also the Bucellarii, an elite brigade established also during the second half of the sixth century also consisting of mounted units.[17] Apart from these (they may have numbered from 2,000 to 3,000), other cavalry units were raised at the same time, while already for Justinian's reign there is good evidence for the establishment of new mounted units along traditional lines – five units of Vandal cavalry (presumably lancers) were established from among the prisoners taken during Belisarius' African campaign; similarly, units of Persian and Armenian cavalry are found, as well as of Ostrogothic cavalry (posted to the eastern front). Other units, of heavy cavalry and *clibanarii* as well as of light cavalry/ archers, seem to have been formed during the fifth and early sixth century.[18]

The increased emphasis upon cavalry was, therefore, a fifth- and especially a sixth-century response to a change in the empire's overall strategic situation, a response which may well have increased in pace from the middle years of the sixth century. Yet while the emphasis in the tactical formations and battlefield situations discussed in the *Strategikon* is placed upon the cavalry, the chapter dealing with combating barbarian and foreign peoples makes it quite clear that infantry continue to play an important role. The chapter on infantry formations, devoted specifically to this arm, begins by noting that infantry training and discipline have been greatly neglected in recent times, and that the purpose of the section is to redress the balance. The point is reinforced by the section on infantry tactics in the mid-sixth-century anonymous treatise on strategy, which merely paraphrases a number of ancient authorities and describes in effect a Macedonian phalanx rather than any formation employed in East Roman armies.[19] Yet at the same time this treatise views cavalry primarily as a screen in front of the main infantry battle line, or as flank cover or pursuit troops.

This apparent emphasis on cavalry, which in fact takes the infantry more or less for granted, actually suggests an effort to ensure that Roman commanders take cavalry more seriously into account in the strategic context for which the *Strategikon* was written – against the Slavs, and more particularly the nomadic Avars. In the latter text, for example, while the emphasis on cavalry formations is clear, only one chapter (Chapter III) actually assumes that cavalry alone are involved. The other chapters deal with mixed formations, with sieges (in which infantry would normally play the central role) or with contexts in which cavalry would as a matter of course be employed against an enemy such as the Avars – surprise raids into enemy territory, ambushes and related undertakings. The author of the *Strategikon* also notes that mounted troops should anyway be dismounted and fight as infantry wherever the situation demands, as occurred at Solachon near Mardin in 586.[20]

Infantry were thus by no means an insignificant element in late Roman armies of the sixth and first half of the seventh centuries. In the wars with the Persians, whose own infantry were often quite numerous (if not particularly well-trained),[21] as well as in the Balkans, infantry could not be ignored: in some situations they were essential. It was infantry units who carried out garrison duties, manning both major defensive installations as well as minor outposts and fortlets. In addition, much of the fighting in the densely wooded and hilly Balkan regions depended upon infantry, particularly when opposing the tactics of the various Slav tribes which the *Strategikon* describes. Ambushes were usually carried out and defiles had to be held or seized by troops on foot, and difficult tracks and pathways that could not be followed by mounted troops were accessible only to infantry. And where battles had to be fought in difficult terrain, it was advised that cavalry units be dismounted and drawn up in infantry formation to make the best use of the available resources.[22] In a number of battles, infantry seem to have formed up in a solid line behind the cavalry units, acting as both a reserve and as a defensive wall behind which the cavalry could shelter. There are still examples of infantry formations forming up in solid ranks with linked shields to drive an already retreating force back,[23] but the general tendency by the early seventh century would thus seem to be one in which infantry are increasingly passive and defensive, serving both as a reserve once the enemy has been repulsed or turned and a safe haven for defeated or withdrawing Roman cavalry units.

Infantry in the line of battle c. 640–900

Delbrück asserted uncompromisingly that a disciplined infantry was non-existent in the Byzantine world.[24] Yet neither the Persian nor the Arab wars were conducive to any sudden transfer of attention away from infantry towards cavalry. Infantry continued to play an important role in the battles fought against the early Islamic armies, which were themselves made up predominantly of infantry, troops whose use of camels and horses gave them greater mobility than their foes but who fought for the most part on foot.[25] But thereafter the highly mobile nature of the warfare which dominated Byzantine–Arab relations gave the Arab mounted infantry an advantage over traditionally outfitted Roman infantry. Byzantine tactics and strategy had to respond to the nature of the threat from the raiders, and the fact that those contingents from the main field armies of the second half of the seventh and the eighth centuries were referred to as *kaballarika themata* – "cavalry armies" – illustrates the nature of the reaction. The empire certainly continued to employ infantry, and they continue to appear in the sources – when the types of troops involved are specified at all – in their traditional role. Infantry units played an important part in the campaign against the Bulgars in 678/9, for example, and in the guerrilla warfare along the eastern frontier in the later ninth and tenth centuries (and presumably before this) were a recognized element of the provincial armies in official and semi-official sources. But here, their role was confined primarily to guard-post duties, garrisoning forts and watchtowers situated at key points, or waiting in ambush for enemy forces shepherded along before the pursuing cavalry units.[26]

Leo's *Tactica* makes it clear that infantry – both heavy and light troops – continued to function, and they are assigned a role in the mixed tactical formation he goes on to describe. Although derived from the *Strategikon*, the information has nevertheless been brought up to date to a degree.[27] What Leo tells us, however, does not give us much information on the real degree of participation of infantry in the Byzantine armies of the period. Infantry certainly played a role in the wars against both Bulgars and Arabs during the campaigns of the eighth and ninth centuries, but the vast majority of descriptions of battles for the period *c.* 650–800 which appear in the narrative historical sources make virtually no mention of them. Perhaps more significantly, the few technical references to types of provincial soldiery which date to the period before the middle of the tenth century make no mention of them either. An account drawn from ninth-century information describing provincial field armies mustered to meet the emperor on their way to campaign in Syria assumes that they are composed of cavalry; official and semi-official regulations about the minimum property required for the maintenance of soldiers refer only to regular thematic cavalry or to sailors of the provincial fleets. Infantry are not classed, in this context, as soldiers at all.[28]

This absence is at first sight surprising, but reflects perhaps two features of the evolution of Byzantine tactics up to the tenth century. First was the nature of the thematic armies themselves, whose increasingly seasonal campaigning, localized recruitment and physical dispersal were not conducive, were indeed antithetical, to the maintenance of line infantry discipline and order. Infantry of this type were not suited to formal battlefield formations and manoeuvres, although garrison duties and irregular skirmishing warfare in broken country, lying in wait for hostile forces, would have been within their competence.

Secondly, when we have evidence, this is precisely what we find the thematic infantry doing. Although the numbers of the standing forces in each district are unknown – perhaps 4,000 or more in the larger *themata* as Leo's *Tactica* prescribes – the occasional references to the *epilektoi* of each *thema* make it clear that these are usually cavalry.[29] And while this limited material shows that much of the provincial cavalry suffered similar defects to the infantry in respect of organizational discipline, the nature of warfare – raids, harassment of invaders and so forth – inevitably gave them greater prominence, significance and importance. Yet the author of the treatise on skirmishing or guerrilla warfare notes on several occasions that the enemy cannot be defeated without an adequate force of Roman infantry to press home attacks on their encampments, occupy the defiles and ambush the withdrawing enemy columns, and so on.[30] This reflects the fact that the attacking forces themselves were often composed of large numbers of infantry, which made their raids the more dangerous, since they were better able to pursue the rural population to their fastnesses, pillage and ravage their villages and homesteads, and resist Roman cavalry attacks on their encampments.[31]

Moreover, the nature of the warfare adopted deliberately by the East Roman government in the period from c. 640 until well into the eighth century – avoiding direct confrontation wherever possible – will not have promoted battlefield confidence, tactical cohesion and discipline, especially among infantry units, a tendency which will further have reduced their relevance and effectiveness in battlefield contexts. The treatise on skirmishing warfare, although written in the second half of the tenth century, reflects quite clearly the traditional form of warfare which had dominated the eastern frontier in the second half of the ninth century and up until shortly before the time of writing. Thus it becomes quite clear that the regular thematic infantry were regarded as potentially unreliable, undisciplined and easily demoralized. They would attack an enemy camp when ordered to do so less because they were brave soldiers than because they were eager for booty; they were slow moving and might hold up the commander's main operation; in line-of-battle, in an attack upon an enemy formation, for example, cavalry soldiers and officers were to be drawn up in their rear to ensure they pressed home the attack, maintained order and did not try to flee. The commander had to be attentive to their morale, encouraging them before any combat with harangues, promises of rewards and so forth, to keep them from melting away.[32] The mass of the infantry were slow and difficult to muster in time, and relatively poorly equipped: the heavy infantry were equipped with shields and spears, light troops with bows, javelins or slings, although they could also be sent on ahead with cavalry units and were regarded as more useful in this type of warfare.[33] The general impression is thus that infantry seem to have had very low status compared with mounted troops, and the loss of his horse was a social as well as a disciplinary disaster for the cavalryman, especially if he then had to serve with the infantry.[34]

Nevertheless, they continued to play a role, sometimes an important one. Thus we read of the involvement of the Roman heavy infantry alongside the cavalry during a campaign in southern Italy in the 880s, for example, and the campaigns led by Basil I in the 870s against both Arabs and Paulicians in eastern Anatolia involving the besieging and capture of fortresses and other strongholds cannot have been carried out without a substantial force of effective infantry.[35] While Leo's account in the *Tactica* of the armament of the heavy infantry is drawn from that of the *Strategikon* of Maurice, and is unlikely to have applied to the average peasant conscript, certain details not given in the older treatise suggest an attempt to describe contemporary arms: the large, round shields, for example, as well as the battleaxes, which do not appear in the *Strategikon*. More realistically, where both the *Tactica* and the mid-tenth-century *Sylloge taktikon* prescribe either mail or lamellar armour (the lamellar of either iron or horn), and if this is not possible then padded garments of cotton or coarse silk, the later treatise ascribed to the emperor Nikephros II Phocas, the *Praecepta militaria*, lists only the latter. Given that far greater attention was paid to the heavy infantry at this time than in Leo's time or earlier, it seems that the infantry were expected to possess only the most basic, and least costly, protective equipment.[36] It should also be borne in mind that the relationship of infantry to cavalry in Leo's *Tactica* reflects the balance in the *Strategikon* of Maurice on which it was based, and this may not necessarily reflect the actual situation of the period after the first half of the seventh century. But Basil I (867–86) is also credited with a major effort to improve the efficiency of the army, inaugurating better training than had apparently been the case before his reign, and the possibility that he was responsible for an improvement in infantry training, effectiveness and status should not be discounted.[37]

The fate of the East Roman infantry after the middle of the seventh century thus reflected the empire's overall strategic and political-military situation during the period after the first Arab conquests, and, to a degree, the shifts in social relations in the provinces that these changes stimulated. It produced, in effect, a vicious circle of declining discipline and battlefield effectiveness, on the one hand, coupled with an increasing need for an irregular infantry force in ambuscades, garrison and guard duties, and so forth, and a correspondingly decreasing ability to function effectively as battlefield troops. That this was indeed the case is suggested by the efforts made by the generals of the middle of the tenth century to revive a proper, heavy line infantry element in their armies. We will return to this below.

Preparing for battle

As we have seen in an earlier chapter, avoidance of battle was an integral part of Byzantine field strategy, both in the hit-and-run warfare of the frontier which characterized the eastern theatre until the middle of the tenth century, and in larger-scale campaigning. Until the odds were clearly in favour of the Byzantine commander and his forces the military handbooks stressed that combat should be avoided wherever possible. But while the sources often give reasonably detailed accounts of the course of a particular campaign, they very rarely offer any detail of battles, although they sometimes provide a few descriptive remarks on a particular event – as when, for example, the emperor Theophilos was cut off from his guards at the battle of Anzen, near Dazimon, in 838, and had to cut his way through the Turk horse archers of the enemy forces to make good his escape.[38]

The military treatises give us a good deal of information about the preparations to be made before battle was joined and the tactical ploys that were to be put into practice when various circumstances applied and in the context of fighting enemies of varying cultural and military-technological background. The extent to which these tactical prescriptions were actually applied at any given time is difficult to know, since chroniclers' accounts of battles are not usually precise or clear enough to make the connection. But it has been shown that in the tenth and eleventh centuries at least the military treatises were indeed followed by a majority of commanders (and that it was assumed that they would be followed) in matters such as order of march, logistical arrangements, setting up and deploying out of marching camps, and so forth; it has also been shown that the tactics developed by Nikephros II in the 950s and 960s, accurately described in the so-called *Military Precepts* of that emperor, were followed by his subordinates and successors.[39] On the other hand, much of the information about battle order in some of the treatises relates quite clearly to Roman or Hellenistic practice and theory, so that without corroborating information it is difficult to know to what extent Byzantine commanders actually employed the tactical formations which are described, and to what extent they merely used these collections as precedents and general guidelines. That they were indeed used and read quite widely, certainly in the tenth and eleventh centuries, there is no doubt. Ninth- and tenth-century emperors were advised to take some with them, although it is interesting that Roman manuals, rather than any contemporary works, are listed; Basil II is reported to have perfected his generalship and soldierly skills both through the perusal of such literature and personal experience; the writer and general Kekaumenos recommended their use explicitly, and in a typically Byzantine combination of reading matter: "When you have free time, and are not occupied with military affairs [or: the business of a general], read strategic works and books, histories and the books of the Church", while the general John Doukas similarly is known to have been greatly interested in them. Andronikos Doukas, his son, is reported to have been equally well-read in such matters. Incidental evidence suggests that in many cases commanders attempted to compensate for the predictable confusion and slowness of communications in battle by drawing up appropriate battle plans in advance. Thus for the 1060s the emperor Romanos IV is reported by an eyewitness to have assembled his generals and gone over the battle plans before the confrontation at Mantzikert, tactical plans were discussed before the battle with the Hungarian forces in the campaign of 1167, and the emperor Michael IV's expedition against the Bulgar rebels in 1040 is described as following the proper rules of strategy, advancing in the correct order, pitching camp according to the regulation method, and so on. In contrast, the same writer notes that another general failed to halt and take stock of the situation, or to draw up any battle plan at all, and was heavily defeated as a result.[40]

The preparations before battle are described in detail in several treatises, notably the *Strategikon* of Maurice, the *Tactica* of Leo VI and the *Praecepta* of Nikephros II, and while the measures are more or less the same – commonsense precautions, in fact – in all three cases, the *Tactica* of Leo follows its model the *Strategikon* very closely. The prerequisite for battle was an appropriately advantageous situation for the Romans, since it was assumed that battle would always be avoided where this had not been secured. Whether this lay in greater numbers, a superior position with adequate supplies, good defences, surprise or a combination of these elements depended upon the particular circumstances. But given these, then the commander was to make sure in the first instance that his lines of retreat were secure and that his camp could withstand an attack should his troops be driven back. This also involved ensuring in particular adequate water and forage for the horses, as well as the security of the camp during the battle.[41] All the while, of course, scouts should be in constant visual contact with the enemy, preferably not being seen themselves, so that the commander was informed up to the last minute as to the enemy's movements and possible intentions. When marching out to battle, scouts and light troops should be deployed ahead of the main body, the field of battle itself should be thoroughly reconnoitred for possible traps or ambushes, while he himself should select places appropriate to such actions should they be deemed necessary. Cavalry troops should be accompanied by the minimum of baggage, and remounts should be taken only for a small number of men – the rest were to be left securely in the camp and under guard. Enough provisions should be taken for man and horse for the duration of the action, with a reserve in case some soldiers should become separated from their units. Spare weapons and arrows for bows should be taken on pack-animals and accompany the units to their first positions.[42]

Once these basic requirements had been met, the general should issue orders to the division and unit commanders about the coming action, and determine the order of march and the initial deployment. The treatises offer a variety of deployments for infantry divisions, for cavalry forces and for mixed armies, with recommendations as to when they should be employed, how the different elements were to be coordinated, where the commander should establish his position, and how the orders are to be communicated (by flag, horn or by messenger). Particular stress was placed on the maintenance of discipline if the enemy was driven back, so that no hasty pursuit should take place which might lead into an ambush. Equally, the tactic of false retreat or panic is described and the conditions suitable for its use, the preparations that needed to be taken beforehand and so forth. There are many examples in the sources, both of Roman troops employing a feigned retreat to ambush the enemy – as in Narses' campaign in Italy in 553/4, for example, where 300 Roman troops defeat 2,000 Franks employing this tactic, or, as in 1070 and with less disciplined or inexperienced troops, units under Manuel Komnenos fighting the Seljuk Turks rashly pursued the apparently retreating enemy, only to fall into an ambush and be cut to pieces. The tactic is described particularly clearly by Leo the Deacon for the year 970, when the general Bardas Phocas, sent to face the Rus' and their steppe allies, the Pechenegs, who had crossed the imperial frontier, realized he could not face such a large force directly. He devised a plan whereby one of his commanders, John Alkasseus, would march up to the Pecheneg division of the enemy force, appear to be taken by surprise, and fall back in feigned panic. Bardas had meanwhile laid an ambush, and when the Pecheneg forces fell into the trap they were completely routed.[43]

Following the model established by Hellenistic and Roman military writers, Byzantine military texts offer a full range of advice to the general. But in each of the three handbooks referred to – as well as in those which dealt less specifically with battlefield situations, such as the later tenth-century treatises on campaign organization or on skirmishing warfare – the contemporary situation is taken into account, sometimes in great detail. In all the theatres in which Roman forces were engaged, their tactics needed to take account of the different styles of fighting and tactical traditions of the peoples with whom they were dealing, and the *Strategikon* is eloquent testimony to the importance which Roman tactical thinking attached to understanding one's enemy properly. The same sentiments were repeated in the *Tactica* of Leo VI and the later eleventh-century *Strategikon* of Kekaumenos. Both the *Strategikon* and Leo's *Tactica* describe the tactics, customs and fighting styles of several barbarian peoples neighbouring the empire, for example, and although Leo again derives much of what he has to say from Maurice, he does attempt to update the information to take account of more recent developments. During the days preceding battle the commander should endeavour to collect and verify as much information as possible about enemy intentions, numbers and dispositions, through spies and scouts, enemy deserters and captured soldiers. Familiarity with the terrain was essential: only where it was favourable to the Roman forces should battle be offered.

Maurice's *Strategikon* dealt in detail with four such peoples: the Persians, the "Scythians" (Avars, Turks and other Hunnish peoples), the "Light-Haired peoples" (Franks, Lombards and others) and the Slavs and Antes. In each case, a caricature of the cultural make up of the people or peoples in question opens the chapter, accompanied by a series of explanations for their behaviour and moral constitution which precedes the details of their tactical arrangements and usual battle formation. But each such description is accompanied by suggestions for the best ways with which to counter and defeat the enemy formation, and in both treatises, however much Leo depends upon his sixth-century exemplar, the need to know and to understand one's enemy, and especially not to underestimate him, is quite clearly expressed. It has been observed, however, that although it is not the first treatise to note that the Romans should be familiar with the tactics of their enemies, the *Strategikon* is nevertheless the first to go into such detail, and this reflects in part the fact that the fighting methods in question had already become part of the late Roman tradition, and in part the fact that they reflected, so to speak, the two or three "models" of tactical and battlefield organization which the commander of a Roman army could opt to employ.[44] Thereafter it is the treatise on guerrilla strategy and tactics which provides the most detailed account of how to deal with the enemy along the eastern front, while the manual on campaign organization describes warfare in the Balkans, although in this case enemy tactics are only discussed in terms of generalizations about not falling into ambushes, and related topics.[45]

Once battle was imminent, the troops were enjoined to remain as silent as possible while drawn up in their ranks – the idea being that the enemy would be unnerved by the utter silence and discipline of the Roman lines (that this was indeed practised on occasion is clear from a description given by Theophylact

Simocatta of a battle fought between Romans with Persian allies against Persian rebel forces in 591). Leo's *Tactica* maintains the same injunction.[46] They had already had their standards blessed by the clergy accompanying the army, and may also have participated in holy liturgy to purify their souls and to pray for victory. The war cry had been shouted on leaving camp. According to Maurice's *Strategikon*, clergy and officers were to shout "Kyrie eleeson" (Lord have mercy), and the men were to shout three times in response, unit by unit, "Deus nobiscum" (God with us), as they left the camp. Once drawn up in their positions, no unnecessary movements were to be undertaken, soldiers and subordinate officers were to await the orders to advance and be prepared to resist the enemy's attack in the appropriate manner (according to whether it was by arrow, frontal assault or whatever). Only when they were on the point of clashing with enemy soldiers was the battle-cry to be shouted again, in an attempt to unnerve the enemy. In practice, of course, the use of a battle-cry or war chant depended very much on the circumstances – there are several examples of soldiers who, having secretly been able to surround an enemy force, were then encouraged before the attack to make the maximum noise in terms of both regular war cries, trumpet blasts and drum beats, and blood-curdling yells to terrify the enemy, especially if the Romans were fewer in number, and this is something which the treatises also recommend. Thus the smaller Roman force terrified the Paulician army encamped at Bathys Ryax before charging down from the surrounding hills to annihilate it in 878, while as his troops marched in dense line-of-battle order against the enemy, John Tzimiskes ordered a similar effect to cowe the Rus' forces at Preslav in 970.[47] Other war cries were also used, of course: for the battle in 878, the soldiers cried in unison "the Cross has conquered". In the middle of the tenth century, the troops were instructed to utter a slightly different variant: "Lord Jesus Christ, our God, have mercy on us. Amen".[48] The extent to which these battle-cries were employed across the whole army is difficult to ascertain: particularly where non-Christian allies or mercenaries were involved, for example, or even more clearly in the case of Muslim auxiliaries or mercenaries (as in the later eleventh and twelfth centuries, when the empire employed considerable numbers of Turk soldiers), it is unlikely that the obviously Christian war cries were demanded from any but the indigenous Byzantine soldiers.

As we shall see, maintaining order even when the enemy had been defeated was regarded as essential, and numerous examples of defeats where the enemy had suddenly turned on a disorganized rabble of pursuing troops are found in the narrative histories. Equally, preventing troops from running off to sack the enemy camp or chase booty was a major concern. In both cases, severe punishments were prescribed for such dereliction of duty; the military treatises insist on these points repeatedly, as they insist upon the fair distribution of booty in an orderly manner after victory has been secured. Again, the historical accounts of the period provide examples (as they do also of the anger and mutinous response provoked by an unfair distribution of booty).[49]

Battlefield formations and field tactics

The hallmark of Roman and Byzantine field tactics was the ordered line of battle – again and again both the military treatises and the narrative histories stress the impact of Roman order on the enemy host.[50] The basic formation for Byzantine armies from the later sixth century onwards was, according to the military handbooks, a tripartite line – left, centre and right – with flank-guards and outflanking units on the left and right wings respectively, and with a second line and a third, reserve line, behind the front line. The general himself should have a small reserve attached to his person, which could be despatched as appropriate to strengthen the attack or the defence. Units could also be concealed behind the flank of the first or second line, both to cover these from an outflanking move or an ambush, as well as to sweep around the enemy's line to take them in the rear. In the later sixth century, the relative strength of the different categories of unit was reflected in the depth of their line: thus the elite cavalry units of the Optimates had a depth of 5–7, those of the *vexillationes* and Illyrikianoi 7–8, whereas the regular cavalry were to be 10 deep. The distances between the lines, and at which the army should draw up to face the enemy, were multiples of the standard rule-of-thumb measure on the battlefield, the bowshot (up to about 120 m in respect of aimed penetrative range, up to 330 m for maximum carry).[51]

The extent to which these precise tactical distinctions were maintained after the middle of the seventh century is impossible to say. The merits of having more than one battle line continued to be recognized, and they were not just tactical: the fear that the front line might turn and run was ever present, and Byzantine treatises clearly took this into account when describing the various formations a commander might employ. But it is equally apparent from Leo's *Tactica*, as well as from later writers, that the Byzantine battle order for cavalry, consisting of two clearly separated lines which could strike the enemy's front in succession, was regarded as an essential element in the Roman potential for victory, and clearly differentiated the imperial forces from their opponents. Given that many units, relocated in their new bases in Asia Minor from the later 630s, retained their unit identity well into the tenth and even eleventh century, it seems entirely possible that the older tactical traditions also survived, since the unit organization of the sixth century reflected precisely this type of battle order. An obvious advantage of the clearly separated double battle line was that if the army had to fall back the van could face about to keep the enemy at bay or counter-attack, while the rear could face about to ward off outflanking attacks by an enemy force. This is exactly what seems to have been intended by Romanos IV as he ordered the withdrawal of his double battle line at Mantzikert (in a description which closely parallels the account of the march in battle order in the sixth-century *Strategikon*); the failure was a result of the second line continuing to retreat when the first line halted to counter-attack. A similar formation appears to have been employed by Alexios I in 1078 at the battle of Kalvrytai. The continuity of this double-line tradition in Byzantine practice, reinforced perhaps by the advice of the military handbooks as well as by custom, is very likely.[52]

Both the *Strategikon* and the later *Tactica* of Leo provide descriptions and advice on standard battle formations for both infantry and cavalry. The *Strategikon* reflects already a shift in Roman battle tactics as the empire responded to the influence of the Avars and other nomad peoples it had had to face during the later sixth century, noting that the greater the degree of subdivision of the various units, the more flexible the battle formation. The "older military writers", it is reported, emphasized this; yet the writer notes also that the Avars and Turks "do not draw themselves in one battle line only, as do the Romans and Persians, staking the fate of tens of thousands of horsemen on a single throw. But they form two, sometimes even three lines, distributing the units in depth."[53] The *Strategikon* stresses that cavalry commanders should approach battle in a more sophisticated way. It prescribes a variety of basic formations, depending upon numbers, designed to meet various eventualities in the field. In each case, two battle lines are ordained, the first line with outflankers on the right and flank guards on the left, and with a third line made up of the baggage train, reserve horses and two bodies of rearguards behind the flanks.[54]

The extent to which this description marks a real change in tactics is difficult to assess. There is no reason to doubt that, whatever their tactical administrative structure, Roman forces will always have been drawn up in such a way as to provide flank guards, a reserve or rearguard, and the main battle line, normally divided into left, centre and right. But the fact that it is explicitly remarked that the Romans (at least in the context of fighting the Persians) drew their forces up in an undifferentiated line receives partial support from the much earlier work of Vegetius, who describes the Roman main battle line without distinguishing any clearly differentiated tactical (cohort) subdivisions within it.[55] This probably reflects a general tendency in Roman warfare when facing foes such as the Persians in the east, who similarly drew their forces up in a single body (as described in the *Strategikon*), especially in respect of cavalry armies of lancers such as those deployed at an earlier date by the Sarmatians and later the Goths as well as the Persians. The only concession to a second battle line in Vegetius is his reference to a reserve, behind the main line, near the wings and centre. But this is clearly intended only as a reserve, as an element that can be committed defensively to fill gaps in the Roman line, or offensively when the battle is already turning in favour of the Romans.[56]

Accounts of battles in the *Histories* of Theophylact Simocatta, for example, describing the wars of the last quarter of the sixth century, are usually too vague to be of help, although the description of a great Roman victory over the Persian king Chosroes I in 574 suggests that it was the depth of the main battle line which won the day for the Romans and thus that both armies deployed in a single line. Similarly at the battle of Solachon in 586 the Roman and Persian forces are clearly described as being arrayed in three divisions organized in a single battle line. Another account of the preparations for battle against the Avars in 598 likewise suggests that the Roman forces, while divided into left and right wings and centre with baggage train behind (and probably small units of men behind the flanks to cover against enemy outflanking movements), had no separate rearguard or second line.[57] But Theophylact's descriptions are heavily rhetorical, and it is very difficult to know whether any reliance can be placed upon them. From the earlier reports of Procopius of Caesarea and Agathias, however, it seems that Roman armies were regularly drawn up in a single main battle line, with only a small reserve posted with the commander, although with flank-guards and outflankers on the wings. Such appears to have been the case in Narses' victory over the Goths at the battle of Taginae/Busta Gallorum in 552, and also at a battle on the Volturno river in 554 when a single battle line, with the usual centre and wings, was made up of troops arrayed in a fairly deep formation, the ranks armed differently according to their position in the line and their armament. In this battle, Narses also held back two small reserves behind the wings to outflank the Frankish forces. Again, the account is confused, but does seem to reflect a standard practice, and the description here matches closely that given in the earlier treatise of Vegetius.[58] Ammianus' accounts of the battles of Strasbourg in 357, fought by the later emperor Julian against the Alamanni, and of Adrianople in 378, when the Goths defeated and killed the emperor Valens, suggest that little had changed. In both cases, the Roman forces were drawn up in one main battle line – infantry in the centre and cavalry on the wings with a reserve behind.[59]

The single Roman main battle line appears to have evolved from the third and fourth centuries in response both to the conditions which evolved in the civil wars of the third century, and to the increasing pressure and numbers of barbarian attacks. It seems to have involved the drawing closer together of the tactical sub-units of the legions, the cohorts, and the redistribution of the various specialized elements from a cohort-based to a linear arrangement. It is almost certain that different commanders will have drawn up their forces differently according to the situation and the nature of the enemy, so that it would be dangerous to generalize. The description given by Vegetius, however, drawn from several Roman sources, and reflected in both the second-century military writer Arrian and the fourth-century Ammianus, does make it fairly clear that the tactical divisions within the legions no longer took the form of a division on the basis of cohorts, as in his "ancient" legion,[60] but on the basis of a dense linear formation: heavily armed and protected soldiers in the first rank, with archers and other troops equipped with missiles behind them, and a further rank of experienced and armoured soldiers behind them. This gives a standard formation drawn up six deep, with six feet between each rank. Cavalry were posted to the rear and on the wings, and flank-guards were held behind the wings for defensive or offensive movement.[61] Cavalry formations appear to have been arranged in the same manner – separate centre and flank divisions organized in an extended line up to eight deep, with no second line to follow up and with minimal reserves.[62]

This arrangement, as long as it was properly covered on the flanks, and with the baggage and spare mounts drawn up in the rear with a small rear-guard, appears to have been the standard line-of-battle formation employed in the wars against the various Germanic peoples in the west and the Persians in the east, judging from the comments in the *Strategikon*. The latter, however, is speaking in particular about cavalry formations drawn up in a single deep line, and it is this tactic especially which the author suggests should be abandoned in favour of a more flexible, if less dense, array. As the text makes clear, this was chiefly to enable Roman armies more effectively to oppose their steppe enemies the Avars, whose battle array was similarly broken up (by clan and kinship groups) and was clearly perceived to be much better as a result (see Fig. 6.1).

Tactics and the thematic armies

The evidence for the pre-eminence of cavalry in the period from the middle of the seventh century onwards is, as we have seen, persuasive: the fact that the provincial armies are sometimes referred to as "the cavalry armies" (*ta kaballarika themata*) is itself indicative. There is no reason to doubt that there continued to be substantial infantry elements in each thematic army, but they remain more or less invisible in the sources, presumably employed as garrisons, frontier and fortress guards and so on. The *Tactica* of Leo assumes that the army confronting the Arabs along the frontiers will usually be of cavalry. Where infantry are present, they are used both to shield the cavalry in the opening phases of battle as well as to complement the cavalry in attacking a defended position.[63] But the effectiveness of infantry and cavalry clearly depended as much upon discipline and a workable command structure as it did upon weapons and mounts or *esprit de corps*. And it seems that it was discipline in particular which suffered in the East Roman army during much of the period from the seventh to the tenth centuries – indicative is the fact that the *Tactica* of Leo recommends that dismounted cavalry troopers should not have their horses tethered too close in case they panic and abandon their position in the line for their horses, and that the commander should take care to reinterpret in a positive light any signs and portents circulating in the camp which may lead to the demoralization of the soldiers. By the same token, the *Tactica* notes that brave soldiers often die precisely because they do not obey their officers, and rush to attack the enemy without order.[64]

Order, discipline and the coherence these generated, reliance on collective effect rather than on individual prowess, these were the characteristics which the Byzantines considered differentiated them and their methods of waging war from their enemies. The tactical infrastructures described in Chapter 4 above were an essential element in this: right up until the end of the empire units were organized into subdivisions placed under junior officers in a chain of command which made the coherent management of often very disparate forces at least feasible – an essential in such a multi-ethnic army. Such qualities as discipline and order are frequently repeated in all the military treatises, and they are alluded to also implicitly as well as explicitly in some of the narrative histories. The differences between Byzantine order and discipline and Frankish haste and indiscipline, for example, described in the *Strategikon* of Maurice and repeated by Anna Komnene in the early twelfth century, typifies this perspective. In reality the Frankish leaders of the twelfth century were often able tacticians who outwitted the supposedly more subtle Byzantines; and as will become clear, the mere existence of a military disciplinary code and the assumption of Roman discipline is no proof that such discipline was always enforced, or indeed enforceable: context and the quality of leadership were crucially important prerequisites for effective discipline. But while the Byzantine view of themselves and their enemies was laden with value judgements, it nevertheless indicates the centrality of military discipline and Roman tradition in Byzantine military thinking.[65]

It is notable, to begin with, that Byzantine armies confronted Arab forces in the field on only relatively few occasions between *c.* 640 and 680. That this reflected deliberate strategic thinking – and then custom or habit – is very probable, but it may also reflect tactical advantages held by the Arab armies, in particular the greater use of infantry archers (but who travelled on horse or camel along with the cavalry). Whether the fact that avoidance of battle appears to have been the norm between the years 640 and 680 is merely a reflection of partial sources is impossible to say. They certainly recount hardly any open encounters between the two sides in these years. Byzantine successes were limited to the recovery of fortresses in Anatolia or along the Taurus occupied by the Arabs (such as Amorion, taken in 669 and recovered during the winter of the same year), to the ambush and defeat of one of the Arab columns involved in the attacks on Constantinople between 674 and 678 (probably in the last year of the "siege"), and to the successful defence of Constantinople itself during this period.[66]

After this date, and the brief period of Byzantine offensive action in the 680s and early 690s (exploiting the internal troubles within the caliphate), imperial armies registered some limited successes, but were clearly barely holding their own. Against the Slavs in the Balkans in 687/8 and, in Cilicia, against the limited garrisons which had been left to defend the region during the involvement of the caliph's forces in Iraq, imperial armies were able to win some victories. Yet the defeat at the hands of the numerically inferior Bulgars in 678/9 implies significant weaknesses in the imperial field armies. In 691/2 a major battle was fought near Sebastoupolis in Armenia II between the combined field armies with conscripted Slav infantry and an Arab invasion force, and although the battle went at first in the Byzantines' favour, the desertion of the Slavs brought disaster and rout to the imperial forces.[67] A series of notable successes was achieved by Herakleios, brother of the emperor Tiberios Apsimar (698–705) in the years between 697/8 and 702/3, who was appointed to the position of *monostrategos*, commander of all the frontier cavalry divisions in Cappadocia, and who was thus able to coordinate the efforts of local forces from the armies of Anatolikon and probably from other *themata*. Thereafter, Arab raids and incursions recommence on a regular basis, accompanied once again by the Byzantine policy of avoidance until well after the defeat of the great siege of Constantinople in 717/18. Only gradually did the imperial forces begin to face up to invading Arab troops. The success of Herakleios may suggest that it was primarily the command structure and the nature of the military leadership that was to blame for the failures to contain Arab raiders effectively, rather than the fighting capabilities of the troops.[68]

The policy of avoidance which appears to mark the years 640–80 reflects, in all likelihood, both the bitter experiences of the war against the Arabs in Syria and Palestine in the 630s (and Heraclius' order to avoid open battle: see Chapter 3 above), as well as the strategic difficulties of covering the long frontier. The imperial forces relied upon their fortified centres behind the Taurus/Anti-Taurus, none of which was taken and held permanently by the Arabs, and upon the policy of harassing and ambushing enemy troops as they withdrew. It may often have been encouraged by an imbalance in numbers, and low morale may have played a role: the frequent defeats meted out to the Roman forces in Italy by the Gothic leader Totila after Belisarius' recall certainly had this effect, as Belisarius himself is reported to have noted in a letter to the emperor. At the same time, what was perceived as the political deterioration of the empire promoted a certain amount of discontent among the different provincial armies and their officers, so that the period from *c.* 695 to after the accession of Leo III in 717 was one of frequent *coups d'état* involving thematic units.[69]

Those successes which were achieved often resulted from the involvement of the imperial government, for example when Herakleios was appointed as *monostrategos*, as noted already, or when the emperors Leo III and Constantine V themselves led counter-attacks against a substantial Arab army which entered Roman territory in 739/40 and split up into three columns, defeating one of them. When local troops were successful, the limited evidence suggests that it was because they were able to ambush and cut off the invading forces rather than face them in open battle (as in the defeat of an Arab force in 677/8 referred to already).

One of the effects of this strategy was, however, to deprive many imperial field units of any formal or regular line-of-battle experience for more than a generation. And where this was the case, it must in turn have had fairly dramatic consequences for field discipline, battle training, the ability to carry out manoeuvres while under attack, and so forth. It is entirely probable that a further consequence was the disappearance of any semblance of consistency in the arming and equipping of the soldiers. There is very little evidence to go on, but when an official text of the eighth century refers to the provincial cavalry soldier as possessing a horse, weapons and, perhaps, a *lorikion* (mail shirt or equivalent), it is clear that considerable variations in both equipment and financial situation existed among the soldiers.[70] Other evidence for the later eighth and ninth centuries suggests that the general standard of equipment and armament in the seasonally mustered provincial armies was not high, and increasingly the core units of the *themata* are mentioned as the most important elements. The field armies of the late Roman period had thus been transformed into a provincial militia. Leo's *Tactica* recommends that the general should train and exercise the troops into a warlike state during winter months or other times whenever an opportunity presented itself, suggesting that these were the only times at his disposal in this seasonal campaigning tradition (in contrast to passages in the *Strategikon*, where the winter camp is the time for re-equipping the troops, but where military exercises should take place on a constant and regular basis). Ninth-century hagiographies show that the *adnoumion*, or muster, following which some training and drilling would take place, occurred on a yearly basis, and this also remained true of the ordinary thematic contingents in the tenth century, although even this muster fell into desuetude with the increase in emphasis on full-time and mercenary units.[71] How rapidly this transformation occurred is impossible to say with certainty, but the establishment of a full-time standing force in the 760s by Constantine V suggests the point at which the emperors took action to address the problem.

It is not always easy to say from the vague accounts in the sources whether indiscipline was the fault of the soldiers or their officers. During a campaign against the Bulgars in 707/8, for example, the cavalry *themata* suffered a defeat because they failed to set piquets and guard the camp carefully, and were caught by surprise while scattered to collect forage for the horses. This was most probably the fault of the officer commanding. In the same year, a disorganized Byzantine attack on an invading Arab force was defeated with losses. In 788/9 the *strategos* of Thrace, Philetos, failed to take adequate precautions during a campaign along the Strymon and was ambushed, losing his own life in the defeat. Theophanes records that Constantine VI was defeated when he engaged the Bulgar forces at Markellai in 791/2 because he attacked "without plan or order", suggesting that the opposite was generally the case.[72] In 808/9 the Bulgars were able to surprise the Byzantine forces of several *themata* on the Strymon and capture the salaries of the armies, 1,100 pounds in gold coin, which had just been delivered. The fact that the officers in question later asked the emperor's pardon strongly suggests that it was their incompetence which was responsible. In the 880s the general in charge of a hitherto successful thematic field army on campaign against Tarsos failed to cover his advance with forward scouts and failed to entrench his camp and set a proper watch, with the result that his forces were surprised and routed, he himself being killed in the attack.

It is clear from these examples that in the normal run of things Byzantine armies advanced to fight in regular divisions and ordered lines of battle, and were both reasonably well-disciplined, and superior in numbers and equipment to the Bulgars: in 795/6 the Bulgar forces withdrew through the woods when confronted by the Byzantine forces in full battle array led by Constantine VI, and it was clearly widely recognized by the Byzantine officers and soldiers that they would normally defeat the Bulgars on open ground – most Byzantine defeats occurred when the imperial forces were either caught off guard, as noted already, or boxed in one of the defiles through the mountains when attempting to enter or leave the Bulgar heartland. The catastrophe of 811, when the forces of Nikephros I were caught in such a situation, as well as in inadequately defended or guarded encampments, is unusual only in its magnitude. The battle of Versinikia in 813, fought in the open where the Romans' order and discipline gave them an initial advantage, was clearly expected by the officers present to result in an imperial victory until, as the result (apparently) of a plot, a division of the army withdrew (in fact, pretended to flee) under the eyes of a smaller Bulgar force, leading to a real rout of the remaining units. Moreover, as the consequence of petty jealousies between the two commanding officers of imperial forces in southern Italy in the 880s, a Byzantine force which was actually winning the battle was forced to abandon the field when one commander failed adequately to support his colleague whose troops were being pushed back by a fierce enemy attack. Before the battle of Acheloos in 917, the field army of *tagmata* and *themata* was drawn up in order, unit by unit, prior to advancing against the Bulgar forces. An orderly line of battle and the clear division of the army into independent corps consisting of several smaller divisions are attested throughout, and clearly continued to be the basis upon which Byzantine armies were disposed for battle, however able the commanders were.[73]

Examples of indiscipline among the soldiers in battlefield contexts (as opposed to soldiers' activities in rebellions or attempted coups) are rarely mentioned in the sources. The state of the army's morale in general was always a cause for concern: the *Strategikon* of Maurice, followed by Leo's *Tactica*, advises that acts of insubordination or indiscipline immediately preceding a battle should be ignored by the officers in case the troops should be demoralized or alienated by the usual punishment. This tells us two things. In the first place, it suggests that discipline was indeed enforced by punishment, although whether of the severity or consistency described in the various versions of the so-called "military laws" is unclear. But it also tells us that the morale of the armies could be fairly fragile, and that commanders needed to pay considerable attention to the psychological state of their soldiers. We have already alluded to this question above. Armies could panic for a number of reasons, and Maurice's/Leo's advice makes it clear that Byzantine officers were aware of the fact. They could also refuse to fight, and certainly complained and grumbled when ordered to carry out unpopular tasks. In 813, when Michael I (811–13) transferred thematic troops from Anatolia to Thrace preparatory to fighting the Bulgars, the eastern soldiers complained vociferously about the unseasonably early move and were thereafter easily manipulated by certain officers not to cooperate with the emperor's orders.[74]

As far as the evidence permits us to draw any conclusions about battlefield tactics in the period up to the tenth century, therefore, we may say with some confidence that heavy infantry generally played a secondary role, that the

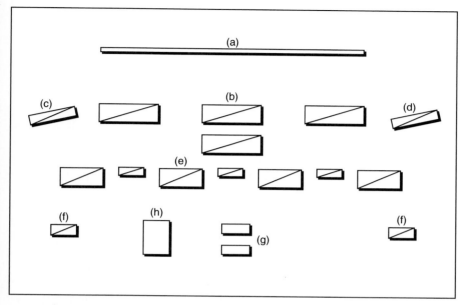

(a) light cavalry screen (b) first line (c) flankguard
(d) outflankers (e) second line (with gaps covered) (f) rearguard
(g) remounts (h) baggage

Figure 6.1 Tactical deployment of cavalry field army *c.* 600.

provincial cavalry were, for the most part, light-armed lancers consisting of a core of more or less permanent and better armed and trained units supported by an irregular militia, and that with the establishment of a central elite force at Constantinople in the second half of the reign of Constantine V, these provincial armies would frequently have been strengthened by the presence of (probably) heavier cavalry. In ninth-century defeats, for example, it was frequently only the *tagmata* which held their position when other (thematic) units began to retreat or break up, and by the same token, a retreat of tagmatic units seems often to have sown panic among the provincial forces. As the empire adopted a more aggressive posture, especially from the middle of the ninth century, so increasing numbers of indigenous and foreign mercenary units – *tagmata* – appeared to further bolster the "professional" element in the provincial and especially the central field armies: as we have noted in Chapter 3 above, such units were recruited, either permanently or for the duration of a particular campaign, by most of the emperors of the ninth century. We may assume that discipline and training among the permanent forces would have been reasonably good, less so among the seasonal troops. Leo's *Tactica* makes this very clear: in noting that the selected cavalry force of a *thema* usually numbers only 4,000 (if possible), he remarks that this is "on account of the lack of drill, neglect and fewness of the soldiers which currently prevails".

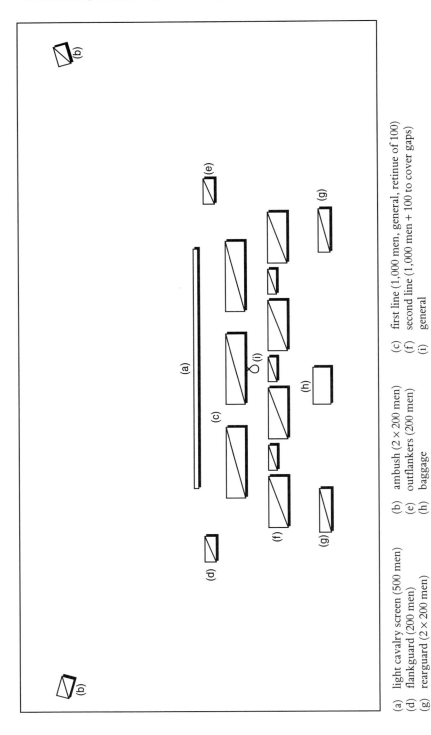

(a) light cavalry screen (500 men)   (b) ambush (2 × 200 men)   (c) first line (1,000 men, general, retinue of 100)
(d) flankguard (200 men)   (e) outflankers (200 men)   (f) second line (1,000 men + 100 to cover gaps)
(g) rearguard (2 × 200 men)   (h) baggage   (i) general

Figure 6.2 Tactical deployment of a thematic cavalry force of 4,000 men *c.* 900.

These 4,000 make up the real army (Leo calls it the "military division" – *stratiotikon thema*); the rest of the registered "soldiers" from the *thema* (now used in the sense of administrative province) should be assigned to other, less demanding tasks. This clearly includes the infantry (see Figures 6.1 and 6.2).[75]

The question of archery

One of the obvious results of the warfare and strategy pursued by the empire over this period, and a reflection of the tactics and fighting techniques of its enemies, however, seems to have been a real decline in effective mounted archery. Archery is a skill requiring constant practice, training and exercise, mounted archery even more so, as something not found naturally among most sedentary societies. It is notable that the great majority of archer units, both foot and horse, in the Roman army before the fourth century were from allied peoples or in auxiliary units drawn from regions where an established tradition of archery existed. Otherwise it has to be maintained through deliberately fostered training – as in the case of the archer-cavalrymen of the sixth century, and as explained and described in detail in the *Strategikon* of Maurice, or in the mid-sixth-century anonymous treatise on strategy. It is notable, for example, that the Roman archers of the sixth century were taught the Hunnic or steppe release using the thumb together with the index and middle fingers, rather than the Mediterranean release employing the first three fingers, although both releases were clearly known: the *Strategikon* states that archers could shoot using either the Roman (i.e. the Hunnic) or the Persian method. It is likely that unless the Hunnic draw were specifically maintained and practised, it would fall out of use and be replaced by the culturally more usual release. It is not mentioned specifically in the tenth-century treatises, and the *Tactica* of Leo, in paraphrasing this section from the *Strategikon*, omits this detail, but the fact that Leo the Deacon, commenting upon the training imposed upon his soldiers by Nikephros Phocas, remarks that Nikephros taught his soldiers "to draw the arrow to the chest" suggests that in all probability it was the Mediterranean release which had reasserted itself.[76] One of the advantages competent archery brought the Roman armies against the Goths in Italy or the Vandals in Africa, for example, was the ability to wear down and harass the enemy force from a distance before allowing the main battle lines to meet, an advantage noted on several occasions by Procopius. Against the Persians, who used massed archer formations, it at least gave the Roman forces the possibility of replying in kind to the same tactic used against themselves. While against highly mobile steppe peoples, such as the Avars, going into battle without adequate mounted archery in particular would have left the Romans at a permanent disadvantage in most situations.[77]

The armies of the early Islamic conquests seem to have included substantial numbers of foot archers, and their effectiveness, aided by the high degree of mobility and flexibility of their armies in the early conquests, seems to have been a key factor in their victories against Roman and Sassanid forces. At the battle of the Yarmuk in 636, during the opening phases of which the Muslim forces held prepared defensive positions, it may have been archery which broke up Roman efforts to dislodge them.[78] In contrast, we may reasonably suspect that the numbers of effective mounted archer/lancer units in the Roman army was never great, and that the commanders of the various field divisions were able to maintain a high level of efficiency and competence only with great difficulty and constant attention to the issue. There is no evidence that archery played any significant role on the Byzantine side against the Islamic conquerors in the 630s. This is not to say that the Byzantines abandoned archery altogether: there must always have been some mounted archers, and the provincial infantry troops probably included substantial numbers of men equipped with bows. Leo's *Tactica* and the mid-tenth-century *Sylloge taktikon* assume, following almost exactly the description in the *Strategikon* of Maurice, that the cavalryman has a bow, quiver and arrows, which probably can be taken to mean that many cavalry soldiers were indeed so equipped. Yet the treatise on skirmishing has the cavalry dismount to use their missile weapons, and assumes that each trooper will muster with his preferred weapons, suggesting that the bow was by no means universally present.[79]

The limited evidence from other Byzantine sources – casual references to soldiers' equipment in non-technical texts – ignores archery almost entirely: the standard panoply was lance, sword, helmet and shield alone. And the evidence from both the Balkans and the eastern theatres in the later seventh century and after suggests that the empire's enemies relied upon exactly the same weaponry, with minor variations. The sources mention the sling as often as they mention the bow (as when, in 811, the emperor Nikephros I marched against the Bulgars with the cavalry *themata* and a mass of peasant conscripts equipped with clubs and slings only).[80]

In contrast, that the Byzantines experienced great difficulties when confronted by effective archery is evident from the account of the victory of the Muslim forces over the emperor Theophilos in 838 at the battle of Anzen (near Dazimon), when one source at least notes that the Romans were sorely afflicted by the horse-archery and tactics of the Turk contingent. By the time the emperor Leo VI commissioned his *Tactica*, the situation does not seem to have greatly improved: he notes the complete decline in Roman archery, and the defeats which were a result, and commends that all Roman recruits practise with the bow. The mounted lancer/archer he describes is taken directly from the sixth-century *Strategikon*, and while it certainly represents some cavalry troops of his own time, is unlikely to have reflected the generality in the provincial armies.[81]

The result of these considerations is that the Byzantine composite lancer/horse archer is probably something of a myth.[82] When archery once more appears to be an important element in the imperial forces, it is clear that tenth-century emperors attempted not to reintroduce the composite archer-lancer, but rather to establish and promote more effective bodies of infantry archers, a development which goes hand in hand with the general revival of interest and importance attached to infantry in general from the 940s and 950s on. They also recruited increasing numbers of mercenary soldiers from a variety of neighbouring peoples, including Magyars and other steppe peoples to the north, adepts at mounted archery. Indigenous units certainly included lancers equipped with bows, both in the provinces and in the elite forces based in and around Constantinople: a tenth-century letter refers to the panoply of a cavalry-man in the *themata* as consisting of horse, bow and quiver, and helmet. Preparations for the equipping of archers were undertaken before the expedition against the Syrian coast and Crete in 910–11: an official record notes that 500 mercenary soldiers, who knew how to handle the bow, were to be recruited from the Anatolikon region. The document states that cavalrymen would be preferable. In the late tenth-century treatises, although it is clear that archers were an integral element in the field army, they were by no means predominant. Nikephros Ouranos specifies that approximately one-third of the infantry should be light-armed archers, in the light cavalry, the proportion varied from one-third to one-quarter according to tactical dispositions, and in the regular cavalry the proportion of mounted archers was about 40 per cent.[83]

While mounted archers were thus a significant element, they did not represent the standard Byzantine cavalry soldier, who was reflected rather in the lancers of the provinces. Further, they seem often to have dismounted to use their bows, as the treatise on skirmishing warfare, harking back to earlier practice, also implies. Mounted archery never became a dominant element in the Byzantine army, and was provided for the most part by foreign contingents who were recruited specifically to provide it. Even in the 930s Byzantine forces could be defeated by armies of mounted archers although, as in the sixth century, the intelligent deployment of Byzantine mounted and foot archery against non-archers was usually effective.[84] And the longer-term results were to be seen in the middle of the eleventh century, when the Pechenegs and then the Seljuks were able (although not very often) to break up Byzantine battle formations using traditional nomad tactics. The imperial response was to increase the number of such troops they themselves employed, either hiring them directly as mercenaries or, as in the case of the Pechenegs, having defeated them, adopting them en masse under an obligation to serve in the imperial forces on a regular basis. The only evidence for the development of a tactical formation to deal specifically with such archery comes from Anna Comnena's account of an oblique line of battle evolved by her father in the early twelfth century, involving also an infantry square for the march, and probably returning to an earlier tactical formation of the pre-Mantzikert period.[85]

The tactical revolution of the tenth century

The treatises on strategy and tactics of the middle and later tenth century show that substantial changes in tactics had occurred by the 960s and 970s. These changes reflected primarily the much more offensive character of imperial policy, especially in the eastern theatre, the need to recruit more professional soldiers, and the need to operate effectively and aggressively on campaigns which required more than merely seasonally available forces. They are realized in two ways. First, the revival of a corps of disciplined, effective line-of-battle infantry which could confront enemy infantry and cavalry, support their own cavalry, march long distances and function as garrison troops away from their home territory on a permanent basis. Second, the introduction of a corps of heavily-armoured lancers which could operate in conjunction with the infantry, which would add weight to the Byzantine attack, and which would substantially increase the aggressive power of the Byzantine cavalry. Whereas the evolution of tactics in the period from the later sixth to the early tenth centuries has received very little attention, these developments have been the subject of several excellent studies, the results of which can be summarized here.

The first evidence for a change in tactical formations comes from the mid-tenth-century treatise known as the *Sylloge taktikon*, the "Recapitulation of Tactics". In this tract, which includes also substantial extracts or summaries from ancient authorities as well as paraphrases from the *Tactica* of Leo VI, there appears a new formation of infantry soldiers, equipped with a thick-stocked, long-necked javelin or pike called a *menavlion*, probably similar in form to the Roman legionary *pilum*.[86] Their task is to engage and repulse enemy heavy cavalry – cataphract – attacks. According to the *Sylloge*, there are to be some 300 such *menavlatoi* who are drawn up in the intervals between the various infantry platoons making up the main line, from which position they are to venture forth and form a line or wedge and break up the enemy attack. By the time of the *Praecepta*, in contrast, in which the infantry had been reorganized into taxiarchies of up to 1,000 soldiers, there were 400 spearmen, 300 archers, 200 light infantry (with slings and javelins) and 100 *menaulatoi* in each such unit, but the task allotted the last group was the same as in the *Sylloge*.[87]

It is quite clear that a major change in the role of infantry had been stimulated by the changed political-military situation of the tenth century. In marked contrast to the late sixth-century *Strategikon*, which deals with the infantry as an afterthought, the *Praecepta* dedicates its first two chapters to the infantry formations. It is also clear from the figures given for a major field army that the importance of infantry was well acknowledged, and that they were numerically a crucial element of the army, far more central to the sort of campaigning strategy and battlefield tactics practised in the later tenth century than they had been in the nearly three centuries preceding. Not only did infantry form a major element, but in contrast again to the period of cavalry dominance which lasted until the tenth century they outnumbered the latter by 2 : 1 or more. They were divided by weapon in each taxiarchy, as already noted, and the exact instructions set out by the *Praecepta* testifies to the greatly improved discipline and training which such troops were expected to display. Historians of the second half of the tenth century praise both Nikephros II and John I Tzimiskes for their training and the rigorous discipline they enforced, while the *Praecepta* sets out the stages of training through which individual soldiers, units and then the whole army should be put. The new prominence of infantry in the warfare of the period is emphasized by the fact that the whole infantry force was placed under the command of a single senior officer, the *hoplitarches* (or *archegetes*), who was responsible below the commander-in-chief of the expeditionary force for their training, field discipline and effectiveness in battle – a post not dissimilar to that of the original *magister militum peditum* of the reforms of Constantine I over six centuries earlier.[88]

Yet the weaknesses of infantry, especially when facing heavy cavalry, were recognized and understood: the basic formation for the battle line was a hollow square or rectangle – the precise shape depended on the terrain – intended to deal with encircling attacks from enemy cavalry, as a refuge for the Byzantine cavalry should their attack be thrown back, and – importantly – as a means of preventing the infantry themselves from turning to flight.[89] As we have seen in Chapter 5 above, it has been shown that this was a fairly recent development, perhaps dating from the second quarter of the tenth century during the first great offensive campaigns of the period. That the Byzantine texts themselves make this clear illustrates the fact that the infantry had usually been, as surmised above, drawn up in a deep line, and with only a limited offensive role in battle. More importantly, in spite of their new role, the treatises of the 950s and 960s make it fairly apparent that the cavalry were still regarded as the main offensive arm in battle – the infantry remained as a refuge, as a mobile base for the mounted units and as follow-up troops in the event of the enemy being put to flight. This is, in itself, good indirect evidence of the pre-eminence of cavalry and the very reduced role of infantry in the preceding centuries.[90]

Although Roman and Hellenistic treatises describe square formations, especially for contexts when the enemy might employ an encircling tactic, it is clear that this tenth-century Byzantine formation was something relatively new. It is mentioned briefly in the *Tactica* of Leo as a formation for dismounted cavalry who have been repulsed or defeated, used to protect the baggage and mounts as the army withdraws in order from a superior enemy force. But this is clearly a particular case.[91] From the description given in the *Praecepta* of Nikephros, it appears to be very similar to the basic layout of the standard marching camp, suggesting that the increased demand for heavy infantry formations in the offensive warfare of the period had been met by taking a traditionally somewhat unreliable force and employing an essentially defensive field formation which provided both solidity and security in defence or on the march, which could serve as a mobile base and a refuge for lighter troops and cavalry, and yet which could also be transformed by a few simple manoeuvres into a solid attacking formation.

This development appears to reflect Byzantine commanders intelligently applying tactically flexible measures to the materials that were at their disposal. Under good leadership, and increasingly as a tradition of discipline combined with effective field actions takes hold, we may assume that Byzantine infantry units, especially those made up of more or less full-time soldiers, recovered some of their former "Roman" attributes: good morale, tactical cohesion, *esprit de corps* and battlefield discipline. The evidence mentioned already, especially from the accounts of the wars of the 950s to the 970s, makes this much clear. At the same time, this is a reflection of the recruitment of good infantry from among certain warlike peoples within the empire, notably Armenians (although Slavs, Lycaonians and Isaurians also seem to provide infantry units). Infantry always remained lower in status than cavalry, and their equipment always seems to have been relatively poor. Yet the warfare of the tenth century demanded at the least a uniformity in respect of function as well as tactical specialism, so that in general we may say that the Byzantine heavy and light infantry formations of this period would have acted and been employed in battle and on campaign much more like the regular infantry units of the late Roman era than their predecessors of the ninth or eighth centuries. Thereafter, and well into the eleventh century, Armenian infantry seem to have represented the best foot soldiers in the imperial armies.[92]

As well as this transformation in the role of infantry (if not all, then certainly those core elements regularly called up for campaign or recruited from mercenary sources), a major change also took place within the cavalry forces of the empire. In addition to the presence of heavy and light cavalry on the battlefield and on campaign, a new arm now appears, the heavily armed *klibanarios* or *kataphraktos*, a heavy cavalry trooper armed from head to foot in lamellar, mail and quilting, whose horse was likewise protected – face, neck, flanks and forequarters were all to be covered with armour to prevent enemy missiles and blows from injuring the cavalryman's mount. Such cavalry were the elite of the army, and were, of course, extremely expensive. They formed up in a broad-nosed wedge, and their primary function was, supported by the regular lancers and other cavalry, to smash through the enemy's heavy cavalry or infantry line, break up his formation, and permit the supporting horse to turn the flanks of the severed lines. But they were very few in number: the *Praecepta* specifies a maximum formation of just over 500 for a large wedge, only two-thirds of whom would be real *klibanarioi/kataphraktoi*, the rest consisting of more lightly armed mounted archers. Since this description is intended to apply to the main field army operating in the east at any given time, this provides some perspective on the numbers involved (see Figure 6.3).[93]

A number of sources, both Byzantine and Arab, attest to the impressive effects of this formation on enemy troops – one Arab writer remarks that the horses were armoured so that they appeared to advance without legs. The wedge formation may have been a particular innovation of Nikephros Phocas, although this is not certain. But the renewed emphasis on both regular infantry and upon heavily armoured cavalry units certainly predates him by at least half a generation – the Arab poet referred to above was describing a battle fought in 954, for example, while the *Sylloge* was compiled in the late 940s or early 950s and already attests to some of the changes. The reintroduction of a corps of very heavily armoured cavalry, or at least their greater prominence in

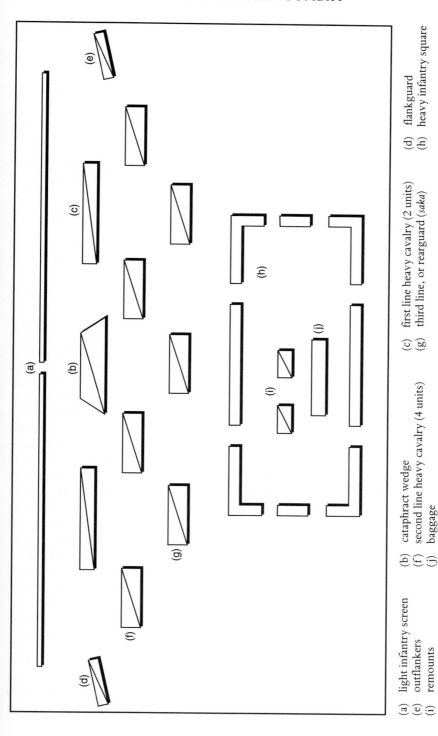

Figure 6.3 Tactical deployment of a combined infantry and cavalry force army, including cataphract wedge, *c.* 960.

(a) light infantry screen	(b) cataphract wedge	(c) first line heavy cavalry (2 units)	(d) flankguard
(e) outflankers	(f) second line heavy cavalry (4 units)	(g) third line, or rearguard (*saka*)	(h) heavy infantry square
(i) remounts	(j) baggage		

the cavalry line of battle, may again date to the campaigns of the general John Kourkouas along the eastern front in the 920s, 930s and 940s.

The transformation in the performance of the Byzantine army seems to date from the last years of Constantine VII when, in response to his own disappointment at the defeats the army was suffering at the hands of the Hamdanid emirs of Aleppo and some forthright criticism from the general Nikephros Phocas (later emperor), he dismissed the latter's father as commander-in-chief in the east, replacing him with his own son. Nikephros appears immediately to have instigated a major programme of training and drilling the troops in an effort to re-establish a disciplined fighting force with high morale and good battlefield skills. His success, reflected partly in the treatise ascribed to his hand, the *Praecepta*, and in the successful warfare of the next 50 or so years, is evident. It also illustrates the relatively poor levels of training and tactical discipline of the Byzantine armies up to that point (however well they may otherwise have compared with the armies of the Bulgars, for example), with the exception perhaps of the elite *tagmata* and when a particularly able commander was at their head, such as John Kourkouas.[94]

Tactical cohesion and order, always a key element in Byzantine ideas on successful battlefield performance, were among the foremost concerns of the commander. Infantry and cavalry forces in the main battle lines were ordered to keep an eye on their unit and divisional standards, and to maintain the line evenly and unbroken, advancing at the same pace. No individuals should leave the line to attack the enemy until the general advance was sounded; even soldiers who charged the enemy successfully were to be punished if they abandoned their position, for this directly endangered the cohesion and therefore the strength and solidarity of the line. While as we have seen these remained standard practice throughout the Byzantine period, the tenth-century historians' accounts agree with the treatises of the period in stressing these aspects. The order and cohesion of the Roman forces is mentioned by several writers, as in the battle before Tarsos in 965, between the well-ordered battle line of the Roman forces under Isaac I Komnenos in 1059 and the Pechenegs (Psellos remarks on the Pechenegs' dismay at the unbroken line of Roman shields facing their assault), or the battles fought by Romanos IV against the Turks in 1070 (where, in spite of the criticisms of poor generalship and lack of discipline among the troops made by the contemporary eyewitness Michael Attaleiates, Roman units seem still to have fought and marched with order and cohesion). The harsh tactical discipline imposed on his forces by Basil II was singled out for praise by the slightly later writer Michael Psellos, but was only exceptional in its rigour. Alexios I imposed a similar order on his battle line, in which no one was to advance in front of the line as it moved and where cohesion and solidarity were the key elements.[95]

The increased degree of specialization which these developments reflect illustrates the nature of the Byzantine offensive in the west as well as, and especially, in the east. Combined with an effective screen of light cavalry who could both harass enemy forces on the move and cover the advance of the heavy cavalry and protective infantry formations, the Byzantine armies proved their effectiveness in the long series of victories lasting through the second half of the tenth century and into the eleventh. There were, of course, defeats too, sometimes the result of the incompetence or inexperience of the commander, sometimes of the greater tactical skill of the opposing commander or the better morale of his troops.

Yet no sooner had the military expansionism of the tenth century achieved its immediate strategic aims than a change in strategy at the local level can also be observed. With the conquest and absorption of Bulgaria and the Balkans up to the Danube, the empire met with the newly stabilized power of the Magyars to the north and west, while in the east, the growing power of the Fatimids on land and at sea meant similarly the need to stabilize the frontier. This was initially done under Basil II by the creation of buffer states around the empire's borders and by the attempt to establish recognized spheres of interest. In this new context, offensive warfare involving the crushing of major enemy field armies was no longer the focus. Instead, raiding across the frontier, patrols to check hostile activity and the establishment of well-fortified garrison posts became the priorities. In the Balkans in particular, controlling routes of access, maintaining internal security and political control, and garrisoning strongpoints and administrative and strategic centres rendered the expensive heavy cavalry squadrons redundant. Regular heavy cavalry continued to be a key element in the Byzantine forces, of course. At the battle of Troina in Sicily, in 1040, the Byzantine heavy cavalry fought alongside a contingent of Norman and other heavy cavalry (all apparently sent by their lords at the behest of the commanding general George Maniakes). Whether the Byzantine cavalry were as heavily armed as the *klibanophoroi* is unknown, but the source which recounts the battle stresses the impact of the Roman charge, which demolished the Arab battle line at the first attack. Shortly after, when Constantine IX celebrated his victory over George Maniakes in 1043, the elite heavy cavalry – described as *kataphraktoi* – took part in the triumph. The extent to which a lay witness such as Psellos knew how to differentiate between the *klibanophoroi* and regular heavy cavalry is unclear. The special heavy cavalry who made up the shock-delivering wedge of the treatise ascribed to Nikephros Phocas disappear from the sources after they are mentioned in the treatise of Nikephros Ouranos, thus during the middle years of the reign of Basil II, although there is no reason to think, in the context of Basil's wars, that they were disbanded at that time. But they may well have been stood down during the middle years of the eleventh century – possibly during the reign of Constantine X (1059–67), whom Attaleiates blames for many of the problems faced by Romanos IV – with the result that when heavily armoured cavalry were needed later in the century they were recruited mostly from mercenary sources, in particular from the Normans of southern Italy – whose tactics may themselves originally have derived from the Byzantine model.[96]

The tactics of the imperial forces during the eleventh century evolved out of this late tenth-century context. Warfare against the Saracens of southern

Italy, against the Pechenegs and Uzes (Turks) in the Balkans and, after 1071 and the defeat at Mantzikert, the Seljuks in Anatolia demanded for the most part lightly armed cavalry to track and harass and eventually bring the enemy to battle, and infantry to control key strategic points and refuges. Increasingly, as the government preferred to rely upon mercenary forces both foreign and indigenous, the uniformity of the forces must have given way to a diversity of ethnic fighting styles and armaments. This is not to say that diversity was new: on the contrary, the tenth-century field armies had been remarkable for the great number of races which composed them, as Arab commentators noted: the poet al-Mutanabbi commented upon this facet of the Byzantine armies, and noted that there were so many languages in the ranks that interpreters were needed to transmit the commanders' orders.[97] By the same token, footsoldiers remained an important and active element in the imperial forces. The infantry corps formed an important section of the campaign army in Cilicia in 1137, while heavy infantry are mentioned on many occasions as key elements in the Byzantine battle line: infantry formed a substantial part of the army which recovered Corfu from the Sicilian Normans in 1148. At a battle with the Hungarian army in 1167 the outcome was decided by the decisive charge of the Roman infantry division, and the vanguard which forced its way through the Turkish forces at Myriokephalon was of infantry. The renewed significance of infantry reflects the changes which took place in the tenth century, and the need to have a solid bulwark which could resist enemy heavy cavalry attacks and form a solid battlefield base from which the Roman cavalry could retaliate. Such changes were not confined to the Byzantine world alone, of course: western and Muslim armies were also part of the process. Not only did Crusader armies include substantial numbers of infantry spearmen and footsoldiers of varying levels of competence and training, but an important proportion of the foreign mercenaries recruited into the Byzantine forces during the twelfth century were also of infantry.[98]

The drilling, training and exercising of the troops were the factors that had forged such an effective war-machine, a process which, as noted above, seems to have been instigated in the mid-950s, when Nikephros Phocas was appointed to reform and command the armies in the east. All the treatises place great emphasis upon exercising and drilling the troops in a variety of field manoeuvres and in developing their endurance, an emphasis which the narrative histories of the time corroborate, and to which they attribute numerous victories. Michael Psellos remarks on the superb discipline of Bardas Skleros' cavalry, who were able even under heavy attack and while withdrawing to wheel about, counter-charge and drive their enemies from the field.[99] Without such drilling, without the regular discipline imposed by proper military exercises, the tactical competence of the field armies could not last long. Under able commanders such as George Maniakes and Katakalon Kekaumenos in the 1030s and 1040s, an army of foreign and indigenous mercenaries and some provincial levies could still achieve victories over a variety of enemies: the battle order employed by Romanos IV in his campaign in 1070 involved the traditional two battle lines divided into several smaller divisions with flanking and outflanking units in support, while all the sources refer regularly to the Byzantine forces organized into three main divisions with rearguard and vanguard.[100] The advantage held by the Roman infantry was, until the later eleventh century and possibly into the twelfth, in their better tactical training: Michael Psellos notes with some contempt that the emperor Romanos III thought numbers counted for more than skill and discipline; Choniates and Kinnamos refer on several occasions, as do the historians of the eleventh and tenth centuries, to the training and exercising of the troops in field tactics and fighting skills which may have given them a slight advantage, when well led, over their enemies.[101] But financial cuts, the fiscalization of military service and the reduction in the military budget, together with the increasing dominance of foreign mercenaries, all took their toll. Attaleiates, who as a leading official concerned with military affairs during the reign of Romanos IV accompanied the emperor on several campaigns, was particularly scathing about the results of fiscal stringency for the readiness, morale and equipment of the imperial armies, as well as the competence and ability of many of the leading officers. The military failures of the period were, for him, directly attributable to such administrative parsimony and short-sightedness.[102]

The end of "Byzantine" tactics

While mercenary units of professional soldiers – whether the warrior-tribesmen of the steppe peoples or the mounted lancers of the Normans – continued to fight with order and discipline according to their own traditions and battlefield loyalties, the units of the imperial armies seem to have been neglected during the middle years of the eleventh century to the extent that, when the emperor Romanos IV set out on campaign to Syria in 1068, he had to spend some time and energy in recruiting new units and training them to fight effectively. The contemporary chronicler Michael Attaleiates paints a pitiful picture of the state of the thematic levy that was raised before the campaign of 1071, and gives the impression that much of the imperial army was militarily of little value. He states that the soldiers raised from the provinces on the basis of their traditional military obligations were quite unfitted for warfare, having been neither mustered nor having been paid or supplied with their traditional provisions for many years. The older men, who had some experience of fighting, were without mounts and equipment; the newer draftees had no experience at all and were quite without training,[103] and the emperor had to mix them with the more experienced soldiers.[104]

The army was a mixture of regular mercenary units from the different parts of the empire and the older thematic soldiers. The "five *tagmata* of the West", perhaps because they had been less neglected than their eastern counterparts, were classed by Attaleiates alongside the western mercenaries in respect of their military value.[105] No mention is made of their eastern detachments, but the poor state of the eastern forces stems in part from the effects of the civil wars of 1047–8 and 1057. The distinction between the two commands was re-established under the Komnene emperors.[106]

But while Mantzikert was a defeat, the campaigns of Romanos IV in the late 1060s which culminated there were by no means failures. Indeed, the account of Attaleiates, who was an eyewitness, attests to a surprising degree of discipline and competence, with regularly entrenched and fortified camps, considerable tactical order and well-organized lines of supply. This should, perhaps, not surprise us: according to Psellos, Isaac I had revived the traditions of strict discipline and tactical order which central government neglect had threatened, and his forces were both effective and successful in battle.[107] It was the localized incompetence or communications failures, combined with treachery and desertion, which brought about the downfall of Romanos IV's division at Manzikert: the campaign was a strategic failure, but tactically was hardly the disaster it has frequently been made out to be, in spite of the rhetorical flourishes of Attaleiates and others (whose description of the run-down army was intended as much as anything to shift the blame for failure onto the shoulders of the imperial predecessors of Romanos IV).[108]

Nevertheless, the old army was rapidly disappearing. The government of Michael VII could raise only a few hundred troops to march against Roussel de Bailleul in 1073, relying mostly on Turkish allies. By the time of Alexios I's desperate efforts to re-establish imperial authority in the Balkans and northwest Asia Minor, his army consisted almost entirely of mercenaries, and in the sense that these fought with their own weapons and methods, albeit under Byzantine command, we may say that "Byzantine" tactics, in the sense that this term represents something particular and different from those of other peoples, died with the older imperial and thematic armies during the eleventh century. Thereafter, as is clear from the sources, the empire became much more closely integrated into the tactical world of the lands around it: Seljuk, Pecheneg or Cuman horse archers, Norman, German and "Frankish" knights, Bulgarian and Anatolian light infantry, Georgians and Alans from the Caucasus, supplemented by small contingents of imperial guards – mostly recruited from outside the empire, such as the Varangians (from the 1070s chiefly made up of Anglo-Saxons and their retinues abandoning Norman England) – this was the "Byzantine" army of the twelfth century. In spite of attempts by Alexios I and John to re-establish an indigenous army, the armies of the twelfth century were predominantly composed of non-Byzantines. Under Manuel I, the tendency to adopt western heavy cavalry tactics was further stimulated by the emperor himself, who re-equipped many indigenous units in western style and had them trained appropriately. The result was an army whose tactics were no different from any other multi-ethnic, polyglot mercenary army. Niketas Choniates notes the harangue of the commander of the imperial troops fighting against the Hungarians in 1167, who remarks that the formation, military equipment and training are the same for both sides; the difference lay in the Byzantines' better order and tactical dispositions.[109]

There are no military or technical tactical treatises after the later tenth century, although the so-called *Strategikon* of the general Kekaumenos, penned probably in the 1080s or 1090s, reflects the tradition, if in a very generalized and anecdotal form. Byzantine tactics are "Byzantine" only insofar as they represent the fighting techniques of soldiers under Byzantine command; but the extent to which the Byzantine battle formation of the later tenth and eleventh centuries was maintained – regardless of the claim of Kekaumenos that it is superior to all others – remains unclear. What the empire did not possess – heavily armoured western knights – it hired, although there was an attempt under Manuel I to establish a small force of Roman cavalry armed and equipped in the western manner. But by the end of Manuel's reign, although there is precious little clear evidence, Byzantine light infantry and cavalry must have been remarkably similar to their Turkish and Bulgar counterparts, while Byzantine heavy cavalry were modelled on, or hired among, western knights.[110]

Byzantine field dispositions in the 1070s seem still on occasion to have retained an element of the traditional East Roman order of battle. But was there any real difference between the armies of the twelfth-century emperors and their foes, except for the multi-ethnic character of their forces? Choniates describes the battle lines of Byzantine and Hungarian forces in 1167: the imperial troops were drawn up in three main divisions – right, centre and left, with a second line of flanking units behind the wings. Kinnamos distinguishes also the different units – Cumans and Turks, together with some western mercenary knights, made up one division; three Roman taxiarchies, together with archers and some heavily armed Turks and four further taxiarchies two other divisions. A further section of the battle line consisted of elite Roman, German and Turk cavalry, together with the commander-in-chief with a body of allied Serbs and the Lombard mercenary cavalry. Choniates notes that the Hungarian commander had also drawn up his force in three divisions, yet goes on to say that he did not separate the infantry from the cavalry clearly, suggesting that the imperial forces were drawn up in their squadrons and taxiarchies in the traditional manner, a point reinforced by one or two other descriptions and by the fact that John II ordered his forces by division, according to ethnicity, weaponry and so forth. A similar arrangement for the Roman forces in Cilicia in the 1160s under Andronikos Komnenos is described also, although the sources generally depict both the Roman armies and their opponents as drawn up in three divisions.[111]

The distinctiveness of Roman armies in the field, where this continued to be maintained, seems to have depended on the subdivision of the main divisions into separate units and companies, with the taxiarchy as the basic tactical-administrative entity, an arrangement which should have given greater tactical flexibility. Anna Comnena's accounts of her father's battles with the Pechenegs, Cumans and Turks frequently stress the order and discipline of the Roman (including their mercenaries') lines. When Andronikos Komnenos confronted the Cilician Armenians in 1166, in contrast, he appears to have deployed his forces in a more rigid formation, whereas the Armenian commander Thoros arranged his army in a large number of linked companies and, with the assistance of several ambuscades, put the Roman army to flight. But in general, the imperial armies appear – when the sources give any details – to have a more flexible tactical arrangement than their foes. This appears to have been the case in the 1160s still, if the historians' accounts of engagements with the Hungarians and Turks are to be relied upon. But such arrangements clearly depended also on the skill and knowledge of the general: it is significant that the emperor Alexios gave quite explicit instructions to his generals on occasion on how to deploy the army on the field.[112]

There is evidence that the Byzantine infantry and cavalry dispositions which were evolved from their experience in dealing with mounted archers, both the Turks who fought for the Syrian emirates and for the caliphate in the tenth and early eleventh centuries and the Seljuks from the 1060s and afterwards, continued to be employed thereafter, and retained a certain distinctiveness. Anna Comnena describes an oblique hollow square formation adopted by Alexios, which she (and the emperor himself) claimed was quite new and designed to respond to the Turkish tactic of attacking in a series of loosely formed groups and from all sides in order to break up the enemy battle line or column. Such tactics were particularly effective against troops marching in column.[113] Yet the square formation, whether on the battlefield or on the march, was in fact not new, as we have seen (see Chapter 5 above). It was in use from the middle of the tenth century at least if not before, at the end of the tenth century and into the eleventh during the reign of Basil II, and it probably continued to be employed when the situation demanded thereafter.[114] It is possible that, with the destruction or melting away of the regular field and thematic armies in the period between 1071 and the early years of Alexios' reign, it had been abandoned, simply because the empire's forces had come to consist almost entirely of mercenaries, often under their own officers or leaders. In this case, it may be that Alexios was rediscovering (or reintroducing) something with which he might have been familiar from his youth (although he had not fought at Manzikert, he had later been entrusted with the command in the expedition against Roussel de Bailleul in 1073). That the formation worked well is suggested by the fact that it was adopted by the Crusader forces in the east thereafter, where Muslim historians commented on its effectiveness (although whether it was adopted and adapted directly from the Byzantine formation remains unclear), while Choniates' account of the events of 1159 makes it clear that the Byzantine marching order was usually invulnerable to Turkish attack, suggesting the likelihood that Alexios' formation continued to be employed thereafter against enemies such as the Seljuk light horse archers.[115]

Morale and leadership

It remains to comment briefly on two aspects of any army's performance which always play a fundamental role: the competence and ability, as well as the personality, of its commanders, and the related question of the confidence in themselves and their abilities, as well as in their leaders, displayed by the soldiers. We have already noted several examples of troops panicking or refusing to go into action when signals or movements were misconstrued, when officers failed to dress the battle formation suitably, or when the soldiers had no confidence in their leaders. And these issues were clearly recognized by writers on military matters such as Leo VI in the *Tactica*. The psychological state of the soldiers was always a key factor, and the importance of haranguing the troops before battle was widely acknowledged and practised.[116]

It is quite clear that Byzantine armies, when well-led and motivated, could win in even the most difficult situations. But their fighting abilities were compromised by incompetent officers, as we have already noted in examples stretching from the seventh through to the eleventh centuries; by lack of discipline and unit cohesion, another major contributory factor; and by the lack of confidence encouraged by the presence of one or both of these factors. Rumours that the commanding officer had fallen, whether true or not, generally led to panic and rout, as in 678 when Constantine IV's standard was observed leaving the field (he was suffering an attack of gout) promoting panic and flight, or as in 917 when the imperial forces under Leo Phocas had driven back the Bulgars in the first phase of the battle and the commander dismounted to refresh himself. Unfortunately, his horse bolted and, seeing the riderless animal and thinking he had been killed, the cavalry began to panic and turn back from the pursuit, enabling the tsar Symeon to reassemble his forces and counter-attack. In 998 the Byzantine forces had begun the pursuit of the defeated Fatimid forces near Apamaea in Syria when the commander, Damianos Dalassenos, *doux* of Antioch, was killed. Demoralization set in, the Fatimid troops rallied, and victory turned into rout. In 1071 during the engagement at Manzikert, Romanos IV gave the order to withdraw in order: while his own division understood this correctly and began the orderly retreat, more distant contingents saw the imperial standard facing about and assumed the emperor had been driven back or killed, and began to panic and flee. Again, in 1177, when their commander (Andronikos Angelos) abandoned his command during the night, the army fell into a disorderly retreat when he could not be seen the next day, to be halted only by the quick action of the second-in-command Manuel Kantakouzenos.[117] And it was precisely because of this that the treatises recommend that the commander not endanger himself by fighting in the front line. Of course, many leaders ignored this advice, even emperors – John Tzimiskes joined his cavalry in a charge against the Rus' at Dorostolon, for example; Alexios I himself fought a single combat with a Cuman horseman before both armies and won; and the young Manuel Komnenos rashly attacked the enemy, fortunately with success (but was later punished by his father John II); while more notoriously the *patrikios* Leo, commander of Adrianople when it was besieged by the Bulgars in 921, was nicknamed "stupid Leo" for his frequent personal attacks on the enemy forces: personal involvement of the commander was not necessarily either sensible or laudable.[118]

But good morale and forceful leadership might just as easily hold troops together when all appeared to be lost: although the reports of the event are unclear, the imperial *tagmata* appear to have stood and been massacred when their camp, with the emperor Nikephros I, was attacked by surprise by Bulgar forces in 811; in 813 the army of the newly crowned emperor Leo V, weakened and dispirited by recent defeats, was again put to flight by a Bulgar army. But seeing the disarray of the Bulgar troops in pursuit from the hill on which he and his guards had taken station, the emperor mounted a sudden counter-attack, taking the Bulgars completely by surprising and snatching victory from defeat. In 838, it was the elite tagmatic officers along with Kurdish units which had recently fled from the caliphate who stood, isolated and surrounded, to defend the emperor when the rest of the army had been driven off.[119] Clearly, *esprit de corps*, unit identity, kinship loyalties, as well as an especially cultivated loyalty to the emperor, may all have played a role in such situations.

Leadership was not the only factor, therefore, but it was certainly crucial. It is noticeable, for example, that thematic provincial loyalties focus on particular generals; indeed, in battle it was to the divisional commander that soldiers looked for leadership, less so the commander-in-chief: on several occasions it is clear that whole divisions of thematic soldiers simply disregarded the orders or needs of the commander-in-chief, preferring instead to follow their own officer – whether he decided to fight against superior odds, or withdraw even if the battle was going well. Thus at Versinikia in 813 the Macedonian and Thracian contingents on the one flank attacked and began to drive back their Bulgar opponents, while the Anatolikon and (probably) Cappadocian divisions on the other flank, under their commander Leo, began to withdraw, followed by the central divisions (Opsikion, Armeniakon and others). Yet once engaged, the units from Thrace and Macedonia under the *strategos* John Aplakes fought on after they were surrounded, until they were cut to pieces. In 878 in eastern Asia Minor, the two divisions of Charsianon and Armeniakon argued about which deserved the greater battle honours, and each followed its own commander loyally; and we have already seen other examples where officers and the troops under their command failed or refused to support their colleagues.[120] Such specific divisional loyalties (not always a reflection of the competence of the officer in question) had evolved over the period from the establishment of the field armies in Asia Minor, and had on several occasions plunged the empire into civil war – particularly clear divisional loyalties can be seen in the events of the years 698–718, for example, the war between Constantine V and Artavasdos in 741–2 and in the civil war between Michael II and Thomas the Slav in the early 820s. The importance of the soldiers' respect for and loyalty to their own commanders was crucial to these developments.[121] But such loyalties also had a positive aspect. Indeed, the value of placing men from the same communities and of the same kin together in the ranks was clearly recognized, and many military treatises – from the Roman period on – recommended that the general make use of this to strengthen his line. Loyalty to officers from one's own region or army also had its positive side, as when the general Nikephros Botaneiates, following a defeat at the hands of the Pechenegs in 1048 and the break-up of the other Byzantine corps, was able to keep his own forces together in a coherent and tightly disciplined division, and over a period of eleven days march his way back to Adrianople under constant attack.[122]

This fundamental element was certainly recognized by the Romans and Byzantines: Leo VI makes it abundantly clear throughout the *Tactica* that the behaviour and attitudes, knowledge and judgement of the commander of an army was a crucial ingredient in its success or failure. Behind the long list of moral virtues and characteristics which the good general should cultivate one can see the intelligent employment of charisma and personal dynamism which, harnessed to Leo's notion of a "scientific" approach to warfare, were to impose loyalty and discipline on the soldiers, attract the respect and obedience of the officers, and inspire the soldiers to fight bravely. Such virtues are mentioned in earlier treatises, but the *Tactica* devotes a great deal of time to them, frequently repeating itself in order to emphasize the point: emperors were as conscious as everyone else of the dangers posed either by a mutinous army or a disloyal general. Good commanders themselves recognized the importance of their own popularity, and actively encouraged it by regular issues of largesse – indeed, an imperial treatise on campaigns makes it clear that traditional and regular issues of cash and gifts were an essential part of the relationship between commander and soldiers.[123]

Of course, a successful commander with a good record of victories inevit-ably attracted the enthusiasm and loyalty of the soldiers, and success was also conducive to good discipline or the ability to enforce it without demur: Leo VI, following the *Strategikon* of Maurice, suggests that officers should not be too harsh in their application of the disciplinary code, and should take especial note of the context in case the troops should react badly or be demoralized, suggesting that the officers may often have had a fairly tenuous authority over their soldiers at times (and as borne out by some of the evidence we have reviewed already). In contrast, Nikephros Phocas' popularity enabled him to impose draconian measures where he thought an example should be made, measures which appear to have been accepted without complaint from the soldiers.[124] Such differences were clearly understood: military officers them-selves certainly recognized the differences between their individual talents on occasion, so that Leo the Deacon, chronicling the events of the months leading up to the accession of Nikephros Phocas as emperor, has the *patrikios* Marianos point out to another high official that John Tzimiskes is the next-best-loved general after Nikephros, and that the soldiers would follow them anywhere, whereas they would not be so inclined towards himself – competent a general though he was while in command in the west.[125] By the same token, Michael Psellos remarks that the rebel general Bardas Skleros excited a fierce loyalty among his troops, whereas Skylitzes remarks that the general George Maniakes, popular though he was, had a reputation for intemperate and harsh behaviour with regard both to his fellow officers and his soldiers.[126]

The one feature that can, in the right circumstances, make up for incompetent leadership is, of course, discipline and training. This ought to be essential regardless of the context, of course, and all able military leaders, from Belisarius, Narses, Priscus and Philippicus and Maurice in the sixth century, through Heraclius, Constantine V, Basil I to the soldier emperors of the tenth century, knew this. Yet it is clear that it was difficult to maintain a uniform degree of unit cohesion and discipline in Byzantine armies after the sixth century, hence the references in the sources to the efforts of good commanders occasionally trying to address the problem. The main reasons for this we have already outlined: the increasingly localized and seasonal aspect to the armies from the 640s, in conjunction with the decline in status and military value of infantry, the lack of anything other than token training on a regular basis, and the preference for irregular warfare wherever possible. Only the especially recruited mercenary units, such as the imperial *tagmata* and to a lesser extent the "core" thematic contingents (where they can be identified), seem to have maintained an *esprit de corps*. In such a context, therefore, good leadership becomes even more crucial, and it is hardly surprising that the empire's ability to go on to the offensive in the middle of the tenth century was accompanied both by the rise of a number of extraordinarily capable military commanders, and their insistence upon a more rigorous discipline and training programme for the armies than had usually been the case. The ability of commanding officers to impose their will on their forces and maintain a strict discipline was, of course, particularly important in the later tenth and eleventh centuries, when the multi-ethnic character of the Byzantine armies was especially marked. It is precisely the lack of such leadership and discipline which Michael Attaleiates bemoans in the 1060s, a lack which led, in his view, to the defeats which he records under Constantine X and Romanos IV.[127]

Leadership and discipline together could achieve a great deal even in the most adverse circumstances, as when the general Nikephros Botaneiates kept his units together under constant attack while on the retreat from a defeat, or as when imperial troops under Romanos IV, an able and popular general, were able to entrench and fortify their camp while under attack from the Arabs in the campaign of 1068.[128]

Thematic solidarity within divisions, and the discipline and cohesion which this encouraged, was sometimes an adequate replacement for universally applied and enforced training. Combined with competent leaders – as under the successful commanders of the seventh to later ninth centuries – Byzantine armies were frequently able to win great victories or stave off impending disaster. But only from the middle of the tenth century does a regular system of discipline and training seem to have become an expected aspect of imperial field-army service. Even then, of course, and with the best-disciplined and battle-hardened troops, competent leadership was an essential: after the successful landing on Crete in 961 and the penning in of the enemy forces in Chandax, Nikephros Phocas sent his trusted general Nikephros Pastilas inland with a small force to scout and report back on enemy dispositions.

Yet in spite of his experience, he allowed his column to disperse – attracted by the richness of the plunder and the absence of the enemy forces – and was subsequently ambushed and heavily defeated. The eleventh-century general Kekaumenos includes a number of examples of careless generalship in his *Strategikon*.[129] As R.C. Smail noted in his account of the warfare of the Crusades, the results of a battle, even with well-trained and disciplined troops, was in the end unpredictable: "the interplay of morale, individual prowess and good fortune" was the ultimate arbiter. The difference between the good general and the bad general, however, as Leo VI points out in his *Tactica* and as is implicit throughout all Byzantine writing on military affairs, was that the former understood this, behaved in a manner appropriate to the circumstances, and made sure his dispositions could cope with sudden surprises or changes in the conditions of battle. It was precisely the task of a good general to engage only when the circumstances were optimal for a favourable outcome.

CHAPTER SEVEN

Warfare and society

The impact of war: the physical environment

It remains to survey the ways in which warmaking, fighting and the presence of soldiers affected medieval East Roman society, and to examine the physical and cultural environments as they were influenced and determined by these factors.

The military and the provincial populations

The East Roman empire from the seventh century until its disappearance in the fifteenth was, as we have seen in an earlier chapter, in an unenviable strategic position. It had to organize for almost constant warfare on one front or another, and this had enormous implications for the whole population, not just those living adjacent to the frontiers. Warfare was for much of society for considerable periods of time an entirely "normal" element in day-to-day existence, a fact borne out by the constant presence of the topic in personal letters, for example, even in those of the most important members of the ecclesiastical establishment.[1] The impact of warfare manifested itself in several ways. Not only was the population directly affected by hostile activity, it was also subject to the effects of the presence of soldiers of the East Roman forces, whether on campaign or not. The very existence of an army, and the need to supply and provision it and to provide materials and livestock for it when it was on campaign, all contributed. We have already discussed the extensive and burdensome logistical demands of the army, and although few specific examples of the effects of these demands upon the civilian population are revealed in the written sources, enough is known to hint at its magnitude. The burden of supporting soldiers passing through on campaign had always been onerous as many late Roman sources show. This was not just a question of demands made by the army on local populations, but also of the fact that state intervention into local exchange relations on such a large scale could adversely affect the economic equilibrium of an area. In the fourth, fifth and sixth centuries there is good evidence of the distortion of prices as a result of such state activity, either through the fixing of artificially low prices for the sale of produce to the army thus harming the producers, or by sudden heavy demand driving prices for those in the private sector upwards. A graphic account of such effects is given in the Syriac *Chronicle* of Joshua the Stylite, written probably in 506–7, narrating events surrounding the Persian and Roman sieges of Amida during the Roman–Persian war of 502–6, and the effects of the presence of a large concentration of Roman field units in and around Edessa at that time. Not only was the civil population compelled to bake bread and biscuit for the troops; they were in addition subjected to the plundering and pillaging of those elements (the Gothic *foederati* were singled out in particular) which got out of hand. Evagrios describes a similar situation in the late 580s in the province of Phoenici Libanensis.[2] Even more telling is the evidence of the sixth-century legislation on the situation in Thrace and the combined effects of barbarian inroads and military supply demands on the economy of the region.[3]

The *quaestura exercitus*, through the administrative linkage between the Aegean islands and coastal regions and the Danube zone, represented one response to the problem; although Maurice still ordered his armies to winter on the non-Roman side of the river in 593 and 602.[4] Leo VI recommended that generals carry sufficient supplies with the army and forage on enemy territory rather than prey upon the citizens of the empire.[5] The need to avoid harming the provincials by permitting the army to forage and extract supplies without proper administrative controls is often repeated – although even where such controls were established, the presence of a large force of soldiers, their animals and their followers will rarely have been welcome.[6] In Byzantine territory, and presumably when the army arrived in a district which was not warned in advance, troops were sent out to purchase corn and other requirements from the local populations, as occurred during the Manzikert campaign of 1071, for example, where an eyewitness account reports the sending off of a detachment to purchase corn, or of the rearguard lagging behind the main body of the army to protect those sent to purchase supplies.[7] Regardless of the behaviour of the soldiers, as we have seen, this could still distort prices and market relationships, but even on Byzantine territory the depredations of soldiers were difficult to restrain, as in the locality of Krya Pege in 1071, where Roman and mercenary forces cause much damage in their search for supplies and fodder.[8] And whether or not the army was engaged in fighting the enemy, whole communities or individuals might still suffer at the hands of unruly or poorly disciplined soldiers. The monks of the island of Gymnopelagesion in the Aegean were forced to abandon their home in the tenth century as a result of the constant requisitioning of their livestock and other produce by passing vessels of the imperial fleet; the damage inflicted by the poorly disciplined troops of Nikephros II while in Constantinople has been alluded to already; Armenian soldiers, notorious (according to the Greek sources at least) for their wayward conduct and indiscipline, were deeply unpopular with the provincial populations in the tenth and eleventh centuries; and in an eleventh-century source, we read of a local girl who had been robbed by a unit of Armenian troops passing through. Soldiers were always a potentially dangerous body, and a very different view of them emerges when the sources are examined more closely. Choniates notes that Roman troops could be either poorly disciplined on occasion, or ravage imperial territory for their supplies, or both. Either way, the ordinary population suffered.[9] Isaac I was thoroughly aware – as a soldier himself – of the dangers of having his troops in Constantinople, and a contemporary sums up the general attitude to their presence wherever they were found when he speaks of "the troublesome presence of soldiers".[10]

Provincial administrators did try to minimize the effects of passing military forces and one should not exaggerate the problem, although in the last years of Manuel I Komnenos and afterwards it seems to have grown as central government authority waned. Several letters of the ninth–twelfth centuries appeal to state officials against the burden imposed upon them, or their clients, through the imposition of *mitaton* and related expenses; these are on several occasions related explicitly to the effects of the presence of soldiers on campaign. And while we must allow for some degree of hyperbole on the part of the more privileged and literate elements in society, some of the complaints are on behalf of those less fortunate than the writers themselves. Extraordinary levies in grain were particularly onerous, and there are complaints in letters from the early ninth century through to the twelfth century concerning this and related burdens which resulted either from special requirements of the army for particular campaigns or the regular impositions made by the army in its normal operations. Quite apart from purely military requirements, of course, the local provincial populations had also to support the burden of the public post, the *dromos*, with its system of posting stations and stables, stud-farms and breeding ranches, mule-trains and associated requirements. This system served the needs of both the military and the fiscal administration of the empire, contributing not only to the movement of military supplies but also the rapid transit of couriers, imperial officials of all kinds, as well as important foreigners – diplomatic officials, prisoners-of-war and so forth. Although it almost certainly operated on the same basis before, there is evidence from the eleventh and twelfth centuries of groups of individual households being designated specifically as exempted from regular taxes because they supported the costs of one or more elements in this machinery, just as those registered as soldiers were similarly exempted but bore a corresponding different fiscal burden imposed by the government.[11]

The extent to which the soldiers themselves contributed anything to the local economy or to the physical environment remains very unclear. From a

purely economic point of view, newly paid soldiers might well bring the benefits of their custom to local markets, although with the price-distorting effects
noted already. Soldiers could also contribute to the local economy through
funding the building of churches, for example, as the dedicatory inscription
by a local military officer (a *drouggarios*) for a church in 898 appears to testify.[12]
Unlike the legionary soldiers of the period up to the later second century and
perhaps later, however, soldiers of the East Roman empire seem to have made
only minimal contributions to the built environment, in terms of their work
on roads and bridges, for example. They built their own marching camps, of
course, but these were usually temporary and purely military structures. They
appear to have been involved at times in fortress building, although the
evidence is very thin. Thus the soldiers in Constantine V's Balkan expeditions
probably contributed to the building of the forts with which that emperor
protected the borders of Thrace, while in 808/9 the disaffected forces under
Nikephros I on campaign in Thrace objected to rebuilding the fortifications of
Serdica, which seems otherwise to have been taken as a usual aspect of their
duties on campaign. Some inscriptions from the ninth/tenth and early eleventh
centuries likewise suggest the involvement of soldiers in building and fortification work.[13] Officers in the provinces were normally responsible for maintaining
fortifications, both in towns and fortresses as noted in Chapter 2, the labour
usually being provided through the imposition of the burden of *kastroktisia* on
the local peasantry. Thus an eighth-century inscription notes that a certain
Symeon, imperial *spatharios*, was despatched by the emperors Leo and Constantine to take charge of the repairs to the fortress of Rhodandos on the
southeastern frontier.[14] A number of other inscriptions record the restoration
of fortifications by military officers, and it may be that the soldiers under their
command also contributed.[15] But one concrete example of soldiers involved
in building work implies that, at least by the early twelfth century, this was
unusual: instead of employing or conscripting local people, Alexios I paid his
soldiers an extra bounty for their work for which they had volunteered.[16]

The weight of the state's requirements on the local population can be
seen especially clearly from the later tenth and especially the eleventh century,
from which period a large number of imperial grants of exemption from the
billetting of soldiers, the provision of supplies for various categories of troops
in transit, the provision of horses, mules and wagons for the army, as well
as the delivery of charcoal and timber for military purposes are requested and
awarded. The preparations undertaken by the provincial authorities for the
campaigns of emperors such as Nikephros II, Romanos IV or Manuel I entailed
the requisitioning of large numbers of draught-animals, wagons and foodstuffs,
for example, as well as considerable increase in demands for supplies of all kinds.
For Manuel I's campaign of 1160, for example, large numbers of ox-carts
were requisitioned from the peasant farmers of Thrace; similarly in 1176 the
population of Anatolia was subjected to vast requisitions for the army.[17]

While the incidence of demand may have risen in the later tenth and
eleventh centuries as a result of changes in the way the army was recruited,

paid and supplied, there is no doubt that the military presence was always a heavy burden. From the Roman period through to the twelfth century there is evidence for the continued existence of state obligations such as those named above, as well as those imposed for the maintenance of roads and bridges.[18] The archbishop Theophylact of Ohrid complains in the late eleventh and early twelfth centuries about the oppressive weight of the state demands on church tenants, especially in respect of labour demanded for the repair, maintenance or construction of fortifications (*kastroktisia*). He complains likewise about special conscriptions for the army, which takes men away from an already weakened local population. The agricultural population was cruelly exploited by imperial fiscal officials, to the extent that Theophylact remarks on the flight of many to the forests to escape such oppression. Demands for raw materials, timber and so forth were also a regular item on the state's list of military needs. Such requisitions and demands, the hardship they caused, and the administrative and bureaucratic structures which gave rise to them continued to the last years of the empire to be a major burden on its rural population.[19] And the more effectively powerful landlords, whether secular or monastic, were able to gain exemptions, the greater the burden on the remaining rural population.[20]

By the last years of the twelfth century, and reflecting the weakening of the system of dynastic and clan alliances which had enabled the Komnenos family to govern so effectively hitherto, there occurred also a drastic weakening of central governmental authority over many regions, with provincial governors free to plunder the districts they governed for their salaries and the resources with which to support their own retinues and administration. The best exemplification of the situation that accompanied these developments is found in the letters of Michael Choniates, Metropolitan of Athens in the last 20 years or so of the twelfth century: in spite of reforming efforts by the emperor Andronikos I Komnenos (1183–5), the hardships caused to the ordinary peasantry and the urban population of Athens by the visits of imperial officials and their retinues, the exaction of supplies and livestock for the navy (three times in one year on one occasion) and the inability of the imperial government to ameliorate the situation continued unabated. This situation was not typical for Greece alone: many other regions clearly suffered under similar pressures, among which the needs of the army or navy figured prominently:[21] in certain regions of the empire in the twelfth century the native population preferred the less oppressive rule of the emperor's enemies for exactly the same reasons, and while they were branded by the government and by those who remarked on the phenomenon as traitors to the Roman and Christian cause, the reasons for their attitude and actions is clear.[22]

As well as affecting the local economy, of course, the presence of soldiers affected also local power relationships and the social environment in which they were rooted. In the first case, local military commanders might use their troops to improve their own social and economic situation, by employing them to coerce the population in one form or another. In the period up to the tenth century, provincial military commanders were endowed with authority over considerable resources in manpower and the coercive power vested in their office. This became especially problematic after the ninth century, when military officers in the provinces frequently came from landed families – ninth- and tenth-century legislation explicitly mentions the fact that soldiers are attracted into the "private" service of "powerful" persons, and that officers take soldiers away from their duties and employ them in their own service. The growth of military retinues at this time and thereafter is a basic feature of Byzantine social development.[23] But as often as not, it was the regular troops of a region who harassed and terrorized the local population, even those seconded to the provinces to deal with banditry and brigandage. There is a mass of sixth-century material testifying to this, although there is no reason to doubt that the basic problem continued to exist through the whole period in question. An imperial rescript issued in 527 grants imperial protection to an oratory in Pamphylia from the harm inflicted by soldiers and officers charged with policing the region against brigands; several *novellae* or laws issued in respect of reorganizing provincial administration in both Asia Minor and prov- inces such as Palestine and Arabia refer to similar problems, and in particular the illegal imposition on local people by soldiers and other officials of extra prestations, hospitality and similar demands; Justinian's Edict VIII, issued in 548, refers explicitly to the abuses of soldiers in the provinces (in this case, in the Pontic diocese), as does a petition of 569 in Egypt, addressed to the *dux* of Thebaid, requiring him to put a stop, among several abuses, to those of the state *bucellarii* who had been hiring out their services to private landlords.[24]

The role and influence of soldiers reflected also the ways in which they were recruited and remunerated. This was especially true when, in the second half of the seventh century, the government distributed the soldiers across the provinces so that they could be maintained directly, and at least in part, through taxes raised and redistributed in kind rather than by paying them entirely in cash. In this context, soldiers developed local and regional – thematic – loyalties and identities which could be expressed in military rebellions and internecine conflict, identities which were reinforced as many began to contribute to their own maintenance, drawing on family resources, so that a degree of privatization of military finance evolved, with the local vested interests which such a develop- ment entailed. Soldiers became much more closely involved in the politics of their own regions, and the loyalties that evolved between thematic armies and their commanders – who in the later ninth and tenth centuries were often major landlords in the regions from which their troops were drawn – directly affected the internal politics of the state.[25]

Warfare and the provincial population

Warfare and fighting inevitably damaged both the economy and the social relationships of village and provincial life. Where it caused no damage, it influenced the pattern and tempo of life in many different ways. On occasion, emperors exempted whole provinces from taxation for a specified period to permit them to recover. Tiberius Constantine remitted taxes for a large number of provinces in the late 570s, for example, while Nikephros I undertook several unpopular measures intended both to re-establish the state finances and to repopulate devastated regions in the early ninth century. Other measures might also be taken: the empress Eirene cancelled the campaign payments made in lieu of military service, which were the cause of hardship for widows of registered soldiers, for example.[26]

During the sixth century widespread Persian raiding in Syria and Mesopotamia caused both demographic decline in many regions and brought about the removal of substantial numbers of people as captives to Persia. Refugee populations brought further dislocation to the regions into which they migrated: many people are recorded to have fled westwards before the advance of Persian troops in eastern Anatolia in the 570s, for example. During the seventh century devastation caused both the abandonment of some regions, the deliberate evacuation of others in order to hinder enemy activity, and the movement of refugees from threatened to safe areas. Refugee populations were on the move in the areas affected by the Slav immigration into the regions south of the Danube from the later sixth century on, and later from the affects of Avar and then Bulgar raids and invasions. Some slight evidence of refugees from southern and central Anatolia towards the Black Sea coast and the northwestern regions of the subcontinent can be found in sources of the seventh century, while Theophanes refers to the resettlement in Thrace by Nikephros I of refugees from Asia Minor in 806/7. Given the constant state of insecurity along the frontier zone in Anatolia throughout much of the later seventh, eighth and ninth centuries, such problems must have been commonplace. The effect of the arrival of refugees in a hitherto unaffected area, even in quite small numbers, could be dramatic, causing a shortage of foodstuffs, disruption of local administration and cultural conflict, quite apart from the secondary consequences: violence, disease, further demographic dislocation.[27] The Quinisext council which met at Constantinople in 692 had to legislate for cases where bishops abandoned their flocks and wandering monks and "holy men" distressed the rural populace with their activities, presumably their preaching. Popular literature of the apocalyptic variety may have circulated at times among the literate to further encourage dismay and anxiety and dilute resistance, so that the response of the populations in affected regions was of more than academic interest to the government's war effort. The effects of Seljuk raids on the economy and administration of western Asia Minor in the eleventh and twelfth centuries were similar, stimulating both the flight of populations away from the affected regions and the alienation of some of the population from the imperial government.[28]

Both economic and demographic disruption threatened the control of the government at Constantinople over its resources; it also threatened the church's authority and ability to supervise the Christian communities most affected. In the middle Byzantine period there is good evidence of serious concern on the part of the church with respect to supposed "pagan" practices and folk-beliefs, for example, which posed a challenge to some aspects of church doctrine.[29] Similarly there is both written and archaeological evidence of the flight of populations as well as the movement of settlements (to more defensible locations) from the Aegean islands, the object of the attention of pirates and raiders from the later seventh into the ninth and tenth centuries. Hagiographies of the ninth, tenth and eleventh centuries all make reference to the devastation caused by "barbarian" attacks, and in some cases it seems that areas in Asia Minor first attacked in the seventh century, and regularly thereafter, were still only at the beginning of recovery in the later tenth century. Their pages are filled with tales involving soldiers or warfare, however distant and however unmilitary the story and the context: soldiers, and the possibility of warfare, are a constant background theme in the daily life of Byzantium.[30] In one eighth-century account, the population of the beleaguered fortress town of Euchaita consider abandoning their homes in an effort to locate a less hazardous environment (as did indeed happen in one or two documented cases), and the text speaks almost mechanically in terms of "when the yearly raid of the Saracens came".[31] Indeed, it was not only in literature that the more gruesome effects of warfare were to be seen: the Patriarch Nikephros refers in one of his polemical writings to the bones of the soldiers slain at the battle of Anchialos in 763 which could still be seen there at the beginning of the ninth century.[32]

In some cases, the emperors catered for particular groups by providing for their removal at imperial expense to a safer area, as with the resettlement during the last years of the seventh century in the province of Hellespont of refugees from the island of Cyprus, under the leadership of their bishop.[33] In several other cases, the government pursued a deliberate policy of repopulating areas most seriously affected by enemy invasion or other war-related calamities (plague, famine, etc.). Thus on several occasions during the second half of the seventh and the eighth centuries large numbers of Slavs were forcibly transplanted to Asia Minor, while similarly people from eastern Asia Minor in particular were removed to Thrace. In both cases, a political as well as a fiscal/demographic end was achieved, for the new populations were intended also to be a source of recruits for the army and of fiscal income for the state, as well as representing an element hostile to the depredations of whichever enemy threatened their new homeland. But such activity had important repercussions on the ethnic and cultural composition of the Byzantine world thereafter.[34]

The recovery of the Anatolian provinces of the empire from the raiding and devastation of the later seventh to the early ninth centuries was slow, whereas in Greece and the Peloponnese the process appears to have taken off more rapidly. Comparative evidence suggests that Balkan towns and the economy as a whole were more flourishing, earlier, than in Asia Minor, with some localized exceptions.[35] But the consequences of the defeat at Manzikert and the political vacuum which followed were the more or less unopposed occupation of the western and southern regions, and especially the central plateau, of Anatolia. Although the emperors were able to re-establish imperial power in the western parts, as we have seen (Chapters 2 and 3 above), the dislocation and devastation of the last decades of the eleventh century took their toll, and western Anatolia began to suffer from Turkish raids in the way that southern and southeastern Anatolia had suffered at the hands of the Arabs. Establishing a new frontier facing the plateau took time, and it was not until the reign of Manuel that Byzantine possession was secure and a limit set to the raiding. The process was aided by the traditional policy of transplanting populations: in this case, captured Serbs settled in Bithynia. Western visitors who passed through the region noted the many ruined towns as well as those which had been refortified and rebuilt, and William of Tyre notes that Attaleia, an important military base in the southwest, was so harassed by Turkish raids that it had to be supplied by sea since the populace was prevented from cultivating the rich arable land around the city. While western and northwestern Anatolia had made a substantial recovery by the end of Manuel's reign, a recovery which was the basis for the power of the empire of Nicaea in the first half of the thirteenth century, the long land frontier, the nature and numbers of the nomadic Türkmen raiders, and the limited resources of the empire made a successful long-term defence very problematic. In the event, it was really only after the region had been absorbed into the various Turkish successor states of Anatolia that economic prosperity returned on a more permanent basis.[36]

The recovery of provincial life in both the southern Balkans and Asia Minor which accompanied the empire's adoption of a more offensive military and political stance in the tenth and early eleventh centuries was compromised from the later 1060s and afterwards in Anatolia by the effects of the raids of Seljuk Turk nomads who laid wide tracts of territory waste in their raiding and pillaging expeditions; and even after the re-establishment of a defensible frontier under Alexios I and John II, a situation developed in western Asia Minor and along the divide between the Pontic regions and the Anatolian plateau which was comparable to that which had evolved earlier along the Taurus–Anti-Taurus ranges in its economic and demographic effects: both in respect of the construction of defenses, refortifying strongpoints and the implications this labour had for the provincial population, as well as in the direct economic consequences – loss of livestock, enslavement of populations, destruction of dwellings – similarities in effect can be seen.[37]

The population of the eastern Roman state was never wholly free from the violent and disruptive effects of warfare. Undoubtedly the worst and most extensive devastation occurred during the seventh and eighth centuries, a period during which virtually every province was affected on some occasions, and during which frontier regions were rendered almost unviable economically and socially. Western Anatolia was equally badly affected by the Türkmen raids of the later eleventh and early twelfth centuries. In addition, we should also bear in mind the cycles of endemic disease – especially of bubonic and related types of plague – which regularly devastated the Middle and Near East and Balkan regions throughout the medieval period. A major pandemic affected the population of the empire in the 540s, and returned in smaller but still devastating waves throughout the seventh and eighth centuries – to the extent that the emperor Constantine V had to repopulate Constantinople from the Aegean isles and coastal regions which had been less badly affected. And although it returned on the same scale as the sixth-century attack only in the form of the Black Death in the late 1340s, the region was never entirely free of it. Warfare, especially the movement of refugees accompanied by the destruction of crops and pollution of water supplies, contributed directly to the spread of disease of one sort or another, of course, so that the consequences of a long period of such disruption – as in parts of Anatolia during the later seventh and eighth centuries, for example – must have had very marked results. But the sources provide little detail, and most attempts to estimate the demographic effects of such developments remain highly speculative. Yet local populations were often able to find ways of maintaining a precarious existence, so that when the situation stabilized and peace again came to those areas, urban and rural economies were once again able to develop. This is more true of the Balkans than southern Anatolia, but the flow of Syrian and Armenian immigrants to the latter region in the tenth and eleventh centuries, partly under imperial auspices, certainly assisted the re-establishment of a flourishing provincial agriculture and market relations which were only slowly recovering from three centuries of border warfare.[38]

Paradoxically, while warfare has a disruptive effect on patterns of social and cultural life, it inevitably also stimulates change and new ways of doing things in response. Warfare thus directly influenced the patterns of daily existence, so that distinctive cultural traditions evolved in those areas most regularly affected by military activity and hostile action, most clearly along the Taurus–Anti-Taurus front. These developments were intimately linked with the seasonal nature of the fighting, since the Arab raiders established already in the later seventh century a pattern of spring and summer raids, a pattern which became firmly entrenched in the frontier provinces of both sides, after the abandonment of the Islamic effort to eradicate the empire following the defeat of 717–18 and the transfer of the political capital to Baghdad in the 750s. Here, a distinctive frontier culture and society evolved, not only on the Byzantine side, in the *akritika themata*, the frontier themes, but also on the Arab side, in the regions of the *Thughur* (frontier districts) and the *'Awasim* (the protecting fortresses), which gave rise at one level not only to a value-system and way of life very different from that in the inner provinces, but which also stimulated social relationships, inter-cultural contacts and influences, and an oral tradition very different in many respects from that of "mainstream" East Roman (or Islamic) culture.[39] The differences between life in these regions and in the areas of the empire less affected by the constant fighting was well-understood at Constantinople and, presumably, among all those involved with the warfare.

Such local identities with land and community evolved throughout the empire, but were perhaps most clearly expressed in the frontier *themata*. Here, warfare on both sides of the frontier soon lost its exclusively "religious" and "ideological" character to become an integrated aspect of day-to-day existence and reality, a state which radically affected attitudes to the enemy, diminishing the anxiety and fear of the unknown which the less affected populations and those of the imperial capital felt, replacing these feelings among the soldiers and their leaders with an element of mutual respect for and recognition of the warriors and their achievements. Nevertheless, elements of this military value-system were reproduced in a metropolitan cultural context. For the values and the interest in warfare characteristic of the provincial military elite, with its emphasis on individual bravery and heroism, personal honour and skill with weapons, was reflected also in the accounts of their deeds written by the historians of the tenth and eleventh centuries. Leo the Deacon frequently alludes to this code of conduct in his account of the battles of his main protagonists, Nikephros II and John Tzimiskes: individual combats, hand-to-hand struggles between the heroes of two opposing armies, challenges to resolve whole battles on the outcome of a duel between the two chosen heroes of the Byzantines and their foes, the martial skill and courage of particular leaders, especially the emperors themselves, these are all motifs which reflect not only the reality of the warfare of the period along with the values of those who lead the imperial armies and the social milieu they represented, but also the evolution of a new attitude to the representation of warfare in the literature of this period, generated by the demands of the Byzantine social establishment as well as the preferred self-image of the soldiers themselves. That these attitudes had taken root in Byzantine literate society by the later eleventh century is demonstrated by the admiration shown by some Byzantine writers of the time for Frankish military prowess and bravery (even while they were disparaged as dangerous barbarians).[40]

By the eleventh and twelfth centuries certainly, if not long before, this was being expressed in the form of orally transmitted epic adventures such as *Digenis Akrites* on the Byzantine side of the border, and parallel traditions in both the Arabic and Armenian cultural world. Needless to say, the cultural evolution represented by this world was one variant within a complex whole, with which it continued to have much in common. Nevertheless, there evolve clear contrasts between what might be called "outer provincial", "inner provincial" and metropolitan cultures, of which Byzantines themselves were certainly aware in terms of cultural discourse and sometimes politics, contrasts which were but one of the long-term consequences of this state of constant warfare.[41]

One of the most painful experiences of a population subject to hostile action is that of losing captives to the enemy, either through death or enslavement. The latter was a regular instrument of policy in all Byzantine wars, practised both by the imperial armies on the one hand and by the enemies of the empire on the other. The ransoming of prisoners was an established means for barbarians to obtain cash or gifts – gold and silver coin, precious cloths and so on – in Roman and later Roman times, and generals or rulers who did not ransom captives when the opportunity arose were deeply unpopular.[42] But by the later eighth and early ninth centuries, if not before this time, a regular custom of exchanging prisoners of war at specific points in the "frontier" region had developed, through which Christian and Muslim prisoners were exchanged, not always on a 1 : 1 basis, of course – rank, importance and value to the ransomer played a key role. Non-Christian prisoners were sometimes converted to Orthodoxy, and sometimes simply recruited into the army as mercenaries or regular soldiers, a tradition maintained from Roman and late Roman times.[43]

Philanthropy was in theory the guiding motif of the Byzantines in dealing with prisoners, and neither Islam nor Christianity condone the use of violence to convert, nor the killing of prisoners. But on occasion military leaders in particular adopted a much more pragmatic and ruthless approach. According to the chronicler Theophanes in the early ninth century, the emperor Constantine V publicly beheaded a number of Bulgar captives taken during his victorious campaign in 761/2, a reflection both of Constantine's own policy with regard to the Bulgars and contemporary propaganda. More pragmatically, on two occasions Basil I gave orders to kill prisoners of war, who were proving to be a considerable burden to his army during its homeward march through the mountains. Alexios I refused on humanitarian grounds to execute the large number of prisoners his forces had recently taken, which were presented as a major threat to his army's security, according to Anna's account. The sources, both Byzantine and Arab, furnish many other examples, and it is possible that in such cases both the transmission of information back to the enemy was feared, or some form of sabotage, as well as the danger that the captives might overwhelm the captors or the existence of simple religious prejudice and fanaticism on either side. The treatise on *Skirmishing* recommends that military prisoners either be sent on ahead or, if circumstances are difficult, slaughtered outright, to avoid burdening the army unduly.

The ideological current of the moment appears to have been the major determining factor, however – there is a notable relaxing of attitudes towards Muslim prisoners during the tenth century, when the empire was, on the whole, much more successful in waging war against its Muslim neighbours than had hitherto been the case. Prisoners-of-war were a valuable source of information for both their own side and their captors, of course, and this also affected the way in which they were treated.[44] But more constructive and humane attitudes tended to prevail. In some examples, Muslim prisoners were married to the widows of former imperial soldiers, given land on which to settle and registered – after a "setting-up" period – as regular taxpayers. The loss of friends, relatives, or fellow-subjects of the empire to hostile raiders was a regular occurrence and even taken for granted in many regions of the empire for much of its history. Some of the letters referred to already lament such losses and the fate of those who had been carried off, and collections of miracles of the saints frequently include stories about Byzantine soldiers captured in war and miraculously freed by the saint's intervention.[45]

Sometimes prisoners were faced with a stark choice, especially on the eastern front – convert to Islam or die. And the period of captivity could vary: sometimes it might be permanent, as captives were transported to distant regions of their captors' lands; on other occasions, especially when a ransom could be arranged, it might be fairly short. The son of the *domestikos* of the Scholai, Bardas Phocas, was captured in battle by Saif ad-Daulah in 957, but while being taken back to his captor's headquarters died of an illness contracted en route. The text of the letter of condolence sent by the emir to the young man's father provides a touching insight into the personal psychology of loss and bereavement, albeit from the most privileged levels of society, and illustrates also the mutual respect in which such warriors from opposing sides held one another. The two sons of the commander of the garrison of Antioch, defeated and killed by Fatimid forces in 998, were taken off to Egypt and released only ten years later when a ransom was arranged. But from the point of view of Byzantine observers and participants, the frequent mention of loss of friends and relatives as prisoners to the enemy serves to underline the ubiquity and inevitability of the wars to which their state was irremediably committed. A tenth-century Arab report claims that in one church – perhaps in the frontier districts, the location is not clear – images of famous Muslim war leaders were to be seen alongside those of Byzantine warriors. In fact, this was probably a misinterpretation of a series of frescoes depicting the battles between the two sides. But it is a telling indication of the attitudes to "the war", prevailing on both sides of the frontier regions, which we have discussed.[46]

Death or capture were not the only possible outcomes of warfare, of course. Far more soldiers suffered injury – and perhaps eventual death – from wounds of one sort or another than died in battle, and the basic system of medical care which had evolved in the earlier Roman army seems to have been preserved, although no doubt with modifications and changes over time.[47] The arrangements for those who were wounded were given some priority in the military manuals: in the *Strategikon* of Maurice a small number of soldiers were detached from each unit, referred to as *depotatoi*, whose task was to follow a short distance behind their unit in action to assist wounded soldiers – their mounts were equipped with an extra stirrup to help carry the wounded to safety. The same prescription is repeated in Leo's *Tactica*, although the *depotatoi* are referred to as "those now called *skribones*", and it is difficult to know to what extent the practice continued unaltered. In the later tenth-century treatise on *Campaign Organisation* the wounded were then to be taken back, when the army was returning to imperial territory, with a section of the rearguard, transported on the pack-animals no longer required for the army's supplies, presumably to the next major camp or base. Kinnamos records that during the battle with the Hungarians for the Danube fortress of Zeugminon in 1165 the Roman wounded were taken off by warship and replacements were ferried in by the same means.[48]

The treatment of wounds – just as the study of diseases – was regarded as an important aspect of medical knowledge, and the Alexandrian physician Paul of Aegina, writing in the middle of the seventh century, devoted part of a medical treatise to the problems of extracting arrow-heads (including also a substantial amount of detail on types of arrow-head and shaft), dealing with fractured or broken bones, and related injuries that were typical of fighting.[49] Military surgeons certainly accompanied the army according to the sixth- and tenth-century military treatises, and Procopius describes in detail how they treated various wounds, including the extraction of an arrow-head which had pierced the soldier's face between the nose and the right eye after a battle with the Goths. Another soldier, who received a javelin in the skull, died as a result of the infection which followed its withdrawal, while a third, who received a series of deep cuts in the back and thigh, eventually died from blood loss in spite of the efforts of the physicians. Several other historians also give descriptions of the sorts of wounds incurred by soldiers in battle or of the treatment of wounds, up to the twelfth century.[50] There is no evidence of specifically military hospitals, and if soldiers were not cared for in the general hospitals established at Constantinople and in some provincial centres, they were most probably looked after by their families, assuming that they survived their wounds and the journey and that they had families who could look after them. Choniates mentions that Manuel issued cash from the imperial treasury to cover the expenses of medical treatment for soldiers wounded in the wars with the Turks in Asia Minor in the 1170s. How exceptional this was is impossible to say.[51]

Cities, villages and fortifications

One of the most obvious effects of warfare is to be seen in the architectural heritage of a society, primarily in respect of fortifications and in shifts in settlement patterns and relationships between centres of consumption and areas of production. In the East Roman world such shifts are especially apparent during the seventh century and in the aftermath of the Persian and more particularly the Arab invasions. While these wars were in themselves neither the original stimulus for the transformation of urban life in the late Roman and early Byzantine period, nor the only factor affecting the evolution of fortified inhabited sites during the period from the seventh to the twelfth centuries, they were nevertheless a crucial factor in the form towns and fortresses took and in the pace of their evolution.[52]

In fact, there had been a slow process of transformation in the pattern of late Roman urban society over the centuries preceding both the Persian wars and the Arab conquests which it will be worth very briefly summarizing here. During the Roman period cities – *poleis* or *civitates* – had held a key role in both social and economic relations, as well as in the imperial fiscal administration. They could function as market centres for their district or region or, where ports were concerned, as major foci of long-distance commerce. Some fulfilled all these roles, others remained merely administrative centres created by the state for its own fiscal administrative purposes. All cities were also self-governing districts with, originally, their own lands, and were made responsible by the Roman state for the return of taxes – indeed, where cities in their Mediterranean form did not exist, the Roman state created them, either establishing new foundations or amalgamating or changing the form of pre-existing settlements, providing them with the corporate identity, institutional structure and legal personality of a *civitas*.[53] All cities, with a few exceptions such as Rome and Constantinople, were dependent on their immediate hinterlands for their (usually highly localized) market and industrial functions, where these existed at all, as well as for the foodstuffs on which the urban populace lived. As the society of the empire evolved away from the relationships and conditions which gave rise to and maintained these urban structures, so the cities became the first key institution of the classical world to feel the effects of these changes.

The form which these changes took are complex, but mirror the effects of a growing tension between state, cities and private landowners to extract surpluses from the producers, and the failure of the cities to weather the contradictions between their municipal independence on the one hand, and on the other the demands of the state and the vested interests of the wealthier civic landowners. While many cities were able to maintain themselves and their fiscal role well into the first half of the seventh century in the east, it is clear already by the later fourth century that many did or could not. There were regional variations, but as a result, and over the period from the later fourth to the later fifth century (in the west until the empire disappears as well as in the east), the state had to intervene increasingly to ensure the extraction of revenues, so that the burden of fiscal accountability had been considerably reduced, if not removed entirely, during the reign of Anastasius (491–518).[54] This may even have promoted the brief renaissance in urban fortunes which took place in some eastern cities in the sixth century, but it did not re-establish their traditional independence and fiscal responsibilities.

The physical structure of cities was transformed over the course of the later fifth and sixth centuries, and archaeological evidence has revealed an almost universal tendency for cities to lose by neglect many of the features familiar from their classical structure. Major public buildings fall into disrepair, systems of water supply are often abandoned (suggesting a drop in population), rubbish is dumped in abandoned buildings, major thoroughfares and public spaces are built on, and so on. These changes may not necessarily have involved any substantial reduction in economic or exchange activity in cities, of course.[55] On the other hand, the undoubted decline in the maintenance of public structures or amenities – baths, aqueducts, drains, street surfaces, walls – is suggestive of a major shift in the modes of urban living: of both the object of the investment of wealth, and of finance and administration in particular. And from the middle of the seventh well into the ninth century the only evidence for building activity associated with provincial urban contexts concerns fortification work and the construction or repair of churches or buildings associated with monastic centres.[56]

By the early years of the seventh century all the evidence suggests that cities as corporate bodies were simply less well-off than they had been before about the middle of the sixth century. There may have been as much wealth circulating in urban environments as before, with the difference that the city as an institution had only very limited access to it, having lost their lands and the income from those lands. During the later sixth century in particular the local wealthy tended to invest their wealth in religious buildings or related objects (so that there was an evolving pattern of investment as much as there was a decline). In addition, the church was from the fourth century a competitor with the city for the consumption of resources. And however much their citizens might donate, individually or collectively, this can hardly have compensated for this loss.[57] Indeed, such contributions became the main source of independent income for many cities. The archaeological data suggests a shrinkage of the occupied area of many cities during the sixth century, and even an increasing localization of exchange activity; but again, this does not have to mean a change in their role as local centres of such exchange.

The survival of urban settlements during and after the Arab invasions – thus from the 640s until the 750s – owed much to the fact that they might occupy defensible sites, as well as be centres of military or ecclesiastical administration. But endemic warfare and insecurity, economic dislocation and social change meant that the great majority played a role peripheral to, and derived from, the economic and social life of the countryside, and reflected if anything the needs of state and church. The invasions of the seventh century dealt what was simply the final blow to an institution that was already in the process of long-term transformation.[58]

Fortifications serve several purposes: to protect populations and/or soldiers and their supplies, equipment and armaments, to act as refuges for civilian populations in times of need, and to provide safe bases for soldiers from which to protect the surrounding countryside or a particular route or crossroads of strategic value, as well as to serve as a deterrent to hostile attack and as defended watch-posts to warn of invasion and perhaps to delay the enemy advance, or to function as bases from which raids or attacks against enemy installations might also be mounted. Each of these functions demands different sorts of defensive works, of course, depending upon size, location, availability of supplies of food and water, proximity to similar defensive structures, the possibilities of relief when attacked, and so forth. The Roman state had a long and sophisticated tradition of fortification, and this was inherited without a break by its medieval East Roman successor.

During the period from the third to the sixth century the Roman world saw a generalized tendency to provide settlements of all sizes with walls and some form of defensive perimeter where there had hitherto been no such defences, a reflection both of a real threat in those areas most affected by external attack, and a changing set of assumptions about what a "city" should look like. In many exposed areas a move from a lowland site to a more defensible situation nearby, or the re-use of older pre-Roman hilltop fortified sites takes place, and although there are a number of reasons for this gradual process in the late Roman period, it increases very dramatically during the later fourth and fifth centuries in the Balkans as a result of the constant threat from Germanic and steppe nomadic barbarians, and again during the seventh century in Anatolia in response to the effects of the Persian and then particularly the Arab invasions and raids. But the contrast between the late ancient *polis* and the middle Byzantine *kastron* should not be exaggerated: of the large number of settled sites which can clearly be differentiated from undefended rural settlements, only a small proportion bore the official or unofficial characteristics of a *polis* in the classical sense. A far larger number were characterized already in the fourth and fifth centuries, and especially in the sixth century, by features normally identified archaeologically and topographically as characteristic of defended centres of population with administrative and military functions, exactly the same, in fact, as the later Byzantine *kastron*.[59] The transformations which occurred did not, except in a relatively small number of cases, involve a universal abandonment of formerly urban sites (*poleis*) in favour of hilltop fortified sites (*kastra*). Rather, it involved a change in the way populations were distributed between such sites, their extent and how they were occupied.[60]

With a handful of exceptions, such as Nicaea, Constantinople and Thessaloniki, most of the major classical cities shrank during the seventh century to the size of their defended citadels, even though the "lower city" of such towns – the main late Roman inhabited area – may have been in many cases still the site of smaller communities. Archaeological surveys suggest that Ancyra shrank to a small citadel during the 650s and 660s, the fortress occupying an area of 350 × 150 metres, the occupied upper town in which it was situated occupying an area not much larger; Amorion, which supposedly had a vast perimeter wall, was defended successfully in 716 by 800 men against an attacking army more than ten times larger, the area of the *kastron* occupying some 450 × 300 metres. The latter survey has also shown that, while the classical/late Roman site was indeed very extensive, with an impressive wall and towers, the occupied medieval areas were thus similar to those of Ancyra. Amastris, mod. Amasra, offers similar evidence, as does Kotyaion, mod. Kütahya, and there are many more formerly major centres which underwent a similar transformation.[61] In some Byzantine texts, mostly hagiographical, there occur descriptions of "cities" with populations inhabiting the lower town.[62] Excavations at Amorion and several other sites show that while the very small fortress-citadel continued to be defended and occupied, discrete areas within the late Roman walls also continued to be inhabited, often centred around a church. In Amorion there were at least two and probably three such areas.[63] Small but distinct communities thus continued to exist within the city walls, while the citadel or *kastron* – which kept the name of the ancient *polis* – provided a refuge in case of attack. Many cities of the seventh to ninth centuries survived because their inhabitants, living effectively in separate communities or villages within the walls, saw themselves as belonging to the *polis* itself.[64] In some cases, the walls of the lower town area were maintained – irregularly, for the most part – in order to provide shelter for larger than usual concentrations of troops. This may have been the case at Amorion, for example. Together with the large number of much smaller garrison forts and outposts of a purely military nature (although sometimes associated with village settlements nearby or below them), such provincial *kastra* (which were also called, confusingly, *poleis* by their inhabitants and by many writers who mention them) and frontier fortresses, generally sited on rocky outcrops and prominences, often also the sites of pre-Roman fortresses, typified the East Roman provincial countryside well into the Seljuk period and beyond, and determined the pattern of development of urban centres when they were able to expand once more during the tenth and eleventh centuries.

There is in the development of late Roman fortification a move from passive, linear defences sufficient to repel relatively primitive, barbarian attackers, to more complex, active defensive arrangements, with large numbers of towers providing intersecting fields of fire and complex gate arrangements. Byzantine fortresses after the seventh century generally involved combinations of protruding towers, angled gates, sometimes including a tower-fortress integrated into an inner curtain wall. The notion of a central stronghold that could continue to resist the enemy after the curtain had fallen and the "lower" defences were taken can be traced back to the Hellenistic period at least in some Anatolian fortresses, and was reflected both in the reoccupation and refortification of many ancient citadels and acropoleis within, or attached to, cities of the Roman period as well as in the construction of tower-fortresses where a natural defensive height was not available (as at Nicaea, for example). The Norman and western keep represents the same idea, given added stimulus in respect of technique and materials, especially in the use of lime mortar, by the Crusaders' experiences in the Balkans, Asia Minor and Syria-Palestine.[65] With the recovery of the empire's economic stability from the ninth century on, many urban centres recovered their fortunes, although their physical appearance was very different from that of their late antique predecessors. On the eastern frontier especially the empire constructed a number of major fortified centres serving chiefly as strategic centres and military bases, rather than centres of local population, fortresses which have only recently attracted the attention of archaeologists and architectural historians and which clearly had a major role in both frontier defence and internal security.[66] Such fortifications closely reflected the strategic networks of the regions in which they were established, both in respect of communications and routes of ingress and egress, as well as – depending upon the region – of economic activity and the movement of resources. Fortifications were an integral element of every town and, as we have seen in Chapter 3 above, the recovery of substantial areas in western Asia Minor during the first half of the twelfth century owes much to the policies of Alexios I, John II and Manuel I in utilizing fortress towns as solid bases which, regardless of the frequency or damage caused by the raids of the Turk nomads from the plateau to the east, could control the countryside and maintain imperial political and fiscal authority.[67] Warfare – and the events of the seventh century in particular

– had a lasting effect on the pattern and form of concentrated settlement in both the Balkans and Asia Minor, a pattern that was further inflected in Asia Minor especially by the Seljuk invasions and the warfare of the twelfth century and after.

The impact of war: the cultural environment

Perceptions and representations of war

We have already seen that, at certain times and under certain conditions, warfare could be glorified, especially by those most involved, soldiers and their leaders. In addition, we have seen that there evolved a range of official and semi-official views about the undesirability and necessity of warfare. But there were many other perspectives on war and fighting, reflecting the attitudes held by the provincial populations, for example, or by the soldiers themselves. The soldiers who called upon the dead emperor Constantine V to return and lead them once more to victory and those whom emperors addressed as their "children" or "fellow-soldiers",[68] those whom Nikephros II wanted declared martyrs should they die in battle against the infidel and those whose bodies were described by Constantine VII as having been wounded for Christ, all had views on what they did, even if they remained for the most part unexpressed, and the regular exhortation to commanders to address their troops in the most stirring language, invoking heroism, bravery, glory, dying for the faith as well as their homeland, suggests that such feelings were both appreciated and deliberately exploited or manipulated by military and political leaders. In the late Roman period, units also had orators appointed from soldiers suitably qualified, whose task it was to urge the troops to bravery by playing on their role as soldiers of God and emperor, a tradition which may have continued into the middle Byzantine period.[69]

By the same token, popular approval and enthusiasm for war could be similarly encouraged, and imperial ceremonial was employed in this respect, especially at Constantinople: triumphal processions, organized on an almost liturgical basis and completely integrated into a Christian thought-world, displays of booty and prisoners, or the acclamations reminding the emperors (and the crowd who were in earshot) of their Christian duty to defend orthodoxy and the empire, all served this end. Noteworthy, for example, is the triumphal entry of John II Komnenos into the city in 1133, when the emperor accompanied a silver-decorated processional chariot bearing the image of the Virgin to whom his victories were ascribed.

Court poets were commissioned to write and declaim verse narratives of the military achievements, courage and other skills shown by emperors in wartime, among the best-known being George of Pisidia's poems on the Persian and other wars of the emperor Heraclius, or that of Theodosios the Deacon on the recovery of Crete by Nikephros Phocas. Members of the political and ecclesiastical elite composed letters in praise of the emperor's deeds in war, slanting the approach according to whether or not the emperor actually campaigned himself or whether he stayed at home. The glorification of military deeds and of individual leaders or rulers formed part of the stock-in-trade of panegyrists and encomiasts, whether on account of an emperor's successes in war, or his pursuit of its antithesis, peace, or indeed both (since in the Byzantine view the one was often necessary for the achievement of the other). Warfare thus had its positive image, since it was an unfortunate but mostly necessary means to a divinely approved end.[70]

But there were other ways in which warfare imposed itself upon the literature and practice of Byzantine culture: in hagiographies, funeral addresses, in speeches in praise of emperors, in sermons and homilies to the congregations of churches, as well as in private letters addressed to individuals in connection with warfare – death, loss of property and so forth. Two homilies of the Patriarch Photios written in 860 describe graphically the terror inspired by a sudden raid by a large Rus' fleet in that year and the damage it caused. A number of letters bewail the effects of warfare – the tears of the orphaned children and widowed mothers, the destruction of crops in the fields, of homes, of monastic communities, the enslavement or death of populations, driving off of livestock and so forth.[71] In a series of letters to the Bulgar tsar Symeon written in the period c. 912–25, the patriarch Nikolaos Mystikos describes graphically the devastation, death, enslavement of the population and other consequences of warfare in Thrace, a picture reinforced by other writers. Other letters of Nikolaos – as well as of other writers – also deal with the effects of the state's demands on the provincial populations for extra supplies and provisions, for hospitality, livestock and equipment, which have already been noted. And although there is often a powerful rhetorical element in many of the letters (frequently designed to show off the author's literary knowledge and skills), they also illustrate the realities of warfare and fighting. With warfare came insecurity and uncertainty: the *Life* of Lazaros of Galesion mentions a former prisoner of war of the Arabs, who informs the saint that his daughter has had no news of him and thinks he is dead or still a prisoner.[72] And although she was writing for a very limited readership, and in a style heavily influenced by classical literary models and motifs, Anna Comnena was also able to provide a graphic description of the effects of warfare on the provinces:

> Cities were wiped out, lands ravaged, all the territories of Rome stained with blood. Some died miserably, pierced by arrow or lance; others were driven from their homes or carried off as prisoners-of-war . . . Dread seized on all as they hurried to seek refuge from impending disaster in caves, forests, mountains and hills. There they loudly bewailed the fate of their friends . . . the few others who survived . . . mourned the loss of sons or grieved for their daughters; one wept for a brother, another for a nephew killed before his time . . . In those days no walk of life was spared its tears and lamentation.[73]

There evolved in addition, and in relation to Islam in particular, an astrological literature, connected also to the apocalyptic tradition, which claimed to foretell the results of wars. Not only this, but some branches of this tradition presented the wars themselves and the political fortunes of the two contestants, Orthodoxy and Islam, as tied together by divine will in a cyclical relationship, where first one, then the other would be victorious. This literature was of such influence that it was believed by some that when, on the basis of the cycle, it was the turn of the other side to be victorious, there was no real point in resisting – fate and divine providence had already determined the outcome.[74] Horoscopes and other forms of predictions were particularly important when fighting and warfare were at issue, since not only the ordinary soldiers but the senior officers were just as interested in trying to predict the outcome of a conflict. As we have seen in an earlier chapter, Leo's *Tactica* advises generals to beware of the misinterpretation of signs and portents among the soldiery, and to make sure that they spread favourable predictions to avoid demoralizing the soldiers. On imperial expeditions, emperors were advised to take along not just military handbooks and literature relevant to the practice of war, but also astrological and horoscopic books which would assist them in foretelling the outcome. The emperor should take "an oneirocritical book; a book of chances and occurrences; a book dealing with good and bad weather and storms, rain and lightening and thunder and the vehemence of the winds; and in addition to these a treatise on thunder and a treatise on earthquakes, and other books, such as those to which sailors are wont to refer."

One or two examples of this tradition occur in the narrative sources, as when the emperor Constantine VI was told by the court astrologer that if he attacked the Bulgar army facing him at Markellai in Thrace he would win, although several of the generals, who considered their tactical situation unsound, advised against this. Constantine duly attacked, and his army suffered a serious defeat. In spite of the powerful influence of Christian theology and dogma, pre-Christian traditions of this sort continued to have a certain influence. Alexios I reached a decision by writing down two possible courses of action on separate bits of paper, leaving them on the altar of a church during a night of prayer, and waiting to see which one God's will directed the priest to pick up first on entering the building the next morning. The emperor Manuel I reportedly placed considerable emphasis on astrology and its predictive potential in such contexts, with similar unfortunate consequences.[75]

The impact of warfare on literature was most obviously reflected, of course, in military writings. But warfare also marked the chronicle and historiographical literature, partly because it was the stock-in-trade of the traditional historical models: whether Thucydides or Procopius, the deeds of military leaders and emperors in war, the bravery of the soldiers, the hard-fought campaigns, all played a central role in the construction of the narrative, and this remained true to the end of the Byzantine period. Being "at war" was the usual situation for the Byzantine world for much of its history, and the fact that wars were fought in order to achieve a state of peace meant that the wars of the Romans could usually be presented in a positive light, as serving not just the ends of individual war-leaders and rulers, but of the Roman empire and its people as a whole, hence also of God in his struggle with the forces of evil on earth. The vocabulary of warfare permeated theological and religious literature, too, so that monastic communities were described as regiments of spiritual fighters for the faith, and the struggle of the church against evil (and heterodoxy) was phrased in terms of a military campaign, in which the weapons of prayer, contemplation, spiritual purification were part of the armoury of the East Roman Church. Such motifs can be traced to the very beginnings of Christianity, of course, and indeed early Christians who argued against Christian participation in fighting had argued precisely that the Christian community fought a spiritual war for the benefit of the Roman state.[76] Equally, however, the benefits of peace were emphasized, both in letters to foreign rulers and in political discourse in general since, as was noted in Chapter 1, the emphasis upon either war or peace, and the appropriate characterization of the enemy at any given time, depended upon pragmatic political demands and priorities as much as it did upon abstract and theoretical arguments.[77] Peace was always the ultimate aim, even if warfare were necessary to secure it.

Outside these more literate milieux, however, attitudes clearly varied dramatically by context. At a distance, warfare was something to be anxious about, to hope to avoid and to pray for success in. A seventh-century fragment of a touching prayer for deliverance from the Arabs and military success for the army survives from Egypt, for example, which testifies eloquently to this, while numerous inscriptions bear witness to the attitudes of the provincial population in Syria and Palestine during the sixth-century wars with Persia.[78] The population of fortress towns and villages bore the brunt of both enemy and imperial activity: they were liable to lose their crops and their livestock, quite apart from their lives or their personal freedom, to the one, while they were subject to both fiscal demands and, more immediately, to forced evacuation from their homes when the local military commander decided they were too inviting a target for the enemy raiders. When enemy raids were expected in the ninth and tenth centuries, and probably before, officers referred to as *ekspelatores* were instructed to go from village to village and bring the population and their movables to safety in the fortresses and refuges in the hills or elsewhere. Indeed, the threat to the population in some areas, such as Cappadocia, was such that they took to living in caves in the hills, where vast underground complexes were established, veritable troglodyte communities whose vestiges can still clearly be seen today.

Over the longer term, this situation must have affected the nature of social ties as well as the structure of agricultural and pastoral activity, although we have very little evidence for the forms through which these effects were manifested. Some epigraphic and archaeological evidence from the region of medieval Barata (anc. Gaianoupolis, mod. Maden Şehir) in Lykaonia, southeast of Ikonion, may be characteristic. Here the easily defended upper town at the site of a city of the Roman period was reoccupied from the seventh to the ninth centuries, dated by several small churches, and suggests the sort of settlement to which much of the rural population of such a region would have recourse in time of attack. Inscriptions, probably eighth or ninth century, hint at the centrality of warfare in the lives of those who lived there: "Here lies Mousianos, who endured many wounds", for example, or "Here lies Philaretos Akylas, who died in the war on May 30th in the 4th indiction". The simple reference to "the war" is testimony enough to its endemic quality.[79] Soldiers and their families were no more exempt from these effects than the rest of the population, of course. The parents of young men drafted into the army or called up to fulfil their military service wept and lamented as they took leave of their sons; the more privileged were able to deploy powerful contacts to have their sons released from serving in the army, on grounds of economic hardship, for example.[80]

Some no doubt ran away, and desertion was clearly a problem, as in any army at any time. The military treatises frequently refer to the issue, and provincial officials had instructions to arrest and confine all those who failed to turn up in time for the muster held at the beginning of the campaigning season. The regular muster and updating of the military register was essential in helping to minimize desertion, as the treatise on campaign organization makes clear. The guardsman Ioannikios, a soldier in the elite Exkoubitoi regiment, decided to desert his unit after the defeat at Markellai in 796 (after some 23 years of service and at the age of 43) in which his unit was badly mauled. Although he became a monk, he was forced to flee from former comrades on at least one occasion years later when he was recognized – testifying also to the effectiveness of military discipline. But desertion was not uncommon: some soldiers ran away to become monks, where they would be able to conceal themselves under a new identity; others may have tried simply to return to their homes and families. But desertion was treated very harshly, as the military codes make clear and as the occasional testimony of the narrative sources also shows: in southern Greece in 880 the crews and soldiers of the Byzantine ships facing an Arab raiding force deserted their posts and fled. They were tracked down, captured, paraded with ignominy through Constantinople and impaled.[81]

The army in society

Group identity and solidarity

Warfare was thus part of day-to-day existence in different regions of the empire at different times, in some districts for much of the time. But while soldiers and warfare thus represented a ubiquitous element within the Byzantine world, war and the military were allotted a particular and carefully defined place in the Byzantine order of things. Throughout the empire's history, soldiers represented only a specific and specialist aspect of the state's organizational arrangements. There was no military caste, and soldiers were perceived as neither a social class, permanently differentiated from the rest of society by function, status and social code, nor again as a citizen body under arms (although this definition occasionally found favour in expressions of the theory of the East Roman state). On the contrary, the Byzantine army was perceived as a distinct branch of the state apparatus, composed of subjects of the emperor, equipped and supported by the state through its taxes, recruited and paid to carry out a specific and limited set of tasks. The remarks of both Leo VI, in the *Tactica*, and Constantine VII in his legislation make the point clearly: "as the head is to the body, so is the army to the state". It was differentiated functionally, but not socially (although, inevitably, such a differentiation in function had social implications and effects).[82]

Soldiers were everywhere in society: assisting tax-collection, maintaining and imposing law and order and internal security – defined in the broadest sense, of course – enforcing imperial religious policies, travelling through the provinces in groups or individually on imperial business, sometimes regarded with deep suspicion and even hatred by the local populace upon whom they were billetted or whom they attempted to coerce, sometimes treated sympathetically.[83] This is not to suggest that soldiers or "the army" were in any way a single, undifferentiated bloc: on the contrary, there were numerous functional, regional, tactical and social demarcations between different divisions and, in some cases, within individual units. Nor is this to suggest that society should be viewed as in any way "militarized", in the sense that everything was dominated by the army and by military needs. But even with the considerable degree of integration of some soldiers into local society and the pattern of non-military life, the distinctive function and presence of soldiers in East Roman society is nevertheless apparent in the sources, and is reflected also in the fact that it was always possible to draw a line between the "military" and the "civil" in law, and by the fact that the bearing of arms was, at least in theory and throughout Byzantine history, confined to soldiers only.[84]

From the time of Justinian I arms production had been a state monopoly, and the bearing of arms had long before this been prohibited to private citizens. Only in exceptional circumstances were private citizens armed, as when they had to defend their town against attack, for example. Weapons and military equipment were kept in state armouries, guarded by soldiers or watchmen. After the middle of the seventh century, even though there is good evidence that the system of state arms factories broke down, that the production of weapons became more diffused and that private households may well have possessed weapons, especially in those areas most frequently attacked, these restrictions seem still to have applied. In a tenth-century commentary on earlier late Roman legislation, it is asserted that laws intended to uphold public peace and law and order, and which prohibit the private possession or use of weapons, were still respected.[85] By the same token, the export of weapons was strictly prohibited, although once more it is impossible to know the extent to which such prohibitions – repeated in late ninth- or tenth-century codifications derived from sixth-century legal collections – were actually enforced or, indeed, enforceable. The government at Constantinople clearly was able to enforce the prohibition on the export of certain commodities, such as particular types of silk garment. How far this applied to weapons is not known, although in the sixth century, at the beginning of our period (and provided the authorities knew whom to search), the regulations could be enforced: Avar emissaries who purchased weapons in Constantinople while on a diplomatic mission in 562 later had their purchases confiscated.[86] Weapons were certainly sent as gifts to foreign potentates, and when necessary the empire was willing to send weapons on a larger scale to its allies – as in 1161–2 when Manuel I sent weapons to help the pro-imperial party at the Hungarian court.[87]

By the same token, and according to Procopius in the sixth century, soldiers were normally permitted to carry only a sword in civilian contexts, and the sources record one or two incidents suggesting that such prohibitions were generally respected throughout the Byzantine period. Thus the Rus' traders and warriors who visited Constantinople were forbidden by treaty to carry weapons at all in the city, while Basil I protested to Louis II in 871 about the Frankish emissaries and their retinue who walked about the streets of the city fully armed harming citizens and animals alike.[88] Equally, Byzantine soldiers who had been dismissed or retired surrendered their weapons to the state, while newly recruited soldiers were provided with weapons through the military administration: it was never assumed that they came with their own weapons – although whether this applied to weapons which might have a use in non-military contexts (as the bow for hunting, for example) is not clear.[89] How far these regulations, if that is indeed what they were, were actually and always observed is imposible to say. But that this was at least the case in theory is in itself important enough.

The clear insistence upon a separation of warlike from non-warlike dress, activities and behaviour highlights the very special position awarded to soldiers and to warfare within the East Roman order of things. Partly inherited from Roman civil legal tradition, partly from the Christian view of warfare, it serves to reinforce the distinction made between war – regrettable but necessary – and peace, ideally the "normal" state of affairs. But the very omnipresence of warfare around the empire's frontiers, frequently penetrating deep into its territory, made the maintenance of a distinction and a balance more important than ever. In his letter confirming the acts of the sixth ecumenical council of the church sent to the Pope in 687, the emperor Justinian II includes among those whose confirmation is attached the various field armies based in the provinces, as well as the palatine guards regiments: these are his armed forces, his to command through his appointment by God, to defend the Orthodox faith and the Chosen People.[90] Leo VI and Constantine VII may reflect a particular context and moment when they attempt their definitions of the role of the army in relation to other elements of society. But their purpose is the same: to frame, delimit and control warfare and, by extension, any sort of armed violence, which should remain the prerogative of the state, which is to say the emperor chosen by God, in defence of the Christian Roman *oikoumene*.

And even with the rise of a more self-conscious "warrior" mentality among certain elements of the provincial elite during the tenth century and after and, perhaps more artificially, in court society during the middle years of the twelfth century, this attitude remained unchanged.[91] Warfare, the use of weapons and military matters in general were the occupation of a distinct group, specifically delegated by the state – by the emperor – to defend the Roman world and its Orthodox inhabitants from those who would harm it.

The conditions under which soldiers served, and the social status and esteem attached to their role in state and society as a whole, varied across time and in terms of attitudes in different sections of society. However much individual attitudes to soldiers may have varied, soldiers had a relatively privileged position in comparison with the ordinary inhabitants of towns or countryside. They also constituted an identifiable group within society.[92] To begin with, the Roman tradition of distinctive military dress, with units defined by uniform and colour, and shield decorations, as well as by regimental standards or their equivalent, seems to have continued to the end of the empire. Units were thus differentiated one from another in battle or on the march, and were also seen to be different, in smaller groups or as individuals, when on service in a more civilian context. Foreign units – such as the Varangians, for example – were even more distinctive. The extent to which differences in dress could be used to distinguish the various corps or divisions from one another is not clear: emblems and banners certainly differed and were employed as a means of signalling certain commands to the soldiers in each unit; units may also have had distinctive shield decorations. In units with a particular identity – the *tagmata*, for example, and other elite units – such distinctions appear to have been preserved and encouraged. Whether the same was the case in the thematic divisions is unclear.[93]

There were, of course, considerable differences in economic status and situation between and among soldiers. Nevertheless, Byzantine armies until the later tenth and early eleventh centuries were relatively homogeneous, a reflection partly of their juridical status, partly of the fact that the armies were very much rooted in local society, recruited regionally from peasant communities and officered to a great extent by local men. This applied to a degree also to the many foreign mercenary soldiers who were assimilated into Byzantine-led units, even where they constituted distinct groups within such units, such as the Chazars and Pharganoi in the Hetaireia, for example. Likewise non-Byzantine soldiers recruited from foreign refugee settlers, such as the Kurds under Theophilus or the Bedouin Banu Habib under Constantine VII, were settled and subjected to the same conditions of fiscal and civil administration as native Byzantine populations.[94]

This homogeneity was reinforced by the juridical privileges which came with the position of soldier. Property acquired through their military service was from Roman times on protected by a special status. All property belonging to soldiers (as well as to certain other categories of state official) was protected by state law under the principle *in integrum restitutio*, by which the state undertook to make good property lost or damaged as a result of the owner's absence on public service. This underlies the principle of restitution enshrined in the tenth-century legislation dealing with soldiers' lands. The active troops received donatives and a share of booty (in theory, at least).[95] There were also day-to-day advantages to being a soldier, particularly in the area of fiscal privileges: soldiers and their immediate family (and thus any property directly owned/held by them) were always exempted from extraordinary fiscal burdens or corvées. In the late Roman as well as the Byzantine period, they paid only the basic state demands, up to the later seventh century the land tax, later the land-tax and the hearth-tax, or *kapnikon*. The difference between the middle Byzantine "military" and "civil" household was not really of medieval origin, but lies in the usual Roman distinction drawn between those groups who enjoyed specific immunities in respect of certain state demands, and those who did not.[96]

The privileges of military status and the principle of restitution of property thus gave soldiers a particularly advantageous position. In addition to this they, and their immediate dependents, had the right to have cases tried by their own commanders for offences relating to their duties or committed against them. In the late Roman period, soldiers also had the privileges of "prescription of forum", by which accused persons could refuse in many situations to appear before any court but their own, even for criminal offences. But these do not seem to have survived.

These official privileges are reflected in legal codifications and imperial legislation, as well as in military treatises. In reality, soldiers were sometimes treated rather differently, depending upon the actual status and position of the soldiers in question and the conditions of the time. Thus there is a reasonable amount of indirect evidence for certain categories of soldier in the provinces being victimized by imperial officials and by powerful landlords or other such persons. The author of the treatise on guerrilla strategy complains that soldiers' rights were being violated by civil officials, and makes clear reference to the oppression of soldiers by provincial authorities. Since many soldiers were actually quite well-to-do, it is difficult to know to what extent this complaint merely reflects the prejudice of the author.[97] A number of other texts give the same impression. But as we have already noted, the situation was easily reversed when large numbers of troops descended on a region, or when local officers exploited their authority against the local populace.[98]

The conditions of military service

Recruitment into the armies of the late Roman period was subject to a number of qualifications. Certain groups – including those of servile status, *curiales* (those with hereditary obligations to serve as town councillors) and adscripted *coloni* (dependent peasants registered for tax along with their tenancies) – were excluded, although legislation concerning them suggests that many often succeeded in joining up. In addition, heretics and certain other religious groups, such as Samaritans, were prohibited from military status. The minimum age for enlistment, set out in laws of the fourth and fifth centuries, appears still to have been 18; and although no upper age-limit is prescribed in the sixth-century sources, some texts assert that those over the age of 40 were not eligible. A fourth-century law specifies a minimum height for recruits of 5 feet 7 inches, but again no sixth-century legislation repeats this, and it may have lapsed. New recruits were inspected by the responsible officers of the unit to which they were admitted, and put on the payroll once a warrant had been received from the central department responsible (issued in exchange for the request from the unit itself). The basic period for which men enlisted appears to have been still in the later sixth century, as earlier, 18 or 20 years, although men could be invalided out as a result of illness or injury.

The provisions for veterans seem by the middle of the sixth century to have been less generous than those described in the legislation from the fifth century and earlier – soldiers no longer received land or discharge bounties, for example. But all received certain extended fiscal privileges and exemptions from compulsory public services. The emperor Maurice is reported to have reintroduced more generous provision: discharged soldiers were given a small state allowance and provided with housing in cities; he also revived a regulation permitting the sons of soldiers killed in action to succeed to their father's rank and pay.[99]

The sources for recruitment and length of service for the period after the middle of the seventh century are much less informative. There is good evidence to believe that the minimum age for recruitment in the ninth and tenth centuries was still 18, the maximum 40, although service beyond the age of 40 was common – we know of at least two examples of soldiers who served in either tagmatic or thematic armies until the ages of 43 and 48. From the report of the Arab geographer Ibn Khurradadhbih, the minimum period of service in the themes appears to have been 12 years, but there is no way of knowing how accurate this information is. Some sources refer to soldiers who were now too old for service, but still physically active, so there probably was a statutory or standard age for retirement, possibly 52 to judge from some hints in ninth-century texts. On the other hand, sixth-century legislation setting out the minimum period of service at 20 years was retained in the tenth century, although again there is no way of knowing the extent to which this was actually applied, still less known to those responsible. Other texts, particularly from the later eleventh century, suggest that many stayed on – officers in particular – long after their useful career was over, thus adversely affecting the military capacity of their unit. Leo VI notes that officers should select from those registered in each *thema* those best suited for active service, and this probably took account of age as well as other attributes.[100]

There were probably considerable differences between the requirements demanded of recruits to "professional" units, such as the *tagmata*, and the regular thematic armies. Whereas many of the regulations governing admission to the former seem to have been retained from the late Roman legislation, thematic soldiers were required merely to appear at the regular muster parade (once a year for each *drouggos*) appropriately equipped, that is with mount, provisions for a certain number of days, shield and spear. In the provincial armies, defensive armour and more expensive items, such as swords, were seen as a bonus rather than as regular items borne by all soldiers. Regulations such as those dealing with the height of recruits will have been difficult to impose at a time when available manpower was limited, although, as noted already, Leo VI emphasizes that the selection of soldiers for campaign service should take account of suitability in respect of wealth, age and physical fitness, and this probably reflects long-standing practice. There were substantial differences between the better-off thematic soldiers and the less fortunate: of the former, the sources relate several stories of how they were able not only to equip and provision themselves, but could afford to contribute to the arming and mounting of their less well-off comrades.[101]

While no evidence for demands in respect of height or other qualifications appears in the later sources, and given the nature of the pool from which soldiers would be selected are unlikely to have been practicable, it is very likely that prohibitions on heretics (where they could be recognized) were still applied. Late Roman ordinances on the prohibition on priests and monks joining the ranks were retained, as well as on those convicted of adultery or similar crimes, those who had already been dishonourably discharged, and so forth. Again, however, it is very difficult to know to what extent such regulations were observed. We will probably be correct to assume that Leo VI's injunction, that the thematic officials and the *strategos* were to choose those whom they felt were best suited to enlistment, was the norm after the middle of the seventh century, and that most of the formal regulations of the Roman period had become irrelevant by this time.

The application of such regulations was in any event not possible in respect of foreign units, especially Muslims, Franks and others outside the sphere of Byzantine religious-political control. Nor can it have applied to others, such as Armenians, who may often have belonged to the Armenian Monophysite community. Presumably a certain degree of economy was practised by the authorities in this respect, and the further away from Constantinople, the more likely will this have been. Given the much greater variety from the ninth century in the origins, military value and contexts in which soldiers for different types of unit were recruited, there is likely to have been an equal diversity in their conditions of enlistment and service: simple thematic soldiers and soldiers of the imperial *tagmata* were already different in this respect, and the admission of foreign units in various forms, as well as the short-term recruitment of mercenary soldiers for specific campaigns, will have added to this variety.

Once enlisted, all soldiers paid by the central fisc – either as *tagmata* or in the *themata* – were registered in the military rolls, or *kodikes*, held in their province and in the government department responsible, the military *logothesion*, at Constantinople. Foreign units employed as mercenaries under their own officers could be treated in the same way and registered in the central department, or alternatively paid through their leaders, who would receive a lump sum at regular intervals to be distributed to the men. Both methods were employed in the later tenth and eleventh centuries, the former for the Varangians, for example, the latter for the various Frankish contingents who fought for the empire in the 1060s and 1070s.[102]

Leave was granted in the sixth and early seventh century on a rotational basis, and for periods of between 30 days and three months, depending upon the situation of the unit in question – whether on active service, for example, or in winter quarters. The number of men who could be absent at any given time was restricted in theory to 30, and officers who permitted more men to be away could be punished. The same regulations are repeated in the late ninth-century codification of the Justinianic material and in Leo's *Tactica*, although whether they were observed, and to which types of unit they were applied, is not known. Most probably such rules were used for the full-time tagmatic troops, at least where they were indigenous Byzantine units; they would hardly have been relevant to the militia-like thematic contingents, at least once the majority had begun to evolve away from being full-time field forces.[103]

Upon retirement soldiers received no state benefits other than their pro-tected fiscal-juridical status. There is no evidence for any system of state pen-sions or annuities such as existed at the end of the sixth century and, probably, up to the middle of the seventh century, and it is likely that the conditions of the seventh century made such arrangements financially impossible for the hard-pressed government. For the ordinary soldiers of the field armies in the provinces, the state's acceptance and probable encouragement of their deriving support (provisions for a limited period, equipment and weaponry, mounts) directly from their own households in the regions where they had come to be based was a reflection of this situation, and resulted by the later eighth century – if not long before – in the majority of thematic soldiers holding landed property from which their duties could be supported. In such a situation, the state will hardly have needed to cater for veterans, since retirement to their farms will have been taken for granted. This certainly applied also to some tagmatic soldiers of whom we hear in the tenth-century sources, for neither was any provision made for them in this respect.

Many soldiers, particularly those who hired themselves as mercenaries, whether they were with or without property in their homeland (either in the empire or elsewhere), would undoubtedly have served in order to save cash and other forms of wealth, gained from their (often substantial) salaries and from imperial largesse, as well as – importantly – from booty, and would have invested this in land or other forms of security on retirement. Less well-off thematic soldiers may similarly have profited from their military service, although the evidence for the impoverishment of substantial numbers of those who were subject to a military obligation – *strateia* – is considerable, and shows that the government had to take action at irregular intervals to redress the situation. The state could also reward soldiers for bravery or meritorious service with grants of land, particularly in depopulated regions or where the original tenants or owners had died or abandoned the properties in question. Some retired guardsmen appear in the early eleventh century as owners of considerable properties, including mills and other facilities.[104]

A popular form of retirement for many who had completed their service in the army (as well as for those who were trying to avoid conscription or who had deserted) was to enter the monastic life. Although most of the evidence concerns senior officers, there is nevertheless some information on ordinary soldiers opting for this mode of retirement, especially those without dependants. Although official regulations forbidding serving soldiers to join a monastery were repeated from the late Roman legislation, the evidence from some saints' lives suggests that this sometimes happened. As well as providing a degree of economic security, of course, adopting the monastic life also catered for the spiritual well-being of the individuals concerned, since it offered a means whereby the soldier could atone for the sins he had committed while serving the emperor, an issue we have already discussed briefly in Chapter 1 above. The numbers entering monasteries among the middling officers of the provinces was substantial enough for an Arab historian to remark on the fact, and to note that those who pursued this life forfeited their state *rhogai* – their "pension" (a continuation of their cash salary, to which they were entitled as bearers of an imperial title) – after their retirement from active service.[105]

Discipline

Constant drill is of the greatest value to the soldier.

Nature produces but few brave men, whereas care and training make efficient soldiers.[106]

As has already been pointed out above and in Chapters 5 and 6, levels of discipline appear to have varied enormously but were a central cause of concern to commanders and to the authors of all the military treatises. The author of the *Strategikon* explicitly states that discipline had partially broken down in the imperial field army, and that his treatise was designed to address the issue.[107] The numerous instances of mutiny and unrest among the provincial, thematic, armies in the seventh–ninth centuries, and the examples of troops panicking when the commander was thought to have been killed or injured attest to the very labile psychological state of these forces. The maintenance of discipline and, therefore, of morale was a key concern of the writers of military treatises, and all pay considerable attention to questions of how to prevent indiscipline breaking out in the ranks (especially while encamped or when the troops were inactive), and how to avoid letting the troops lay waste one's own territory and damage the interests of the rural populace on the Roman side of the border. In the latter case, however, there is some incidental evidence to show that this was not always achieved. The so-called "military laws", based on traditional Roman codes of discipline, repeated and revised in the *Strategikon* of the late sixth century, and reproduced in the eighth and tenth centuries, set out a clear code of conduct and discipline, with appropriate punishments for transgressors.[108]

The extent to which such discipline was actually enforced is unclear. It was chiefly the most able commanders and leaders who were the most likely to effectively apply military discipline, a reflection both of their charisma and the confidence placed in them by the soldiers. This was recognized in the military treatises, too. Financial generosity, either on the part of individual commanders or officers or the government, was a crucial ingredient in encouraging soldiers to follow orders and accept the discipline necessary for effective fighting.[109] Byzantine armies demonstrated, at different times and in different contexts, the most extreme degrees of bravery and commitment on the one hand, and the most abject incompetence and indiscipline on the other. Successes clearly generated a high level of morale and self-confidence (as in the tenth and early eleventh centuries); failure and defeat produced low morale and defeatism, as the sources for the military events of the later seventh century appear to suggest. But in all cases – most spectacularly under Heraclius against the Persians, for example – the example of an effective leader was essential.[110]

The variability of conditions among Byzantine troops is reflected in their cohesion and effectiveness. A strict code certainly prevailed in elite units such as the imperial *tagmata*, for example, and in units which had a particular loyalty to their commanding officer. One account tells of an officer who was upbraided by the emperor himself for his unkempt appearance while at his post in the palace. Discipline was probably least effective in the militia-like thematic forces. On another occasion, and in contrast, we read of a group of drunken Varangians attacking the emperor Nikephros III Botaneiates. For the mass of the regular provincial soldiers, it seems probable that the events and contingent changes of the middle of the seventh century marked an important watershed in the erosion of traditional, effective Roman military discipline, while the military revival of the later ninth and especially of the tenth century was certainly marked by the revival of a more rigorous disciplinary code.[111]

Discipline was reflected in two ways: day-to-day behaviour while on duty, about which the sources tell us very little; and cohesion and effectiveness in action, which we have already discussed in Chapters 5 and 6. Leo VI notes in his *Tactica* (following the *Strategikon* of Maurice) that soldiers of the thematic armies should, wherever possible, be brigaded in units of men from the same villages and districts to stiffen morale and encourage them to stand firm in the line of battle. Tactical formations designed to provide maximum cohesion and solidity – especially the infantry square described in tenth-century manuals – reflected also concerns that troops might panic and attempt to flee at the point of an enemy attack; evidence for the issue of imperial largesse – usually just before a campaign, and associated with the possibilities of booty – demonstrates the efforts made by commanders to ensure good order and the obedience of the soldiers. Drilling and exercising the troops was strongly emphasized in all the military manuals, and is specifically mentioned by chroniclers in connection with successful commanders, especially emperors.

In one or two cases we have some evidence of the real exercises carried out by the soldiers. Thus George of Pisidia, Heraclius' panegyrist, refers to his extensive drilling and training of the troops in preparation for the struggle against the Persians; a collection of miracles of St Anastasius the Persian, the scene of which was set in Palestine in the first half of the seventh century, refers to the regular yearly military exercises and games which took place in March, although the *Tactica* of Leo implies that these were no longer held on the same basis. And as already noted, the chroniclers record that both Nikephros II Phocas and John Tzimiskes drilled their troops rigorously and regularly, while the military games and mock battles put on by Nikephros Phocas in the hippodrome at Constantinople in the 960s so terrified the population that a panic occurred which claimed many lives.[112]

But whatever the textbooks said about the value of such exercises, Byzantine commanders – at least, the more able – were usually aware of the limitations of the different sorts of troops under their command. The treatise on warfare compiled by Nikephros Phocas sets out quite simple, easily managed tactical manoeuvres for the great bulk of the thematic infantry, who were on the whole not well-equipped and potentially unreliable. In contrast – and as with the elite cavalry units of the later sixth century depicted in the *Strategikon* – the well-trained and equipped heavy cavalry and tagmatic units were expected to implement quite complex manoeuvres, frequently under enemy attack, on the battlefield. Skills and training, discipline and morale went hand in hand. When well-led and properly prepared, Byzantine forces were able to perform well under often very adverse conditions – accounts of armies withdrawing in good order into camp, or even entrenching while under attack, demonstrate this quite clearly. Military discipline certainly varied in its effectiveness and maintenance, but it is also clear that the East Roman army functioned on the basis of an essentially Roman organizational structure. Even in the twelfth century it was discipline and a code of military conduct, rather than kinship or any other principle, which was the key to the soldiers' solidarity in battle and on campaign.[113]

Social differentiation

While the term "soldier" had only one meaning in a purely military context, it encompassed men of a variety of different social and economic backgrounds. Little is known of the social origins of soldiers in the seventh and eighth centuries, although there can be no doubt that the majority, as in the preceding period, were of fairly humble status. But the better-off ordinary soldiers among the thematic armies in the ninth and tenth centuries appear to have held a relatively high position in their communities.

Military (specifically tactical) function also played a role, however: poorer mercenary recruits to the expensively armed heavy cavalry of the armies of

Nikephros Phocas and John Tzimiskes (mostly composed of wealthier thematic soldiers or mercenaries) may well have been able to improve their social
position in their own communities through their military service. Border
garrisons and watchtowers were manned by local forces on a rotational basis,
and by men of relatively humble status, some serving on the basis of a *strateia*,
others on the basis of a salary paid by the military authorities, others as
draftees to the *apelatai*, regular thematic soldiers who had become impoverished. Indeed, the status of these soldiers is interestingly reflected in the fact
that the word used of them came also to mean "bandits", and was associated
very closely with the marginal society of the borderlands, a society in which
immigrants and newcomers sought to exploit the insecurities of frontier existence.[114] Such men were socially far inferior to the wealthy heavy cavalrymen
of the themes, or indeed the mercenaries paid by the state. Nevertheless, as
enlisted men they all shared the same juridical status and privileges, in theory.

In some texts, soldiers are regarded as belonging to the wealthy and/or
the oppressors of the rural smallholders: Theophanes, for example, contrasts
the enlisted soldiers with the poor; a tenth-century chronicle, describing the
effects of the legislation of Constantine VII, lists soldiers alongside high imperial officers and administrators in contrast to the *penetes* or poor, and it may be
that the reference is to the wealthier category of registered *stratiotai* who could
afford to provide their own provisions.[115] In contrast, in much imperial legislation, ordinary soldiers are often classed along with less well-off peasants, and
it is difficult to know if this represents a general view or reflects the conditions of the tenth century, when the thematic soldiers' economic position was
threatened in many areas by powerful landlords: according to imperial legislation of the reign of Constantine VII, the situation of "soldiers" had worsened
in the years before 959, the latest date for the issue of the document. Yet
according to another legal text of the same period (dated to 947), soldiers
occupied quite a privileged position in the hierarchy of the rural community.
Another piece of imperial legislation dated to the period 963–9 notes that the
"modest ways of *stratiotai*" might include the possession of vineyards, mills,
barns and so forth. While it appears that many soldiers registered in the thematic
rolls were well-off compared with much of the rural population, the sources
themselves were clearly faced by a wide variety of different types of soldier,
which led to a number of contradictions or paradoxes in their descriptions
(and in modern historians' debates).[116]

The sale-value of the property thought necessary for the maintenance of
a thematic cavalry soldier was 4 or 5 lb gold (288–360 *nomismata*) in the first
half of the tenth century; that of a soldier/sailor of the naval *themata* 2–3 lb
gold. This was a substantial small estate rather than an average poor peasant's
holding, and reinforces the idea that the theme soldiers whose property reached
this value were relatively well-off, a rural elite. But there is evidence to show
that in the later tenth and eleventh century, the holding of a peasant tenant
varied considerably, and suggests that many of those *stratiotai* who were in
possession of land valued at 4 lb of gold were not necessarily all that better off

than many non-military households: the figure of 4 or 5 lb gold is a figure that, according to the texts, "ought" to be sufficient: in reality, there was very probably a great deal of variation. We may guess that the advantages of registering as a soldier brought social advantages too, just as had been the case in the late Roman period, for a law of Constantine VII makes it clear that individuals were still registering themselves and their properties. This would hardly have been the case had it not still brought significant social and economic advantages. According to the legislation of Nikephros II, property to the value of 12 lb gold was necessary for maintaining one of the new heavy cavalry which were the centrepiece of his field army, along with his servants or esquires. This really did represent a substantial property, and although it is unlikely that many individual soldiers actually possessed such a property, it illustrates the expense of fitting out these costly units of shock troops who were attended by several "esquires" to help them with their equipment and arms.[117]

There was thus a great deal of variation in social and economic terms, and therefore in respect of the conditions under which they served the empire, among the soldiers. The legislation of Nikephros II may itself have served to widen the gap between the wealthier and poorer soldiers. The extent to which their juridical status gave poorer soldiers a slightly higher social position than non-soldiers in anything other than legal fiction is impossible to say. But the fiscalization of the *strateia* – the demand of a cash sum from those listed on the military registers instead of military service itself – the increasing neglect of the regular theme forces and the corresponding increase in units of professional, full-time soldiers must have brought a decline in status for the former, and it may be this which is reflected in the complaint of the anonymous author of the treatise on skirmishing warfare about the treatment meted out to provincial soldiers.[118]

The position of thematic soldiers as a special category began to decline from the tenth century. The category of military lands continued to exist throughout the eleventh century, although the obligation to military service, the *strateia*, came to represent merely one fiscal obligation among several. With the use of the device of *pronoia* to maintain soldiers (occasionally in the eleventh century, increasingly during the second half of the twelfth century and after), and with government reliance on salaried tagmatic units of both Byzantines and foreigners, alongside foreign mercenaries under their own leaders, the peasants who had previously supplied the core of the theme armies were no longer differentiated from the mass of the rural population, which by the twelfth century served merely as a resource upon which the empire's predominantly foreign mercenary forces drew for their maintenance and support. Such changes clearly had important consequences for the popular perception of soldiers, and for soldiers' views of their own relationship with the indigenous population.[119]

During the period from the middle and later seventh century to the early or middle tenth century, many, and at some times most, soldiers were Byzantines, drawn from the provincial rural populace, with roots in their home districts and serving in units composed for the most part of other men from the same regions. This is reflected in the pattern of provincial rebellions and factionalism, for example, which is closely associated with thematic and provincial identities until the eleventh century. With the replacement of this arrangement during the eleventh century (with some minor exceptions) by one in which most soldiers were certainly not local, and at some periods mostly not Byzantine, soldiers became an alien element imposed from the outside upon an exploited rural or urban population, and military service was institutionally and socially deracinated. For the government, this had certain advantages. As long as the soldiers were paid properly and on time, they were in many ways politically more reliable and less inclined to become embroiled in Byzantine politics: there is no evidence for any serious mutinies or rebellions instigated by the empire's foreign mercenary armies between 1081 and 1185, for example, which would seem to confirm this contention.[120]

On the other hand, the perception of soldiers as oppressive outsiders did not change, and may have intensified, as the foreign element came to predominate. Suspicion of foreigners was an element in Byzantine culture in any case, and suspicion of foreign soldiers is evident already in the late eleventh-century *Strategikon* of Kekaumenos.[121] The attitude to the western armies of the First and Second Crusades, in which their bravery was often admitted but according to which their greed, lack of discipline and ignorance are often stressed, are foreshadowed in a somewhat different context in the chapter on the empire's foreign enemies in the late sixth-century *Strategikon* of Maurice and the revised version thereof in Leo's *Tactica*. Anna Comnena's *Alexiad* typifies such views and the many paradoxes they entailed, which – in spite of the changing nature of Byzantine relations with, and greater awareness of, foreigners – remained a significant feature of both literate and less literate culture.[122]

Whether the predominance of foreign soldiers on Byzantine territory materially affected attitudes to soldiers in general is difficult to judge, however: Attaleiates notes that in the Mantzikert campaign it was the foreign mercenary units who caused most damage in their foraging expeditions, although he by no means exempts the Byzantine contingents. But those who suffered, or were liable to suffer, from the presence of imperial troops, probably did not discriminate, since the end result was the same, and eleventh and twelfth-century exemptions from state burdens associated with the army drew no distinction between foreign and Byzantine troops in this respect. Indeed, it appears that when the Frankish mercenary leader Roussel de Bailleul and his followers seized control of Amaseia and the Armeniakon region in 1073, his administration was certainly no less and was probably more popular than that of Constantinople: local opposition to him is not recorded, whereas the population of Amaseia were prepared to pay a considerable sum to the representative of the imperial power in 1075 to save him from being blinded, and showed a degree of hostility to the imperial forces.[123]

But soldiers continued to enjoy a particular legal status, whether foreign or Byzantine: in respect of privileges and fiscal exemptions it was the name

and title of soldier which continued to be crucial, regardless of social background. The emperor Alexios I praised those knights and footsoldiers who died
during the course of the First Crusade as "blessed . . . since they met their end
in good intent. Moreover, we ought not to regard them as dead, but living
and transported to life everlasting and incorruptible" – sentiments echoed in
the treatise on skirmishing warfare over a century earlier. The flowery pre-
faces to imperial grants of revenue, *pronoia*, composed during the twelfth
and thirteenth centuries and later illustrate the important position held by the
better-off class of soldiers, mounted "knights" with retainers and their own
armed followers, in the esteem of the government, and while they reflect
contemporary trends in the social evolution of the later empire, reveal also the
longer-term attitude to warfare in defence of Orthodoxy and the fundamental
role of soldiers in the struggle to protect the empire which we have already
traced to before the late Roman period.

> Why then shall we not reward our soldiers and warriors, who fight
> for us and face the barbarian with danger so that we may continue to
> live without peril . . . ?[124]

Officers

Officers were drawn from a wide variety of backgrounds in the later Roman
period: many seem to have worked their way through the ranks, and indeed
this seems to have applied throughout the middle Byzantine period too. The
highest ranking posts generally fell to those from more privileged social and
economic backgrounds, of course, although there are some notable exceptions.
Promotion to lower officer ranks – "non-commissioned" posts in modern
parlance – in the late Roman armies generally occurred through long service
and/or meritorious conduct, and involved advances through the various grades
above the individual concerned, but interest and patronage also played an
important role.[125] The same appears to have been true of the Byzantine armies,
where several references to promotion through merit, sometimes to commissioned rank, are preserved, and where a tenth-century imperial speech refers
explicitly to promotion as a means of rewarding brave or competent soldiering.
Officers were supposed to make recommendations for promotion as they
appeared relevant, and pass them on to their superiors. Again, the soldier
advanced his career by moving upwards through the grades at his disposal;
ordinary soldiers were regraded, officers were given independent commands,
commanders of *themata* or other districts received the command of a *tagma* or
similar position, and so forth.[126] A ninth-century biographical account of a
particular soldier, a certain Kallistos, who was executed after his capture by
the Arabs and refusal to renounce his religion, describes how he rose by merit
and by coming to the emperor's attention. From the rank of a junior officer in
one of the palatine regiments he was promoted to the position of *komes* in the
imperial Scholai. Promoted into the corps of imperial *spatharioi* attendant upon

the emperor, he was later given command of an independent *tagma*, that of the so-called Ethiopians, and eventually appointed to the position of *tourmarches* in the Anatolikon *thema*.[127]

Other accounts describe similar careers, both for Constantinopolitan units and for the *themata*. But the great majority of officers for whom the sources provide information seem to have come from relatively well-off social backgrounds, as in the late Roman period: this was inevitable, given the advantages attached to the possession of a certain degree of literacy, the ability of such men to pay their way and support their greater outgoings (and, in the *themata* certainly, provide for the poorer soldiers in their units) and, especially in respect of obtaining imperial dignities, an essential symbol of their status, pay the relevant fee or bribe to the officials responsible. In the provinces, it is clear that a recognizable stratum of officers and state officials evolved, possessing both land and influence, able to exercise patronage and build up their own retinue and clientele, and also receive the education and experience from their kin and family for life in imperial military service. In at least one case the sources record a *drouggarios* whose son likewise followed him to attain the same position in the same *thema*, and incidental evidence suggests that this was entirely usual.[128] Another case, of a certain Eudokimos, is similar to that of Kallistos. Coming from a wealthy Cappadocian family, he was educated at Constantinople, and on completing his studies received the dignity of *kandidatos* and an appointment to a command, first in Cappadocia and later in Charsianon.[129] At a more humble level, the example of the junior *domestikos* Benjamin, in Bithynia in the early ninth century, again illustrates how careers might run in families, for his son Constantine joined the *scholai* in his father's footsteps, initially as a trooper rather than an officer.[130] A further example is furnished by the example of a certain Leo, from a well-off provincial family from Galatia. He was enrolled into one of the *tagmata* at Constantinople at the age of 25 and seems to have been appointed to the rank of a *komes* in charge of one of the units within the regiment.[131] Background, education and the connections available through relatives in the military or at court were key elements in such careers. At the level of the individual unit or squadron it appears thus to have been merit and competence which determined, to a large extent, arrangements for appointments to junior and middling commands or positions of authority.[132]

At the higher level, the administrative machinery was dominated more clearly by the wealthy families and their protégés, whether in civil or military affairs. In the provinces, although literacy was an important aspect of the culture of anyone who aspired to positions of rank and was a *sine qua non* for a clerk or a member of any government bureau, it was less important to a military officer: familiarity with the land, local society, the enemy and the soldiers themselves were the key requirements – although the sons of the wealthy and powerful tended to have an education and thus possess a good degree of literacy in any case. By the later ninth century, they and their clients came to exercise a virtual monopoly over leading provincial military posts, the result of a long, carefully nurtured tradition of military service and a close-knit

271

system of inter-family patronage and clientship. Yet social mobility – facilitated through merit, connections or both – remained always a significant aspect of the way in which East Roman society worked. Several key figures during this period rose from the most lowly of positions to high office, raising in the process the position, wealth and status of their own families – the emperors Michael II, Leo V and Basil I are but the most obvious cases. By their very success, of course, such figures attracted (and usually deliberately promoted), the attention of chroniclers and historians. They were typical, therefore, insofar as they provided examples of what was always theoretically possible in a meritocratic, but still fairly clearly stratified, society. It was only exceptional cases who by good luck or favour managed to break through the barriers of social and educational status.

The senior military officers came chiefly from two sources: in the first place from among the wealthy provincial landowners, families which had gained power and wealth over several generations by virtue of the appointment of their members to local commands; and secondly from among the less wealthy group which provided men such as the officers already described. In the provinces, the former group was in the best position, for it had in addition to its landed resources the support also of the local population, the soldiers from which often placed greater faith in the local officers, men whose abilities and qualities were known, as well as their failings, than in strangers appointed centrally. The frequent provincial risings in support of locally raised officers, especially in the period from the eighth to later tenth centuries, provides ample support for this.[133] Such provincial officers were also the product of generations of experience, and were thus the best qualified to carry on the military policies of the government. The hold on high military commands exercised by this clique is best illustrated by the officers of the imperial *tagmata*, for their commanders were appointed consistently (although there are some exceptions) from a small group of families, including those of Doukas, Skleros and Phocas and their relatives or their clients.

Most senior officers were also "career soldiers", men who started out with the advantages of both an education, a patron and military experience, and who rapidly attained the leading commands in the capital or the provinces. Many senior tagmatic officers appear to have begun their careers as provincial commanders, for example, progressing from there to a court post, and thence to command of an elite regiment or a theme army. The high-ranking commander Manuel, who had been a *protostrator* under Michael II and then *strategos* of the Anatolikon theme, became *domestikos* of the *Scholai* under Theophilos, while Andreas, of Turkic background, had been deputy commander of the Opsikion before his promotion to command the Scholai.[134] A good example is provided by the family of the empress Theodora, wife of Theophilus: the daughter of a *drouggarios* of the Paphlagonian theme, respected and wealthy, she obtained for her brothers Bardas and Petronas important military and administrative posts. The former later became logothete of the Drome, while Petronas became first commander of the imperial *vigla*, then *strategos* of the

Thrakasion theme and, finally *domestikos* of the Scholai, while Bardas had also held this last post for a while. The latter's son Antigonos later succeeded Petronas as domestic at the end of Michael III's reign.[135] The earliest commanders of the palatine guards units appear likewise to have come from leading provincial families with strong military connections. Alexios Mousele, the first *drouggarios* of the *vigla*, came from an Armenian aristocratic military background, as did other commanders of the time, men such as Bardanios, *domestikos* of the Scholai under Constantine VI, Niketas Triphyllios, *domestikos* of the Scholai under Eirene and supporter of Nikephros I, and so on. The first commander of the Hikanatoi, established by Nikephros I, Peter, was the son of a wealthy family: his father had been a *patrikios* and *strategos*, and Peter had apparently been appointed to the post of *domestikos* of the Scholai sometime after Nikephros' accession in 802. Peter's career – holding one of the highest military commands in the empire at the age of about 25 – is illustrative of the advantages which the wealthy, privileged "military" families possessed through patronage and family influence.[136]

But during the tenth century the growth of the middle Byzantine provincial elite meant that the meritocratic principles governing middling and senior military appointments appear to have been substantially compromised. By the time of Leo VI, leading military commanders were able to an increasing extent to keep important posts "in the family", a result both of the immense power of the leading military families by this time – whose support no emperor could afford to lose – and the complete dependence of the government on these men at a military level. The history of the Phokades during the tenth century provides the best-known example, but even a relatively unknown family could barter for posts. The tenth-century Arab historian Ibn Hawkal remarked that the *tourmarchai* of the imperial army were all members of what he calls the aristocracy, suggestive of the visibility of these lines of social demarcation.[137] By the twelfth century, this was the norm, and although it was still possible to rise through the ranks and on the basis of good soldiering, birth and social status played an increasingly significant role in determining appointments to positions of leadership in the army.

Although it is often dangerous to over-schematize, it is nevertheless possible to determine the social strata from which officers and men were drawn at different periods. The mass of the soldiers were drawn from the uneducated rural populations of the empire and its neighbours. The great majority of these remained in the ranks, a few attaining the lower echelons of the officer hierarchy: dekarch, pentekontarch and kentarch, occasionally rising higher to positions such as *komes*. But we should be careful to distinguish within this group a series of sub-strata, in which mounted thematic soldiers – those who could afford a horse and a spare mount, for example – were probably a good deal better off than the simple registered footsoldiers of the provinces. And by the tenth century, the heavy cavalryman, if he was not a mercenary equipped by the state, may often have been a substantial small-scale landowner. Indigenous mercenaries, especially cavalrymen, initially recruited and equipped by the state, might improve their social and economic situation through their military service, of course, if they served long enough to amass sufficient savings in terms of salary and booty: the examples noted already, of retired soldiers owning or part-owning mills and land, are indicative.[138]

The less easily distinguished middle group of officers was drawn largely from economically comfortable and often very well-off families in Constantinople or the provinces. They could afford an education for their children, exploit family contacts and networks, and obtain commissions for them, either in the civil service or the military. But they were also drawn from the sons of the aristocracy. Many of the wealthier "military families" may have developed and extended their clientele and their fortunes from this sort of basis. And it seems that by the early twelfth century the majority of middling and many junior officers in East Roman units were drawn from such backgrounds – certainly, Anna Comnena's epithets for such men regularly involve terms such as "of noble birth" or "well-born".

The most easily recognized group of senior officers belonged, with some exceptions, to a wealthy, landowning elite, a group which evolved during the tenth and eleventh centuries into an aristocracy, and whose families generally had a tradition of service in one sphere or another of the state administration. Even at this time, however, a degree of social mobility at the middle levels of society continued to exist, which continued well beyond the growth of "aristocratic" identities in terms of kin and family in the eleventh century – elite exclusivism only seems to have dominated at the very highest levels, those in which the emperors themselves had a direct interest: the *doukes*, *domestikoi*, *strategoi* and so forth, in both army and navy. And even here there were notable exceptions.[139] The existence of an administrative bureaucracy hindered the evolution of the sort of relatively impermeable social divisions such as began to crystallize in the medieval west, and it continued to be possible – by whatever means – to move up through society. Service in the army, along with service in the civil apparatus of the state and in the church, was one way through which this could be achieved.

The degree to which warfare was fundamental to the fabric of late Roman and Byzantine society and its historical development should by now be abundantly clear. Social values and cultural attitudes, the physical appearance of the Byzantine countryside, the fiscal and administrative organization of the state, themes of both literature and art, all were directly influenced by the beleaguered situation of the medieval East Roman state and its need for defence. In this last chapter, I have tried to point to the connections between the cultural development of Byzantine society and its military situation, in the hope that the close relationship between social and cultural evolution and the different elements analyzed in the preceding sections will the more readily be appreciated. A great deal more can be said, and there is much that remains to be done in this respect. But the importance of looking at all these elements in close relation to one another will, I hope, need no justification.

Warfare and society in Byzantium: some concluding remarks

That warmaking and all that it entailed were integral aspects of Byzantine culture and social-economic organization is undeniable. In the foregoing discussion I hope I have been able to demonstrate the extent to which this was the case, and to suggest that only by taking these factors into account can we properly comprehend the spirit as well as the structure of Byzantine civilization. In examining Byzantine military organization in its social and cultural context, we can perhaps perceive the solution to the paradox presented at the beginning of this volume. For here we have a society in which war was condemned, peace extolled, and fighting was to be avoided at all costs, but which was nevertheless the inheritor of the military administrative structures and, in many ways, the militaristic ideology of the expanding pre-Christian Roman empire in its heyday. Yet, through the blending of Christian ideals with the political will to survive, the late Roman Christian society of the eastern Mediterranean/south Balkan region generated a unique culture which was able to cling without reservation to a pacifistic ideal while at the same time legitimate and justify the maintenance of an immensely efficient, for the most part remarkably effective, military apparatus.

In its self-awareness and in its constant effort to present and rationalize this paradox, East Roman culture evolved what was, in many respects, a remarkably modern political-theoretical rationale, in which philanthropy merged with the practical demands of medieval Realpolitik to harness both the pacific and the militaristic elements of the society – reflected in the culture of monasticism on the one hand and of the provincial military elite on the other. The fact that retiring soldiers so frequently took up the monastic life as a means both of securing their future economically and physically, as well as of recovering spiritual well-being and working towards the remission of their sins, is an indication of this – however much, in reality, the individuals themselves may have harboured a less refined notion of their actions.

East Roman military administration remained, until the twelfth century, far in advance of that of its nearest neighbours, even though that of the Muslim states and principalities to the east was also very sophisticated. But the continued centralization of fiscal structures and consequent control over resources in materials and men (both politically and economically) gave the Byzantine government an advantage which none of its foes enjoyed. As long as the central government maintained its grip on the tax-extracting (or resource-extracting) machinery of the state, it was able to direct resources according to the requirements of defence or offence, and in accordance with the overall interests of the empire, to the best effect, in theory if not always in practice. Efficacious use of resources in men and matériel depended, of course, on those in authority recognizing where the priorities lay and not having to fight for their point of view to be implemented. That this was not always the case the political history of the Byzantine empire all too frequently shows.

Yet the organizational edge which Byzantine forces had over their enemies was maintained well into the twelfth century, when the predominance of non-Byzantine mercenary forces becomes particularly clear. Attitudes also played an important part, and effective military organization owed something to the consciousness, not only of Byzantine military officers, but of civilians with no practical military experience as well, of a long and honourable tradition of military writing. This was in turn combined with the historical awareness, cultivated in the upper levels of literate Byzantine culture in both Constantinople and the provinces, of the past achievements of East Roman armies. But it was not just the knowledge of a catalogue of achievements. Much more importantly, the historical narratives and the military manuals offered reasons for these achievements: order, discipline and tactical cohesion in battle; well-planned logistical arrangements; and strict adherence to Orthodoxy and clear awareness of the crucial importance of divine support.

From Roman times on the values and the achievements associated with these characteristics are repeated time and again and, as we have seen, recur throughout Byzantine texts. And while it is clear that there were considerable periods when discipline, tactical order and competent field manoeuvres in combat situations were neglected, it is equally apparent that it was in particular the existence of this tradition of military writing and this sense of history which kept the precepts (and associated successes) of the writers of tactical and strategical treatises in mind, and which enabled commanders to revive, strengthen and enforce a code of military discipline, training and tactical skills.

The East Roman world was not alone in this element of literacy and historical consciousness, of course. The Islamic world, too, generated a complex, sophisticated and multi-faceted secular literary culture, in which the writing of military and tactical/strategical treatises also had a place; and from the twelfth century, western Europe began rapidly to evolve its own literary self-consciousness and awareness and to rival and overtake the East Roman world in organizational and technical structures. But it was this factor in combination with its particular political and administrative contours which differentiated East Roman culture from its neighbours until that time. As long as the central government was able to control and direct the resources to maintain the defensive arrangements appropriate to the situation, and as long as the strategic arrangements were equal to the international military and political context, East Roman armies were able to maintain, however precariously at times, an effective control over their own territories. And there can be no doubt that central control of this sort, however modified and occasionally weakened by circumstances, was maintained more consistently between the sixth and twelfth centuries in the Byzantine world than in the caliphate, which already by the second half of the ninth century was beginning to fragment politically and ideologically.

The geographical situation of the empire offered, in this respect, both disadvantages and advantages. In the former case, the fact that potentially hostile powers were to be found on at least two, and usually three, fronts (Balkan, Syrian/Anatolian and maritime) meant that resources were always spread very thinly. In the latter, the mountain ranges which protected the Anatolian territories of the empire, together with the associated climatic conditions, appear to have discouraged attempts from the Arab Islamic powers to the south to occupy the areas beyond the Taurus–Anti-Taurus frontier zone, except very occasionally and, ultimately, unsuccessfully. And even when fortresses on the Byzantine side of this zone were seized and occupied, the Byzantine riposte was usually rapid and effective, inhibiting any longer-term build-up of military strength on the part of the invaders. In the Balkans, the situation was by no means so clear cut, but on the other hand neither the empire nor its closest powerful neighbour, the Bulgar state, enjoyed a natural boundary (until the empire extinguished Bulgar independence and recovered control of the regions up to the Danube in the late tenth century), and the political imbalance between the two was never as marked as between the Umayyad and Abbasid caliphates at the height of their power (c. AD 660–740 and 780–840) and the empire.

This difficult strategic situation encouraged an extremely close involvement with the demands of international diplomacy, of course, without which the empire would quickly have foundered. In turn, this stimulated the consolidation fairly early on of a relatively consistent, albeit conjuncture-bound, general strategy for the empire. Naturally, this was not written down, nor was it necessarily constantly present in the thoughts of the empire's political leaders and their advisers. But it possessed a certain momentum and direction of its own. Complex institutional arrangements, particularly those with which we are concerned here, evolve certain well-worn methods for achieving certain ends, and it is usually only in times of major crisis and organizational upheaval that such methods can be substantially altered. This is what happened during the seventh century, of course, and again, although on a more gradual scale, from the middle of the eleventh and into the early twelfth centuries. The ramified relationships between armed forces and their requirements, the resources available in different regions of the empire at any given time, as well as important features of the practice of diplomacy (such as time required for the diffusion and transmission of information, for example, or in respect of the movement of soldiers and matériel), as well as the psychology of the situation, these are all factors which played a role, and of which the government at Constantinople had to be aware in order to make any meaningful calculations of its own when confronted by a threat. Such factors in turn imposed their own demands – in time, in resources, in the pace of recruitment and dispositions of troops, and so forth – upon the state, operating in effect according to their own, institutionally determined agenda. Thus, while the administration and rulers at Constantinople acted according to their own, context-bound understanding of the political and strategic needs of the moment, they also worked within a framework which imposed itself upon them in respect of how policy and strategy were realized in practice.

One of the most important aspects of Byzantine diplomatic and military manoeuvring – thoroughly legitimated in all the military treatises – was the avoidance of fighting wherever possible, as we have seen. Strategy was designed not just to protect the state with physical force; a primary feature of imperial strategic thinking was to deter possible aggression by making the potential losses on the part of the aggressor appear unacceptable before the first blow was struck. The policy of avoidance which characterizes warfare in Asia Minor in the period c. 650–730 was certainly forced upon the empire by the situation, but the empire's political and military leaders were able over several generations to turn this into a positive feature, so that regular raids and invasions became less and less profitable, to the point indeed where, by the later eighth century, they had as much a symbolic significance for the Arabs as any worthwhile political or even economic value. This was not necessarily a reflection of a continuity in strategic decision-making over the longer term (although it may have been – there is no real evidence), but it certainly represented the ways in which the empire's military and fiscal structures responded, the methods through which individual emperors and their military commanders were able in the circumstances to exploit the resources at their disposal, and the realization that it was an appropriate way of defending the state's territorial integrity. In the Balkans, displays of imperial military might served similarly to dissuade planned hostile attacks, or to encourage – as in the situation during the 860s – the development of a particular political-cultural alliance. Such a policy was encouraged by the fact that, in contrast to the situation in the east, it was the empire which, generally, had a greater availability of resources, even if manpower was always a problem. This relative superiority – expressed both tactically on the battlefield and in terms of logistical arrangements – was frequently employed to discourage aggressive action.

Deterrence could also take a more militarily active role, however: punitive expeditions, intended to destroy the opponent's will to fight in the future as well as his resources and his organization for warfare, were also a feature of Byzantine strategy – most obvious, perhaps, in the Bulgarian expeditions of the emperor Constantine V, but evident also in the raiding which Byzantine commanders carried out along the eastern frontier at various times. The dangers inherent in this approach, however – that an equally powerful response might be provoked, with consequences for the empire's own military and economic situation – meant that such action was usually undertaken only when the enemy was in no condition effectively to respond. The intelligent exploitation of political difficulties inside the hostile polity, and the crucial importance of the various means for collecting and assessing information at the government's disposal, becomes especially clear here.

Byzantium thus possessed an effective military organization, based upon an efficient and, above all, highly centralized fiscal system. An intelligent, effective and flexible diplomatic and political strategy, combined with a powerful sense of its own identity and the values it represented, enabled it to survive, even flourish, in a highly disadvantageous strategic situation for some six centuries. Its political and military demise followed inevitably from the combination of a series of factors during the twelfth century and after: first, a long-term change in the international political situation, which saw the appearance to the north and west of a number of rival, and often hostile, political formations of equivalent technological, organizational and, above all, economic potential, a situation that had not arisen before this time; second, the loss of the Taurus–Anti-Taurus ranges as a natural political barrier in the southeast, as it was outflanked by the Turkish occupation of Asia Minor from the east in the later eleventh century; third, and perhaps most importantly, major changes in the distribution of political and economic power within the empire, as the growth of a self-aware political, economic and cultural elite challenged the government's absolute authority over the distribution and consumption of provincial resources. Together, these factors weakened the military organization of the state in the short term, reduced the government's ability to respond to external threats by an appropriate manipulation of resources in both the short and long term, and created a competition for central power within the elite – with consequent consumption of precious resources in internecine conflicts – which fatally weakened the government's ability to maintain a consistent foreign policy and defensive strategy. Most of the results of these developments become apparent only during the thirteenth century, but the last fifteen or so years of the twelfth century, culminating in the Fourth Crusade and the partition of the empire, point the way of things to come.

The effects of constant warfare, of the ever-present need to maintain a substantial military force with which to defend itself, were felt directly by the mass of the ordinary people of the empire in particular, and especially by the peasantry who constituted the greater part of the population. For it was they who bore the burden of maintaining these forces, whose lives were in part regulated by the timetable and often exceedingly oppressive, if not ruinous, demands of the state's fiscal apparatus, quite apart from the effects of warfare and raiding on the provincial economies of the empire at different times. Byzantine society was thus moulded in its institutional forms and in the ways in which it could evolve and develop by factors associated with warfare, and this gives the study of its military and corresponding fiscal organization a particular importance. Byzantium was a society organized for war, yet it was not, in its general aspect, a warlike society, at least not in any traditional sense. It was a society in which the language and vocabulary of warfare permeated both secular and religious literature as well as oral culture in various ways, yet in which warfare was universally seen as evil, even by the soldiers most actively involved. It was also a society which knew what it was defending, and why; and herein, perhaps, is to be found the psychological aspect of its success. The strength of the imperial ideology, in the various forms through which it was effective in society as a whole, was crucial. The certainties which this system of beliefs and values presented to the literate cultural and political elite, the close relationship between the church, as the formal representative of Orthodox Christianity – firmly rooted in the hearts and minds of the ordinary population – and the emperors, and the ideological motivation thus generated to maintain the state in existence, certainly bear some of the credit for the survival of the East Roman empire. Together with the factors already outlined, this made the East Roman state, with its armies, its military administration and its methods of waging and avoiding warfare, such a significant actor on the medieval historical stage for so long.

APPENDIX 1

Weights and loads

In order to calculate the relative value of the amounts of grain mentioned in the various sources as provided by the thematic authorities for various expeditions, as well as the numbers of animals required to transport a specific quantity of supplies for men and animals over a specific period of time, the value of the measures which are used must first be established, and this is still to a degree problematic, in spite of the work of several specialist scholars. Such calculations depend on a range of variables which have aroused a great deal of disagreement. The measure used in the majority of texts dealing with grain from the middle Byzantine period is the *modios*, but since there were several different *modioi*, and since the relationship between the various *modioi* and other measures, such as the *litra* (the Roman pound), on the one hand and, on the other, late ancient values for weight and volume such as the *artaba* remain unclear, it is not possible simply to read off the values from the texts in question.

Most of the information on the relationship between the *artaba* and the *modios* for the late Roman period comes from Egyptian documents, and although there are some difficulties (because of the variety of equivalences given in different localities), an equivalence of 4.5 basic (or "Roman") *modioi* or 3.3 *modioi xystoi* to the *artaba* can be derived from fiscal documents of the fifth and sixth centuries; nevertheless there are several other equivalences, depending on which of the various *modioi* are meant.[1] The issue is complicated by the fact that the *modios* is a measure of volume or capacity, and that in consequence it is difficult to extrapolate a weight in order to calculate the results of any conversion from grain to flour and thence through the baking process to bread. Equivalences between volume and weight must therefore remain averages, the more so since different types of grains weighed differently and were of different density, so that a *modios* of barley is by no means the same quantity, by weight or by product, as a *modios* of wheat.[2] Matters are further complicated by other factors, in particular the variable value of the

281

Roman pound (calculated at 327.45 g in the late Roman period), which in the middle Byzantine period had fluctuated to a mean of as little as 320 g in the ninth to the tenth centuries, thus further reducing the weight-value of the *modioi* in question.[3] The *annonikos modios* has been calculated at 26.6 Roman pounds (at 320 g to the pound, i.e. 18.75 lb avoirdupois/8.7 kg).[4] This was probably the *modios* used to calculate the military *synone*, a conclusion based on calculations using middle Byzantine figures for pack-animal loads.

The approximate maximum weight a horse or mule can transport over reasonably long distances is about 250 lb (114 kg),[5] and a little more over short stretches, although the optimum has generally been set at about 200 lb in modern and immediately pre-modern pack-trains.[6] In the late third-century Edict of Diocletian (14.11) a load of 200 Roman pounds (65.49 kg/144 lb) is prescribed; a sixth-century source gives mules a total burden of 156–66 Roman pounds (110–16 lb/50–3 kg).[7] Similar limits are established by the imperial legislation on the public post.[8] A mid-tenth-century Byzantine text gives somewhat higher levels, as we have noted in Chapter 5 above: three categories of load are specified: (a) saddle-horses carrying a man (presumably not armoured and carrying military panoply) and their own barley were loaded with four *modioi* each – 106 Roman pounds = 75 lb (34 kg); (b) unridden saddle-horses carried eight *modioi* – 212 Roman pounds = 150 lb (68 kg); and (c) pack-animals loaded with barley carried ten *modioi* – 265 Roman pounds = 187 lb (85 kg).[9] Thus the maximum permitted load for an animal in the imperial baggage train in the ninth and tenth centuries was set at 10 *modioi* without the pack-saddle (*sagma*) and harness which, according to the legislation of the fourth–sixth centuries, weighed approx. 50–60 Roman pounds (35–42 lb/16–19 kg, equivalent to 51–62 Byzantine pounds).[10] Using the larger *thalassios modios* of 40 Byzantine pounds as a basis for calculations, the result would be an impossibly heavy load of 450 Roman pounds, or 144 kg/319 lb avoirdupois. Using the smaller *annonikos modios* of 26.6 Byzantine pounds, the load would weigh some 266 Byzantine pounds, and with the pack saddle, a total of 316 pounds, i.e. *c.* 101kg/223 lb. Given the various weight limits decreed in the different late Roman and Byzantine sources referred to, these results strongly suggest the *annonikos modios* as the basis for calculation of middle Byzantine military supplies. The figures tally also with those generated by scholars who have studied late Roman or Hellenistic transportation, especially the loads carried by horses and mules. No single figure for "average" loads has been produced, however, for several reasons. First, the exact meaning of, and the relationship between, the weights and measures used by ancient and medieval writers are still debated; second, the size of the animals plays an important role – the carrying capacity of a mule or horse is in direct relationship to the weight and stature of the animal – the smaller the animal, the less they can carry and the more of them that may be required. Lastly, local variations in climate, ground and so on also played an important role, and these factors are hardly ever mentioned in connection with the use of animals in warfare.[11] For the purposes of the present discussion, I have used the tenth-century Byzantine figures, modified where appropriate (or where relevant information is lacking) by more recent analyses of the capacities and needs of these animals in military contexts.

In the estimates below, therefore, I will take the average weight for a horseman to be 154 lb (70 kg) and, based on Roman information, the weight of his accoutrements as a further 6 kg for clothing, 14 kg for a mail shirt, 1.4 kg for a helmet, 5.5 kg for a light shield, 2 kg for a spear, 1 kg for a light sword or sabre and 12 kg for a military saddle and harness.[12] The total thus amounts to some 112 kg (approx. 246 lb). A horseman thus equipped would not be able to carry much extra weight without damaging his mount – a maximum of 3–4 kg (between 6 and 9 lb), sufficient for three–four days' supplies for himself, or about one day's worth for both himself and his mount: note that both the late sixth-century *Strategikon* and the tenth-century treatise on *Skirmishing* recommend that cavalry soldiers carry three to four days' supply with them in their saddle bags.[13]

As far as concerns the pack-animals and unridden spare mounts, I will take for the latter the maximum load specified in the tenth-century military treatise on imperial expeditions, that is 8 *modioi* – 212 Roman pounds or 150 lb (68 kg) – which, together with a military saddle of about 10–12 kg makes a total of some 80 kg (or with the heavier framed pack-saddle, or *sagma*, which weighed between 50 and 60 Roman pounds, 35–42 lb/16–19 kg, a total of about 84–7 kg).[14] I will also assume that, under certain conditions, the spare mounts accompanying cavalry units will have been used to carry provisions and supplies, but that the lower figure given in the treatise reflects the practice of keeping their loads light so that they do not lose spirit or become worn out.[15]

For the regular mules and pack-horses, the same treatise specifies a load of 10 *modioi*, i.e. 265 Roman pounds = 187 lb (85 kg) which, with pack-saddle and harness, would thus amount to some 100–2 kg (227 lb). This is not the maximum, and since the average capacity has been estimated from other historical examples to have been slightly higher, I will take the standard figure of 250 lb (113.6 kg) as the maximum weight that could be borne, including saddle and harness, so that the average load carried would amount to approximately 96 kg (211 lb) (making 112–115 kg with the pack-saddle).

APPENDIX 2

Feeding armies: grain

The question of the quantities of grain the army required for its soldiers and livestock is complicated by several factors, in addition to a relative sparseness of detailed statistical evidence, especially from the middle Byzantine period. In particular, the values of the weights and measures used in Byzantine texts, as well as the more detailed and informative material from the late Roman period and before, are still by no means generally agreed. In addition, the technology of milling and baking, and the types of grains involved, present several problems. I have assumed in respect of the figures which are given in the sources that they refer to unmilled grains, except in one or two cases where flour is actually stated to have been supplied. In general, flour would be too easily damaged by weather and transportation, and the assumption in some texts that handmills were taken would tend to confirm this. In the following section, I have attempted briefly to survey the evidence for this aspect of military undertakings in order to provide a basis for calculations about the relationship between the needs and rate of consumption of the army, on the one hand, and the distances covered and duration of marches on the other.

As noted in Chapter 5, soldiers were issued with, or themselves milled and baked, two main varieties of bread: simple baked loaves, and double-baked "hard tack", referred to in late Roman times as *bucellatum* and by the Byzantines as *paximadion* or *paximation*. The hard tack kept better and much longer, was easily produced in field conditions, and required a relatively unsophisticated milling and baking technique.[1] Hard tack could be baked either in field ovens – *klibanoi* – or simply laid in the ashes of camp-fires: the latter technique was no doubt employed when speed of movement was a priority, as the tenth-century *Sylloge tacticorum* specifies.[2]

One document states clearly that 80 Roman pounds of "dry" bread (i.e. 25.6 kg/56.3 lb) could be baked from 1 *artaba* of wheat.[3] One *artaba* of wheat is the equivalent of 3.3 *modioi xystoi* at 26.6 Roman pounds, that is to say 87.78 Roman pounds (28.7 kg/63.2 lb).[4] Now, in pre-modern milling, which was less efficient than industrial techniques, a greater proportion of bran and wheatgerm would be included in the flour, and in field or campaign conditions, the grinding process would tend to be both more rapid and produce a far less refined flour. After grinding, an average return in flour of between 75 and 90 per cent on weight of grain would result, somewhat higher than the 72 per cent produced by modern milling and extractive processes. In the case in hand, and assuming the least favourable conditions for grinding, 1 *annonikos modios* of grain (26.6 Roman pounds) would produce between 20 and 24 Roman pounds of flour.[5] In modern baking, a return of at least 2 : 1 on weight of flour : bread is usual, since rolling and milling techniques produce a greater amount of damage to the starch elements, which in turn increases water absorbency and water retention capacity, and thus overall weight. In ancient and medieval bread-making, although fine white bread (using only some 75 per cent of the product of grinding and milling) was certainly produced for the luxury market,[6] the degree of water absorption was much less, especially in the case of *bucellatum* and biscuit (hence the description of some Egyptian bread in papyrus documents as "dry" bread). Thus the return on flour per weight of dough produced was lower, varying from 1 : 1 to 1 : 1.75, depending on the type of grain milled, the degrees of refinement of the milling process and other variables.[7]

The ratio of 1 *artaba* to 80 Roman pounds of bread bears these figures out: as we have seen, 87.78 Roman pounds of wheat, after milling (i.e. the loss of an average of *c.* 20 per cent of weight, leaving *c.* 75 pounds of flour) and baking, produced only 80 pounds of bread. Specific figures are given in a set of records relating to a sea-borne expedition in the year 911, and these are illustrative of the quantities involved in organizing a major expeditionary force.

A total of 40,000 *modioi* of barley (20,000 each from Thrakasion and Anatolikon/Kibyrrhaiotai) and 40,000 *modioi* of wheat, as well as 60,000 *modioi* of flour was to be supplied, in addition to further unspecified quantities of *paxamation*, wheat and flour. It is not stated whether the flour is wheat flour or barley flour (or even millet),[8] but it is possible that the unspecified quantity of wheat required from the Anatolikon region was the same as that provided by the Thrakasion (as was the case with the barley). Leaving aside the unspecified quantities for the moment, the 40,000 *modioi* of wheat and 60,000 *modioi* of flour would total, after the milling of the wheat (i.e. deducting an average 15 per cent from the weight of the wheat as loss through grinding), some 34,000 + 60,000 = 94,000 *modioi* of flour. Assuming the *annonikos modios* is meant (which is probable, but by no means certain), this gives us some 2.54 million Roman pounds of flour (817,000 kg/1,762,500 lb), which would bake into *c.* 2.6 million Roman pounds of bread (approx. 818,000 kg/1,770,000 lb). The total personnel involved in the expedition amounted to some 46,964, including all the oarsmen and sailors; assuming the minimum requirement of 1.3 kg of bread per day per man (just under 3 lb), this is enough only for 12 days maximum. The probability is, therefore, that these provisions were to be baked into hard tack and were supplied to only a portion of the army, and that other supplies were to be collected both en route and in enemy territory. The method for calculating the ratio of supplies to men and to duration of expedition is given below, in Appendix 3.

APPENDIX 3

Daily rations

In the following tables, I present some calculations for field forces of different strengths and in different hypothetical circumstances, using as material the weights and measures arrived at in the preceding appendices, and taking as the standard weight of the ration of a soldier, excluding water, 1.3 kg *per diem*. For horses and mules, which require roughly the same weight as each other in hard feed (grains) and forage, I will take a low 2.2 kg as a field ration in grain, with a further 6.8 kg in forage – grass or hay, although in reality, working animals should receive a somewhat more generous ration than animals at rest. It is worth noting that the tenth-century text dealing with imperial military expeditions remarks that, while the animals of the imperial cortège are in Roman territory, the so-called imperial horses – higher quality animals – were to be fed a threefold ration per day and the rest a double ration. This suggests that a single ration (*tage*) was a fixed quantity, and that it was low: to feed the animals properly it needed to be administered in multiple units. It might also suggest that the single (i.e. the smallest practicable) ration was that which was normally used on campaigns, since otherwise there would have been no need to be so specific about the imperial animals.[1] It should be emphasized at the outset that in all cases slightly different figures could be employed. In this case, I have taken deliberately low estimates of the size of rations issued, to illustrate the nature of the logistical issues facing Byzantine commanders. Taking a higher weight for the load per animal would have the effect of decreasing very slightly (but not by much) the total number of transport animals required for the different-sized forces taken as examples; taking a larger ration would correspondingly increase the total weight needed to be transported, and thus the number of pack-animals.[2]

The examples are all somewhat artificial illustrations, of course. In reality, armies – especially larger ones – would have to face all the conditions described in the process of a single extended campaign, so that the solution to a logistical problem will be found by combining different sets of circumstances in the different areas where field operations took place.

The calculations will be based on a series of equivalences, as follows:

Standard weight of armed
  cavalryman with harness: 112 kg   ration: 1.3 kg
Standard load carried by
  unridden remount: 68 kg   ration: 2.2 kg (+ 6.8 fodder)
Standard load carried by
  pack-animal: 96 kg   ration: 2.2 kg (+ 6.8 fodder)

I will assume further that the proportion of remounts to ridden horses is approximately 1 : 4 (see the appropriate remarks in Chapter 5), and that the ratio of pack-mules to soldiers (carrying tents, kitchen utensils, hand-mills, etc.) was approximately 1 : 50. This is certainly too low an estimate for animals carrying supplies, of course: Leo VI notes that infantry should be accompanied by one pack-animal for each group of 16 soldiers, and *in extremis* (i.e. shortage of animals), one for every 32 soldiers, to carry their provisions for up to 10 days should they be sent on ahead of the main column and slower (wheeled) baggage. Since the maximum load such animals could carry was about 96 kg, possibly 100 kg, excluding the pack-saddle, this suggests a rather small basic ration allowance for the soldiers: 96 kg ÷ 16 men = 6 kg per man. Spread over 8 days this produces a mere 0.75 kg, just over half the standard 1.3 kg basic ration generally assumed, and suggests that the soldiers must also have been expected to forage for themselves to supplement this meagre fare.[3]

The basic equation for establishing the relationship between the size of an army, the number of pack-animals and quantity of provisions it requires, and the number of days it can be kept in the field, was established by Engels in his analysis of the strategy of Alexander the Great, in which he also took into account the need to transport water, since much of Alexander's campaigning took place in relatively arid regions. Here I will employ a slightly simpler equation:

$$N = \frac{(a + b + c + d)\, y}{(x - z)\, y}$$

where N = the number of pack animals required, a = the sum of the soldiers' provisions in kg, b = the sum of the horses' rations in kg, c = the sum of the rations of the pack-mules, d = the sum of the rations of the remounts that also carry provisions; x = the average load carried, z = the standard ration of the animals carrying the provisions, and y the duration of the expedition in days.[4]

Let us begin with A, a small cavalry force of 1,000 men accompanied by 250 spare horses. They require 1,000 × 1.3 kg + 1250 × 2.2 kg per day, i.e. 1,300 +

2,750 = 4,050 kg per day. This sum is then multiplied by the number of days and divided by the weight in kg carried by each pack-animal, minus its own daily ration. For the sake of the example, I have calculated up to the 24th day, since that is the length beyond which the tenth-century evidence suggests troops could no longer be supplied from what was brought with them.[5] As emphasized in Chapter 5, in addition, the question of how many mules and pack-horses were actually available to the army is impossible to answer. But it is unlikely that many thousands will have been easily acquired, except for campaigns planned well in advance.

The result is as follows, assuming the remounts themselves carry no provisions:

Days	Total of provisions	Load minus ration per animal	Number of mules required
1	$N = 4,050 \times 1 = 4,050$	$\div\ 96 - 2.2 \times 1$	$=\ \ \ \ 43$
2	$4,050 \times 2 = 8,100$	$\div\ 96 - 2.2 \times 2$	$=\ \ \ \ 88$
5	$4,050 \times 5 = 20,250$	$\div\ 96 - 2.2 \times 5$	$=\ \ \ 238$
10	$4,050 \times 10 = 40,500$	$\div\ 96 - 2.2 \times 10$	$=\ \ \ 547$
15	$4,050 \times 15 = 60,750$	$\div\ 96 - 2.2 \times 15$	$=\ \ \ 964$
20	$4,050 \times 20 = 81,000$	$\div\ 96 - 2.2 \times 20$	$=\ 1,558$
24	$4,050 \times 24 = 97,200$	$\div\ 96 - 2.2 \times 24$	$=\ 2,250$

If provisions were carried on the 250 remounts, each horse would carry some 68 kg (× 250) making a total of 17,000 kg. Both men and horses could be maintained for up to 4 days from these supplies; at the same time, the soldiers themselves could carry a day's supplies for themselves and their mounts, extending this initial period to some 5 days at the outside.[6] With the provisions carried on 1,558 mules, in addition, they could provide themselves with food to last about 24 days altogether. Whether such small forces had access to such relatively large numbers of pack-animals is open to question, however, since it is clear that even the imperial *metata* were unable to provide all the animals for the imperial baggage train of over 1,000 horses and mules in the ninth and tenth centuries.[7]

Applying the same calculations and conditions to larger armies, we obtain the following results for B, an army of 4,000 cavalry with 1,000 remounts, and C, an army of 10,000, made up of 6,000 infantry and 4,000 cavalry accompanied by 1,000 remounts:

B: 4,000 men × 1.3 kg per day + 5,000 horses × 2.2 kg per day = 5,200 + 11,000 = 16,200

Days	Total of provisions	Load minus ration per animal	Number of mules required
1	$16,200 \times 1 = 16,200$	$\div\ 96 - 2.2 \times 1$	$=\ \ \ 173$
2	$16,200 \times 2 = 32,400$	$\div\ 96 - 2.2 \times 2$	$=\ \ \ 354$

5	$16,200 \times 5 \ = 81,000$	$\div 96 - 2.2 \times 5$	$= \ \ \ 953$
10	$16,200 \times 10 = 162,000$	$\div 96 - 2.2 \times 10$	$= 2,190$
15	$16,200 \times 15 = 243,000$	$\div 96 - 2.2 \times 15$	$= 3,858$
20	$16,200 \times 20 = 324,000$	$\div 96 - 2.2 \times 20$	$= 6,231$
24	$16,200 \times 24 = 388,800$	$\div 96 - 2.2 \times 24$	$= 9,000$

If provisions were carried on the 1,000 remounts, each horse would carry some 68 kg ($\times$ 1,000) making a total of 68,000 kg. Both men and horses could be maintained for up to 4 days from these supplies; at the same time, the soldiers themselves could carry a day's supplies for themselves and their mounts, extending this initial period to some 5 days at the outside. With the provisions carried on 6, 231 mules, in addition, they could provide themselves with food to last the full 24 days noted in the sources.

C: 10,000 men $\times$ 1.3 kg per day + 5,000 horses $\times$ 2.2 kg per day = 13,000 + 11,000 = 24,000

Days	Total of provisions	Load minus ration per animal	Number of mules required
1	$24,000 \times 1 \ = 24,000$	$\div 96 - 2.2 \times 1$	$= \ \ \ \ 256$
2	$24,000 \times 2 \ = 48,000$	$\div 96 - 2.2 \times 2$	$= \ \ \ \ 524$
5	$24,000 \times 5 \ = 120,000$	$\div 96 - 2.2 \times 5$	$= \ \ 1,412$
10	$24,000 \times 10 = 240,000$	$\div 96 - 2.2 \times 10$	$= \ \ 3,244$
15	$24,000 \times 15 = 360,000$	$\div 96 - 2.2 \times 15$	$= \ \ 5,715$
20	$24,000 \times 20 = 480,000$	$\div 96 - 2.2 \times 20$	$= \ \ 9,231$
24	$24,000 \times 24 = 576,000$	$\div 96 - 2.2 \times 24$	$= 13,334$

These figures assume that the infantry carry nothing but their arms and clothing, however, which is probably unlikely to have been the case very often. Where infantry are present, and where the cavalry remounts are employed to carry extra provisions, the first stages of any march can be covered by the horsemen themselves, as we have seen (up to 4 days). Infantry can in turn carry up to 20 days' worth of supplies if necessary. If we subtract the infantry portion (6,000 $\times$ 1.3 per day = 7,800 kg) from the above calculations, we arrive at the same figures for mules as in an army with only 4,000 cavalry and 1,000 remounts. If we then add in mules carrying items of siege equipment, tents and other paraphernalia, as well as a quota of camp attendants and followers (both servants and specialist armourers and weapons makers) an expedition of up to 20 days is logistically quite feasible. How many attendants there were needed for the pack-animals is unclear – one tenth-century source suggests 1 man per 10 mules or 20 pack-horses. During imperial expeditions in the later ninth and tenth centuries, the mules of the imperial baggage were each accompanied by an individual muleteer drawn from the special corps of the Optimatoi, although these were clearly exceptional circumstances.[8] Armies substantially larger than this would rapidly lose in flexibility and speed.

Contexts in which the army will have needed to provide all its hard fodder for the horses and all the rations for the men from supplies acompanying the expedition will usually have involved leaving imperial territory. But even inside the empire there exists a relationship between troops and pack-animals which determined the possibilities for long-distance movement, as these following examples show. In the next example, I have calculated the figures for an army in which all food, forage and hard feed for the animals was available along the route, conditions which might be met on occasion within the empire, or on enemy territory when the Roman commander had the advantage of surprise and the appropriate season.

D: 1,000 men × 1.3 kg per day = 1,300 kg per day

250 remounts each loaded with 68 kg = 17,000 kg will provide enough rations for about ten days (17,000 ÷ 1.3 = 13,076 ÷ 1,000 = 13 kg per man, i.e. 1.3 per man per day). Thereafter extra mules with rations will be required. By the same token, a force E of 4,000 cavalry with 1,000 remounts carrying rations for the men only will be able to transport some 96,000 kg of provisions, enough for the men for about 14 days; a similar cavalry force, accompanied by 6,000 infantry F, and with the infantry carrying their own provisions, will have needed fewer extra pack-animals to stay in the field for up to three weeks or more.

Examples A and D are probably most typical in respect of the defensive warfare in the frontier regions of Anatolia, where the Byzantine forces could rely on local support and provisioning. In contrast, there must have been occasions when imperial armies had to take not only their basic rations in grain feed, but also green fodder or hay and possibly water as well. But under these conditions the army will have been able to provide for only a couple of days at the outside, as example G, for an army of 4,000 cavalry and 1,000 remounts accompanied by 80 mules with tents and other equipment, will illustrate. Here, the rates for provisions are slightly different: 1.3 kg per day for the men, but 9 kg for the animals (2.2 kg basic grain feed, 6.8 kg hay or green fodder). Assuming the spare horses were employed to carry some of this material and that the cavalry soldiers' mounts were also loaded with supplies for the men for up to 3 days, 1,000 horses would transport 68,000 kg of fodder and grain, which would last just under 1½ days for the 5,000 horses and 80 mules at the above-mentioned minimum rate of 9 kg per day. Thereafter, pack-animals would be required to carry the fodder and rations for both men and horses. The total requirements for such a force amount to 4,000 × 1.3 kg per day for the men (= 5,200 kg per day) and 5,080 × 9 kg per day for the animals (= 45,720 kg per day), thus 50,920 kg of provisions per day. The calculation shows the following:

Days	Total of provisions	Load minus ration per animal	Number of mules required
1	$50{,}920 \times 1 = 50{,}920$	$\div 96 - 9 \times 1$	$= 585$
2	$50{,}920 \times 2 = 101{,}840$	$\div 96 - 9 \times 2$	$= 1{,}305$
5	$50{,}920 \times 5 = 254{,}600$	$\div 96 - 9 \times 5$	$= 4{,}992$
10	$50{,}920 \times 10 = 509{,}200$	$\div 96 - 9 \times 10$	$= 84{,}866$

For an army of 10,000, where 6,000 are infantry carrying as much of their own rations as possible, a little more flexibility is possible; but it is clear that, for an army to attempt to carry all its supplies with it – and I have excluded water in this example[9] – for more than a few days was virtually impossible, if only because there were limits on the number of pack-animals available. The law of diminishing returns applies quite mechanically here, as the figure for a 10-day march indicates: the longer the march (and given a constant number of transport animals from start to finish), the greater the portion of supplies remaining each day consumed by the pack-animals themselves, until none is left to distribute elsewhere: by the tenth day in this example, an impossible 84,000+ animals would have been required from the beginning of the march to supply all the needs of the army for the period in question. The "line of logistical impossibility" would be drawn after the fifth day, and even assuming there were enough animals for each horseman to lead one pack-animal, that would mark the maximum duration of a march under these conditions. Engels showed that even on half-rations – extremely dangerous in terms of the fitness of the troops and the problems of disease and malnutrition – Alexander's army could never have moved with its supplies in this manner for more than a couple of days before the animals had consumed their loads.[10]

The relationship between size of army and available pack-animals is clearly a crucial consideration. The illustrations above make it quite clear that small forces of cavalry or mixed cavalry and infantry were both more flexible, faster (because smaller and more coherent) and easier to provision. Larger armies, especially offensive forces intending to undertake sieges, for example, involved a great deal more planning, of course, but also moved more slowly, since carts and wagons were usually also involved. Yet the availability of pack-animals would have placed very clear limits on the size of any army operating on enemy territory where supplies were inadequate. These points are fundamental for any consideration of the issue of numbers and the logistical feasibility of the various forces mentioned for differernt situations by the sources.

Notes

Introduction

1. For historical surveys see P.R.L. Brown, *The World of Late Antiquity* (London, 1971); George Ostrogorsky, *History of the Byzantine State* (Oxford, 1968); *The Cambridge Medieval History*, IV: *The Byzantine Empire*, 2 parts, revised edn J.M. Hussey (Cambridge, 1966); M. Whittow, *The Making of Orthodox Byzantium, 600– 1025* (London, 1996); M. Angold, *The Byzantine Empire 1025–1204. A Political History* (London, 1984). For the seventh century as a period of transformation, see J.F. Haldon, *Byzantium in the Seventh Century: The Transformation of a Culture*, 2nd revised edn (Cambridge, 1997).
2. A useful introduction in English to the history of Byzantine studies can be found in the opening section of Ostrogorsky's *History of the Byzantine State*.
3. Hans Delbrück, *History of the Art of War*, II: *The Barbarian Invasions*, trans. Walter J. Renfroe, Jr (Lincoln/London, 1990), pp. 339–83; III: *Medieval Warfare*, pp. 189– 202 with 203–15 (on the Arabs). Oman's work – *The Art of War in the Middle Ages, A.D. 378–1515* – was originally published in 1885, then republished in an up-to-date version and edited by J.H. Beeler in 1953 (Ithaca, NY), and is now available in paperback. For an alternative, often dogmatic, but nevertheless still insightful approach to the relationship between warfare and society, see also J.S. Rasin, *Geschichte der Kriegskunst* (Berlin, 1959), originally published in Russian in the late 1940s and marred by the political and ideological exigencies of its time.
4. Among the more reliable older accounts are: *The Cambridge Medieval History*, IV: *The Byzantine Empire*, part 2 (Cambridge, 1967), pp. 35–50; the chapter by W. Ensslin, in N.H. Baynes and H. St L.B. Moss (eds), *Byzantium: An Introduction to East Roman Civilization* (Oxford, 1969), pp. 294–306. Only one Greek scholar devoted a monograph to the subject, but the work was heavily marked by romantic Hellenism and a nationalist perspective: see N. Kalomenopoulos, *The Military Organisation of the Greek Empire of Byzantium* (Athens: S.K. Blastos, 1937 (in Greek)), which refers throughout to "our" empire!
5. Good detailed treatments can be found in A. Toynbee, *Constantine Porphyrogenitus and His World* (London, 1973), pp. 282–322 (the army), 323–45 (the navy); Whittow, *The Making of Orthodox Byzantium*, pp. 113–26, 165–93, 323–5.

6. As well as the work of these writers, of course, there are a number of other scholars who have devoted single articles to a particular aspect of Byzantine military history. Many of these will be mentioned as appropriate in the chapters which follow. Among the more important is the Russian scholar Vassili Kucma, but his work is written for the specialist Byzantinist and is anyway not translated. See, for example, V.V. Kucma, "Komandniyi sostav i ryadovye stratioty v femnon vojske Vizantii v konce IX–X v" [Commanding officers and rank-and-file soldiers in the theme armies in Byzantium, late 9th–10th centuries], in *Vizantijskie Ocerki* (Moscow, 1971), pp. 86–97.

7. Mark C. Bartusis, *The Late Byzantine Army. Arms and Society, 1204–1453* (Philadelphia, 1992); Warren Treadgold, *Byzantium and Its Army, 284–1081* (Stanford, CA, 1995).

8. See Walter E. Kaegi, Jr, *Byzantine Military Unrest 471–843: An Interpretation* (Amsterdam, 1981); and my review in *Byzantinoslavica*, 44, 1983, pp. 54–7.

9. The near exception is the discussion of F. Trombley, "Warfare and society in sixth-century Syria", *BMGS*, 21, 1997, pp. 154–209.

10. The best survey and analysis of the manuscript tradition is by Alphonse Dain, "Les stratégistes byzantins", *Travaux et Mémoires*, 2, 1967, pp. 317–92, but see also, for context and historical development of the genre, H. Hunger, *Die hochsprachliche profane Literatur der Byzantiner*, 2 vols (Handbuch der Altertumswissenschaft, XII, 5.1 and 2 = Byzantinisches Handbuch, 5, 1 and 2) (Munich, 1978), "Kriegswissenschaft", pp. 323–40.

11. For a good survey of the nature of Byzantine hagiography, its origins, characteristics and functions, see J. Dümmer, "Griechische Hagiographie", in F. Winkelmann and W. Brandes (eds), *Quellen zur Geschichte des frühen Byzanz* (Berlin, 1990), pp. 284–96 and the relevant sections in *The Cambridge Medieval History*, IV, part 2.

12. See, for example, C. Foss and D. Winfield, *Byzantine Fortifications. An Introduction* (Pretoria, 1986).

13. See M.C. Bishop and J.N.C. Coulston, *Roman Military Equipment from the Punic Wars to the Fall of Rome* (London, 1993), esp. pp. 122–82; and P. Southern and Karen R. Dixon, *The Late Roman Army* (London, 1996), pp. 89–126.

14. See T. Kolias, *Byzantinische Waffen* (Byzantina Vindobonensia, XVII) (Vienna, 1988).

15. K. Armstrong, *Holy War. The Crusades and Their Impact on Today's World* (New York, 1988), p. 25.

16. Liudprand, *Antapodosis*, in *Liudprandi Opera*, ed. J. Becker, *Monumenta Germaniae Historica in usum scholarum* (Hanover, 1915), I, 11 (p. 9). Cf. also the translation by F.A. Wright, *Liudprand, Works* (London, 1930), p. 38.

17. The literature on all these aspects of later Roman history is vast. An accessible brief introduction can be found in Brown, *The World of Late Antiquity*. For more detailed analyses, with sources and recent literature, see A.H.M. Jones, *The Later Roman Empire, 284–602: A Social, Economic and Administrative Survey*, 3 vols and maps (Oxford, 1964) henceforth *LRE*; and Haldon, *Byzantium in the Seventh Century*.

18. See in this respect the discussion in John Keegan, *A History of Warfare* (London, 1993), pp. 3–60.

19. It seems now generally to have been accepted that the two opposing camps in this debate – those who argued that warmaking and aggression were entirely culturally

determined, and those who argued in contrast that biogenetic elements were the only crucial factors at issue – have both been overzealous in arguing their one-sided cases. In fact, as anthropologists are increasingly recognizing, violence, aggression and, on a larger scale, warfare are the results of a combination of bio-genetic potentials and socio-cultural stimuli which operate together dialectically. See, for example, the useful discussion of Donald Tuzin, "The specter of peace in unlikely places: concept and paradox in the anthropology of peace", in T. Gregor (ed.), *A Natural History of Peace* (Nashville/London, 1996), pp. 3–33, and other contributions on this theme by Bruce M. Knauft and Leslie E. Sponsel in the same volume. Note also Keegan, *A History of Warfare*, pp. 79–126.

20. For the best detailed analysis of these developments, see Jones, *LRE*, I, pp. 37–111.
21. For a variety of approaches to the state, with more recent literature, see M. Mann, *The Sources of Social Power*, I: *A History of Power from the Beginnings to A.D. 1760* (Cambridge, 1986) (with the helpful review by C.J. Wickham, "Histor-ical materialism, historical sociology", *New Left Review*, 171, 1988, pp. 63–78); W.G. Runciman, *A Treatise on Social Theory*, II: *Substantive Social Theory* (Cam-bridge, 1989) (also reviewed by C.J. Wickham, "Systactic structures: social theory for historians", *Past and Present*, 132, 1991, pp. 188–203); T. Skocpol, *States and Social Revolutions: A Comparative Analysis of France, Russia and China* (Cambridge, 1979); and J.F. Haldon, *The State and the Tributary Mode of Production* (London/New York, 1993).
22. For a useful introduction to what such a project entails, see P.M. Strässle, "Krieg, Kriegführung und Gesellschaft in Byzanz (9.–12. Jh.). Ein polemologischer Erklärungsansatz", *BF*, 19, 1993, pp. 149–69.

Chapter 1   Fighting for peace: attitudes to warfare in Byzantium

1. *Ecloga. Das Gesetzbuch Leons III. und Konstaninos' V.*, ed L. Burgmann (Forschungen zur byzantinischen Rechtsgeschichte, X) (Frankfurt am Main, 1983), proem; English translation in E. Barker, *Social and Political Thought in Byzantium. From Justinian to the Last Palaeologus* (Oxford, 1957), pp. 84–5.
2. See R.F. Taft, SJ, "War and peace in the Byzantine divine liturgy", in T.S. Miller and J.S. Nesbitt (eds), *Peace and War in Byzantium* (Washington, DC, 1995), pp. 17–32.
3. See R.M. Grant, *Augustus to Constantine: The Thrust of the Christian Movement into the Roman World* (London, 1971); and esp. J. Helgeland, "Christians and the Roman army from Marcus Aurelius to Constantine", in *Aufstieg und Niedergang der römischen Welt*, 23, 1 (Berlin/New York, 1979), pp. 724–834; and L.J. Swift, "War and the Christian conscience I: the early years", ibid., pp. 835–68.
4. See J. Helgeland, "Christians and the Roman army A.D. 173–337", *Church His-tory*, 43, 1974, pp. 149–63.
5. There is an excellent discussion in D.L. Jones, "Christianity and the Roman imperial cult", in *Aufstieg und Niedergang der römischen Welt*, 23, 2, pp. 1023–54.
6. For the Christianization of the ruler cult and its longer-term implications, see T.D. Barnes, *Constantine and Eusebius* (Cambridge, MA/London, 1981), pp. 245–60; and N.H. Baynes, "Eusebius and the Christian empire", in N.H. Baynes, *Byzantine Studies and Other Essays* (London, 1955), pp. 168–72. See also the more

detailed analysis of F. Dvornik, *Early Christian and Byzantine Political Philosophy* (Washington, DC, 1966), 2, pp. 614–15, 652–3. For expressions of the hope for peace and a reluctant support for the state and the need to fight wars, see the discussion in Taft, "War and peace in the Byzantine divine liturgy", pp. 29–30.

7. During the reign of Theodosius I (385–95) Christianity became the official religion of the state and non-Christians were excluded from state service – a process which considerably speeded up the process of public acceptance of Christianity, even if pagan cult practices and beliefs continued to inform many aspects of both elite and mass popular culture. See J.L. Boojamra, "The Emperor Theodosius and the legal establishment of Christianity", *Byzantina*, 9, 1977, pp. 385–407.

8. Swift, "War and the Christian conscience", and on Basil's canon and later commentaries, see P. Viscuso, "Christian participation in warfare. A Byzantine view", in Miller and Nesbitt (eds), *Peace and War in Byzantium*, pp. 33–40.

9. For the liturgical texts and their complex history, see P.N. Trempelas, *The Three Liturgies According to the Athens Codices*, Texte und Forschungen zur byzantinisch-neugriechischen Philologie (Athens, 1935) (in Greek), and pp. 185–6 for this passage. On attitudes to warfare within the Christian cultural world, see, for example, the discussion in the introductory chapter of John Keegan's *A History of Warfare*, or the introduction by the editor of the volume, Thomas Gregor, to *A Natural History of Peace* (Nashville, TN, 1996).

10. The most detailed recent discussion of the subject is Athena Kolia-Dermitzaki, *Byzantine "Holy War": The Concept and Evolution of Religious Warfare in Byzantium* (in Greek) (Athens, 1991). Somewhat different perspectives are argued in A. Laiou, "On Just War in Byzantium", in S. Reinert, J. Langdon and J. Allen (eds), *To Hellenikon. Studies in Honor of Speros Vryonis Jr. I* (New Rochelle, NY, 1993), pp. 153–74. In general, see V. Laurent, "L'idée de guerre sainte et la tradition byzantine", *Revue Historique du Sud-Est Européen*, 23, 1946, pp. 71–98; J.R.E. Bliese, "The Just War as concept and motive in the central Middle Ages", *Medievalia et Humanistica*, new ser. 17, 1991, pp. 1–26; and the useful collection of articles in Miller and Nesbitt (eds), *Peace and War in Byzantium*. Holy war or *jihād* in Islam can have for contemporary Islamic society a predominantly peaceful character of the struggle, internal to the self and within Muslim society in general, against evil. But it has historically been appropriated very frequently by political elites as an ideological cloak for short-term political ends (even though in the Qur'ān it is strictly forbidden to wage wars for the sake of acquiring worldy power, glory and so forth), as well as longer-term political-religious motives. Such distinctions were not always appreciated by Muslims themselves, and still less so by the non-Muslim world. See A. Noth, *Heiliger Krieg und heiliger Kampf* (Bonner historische Forschungern, 28) (Bonn, 1966), and W. Madelung, art. "Jihad", in *Dictionary of the Middle Ages*, 13 vols (New York, 1982–9), 7, pp. 110–11.

11. For arguments for a Byzantine notion of holy war, see Kolia-Dermitzaki, *Byzantine "Holy War"*; for alternative views, see N. Oikonomidès, "The concept of 'Holy War' and two tenth-century ivories", in Miller and Nesbitt, *Peace and War in Byzantium*, pp. 62–86. A recent survey of some of this literature is to be found in T.M. Kolbaba, "Fighting for Christianity. Holy War in the Byzantine empire", *Byzantion*, 68, 1998, pp. 194–221.

12. See esp. Barnes, *Constantine and Eusebius*, and H.A. Drake, *In Praise of Constantine* (Berkeley/Los Angeles, CA, 1976); for a brief summary of Eusebius' life and

NOTES

work, see A. Kazhdan et al. (eds), *The Oxford Dictionary of Byzantium* (Washington, DC, 1991), pp. 751–2.

13. See esp. the catalogue of such developments in E. Kitzinger, "The cult of images in the age before iconoclasm", *DOP*, 8, 1954, pp. 109–115; Averil Cameron, "Images of authority: elites and icons in late sixth-century Constantinople", *Past and Present*, 84, 1979, pp. 3–35.

14. See Kitzinger, "Cult of images", p. 111 for texts and discussion.

15. An excellent account of relations between the two states can be found in J.D. Howard-Johnson, "The two great powers in late antiquity: a comparison", in Averil Cameron (ed.), *States, Resources and Armies: Papers of the Third Workshop on Late Antiquity and Early Islam* (Princeton, NJ, 1995), pp. 157–226.

16. See Kolia-Dermitzaki, *Holy War*, pp. 147–52 with sources, and K.G. Holum, "Pulcheria's crusade A.D. 421–422 and the ideology of imperial victory", *Greek, Roman and Byzantine Studies*, 18, 1977, pp. 153–72.

17. The treaty is described in the account of Menander Protector, XI, 206–217 (see R.C. Blockley (ed. and trans.), *The History of Menander the Guardsman* (Liverpool, 1985), pp. 61–87, esp. 71–5 for the details). For a brief account of the wars between Rome and Persia in the sixth century, see Jones, *LRE*, pp. 287–8, 290, 294 (Justinian's reign), pp. 305–6 (Justin II), pp. 307–8 (Tiberius Constantine) and pp. 309–11 (Maurice); Whittow, *The Making of Orthodox Byzantium*, pp. 47–53; and for Maurice's reign in particular L.M. Whitby, *The Emperor Maurice and His Historian: Theophylact Simocatta on Persian and Balkan Warfare* (Oxford, 1988).

18. See Z. Rubin, "The Reforms of Khusro Anushirwan", in Cameron (ed.), *States, Resources and Armies*, pp. 227–97.

19. See in particular Haldon, *Byzantium in the Seventh Century*, pp. 37–40, 281–375.

20. See Haldon, *Byzantium in the seventh century*, pp. 41–7 for sources and more recent literature; see also J.D. Howard-Johnston, "Heraclius' Persian campaigns and the revival of the East Roman empire, 622–630", *War in History*, 6, 1, 1999, pp. 1–44. For the near-contemporary account in the so-called "Easter Chronicle" see *Chronicon Paschale 284–628 AD*, trans. with notes and commentary by M. and M. Whitby (Liverpool, 1989), pp. 142–89.

21. On the cult of the Cross, see: A. Frolow, *La relique de la vraie croix. Recherches sur le développement d'un culte* (Paris, 1961); and the brief summary in *ODB*, pp. 552f. See, for example, the comments in this connection made by the later chroniclers, drawing on near-contemporary sources, esp. Theophanes Confessor (writing in the late eighth century) and Agapius of Manbij (tenth century): Theophanes, *Chronographia*, p. 301 (English trans. by C. Mango and R. Scott, *The Chronicle of Theophanes the Confessor. Byzantine and Near Eastern History AD 284–813* (Oxford, 1997), p. 433); *Kitab al-'Unvan. Histoire universelle écrite par Agapius (Mahboub) de Menbidj*, II. (= Patrologia Orientalis, VIII, 3) (Paris, 1912), p. 460.

22. George's poems exist only in the original Greek and a modern Italian translation, although they have been the subject of much discussion: see A. Pertusi (ed.), *Giorgio di Pisidia. Poemi, 1. Panegirici epici*, Studia Patristica et Byzantina, 7 (Ettal, 1959). Among the works are poems dealing with Heraclius' Persian campaign, on Bonos the *magister* who stood in for Heraclius in his absence from Constantinople, on the restoration of the Cross and on the Avar siege. The account in the *Chronographia* of Theophanes is strongly imbued with a religious fervour: see p. 308 (trans. Mango and Scott, p. 440), for example, when Heraclius orders the troops to spend three days in prayer and spiritual purification. The contemporary

Chronicon Paschale refers to both Persians and Avars as impious enemies of the faith and emphasizes the nature of the struggle between Christians and non-Christians: cf. pp. 169–70, 187ff. (trans. Whitby).

23. See Theophanes, pp. 303, 298 (trans. Mango and Scott, pp. 435–6, 427). Several later emperors similarly used the icon of the Virgin in this way: John I Tzimiskes (against the Bulgars) in 971 (Scylitzes, *Synopsis Historiarum*, p. 310), for example. For the use of other such symbols, see also Cameron, "Images of authority", and "The Virgin's Robe: an episode in the history of early seventh-century Constantinople", *Byzantion*, 49, 1979, pp. 42–56.

24. See Averil Cameron, "The Theotokos in sixth-century Constantinople: a city finds its symbol", *JThS* 29, 1, 1978, pp. 79–108. Relying on earlier sources, the *Chronographia* of Theophanes attributes to Heraclius a harangue in which he asks the soldiers willingly to sacrifice themselves for the sake of their fellow Christians and to choose the crown of the martyrs in return for God's reward (pp. 310–11 (trans. Mango and Scott, pp. 442–3)).

25. The development of East Roman society and culture at this time are traced in detail in Haldon, *Byzantium in the Seventh Century*.

26. For a detailed analysis of the image promoted by Heraclius and his panegyrist George of Pisidia – with its "crusading" elements, its presentation of Heraclius as a new David and its depiction of the struggle between Romans and Persians as one between Christianity and the forces of darkness – see Mary Whitby, "A new image for a new age: George of Pisidia on the emperor Heraclius", in E. Dabrowa (ed.), *The Roman and Byzantine Army in the East* (Cracow, 1994), pp. 197–225.

27. For example, Liudprand, *Antapodosis*, I, 11 (p. 9) (cf. also the translation by F.A. Wright, *Liudprand, Works* (London, 1930), p. 38).

28. See especially L. Kretzenbacher, *Griechische Reiterheilige als Gefangenenretter* (Vienna, 1983).

29. Leo diac., 61. 2f.; and cf. for the eleventh-century P. Gautier, "Typikon du Sébaste Gregoire Pakourianos", *REB*, 42, 1984, pp. 5–145, at l. 1681.

30. See the discussion in J.F. Haldon, *Constantine Porphyrogenitus, Three Treatises on Imperial Military Expeditions (CFHB, 28)* (Vienna, 1990), pp. 245–7 and for details of further literature and sources. For Arabic accounts of the capture of crosses, see, for example, the extracts from the ninth–tenth-century chronicler Tabarī, in A.A. Vasiliev, *Byzance et les Arabes*, II: *Les relations politiques de Byzance et des Arabes à l'époque de la dynastie macédonienne (Les empereurs Basile I, Léon le Sage et Constantin VII Porphyrogénète) (867–959)*, ed. Grégoire, H. and M. Canard (Corpus Bruxellense Hist. Byz. I, II) (Brussels, 1950/1968), pp. 9, 59 etc.

31. Niketas Choniates, I, 179–180 (*Nicetae Choniatae Historia*, ed. J.A. Van Dieten, 2 vols (*CFHB*, 11, 1–2) (Berlin/New York, 1975)); Akropolites, XI, 19.25–20.7 (*Georgii Akropolitae, Historia*, eds A. Heisenberg and P. Wirth (Stuttgart, 1978)).

32. See the still very useful discussion of J. Gagé, "*Stavros nikopoios*. La victoire impériale dans l'empire chrétien", *Revue d'histoire et de philosophie religieuses*, 1935, pp. 370–400.

33. *Strategy* "The Anonymous Byzantine Treatise on Strategy", in G.T. Dennis (ed. and trans.), *Three Byzantine Military Treatises*, text, trans. and notes (*CFHB*, 25 = *DOT*, 9) (Washington, DC, 1985), pp. 10–135, § 4.9–14 (p. 20).

34. See *Skirmishing*, proem. 1 (G. Dagron and H. Mihaescu, *Le traité sur la guérilla (De velitatione) de l'empereur Nicéphore Phocas (963–969)* (Paris, 1986); also Dennis

NOTES

(ed. and trans.), *Three Byzantine Military Treatises*, pp. 144–239 – see p. 147); and Haldon, *Const. Porph., Three Treatises*, Text B, 3, 80–1 and pp. 157, 164.

35. See N. Oikonomidès, "The concept of 'Holy War' and two tenth-century Ivories", in Miller and Nesbitt (eds), *Peace and War in Byzantium*, pp. 62–86.

36. *Skirmishing*, § 24, 8.58–9 (trans. Dennis, p. 235).

37. Constantine Porphyrogenitus, *De Administrando Imperio*, I: Greek text, ed. Gy. Moravcsik, English trans. R.J.H. Jenkins (*CFHB*, 1 = *DOT*, 1, Washington, DC, 1967); II: Commentary, ed. R.J.H Jenkins (London, 1962), § 13. 32–3, 48ff., 76ff., 111ff. (hereafter *DAI*). For the importance of this particular aspect of the imperial symbolism, see the remarks of Shepard, "Information, disinformation and delay", pp. 240f.

38. *Antapodosis*, I, 7; III, 31 (Becker edn, pp. 7f., 88; Wright trans., pp. 35f., 124), for example.

39. See the detailed account in M. McCormick, *Eternal Victory. Triumphal Rulership in Late Antiquity, Byzantium and the Early Medieval West* (Cambridge, 1986).

40. Proem (p. 9, Dennis trans.).

41. For discussion of the seventh-century context, see J.F. Haldon, "Ideology and social change in the seventh century: military discontent as a barometer", in *Klio*, 68, 1986, pp. 139–90 (repr. in J.F. Haldon, *State, Army and Society in Byzantium* (Aldershot, 1995), no. II); and for the eleventh century, Attaleiates, *Historia*, pp. 86–7 and 96–7, 193–7. Cf. also pp. 208–9 and 306–10 for Attaleiates' view that the outcome of battles was determined ultimately by divine judgement.

42. For a tenth-century military service, see A. Pertusi, "Una acolouthia militare inedita del X secolo", *Aevum*, 22, 1948, pp. 145–68; see also services described in tenth-century letters (of Symeon *magistros*): J. Darrouzès, *Epistoliers byzantins du Xe siècle* (Archives de l'Orient chrétien 6, Paris, 1960), nos 83, 88; for military chaplains in the army (from the fifth century at least), see J.F. Haldon, *Byzantine Praetorians: An Administrative, Institutional and Social Survey of the Opsikion and Tagmata, c.580–900* (Poikila Byzantina, 3) (Bonn, 1984), p. 568; McCormick, *Eternal Victory*, esp. pp. 245–52 with sources and literature; and G.T. Dennis, "Religious services in the Byzantine army", in E. Carr et al. (eds), *EULOGEMA. Studies in Honor of Robert Taft, S.J.* (*Studia Anselmiana*, 110) (Rome, 1993), pp. 107–17. According to canon law the clergy were not meant to be associated with warfare at all, either in the battle-line itself or even in the camp. In practice, it is clear that they certainly did accompany armies on campaign, even if the prohibition on their participation in fighting seems to have been observed. Cf. J.-R. Vieillefond, "Les pratiques religieuses dans l'armée byzantine d'après les traités militaires", *Revue des Études Anciennes*, 87, 1935, pp. 322–30. The stark contrast between Byzantine and western practice in this respect is clearly brought out in the *Alexiad* of Anna Comnena, who expresses her horror at the presence of fighting clergy in the Latin armies: *Alexiad*, X, 8.7–9 (Anne Comnène, *Aléxiade*, ed. and trans. B. Leib (Paris, 1945), vol. 3; English trans. E. Sewter, *Alexiad* (Harmondsworth, 1969), pp. 317–18. This particular issue is discussed in greater detail in Kolbaba, "Fighting for Christianity" (note 10 above), where the contradictions in Byzantine practice are also noted: prohibition in canon law, for example, on priests engaged in military activity and actual punishments meted out by the ecclesiastical authorities to those who contravene these regulations contrasted with examples of priests actively fighting to defend their church or flock against barbarians, praised and

commended in the texts in question. It is worth remarking, in addition, that when, in the last century of the empire's existence, the government at Constantinople could no longer adequately support the construction and manning of defensive works in the provinces, monastic houses often took over such obligations in return for exemption from certain taxes. See J.F. Haldon, "Limnos, monastic holdings and the Byzantine state c.1261–1453", in *Continuity and Change in Late Byzantine and Early Ottoman Society*, papers of the 1982 Dumbarton Oaks Symposium, eds A.A.M. Bryer and H.W. Lowry (Birmingham, 1986), pp. 161–215.

43. See, for example, the sixth-century *Strategikon*, a military treatise attributed to the emperor Maurice (although probably written by one of his generals): *Das Strategikon des Maurikios*, ed. G.T. Dennis, trans. E. Gamillscheg (*CFHB*, 17) (Vienna, 1981), II, 18 (also in English trans. as: G.T. Dennis, *Maurice's Strategikon. Handbook of Byzantine Military Strategy* (Philadelphia, 1984), pp. 33f.); Niceph., *Praecepta*, iv, 106–20 (in E. McGeer, *Sowing the Dragon's Teeth. Byzantine Warfare in the Tenth Century* (*DOS*, XXXIII) (Washington, DC, 1995), pp. 3–59 (text), pp. 61–78 (notes)). Other symbols of the faith were also invoked at such moments, with cries of "*Christe boethei*" (Christ aid us) or "*stauros nika*" (the Cross conquers). Contemporary historians mention prayers and liturgies held before battle on numerous occasions.

44. See H. Hunger, *Die hochsprachliche profane Literatur der Byzantiner*, 2 vols (Handbuch der Altertumswissenschaft, XII, 5.1 and 2 = Byzantinisches Handbuch, 5, 1 and 2) (Munich, 1978), 1, pp. 157–65.

45. See H. Hunger, I. Sevcenko (eds), *Des Nikephoros Blemmydes* Basilikos Andrias *und dessen Metaphrase von Georgios Galesiotes und Georgios Oinaiotes. Ein weiterer Beitrag zum Verständnis der byzantinischen Schrift-Koine* (Wiener byz. Studien, 18) (Vienna, 1986), pp. 123–54.

46. See in particular the discussion in A. Kolia-Dermitzaki, "Byzantium at war in sermons and letters of the 10th and 11th centuries. An ideological approach", in N. Oikonomidès (ed.), *Byzantium at War* (Athens, 1997), pp. 213–38; E. Kurtz and F. Drexl (eds), Michael Psellus, *Scripta Minora*, I (Milan, 1936), p. 36.

47. *Alexiad*, XII, 5 (Anne Comnène, *Aléxiade*, ed. and trans. B. Leib (Paris, 1945), vol. 3; English trans. E. Sewter, *Alexiad* (Harmondsworth, 1969), p. 381).

48. See O. Treitinger, *Die oströmische Kaiser- und Reichsideologie nach ihrer Gestaltung im höfischen Zeremoniell* (Jena, 1938/Darmstadt, 1956), pp. 228f.; and on the rhetoric and language of letters in respect of warfare and the empire's enemies, see Kolia-Dermitzaki, "Byzantium at war in sermons and letters".

49. See R. Browning, *Notes on Byzantine prooimia* (*WBS*, 1: Supplement) (Vienna, 1966), p. 23 (i); cf. also p. 29 (o). Cf. H. Hunger, *Prooimion. Elemente der byzantinischen Kaiseridee in den Arengen der Urkunden* (*WBS*, 1) (Vienna, 1964), pp. 243–4 (no. 19)

50. Leo, *Tactica*, proem (*PG*, 107, col. 673C–D).

51. See *Theophylacti Simocattae Historia*, ed. C. de Boor (Leipzig, 1887; revised and emended edn P. Wirth, Stuttgart, 1972), pp. 132–3 (English trans. *Theophylact Simocatta, History*, trans. M. and M. Whitby (Oxford 1986)).

52. This text, as well as that of St Basil already referred to, is discussed in detail in Kolia-Dermitzaki, *Byzantine Holy War*, pp. 126–30.

53. Niceph., *Praecepta*, vi, 31–48.

54. There is a considerable literature on this concept and the various shades of meaning it evoked. See in particular H. Hunger, "*Philanthropia*. Eine griechische

Wortprägung auf ihrem Wege von Aischylos bis Theodoros Metochites", *Anzeiger d. österr. Akad. d. Wissenschaften*, phil.-hist. Kl. 100, pp. 1–20, 1963.

55. Maurice, *Strat.*, viii, 1. 23 (trans. Dennis, p. 81 [23]). The sentiment is repeated in Leo's *Tactica*.

56. Treitinger, *Reichsideologie*, pp. 230ff.

57. See McCormick, *Eternal Victory*, esp. pp. 245–52 for sources.

58. See Attaleiates, *Historia* (*Michaelis Attaliotae Historia*, ed. I. Bekker (Bonn, 1853)), pp. 104ff.

59. For Anna, see G. Buckler, *Anna Comnena* (Oxford, 1929), pp. 141ff; for the wars described by Leo the Deacon of the emperor John I Tzimiskes against the Russians, for example, see Leo diac., *Historiae*, VI, 12–13 (pp. 108–11); and for Nikephros II Phocas, see especially the discussion in Dagron and Mihaescu, *Le traité sur la Guérilla*, pp. 259ff., 284ff.

60. See Treitinger, *Reichsideologie*, pp. 230ff.

61. *Nicholas I, Patriarch of Constantinople, Letters*, ed. and trans. R.J.H. Jenkins and L.G. Westerink (*CFHB*, 6) (Washington, DC, 1973), p. 70f.; Leo, *Tact.*, III, 49, 50.

62. Later tenth-century prayer to be recited by the troops as they march to attack the enemy: see Nikephros Ouranos, *Taktika*, § 61.11 (trans. McGeer, *Sowing the Dragon's Teeth*, p. 127).

63. See Kolia-Dermitzaki, *Byzantine Holy War*, pp. 132–41 for a detailed discussion.

64. Kolia-Dermitzaki, *Byzantine Holy War*, pp. 130–2.

65. The main historical accounts which comment on Nikephros' proposal are those of Skylitzes (later eleventh century), Zonaras, Balsamon and Glykas (twelfth century), and are all discussed by Kolia-Dermitzaki, *Byzantine Holy War*, pp. 136–9.

66. See the discussion in Dagron and Mihaescu, *Le traité sur la Guérilla*, pp. 285–6; and G. Dagron, "Byzance et le modèle islamique au Xe siècle, à propos des Constitutions tactiques de l'empereur Léon VI", *Comptes rendus des séances de l'Académie des Inscriptions et Belles-Lettres* (Paris, 1983), pp. 219–43.

67. See Dagron and Mihaescu, *Le traité sur la Guérilla*, p. 285.

68. See J.A. Munitiz, "War and peace reflected in some Byzantine *Mirrors of Princes*", in Nesbitt and Miller (eds), *Peace and War in Byzantium*, pp. 50–61, and N. Oikonomidès, "The concept of 'Holy War' and two tenth-century ivories", ibid., pp. 62–86, esp. 64–8.

69. On the origins of this group, see Haldon, *Byzantium in the Seventh Century*, pp. 153–72, 395ff.

70. See A.F.C. Webster, "Varieties of Christian military saints: from martyrs under Caesar to warrior princes", *Saint Vladimir's Theological Quarterly*, 24, 1980, pp. 3–35.

71. For a brief survey of this warfare, see Steven Runciman, *A History of the Crusades*, I: *The First Crusade and the Foundation of the Kingdom of Jerusalem* (Cambridge, 1951), pp. 29–33.

72. G. Schlumberger, *Un empereur byzantin au Xᵉ siècle: Nicéphore Phocas* (Paris, 1890), pp. 347–50; the eighth-century (A.H.) Arab writer Ibn Kathīr preserved the text of Nikephros' letter: *Al-Bidāya wa'l-Nihāya*, ed. M. al-Sa'āda (Cairo, 1932), XI, pp. 244–7. For John I Tzimiskes' letter to Ashot, recorded by the twelfth-century chronicler Matthew of Edessa: A.E. Dostourian, *Armenia and the Crusades, 10th to 12th Centuries: The Chronicle of Matthew of Edessa* (Lanham, MD, 1993), pp. 22–32. Although some evidence supports the idea that these war aims were in part fulfilled, recent analysis of the material has shown that it is very unreliable, the

product of later legend and quite uncorroborated. See P.E. Walker, "The 'Crusade' of John Tzimisces in the light of new Arabic evidence", *Byzantion*, 47, 1977, pp. 301–27.

73. See, for example, I. Sevcenko, "Constantinople viewed from the eastern provinces in the middle Byzantine period", in *Eucharisterion: Essays Presented to Omeljan Pritsak = Harvard Ukrainian Studies*, 3/4, 1979–80, pp. 712–47 (repr. in I. Sevcenko, *Ideology, Letters and Culture in the Byzantine World* (London, 1982), no. VI).

74. As well as the French edition, translation and commentary by Dagron and Mihaescu, there is a good English translation in Dennis, *Three Byzantine Military Treatises*, pp. 137–239 (text pp. 144–238), but with no discussion. For a detailed analysis by Dagron, see *Le traité sur la Guérilla*, pp. 259–74. For the recommendation to kill prisoners, see § 11, 4.23–4 (Dennis, ed., p. 184). Examples of this in practice occur in several chronicles: see Chapter 7 below.

75. See *Cecaumeni Strategicon et incerti scriptoris de officiis regiis libellus*, eds B. Wassiliewsky and V. Jernstedt (St Petersburg, 1896/Amsterdam, 1965), p. 20.19–20. There is also a Russian edition with translation: *Soveti i rasskazi Kekavmena: socinenie vizantijskogo polkovodtsa XI veka*, ed., trans. and commentary G.G. Litavrin (Moscow, 1972).

76. See pp. 21.21–22.2; and see below, Chapter 2 on strategy.

77. The values of the tales, and the relationship between the morality of this epic and that reflected in the *Strategikon* of Kekaumenos have been compared and analysed by Paul Magdalino, "Honour among Romaioi: the framework of social values in the world of Digenes Akrites and Kekaumenos", *Byzantine and Modern Greek Studies*, 13, 1989, pp. 183–218. For the history of the text and its social and cultural significance, see also A. Pertusi, "Tra storia e leggenda: Akritai e Ghazi sulla frontiera orientale di Bisanzio", in *XIVe Congrès International des Études Byzantines*, Bucarest, 1971 (Bucarest, 1974), I, pp. 285–382; and esp. N. Oikonomides, "'L'épopée' de Digénès et la frontière orientale de Byzance aux Xᵉ et XIᵉ siècles", *TM*, 7, 1979, pp. 377ff. See also the discussion in A.P. Kazhdan and Ann Wharton-Epstein, *Change in Byzantine Culture in the Eleventh and Twelfth Centuries* (Berkeley/Los Angeles, CA, 1985), pp. 117–18.

78. See Theoph., p. 501 (trans. Mango and Scott, p. 684).

79. See Whittow, *The Making of Orthodox Byzantium*, pp. 150–1. The history of the so-called iconoclastic controversy is complicated by the fact that most of the surviving textual evidence comes from the ninth century or after and is heavily tinged by the point of view of the iconophile, i.e. "orthodox" victors, while iconoclastic texts, or those which might support an iconoclastic point of view, were either edited or destroyed by the iconophiles. See J.F. Haldon and L. Brubaker, *Byzantium ca. 717–843: A Culture Redefined* (Cambridge, forthcoming) and P. Speck, "Ikonoklasmus und die Anfänge der makedonischen Renaissance", in *Varia I* (Poikila Byzantina, 4.) (Bonn, 1984), pp. 177–210.

80. See Haldon, "Ideology and social change in the seventh century", and for a general account from the fifth to ninth centuries, W.E. Kaegi, *Byzantine Military Unrest 471–843: An Interpretation* (Amsterdam, 1981).

81. Soldier saints' cults have been studied by several scholars. See esp. H. Delehaye, *Les légendes grecques des saints militaires* (Paris, 1909). For images of saints on shields, see *Th. cont.*, pp. 180.21–181.2 (battle of Poson, 863). For Psellos' comment, see *Chronographia*, III, 10 (trans. Sewter, p. 44); and for Basil II, see ibid., I, 16 (trans. Sewter, p. 18).

82. See Magdalino, "Honour among Romaioi", pp. 183–218.
83. See esp. the relevant sources, commentary and literature in Haldon, *Const. Porph.*, *Three Treatises*, pp. 245–7.
84. For Constantine VII's harangues to the army and bestowal of divinely blessed talismans upon the army, see H. Ahrweiler, "Un discours inédit de Constantin VII Porphyrogénnète", *Travaux et Mémoires*, 2, 1967, pp. 393–404, at p. 397. See also R. Vari, "Zum historischen Exzerptenwerke des Konstantinos Porphyrogennetos", *Byzantinische Zeitschrift*, 17, 1908, pp. 75–85 – see 83.20–31. For spiritual purification before a campaign, triumphal returns and the central importance of the church see, for example, *Const. Porph.*, *Three Treatises*, (B) 84–91, (C) 724–879 (ninth-century accounts), with commentary and further sources at pp. 164–5; and Leo diac., *Historiae*, VIII, 1 (pp. 128.1–129.8) (processional prayers conducted by John I Tzimiskes in the 970s). For detailed discussion in a wider context, see McCormick, *Eternal Victory*, pp. 237–52.
85. See now P. Magdalino, *The Empire of Manuel I Komnenos, 1143–1180* (Cambridge, 1993), and Kazhdan and Wharton-Epstein, *Change in Byzantine Culture in the Eleventh and Twelfth Centuries*, pp. 99–119. For the coins, see M.F. Hendy, *Catalogue of the Byzantine Coins in the Dumbarton Oaks Collection and in the Whittemore Collection*, IV: *Alexios I to Michael VIII, 1081–1261* (Washington, DC, forthcoming), and P.D. Whitting, *Byzantine Coins* (London, 1973), nos 280–2, 340, for example.
86. For the West: G. Duby, *The Three Orders: Feudal Society Imagined*, trans. A. Goldhammer (Chicago, 1980), pp. 1–57; M. Bloch, *Feudal Society*, 2 vols, trans. L.A. Manyon (Chicago, 1964), 2, pp. 293–311. For Islam, see Ella Landau-Tasseron, "Features of the pre-conquest Muslim army in the time of Muhammad", in Cameron (ed.), *States, Resources and Armies*, pp. 299–336.
87. See Nike-Catherine Koutrakou, *La propagande impériale byzantine. Persuasion et réaction (VIIIᵉ–Xᵉ siècles)* (Athens, 1994), esp. pp. 361–86, and G. Michailidis-Nouaros, "The just war according to the *Tactica* of Leo the Wise", *Symmeikta Sepheriadou* (Athens, 1961), pp. 411–34.
88. On Nikolaos and Symeon, see Kolia-Dermitzaki, "Byzantium at war in sermons and letters of the 10th and 11th centuries", pp. 220–4, 234–7. The best synthesizing discussion of this tradition and its evolution is in McCormick, *Eternal Victory*, pp. 237ff.

Chapter 2 Warfare and the East Roman state: geography and strategy

1. *Strategy*, in G. Dennis (ed. and trans.), *Three Byzantine Military Treatises* (*CFHB*, 25 = *DOT* 9) (Washington, DC, 1985), pp. 1–136 – see § 5.6–10 (p. 21).
2. *Strategy*, ibid., § 5.1–5.
3. Leo, *Tact.*, i, 1–4; cf. Leo., *Tact.*, xx, 58.
4. See further Leo, *Tact.*, proem (= Maurice, *Strat.*, vii A, proem); xii, 3 (= Maurice, *Strat.*, ii, 1 (trans. Dennis, p. 23); and cf. Maurice, *Strat.*, xi, 4.236 (trans. Dennis, p. 126).
5. Cf. Leo, *Tact.*, xii, 4; 126; 128; xiv, 18; xx, 12 (cf. Maurice, *Strat.*, ii, 1; vii A, proem (trans. Dennis, pp. 23, 64)).

6. For the text, see Maurice, *Strat.*, vii, proem (trans. Dennis, p. 65). Similar sentiments occur in all the treatises.

7. Some valuable discussion of the constraints imposed by geopolitical considerations on states can be found in Michael Mann, *The Sources of Social Power*, 1: *A History of Power from the Beginning to A.D. 1760* (Cambridge, 1986).

8. *Strategy*, ed. and trans. Dennis, in *Three Byzantine Military Treatises*, p. 13.

9. Ibid., p. 23.

10. The point has been ably demonstrated, and in detail, by Jonathan Shepard, "Information, disinformation and delay in Byzantine diplomacy", *Byzantinische Forschungen*, 10, 1985, pp. 233–93, the best modern survey of the subject.

11. Shepard, "Information, disinformation and delay in Byzantine diplomacy", pp. 249–67.

12. For an excellent brief introduction to these issues, see W.E. Kaegi, Jr, *Some Thoughts on Byzantine Military Strategy* (Brookline, MA, 1983), pp. 1–18.

13. See D. Obolensky, *The Byzantine Commonwealth. Eastern Europe 500–1453* (London, 1971), p. 16, for example.

14. Liudprand, *Antapodosis*, I, 11 (p. 9); trans. Wright, p. 38.

15. See *De administrando imperio*, proem. 25–7 (p. 47 trans.) (*Constantine Porphyrogenitus, De Administrando Imperio*, I: Greek text ed. Gy. Moravcsik, English trans. R.J.H. Jenkins, new revised edn (*CFHB*, 1 = *DOT* 1) (Washington, DC, 1967); II: Commentary, ed. R.J.H. Jenkins (London, 1962)). See the collection of papers in S. Franklin and J. Shepard (eds), *Byzantine Diplomacy* (Aldershot, 1992); and the important discussion by Shepard, "Information, disinformation and delay in Byzantine diplomacy".

16. For the nature and speed of movement of information under various conditions, see the important discussion in A.D. Lee, *Information and Frontiers. Roman Foreign Relations in Late Antiquity* (Cambridge, 1993), pp. 149–65 and 166–84; and, for the middle Byzantine period, the advice and account regarding information-gathering in *Const. Porph., Three Treatises*, (B) 18–33; also Dagron and Mihaescu, *Le traité sur la Guérilla*, pp. 248–54 on spies and other sources of information. For spies, see in particular N. Koutrakou, "Diplomacy and espionage: their role in Byzantine foreign relations, 8th–10th centuries", *Graeco-Arabica*, 6, 1995, pp. 125–44.

17. For strategy in Justinian's wars, see the still useful discussion of Delbrück, *History of the Art of War*, II, pp. 375–83; for a brief account of Heraclius' Persian war, see M. Whittow, *The Making of Orthodox Byzantium*, pp. 75–81; and on the campaigns: N.H. Baynes, "The military operations of the emperor Heraclius", *United Service Magazine*, n.s. 46, 1913, pp. 526–33, 659–66; 47, 1913, pp. 30–5. For Justin II, see Blockley, *The History of Menander the Guardsman*, pp. 146, 154.

18. See Obolesnky, *Byzantine Commonwealth*, pp. 128–33; Whittow, *The Making of Orthodox Byzantium*, pp. 280–98 and 386–8.

19. Obolensky, *Byzantine Commonwealth*, pp. 128–30; Whittow, *The Making of Orthodox Byzantium*, pp. 260–1, 294–6. There are numerous examples of transfers from east to west and vice versa from the sixth century on. But a clear statement of this principle appears in *Th. cont.*, p. 181.15–18, recounting a campaign in 863: "for when the Bulgars were at peace it was the rule that they [i.e. the armies of Thrace and Macedonia] shared the danger and fought alongside the eastern troops".

20. See Chapter 1 above; but see also Ostrogorsky, *History of the Byzantine State*, p. 297, and Whittow, *The Making of Orthodox Byzantium*, pp. 356–7.

21. On Aleppo, see Wesam A. Farag, *The Truce of Sa'far A.H. 359/December–January 969–970* (Birmingham, 1977). See the summary of developments in these regions, and also of Basil's policies in the Caucasus and Trans-Caucasus regions, in Whittow, *The Making of Orthodox Byzantium*, pp. 379–86.

22. Whittow, *The Making of Orthodox Byzantium*, p. 357.

23. On this defensive thinking, see the remarks of B. Isaac, "The army in the late Roman East: the Persian wars and the defence of the Byzantine provinces", in Cameron (ed.), *States, Resources and Armies*, pp. 125–55 – see 127–8.

24. See W.E. Kaegi, Jr, "Some thoughts on Byzantine military strategy", *The Hellenic Studies Lecture* (Brookline, MA, 1983).

25. See Michael Psellus, *Fourteen Byzantine Rulers*, trans. E.R. Sewter (Harmondsworth, 1966), pp. 66–8.

26. See Whittow, *The Making of Orthodox Byzantium*, p. 294f.

27. *Alexiad*, xii, 5; trans. Sewter, p. 381. Cf. Leo, *Tact.*, ii, 49.

28. For a translation of Pachymeres' text, see D. Geanakoplos, *Byzantium: Church, Society and Civilization Seen through Contemporary Eyes* (Chicago, 1984), pp. 36–7.

29. See Laurent, "L'idée de guerre sainte", pp. 89–90.

30. See N. Oikonomidès, "Byzantine diplomacy, A.D. 1204–1453: means and ends", in Shepard and Franklin, *Byzantine Diplomacy*, pp. 73–88.

31. See C. Mango, *Byzantium: The Empire of New Rome* (London, 1980), ch. 11.

32. From the late eleventh-century *Logos nouthetetikos*, or Book of Advice (in *Cecaumeni Strategicon*, eds. Wassiliewsky and Jernstedt, § 259, p. 103), trans. E. Barker, *Social and Political Thought in Byzantium* (Oxford, 1957), pp. 128–9.

33. See Jones, *LRE*, pp. 462–4; M.F. Hendy, *Studies in the Byzantine Monetary Economy, c.300–1450* (Cambridge, 1985), pp. 164ff.

34. Jones, *LRE*, pp. 462–4; Hendy, *Studies*, pp. 168ff.

35. Hendy, *Studies*, p. 620, with pp. 616–18.

36. Ibid., p. 620.

37. *Const. Porph., Three Treatises*, (B) 3–12.

38. For the *strata Diocletiana* and its strategic significance, see J. Eadie, "The transformation of the eastern frontier, 260–305", in R.W. Mathisen and H.S. Sivan (eds), *Shifting Frontiers in Late Antiquity* (Aldershot, 1996), pp. 72–82. For the general state of the roads by the late fourth and fifth centuries, see *Ch.* xv, 3.4 (AD 412), which refers to "the immense ruin of the highways" throughout the prefecture of the east (*Theodosiani libri xvi cum constitutionibus Sirmondianis*, eds Th. Mommsen, P. Meyer et al. (Berlin, 1905)). Procopius describes a section of the Via Egnatia as almost impassable in wet weather: Procopius, *Buildings*, IV, viii.5. For roads and usacks in the Byzantine period in general, see the comments in I. Ch. Dimitroukas, *Reisen und Verkehr im byzantinischen Reich vom Anfang des 6. bis zur Mitte des 11. Jhs.* (Athens, 1997), pp. 324–31.

39. Via Egnatia: Malchus of Philadelphia, *Fragments*, § 18 (in: *Fragmenta Historicorum Graecorum*, eds C. and Th. Müller, 5 vols (Paris, 1874–85), p. 127); Comentiolus: *Th. Sim. Historia*, viii, 4.3–8 (trans. Whitby, p. 214). For Constantine's remark see *DAI*, § 42.15–18. The difference between the speed of an individual and a body of soldiers is clear from the remark of Theophylact Simocatta in the early seventh century that a somewhat shorter journey – from Drizipera in Thrace (between mod. Lüleburgaz and Corlu) to Dorostolon (Dristra, mod. Silistra) on the Danube – for a field army could take 20 days: see *Th. Sim., Historia*, vi, 6.5

(trans. Whitby, p. 167). For a summary of some evidence for Balkan routes, especially the Via Egnatia, see Dimitroukas, *Reisen und Verkehr*, pp. 341–67.

40. See Haldon, *Byzantium in the Seventh Century*, pp. 92–124.

41. Procopius, *Buildings*, IV, viii.4–9; V, ii.12–14; iii.4–6, 8–10, 12–15; iv.1–4; v.1– 7. But there are a number of problems with Procopius' account, and his reports should not always be taken at face value. See M. Whitby, "Justinian's bridge over the Sangarios and the date of the De Aedificiis", *Journal of Hellenic Studies*, 105, 1985, pp. 129–48; and G. Greatrex, "The dates of Procopius' works", *BMGS*, 18, 1994, pp. 101–14. Localized networks of maintained roads were kept up around many towns since they served to facilitate markets and trade in general; see Dimitroukas, *Reisen und Verkehr*, p. 336.

42. See V. Beševliev, *Spätgriechische und spätlateinische Inschriften aus Bulgarien* (*BbA*, 30) (Berlin, 1964), p. 2, no. 3; and for Constantinople: C. Mango, "The water supply of Constantinople", in C. Mango and G. Dagron (eds), *Constantinople and its Hinterland* (Aldershot, 1995), pp. 9–18 with further literature.

43. See Attaleiates, *Historia*, p. 145.20; Bryennios, *Historiarum libri quattuor*, ii, 14 (p. 169.8); Anna Comnena, *Alexiad*, xv, 4 (trans. Sewter, p. 482).

44. See, for example, the imperial prescriptions incorporated into the fifth-century *Codex Theodosianus*, and repeated or replaced in the sixth-century legislation of Justianian. Cf. *CTh.*, xi, 16.15, 16.18; xv, 3.6; *CJ*, i, 2.5; Just., *Nov.*, 131.5 (*Codex Justinianus*, ed. P. Krüger, in: *Corpus Juris Civilis*, II; *Justiniani Novellae*, in: *Corpus Juris Civilis*, III, eds R. Schöll and W. Kroll (Berlin, 1892–95, repr. 1945–63)); repeated again in the early tenth-century codification, the *Basilika*, v, 1.4; v, 3.6 (*Basilicorum libri LX*, ser. A, eds H.J. Scheltema and N. Van Der Wal, 8 vols (Groningen, 1955ff.)). For local military authorities responsible, see Leo, *Tact.*, xx, 71.

45. The emperor Heraclius is reported to have employed a large pontoon bridge to cross the Bosphorus on horseback in 638: see the account in the Short History of the patriarch Nikephros, compiled in the late eighth century, *Breviarium*, in: *Nicephori Archiepiscopi Constantinopolitani Opuscula Historica*, ed. C. de Boor (Leipzig, 1880), pp. 1–77, at pp. 25–6; ed. and trans. C. Mango, *Nicephorus, Patriarch of Constantinople. Short History* (Washington, DC, 1990), pp. 73–5. Anna Comnena describes a substantial pontoon construction in an account of one of the campaigns of her father, the emperor Alexios I (1081–1118): *Alexiad*, viii, 4 (trans. Sewter, p. 254).

46. See Dagron and Mihaescu, *Le traité sur la Guérilla*, p. 219.

47. Procopius, *Buildings*, IV, viii.4–9.

48. *Th. cont.*, 280.13–14; and cf. J.G.C. Anderson, "The campaign of Basil I against the Paulicians in 872", *Clasical Review*, 10, 1986, pp. 138–9. For the Second Crusade: Odo of Deuil, *De profectione Ludovici VII in orientem*, trans. V. G. Berry (New York, 1948), pp. 102–6. For Manuel I's campaign in 1176, see Chapter 5 below. For Basil II: Psellos, *Chronographia*, I, 32 (trans. Sewter, p. 25); and for advice on campaigning seasons: Nikeph. Ouranos, *Tact.*, §63.1; and see McGeer's comments, *Sowing the Dragon's Teeth*, pp. 255–6. Arab geographers in the ninth and tenth centuries recommended staying only twenty days in Roman territory during a winter raid, because of the lack of forage. See Abū'l-Faraj al-Kātib al-Bagdādī Kudāma ibn Ja'far, *Kitāb al-Harāj*, in: *Bibliotheca Geographorum Araborum*, ed. M.-J. De Goeje (Leiden, 1870/1938), VI, pp. 199–200.

49. The treatises on imperial expeditions note the importance of sending both an advance division to prepare the way and of employing suitably qualified scouts:

see *Const. Porph., Three Treatises*, (B) 116–21; (C) 564–5; and commentary with other sources, p. 171.

50. See: R.W. Bulliet, *The Camel and the Wheel* (Cambridge, MA, 1975); Dimitroukas, *Reisen und Verkehr*, pp. 308–17.

51. See Hendy, *Studies*, pp. 602–13; and Ann Hyland, *Equus: The Horse in the Roman World* (London, 1990), pp. 250–62; on the operations of the postal system in the middle Byzantine period, see V. Laurent, *Le Corpus des sceaux de l'empire byzantin*, II: *L'Administration centrale* (Paris, 1981), pp. 289–99, 487–97.

52. For a good overview of the Roman road system in Asia Minor, see the map edited by W.M. Calder and G.E. Bean, *A Classical Map of Asia Minor* (London: British Institute of Archaeology at Ankara, 1958). For a discussion of the Byzantine material, see K. Belke, "Von der Pflasterstrasse zum Maultierpfad? Zum kleinasiatischen Wegenetz in mittelbyzantinischer Zeit", in N. Oikonomides (ed.), *Byzantine Asia Minor (6th–12th cents.)* (Athens, 1998), pp. 267–84.

53. See for detailed description and analysis of climate and geography: *Greece*, I: *Physical Geography, History, Administration and Peoples*, Naval Intelligence Division, Geographical Handbook Series, BR 516 (Naval Intelligence Division, London, 1944); together with the relevant volumes of the *Tabula imperii Byzantini* (see Bibliography: Primary sources) and the appropriate section on the Balkans in Hendy, *Studies*.

54. For the best short survey of the physical context, see Hendy, *Studies*, and the detailed descriptions and analyses available in the Geographical Handbooks of the Naval Intelligence Division: *Turkey*, I, Naval Intelligence Division, Geographical Handbook Series, BR 507 (Naval Intelligence Division, London, 1942). One of the best and most accessible discussions for an English-language readership remains W.M. Ramsay, *The Historical Geography of Asia Minor*, Royal Geographical Society, Supplementary Papers IV (London, 1890/Amsterdam, 1962), pp. 51–88, and esp. pp. 74–82. The best modern treatment of the Byzantine provincial road system is the series of volumes published as part of the project *Tabula imperii Byzantini* by the Byzantinological section of the Austrian Academy, including an important preliminary volume: F. Hild, *Das byzantinische Straßensystem in Kappadokien*, Veröffentlichungen der Kommission für die TIB 2. Denkschriften der österr. Akad. d. Wiss., phil.-hist. Kl. 131 (Vienna, 1977).

55. The road from Amorion to the southeast along the western edge of Lake Tatta is arid and difficult and seems only rarely to have been used: see Ramsay, *Historical Geography*, p. 199.

56. The routes are discussed in detail by Ramsay, *Historical Geography*, pp. 197–221. Since Ramsay's pioneering study there have been a number of other publications dealing with the Byzantine road system in Anatolia: see J.G.C. Anderson, "The road system of eastern Asia Minor with the evidence of Byzantine campaigns", *JHS*, 17, 1897, pp. 22–30; and E. Honigmann, *Die Ostgrenze des byzantinischen Reiches von 363 bis 1071* (Brussels, 1935). More recently the series *Tabula imperii Byzantini* (Austrian Academy, Byzantine Institut, Vienna) has produced a series of detailed historical-topographical texts analysing and describing all the provinces of the Byzantine empire, accompanied by detailed maps.

57. Ramsay, *Historical Geography*, pp. 218–20 suggests that this is an error for Saniana, since Koloneia in the Pontus, south of Kerasous, is clearly not plausible in respect of the direction of the expeditions involved and the starting point of the provincial armies involved. See F. Hild and M. Restle, *TIB*, 2. *Kappadokien (Kappadokia, Charsianon, Sebasteia und Lykandos)* (Vienna, 1981), p. 207.

58. For all these routes, see Ramsay, *Historical Geography*, pp. 270–81 (passes over the Anti-Taurus); 349–56 (over the Taurus); and Anderson, "The road system of eastern Asia Minor". The tenth-century text *On Skirmishing (De velitatione bellica)* is edited and translated in both Dagron and Mihaescu (eds), *Le traité sur la Guérilla*, and Dennis (ed.), *Three Byzantine Military Treatises*, pp. 137–239 – see § 23. For a brief general assessment of the Byzantine strategy in Asia Minor in the eighth and early ninth centuries, see J.A. Arvites, "The defense of Byzantine Anatolia during the reign of Irene (780–802)", in S. Mitchell (ed.), *Armies and Frontiers in Roman and Byzantine Anatolia (BAR S156)* (Oxford, 1983), pp. 219–36. For the Arab perspective see Ibn Khurradadhbī (Abū'l-Kāsim 'Ubayd Allāh b. 'Abd Allāh b. Khurradadhbīh, *Kitāb at-Masālik wa'l-Mamālik*, in *Bibliotheca Geographorum Araborum*, ed. M.-J. De Goeje (Leiden, 1870ff./1938)), pp. 73–5, 82–3, 85–6.
59. For a detailed treatment of the late Roman frontier from both a military and social-cultural historical perspective, see Lee, *Information and Frontiers*. See also J. Eadie, "The transformation of the eastern frontier, 260–305", in R.W. Mathisen and H.S. Sivan (eds), *Shifting Frontiers in Late Antiquity* (Aldershot, 1996), pp. 72–82; on Byzantine ideas of frontier, see W.E. Kaegi, "Reconceptualizing Byzantium's eastern frontiers in the seventh century", ibid., pp. 83–92; and W.E. Kaegi, "The frontier: barrier or bridge?", in *The 17th International Byzantine Congress. Major Papers* (Washington, DC, 1986), pp. 279–303. Note also D. Obolensky, "The Balkans in the ninth century: barrier or bridge?", in J.D. Howard-Johnston (ed.), *Byzantium and the West c. 850–1200* (Amsterdam, 1988), pp. 47–66.
60. For the best description of warfare in Anatolia in the seventh and eighth centuries see Lilie, *Die byzantinische Reaktion*; for the Arab tendency not to invest time and resources in besieging towns, see the discussion in H. Ahrweiler, "L'Asie mineure et les invasions arabes", *Revue Historique*, 227, 1962, pp. 1–32, at 10f. On the use of delaying tactics, see Shepard, "Information, disinformation and delay", pp. 258–9 for a brief discussion and literature.
61. A. Dunn, "The transformation from *polis* to *kastron* in the Balkans (III–VII cc.): general and regional perspectives", *Byzantine and Modern Greek Studies*, 18, 1994, pp. 60–80.
62. The best discussion is Shepard, "Information, disinformation and delay".
63. See Shepard, "Information, disinformation and delay".

Chapter 3   Protect and survive: a brief history of East Roman strategic arrangements

1. *Strategy*, § 4.15–17. For a useful introduction to the background and context of the development of Roman strategy up to the fourth century, and the establishment of the Diocletianic–Constantinian system upon which developments up to the early seventh century were based, see Edward N. Luttwak, *The Grand Strategy of the Roman Empire. From the First Century A.D. to the Third* (Baltimore, MD, 1976). For Byzantium, see W.E. Kaegi, Jr, *Some Thoughts on Byzantine Military Strategy* (Brookline, MA, 1983), pp. 1–17.
2. On the structure and evolution of the late Roman army from the end of the third/ beginning of the fourth century, see R. Grosse, *Römische Militärgeschichte von Gallienus bis zum Beginn der byzantinischen Themenverfassung* (Berlin, 1920); D. van Berchem, *L'Armée de Dioclétian et la réforme Constantinienne* (Paris, 1952); and

K.R. Dixon and P. Southern, *The Late Roman Army* (London, 1996), pp. 4–38, esp. 15ff. The separation of military from civil command was chiefly the work of Constantine, although begun in places by Diocletian. See Jones, *LRE*, pp. 607–8. For a good discussion of the development of the late Roman army during the period from the third to the fifth centuries, see H. Elton, *Warfare in Roman Europe, AD 350–425* (Oxford, 1996), pp. 89–107; R.S.O. Tomlin, "The army of the late Empire", in J. Wacher (ed.), *The Roman World* (London, 1987/1990), I, pp. 107–33; and R.S.O. Tomlin, "The late Roman empire AD 200–450", in P. Connolly (ed.), *Greece and Rome at War* (London, 1981/89), pp. 249–61.

3. Elton, *Warfare in Roman Europe*, pp. 99–100; Dixon and Southern, *Late Roman Army*, pp. 23–37; Jones, *LRE*, p. 608.

4. For the strategy pursued by the Roman state at different periods along its frontiers, see: J.C. Barrett, A.P. Fitzpatrick and L. Macinnes (eds), *Barbarians and Romans in North-West Europe* (*BAR* S471) (Oxford, 1989); C.R. Whittaker, *Les frontières de l'empire romain* (Paris, 1989). For the eastern frontier, see: B. Isaac, *The Limits of Empire. The Roman Army in the East* (Oxford, 1990); M. Dodgeon and S.N.C. Lieu, *The Roman Eastern Frontier and the Persian Wars, AD 226–363* (London, 1991); P.M. Freeman and D.L. Kennedy (eds), *The Defence of the Roman and Byzantine East* (*BAR* S297) (Oxford, 1986). For the changes in frontier structures in general, see: A.D. Lee, *Information and Frontiers. Roman Foreign Relations in Late Antiquity* (Cambridge, 1993). See also the essays in R. W. Mathissen and H. S. Sivan (eds), *Shifting Frontiers in Late Antiquity* (Aldershot, 1996).

5. Jones, *LRE*, p. 280 with sources.

6. The most detailed analyses of these arrangements is by I. Shahid: see *Byzantium and the Arabs in the Fourth Century* (Washington, DC, 1984); *Byzantium and the Arabs in the Fifth Century* (Washington, DC, 1988); *Byzantium and the Arabs in the Sixth Century* (Washington, DC, 1996). The Ghassanids were Monophysite Christians, which made their relations with those emperors who insisted upon a more inflexibly orthodox religious politics problematic and led to a major schism between empire and Arab allies in the 580s: see I. Shahid, art. "Ghassanids", in *Encyclopedia of Islam*, new edn, II.

7. Haldon, *Byzantine Praetorians*, pp. 119–28.

8. Haldon, *Byzantine Praetorians*, pp. 136–9.

9. See Procopius, *Wars*, III, xi.13–16.

10. See in particular B. Isaac, "The meaning of the terms *limes* and *limitanei*", *Journal of Roman Studies* 78, 1988, pp. 125–47, and *The Limits of Empire*.

11. See: L.M. Whitby, *The Emperor Maurice and His Historian: Theophylact Simocatta on Persian and Balkan Warfare* (Oxford, 1988); L.M. Whitby, "The Persian king at war", in E. Dabrowa (ed.), *The Roman and Byzantine Army in the East* (Cracow, 1994), pp. 227–63; and esp. J.D. Howard-Johnson, "The two Great Powers in late Antiquity: a comparison", in Cameron (ed.), *States, Resources and Armies*, pp. 157–226.

12. For attitudes towards war aims and strategy, see B. Isaac, "The army in the late Roman East: the Persian war and the defence of the Byzantine provinces", in Cameron (ed.), *States, Resources and Armies*, pp. 125–55 – see 125–9. The issue of pay, conditions of service and their effects on the late Roman armies is discussed in Jones, *LRE*, pp. 668–79, 685–6, and the relevant opening sections in Kaegi, *Byzantine Military Unrest*. For a useful discussion, with wider implications, of late Roman strategy on the eastern front, see M. Whitby, "Arzanene in the late sixth

century", in Mitchell (ed.), *Armies and Frontiers in Roman and Byzantine Anatolia*, pp. 205–17.

13. For the fourth and fifth centuries, for example, see the comments in Elton, *Warfare in Roman Europe*, pp. 214–20.
14. *CJ*, X, 27.2 (a. 491–505) (*Codex Justinianus*, ed. P. Krüger (*Corpus Juris Civilis*, II, Berlin, 1919)). See Jones, *LRE*, p. 235.
15. See Haldon, *Byzantine Praetorians*, pp. 164–78, for a detailed discussion of the relevant sources.
16. See in general J.F. Haldon, "Administrative continuities and structural transformations in East Roman military organisation *c.* 580–640", in *State, Army and Society in Byzantium* (Aldershot, 1995), V, pp. 1–20 – see pp. 16–17; and Haldon, *Byzantine Praetorians*, pp. 173–4. On the guardposts and garrisons in Palestine, for example, see Isaac, "The army in the late Roman East", pp. 144–5.
17. See J.F. Haldon, "Seventh-century continuities: the *Ajnād* and the 'Thematic Myth'", in Cameron (ed.), *States, Resources and Armies*, pp. 379–423.
18. For detailed accounts and analyses of the Islamic conquests and the sources, see W.E. Kaegi, *Byzantium and the Early Islamic Conquests* (Cambridge, 1992) and Fred Donner, *The Early Arabic Conquests* (Princeton, NJ, 1981).
19. Haldon, *Byzantium in the Seventh Century*, pp. 212–20.
20. For Italy, see T.S. Brown, *Gentlemen and Officers. Imperial Administration and Aristocratic Power in Byzantine Italy, A.D. 554–800* (Rome, 1984); and for Africa, N. Oikonomidès, "Une liste arabe des stratèges byzantins du VIIe siècle et les origines du Thème de Sicile", *Rivista di Studi Bizantini e Neoellenici*, 11, 1964, pp. 121–30.
21. Haldon, *Byzantium in the Seventh Century*, pp. 54–73, 74–8.
22. See Haldon, *Byzantium in the Seventh Century*, pp. 102–14 for some of the economic consequences; and on Arab and Byzantine strategy at this period, especially the creation of a "no man's land" and the various phases which can be traced in Arab strategy with respect to the empire, see esp. R.-J. Lilie, *Die byzantinische Reaktion auf die Ausbreitung der Araber* (Miscellanea Byzantina Monacensia, 22) (Munich, 1976). For the *themata* and their development, see also Lilie, "'Thrakien' und 'Thrakesion'. Zur byzantinischen Provinzorganisation am Ende des 7. Jahrhunderts", *JöB*, 26, 1977, pp. 7–47; and "Die zweihundertjährige Reform: zu den Anfängen der Themenorganisation im 7. und 8. Jahrhundert", *BS*, 45, 1984, pp. 27–39, 190–201. For Arab forces overwintering, see E.W. Brooks, "The Arabs in Asia Minor (641–750) from Arabic Sources", *JHS*, 18, 1898, pp. 182–208 – see, for example, 185–9. For the Kibyrrhaiotai, see P.A. Yannopoulos, "Cibyrra et Cibyrrhéotes", *B*, 61, pp. 520–9, 1991; and on the evolution of the "naval" *themata* in general, see the useful general survey in A. Toynbee, *Constantine Porphyrogenitus and His World* (London/Oxford 1973), pp. 323–45; E. Eickhoff, *Seekrieg und Seepolitik zwischen Islam und Abendland* (Berlin, 1966); and the relevant sections in N. Oikonomidès, *Les listes de préséance byzantines des IXe–Xe siècles* (Paris, 1972).
23. Haldon, *Byzantine Praetorians*, pp. 228–56; N. Oikonomidès, "L'évolution de l'organisation administrative de l'empire byzantin", *TM*, 6, 1976, pp. 125–52; and esp. H.-J. Kühn, *Die byzantinische Armee im 10. Jahrhundert* (Vienna, 1991).
24. *Theoph.*, pp. 371–2 (trans. Mango and Scott, pp. 517–20).
25. For the significance of these strongholds, see in general the account in Lilie, *Die byzantinische Reaktion*; and for a specific example from the Balkan context, see

A. Stavridou-Zaphraka, "Vodena, a Byzantine city-fortress in Macedonia", in G. Kioutoutskas (ed.), *Edessa and Its Region. History and Culture* (Edessa, 1995), pp. 165–78 (in Greek).

26. For the frontier at this time, and the strategies pursued by both sides, see J.F. Haldon and H. Kennedy, "The Arab–Byzantine frontier in the eighth and ninth centuries: military organisation and society in the borderlands", *ZRVI*, 19, 1980, pp. 79–116; for the wars of the later eighth and first half of the ninth century, see Ostrogorsky, *History of the Byzantine State*; for Leo IV's order, see *Theoph.*, p. 452.6–12 (trans. Mango and Scott, p. 624). See also Lilie, *Die byzantinische Reaktion*, pp. 171–2.

27. See Attaleiates, *Historia*, p. 121; and cf. *Skirmishing*, § 23.

28. See Eickhoff, *Seekrieg und Seepolitik*, p. 198; J. Pryor, *Geography, Technology and War. Studies in the Maritime History of the Mediterranean 649–1571* (Cambridge, 1988/1992), pp. 102–11.

29. See Obolensky, *Byzantine Commonwealth*, pp. 63–5; H. Ditten, *Ethnische Verschiebungen zwischen der Balkanhalbinsel und Kleinasien vom Ende des 6. bis zur zweiten Hälfte des 9. Jahrhunderts*, eds R.-J. Lilie, Ilse Rochow, Friedhelm Winkelmann and I. Sevcenko (*BBA*, 59) (Berlin, 1993), pp. 158–9.

30. For the growth of the *themata*, see Oikonomidès, *Préséance*, pp. 348–54; Winkelmann, *Rang- und Ämterstruktur*, pp. 72–118.

31. During the tenth century a considerable movement of immigrants from Armenia proper into southeastern and southern Asia Minor took place, which led the government at Constantinople to regard these regions as a "lesser Armenia". See Dagron and Mihaescu, *Le traité sur la Guérilla*, pp. 239–45; Kühn, *Die byzantinische Armee im 10. und 11. Jahrhundert*, pp. 61–6.

32. See Kühn, *Die byzantinische Armee im 10. und 11. Jahrhundert*, pp. 165–8; Oikonomidès, *Préséance*, pp. 354–63. For further comment on the Balkan context, see D. Obolensky, "The Balkans in the ninth century: barrier or bridge?", in J.D. Howard-Johnston (ed.), *Byzantium and the West c. 850–1200* (Amsterdam, 1988), pp. 47–66.

33. For Basil's campaign of 995, see J.H. Forsyth, *The Byzantine–Arab chronicle (938–1034) of Yahya b. Said al-Antaki* (Ann Arbor, MI, 1977), pp. 492ff.; for the campaigns and wars of the later tenth century, see Whittow, *The Making of Orthodox Byzantium*.

34. Psellos, *Chronographia*, vi, 83 (trans. Sewter, p. 145); vi, 105 (trans. Sewter, pp. 155–6); vi, 112 (trans. Sewter, p. 159); vii, 10 (trans. Sewter, pp. 213–14).

35. See H. Ahrweiler, *Byzance et la mer: la marine de guerre, la politique et les institutions maritimes de Byzance aux VIIe–XVe siècles* (Paris, 1966), pp. 122–35, 136–63.

36. See Paul Stephenson, "Byzantine policy towards Paristrion in the mid-eleventh century: another interpretation", *BMGS*, 23, 1999; and P. Doimi de Frankopan, "The numismatic evidence from the Danube region, 971–1092", *BMGS*, 21, 1997, pp. 30–9. For the organization of the Balkan provinces at this time – some under direct Roman authority, others administered under Roman auspices by their own lords and local rulers (as in the provinces which later became the central regions of Serbia) – see in particular: L. Maksimovic, "L'organisation du pouvoir byzantin après 1018 dans les contrées reconquises", *ZRVI*, 36, 1997, pp. 31–42 (with Fr. résumé p. 43), with older literature.

37. See P. Magdalino, "The Byzantine aristocratic *oikos*", in M. Angold (ed.), *The Byzantine Aristocracy, IX–XIII Centuries* (*BAR* S221) (Oxford, 1984), pp. 92–111;

and McGeer, *Sowing the Dragon's Teeth*, p. 221f. For thematic soldiers being drawn into the retinues of powerful landlords, see for an example of the relationships of dependence which might develop between local officer-magnates and the soldiers of their theme, *Jus Graecoromanum*, eds I. and P. Zepos, 8 vols (Athens, 1931/Aalen, 1962), I, pp. 225–6 (and Lemerle's commentary, *Agrarian History*, p. 122f.), where soldiers are granted exemptions from military service in return for gifts. Note also Leo, *Tact.*, viii, 26, concerning the secondment of theme soldiers to the personal service of higher officers; and Dagron's comment in *Le traité sur la Guérilla*, p. 282. More detailed discussion in Haldon, "Military service, military lands and the status of soldiers: current problems and interpretations", *DOP*, 47, 1993, pp. 1–67 – p. 48 and n. 119 (repr. in *State, Army and Society in Byzantium. Approaches to Military, Social and Administrative History*, no. VII).

38. Psellos, *Chronographia*, vii, 50 (trans. Sewter, p. 233).
39. Importantly, the bulk of the forces accompanying the emperor Romanos IV at Manzikert appear to have been able to get away relatively intact from the battle; yet they were squandered in the following months as Romanos, now deposed, had to fight for his throne, first in the Armeniakon region and, after a first defeat, again in the region of Tarsos in Cilicia. Thereafter indigenous units were assembled only with the greatest difficulty. See Oikonomidès, "L'évolution de l'organisation administrative de l'empire byzantin"; and the relevant sections in Sp. Vryonis, Jr, *The Decline of Medieval Hellenism in Asia Minor and the Process of Islamization from the Eleventh Through the Fifteenth Century* (Berkeley/Los Angeles/London, 1971).
40. A useful account of these developments can be found in M. Angold, *The Byzantine Empire 1025–1204: A Political History* (London/New York, 1984), pp. 12–26, 92–8. For a good analysis of the development of the role of western mercenaries in Byzantium in the eleventh century, see J. Shepard, "The uses of the Franks in eleventh-century Byzantium", *Anglo-Norman Studies*, 15, 1993, pp. 275–305.
41. Particularly important as an imperial elite unit were the Varangians: see S. Blöndal, *The Varangians of Byzantium. An Aspect of Byzantine Military History*, revised edn B.S. Benedikz (Cambridge, 1978).
42. See Kaegi, *Byzantine Military Unrest*, for the provincial and Constantinopolitan mutinies and rebellions – generally a result of local and inter-provincial political conflict – which mark the period up to the later ninth century; and esp. J. Shepard, "The uses of the Franks in eleventh-century Byzantium", esp. pp. 278ff., 295–305. As Shepard rightly notes, modern western views of the mercenary are strongly coloured by later historical and quite recent experience.
43. See: Kühn, *Die byzantinische Armee im 10. und 11. Jahrhundert*, pp. 243–59 for the *tagmata* of the eleventh century; Oikonomidès, "L'évolution de l'organisation administrative de l'empire byzantin"; and A. Hohlweg, *Beiträge zur Verwaltungsgeschichte des oströmischen Reiches unter den Komnenen* (Miscellanea Byzantina Monacensia, 1) (Munich, 1965), pp. 45ff.
44. Bartusis, *The Late Byzantine army*, pp. 157–90; Magdalino, *The Empire of Manuel I Komnenos*, pp. 123–7, 132–4; Hohlweg, *Beiträge*, pp. 45–82 and, on *pronoia*, pp. 82–93.
45. See Angold, *Byzantium 1025–1204*, pp. 106–11; Magdalino, *The Empire of Manuel I*, pp. 132–7.
46. See the detailed exposition of Byzantine diplomacy and strategic policy under John II, Manuel I and their immediate successors up to 1203–4 in Magdalino, *The Empire of Manuel I*, pp. 27–108; Angold, *Byzantium 1025–1204*, pp. 161–209,

263–96; and J. Shepard, "Byzantine diplomacy A.D. 800–1204: means and ends", in S. Franklin and J. Shepard (eds), *Byzantine Diplomacy* (Aldershot, 1992), pp. 41–71.

47. For these aspects, see Chapters 4 and 7 below.
48. For John's and Manuel's measures, see Choniates, *Historia*, p. 55. See in particular R.-J. Lilie, *Handel und Politik zwischen dem byzantinischen Reich und den italienischen Kommunen Venedig, Pisa and Genua in der Epoche der Komnenen und der Angeloi (1081–1204)* (Amsterdam, 1984), pp. 613–43; Hohlweg, *Beiträge*, pp. 134–57; Ahrweiler, *Byzance et la mer*, pp. 197–225, 271–9; F. Chalandon, *Les Comnène*, 2: *Jean II Comnène (1118–1143) et Manuel I Comnène (1143–1180)* (Paris, 1912, repr. London/New York, 1962), pp. 622–3. In general on Byzantine–Venetian relations and the question of naval power, see the brief survey in D.M. Nicol, *Byzantium and Venice* (Cambridge, 1988), p. 20ff.; and Ahrweiler, *Byzance et la mer*, pp. 255–63.
49. Alexios I established 15 such commands along the Balkan frontier and in Asia Minor, stretching from Abydos around to Seleukeia; John and Manuel established further *doukata*, including those of Thrakesion, Kibyrrhaioton, Kilikia, Malagina, Mylasa and Attaleia. See Kühn, *Die byzantinische Armee im 10. und 11. Jahrhundert*, pp. 168–9.
50. See Magdalino, *The Empire of Manuel I Komnenos*, pp. 98–9, 125–8; Angold, *The Byzantine Empire, 1025–1204*, pp. 256–7, 263–82.
51. Maurice, *Strat.*, viii, 2.38 (trans. Dennis, p. 86).
52. Two writers later than this also give some figures: John Lydus, writing in the sixth century, gives figures for the army of Diocletian, while Zosimus, writing at the end of the fifth century, records figures for the armies of Constantine in his wars with Maxentius and then Licinius. These figures are discussed in detail by Jones, *LRE*, pp. 679–84; R. MacMullen, "How big was the Roman imperial army?", *Klio*, 62, 1980, pp. 451–60; R.P. Duncan-Jones, *Structure and Scale in the Roman Economy* (Cambridge, 1990), pp. 105ff., 214ff.; and Treadgold, *Byzantium and its Army*, pp. 44–59.
53. For the discussion, see Jones, *LRE*, pp. 679–84 and 379, table xv; for lower estimates, see: MacMullen, "How big was the Roman imperial army?"; and Duncan-Jones, *Structure and Scale*, pp. 105–17, 214–21. In fact, the figures for the Diocletianic legions in the *comitatenses* are generally agreed upon by all as being nominally 1,000 strong, and the overall figures for the *comitatenses* are likewise agreed (ranging between 93,000 and 104,000), the main differences of opinion concerning the size of the legions and *auxilia* in the *limitanei*.
54. See Maurice, *Strat.*, iii, 8, 10; *Not. Dig. Or.*, v–ix; *Occ.* v, vii; Vegetius, *Epitome rei militari*, iii, 1, 15.
55. See Procopius, *Wars*, III, xi, 11–12, 19, for Africa; and Agathias, *Historiae*, ii, 4 for Italy. For Illyricum, see Jones, *LRE*, p. 685.
56. For detailed discussion, see Haldon, *Byzantium in the Seventh Century*, pp. 251–3; M. Whitby, "Recruitment in Roman armies from Justinian to Heraclius (*c.* 565–615)", in Cameron (ed.), *States, Resources and Armies*, pp. 61–124, esp. 71–5, 100–2.
57. It has been reasonably estimated that the field army of Africa, as reconstituted under Justinian, may have numbered some 15,000, following the figure for the basic expeditionary force accompanying Belisarius in 533: Procopius, *Wars*, I, xv.11. (I exclude the naval element and the federates who also accompanied the expedition.) No figure is available for Italy, the field army for which was anyway

divided among those districts still held by the empire, but the total may have numbered 15,000.

58. See Haldon, *Recruitment and Conscription*, p. 26.
59. *Theoph.*, p. 451.11f. (trans. Mango and Scott, p. 623).
60. *Theoph.*, p. 447.31f. (trans. Mango and Scott, p. 618). Such variations, of course, reflect the sources used by the original chronicler.
61. Thomas the Slav: *Th. cont.*, p. 55.22f.; Genesius, *Regna*, ii, 5. Many descriptions of campaigns and battles involve the formulaic use of terms such as "*x* myriads" (i.e. 10,000 × ?) for both sides, as at *Th. cont.*, 177.18–22 where opposing forces of three and four myriads are mentioned; it is difficult to know whether these are purely formulaic or reflect the actual numbers involved.
62. *Theoph.*, p. 471.21–7 (trans. Mango and Scott, p. 648).
63. *Theoph.*, p. 447 (trans. Mango and Scott, p. 617). See Treadgold, *Byzantium and Its Army*, p. 64.
64. It is possible that some of the army of Illyricum may have survived and were represented in the naval *themata* which replaced the original Karabisianoi army in the later seventh or early eighth century.
65. The *tagmata* numbered perhaps 2,000–3,000 at this point, and ought not to be included in this calculation.
66. Treadgold, *Byzantium and Its Army*, pp. 43ff.; "Remarks on Al-Jarmi", *Byzantinoslavica*, 44, 1983, pp. 205–12; Haldon, "Kudāma Ibn Dja'far and the garrison of Constantinople", *Byzantion*, 48, 1978, pp. 78–90; *Byzantine Praetorians*, pp. 629–33; F. Winkelmann, "Probleme der Informationen des al-Garmi über die byzantinischen Provinzen", *Byzantinoslavica*, 43, 1982, pp. 18–29.
67. Thus the combined strengths given for the three ninth-century *themata* of Boukellarion, Opsikion and Optimaton, all divisions of the original Opsikion or praesental army, produces a total of 18,000, which would represent a force slightly smaller than the praesental field army based in the same region in the later sixth century. See Ibn al-Fakīh al-Hamadānī, *Description of the Land of the Byzantines*, trans. E.W. Brooks, in "Arabic lists of Byzantine themes", *JHS*, 21, 1901, pp. 67–77 – see pp. 72–7 (written in 903); and Kudāma ibn Ja'far, *Kitāb al-harāj*, pp. 197–98 (see n. 66 above; written in 928–32).
68. Historians differ in their interpretations of this material. A detailed argument for the higher figures is made by Treadgold, *Byzantium and Its Army*, pp. 66–77 (citing his own previous articles on the subject), but there are methodological problems with his approach, and a building up of arithmetical hypotheses not justified by the nature of the sources he employs. Alternative views are expressed in Winkelmann, "Probleme der Informationen des al-Garmi"; Haldon, *Byzantine Praetorians*, p. 629ff.; and "Chapters II, 44 and 45 of the *De Cerimoniis*. Theory and practice in tenth-century military administration", *Travaux et Mémoires* (forthcoming, 1999). Note also Whittow, *The Making of Orthodox Byzantium*, pp. 181–93. In general, I would argue that field armies were very much smaller than most of the medieval figures would suggest, and that the healthy scepticism about figures and sizes of armies which informs much of the work of Delbrück, *History of the Art of War*, II: *The Barbarian Invasions*; III: *Medieval Warfare*, is to be followed.
69. See Harthama b. A'yan, *Mukhtassar Siyasat al-Harb (The Brief Policy of War)*, ed. 'Abd al-R'uf 'Aun (Cairo, n.d.), p. 28. For the attack on the Paulicians (in 872), see *Th. cont.*, 273.14–274.5. The rest of the combined total of the two *themata* can hardly have been more than a few thousand. For other examples, see Chapter 6 below.

70. For a detailed analysis of the figures for the army and fleets in both 910–11 and 949, see Haldon, "Chapters II, 44 and 45 of the *De Cerimoniis*",
71. See J.-C. Cheynet, "Les effectifs de l'armée byzantine aux Xe–XIe s.", *Cahiers de civilisation médiévales, X^e–XIIe siècles*, 38, 4, 1995, pp. 319–35. Cheynet's analysis is both careful and sceptical of the large figures for armies given in some of the sources. But even his estimate is, in my vew, greatly exaggerated: see the references to Delbrück's discussion, and the evidence assembled by R.C. Smail, *Crusading Warfare, 1097–1193*, ed. C. Marshall (Cambridge, 1995), noted below.
72. See sources and discussion in Shepard, "The uses of the Franks in eleventh-century Byzantium", pp. 279–80, 301.
73. Attaleiates, *Historia*, p. 189; see also Bryennios, p. 179 (*Nicephori Bryennii Historiarum libri quattuor*, ed. P. Gautier (Brussels, 1975)).
74. See Cheynet, "Les effectifs". For the small size of the forces available to the government in the 1070s, see Angold, *Byzantium 1025–1204*, pp. 93–6, 109–13.
75. Choniates, *Historia*, pp. 378–9, 384, 386–7, 429–30, 465, 468, 473, 487, for example.
76. The best specific considerations are Smail, *Crusading Warfare, passim*; and Delbrück, *History of the Art of War*, III: *Medieval Warfare*, pp. 197–8, 218–20. See also J. France, *Victory in the East. A Military History of the First Crusade* (Cambridge, 1994), pp. 122–42.

Chapter 4   Organizing for war: the administration of military structures

1. *Strategy*, § 14.3–9 (p. 45).
2. See Leo, *Tact.*, i, 1, 2, 4–8 for a clear exposition of these aspects; and for "logistics", *Tact.*, epilogue, 57.
3. See Maurice, *Strat.*, proem, 10ff. All the relevant sources are discussed in Haldon, "Administrative continuities and structural transformations in East Roman military organisation *c*. 580–640", in *State, Army and Society in Byzantium*, V, pp. 4–7, with further bibliography and sources. See in general A. Müller, "Das Heer Iustinians nach Prokop und Agathias", *Philologus*, 71, 1912, pp. 101–38, and especially R. Grosse, "Die Rangordnung der römischen Armee des 4.–6. Jahrhunderts", *Klio*, 15, 1915, pp. 122–61; Grosse, *Militärgeschichte*, pp. 127–38, 144f.; Jones, *LRE*, pp. 626, 634, 674ff.
4. See Leo, *Tact.*, iv, 2, 6, 9–23 (and cf. Maurice, *Strat.*, i, 3, 4).
5. Ibn Khurradādhbīh (Abū'l-Kāsim 'Ubayd Allāh b. 'Abd Allāh b. Khurradādhbīh, *Kitāb at-Masālik wa'l-Mamālik*, in *Bibliotheca Geographorum Araborum*, ed. M.-J. De Goeje (Leyden, 1870ff.); R. Blachère et al. (Leyden, 1938ff.), VI, pp. 76–85), p. 84; Kudāma (Abū'l-Faraj al-Kātib al-Bagdādī Kudāma ibn Ja'far, *Kitāb al-Harāj*, in *BGA*, VI, pp. 196–9), p. 196; see Leo, *Tact.*, xix, 149.
6. While Leo's *Tactica* simply copies more or less verbatim what the late sixth-century *Strategikon* has to say on these matters, the former does update the technical language to an extent, and provide new information to make that taken from the older source more relevant. The *Strategikon* presents a schema in which the army is divided into brigades (*moirai*) and divisions (*mere*), and regularly uses *drouggos* for both when drawn up in non-linear formation (i, 3.6; ii, 1.6, 2.1; xii, 8.20/7–8). The first reference to a *tourmarches* is for the year 626/7 (*Theoph.*, p. 325.3 (trans. Mango and Scott, p. 453)): George, *tourmarches ton*

Armeniakon; the first reference to a *drouggarios* is to Theodotos, the *megaloprepestatos drouggarios*, who accompanied the *magister militum* Elias on an embassy to the Persian king Siroes in 626 (*Chronicon Paschale*, p. 731.5). It is apparent that *drouggos* had already achieved a semi-official status as the term for a group of *banda* by this time, while *turma*, which had until at least the fifth century meant officially a cavalry troop of some 30 or so soldiers (cf. G. Webster, *The Roman Imperial Army* (London 1969), pp. 146ff.), had evolved and been applied to much larger mounted divisions. Leo notes that the *moirarches* is now usually called a *drouggarios* and the older *merarches* is called *tourmarches* (*Tact.*, iv, 8–9).

7. For a detailed review of this evidence, see Haldon, "Chapters II, 44 and 45 of the *De Cerimoniis*". Note that the *komites* and the *kentarchoi* of the thematic units are listed in a semi-official document of 899, a list of imperial officials according to their position in the hierarchy of offices: N. Oikonomidès (ed.), *Les listes de préséance byzantines des IXe et Xe siècles* (Paris, 1972), pp. 157.11, 161.16.

8. Leo, *Tact.*, iv, 42; and Haldon, "Chapters II, 44 and 45 of the *De Cerimoniis*".

9. This is known from the list of ranks referred to, as well as from a range of other sources. See Haldon, *Byzantine Praetorians*, pp. 294–6 and notes; Southern and Dixon, *The Late Roman Army*, pp. 61–2.

10. See Haldon, *Byzantine Praetorians*, pp. 228–42, 256–97; Oikonomidès, *Préséance*, pp. 119.12–20, 119.28–121.2.

11. See Chapter 3 above.

12. Hendy, *Studies*, pp. 623–5; Haldon, *Byzantium in the Seventh Century*, pp. 227ff.

13. See J. Koder, "Zur Bedeutungsentwicklung des byzantinischen Terminus *Thema*", *JöB*, 40, 1990, pp. 155–65.

14. See Haldon, "Administrative continuities", pp. 10–16.

15. See esp. *DAI*, §50.92–110; II, p. 189.

16. See, for example, *Theoph.*, pp. 364.8, 366.5, 371.9 (trans. Mango and Scott, pp. 507, 511, 517) for the later seventh century.

17. These were located in the *themata* of Boukellarion, Anatolikon, Kappadokia and Charsianon. According to this document, for example, the emperor Leo VI created certain new territorial districts for certain *themata*: thus the new *tourma* of Kommata in Kappadokia consisted of seven *banda*; the new *tourma* of Saniana in the *thema* of Charsianon consisted of three *banda*: *DAI*, § 50.83–110: II, pp. 127ff.

18. For example, *Tact.*, iv, 38, 41, 45, 47, 48, 63.

19. *Tact.*, iv, 39; with iv, 38 and 40.

20. See note 17 above, and *DAI*, § 50.92–100, 101–5.

21. Leo, *Tact.*, iv, 9, 42. For the structure of the naval forces, see Ahrweiler, *Byzance et al mer*, pp. 53–85, 97–111.

22. Haldon, "Chapters II, 44 and 45 of the *De Cerimoniis*".

23. J.F. Haldon and H. Kennedy, "The Arab–Byzantine frontier in the eighth and ninth centuries: military organisation and society in the borderlands", *ZRVI*, 19, 1980, pp. 79–116 – see p. 104 for sources.

24. See Haldon, *Const. Porph., Three Treatises*, pp. 249–50 for further discussion.

25. On the first *kleisoura*, see Lilie, *Die byzantinische Reaktion*, pp. 302–6; Haldon and Kennedy, "Arab–Byzantine frontier", pp. 85–6, 104–6.

26. Oikonomidès, *Préséance*, pp. 342, 344, 349.

27. For Chaldia, see F. Winkelmann, *Byzantinische Rang- und Ämterstruktur im 8. und 9. Jahrhundert* (*BbA*, 53) (Berlin, 1985), p. 107; Oikonomidès, *Préséance*, p. 349.

For Koloneia, see Winkelmann, *Rang- und Ämterstruktur*, p. 114. For the seals and other textual evidence, see Oikonomidès, *Préséance*, p. 349 and n. 345.

28. See the discussion in Kuhn, *Die byzantinische Armee im 10. und 11. Jarhundert*, pp. 158–60 and older literature.

29. Indeed, in the Greek-speaking parts of the empire the Hellenistic and classical terms had never dropped out of everyday usage, being used as equivalents of the "official" Latin technical words: see, for example, J. Wortley, "Military elements in psychophelitic tales and sayings", in Miller and Nesbitt (eds), *Peace and War in Byzantium*, pp. 89–105, at p. 98 (a fourth-century example).

30. For *drouggarokomites*, see Haldon, "Chapters II, 44 and 45 of the *De Cerimoniis*". For reductions in thematic forces at this time, see N. Oikonomidès, "The social structure of the Byzantine countryside in the first half of the Xth century", *Symmeikta*, 10, 1996, pp.105–25.

31. The evidence for these developments is summarized in greater detail by McGeer, *Sowing the Dragon's Teeth*, p. 203; Kühn, *Die byzantinische Armee im 10. und 11. Jahrhundert*, pp. 260–80. For the size of *banda* and "imperial" units, or *allagia*, in the provinces, see Haldon, "Chapters II, 44 and 45 of the *De Cerimoniis*", and A. Dain (ed.), *Sylloge Tacticorum, quae olim "inedita Leonis Tactica" dicebatur* (Paris, 1938), § 35, 4–5.

32. See Kühn, *Die byzantinische Armee im 10. und 11. Jahrhundert*, pp. 273–5, 278–80.

33. For example, Psellos, *Chronographia*, i, 32, 33 (trans. Sewter, pp. 25–6) (of the army under Basil II); vii, 8 (trans. Sewter, pp. 212–13) (of Isaac I's reorganization of the army); see the references in Chapter 6 below.

34. See Bartusis, *The Late Byzantine Army*, pp. 191ff. For officer/NCO grades in the early twelfth century, see Anna Comnena, *Alexiad*, iii, 11. For non-specific references to junior or subordinate officers, see, for example, Choniates, *Historia*, p. 152; for taxiarchies and companies, see Choniates, *Historia*, pp. 23, 102, 153–4 (and cf. pp. 29–30); Kinnamos, *Epitome*, pp. 271–3.

35. Haldon, *Byzantine Praetorians*, pp. 318–23.

36. Detailed discussion of these developments in McGeer, *Sowing the Dragon's Teeth*, pp. 202–11.

37. On all these units see Kühn, *Die byzantinische Armee im 10. und 11. Jahrhundert*, pp. 243–51; also Shepard, "The uses of the Franks in eleventh-century Byzantium", pp. 283–4 and n. 38.

38. For a full treatment, see the work of Kühn, *Die byzantinische Armee im 10. und 11. Jahrhundert*, pp. 164–242, with analysis of the history of the individual commands through the eleventh and twelfth centuries.

39. For the earlier arrangements, see above; and for the Comnenian structures, see Hohlweg, *Beiträge*, pp. 93–134; J. Herrin, "Realities of provincial government: Hellas and Peloponnesos, 1180–1205", *Dumbarton Oaks Papers*, 29, 1975, pp. 253–84; and the brief summary in Magdalino, *The Empire of Manuel I*, pp. 234–5.

40. See Hohlweg, *Beiträge*, pp. 111–17. For reference to the eastern and western regiments, see Choniates, *Historia*, pp. 77, 189, 195, 236.

41. For foreign mercenaries in the second half of the eleventh century, see N. Oikonomidès, "L'évolution de l'organisation administrative de l'empire byzantin", *TM*, 6, 1976, pp. 125–52, esp. p. 144; Hohlweg, *Beiträge*, pp. 64–80. For recruitment of mercenaries: Choniates, *Historia*, pp. 91, 97, 178, 208–9, 233; Kinnamos, *Epitome*, p. 199. For nationalities, see, for example, Choniates,

Historia, pp. 16 (Pechenegs and Serbs), 23, 29–30 (Macedonian, Keltic (i.e. French or German) and Pecheneg troops), 89 (Germans), 97 (north Italians), 178 ("Latins" and Cumans), 233 (Iberians (Georgians), Italians), 245 (Paphlagonians); Kinnamos, *Epitome*, pp. 10 (Lombards, Turks), 14–15 (Turks), 148 (Alans, Franks), 167 (Normans, Turks, Georgians, Alans), 199 (Franks (from the kingdom of Jerusalem), Serbs, "Latins", Armenians, Lombards, Rus', knights from Rhodes), 271 (Cumans, Turks, Germans, Serbs, Italians), 299 (Serbs and Magyars who did not appear in time for the 1176 expediton against Ikonion).

42. See Scylitzes, *Synopsis historiarum*, 484.23–5, 488.49–54, 490.15, 491.28 and 47, 492.64–6.

43. For the thematic *tagmata* recruited from the provinces of the empire, see Kühn, *Die byzantinische Armee im 10. und 11. Jahrhundert*, pp. 251–9 and Hohlweg, *Beiträge*, pp. 80–2. For the various palatine units, see Oikonomides, *Préséance*, pp. 327–333; *ODB*, pp. 2152 (Varangians), 2153 (Vardariotai), 925–6 (Hetaireia); and Hohlweg, *Beiträge*, pp. 45–80.

44. See J.F. Haldon, *Recruitment and Conscription in the Byzantine Army c. 550–950: A Study on the Origins of the stratiotika ktemata* (Sitzungsber. d. österr. Akad. d. Wiss., phil.-hist. Kl. 357) (Vienna, 1979), pp. 20–8, and Whitby, "Recruitment in Roman armies from Justinian to Heraclius (*ca.* 565–615)", in Cameron (ed.), *States, Resources and Armies*, pp. 61–124 for detailed analyses of the sources.

45. For moving forces in the provinces see Chapter 5 below, and see Jones, *LRE*, pp. 623–30, 672–4; J.L. Teall, "The grain supply of the Byzantine empire", *DOP*, 13, 1959, pp. 87–139 – see p. 93f.

46. See Jones, *LRE*, pp. 643–4, based on the rate of pay for African soldiers assumed from Justinian's legislation for the new African prefecture (*CJ*, i, 27.2/ 19–36, a. 534); Elton, *War in Roman Europe*, pp. 120–4. These figures have been emended by Treadgold, *Byzantium and its Army*, pp. 149ff., who argues that they reflect the rate at which *limitanei* were paid, and that, on a variety of grounds, the rate at which troops of the *comitatenses* were paid should be four times greater than it. At first sight this seems reasonable enough, but several arguments militate against this. First, the figures in question relate to the administrative staff of the bureau of the African ducates, and there is no reason to think that such officials, whatever the standing and status of the soldiers whom they administered, would have been paid at a lower rate than their equivalents elsewhere. In the second place, the grades listed are grades associated not with the older establishment of legions and auxiliaries most closely associated with the *riparii* or *limitanei*, but with the fourth-century establishment associated with the *comitatenses* (cf. Jones, *LRE*, p. 674). Yet this distinction should not be stressed too much, for cross-postings between frontier and field armies were not unusual, while a rigid distinction between the categories of troops under the command of a *dux* (commanding *limitanei*) should not be assumed: *duces* also had command over field-army units assigned to their command for various reasons (see the many examples adduced by E. Stein, *Histoire du Bas-Empire*, II: *De la disparition de l'empire d'Occident à la mort de Justinien (476–565)* (Paris/Bruxelles/ Amsterdam, 1949/repr. Amsterdam, 1968), p. 198; Jones, *LRE*, pp. 660–1 for the sixth century). There is in addition no evidence that units posted to the frontiers were paid at a lower rate than field-army troops (see Jones, *LRE*, pp. 661–3), while the figures given in Justinian's legislation for Africa are also confirmed for a *comitatenses* grade in the fourth century (Jones, *LRE*, p. 634).

Finally, it is not correct to assert that the pay of the *limitanei* was "abolished in 545" (Treadgold, *Byzantium and its Army*, pp. 150–1). Justinian did withold, and then temporarily suspend, their pay (see Procopius, *Historia arcana*, xxiv, 12–14), but there is no evidence to suggest that this state of affairs was made permanent, and indeed the reintroduction of *limitanei* to reconquered regions and the continued appearance of fully equipped and operational units of *limitanei* after his reign makes this inherently unlikely (see, for example, the unit *Legio IV Parthica* in the 580s: *Th. Sim.*, ii, 6 (trans. Whitby, p. 51)).

47. Jones, *LRE*, p. 663.
48. There is much disagreement among historians as to the status and value, and more importantly the interpretation to be placed upon, the limited statistical evidence for rates of pay in the middle Byzantine period. Treadgold, *Byzantium and its Army*, pp. 118–57, devotes a good deal of effort to the attempt to establish scales and rates of pay for the army at different times. Some of his results are not entirely implausible, but there is no way of demonstrating that alternative interpretations are not equally plausible. For some criticisms, see R.-J. Lilie, "Die byzantinischen Staatsfinanzen im 8./9. Jahrhundert und die *stratiotika ktemata*", *BSl*, 48, 1987, pp. 49–55.
49. For a detailed analysis, see Haldon, *Byzantium in the Seventh Century*, pp. 232–51, and "Military service, military lands and the status of soldiers". Treadgold, *Byzantium and its Army*, pp. 172–9, argues for such an allocation and distribution of lands from imperial estates, but this remains a guess, and the implications of the later legislation concerning soldiers' lands would not support such a process in the first place.
50. See *Const. Porph., Three Treatises*, (C) 349ff., and commentary, pp. 236–7.
51. Thus the thematic *protonotarioi* (chief fiscal officials), for example, appear only in the first half of the ninth century. Before this, the provinces within each theme had been administered as a group by eparchs, almost certainly the descendants of the older *ad hoc* praetorian prefects, and by proconsuls, the administrative descendants of the older provincial or diocesan governors. See Haldon, *Byzantium in the Seventh Century*, pp. 202ff. with literature and sources.
52. This is particularly clearly reflected in the shift in the meaning of the technical term *synone*: in the sixth century it referred to compulsory levies of foodstuffs in kind; during the seventh–tenth centuries it had the meaning of the regular state imposition on land.
53. For the process of supplying field armies, see below.
54. Leo VI recommends that the general select the well-to-do but unwilling (military) households and demand from them the fully equipped soldier and his mount: Leo, *Tact.*, xviii, 129; xx, 205. See Haldon, *Recruitment and Conscription*, p. 56, and "Military service, military lands and the status of soldiers", p. 32. Instead of personal service, the wealthy *stratiotai* registered on the *kodikes* were to provide the resources for the person who actually fulfilled the service. For recent surveys of the literature and the evidence, see R.-J. Lilie, "Die zweihundertjährige reform: zu den Anfängen der Themenorganisation im 7. und 8. Jahrhundert", *BS*, 45, 1984, pp. 27–39, 190–201; Haldon, "Military service, military lands and the status of soldiers", pp. 20–41; and M. Kaplan, *Les hommes et la terre à Byzance du VIe au XIe siècle. Propriété et exploitation du sol* (Paris, 1992), pp. 231–49. For differences in wealth and status between those registered in the different classes of service, see Zonaras, *Epitomae historiarum*, iii, pp. 506.3ff. (*Ioannis*

Zonarae epitomae historiarum libri XIII usque ad XVIII, ed. Th. Büttner-Wobst (*CSHB*, Bonn, 1897)).

55. See Ibn Hawkal, *La configuration de la terre (Kitab Surat al-Ard)*, trans. J.H. Kramers and E. Wiet (Beirut/Paris, 1964), p. 194; and Haldon, *Recruitment and Conscription*, p. 61f.; Dagron and Mihaescu, *Le traité sur la Guérilla*, pp. 278ff.

56. See *DAI*, § 51.199–204 and § 52; most recently discussed by N. Oikonomidès, "The social structure of the Byzantine countryside in the first half of the Xth century", *Symmeikta*, 10, 1996, pp. 105–25, esp. pp. 108–12.

57. Ibn Khurradādhbīh, pp. 84–5.

58. For example, *Theoph.*, pp. 484–5 and 489 (trans. Mango and Scott, pp. 665 and 672), when Bulgar and Arab forces respectively captured the thematic *rhogai* despatched from Constantinople in 809 and 811. Cf. Scylitzes, *Synopsis historiarum*, pp. 487.34–488.1; Attaleiates, *Historia*, p. 54.1–4 (Bryennios, the *strategos* of Cappadocia and supporter of the successful rebel Isaac Komnenos in 1057, sent to distribute the pay of the Cappadocian units in the Anatolikon, and wishing to issue a more generous payment than that offered by the emperor, seizes the imperial official sent with him, along with the pay for the soldiers).

59. See Ibn Khurradādhbīh, p. 84; *Const. Porph.*, *Three Treatises*, (C) 647–52 and discussion p. 256; Hendy, *Studies*, pp. 183–4, 646–51; Treadgold, *Byzantium and its Army*, pp. 137–8. See also N. Oikonomidès, "Middle Byzantine provincial recruits: salary and armament", in J. Duffy and J. Peradotto (eds), *Gonimos. Neoplatonic and Byzantine Studies Presented to Leendert G. Westerink at 75* (Buffalo, NY, 1988), pp. 121–36. For the four classes of military service, see Zonaras, *Epitomae historiarum*, iii, p. 506.

60. Haldon, *Recruitment and Conscription*, pp. 79–80 and notes; Dagron and Mihaescu, *Le traité sur la Guérilla*, p. 262. Leo VI notes that the thematic administration should arm and equip the less well off but militarily more useful at the expense of the better-off, although the general was encouraged to select the best from among those registered on the thematic *kodix*. See Leo, *Tact.*, iv, 1; xviii, 129f.; xx, 205. This is the process of *syndosis*. In contrast, the whole *strateia* could be commuted, as occurred in the Peloponnese and other western provinces in the reigns of Leo VI and Romanos I on several occasions: see N. Oikonomidès, "The social structure of the Byzantine countryside in the first half of the Xth century", pp. 109–11.

61. For the generalized fiscalization of the *strateia*, see Zonaras, *Epitomae historiarum*, iii, pp. 505.16–506.10; discussion in H. Ahrweiler, "Recherches sur l'administration de l'empire byzantin aux IXᵉ–XIᵉ siècles", *BCH*, 84, 1960, pp. 1–109 – see pp. 22–3; and Kaplan, *Les hommes et la terre*, pp. 252ff.

62. Soldiers of the imperial *tagmata* (who might also be recruited from among regular thematic troops) were also subject to the *strateia* where they were proprietors of land in their own right: see Haldon, *Byzantine Praetorians*, pp. 297–9.

63. See Haldon, *Byzantine Praetorians*, pp. 252, 518. For the Athanatoi (Immortals), see Kühn, *Die byzantinische Armee im 10. und 11. Jarhundert*, pp. 243–6.

64. Haldon, *Byzantine Praetorians*, p. 252; for the Rus' in the expedition of 949, see *De Cer.*, pp. 660.18, 664.15f.; and in general: S. Blöndal, *The Varangians of Byzantium*, ed. and trans. B.S. Benedikz (Cambridge, 1978).

65. See Shepard, "The uses of the Franks in eleventh-century Byzantium", pp. 280–1, who notes that until the second half of the eleventh century such troops are not usually called "mercenaries", but rather the traditional terms – "allies"

(*symmachoi*) or "barbarians/foreigners" (*ethnikoi*) – are used, reinforcing the notion that they often came as official assistance from foreign rulers or lords rather than as freebooters. Only from the 1050s does a Byzantine term for mercenary – *misthophoros* – and its derivatives appear regularly to describe such troops, reflecting the change in the mode of their recruitment.

66. See the Arab writers translated in A.A. Vasiliev, *Byzance et les Arabes*, II: *Les relations politiques de Byzance et des Arabes à l'époque de la dynastie macédonienne (Les empereurs Basile I, Léon le Sage et Constantin VII Porphyrogénète) (867–959)*, eds H. Grégoire and M. Canard (Corpus Bruxellense Hist. Byz. II) (Bruxelles, 1950), 2, p. 333ff.; also McGeer, *Sowing the Dragon's Teeth*, p. 201 and notes 9 and 10 with sources and further literature.

67. For Brindisi, the alliance with Conrad and the Serbian expedition, see Magdalino, *The Empire of Manuel I Komnenos*, pp. 60, 43, 54, with sources; Angold, *Byzantium 1025–1204*, pp. 172, 163 and 175; for local military service: Magdalino, *The Empire of Manuel I Komnenos*, pp. 123–34.

68. Historians are still debating the question of the evolution and rate of development of the *pronoia*. See the discussion in Hohlweg, *Beiträge*, pp. 82–93; Bartusis, *The Late Byzantine Army*, pp. 162–88; Magdalino, *The Empire of Manuel I Komnenos*, pp. 231–3. For a dated but still useful account of military recruitment under Manuel I, see Chalandon, *Les Comnène*, pp. 611–18.

69. See *ODB*, art. "Roga", p. 1801; Haldon, *Byzantine Praetorians*, pp. 307–12 with notes; Shepard, "The uses of the Franks in eleventh-century Byzantium", pp. 284–5 and n. 42. The evidence remains ambiguous. Symeon *magister* notes that the *tagmata* were paid before the Bulgar campaign in 917, when they fought together with the *themata*, although he does not refer to pay for the latter: *Th. cont.*, 388.19–21; Sym. mag., 881.1–3.

70. For discussion, see Haldon, "Chapters II, 44 and 45 of the *De Cerimoniis*".

71. See Hendy, *Studies*, p. 648f. for sources and discussion.

72. See esp. C. Morrisson, "Monnaie et prix à Byzance du Ve au VIIe siècle", in *Hommes et richesses dans l'Empire byzantin* I: *IVe–VIIe siècle* (Paris, 1989), pp. 239–60; J.-C. Cheynet, E. Malamut and C. Morrisson, "Prix et salaires à Byzance (X^e–XVe siècles)", in V. Kravari, J. Lefort and C. Morrisson (eds), *Hommes et richesses dans l'Empire byzantin*, II: *VIIIe–XVe siècle* (Réalités byzantins, 3) (Paris, 1991), pp. 339–74; J. Irmscher, "Preise und Löhne in frühen Byzanz", in *Studien zum 8. und 9. Jarhundert in Byzanz (BbA,* 51) (Berlin, 1983), pp. 23–33.

73. For the Arabic source, see Ibn Khurradādhbīh, pp. 84–5; for the Byzantine list (dated to *c.* 910), see *De Cer.*, pp. 696.10–697.17.

74. See Treadgold, *Byzantium and its Army*, pp. 118–57, with tables of hypothesized scales of pay and detailed discussion of sources.

75. This was a well-established way of rewarding senior persons and those in attendance upon the emperor. Cf. *Const. Porph., Three Treatises,* (C) 250–3, 501–11, and commentary.

76. See Haldon, *Byzantine Praetorians*, pp. 308ff. and "Chapters II, 44 and 45 of the *De Cerimoniis*".

77. This is the main ground for rejecting the notion that a plausible breakdown of the total salary figures for the army, which are available from different periods of the empire's history in the late eighth–tenth centuries, can be achieved, although acceptable round figures may well be more reasonably hypothesized, as Treadgold (*Byzantine State Finances* and "The Army in the Works of Constantine

Porphyrogenitus", etc.) has attempted to do. But to arrive at detailed figures for officers, men and specific units seems to me a dangerous and unconvincing approach, necessitating as it does the entirely hypothetical standardization of structures which has to be imposed upon the evidence. It has been plausibly suggested that the greater proportion of officers to soldiers in the Armenian units reflects the problems of discipline which Byzantine commentators associated with Armenian troops in general: see E. McGeer, "The legal decree of Nikephros II Phocas concerning Armenian *stratiotai*", in Miller and Nesbitt (eds), *Peace and War in Byzantium*, pp. 123–37 (at 135–6); and N. Oikonomidès, "L'Organisation de la frontière orientale de Byzance aux Xe–XIe siècles et le taktikon de l'Escorial", in *Actes du XIVe Congrès Internat. des Études Byzantines* (Bucarest, 1971), I pp. 285–302 (repr. in *Documents et études sur les institutions de Byzance (VIIe–XVe s.)* (London, 1976) XXIV – see pp. 298–9). For some sources on the pay of mercenaries, see Shepard, "The uses of the Franks in eleventh-century Byzantium", and Haldon, "Military service, military lands, and the status of soldiers", pp. 60–1 and n. 147.

78. See J.F. Haldon, "Some aspects of Byzantine military technology from the sixth to the tenth centuries", *BMGS*, 1, 1975, pp. 11–47; T.G. Kolias, *Byzantinische Waffen: ein Beitrag zur byzantinischen Waffenkunde von den Anfängen bis zur lateinischen Eroberung* (Vienna, 1988). Kolias presents a detailed analysis of the written sources and in particular the technical terminology employed, organized by theme: see pp. 37–64 (on body-armour, esp. the terms *lorikion*, *klibanion* and *zaba*), pp. 65–74 (arm- and leg-guards), pp. 75–87 (helmets), pp. 88–131 (shields); for weapons see: pp. 133–61 (swords), pp. 162–72 (axes), pp. 173–84 (maces), pp. 185–213 (lance and spear). See in addition, for the tenth-century, E. McGeer, "Infantry versus cavalry: the Byzantine response", REB, 46, 1988, pp. 135–45 and esp. "*Menaulion – menaulatoi*", *Diptycha*, 4, 1986–7, pp. 53–7; and M.P. Anastasiadis, "On handling the menavlion", *BMGS*, 18, 1994, pp. 1–10. On the stirrup, see also A.D.H. Bivar, "The stirrup and its origins", *Oriental Art*, 1/2, 1955, pp. 61–5; "Cavalry tactics and equipment on the Euphrates frontier", *DOP*, 26, 1972, pp. 273–91 – see p. 286f.

79. By the fourth century helmets with integral neck-guards made from a single sheet of metal had been replaced by composite helmets of two pieces connected by a welded and riveted ridge piece, which also evolved decorative aspects; cheek- and neck-guards were attached via leather straps and the lining of the helmet, although not all such ridged helmets had crests. It is likely that this type derives from a Parthian–Iranian archetype. Other varieties consisted of several segments, some with hinged cheek-pieces and riveted neck-guards. Known as *Spangenhelme*, they derive probably from trans-Danubian models, and were widely adopted during the fifth and sixth centuries. See M.C. Bishop and J.C.N. Coulston, *Roman Military Equipment, from the Punic Wars to the Fall of Rome* (London, 1993), pp. 167–72; S. James, "Evidence from Dura Europos for the origins of late Roman helmets", *Syria*, 63, 1986, pp. 107–34; also D. Nicolle, "Arms in the Umayyad era: military technology in a time of change", in Y. Lev (ed.), *War and Society in the Eastern Mediterranean, 7th–15th centuries* (Leiden/New York/Cologne, 1997), pp. 9–100, nos 164, 166, 167. For archaeological evidence of the types of military accoutrements and weaponry from the late Roman period, see the relevant contributions in Vallet and Kazanski, *L'armée romaine et les barbares*. For earlier Roman cavalry helmets, see the summary in Karen R.

Dixon and Pat Southern, *The Roman Cavalry. From the First to the Third Century A.D.* (London, 1992), pp. 34–6.

80. The long sword, introduced from the later second century, became standard for cavalry and infantry during the third and fourth centuries, although there were several variations on the basic pattern: see Bishop and Coulston, *Roman Military Equipment*, pp. 126–35, 163–5; Dixon and Southern, *The Roman Cavalry*, pp. 48–9.

81. See J.C. Coulston, "Roman archery equipment", in M.C. Bishop (ed.), *The Production and Distribution of Roman Military Equipment. Proceedings of the Second Roman Military Equipment Research Seminar (BAR, S275)* (Oxford, 1985), pp. 220–36; Dixon and Southern, *The Roman Cavalry*, pp. 52–7. For the Hunnic bow, which was that employed throughout the Byzantine and near-eastern world until the twelfth or thirteenth centuries, see Nicolle, "Arms in the Umayyad era", no. 151.

82. *Wars*, I, i.9–15.

83. The battle of Troina, fought in 1040: see *Vita S. Philareti*, in *AS April.*, I, pp. 603–18, at 608.

84. For shield-boss types (conical or domed, with a flanged base, often with an inscription naming the unit), see Bishop and Coulston, *Roman Military Equipment*, pp. 172–3; D. Nicolle, "No way overland? Evidence for Byzantine arms and armour on the 10th–11th century Taurus frontier", *Graeco-Arabica*, 6, 1995, pp. 226–45, at pp. 227–30; and Nicolle, "Arms of the Umayyad era", nos. 158–60. Spiked or semi-spiked bosses were not unusual: see H.W. Böhme, *Germanische Grabfunde des 4. bis 5. Jahrhunerts zwischen unterer Elbe und Loire* (Munich, 1974), and M. Kazanski, "Quelques parallèles entre l'armement en Occident et à Byzance", in *Gaule mérovingienne et monde méditérranéen* (Lattes, 1988), pp. 75–87. For some examples of spiked bosses (probably of East Germanic/Hunnic troops), see F. Vallet, "Une implantation militaire aux portes de Dijon au Ve siècle", in Vallet and Kazanski, *L'armée romaine et les barbares*, pp. 249–58, at figs 2/5 and 6, 3/2 and 14. For shield shapes, sizes and construction (either of laminated wood or joined solid boards, painted or covered with leather or cloth riveted fast) see: Bishop and Coulston, *Roman Military Equipment*, pp. 149–51, 173; Dixon and Southern, *The Roman Cavalry*, pp. 43–7. For the text, see *Strategy*, § 16.16–30.

85. Bishop and Coulston, *Roman Military Equipment*, pp. 141ff.

86. The term *zaba* in the *Strategikon* is used as an equivalent for *lorikion*, although strictly it meant quilted cloth. See Haldon, "Military technology", p. 24 and n. 65.

87. In comparison with the period up to the third century, relatively few examples of late Roman mail and lamellar have been found throughout the empire, especially at frontier sites: see Bishop and Coulston, *Roman Military Equipment*, p. 167 (and cf. pp. 141–5). For horse armour, see Bishop and Coulston, *Roman Military Equipment*, pp. 157–9, 182; J.C. Coulston, "Roman, Parthian and Sassanian tactical development", pp. 60–8; Dixon and Southern, *The Roman Cavalry*, pp. 61–3, 67–70. For bows, bow-cases and quivers, see Haldon, "Byzantine military technology", pp. 21–2 and n. 52; and for illustrations, see Nicolle, "Arms of the Umayyad era", nos 151–7. Probable helmet forms are illustrated in Nicolle, "Arms of the Umayyad era", nos 172, 178, and examples of earlier horse-armour (from Doura-Europos) at nos 189–91.

88. See Nicolle, "Arms of the Umayyad era", nos 193ff.; Haldon, "Byzantine military technology", pp. 14ff. Laced lamellar thigh-guards were excavated at Doura-Europos: see Dixon and Southern, *The Roman Cavalry*, p. 43.

89. *Strategy*, §§ 16, 17; Maurice, *Strat.*, i, 2–3; xii B, 1–5 (and cf. ii, 5.5; iii, 5.14; xi, 2). For a detailed account with other sources, see: Haldon, "Byzantine military technology", pp. 18–24. For the Heruls see, for example, Procopius, *Wars*, III, xi.11–13; Agathias, *Historiae*, i, 2.3, 14.4–6; ii, 7–9; etc. On the arrow-guide carried by the light infantry archers, see D. Nishimura, "Crossbows, arrow-guides and the *solenarion*", *B*, 58, 1988, pp. 422–35; with literature and discussion in P.E. Chevedden, "Artillery in late Antiquity: prelude to the Middle Ages", in *The Medieval City under Siege*, pp. 131–73, at 144, n. 58. An example of a sixth–seventh-century two-piece Byzantine helmet can be seen in the Karak Castle museum, Jordan: see Nicolle, *Medieval Warfare Sourcebook*, 2, p. 22.

90. Haldon, "Byzantine military technology", p. 22, n. 56, and pp. 24–5.

91. See Chapters 2 and 5, with pertinent literature; see also Bishop and Coulston, *Roman Military Equipment*, pp. 183–8.

92. For the period between the later sixth and later ninth centuries, see Haldon, "Byzantine military technology", pp. 25–30, and the useful survey of evidence for Islamic weaponry and armour during the Umayyad period by Nicolle, "Arms of the Umayyad era".

93. For a possible parallel, see Nicolle, "Arms of the Umayyad era", no. 120 (a single-edged proto-sabre from the Altai, sixth–tenth century). For two-edged swords from the western steppe zone, see nos 126–9.

94. See Ch. Diehl, *Peinture byzantine* (Paris, 1933), pl. lxxxii.

95. For a probably Byzantine tenth-century helmet, with the bowl from a single sheet and with riveted strengthening bands and holes for the attachment of an aventail, and for a *kamelaukion*, a leather cap, with neck-guard such as is described in the tenth-century treatises for the majority of infantry, see Nicolle, *Medieval Warfare Sourcebook*, 2, pp. 76–7.

96. A mid-tenth-century treatise describes large, kite-shaped shields for heavy infantry, and it is entirely possible that it is from their contacts with Byzantine troops in Italy, or as mercenaries in the Byzantine armies elsewhere, that western cavalry and infantry began to adopt this type of shield, usually considered an entirely western European development, especially associated with the Normans. See Haldon, "Byzantine military technology", pp. 33–4, and Kolias, *Byzantinische Waffen*, pp. 105–8.

97. Detailed descriptions in Leo, *Tact.*, v, 2–3; vi, 1–8, 11, 25–7, 30, 32, 34; vii, 3; xiv, 84; xix, 57; *Syll. Tact.*, §§ 38, 39; Niceph., *Praecepta*, i; iii; iv. See also Haldon, "Byzantine military technology", pp. 30–41; McGeer, *Sowing the Dragon's Teeth*, pp. 202–17. For the effects of the mace and its use, see Dennis, "The Byzantines in battle", p. 168 with references. For metal plates on hooves, see *Vita S. Philareti*, in *AS April.*, I, pp. 603–18, at 608, describing East Roman cavalry in action in Sicily in 1040.

98. See Haldon, "Byzantine military technology", p. 39; Kolias, *Byzantinische Waffen*, pp. 214–38.

99. On all these issues, see Kolias, *Byzantinische Waffen*, pp. 239–53, who surveys the discussion and recent literature on the subject, although believes that the hand-held crossbow probably was used in Byzantium in the period from the seventh to the eleventh centuries.

100. See *Nicephori Bryennii Historiarum libri quattuor*, ed. P. Gautier (Brussels, 1975), pp. 264–7, and cf. Kolias, *Byzantinische Waffen*, pp. 207–8.

101. Relevant literature and non-Byzantine sources are in Haldon, "Byzantine military technology", and Kolias, *Byzantinische Waffen*. In her important article

analysing the types of weaponry depicted in the Madrid Skylitzes, Ada Hoffmeyer also began the work of establishing a pictorial typology of helmets, sword-hilts and so forth which may serve as a starting point for future work. Unfortunately, the absence of adequate material data from museums and elsewhere limits the value of the work to the source material of pictorial representation alone: see A. Hoffmeyer, "Military equipment in the Byzantine manuscript of Scylitzes in the Biblioteca Nacional in Madrid", *Gladius*, 5, 1966.

102. For a detailed presentation of the evidence from these non-Byzantine contexts, see the discussion and literature in Haldon, "Byzantine military technology"; and Nicolle, "No way overland?". On the *klibanion* and its form, see T. Dawson, "*Kremasmata, kabadion, klibanion*: some aspects of middle Byzantine military equipment reconsidered", *BMGS*, 22, 1998, pp. 38–50.

103. See Hoffmeyer, "Military equipment in the Byzantine manuscript of Scylitzes" for a discussion of the eleventh-century material and the manuscript illustrations.

104. See Choniates, *Historia*, p. 366. The words were uttered by the captured Norman general count Baldwin, and were intended to flatter the emperor Isaac Angelos that earlier Roman failures were not due to the emperor himself.

105. For Procopius' account, see *Wars*, V, xxi.19. For a general survey with further literature and discussion of the relevant evidence and texts, see P.E. Chevedden, "Artillery in late Antiquity: prelude to the Middle Ages", in Corfis and Wolfe (eds), *The Medieval City under Siege*, pp. 131–73. On the tenth-century Byzantine texts, see Sullivan, "Tenth-century Byzantine offensive siege warfare", pp. 179–200.

106. For Procopius' account, see Procopius, *Wars*, V, xxi.14–18. See also Chevedden, "Artillery in late Antiquity", pp. 148 and 160–3; and K. Huuri, "Zur Geschichte des mittelalterlichen Geschützwesens aus orientalischen Quellen", *Studia Orientalia (Soc. Orient. Fennicae)* 9/3, 1941, pp. 51–63, 212–14. Huuri (p. 80, and n. 2) thinks that a passage in Heron of Byzantium may indicate knowledge of torsion weapons, but the issue needs further clarification. For further discussion (in favour of tension as opposed to torsion after the fifth century) see W.S. Tarver, "The traction trebuchet: a reconstruction of an early medieval siege engine", *Technology and Culture*, 36, 1995, pp. 136–67 at p. 142 and n. 36; and R. Rogers, *Latin Siege Warfare in the Twelfth Century* (Oxford, 1992), esp. pp. 254–73.

107. For *toxobolistrai* with windlasses and without, see *De Cer.,* pp. 669.21–670.1 and 670.10–11. See also, for example, Maurice, *Strat.*, xii B, 6.8–9; 21.13; Leo, *Tact.*, v, 7; Niceph., *Praecepta*, v, 3; and esp. the naval treatises of the tenth century: ed. Dain, *Naumachica*, i, 60 (= vi.57); vii, 122.3, 10, 11. For examples from historiographical works, see: *Theoph.*, p. 384 (for the year 716, see trans. Mango and Scott, p. 534); *Th. cont.*, p. 298.16. See also McGeer, *Sowing the Dragon's Teeth*, p. 65 (comm. to Niceph., *Praecepta*, i, 15).

108. Leo, *Tact.*, v, 7; vi, 27; xiv, 83; xv, 27; cf. also *De obsid. tol.* § 14 (p. 480), and Niceph., *Praecepta*, i, 15.151; *De Cer.*, p. 671.2. Cf. also Maurice, *Strat.*, xii B, 6.8, where wagons with *ballistae* swivelling to both sides are listed. See Chevedden, "Artillery in late Antiquity", pp. 137ff.; Sullivan, "Tenth-century Byzantine offensive siege warfare", p. 199 with references.

109. For the *Tactica* descriptions, see Leo, *Tact.*, xiv, 83; xv, 27. See Chevedden, "Artillery in late Antiquity", pp. 154–63 for the late Roman sources and their interpretation (Proc., *Wars*, V, xxi.14–18; *Anon. de rebus bellicis*, § vii, in E.A. Thompson, *A Roman Reformer and Inventor* (Oxford, 1952)).

110. See the sources and discussion in Haldon, "Chapters II, 44 and 45 of the *De Cerimoniis*", also Sullivan, "Tenth-century Byzantine offensive siege warfare", p. 199, n. 51.
111. See D. Nicolle, *Medieval Warfare Source Book*, 1, pp. 50, 99; 2, pp. 47, 85.
112. See J. Needham, "China's trebuchets, manned and counterweighted", in B.S. Hall and D.C. West (eds), *On Pre-Modern Technology and Science: Studies in Honor of Lynn White Jr.* (Malibu, CA, 1976).
113. See P. Lemerle, *Les plus anciens recueils des miracles de S. Démétrius et de la pénétration des Slaves dans les Balkans*, I: *Le texte* (Paris, 1979), §151 (p. 154.9–17). The machines were described also as very tall: §139 (p. 148.27–8) and §255 (p. 214.24). For other references to such machines cf., for example, the mid-tenth-century treatise on withstanding sieges, *De Obsidione toleranda*, ed. H. Van Den Berg (Leiden, 1947), §14 (p. 48) and §66 (p. 56); Leo, *Tact.*, xv, 27 (= Maurice, *Strat.*, x, 1.49–56, which, however, refers simply to *petroboloi* without specifying the type); and for the beam-sling stone-thrower and later counterweight trebuchet in general, see D.R. Hill, "Trebuchets", *Viator*, 4, 1973, pp. 99–116 (although the author is not aware of the account in the *Miracula Demetrii*); and W.S. Tarver, "The traction trebuchet: a reconstruction of an early medieval siege engine", *Technology and Culture*, 36, 1995, pp. 136–67.
114. Cf. *Chronicon Paschale*, p. 719.22 (trans. Whitby, p. 174). In the medieval western sources for the period immediately preceding the First Crusade one of the standard terms for a stone-throwing device was *petraria*, which is now generally understood as referring to a traction-powered lever device. Whether the Latin term follows an earlier Greek term or evolved independently remains unclear. But equivalence of usage is clearly not to be sought in this context. By the same token, efforts to elaborate a consistent usage in the Latin terminology have met with little success – the western sources use terms such as *mangana* and *mangonella* of both traction-lever devices and for "artillery" in general. See the useful survey of the literature and current debate in R. Rogers, *Latin Siege Warfare in the Twelfth Century* (Oxford, 1997), pp. 254–73.
115. For these, see *De Cer.*, pp. 670.12, 673.2–3.
116. *Leonis Grammatici Chronographia*, ed. I. Bekker (*CSHB*, Bonn, 1842), pp. 335–62, at 347.13–18).
117. Lemerle, *Les plus anciens recueils des miracles de S. Démétrius*, § 206 (p. 187.23), § 209 (188.14–15).
118. See Hill, "Trebuchets", p. 103f. with the available evidence from Arabic sources. For the Skylitzes illustrations, see Estopañan, *Skyllitzes Matritensis*, I, fol. 151 b (with commentary, pp. 159–60) and fol. 166 (commentary, pp. 170–1); A. Grabar and M. Manoussacas, *L'illustration du mansucrit de Skylitzès de la Bibliothèque Nationale de Madrid* (Venice, 1979), figs 193 and 213, with commentary, pp. 88, 93. For the date, see N. Wilson, "The Madrid Skylitzes", *Scrittura e civiltà*, 2, 1978, pp. 209–19. That the *tetrarea* and *labdarea* were beam-sling devices is confirmed by the fact that the leather and iron slings for them are also listed in the same document: *De Cer.*, pp. 671.3, 673.6.
119. See Nicolle, *Medieval Warfare Source Book*, 1, p. 150 (mid-thirteenth-century ms.); 2, p. 236 (twelfth-century ms.).
120. See, for example, Heron's *Belopoeica*, in C. Wescher, *Poliorcétique des grecs. Traités théoriques, récits historiques* (Paris, 1867), pp. 71–119 at p. 85 (also in R. Schneider,

Geschütze auf handschriftlichen Bildern (Ergänzungsschrift zum Jahrbuch der Gesellschaft für Lothringische Geschichte und Altertumskunde, II) (Metz, 1907), pp. 34–62, with German trans. pp. 35–63); and the Anonymous, *Poliorketika* (ed. Wescher, *Poliorcétique des grecs*, pp. 197–279), pp. 256.16–257.2.

121. See *De Cer.*, pp. 670.12, 671.1–3, 672.16, 673.6, Niceph., *Praecepta*, v, 3; v, 5. The anonymous *De obsidione toleranda*, §14 (p. 48) differentiates between *magganika* and *cheiromaggana*; see also *De obsid. tol.*, §66 (p. 56). The confusing use of a single term to denote several different types of engine occurs also in the Arabic sources, where *manjaniq* (from the Greek) can mean either both tension-driven and beam-sling devices, interchangeable with another common term, ʿ*arrāda*. See Hill, "Trebuchets", pp. 99–101. Cf. Kekaumenos, *Strat.*, where *magganika* means simply "artillery", usually mounted on walls or towers for defensive purposes (and therefore probably, although not certainly, tension-powered bow-ballistae): §75 (p. 28.16), §79 (p. 30.33), §81 (p. 32.17).

122. For example Maurice, *Strat.*, xii B, 6.9 (*ballistrarioi* = Leo, *Tact.*, vi, 27, where Leo updates the text and replaces *balliustrarioi* with *magganarioi*); *De Cer.*, p. 661.5–6 (*magganarioi* accompanying a small expeditionary force to Italy in 935); Leo diac., *Historia*, i, 9 (p. 16.21) (*technitai* for the siege engines with Nikephros Phocas' army besieging Chandax on Crete).

123. R. Payne-Gallwey's full-scale reconstruction of an *onager* weighed two tons: see *The Crossbow, with a Treatise on the Ballista and the Catapult of the Ancients*, 2nd edn (London, 1958), Appendix. For some of these issues in relation to neighbouring Islamic cultures, see Cl. Cahen, "Les changements techniques militaires dans la Proche Orient médiéval et leur importance historique", in V.J. Parry and M.E. Yapp (eds), *War, Technology and Society in the Middle East* (London, 1975), pp. 113–24.

124. For a detailed discussion of the sources, with further literature, see J.F. Haldon and M. Byrne, "A possible solution to the problem of Greek fire", *BZ*, 70, 1977, pp. 91–9. For alternative views, see E. Pászthory, "Über das 'Griechische Feuer'. Die Analyse eines spätantiken Waffensystems", *Antike Welt*, 17, 1968, pp. 27–37 (arguing that the device was saltpetre-based); and Th. K. Korres, *Liquid Fire* (Thessaloniki, 1989) (in Greek), arguing that it was not a "flame-thrower"-type weapon, but rather consisted of containers filled with petroleum hurled from catapults). For further comments and discussion, see Haldon, "Chapters II, 44 and 45 of the *De Cerimoniis*". On the evidence for the use of a similar device by the Arabs, see V. Christides, *The Conquest of Crete by the Arabs (ca. 824)*. *A Turning Point in the Struggle between Byzantium and Islam* (Athens, 1984), pp. 29–32, 63–6, 92, and "Naval warfare in the eastern Mediterranean (6th–14th centuries): an Arabic translation of Leo VI's *Naumachica*", *Graeco-Arabica*, 3, 1984, pp. 137–48 at pp. 138–9; see also V. Christides, "Two parallel naval guides of the tenth century: Qudama's document and Leo VI's *Naumachica*", *Graeco-Arabica*, 1, 1982, pp. 51–103.

Chapter 5 The army at war: campaigns

1. There was a system of yearly allowances to provide for weapons. On all these issues, see Haldon, *Byzantine Praetorians*, p. 117f. and notes; Jones, *LRE*, pp. 834–9.

2. On which see Jones, *LRE*, pp. 830–4; Hendy, *Studies*, pp. 602ff.
3. On transport of arms and weapons, see: Haldon, *Byzantine Praetorians*, p. 114 and notes.
4. See J.F. Haldon, "Synone: re-considering a problematic term of middle Byzantine fiscal administration", *Byzantine and Modern Greek Studies*, 18, 1994, pp. 116–53 (repr. in *State, Army and Society in Byzantium*, VIII) for the textual evidence and further discussion.
5. Haldon, *Byzantine Praetorians*, pp. 318ff.
6. Haldon, *Byzantine Praetorians*, pp. 319–21 with notes 972–7.
7. The different points of view in the debate are evaluated in Haldon, *Byzantium in the Seventh Century*, pp. 232–44, and "Military service, military lands and the status of soldiers", pp. 15–18.
8. For soldiers providing their own armour and weapons, see: Haldon, "Military service, military lands and the status of soldiers", pp. 21–3. For the compulsory contracting out of weapons production, see, for example, *De Cer.*, p. 657.12–14 (*strategos* of Thessaloniki to provide 200,000 arrows, 3,000 spears, and as many shields as he could manage), p. 657.15–17 (the *krites* – civil governor or judge – of Hellas to prepare 1,000 spears), p. 658.17–22 (the *strategos* of Samos to obtain cash to pay for the production of nails for the ships).
9. See, for example, *De Cer.*, pp. 672.1ff., 676.18ff. and cf. *Const. Porph., Three Treatises*, [C] 131–5.
10. See P. Magdalino, "The *chartoularata* of northern Greece in 1204", in E. Chrysos (ed.), *The Despotate of Epeiros* (Arta, 1992), pp. 31–5 (in Greek). For some useful comparative material on studs and horse-breeding in general, see C. Gladitz, *Horse Breeding in the Medieval World* (Dublin, 1997), esp. pp. 116f., 129ff.
11. See on all these issues J.F. Haldon, "The organisation and support of an expeditionary force: manpower and logistics in the middle Byzantine period", in N. Oikonomidès (ed.), *To empolemo Byzantio (Byzantium at war)* (Athens, 1997), pp. 111–51.
12. For remounts in the *cursus publicus*, see *CTh.*, viii, 5.34, a. 377; and for ratios of remounts in the military treatises, see: *Strat.*, v, 2.1ff.; v, 4.3ff. (Leo, *Tact.*, x, 7, 12); *Skirmishing*, §14.35–6 (trans. Dennis, p. 193); Niceph., *Praecepta*, i, 17; iv, 1 (and on not having excessive spare horses on raids: iv, 7). See also *Const. Porph., Three Treatises*, (C) 389–91. For Heraclius' cavalry, see: *Chronicon Paschale*, p. 732.11–14 (trans. Whitby, p. 186). More detailed comparative material can be adduced from the earlier Roman period: see Dixon and Southern, *The Roman Cavalry*, pp. 156–62. A good modern treatment of Heraclius' campaigns can be found in J.D. Howard-Johnston, "Heraclius' Persian campaigns and the revival of the East Roman Empire, 622–630", *War in History*, 6, 1, 1999, pp. 1–44.
13. See *Const. Porph., Three Treatises*, (B) 101–6; (C) 347–58.
14. See Oikonomidès, *Préséance*, p. 315; *Const. Porph., Three Treatises*, pp. 167 and 236; and on the various fiscal departments, see: *Const. Porph., Three Treatises*, pp. 168 and 236 with literature; and Oikonomidès, *Préséance*, pp. 313ff.
15. For the origins of the *protonotarioi*, see Haldon, *Byzantium in the Seventh Century*, chapter 5.
16. *De Cer.*, pp. 651–78.
17. The issue of where the state obtained iron ore remains unresolved. Localized extraction of ore from regions where it was found was certainly one source, and a number of late exemption documents excuse certain private (usually monastic)

landlords from paying their share of a levy in iron or iron products (such as nails or finished weapons). One tenth-century example refers to the extraction of iron ore from the ore-bearing sands along the southern coast of the Black Sea, in Bithynia. See Haldon, *Praetorians*, pp. 593–4, and cf. L.G. Westerink, *Nicétas magistros, Lettres d'un exilé (928–946)* (Paris, 1973), no. 5. 19ff.; and J.C. Edmondson, "Mining in the later Roman empire and beyond", *JRS*, 79, 1989, pp. 84–102; S. Vryonis, "The question of the Byzantine mines", *Speculum*, 37, 1962, pp. 1–17.

18. It is clear from the middle Byzantine evidence that the *dromos* was a major element in the state's operations. Originally under the authority of the Praetorian Prefects, by the 760s, and probably by the middle of the seventh century, it was an independent department under its logothete, a high-ranking officer for whom numerous seals survive (see V. Laurent, *Le Corpus des sceaux de l'empire byzantin*, II: *l'administration centrale* (Paris, 1981), pp. 195–243; Oikonomidès, *Préséance*, pp. 311–12; Hendy, *Studies*, p. 608 and n. 238). The operations of the *dromos* were closely associated with those of the *logothetes ton agelon* (logothete of the herds), the officer in charge of the imperial stud ranches, in particular the *metata* of Asia and Phrygia (Oikonomidès, *Préséance*, p. 338; Laurent, *Corpus*, II, pp. 289ff.). He was also associated with the supplying of horses and pack-animals to the army, although he can have provided only a small proportion of the total needed, and for the imperial household and stable service (see *Const. Porph., Three Treatises*, pp. 161 and 184. Animals belonging to the *metata* for the use of the military baggage train or the imperial cortège were strictly excluded from private use and were branded or given an identifying marker to make sure they were not purloined by individuals in this way. Cf. the late sixth-century bronze marker plaques for animals of the public post, bearing the inscription: 'Animal belonging to the sacred *armamenton*, by imperial decree not to be conscripted for *aggareia*' *(Année épigraphique*, 1992, no. 1825, 1945; and cf. D. Feissel, in *BCH*, 116, 1992, p. 397).

19. *De Cer.*, p. 659.7–12. For the Damietta expedition, see: Choniates, *Historia*, pp. 160–1, 164. For the *megas doux*, see: Magdalino, *The Empire of Manuel I*, pp. 234–5.

20. § 21.21–23 (trans. Dennis, p. 302f.); cf. *Const. Porph., Three Treatises*, (C) 347–52.

21. For example, Attaleiates, *Historia*, pp. 118.4–5, 151.9 (1071). Cf. Leo diac., *Historiae*, x, 8 (p. 171.19–21).

22. For the fifth century, see: Vegetius, *Epitome rei militaris*, iii, 3; for the tenth-century, see: *Const. Porph., Three Treatises*, (C) 557–9.

23. *Campaign Organisation*, § 21.36–42 (trans. Dennis, p. 302f.). For the effects on the local population, see Chapter 7 below.

24. *Campaign Organisation*, §§ 21, 32; *Skirmishing*, § 16.1 (trans. Dennis, p. 200).

25. See esp. P. De Jonge, "Scarcity of corn and corn prices in Ammianus", *Mnemosyne*, 4 ser., 1, 1948, pp. 238–245; see Jones, *LRE*, p. 629, on the effects of the presence of a large expeditionary force at Edessa in 503 and 504 (while an exception, the example is nevertheless useful in giving some idea of the problem the presence of a large army created), and 630 for the evidence for price-fixing. For Thrace, see *CJ*, X, 27.10 (a. 491–505). On compulsory purchase and fixed prices see Haldon, "Synone". For Maurice's order and the context, see Kaegi, *Byzantine Military Unrest*, pp. 106–13.

26. *Tactica*, ix, 1–3; xvii, 36.

27. For example, Maurice, *Strat.*, i, 9.

28. The wealthy and powerful were most likely to succeed in gaining exemption: cf. a letter of the general Nikephoros Ouranos to the *krites* of the *Thrakesion* theme appealing for exemption from *mitaton*, which he claimed was crippling his household (J. Darrouzès, *Epistoliers byzantins du Xe siècle* (Archives de l'Orient chrétien, 6) (Paris, 1960), no. 42.241–2); or the letter of the patriarch Nikolaos Mystikos on behalf of the widow of a *drouggarios* of the *Vigla*: Darrouzès, *Epistoliers*, no. 31.120–1. See especially *Nicholas I, Patriarch of Constantinople, Letters*, eds and trans. R.J.H. Jenkins and L.G. Westerink (*DOT*, II) (Washington, DC, 1973), nos. 92.10–26, 94.31–40 (extraordinary impositions for the Bulgarian war), 150, 183 (concerning the imposition of military burdens and renewed general imposition of extraordinary levies on church lands and clerics). For Choniates' remarks, see *Historia*, p. 209.

29. See *CTh.*, xi, xvi, 15.18 (laws of 382 and 390); and A. Harvey, *Economic Expansion in the Byzantine Empire 900–1200* (Cambridge, 1989), pp. 105–9 for the tenth- and eleventh-century Byzantine equivalents.

30. For the naval arsenal in Constantinople, see N. Oikonomidès, "*To kato armamenton*", *Archeion Pontou*, 26, 1964, pp. 193–6.

31. Psellos' letter describes the plight of a widow subject to the *epidosis monoprosopon*; see K. Sathas, *Mesaionike Bibliotheke*, 7 vols (Venice, 1872–94), V, p. 363. For the anonymous *Logos nouthetetikos*, see *Cecaumeni Strategicon*, eds Wassiliewsky and Jernstedt, pp. 103.33–104.2. In fact it is probable that Kekaumenos himself wrote the treatise.

32. In the later Roman period the experience of the provinces of Thrace illustrate the effects of a constant military presence, for since they could not afford to supply the troops through the usual system, a permanent *coemptio* or compulsory purchase had to be enforced. See *Codex Justinianus*, X, 27.2/10.

33. Although this increase may have set in some time before this date, when the first document to list such units which has survived was issued. See Oikonomidès, "L'évolution de l'organisation administrative de l'empire byzantin", p. 144.

34. See A. Harvey, "The land and taxation in the reign of Alexios I Komnenos: the evidence of Theophylact of Ochrid", *REB*, 51, 1993, p. 146.

35. See, for example, for Romanos IV, Attaleiates, *Historia*, pp. 117.1, 126.5, 134.13–14, 140.7–8; etc. For the basic shape of the administration of the state under the Komenoi, see Magdalino, *The Empire of Manuel I Komnenos*, pp. 228–30, and the older discussion in Chalandon, *Les Comnène*, pp. 620–1. For Constantine IX's recruitment and equipping of an army, see: Psellos, *Chronographia*, vi, 112 (trans. Sewter, p. 159). For the role of the *vestiarion* and the *eidikon*, see *Const. Porph., Three Treatises*, s.v., and Haldon, "Chapters II 44 and 45 of the *De Cerimoniis*".

36. See: Oikonomidès, *Préséance*, pp. 344ff., 354–63; "L'évolution de l'organisation administrative de l'empire byzantin", pp. 135–41, 148ff.; and P. Magdalino, "Justice and finance in the Byzantine state, ninth to twelfth centuries", in Angeliki E. Laiou and Dieter Simon (eds), *Law and Society in Byzantium: Ninth–Twelfth Centuries* (Washington, DC, 1994), pp. 93–115.

37. For the development of Byzantine strategy see Lilie, *Die byzantinische Reaktion*.

38. See *Const. Porph., Three Treatises*, (C) 618–16; for the sites and their locations, see commentary, pp. 254–5 with literature. For the inscription, probably originally located at Acrocorinth, see Ann Philippidis-Braat, "Inscriptions du IXe au XVe siècle", in D. Feissel and Ann Philippidis-Braat, "Inventaires en vue d'un recueil des inscriptions historiques de Byzance. III. Inscriptions du Péloponnèse

(à l'exception de Mistra), II", *Travaux et mémoires*, 9, 1985, no. 9, pp. 267–395, inscript. no. 41, pp. 299–300.

39. For an excellent survey of intelligence-gathering operations and methods, see N. Koutrakou, "Diplomacy and espionage: their role in Byzantine foreign relations, 8th–10th centuries", *Graeco-Arabica*, 6, 1995, pp. 125–44; and for a brief introduction to middle Byzantine campaign organization, see H. Ahrweiler, "L' organisation des campagnes militaires à Byzance", in V.J. Parry and M.E. Yapp (eds), *War, Technology and Society in the Middle East* (London, 1975), pp. 89–96.

40. See *Theoph.*, pp. 462, 473 (trans. Mango and Scott, pp. 636, 651). For the camps, see *Const. Porph., Three Treatises*, (A), and commentary, pp. 155–7; G. Huxley, "A list of *aplekta*", *Greek, Roman and Byzantine Studies*, 16, 1975, pp. 87–93. For the location of Malagina on the Sangarios, see C. Foss, "Byzantine Malagina and the lower Sangarios", *Anatolian Studies*, 40, 1990, pp. 161–83 (repr. in *Cities, Fortresses and Villages of Byzantine Asia Minor* (Aldershot, 1996) no. VII). Following S. Şahin (*Katalog der antiken Inschriften des Museums von Iznik (Nikaia)* II, 3 (Bonn, 1987), pp. 22f. and 150), Foss suggested that the base at Malagina was already established by the time of compilation of the so-called Apocalypse of Pseudo-Methodius, since it is mentioned there among the places at which an Arab force would winter in preparation for the attacks on Constantinople in the period 674–8 (A. Lolos (ed.), *Die Apokalypse des Ps.-Methodios* (Meisenheim a. Glan, 1976), xiii, 7). But this section of the text has been shown to be a much later interpolation (late eighth or early ninth century), so that this early date must be abandoned: see W.J. Aerts, "Zu einer neuen Ausgabe der 'Revelationes' des Pseudo-Methodius (syrisch-griechisch-lateinisch)", in W. Diem and A. Falaturi (eds), *XXIV. Deutscher Orientalistentag: ausgewählte Vorträge* (Stuttgart, 1990), pp. 123–30, esp. 129–30.

41. *Const. Porph., Three Treatises*, (A).

42. See Haldon, in *Const. Porph., Three Treatises*, pp. 155–7; and for the parade and assemby ground outside the land walls, see *Const. Porph., Three Treatises*, (C) 742–5, 827–31 and commentary. For the other reviewing and parade grounds, see T. Louggis, "The review of armed forces before campaign", in N. Oikonomidès (ed.), *Byzantium at War, 9th–12th Centuries* (Athens, 1997), pp. 93–110 (in Greek); for those of the Comnene emperors, see: Choniates, *Historia*, pp. 20, 33–4, 37, 280; Kinnamos, *Epitome*, pp. 38, 66, 294, 297, 299 (Lopadion); Choniates, *Historia*, 89, 101, 104; Kinnamos, *Epitome*, p. 127 (Pelagonia); Choniates, *Historia*, 280, 450, 487, 496, 499; Kinnamos, *Epitome*, p. 191 (Kypsella).

43. *Const. Porph., Three Treatises*, (B) 148–50.

44. Details in *Const. Porph., Three Treatises*, (C) 420ff.; *Campaign Organisation*, §§ 1–5.

45. Discussed in detail, with references, by McGeer, *Sowing the Dragon's Teeth*, pp. 349–52. See *Strategy*, § 28; Maurice, *Strat.*, xii B, 22; Leo, *Tact.*, xi, esp. 16–17, 29. For a sightly different layout, see: Niceph., *Praecepta*, v; *Campaign Organisation*, § 1.

46. See below, and also Chapter 6 below.

47. See, for example, Leo diac., *Historiae*, i, 3, 9; iii, 10; iv, 3; iv, 10; iv, 11; ix, 1; x, 8, 9; Attaleiates, *Historia*, pp. 109.5–7, 117.11ff., 118.13ff., 119.12f., 120.9–10, 151.8–10. For discussion and sources see McGeer, *Sowing the Dragon's Teeth*, pp. 347–57. For Theophylact, see *Historia*, vi, 6.5 (the distance from Heraclea in Thrace to Drizipera was 4 camps; that from Drizipera to Dorostolon on the Danube

was 20 camps). The tenth-century treatise on *Skirmishing* likewise speaks of marches in terms of a day or the distance between two camps: see, for example, § 22.15; § 23.2. For rates of march see below.

48. Attaleiates, *Historia*, pp. 111–13; cf. 117.22–118.13; Scylitzes, *Synopsis historiarum*, pp. 470.69–70, 470.87–471.7, 467.11–12, 469.48–50. For Anna's remark, see *Alexiad*, i, 4. Attaleiates (*Historia*, p. 126.4) also refers to a clearly atypical occasion when the emperor Romanos IV did not entrench his camp. For John II, see Choniates, *Historia*, pp. 20, 22; for Manuel, see Choniates, *Historia*, pp. 176, 178–9, 181–2, 187 (and cf. p. 195); see also Kinnamos, *Epitome*, p. 56.

49. For example, the Turkish army in 1138 (Choniates, *Historia*, p. 21). The German forces did not entrench their camp in 1147 because they were on Roman territory: Choniates, *Historia*, p. 64. For Psellos on the Pechenegs, see *Chronographia*, vii, 68 (trans. Sewter, p. 242).

50. See Chapter 6 and McGeer, *Sowing the Dragon's Teeth*, pp. 358–9, who cites several examples such as that reported by the chronicler Michael Attaleiates, 32.6–33.10 about the inexperienced commander of an expedition under Constantine IX against the Pechenegs in 1049, who failed to encamp or rest his troops with disastrous results. For Kantakouzenos (in 1186), see Choniates, *Historia*, p. 375; for the base camp, see Choniates, *Historia*, p. 195.

51. On these state impositions, see: *ODB*, pp. 131, 1385; Haldon, *Byzantine Praetorians*, pp. 599–601, n. 993; and Hendy, *Studies*, pp. 610–11. For the hagiography, see Haldon, *Byzantine Praetorians*, p. 327 and n. 1006.

52. *Const. Porph., Three Treatises*, (B) 107–15, 134ff.; (C) 474ff.; *Campaign Organisation*, § 10.

53. *Const. Porph., Three Treatises*, (B) 128–33; (C) 512–23, 561ff.; *Skirmishing*, § 16.1–13; *Campaign Organisation*, §§ 15, 17. See now the discussion of McGeer, *Sowing the Dragon's Teeth*, pp. 330–47. For materials to be taken, see: *Const. Porph., Three Treatises*, (B) 40–2; Leo, *Tact.*, iv, 55, 56; vi, 21, 27; ix, 37; x; cf. *Skirmishing*, i, 14; ii, 1. For Subordinate officers not to take tents, see *Campaign Organisation*, § 17. For siege materials and artillery, see: Leo, *Tact.*, iv, 56; v, 7; 27; vi, 21; 27; Maurice, *Strat.*, xii B, 6.8–9; 21.13; Niceph., *Praecepta*, i, 15; and the discussion in this chapter, below.

54. For order of march, see esp. *Campaign Organisation*, §§ 9–14. On the advance scouts, route-finders and camp surveyors, see: Leo, *Tact.*, ix; xii, 56; *Campaign Organisation*, *passim*; *Const. Porph., Three Treatises*, (B), and (C) 440ff. Leo's advice is taken largely from the *Strategikon* of Maurice, but is corroborated by the later, more independent treatises. For the *mensouratores*, see *Campaign Organisation*, i, 45–50 (trans. Dennis, p. 249), and McGeer, *Sowing the Dragon's Teeth*, p. 348. The *mensores* of the Roman army of the Principate were chosen on the basis of one man from each tent group – *contubernium* – and ten from each cohort.

55. Choniates, *Historia*, pp. 180–2. See the clear account in Hendy, *Studies*, pp. 146–54, esp. 149–51.

56. Vegetius, *Epitome rei militaris*, iii, 6; Maurice, *Strat.*, i, 9; ix, 3–5; v, 5; vii B, 9.

57. See McGeer, *Sowing the Dragon's Teeth*, pp. 257ff. For the order of march in 1176, see Choniates, *Historia*, p. 180; and for Alexios' order of march, see Anna Comnena, *Alexiad*, xv, 6, 7 (trans. Sewter, pp. 480–7, 491).

58. See: *Const. Porph., Three Treatises*, (B) 107–50; (C) 479–96, 561–9 (information taken from the campaigns of Basil I and Leo VI); and esp. (C) 420–42, 540–3 on

camp security; *Campaign Organisation*, §§ 10, 12–15; Niceph. Ouranos, *Tactica*, §§ 63–4; and the discussion in McGeer, *Sowing the Dragon's Teeth*, pp. 332–41. For Alexios' use of fifes, see Anna Comnena, *Alexiad*, xv, 7 (trans. Sewter, p. 491).

59. Smail, *Crusading Warfare*, pp. 156–62, and esp. 198–9, and pp. 168–74 on Bohemund's tactical skills and intelligence. On Byzantine advice to the Crusaders, see Anna Comnena, Alexiad, x, 10, 11 (trans. Sewter, pp. 326, 329–30). For the Muslim comment (from al-Mankali), see McGeer, *Sowing the Dragon's Teeth*, pp. 278–9.

60. See Haldon, *Byzantine Praetorians*, pp. 223–6; *Const. Porph., Three Treatises*, (C) 312–70.

61. *Const. Porph., Three Treatises*, (C) 512–23.

62. For pack-animals, see, for example, Niceph., *Praecepta*, i, 14 and ii, 1. On wagons, see Choniates, *Historia*, p. 179, for the campaign force of 1176, which moved very slowly due to the siege train and baggage which was taken along.

63. *Tact.*, vi, 29.

64. McGeer, *Sowing the Dragon's Teeth*, pp. 211–12, 300–2, 331–2.

65. See Ibn Khurradādhbīh, 83, 85; and *Const. Porph., Three Treatises*, (C) 347–52.

66. It is worth noting for comparative purposes that the marching camps of the general Agricola during his campaign in eastern Scotland in AD 83–4 were established at distances of between 10 and 13 miles apart: D.J. Breeze, "The logistics of Agricola's final campaign", *Talanta*, 16–19, 1987–8, pp. 7–22. For further remarks on rates of movement in general, see I. Ch. Dimitroukas, *Reisen und Verkehr im byzantinischen Reich vom Anfang des 6. bis zur Mitte des 11. Jhs.* (Athens, 1997), pp. 299–305.

67. See the discussion in McGeer, *Sowing the Dragon's Teeth*, pp. 340–1; and *Skirmishing*, xiii, 2 (Dagron and Mihaescu, *Le Traité sur la Guérilla*, p. 79; trans. Dennis, p. 189).

68. See *Th. cont.*, p. 280, and this chapter, below. The road is discussed in F. Hild, *Das byzantinische Straßensystem in Kappadokien (TIB, 2)* (Vienna, 1977), pp. 134–5 and map 14.

69. For similar exercises, see esp. F. Maurice, "The size of the army of Xerxes in the invasion of Greece, 480 B.C.", *Journal of Hellenic Studies*, 50, 1930, pp. 210–35; and D. Engels, *Alexander the Great and the Logistics of the Macedonian Army* (Berkeley, CA, 1978), pp. 154–5, 131–3. I have on the whole erred on the conservative side in estimating both the space occupied by a row of men or horses and the time-lapse between rows setting out.

70. On these issues in general, see M. Van Crefeld, *Supplying War: Logistics from Wallerstein to Patton* (Cambridge, 1977), p. 29, and Engels, *Alexander the Great and the Logistics of the Macedonian Army*, pp. 154–6, for detailed figures and averages derived from the marches of Alexander's army across Greece, Anatolia, Iran and into northern India. For the Roman rate, see Vegetius, *Epitome de rei militari*, i, 9. See G. Watson, *The Roman Soldier* (London, 1969), pp. 54–5, and Elton, *Warfare in Roman Europe*, pp. 244–5 for further discussion and evidence. For Procopius' figure, see *Wars*, IV, xiii, 32–3. For more recent examples, e.g. the campaigns of Frederick II of Prussia in 1757–8, see Van Creveld, *Supplying War*, pp. 28–9. Compare the rates of movement for individuals and large armies mentioned in Chapter 2 above (see note 39). The distance covered depended on the terrain as well as the need to move rapidly or not. Thus the general Priscus

took four days to cover the 33 miles (50 km) between Heraclea in Thrace and Drizipera (nr. mod. Büyük Karıştıran, southeast of Adrianople), at an average rate of 8.25 miles (12.5 km) per day, yet covered the much more difficult route from Drizipera up to Dorostolon (Silistra) on the Danube, some 280 miles (425 km) by the most direct routes, in 20 days, an average marching speed of 14 miles (21.2 km) per day, very fast indeed, perhaps reflecting the fact that his army was mostly mounted. See *Th. Sim. Historia*, vi, 6.5. In the thirteenth century, Akropolites records marches of 66 miles (100 km) in four 'stations' or days, an average of 16.5 miles (25 km) per day, and refers also to the "usual" daily march: see *Georgii Acropolitae Opera*, I, ed. A. Heisenberg (Leipzig, 1903), p. 120; and cf. pp. 119 and 126. Note that the daily rate of travel for a single mounted traveller was considerably greater, the standard daily rate being reckoned at some 31 miles (47 km): see E. Schilbach, *Byzantinische Metrologie* (Handbuch d. Altertumswiss, xii, 4 = Byzantinisches Handbuch, IV) (Munich, 1970), pp. 33–4, 36.

71. For Basil II, see J.H. Forsyth, *The Byzantine–Arab Chronicle (938–1034) of Yahya b. Said al-Antaki* (Diss. Univ. Michigan, 1977), pp. 492ff. In fact, the Arabic sources differ widely on the size of Basil's original force. Nevertheless, the rate of attrition attributed to the column is at least indicative. For the night-march, see Kinnamos, *Epitome*, 195–6; and for Manuel's march to Claudioupolis, see Choniates, *Historia*, pp. 197–8.

72. See Choniates, *Historia*, pp. 178–9; R.-J. Lilie, "Die Schlacht von Myriokephalon (1176)", *Revue des Etudes Byzantines*, 35, 1977, pp. 257–75. For detailed discussion of the routes taken by the forces of the First Crusade, see J. France, *Victory in the East. A Military History of the First Crusade* (Cambridge, 1994), pp. 185–92.

73. For Roman rates, see Vegetius, *Epitome de rei militari*, i, 19; Ammianus Marcellinus, *Works*, xvi, 2.8; xvii, 9.2; and Elton, *Warfare in Roman Europe*, pp. 115–16; see Watson, *The Roman Soldier*, pp. 62–6, for figures and evidence. Cf. also Dixon and Southern, *The Roman Cavalry*, pp. 91–3. For the sixth century, see Procopius, *Wars*, III, xiii.15; Maurice, *Strat.*, i, 2.4, 9.2; v, 4.

74. I will take the figure of 1.3 kg as the average ration for a soldier for the purpose of the calculations in Appendix 3. For the tenth-century text, see *Skirmishing*, § 8.2.

75. See K.D. White, *Roman Farming* (London, 1970), and for Byzantium from the seventh century, see J.L. Teall, "The grain supply of the Byzantine empire", *DOP*, 13, 1959, pp. 87–139, at pp. 117–32. On nutritional values, see P.J. Reynolds, *Iron-Age Farm: The Butser Experiment* (London, 1979). On the size and value of Roman military rations, see L. Foxhall and H.A. Forbes, "Sitometreia: the role of grain as a staple food in classical Antiquity", *Chiron*, 12, 1982, pp 41–90; C.E.P. Adams, "Supplying the Roman army: *O. Petr.* 245", *Zeitschrift für Papyrologie und Epigraphik*, 109, 1995, pp. 119–24. For comparative statistics, see: Van Creveld, *Supplying War*, pp. 24, 34; V. Aksan, "Feeding the Ottoman troops on the Danube, 1768–1774", *War and Society*, 13, 1, 1995, pp. 1–14; Engels, *Alexander the Great and the Logistics of the Macedonian Army*, pp. 123–6. From the seventh century, a species of hard wheat appears to have been introduced and spread throughout the eastern provinces of the empire (see esp. A.M. Watson, *Agricultural Innovation in the Early Islamic World* (Cambridge, 1983), p. 20), and this brought certain advantages. Hard wheats have a protein content of some 11–15 per cent compared with the 8–10 per cent of soft wheats, and

produce a flour better suited to bread-making. Note that the figures given by Engels, *Alexander the Great and the Logistics of the Macedonian Army*, pp. 126–7, in fact overestimate the weight of grain required, since he ignores the considerable differences between the nutritional values of the ancient grains which would have been used, and modern grains upon which his calculations were based.

76. See Niceph., *Praecepta*, ii, 1.
77. Ibn Khurradādhbīh, 83, 85.
78. Engels, *Alexander the Great and the Logistics of the Macedonian Army*, p. 112f.
79. For the late Roman period, see R.W. Davies, "The Roman military diet", *Britannia*, 2, 1971, pp. 122–42; and Jones, *LRE*, p. 628f. For the Byzantine military diet, see T. Kolias, "Eßgewohnheiten und Verpflegung im byzantinischen Heer", in W. Hörandner, J. Koder, O. Kresten and E. Trapp (eds), *Byzantios. Festschrift für Herbert Hunger zum 70. Geburtstag* (Vienna, 1984), pp. 193–202, at 197–9.
80. *Sylloge tacticorum*, § 57.2.
81. See: *Sylloge tacticorum*, § 38.12 (and Maurice, *Strat.*, xii B, 6.5; Leo, *Tact.*, vi, 27; v, 6); and Davies, "Roman military diet", p. 126 and n. 31. As Davies notes, handmills can be operated with considerable efficiency: experiments with handmills from the Roman fort at Saalburg demonstrated that 4–6 men could mill up to 220 pounds of grain into flour in one hour: cf. *Saalburg-Jahrbücher*, 3, 1912, pp. 75–95.
82. See Teall, "The grain supply of the Byzantine empire", pp. 91–2, 99–100.
83. Davies, "Roman military diet", pp. 126ff., and Kolias, "Eßgewohnheiten", pp. 199–200.
84. See *Campaign Organisation*, § 21.22–23 (trans. Dennis, p. 302f.).
85. The calculation is based on figures discussed in the appendices. The equation in this case includes the following elements:
  (a) To find out how much the remounts carry and how long this will supply the army: (9,200 horses × 2.2 [total requirement per day] = 20,240 kg) ÷ (1,000 horses × 68 [total carried by spare horses] = 68,000 kg) = 3.35 days' worth of provisions carried on remounts.
  (b) To find how many pack-animals are required to extend the march, multiply the total number of animals to be fed by the amount of their daily requirement (i.e. 9,200 × [2.2 kg × 18] = 364,320), multiplied in turn by the number of days of the march, and divide the result by the weight of a pack-animal's load minus its own fodder requirement multiplied by the number of days involved (96 − [2.2 × 18] = 56.4: thus we have 364,320 ÷ 56.4 = 6459.57, i.e. 6,460 animals.
86. See Ann Hyland, *Equus. The Horse in the Roman World*, p. 90; followed by Dixon and Southern, *The Roman Cavalry*, pp. 208–17, esp. 210–11. Hyland underestimates the amount of barley required, however: see Haldon, "The organisation and support of an expeditionary force", pp. 126–7 with note 57.
87. The modern equivalent of 12 horses per acre reflects different priorities for animals bred under modern conditions. See I.P. Roberts, *The Horse* (New York, 1905), pp. 360ff. For water requirements, see: Hyland, *Equus*, p. 96; Engels, *Alexander the Great and the Logistics of the Macedonian Army*, p. 127. See also Gladitz, *Horse Breeding in the Medieval World*, pp. 127–8 and further literature.
88. *Const. Porph., Three Treatises*, (C) 411–14. Similar figures can be derived for the medieval West: see B.S. Bachrach, "Animals and warfare in early medieval Europe", in *L'Uomo di fronte al mondo animale nell'alto Medioevo* (Settimane di

Studio del Centro Italiano di Studi sull'alto Medioevo 31) (Spoleto, 1983, 1985), pp. 707–51 – see pp. 716–20. These are lighter than standard loads in more recent times: see W.B. Tegetmeir, *Horses, Asses, Mules and Mule Breeding* (Washington, DC, 1897), p. 129.

89. *Const. Porph., Three Treatises*, (C) 549–53. I have converted the weights from the original measure, in *modioi*, although scholars disagree over some of the equivalences. The weight 114–20 kg represents the approximate maximum a standard horse or mule (I exclude special breeds and modern strains) can carry over any distance – in Roman/Byzantine measures, 282 Roman pounds. On breeds of horse, see A. Hyland, *The Medieval Warhorse: From Byzantium to the Crusades*, 2nd edn (Stroud, 1996). On the carrying capacity of horses, ponies and mules, see W.C. Schneider, "Animal laborans. Das Arbeitstier und sein Einsatz im Transport und Verkehr der Spätantike und des frühen Mittelalters", in *L'Uomo di fronte al mondo animale nell'alto Medioevo*, pp. 457–578, at 493–554. On the weight of pack-saddles, see *CTh.*, viii, 5.47 and *CJ*, xii, 50.12; and for concern over loads, see *CTh.* viii, 5.8, 17, 28, 30, for example. For further comment on mules, horses, donkeys and camels, see Dimitroukas, *Reisen und Verkehr*, pp. 317–24.

90. On all these details, see *Const. Porph., Three Treatises*, text (C); McGeer, *Sowing the Dragon's teeth*, pp. 349–358. For the pasturage, see Abū'l-Faraj al-Kātib al-Bagdādī Kudāma ibn Jaʿfar, *Kitāb al-Harāj*, in *Bibliotheca Geographorum Araborum*, ed. M.-J. De Goeje (Leiden, 1870/1938), VI, pp. 199–200.

91. For the late Roman arrangements, see the discussion in W.E. Kaegi, "Variable rates of change in the seventh century", in F.M. Clover and R.S. Humphreys (eds), *Tradition and Innovation in Late Antiquity* (Madison, WI, 1989), pp. 191–208; and "The *annona militaris* in the early seventh century", *Byzantina*, 13, 1985, pp. 591–6. For the *protonotarioi* and their stores, see *Const. Porph., Three Treatises*, (B) 101–6; (C) 145–7, 345–52, 395–7.

92. *Const. Porph., Three Treatises*, (C) 392–4, and commentary (p. 238f.).

93. See the discussion and figures presented in Engels, *Alexander the Great and the Logistics of the Macedonian Army*, pp. 18–22. The arrangements made by the Ottoman government for the provisioning of its armies, while involving much greater numbers and a wider resource-base in respect of the sources of state revenue, were nevertheless very similar to the traditional Byzantine practices described here. The nature of the logistical problem, especially in terms of the expenses of transporting grain for the army and its animals, are graphically described in Rhoads Murphey, *Ottoman Warfare, 1500–1700* (London, 1999), pp. 65–103.

94. Maurice, *Strat.*, I, 9.12–17 (= Leo, *Tact.*, ix, 6–7, slightly emended and expanded).

95. Procopius, *Wars*, I, viii, 4–5.

96. See Attaleiates, *Historia*, pp. 107.23–108.1, 126.14–15; and for the damage to the region of Krya Pege (Bathys Ryax), northwest of Sebasteia, see Attaleiates, *Historia*, p. 146.18–22. For the ruinous consequences of the army's presence in Thrace in 812/13, see *Theoph.*, 500 (trans. Mango and Scott, p. 684).

97. Leo, *Tact.*, xiii, 16; xvi, 36; *Campaign organisation*, § 21.22–3 (trans. Dennis, p. 302f.); Kudāma ibn Jaʿfar, *Kitāb al-Harāj*, p. 199.

98. See, for example, *Strategy*, § 26; Maurice, *Strat.*, v, 3; vii, A 9; *Skirmishing*, § 5.1; *Campaign Organisation*, § 10.46–7; § 13; Nikeph. Ouranos, *Tactica*, § 63.9. For the failure of the guides in 594, see *Th. Sim.*, vii, 5.5–7.

99. For Romanos IV, see Attaleiates, *Historia*, p. 136.5–8, and the examples discussed by McGeer, *Sowing the Dragon's Teeth*, pp. 357–8. For Basil I, see *Th. cont.*, pp. 267, 269–70; for Tyana in 708/9, see *Theoph.*, p. 377 (trans. Mango and Scott, p. 525f.). See, for example, Leo, *Tact.*, xvii, 36 for warnings about taking supplies in case the enemy has destroyed them in the localities through which the army passes. Such warnings are repeated in most of the treatises.

100. For John Tzimiskes, see Leo diac., *Historiae*, x, 2; for the campaign of 1130, see Kinnamos, *Epitome*, pp. 12–13; for Damietta in 1169, see Choniates, *Historia*, p. 164; for the Ikonion (Myriokephalon) campaign see Choniates, *Historia*, pp. 178–9; and for warnings about polluted water and grain, see Maurice, *Strat.*, ix, 3.122–7 (with an example from the Persian wars). See *Theoph.*, p. 452 (trans. Mango and Scott, p. 624) for the invasion of 778/9 (and cf. Maurice, *Strat.*, vii, proem. 27–9 (trans. Dennis, p. 64f.)); for Masalmas' army, see *Theoph.*, p. 390 (trans. Mango and Scott, p. 540). For the sources and further discussion of the Arab expedition of 782, see: E.W. Brooks, "Byzantine and Arabs in the time of the early Abbasids, 1", *EHR*, 15, 1900, pp. 737–9; L.A. Tritle, "Tatzates' flight and the Byzantine–Arab peace treaty of 782", *Byzantion*, 47, 1977, pp. 279–300.

101. For the defeat of the Paulicians in 873, see Genesius, 272; for the campaign of 707/8, see *Theoph.*, p. 376 (trans. Mango and Scott, p. 525). For Basil II's expedition in 986, see Leo diac., *Historiae*, x, 8. For advice on the dangers of foraging, see: Maurice, *Strat.*, vii, B 10; viii, 2.75; ix, 3.50–61; Leo, *Tact.*, xiv, 16; *Campaign Organisation*, § 10.38–42; §§ 22–4; and for Manuel's strategy in 1175, see Choniates, *Historia*, pp. 176–7.

102. For example, *Strategy*, § 35.33–5; *Skirmishing*, § 6.4–5; § 9.9, 11, 13; § 16.5–7.

103. On purchasing supplies locally, see, for example, *Campaign Organisation*, § 10.38–42. For the effects on the local population, see above, and Chapter 7 below; see also Maurice, *Strat.*, i, 9.47–54; Leo, *Tact.*, ix, 1–3; xvii, 36.

104. *Theoph.*, 308, 309, 312 (trans. Mango and Scott, pp. 440, 441, 444).

105. *Theoph.*, 311–12 (trans. Mango and Scott, p. 443).

106. *Theoph.*, 317–19 (trans. Mango and Scott, p. 448f.).

107. For example, See *Theoph.*, 314 (Mango and Scott, p. 445), where Heraclius marches back over the Halys to the region of Sebasteia (although Theophanes' chronology is out of order at this point in his narrative: see Mango and Scott, p. 446, n. 10). Cf. *Chronicon Paschale*, pp. 731–2 (trans. Whitby, p. 186), where in his own despatches the emperor describes how his army had moved down from the Zagros mountains to winter at Ganzak, and thus escaped the severe conditions which would otherwise have harmed it.

108. *Strat.*, viii, A 30.

109. *Th. cont.*, 278; *Const. Porph., Three Treatises*, (C) 512–17.

110. *Campaign Organisation*, § 21.33–5 (trans. Dennis, p. 305).

111. See *Th. cont.*, pp. 272–6; Genesius, *Regna*, pp. 121–6 (for the year 873); *Th. cont.*, pp. 179–83; Genesius, *Regna*, pp. 94–7 (for the year 863); Skylitzes, *Synopsis historiarum*, p. 139.

112. *Skirmishing*, § 9.41–56 (trans. Dennis, p. 171); § 16 (p. 201f.).

113. For the events of 772/3, see *Theoph.*, p. 447 (trans. Mango and Scott, p. 617); for those of 778, see *Theoph.*, p. 451 (trans. Mango and Scott, p. 623); for those of 781/2, see *Theoph.*, p. 456 (trans. Mango and Scott, p. 629). See also Brooks, "Byzantines and Arabs in the time of the early Abbasids, 1", pp. 737–9, and Tritle, "Tatzates' flight and the Byzantine–Arab peace treaty of 782", pp. 279–300.

For the events of 770/1, see *Theoph.*, p. 445 (trans. Mango and Scott, p. 615); for those of 787/8, see *Theoph.*, p. 463 (trans. Mango and Scott, p. 637); for those of 878, see: *Th. cont.*, pp. 284–5; Genesius, *Regna*, pp. 114–15.

114. See Chapters 2 and 3 above.
115. *Tact.*, xviii, 127, 134, 143ff., for example.
116. See the commentaries of Dagron and Mihaescu, *Le traité sur la Guérilla*, pp. 215ff., and McGeer, *Sowing the Dragon's Teeth*, pp. 332–8; cf. *Campaign Organisation*, §§ 10, 12–15, and in general *Const. Porph., Three Treatises*.
117. See J.F. Haldon and H. Kennedy, "The Arab–Byzantine frontier in the eighth and ninth centuries", esp. pp. 105ff.
118. See: Dagron and Mihaescu, *Le traité sur la Guérilla*, pp. 248–50; McGeer, *Sowing the Dragon's Teeth*, p. 331.
119. The treatise consists of 25 chapters in all dealing with every aspect of this strategy and the tactics accompanying it. For detailed analysis and discussion, see Dagron and Mihaescu, *Le traité sur la Guérilla*, pp. 161–71, 177–93.
120. *Skirmishing*, §§ 4, 6.
121. § 7.
122. §§ 3–5, 8–11. Needless to say, the Romans were not always able to respond successfully to such attacks, and there are many examples where Roman preparations failed to produce the desired results, or where the Muslim commanders were able to outwit and out-general the Roman commanders. See J. Howard-Johnston, "Byzantine Anzitene", in Mitchell (ed.), *Armies and Frontiers in Roman and Byzantine Anatolia*, pp. 239–90, esp. 241–5, a brief analysis of a successful raid into Anzitene in eastern Asia Minor mounted by the emir Sayf ad-Daula in 956.
123. See § 12 for surpise attacks, and § 3, with n. 2 on p. 157, for Ali's defeats. For analysis of the "guerrilla" strategy described in detail in the treatise, see Dagron and Mihaescu, *Le traité sur la Guérilla*, pp. 195–237.
124. See *Skirmishing*, §§ 2.3, 7.1. *Trapezites* derives from a Persarmenian word, *darpaspan*; the Greek version of the term, meaning "banker", may be a play on words: banker – rogue/trickster – robber/bandit. *Tasinarios* is a transliterated Armenian term meaning one of a group of ten. *Chosarios* derives from a Bulgar term for robber, and evolves into the later *Hussar*. See Dagron and Mihaescu, *Le traité sur la Guérilla*, pp. 252–7, with sources and further literature.
125. See McGeer, *Sowing the Dragon's Teeth*, pp. 212, 300; and *Campaign Organisation*, § 18.
126. See especially the vivid account, with sources and further literature, in Vryonis, *The Decline of Medieval Hellenism in Asia Minor*. For the twelfth century, see Choniates, *Historia*, pp. 124–5, 194–5.
127. Thus John I arranged for large quantities of grain and feed for the horses to be brought to Adrianople at the end of 971, preparatory to his campaign against the Rus' in the following year: Leo diac., *Historiae*, pp. 126–7.
128. See, for example, *Const. Porph., Three Treatises*, (A); and cf. Leo diac., *Historiae*, p. 36 (where Nikephros Phocas sets up his HQ in Cappadocia and summons thence all the troops, who arrive over several days in successive bodies, to be trained and exercised in weaponry and tactical manoeuvres), and pp. 53–4 (for 964, where the troops are stood down for the winter and ordered to report again for the spring campaigning season in the next year with full equipment). Much the same procedure is implied for Basil I before his campaign against Melitene in 873 (*Th. cont.*, p. 278).

129. For the siege of Amida, see W. Wright, *The Chronicle of Joshua the Stylite* (Cambridge, 1882/Amsterdam, 1968), § LVI (p. 45); for Nikephros Phocas, see Leo diac., *Historiae*, ii, 6 (p. 24).

130. See *Theoph.*, p. 376 (trans. Mango and Scott, p. 525), 432–3 (trans. Mango and Scott, p. 599), 436 (trans. Mango and Scott, p. 603), 437 (trans. Mango and Scott, p. 605), 446–7 (trans. Mango and Scott, pp. 616–17), 447–8 (trans. Mango and Scott, pp. 618–19) (cf. Niceph., *Short history*, § 36; § 73; § 76; § 82); Leo. diac., *Historiae*, 129.

131. See, for example, Maurice, *Strat.*, v, 1–3; *Campaign Organisation*, § 15; § 17.

132. See the advice in *Campaign Organisation*, § 21.18–42; for the personnel accompanying a wagon train, see Maurice, *Strat.*, xii, B. 6, 7 (= Leo, *Tact.*, vi, 27–8). A good example of an advance force is given in *Th. cont.*, p. 278, on Basil I's campaign of 878.

133. *Campaign Organisation*, § 10.46–63. For Myriokephalon, see above. In most examples where a Byzantine force was caught in a pass or defile, either on its way to attack an enemy or on the march home, the baggage and supply trains were lost, as with Basil II's withdrawal from Bulgaria in 986: see Leo diac., *Historiae*, x, 8.21–4.

134. *Skirmishing*, § 10.7–9.

135. *Const. Porph., Three Treatises*, (B) 1–17, 39–42; (C) 116–20; *Campaign Organisation*, § 18; Nikeph. Ouranos, *Tactica*, § 63.1. For the sixth century, see *Strategy*, §§ 19, 26, 27.

136. See, for example, *Campaign Organisation*, § 19.

137. *Campaign Organisation*, §§ 1, 6, 7, 30.

138. Nikeph. Ouranos, *Tactica*, § 63.4–6; *Campaign Organisation*, § 21.43–65.

139. *Th. cont.*, p. 267.5–10, 278ff.

140. For example, from the sixth century, see: *Strategy*, §§ 9.37–9, 10; Maurice, *Strat.*, x, 1.8–10; from the tenth century, see: *Campaign Organisation*, § 21.3–17; Nikeph. Ouranos, *Tactica*, § 65.1, 3, 7–10. The tenth-century *De obsidione toleranda* is devoted to resisting sieges and presents many of the same basic strategems from the point of view of those who have to predict and resist them. But the emphasis on supplying the besieged force and civilian population and on making sure that there is a suitable water supply is still strong: see *Anonymus De obsidione toleranda*, ed. H. Van Den Berg (Leyden, 1947), pp. 45–57. For further discussion, see also E. McGeer, "Byzantine siege warfare in theory and practice", in Ivy A. Corfis and Michael Wolfe (eds), *The Medieval City under Siege* (Woodbridge, 1995), pp. 123–9.

141. For lists, see: Leo, *Tact.*, xv, 29–34; Nikeph. Ouranos, *Tactica*, § 65.22; *Campaign Organisation*, § 27.6–9. For ancient writings, see: Leo, *Tact.*, 28; *Campaign Organisation*, § 27.9–11; Nikeph. Ouranos, *Tactica*, § 65.25.

142. Most of Leo, *Tact.*, xv, on siege warfare, is copied from Maurice, *Strat.*, x, but confirmation of the essential continuity of practice is found in the later tenth-century manuals, especially the *Tactica* of Nikephros Ouranos, and in the eleventh-century anecdotes about similar matters recounted in the *Strategikon* of Kekaumenos: see, for example, §§ 73–85 (eds Wassiliewsky and Jernstedt).

143. Leo diac., *Historiae*, iv, 58–60.

144. Kekaumenos, *Strat.*, § 80.

145. See P. Leriche, "Techniques de guerre sassanides et romaines à Doura-Europos", in F. Vallet and M. Kazanski (eds), *L'Armée romaine et les barbares du IIIe au VIIe*

siècle (Mémoires de l'Association Française d'Archéologie Mérovingienne, 5) (Paris, 1993), pp. 83–100, at 84–5, with Figs 3 and 5; and for Dara, see Procopius, *Works*, II, xiii.20–8.

146. Nikeph. Ouranos, *Tactica*, § 65.25 (with details of the method in sections 20–4).
147. For the siege of Adrianople see: *Th. cont.*, pp. 68–9; Scylitzes, *Synopsis historiarum*, p. 39; for Basil's sieges, see *Th. cont.*, pp. 267, 269–70.
148. For 883, see *Th. cont.*, pp. 287–8 (the early tenth-century Arab historian Tabari's version of events is more detailed and shows up the commanding officer's carelessness and incompetence: it is translated in Vasiliev, *Byzance et les arabes*, II, 2, p. 9); for 828, see *Th. cont.*, pp. 79–80, and the accounts repeated in McGeer, *Sowing the Dragon's Teeth*, p. 358.
149. See Leriche, "Techniques de guerre sassanides et romaines", p. 85 and Figs 5 and 6. Such ramps were called *agestai* in Greek (cf. Procopius, *Wars*, II, xxvi.29; Maurice, *Strat.*, x, 1.55), from the Latin *ag(g)er/aggestus* (cf. Vegetius, *Epitome*, iv, 15 (trans. Milner, p. 121, with references to Ammianus)).
150. See: Procopius, *Wars*, I, vii.14–15; Wright, *The Chronicle of Joshua the Stylite*, § L (p. 39); § LIII (pp. 53–4).
151. See: Vegetius, *Epitome rei militaris*, iv, 15; Procopius, *Wars*, I, vii.14–16; II, xxvi.23–5; Kekaumenos, *Strat.*, § 81 (Basil at Moreia); § 82 (Symeon). Kekaumenos repeats the story in Proc., *Wars*, II, xxvi, in § 83.
152. See: Vegetius, *Epitome*, iv, 14–23, and cf. Procopius, *Wars*, V, xxi.6–13; *Strategy*, §§ 13, 16–17, 61–135; *Campaign Organisation*, § 27.5–7; Kekaumenos, *Strat.*, § 79. For the *laisas* or *lesas*, see the discussion, with sources, in E. McGeer, "Tradition and reality in the *Tactica* of Nikephros Ouranos", *DOP*, 45, 1991, pp. 130–40, at 135–8. For the rams for tortoises, see the list for the 949 Cretan expedition in *De Cer.*, p. 671.4–5.
153. See D. Sullivan, "Tenth-century Byzantine offensive siege warfare: instructional prescriptions and historical practice", in Oikonomidès (ed.), *Byzantium at War*, pp. 179–200 – see p. 181f.
154. See Leo, *Tact.*, v, 7 and cf. Maurice, *Strat.*, xii B, 6.8–9.
155. For the disaffected engineer, see *Theoph.*, pp. 485, 498 (trans. Mango and Scott, pp. 665, 682); for Michael II's siege of Thomas, see *Th. cont.*, p. 68.13–17.
156. Three wooden siege towers with iron fittings were built for the Roman siege of Amida in 503, but were burned when the army withdrew to pursue a Persian force. See: Wright, *The Chronicle of Joshua the Stylite*, § LVI (p. 45); for Martyropolis, See *Ioannis Malalae Chronographia*, ed. L. Dindorf (Bonn, 1831), p. 470 (Eng. trans. *The Chronicle of John Malalas. A Translation*, by E. Jeffreys, M. Jeffreys and R. Scott et al. (Byzantina Australiensia IV) (Melbourne, 1986), p. 273f.); for Rome, see Procopius, *Wars*, V, xxi.3–4; 14 (Belisarius' siege of Rome); for the siege of 626, see *Chronicon Paschale*, p. 720.1–3 (trans. Whitby, p. 174); for the siege of Thessaloniki, see P. Lemerle, *Les plus anciens recueils des miracles de S. Démétrius et de la pénétration des Slaves dans les Balkans*, I: *Le texte* (Paris, 1979), pp. 45–241, at pp. 180ff.; for the siege tower fittings listed in the documents relating to the Cretan expedition of 949, see *De Cer.*, p. 670.10–11 ("for attacking fortresses, a wooden tower, tortoises, . . ."). The illustration accompanies the text of the tenth-century treatise on poliorcetics ascribed to Hero of Byzantium, in Ms. Vat. gr. 1605, fol. 185: see Sullivan, "Tenth-century Byzantine offensive siege warfare", pp. 180, 193–4, and esp. 197. For Alexios I, see Anna Comnena, *Alexiad*, vi, 1 (trans. Sewter, p. 181) (and note that Robert

Guiscard had built a similar tower at the beginning of the siege of Dyrrhachium: *Alexiad*, iv, 1 (trans. Sewter, p. 135; and cf. iv, 5 (trans. Sewter, p. 143)). The list could be greatly extended, but these examples provide a general indication.

157.   For Islamic siege technology, see D. Nicolle, *Medieval Warfare Source Book*, 2: *Christian Europe and its Neighbours* (London, 1996), pp. 46–7, 85; for western siege techniques and equipment of the tenth–twelfth centuries, see J. France, "Technology and the success of the First Crusade", in Y. Lev (ed.), *War and Society in the Eastern Mediterranean, 7th–15th Centuries* (Leiden/New York/Cologne, 1997), pp. 163–76, at 171–3. See, for example, Scylitzes, *Synopsis historiarum*, p. 34.89–93, for *helepoleis* used by the army of Thomas the Slav during the siege of Constantinople in 821.

158.   *De Cer.*, pp. 670.10–671.5, 672.16–673.6 (all items relating directly to artillery and siege equipment).

159.   See S.C. Estopañan, *Skyllitzes Matritensis*, I (Barcelona/Madrid, 1965), fols. 32v.a, b, 59v, 72, 100v, 101v, 127a, 142a and many others; for the trebuchets, see 151b and 166; for discussion, see Chapter 6, below.

160.   This is a complex and still unresolved issue. See Chapter 4 above, for further literature and sources.

161.   See J.F. Haldon and M. Byrne, "A possible solution to the problem of Greek Fire", *BZ*, 70, 1977, pp. 91–9, and Chapter 4 above for the naval projector and the hand-held projector. On incendiary weapons in general, see Nicolle, *Medieval Warfare Source Book*, 2, pp. 45–6, 85.

Chapter 6   The army at war: combat

1.   See, for example, the remarks in Smail, *Crusading Warfare*, pp. 165–6, and esp. J. Keegan, *The Face of Battle* (London, 1976/1996), pp. 36–54. For some attempts to re-establish the course of particular engagements, see: S. McGrath, "The battles of Dorostolon (971). Rhetoric and reality", in Miller and Nesbitt (eds), *Peace and War in Byzantium*, pp. 152–64; J.-C. Cheynet, "Mantzikert: un désastre militaire?", *B*, 50, 1980, pp. 410–38; N. Tobias, "The tactics and strategy of Alexius Comnenus at Calvrytae, 1078", *Byzantine Studies*, 6, 1979, pp. 193–211; J.W. Jandera, "The battle of the Yarmuk: a reconstruction", *Journal of Asian History*, 19, 1985, pp. 8–21; Kaegi, *Byzantium and the Early Islamic Conquests*, pp. 112–44.

2.   See Elton, *Warfare in Roman Europe*, pp. 105–6.

3.   Classically overstated in Oman, *The Art of War in the Middle Ages*, pp. 4–5; more moderately in Delbrück, *History of the Art of War*, ii, pp. 269–84; still repeated in A.D.H. Bivar, "Cavalry equipment and tactics on the Euphrates frontier", *DOP*, 26, 1972, pp. 271–91. For a modern analysis, see T. Burns, "The battle of Adrianople: a reconsideration", *Historia*, 22, 1973, pp. 336–45.

4.   See Elton's discussion, *Warfare in Roman Europe*, pp. 80–2, 105–6. On the evolution of heavy cavalry, see: J.W. Eadie, "The development of Roman mailed cavalry"; Bivar, "Cavalry equipment and tactics on the Euphrates frontier", pp. 274–81; and esp. J.C. Coulston, "Roman, Parthian and Sassanian tactical developments", in P. Freeman and D. Kennedy (eds), *The Defence of the Roman and Byzantine East* (*BAR*, S297 (i)) (1986), pp. 59–75, at 60. Vegetius' complaints about the decline in infantry effectiveness (*Epitoma rei militaris*, i, 20; iii, 26) are

difficult to assess. Possibly there was a reduction in field-army discipline; equally, however, comparison with supposedly "good old days" is notoriously liable to misrepresent the past in the light of the ideological priorities of the present.

5. Figures and analysis in D. Hoffmann, *Das spätrömische Bewegungsheer und die Notitia Dignitatum* (= Epigraphische Studien, 7/i), (Düsseldorf/Cologne, 1969), with comments in Elton, *Warfare in Roman Europe*, pp. 106–7.

6. See P. Coussin, *Les armes romaines: essai sur les origines et l'évolution des armes individuelles du légionnaire romain* (Paris, 1926), pp. 480–92; Elton, *Warfare in Roman Europe*, pp. 107–14, does not discuss the changes of the late second–third centuries, and draws no conclusions in this respect with regard to tactical structures.

7. For infantry charging cavalry, see, for example, Ammianus, *Works*, xxxv, 1.16. On the political context and relations between Rome and the new Sassanid kingdom from the 230s, see J.D. Howard-Johnston, "The two Great Powers in late Antiquity: a comparison", in Cameron (ed.), *States, Resources and Armies*, pp. 157–226, at 158–62, and on the Sassanid elite, pp. 220–4. For the relative size of the Sassanian heavy cavalry forces, see the appropriate discussion in A. Christensen, *L'Iran sous les Sassanides*, 2nd edn (Copenhagen/Paris, 1944); the remarks of Bivar in "Cavalry equipment and tactics on the Euphrates frontier", pp. 278–9; the discussion of Z. Rubin, "The reforms of Khusru Anushirwan", in Cameron (ed.), *States, Resources and Armies*, pp. 227–97, esp. 279–91.

8. See: *Strat.*, proem, 2–3; xii, B 1. pr. (specifically dealing with infantry); the references in Haldon, *Byzantine Praetorians*, p. 107 and n. 76; for the general context, see Kaegi, *Byzantine Military Unrest*, pp. 41–119.

9. See for references to traditional Roman discipline: Agathias, *Historiae*, i, 16.9; v, 18.11; and below.

10. Agathias, *Historiae*, ii, 1.2: Narses drills the troops at Rome. And see: *Th. Sim.* iii, 12.7 (the Roman general Justinian pays attention to discipline and training in the eastern theatre); Agathias, *Historiae*, I, 16.9.

11. Procopius, *Wars*, I, xviii.44–8; viii, 29–32, *35*; Agathias, *Historiae*, ii, 1–14; iii, 26–7 (and cf. Vegetius, *Epitome rei militaris*, ii, 15ff.). For discussion of sixth-century Roman tactics and the relationship between infantry and cavalry forces, see C.M. Mazzucchi, "Le ΚΑΤΑΓΡΑΦΑΙ dello *Strategicon* di Maurizio e lo schieramente di battaglia dell'esercito Romano nel VI/VII secolo", *Aevum* 55, 1981, pp. 111–38 – see pp. 132–5.

12. Procopius, *Wars*, IV, xi.37 (North Africa); Agathias, *Historiae*, ii, 9.1–2; Evagrius, *Ecclesiastical History*, v, 14 (Bohn trans., p. 439). For Theophylact's accounts, see *Th. Sim.*, v, 9.5–7, 10–11; vi, 9.15.

13. Procopius, *Wars*, V, xxviii.22–9. In the event, they did not stand when attacked by the Gothic troops, but the underlying assumption is that they would normally be expected to have done so, and that Belisarius was wrong to assume the reverse.

14. For Belisarius' scepticism, see the description of the battle at Daras in 530, where the Roman forces defend their positions with a trench (*Wars*, I, xiii) and the example noted already at Rome (*Wars*, V, xviii); for the speeches, see *Wars*, I, xiv.13–20, 21–7. For Roman and Persian archery, see Procopius, *Wars*, I, i.12–13; IV, xix.23; V, xxvii.27; V, xxix.17–19; *Th. Sim.*, iii, 14.5–8. The point is emphasized in Maurice, *Strategikon*, xi, 1.15–17, 29–32, 41–2, 59–63, 66–70.

15. As for example in the campaign of 594, where the Roman cavalry are the main actors against the Slavs and Avars, both in field actions and in attacking enemy

encampments, but where a force of regular infantry was certainly present, see *Th. Sim.*, vii, 2.1–9; 3.8.

16. See, for example, Procopius, *Wars*, V, xxvii.1–2 (1,600 light horse); VI, v.1 (3,000 Isaurian infantry, 1,000 regular cavalry, 800 Thracian cavalry, 300 "other" cavalry). For a detailed analysis of the wars in Italy, see A. Pertusi, "Ordinamenti militari, guerre in Occidente e teoria di guerra dei Bizantini (secc. VI–X)", in *Ordinamenti militari in Occidente nell'alto medioevo* (Settimane di Studio del Centro Italiano di Studi sull'alto Medioevo XV, 1967) (Spoleto, 1968), 1, pp. 631–700. For the wars against the Avars, see the account in Whitby, *The Emperor Maurice and His Historian*. On the battles in question, for Ad Decimum, see Procopius, *Wars*, III, xix.11–33 (although the battle is an exception in that Belisarius had only his fortified camp as a base, and needed to ensure that it was quite safe, so that the whole infantry force, the army's baggage and spare weapons, as well as Belisarius' wife were left there); for Tricamerum, see *Wars*, IV, iii.4–9; Melitene, see *Th. Sim.*, iii, 142–8 (the battle is probably a rhetorical invention of Theophylact, but the underlying assumptions about the composition of the armies can be accepted as reflecting real battlefield experience: see Whitby, *The Emperor Maurice and His Historian*, p. 95 and n. 65); on the Nymphios, see *Th. Sim.*, i, 9.7–11; on Solachon, see *Th. Sim.*, ii, 3.1–4.7; on the Araxes (in 589), see *Th. Sim.*, iii, 7.17; in 600, see *Th. Sim.*, viii, 2.10–3.10 (cavalry are not specifically mentioned, but the context of the battles against the mounted Avars would suggest this, even if the Roman forces were dismounted in the first engagement, forming a square about their encampment). For Heraclius' campaigns, see *Theoph.*, pp. 306–27 (trans. Mango and Scott, pp. 438–55), with J. Howard-Johnston, "The official history of Heraclius' Persian campaigns", in E. Dabrowa (ed.), *The Roman and Byzantine Army in the East* (Cracow, 1994), pp. 57–87.

17. Haldon, *Byzantine Praetorians*, pp. 97–102 with sources and discussion.

18. See Jones, *LRE*, pp. 655 and 659, with sources.

19. *Strat.*, xi, 1.42, 2.66–8, 85–8, 4.69–74, 141–61. For infantry, see xii B, proem. For the earlier tract, see *Strategy*, §§ 15–16, 21–5, drawn chiefly from Aelian and Arrian.

20. See *Strat.*, xii B, 13; viii, 2.85; and xii A, 1–7 for mixed formations. Cf. *Strategy*, § 36.9–20 (trans. Dennis, p. 111). And although the author of the *Strategikon* laments the lack of attention paid to infantry formations, it should be remembered that he makes almost the same complaint of the armies in general – including, therefore, the cavalry – in the introduction to the treatise: pr. 10–14. The emphasis on cavalry may equally reflect the author's own preferences: he assumes that commanders may choose where they place the emphasis in numbers – advice to those who prefer infantry over cavalry, and vice versa, is given even-handedly (xiii, 2.20–1). For the battle of Solachon in 586, where the opposing cavalry units were locked in stationary combat, the Roman cavalry were ordered to dismount and force the enemy cavalry back, which they did successfully: *Th. Sim.*, iii, 4.5–7.

21. See the remarks of Procopius, *Wars*, I, xiv.25–6.

22. See the detailed discussion in Dagron and Mihaescu, *Le traité sur la Guérilla*, pp. 190–3; for dismounted cavalry, see Maurice, *Strat.*, xi, 1.

23. As at Phasis in Lazica in 553, for example: Agathias, *Historiae*, iii, 26.3–7, 27.6–7. The infantry forces included units of Sabir (Hunnic) and Tzan heavy infantry and Isaurian slingers and javelin men.

24. *History of the Art of War*, ii, pp. 193, 197. On Arab mobility and use of horses and camels to move infantry troops at great speed, see D.R. Hill, "The role of the camel and the horse in the early Arab conquests", in V.J. Parry and M.E. Yapp (eds), *War, Technology and Society in the Middle East* (London, 1975), pp. 32–43.

25. See N. Fries, *Das Heerwesen der Araber zur Zeit der Omaijaden nach Tabari* (Tübingen, 1921); *Encyclopaedia of Islam*, IV (new edn, Leiden/London, 1978), art. "Kaws" (archery), pp. 795–803; Donner, *The Early Arabic Conquests*.

26. See *Theoph.*, pp. 358–9 (trans. Mango and Scott, pp. 498–9). For the role of thematic infantry in frontier warfare, see Dagron and Mihaescu, *Le traité sur la Guérilla*, pp. 190–3.

27. *Tact.*, vi, 24–5; vii, 3–5, 53–7 (based on various sections of Maurice, *Strat.*, xii B); note esp. *Tact.*, xiv, 66–70 (= *Strat.*, xii B, 11–12).

28. See *Const. Porph., Three Treatises*, (C) 443–50; *De Cer.*, p. 695.14–18; and N. Svoronos, *Les novelles des empereurs macédoniens concenant la terre et les stratiotes*, ed. P. Gounaridis (Athens, 1994), no. 5, 118 (A.1). See the commentary in Haldon, *Recruitment and Conscription*, pp. 41ff. Only the later historian John Zonaras makes it clear that infantry were part of the thematic register, listing them alongside heavy cavalry, regular cavalry and sailors/marines. See *Epitomae historiarum*, iii, p. 506.

29. See Leo, *Tact.*, xviii, 143, 149, 153–6, and cf. *Theoph.*, p. 452.10 (trans. Mango and Scott, p. 624), for thematic groups of 3,000 *epilektoi* ordered to harass enemy forces in 778/9. For further discussion and sources, see Haldon, *Byzantione Praetorians*, p. 219f. and notes.

30. *Skirmishing*, iii, 2–4; ix, 14; x, 19–20; xxiii, 2–3; xxv, 1. Compare with Leo, *Tact.*, xviii, 134.

31. See Leo, *Tact.*, xviii, 115, 138; *Skirmishing*, x, 1; 16; xx, 11 (and cf. vii, 2; xv, 2 on the importance of finding out whether infantry were involved in the enemy raid); see also the discussion in Hill, "The role of the camel and the horse".

32. *Skirmishing*, x, 16–17; xxiv, 6 (greed for booty); x, 2, 5, 8; xiv, 7 (slow moving); xxiv, 4 (their unreliability and indiscipline in battle); xxiii, 3–4 (morale).

33. *Skirmishing*, iii, 3; x, 16; xxiii, 6; xxiv, 5. Cf. Leo, *Tact.*, xx, 206.

34. See Haldon, *Byzantine Praetorians*, p. 299 and n. 894; Dagron and Mihaescu, *Le traité sur la Guérilla*, p. 185 and n. 20. See also the indications in A. Kazhdan, "Hagiographical Notes 2: On horseback or on foot? A 'sociological' approach in an eleventh-century Saint's Life", *B*, 53, 1983, pp. 544–5.

35. For the campaign in Italy, see *Th. cont.*, p. 305; for Basil's campaigns in the east, see *Th. cont.*, p. 269ff.

36. Leo, *Tact.*, vi, 25; 26 (Maur., *Strat.* xii B, 4–5). See *Syll. Tact.*, § 38.4 and Niceph., *Praecepta* (ed. and trans. McGeer), i. 14–20, with the comments of McGeer, *Sowing the Dragon's Teeth*, pp. 184–5 and 204–5.

37. See *Th. cont.*, p. 265, where improved discipline and more rigorous military training and exercises are mentioned. But the source in question was commissioned by his grandson, the emperor Constantine VII, and aims explicitly to improve Basil's image in the eyes of later generations.

38. See Genesius, *Regna*, pp. 48–9 (with pp. 65–6); *Th. cont.*, pp. 127–9 (with pp. 113f., 116–18); A.A. Vasiliev, *Byzance et les Arabes*, I: *La dynastie d'Amorium (820–867)*, eds H. Grégoire and M. Canard (Corpus Bruxellense Hist. Byz. I), (Bruxelles, 1950), pp. 331–4, with Arab sources at pp. 275, 299–301) and further sources and literature.

NOTES

39. For General discussion, see: McGeer, *Sowing the Dragon's Teeth*, pp. 253–328; T. Kolias, "Byzantine military tactics: theory and practice", in Oikonomidès (ed.), *Byzantium at War*, pp. 153–64, esp. pp. 155–6, 158–160. See also the discussion of this genre in H. Hunger, *Die hochsprachliche profane Literatur der Byzantiner* (Handbuch der Altertumswissenschaft xii, 5.1 and 2 = Byzantinisches Handbuch 5, 1 and 2), (Munich, 1978), 2, pp. 323–40.

40. *Const. Porph., Three Treatises*, (C) 199 (listing Syrianos and Polyainos); for Basil, see: Psellos, *Chronographia*, I, 33 (trans. Sewter, p. 26); Kekaumenos, *Strategikon*, pp. 10.24, 14.1f., 15.14f., and esp. 19.13–19. For the *caesar* John Doukas (during the reign of Michael VII Doukas (1059–67)), see Psellos, *Chronographia*, vii, 4.16 (trans. Sewter, p. 287), and for his son Andronikos, see Niceph. Bryennios, *Historiarum libri quattuor*, I, 16 (p. 115.12–13). See Kolias, "Byzantine military tactics", pp. 158–9. Michael Attaleiates noted the battle-planning session in the imperial tent of Romanos IV, and in an earlier episode the disastrous failure of the Byzantine commander in 1049 to prepare his commanders: *Historia*, 113.8, and 32.6ff. For Michael IV's expedition in 1040, see Psellos, *Chronographia*, iv, 43–4 (trans. Sewter, p. 77). For the battle in 1067, see Choniates, *Historia*, p. 152.

41. See Chapter 5, above, and the summary of the prescriptions on battlefield preparations in G.T. Dennis, "The Byzantines in battle", in Oikonomidès (ed.), *Byzantium at War*, pp. 165–78.

42. See Chapter 5, above, on the baggage train, and Maurice, *Strat.*, i, 2.83–85 (= Leo, *Tact.*, vi, 21); v, 1–5; Niceph., *Praecepta*, i, 14; ii, 11–14. See Leo, *Tact.*, xiii: "Concerning the day before battle". On spare arrows, see below.

43. Maurice, *Strat.*, ii, 1–20 and iii, 1–16; iv, 1–3 (mostly repeated in Leo, *Tact.*, vii, x and xiv); Niceph., *Praecepta*, i, 5–17; ii, 8–18; iv, 1–20. See Agathias, Historiae, i, 22.1–7, and, for the events of 1070, see Zonaras, *Epitomae historiarum*, iii, pp. 694–5. For the battle in 970, see Leo diac., *Historia*, vi, 109–111. The tale is illustrated in the twelfth-century Skylitzes manuscript: see Estopañan, *Skyllitzes Matritensis*, I, fols. 161–2 b.

44. For the Persians, see Maurice, *Strat.*, xi, 1 (with variations, on the Arabs = Leo, *Tact.*, xviii, 23–4, 110–42); for the Scythians (Turks), see *Strat.*, xi, 2 (= Leo, *Tact.*, xviii, 42–76); on the Franks, Lombards and western peoples, see *Strat.*, xi, 3; *Tact.*, xviii, 80–98; and on the Slavs, see *Strat.*, xi, 4; *Tact.*, xviii, 99–108. For the tactical models implicit in the *Strategikon*, see the discussion of G. Dagron, "Modèles de combattants et technologie militaire dans le *Stratègikon* de Maurice", in Vallet and Kazanski, *L'armée romaine et les barbares*, pp. 279–84.

45. Byzantine descriptions of their enemies, along with the cultural knowledge and assumptions which such descriptions reflect, are discussed in detail in J. Wiita, *The Ethnika in Byzantine Military Treatises* (Ann Arbor, MA/London 1977). See also the discussion of G. Dagron, "Ceux d'en face: les peuples étrangers dans les traités militaires byzantins", *Travaux et mémoires*, 10, 1987, pp. 207–32.

46. *Th. Sim.*, v, 9.5–7; Leo, *Tact.*, xx, 204.

47. On blessing the standards and other religious observances, and the role of military "chaplains", see: Leo, *Tact.*, xiii, 1 (= Maurice, *Strat.*, vii A, 1), A. Pertusi, "Una acolouthia militare inedita del X secolo", *Aevum*, 22, 1948, pp. 145–68; Haldon, *Byzantine Praetorians*, p. 568; McCormick, *Eternal Victory*, pp. 245–52; G.T. Dennis, "Religious services in the Byzantine army", in E. Carr et al. (eds), *EULOGEMA. Studies in Honor of Robert Taft, S.J.* (*Studia Anselmiana* 110) (Rome,

1993), pp. 107–17. For the advice to use loud war-cries to frighten the enemy, see, for example, Maurice, *Strat.*, viii, 2.46; cf. *Th. cont.*, pp. 273–4; Leo diac., *Historia*, viii, 4 (p. 133.4–11). For the use of drums to disturb or cowe the enemy, cf. Leo diac., *Historia*, i, 11 (and cf. ii, 6; vi, 13, etc.).

48. *Strat.*, ii, 18; Niceph., *Praecepta*, iv, 11.
49. See: Dennis, "The Byzantines in battle", pp. 177–8; McGeer, *Sowing the Dragon's Teeth*, pp. 320–7, both with illustrative material from the sources.
50. Dennis, "The Byzantines in battle", pp. 175–6.
51. See *Sylloge tact.*, § 43.11, and the detailed discussion in Kolias, *Byzantinische Waffen*, pp. 220 and 229–38, on shooting techniques and the various releases employed or recommended.
52. See Maurice, *Strat.*, ii, 6; iii, 8; followed but updated in Leo, *Tact.*, xviii, 143–9. The comment of the eleventh-century general Kekaumenos (10.27–28): "the Roman battle-order is better than all others", probably refers to this arrangement rather than to the hollow square formation evolved during the middle years of the tenth century: see below. For a useful detailed account of Mantzikert, see A. Friendly, *The Dreadful Day: The Battle of Manzikert, 1071* (London, 1981). The main sources are Attaleiates and Psellos, although the latter's account is especially biased against the emperor. For Alexios in 1078, see N. Tobias, "The tactics and strategy of Alexius Comnenus at Calavrytae, 1078", *Byzantine Studies/Etudes byzantines*, 6, 1979, pp. 193–211.
53. *Strat.*, ii, 1.
54. *Strat.*, iii, 8–10. See Dennis, "The Byzantines in battle", pp. 169–70.
55. *Epitoma rei militaris*, iii, 14–26.
56. *Epitoma rei militaris*, iii, 17.
57. *Th. Sim.*, iii, 14.2–8. In fact the account is probably fictional, but it must nevertheless reflect what the author understood of Roman tactics: see Whitby, *The History of Theophylact Simocatta*, p. xxii. For the battle order in 586, see *Historia*, ii, 3.1–4.11; and in 598, see *Historia*, vii, 14.2–3.
58. Procopius, *Wars*, viii, 29–32; Agathias, *Historiae*, ii, 8.1 (and cf. iii, 26.8). For brief analyses, see Delbrück, *History of the Art of War*, ii, pp. 351–61, 369–74.
59. Both are discussed briefly, with further literature and discussion of the sources, in Elton, *Warfare in Roman Europe*, pp. 250–6. See also Delbrück, *History of the Art of War*, ii, pp. 261–84.
60. See Arrian (*Flavii Arriani quae exstant omnia*, ii: *Scripta minora et fragmenta*, ed. A.C. Roos (Leipzig, 1928), *Ektaxis kata Alanon*, pp. 177–85), pp. 12–26; and Ammianus Marcellinus, *Works*, xiv, 6.17. For Vegetius' description of the legion of the Principate, drawn from the (mostly lost) work of the first-century general Frontinus, see *Epitoma rei militaris*, ii, 15ff. The basic formation of the legion consisted of two lines each of five cohorts, with a space between each unit, and the second line arrayed in such a way as to cover the gaps between the cohorts of the first line. See G. Webster, *The Roman Imperial Army* (London, 1969), pp. 221–3. This tactical order had clearly been abandoned by the fifth century, and probably long before.
61. *Epitoma rei militaris*, iii, 14–15.
62. See J.C. Coulston, "Roman, Parthian and Sassanian tactical development", in Freeman and Kennedy (eds), *The Defence of the Roman and Byzantine East*, pp. 59–75; Eadie, "The development of Roman mailed cavalry"; R. Tomlin,

"The late Roman Empire AD 200–450", in P. Connolly (ed.), *Greece and Rome at War* (London, 1981), pp. 249–61.

63. For example, *Theoph.*, pp. 376 (AD 707/8), 383 (AD 713/14), 445 (AD 770/1), 446 (AD 770/1), 447 (AD 772/3) (trans. Mango and Scott, pp. 525, 534, 615, 617, 618). For Leo's assumptions, see *Tact.*, xviii, 141, 143–53 for the regular thematic cavalry force of 4,000; xii, 26. For cavalry with infantry, see *Tact.*, ix, 48; xiv, 70–1.

64. *Tact.*, ix, 48; xx, 78, 176.

65. Maurice, *Strat.*, xi, 3. For Normans outwitting Byzantines, see Anna Comena, *Alexiad*, v, 4, 5, for example. Cohesion and solidarity were constant features of the battle order – see Maurice, *Strat.*, iii, 5; and cf. Psellos, *Chronographia*, i, 33 for Basil II's standing orders in this respect. See the remarks of T. Kolias, "Byzantine military tactics", pp. 161–2.

66. *Theoph.*, pp. 372, 411 (trans. Mango and Scott, pp. 520, 571). See Lilie, *Die byzantinische Reaktion*, pp. 113, 115–16, 152. For absence of battles, see Lilie, *Die byzantinische Reaktion*, p. 92 and the evidence discussed at pp. 60–82. Tabari reports a Byzantine defeat, in which the Roman commanders were killed, for the year 661/2, but the other sources do not corroborate this: see E.W. Brooks, "The Arabs in Asia Minor (641–750) from Arabic sources", *JHS*, 18, 1898, pp. 184; Lilie, *Die byzantinische Reaktion*, p. 69. For Amorion, see Lilie, *Die byzantinische Reaktion*, pp. 72–4, and for the "siege" of 674–8 and associated fighting, pp. 76–9.

67. For discussion and sources, see Lilie, *Die byzantinische Reaktion*, pp. 99–112.

68. See the detailed account in Lilie, *Die byzantinische Reaktion*, pp. 112–33, 143–55, with analysis at pp. 155–62.

69. Procopius, *Wars*, VII, v. 5. For the political and ideological context, see Haldon, *Byzantium in the Seventh Century*, pp. 355–75, and the discussion in Kaegi, *Byzantine Military Unrest*, pp. 186–208.

70. Haldon, *Recruitment and Conscription*, pp. 67–72; *Byzantium in the Seventh Century*, pp. 242ff.

71. Leo, *Tact.*, vii, 2; cf. Maurice, *Strat.*, i, 2.5, 87; vi, 1.9. For the annual muster, see Haldon, *Recruitment and Conscription*, p. 63; Dagron and Mihaescu, *Le traité sur la Guérilla*, p. 273 and n. 45, p. 274.

72. *Theoph.*, pp. 376, 377, 464, 467 (trans. Mango and Scott, pp. 525, 526, 638, 643).

73. For the defeat of 808/9, see *Theoph.*, pp. 484–5; for the Bulgar withdrawal, see *Theoph.*, p. 470 (trans. Mango and Scott, pp. 665, 646); for the defeat near Tarsos, see *Th. cont.*, pp. 287–8 (and cf. Tabari, trans. Vasiliev, *Byzance et les arabes*, II, 2, p. 9, for the Arab historians' account). For the defeat of 811, see *Theoph.*, pp. 490–1 (trans. Mango and Scott, p. 672f.); I. Dujcev, "La chronique byzantine de l'an 811", *TM*, 1, 1965, pp. 205–54; text pp. 210–16. For discussion, see Bury, *Eastern Roman Empire*, pp. 344–5. For Versinikia, see Bury, *Eastern Roman Empire*, pp. 350–1, with sources; and for Roman assumptions of superiority on open ground, see *Scriptor incertus de Leone Armenio*, in *Leonis Grammatici Chronographia*, ed. I. Bekker (*CSHB*) (Bonn, 1842), p. 338. For Acheloos and the formation of the battle line in the plain of Diabasis, see Scylitzes, *Synopsis historiarum*, p. 203.81–96. Jealousies between commanders or thematic divisions often bedevilled imperial field operations: see Kaegi, *Byzantine Military Unrest*. For this particular case, see *Th. cont.*, pp. 305–6.

74. Maurice, *Strat.*, viii, 1.15; Leo, *Tact.*, xx, 18; and cf. *Tact.*, ix, 48; xx, 78; xx, 176. For the "Military laws" (*Nomoi stratiotikoi*), see Chapter 7 below. For the events of 813, see *Theoph.*, p. 500 (trans. Mango and Scott, p. 684), and Kaegi, *Byzantine Military Unrest*, pp. 248–50.

75. Haldon, *Byzantine Praetorians*, pp. 318–25. For evidence for the superior fighting skills of the *tagmata*, see Haldon, *Byzantine Praetorians*, 254–5; and for Leo's comment on the state of the armies, see *Tact.*, xviii, 153, 149.

76. *Strat.*, i, 1–2; *Strategy*, §§ 44–7. For Nikephros Phocas, see Leo diac., *Historia*, iii, 9.23. But Leo frequently uses phrases and expressions from classical sources, which should alert us to the possibility that his descriptions are not necessarily to be taken at face value – his account of Nikephros' siege of the Muslim stronghold at Chandax (Candia) on Crete is taken directly from an account in Agathias of the siege of Cumae by Narses: see the examples cited in D. Sullivan, "Tenth-century Byzantine offensive siege warfare: instructional prescriptions and historical practice", in Oikonomides (ed.), *Byzantium at War*, pp. 179–200 at 181f. There is a considerable literature on ancient and medieval archery. In general on Roman archery, see S. James, "Dura-Europos and the introduction of the 'Mongolian release'", in *Roman Military Equipment: The Accoutrements* (*BAR*, S336) (Oxford, 1987), pp. 77–84. See also the section on archery in Kolias, *Byzantinische Waffen*, pp. 214–38, with literature.

77. Procopius, *Wars*, V, xxvii.27–9. For the archery duels between Roman and Persian forces on the eastern front, cf. *Wars* I, xiv.35–7 and I, xviii.31–4, where the armies confronted each other for several hours before finally coming to hand-to-hand combat. The Roman forces were advised to get to grips with the Persians before they had time to inflict too many casualties through archery: Maurice, *Strat.*, xi, 1.54–63. See also note 13 above.

78. See Kaegi, *Byzantium and the Early Islamic Conquests*, pp. 120–31.

79. Leo, *Tact.*, vi, 2–3; *Sylloge Tacticorum*, ed. Dain, § 39.4 (cf. Maurice, *Strat.*, i, 2; *Skirmishing*, viii, 4, 5; x, 5).

80. See Haldon, *Recruitment and Conscription*, pp. 67 and 72, n. 127.

81. For the battle of Anzen, see Bury, *Eastern Roman Empire*, pp. 264–5; Treadgold, *Revival*, pp. 300–1 and n. 410. For Leo's remarks on the damage caused by the lack of competent archery, see *Tact.*, vi, 5; xi, 49; and cf. xviii, 131. The general recommendation ("all Roman recruits up to the age of 40 to be ordered to carry bows and quivers, regardless of the level of skill they have attained") is taken verbatim from *Strat.*, 1, 2.28–30. Leo's specific point about the decline in archery and the evils which have resulted from it are contemporary, and can be assumed to reflect the actual situation. For his description of the mounted lancer/archer, see *Tact.*, vi, 1–13 (with certain changes = *Strat.*, i, 3–58).

82. It might be objected that the picture derived from the sources reflects the less informative nature of the material covering the period from the seventh to the mid-tenth century. But the evidence referred to above is detailed enough to support the contention made here.

83. For the letter, see Darrouzès, *Épistoliers*, ii, 50. For the documents of 910–11, see *De Cerimoniis*, pp. 657.12–13, 17–18, 657.20–658.4. The *strategos* of the theme of Thessaloniki and the commander of Evrippos in Hellas were each to prepare 200,000 arrows for the army, enough at the standard rate of issue given in the military treatises (50 extra arrows per man) for some 5,000 men for one engagement. This quantity probably represents the reserve stock provided by

the commander – the same number of arrows is specified for this purpose in the *Tactica* of Nikephros Ouranos, written in the 990s. For the supply of arrows to soldiers, see, for example, Maurice, *Strat.*, i, 2; xii B, 5; 6; Leo, *Tact.*, vi, 2; Niceph., *Praecepta*, i, 4; Nik. Ouranos, *Tactica*, § 56.4. For the supply of spare (referred to as "imperial") arrows, see Nik. Ouranos, *Tactica*, § 56.14; and for the proportion of archers to lancers and others, see Nik. Ouranos, *Tactica*, § 56.4; 8; § 60.6; § 61.2 (and cf. Niceph., *Praecepta*, iv, 1–4). See the detailed analysis in McGeer, *Sowing the Dragon's Teeth*, pp. 206–8, 212–14.

84. As in the opening stages of the battle of Versinikia in 813, for example, where Byzantine archery caused considerable confusion among the Bulgar ranks (see Scylitzes, *Synopsis historiarum*, p. 6.82–90).

85. See in general W.E. Kaegi, "The contribution of archery to the conquest of Anatolia", *Speculum*, 39, 1964, pp. 96–108, but also J. France, *Victory in the East*, pp. 148–9 and note 27, who suggests that Kaegi may have exaggerated the effects of Seljuk archery on Byzantine troops. For Alexios' special formation, see Anna Comnena, *Alexiad*, xv, 3 (trans. Sewter, p. 480), and below.

86. There is some debate on the exact form and dimensions of the *menavlion* or *menavlon*: see E. McGeer, "Infantry versus cavalry: the Byzantine response", *REB*, 46, 1988, pp. 135–45, and esp. "*Menaulion – menaulatoi*", *Diptycha*, 4, 1986–7, pp. 53–7, who sees it as an exceptionally thick and solid spear; and M.P. Anastasiadis, "On handling the menavlion", *BMGS*, 18, 1994, pp. 1–10, who sees it rather as a short javelin with a long iron head and point. In texts prior to these, the *menavlion* is treated as an ordinary javelin – Lat. *venabulum*: see J.F. Haldon, "Some aspects of Byzantine military technology from the sixth to the tenth centuries", *BMGS*, 1, 1975, pp. 11–47 at 33.

87. Detailed discussion in McGeer, "Infantry versus cavalry".

88. These changes, and the sources which provide the evidence, are discussed in detail in McGeer, *Sowing the Dragon's Teeth*, pp. 202–11. See also Dennis, "The Byzantines in battle", pp. 170–3.

89. See McGeer, *Sowing the Dragon's Teeth*, pp. 257ff.

90. See, for example, *Syll. Tact.*, § 47.19; Niceph., *Praecepta*, i, 5–7, 12, 16; ii, 5, 9–10, 14–17.

91. As, for example, Leo, *Tact.*, xiv, 24.

92. Description and sources in McGeer, *Sowing the Dragon's Teeth*, pp. 203–11, 257–80. For Armenian infantry in the eleventh century, see, for example, Attaleiates, *Historia*, pp. 109.9, 113.13, for the late 1060s; and for their importance in general, see also E. McGeer, "The legal decree of Nikephros II Phocas concerning Armenian *stratiotai*", in Miller and Nesbitt (eds), *Peace and War in Byzantium*, pp. 123–37, esp. 134–7.

93. See especially the prescriptions in Niceph., *Praecepta*, iii, 1–11 (on *kataphraktoi*); iv, 1–20 (deploying cavalry with and without infantry); Nikeph. Ouranos, *Tactica*, § 57.13; § 60.1–11.

94. See Zonaras, *Epitomae historiarum*, iii, pp. 492–3, for example, with the discussion of McGeer, *Sowing the Dragon's Teeth*, pp. 178–80.

95. Cf. Maurice, *Strat.*, iii, 5; Niceph., *Praecepta*, ii, 4–12; iv, 11–12; and for the accounts of the battles of Dorostolon, see Leo diac., *Historia*, viii, 9–10; ix, 1–8. For Tarsos, see Leo diac., *Historia*, iv, 3 (59); for Isaac Komnenos, see Psellos, *Chronographia*, vii, 70 (trans. Sewter, p. 243); and for the battles in 1070, see Attaleiates, *Historia*, pp. 114, 126, 160. For Basil's discipline, see Psellos,

Chronographia, i, 33 (trans. Sewter, p. 26); and for Alexios, see Anna Comena, *Alexiad*, vii, 3 (trans. Sewter, p. 224).

96. These developments are described in greater detail in McGeer, *Sowing the Dragon's Teeth*, pp. 280–317. For the Byzantine influence on the Normans, see Chapter 4 above. For the use of light cavalry screens to harass the enemy with archery and to cover the movements of the main force, see Dennis, "The Byzantines in battle", pp. 172–4 with examples and sources. For the battle of Troina, see the eleventh-century *Vita S. Philareti*, in *AS April*. I, pp. 603–18, at 608 (on which see Beck, *Kirche und theologische Literatur*, p. 582).

97. See Vasiliev and Canard, *Byzance et les arabes* ii, 2, p. 333, and Chapter 4 above.

98. See: Kinnamos, *Epitome*, p. 18; Choniates, *Historia*, pp. 77, 156, 180. For Roman troops being exercised and trained (the texts do not specify either infantry or cavalry), see, for example, Choniates, *Historia*, pp. 12 (in 1120) and 126 (training at Lopadion under Manuel I). For footsoldiers in Crusader armies, see Smail, *Crusading Warfare*, pp. 115–20. Note also Chalandon, *Les Comnène*, pp. 618–19.

99. See, for example, the various occasions preceding a campaign when Nikephros II or John I exercised and drilled their forces mentioned in Leo diac., *Historia*, ii, 24; iii, 36, 50–1; vii, 127; and the discussion of McGeer, *Sowing the Dragon's Teeth*, pp. 217–22. For Skleros' cavalry in action, see Psellos, *Chronographia*, I, 13 (trans. Sewter, p. 16).

100. Attaleiates, *Historia*, p. 111. At the battle of Troina in 1040 the imperial forces attacked in three divisions: see *V. Philareti* (cited n. 96 above), 608. The term in the Latin text for "division" is *acies*, which normally meant this rather than a battle line as such. See Smail, *Crusading Warfare*, pp. 114, 175. The instances of writers referring to left and right flanks, centre or vanguard, and re$\rightarrow$guard, are too numerous to list. But note Psellos, *Chronographia*, vii, 68 (trans. Sewter, p. 242), who notes that the Pechenegs (unusually) do not thus divide and order their forces.

101. Psellos, *Chronographia*, iii, 8 (trans. Sewter, p. 43). For other examples, see Choniates, *Historia*, pp. 12, 29–30, 77; Kinnamos, *Epitome*, p. 126.

102. Attaleiates, *Historia*, pp. 78–9, 93.5–11 and 103 on the disastrous economic policies of Constantine X (1059–67) and 114.23–116.3 on the poor quality of the generals and officers.

103. Attaleiates, *Historia*, pp. 78.23–79.6, 93.5–11; Cedrenus, *Compendium historiarum*, ii, 668–9.

104. Attaleiates, *Historia*, p. 104.13–20.

105. Attaleiates, *Historia*, pp. 122.7ff., 123.8–10. Cf. 104.16–18 (new officers and soldiers brigaded with experienced western units: this was not unusual when a commander wanted to reorganize his forces and stiffen their morale. Thus Isaac I distributed the steady and reliable men among the other units, making promotions and rewarding those of ability appropriately. Basil II similarly made sure that junior and middling officers filled the posts appropriate to their ability and experience: see Psellos, *Chronographia*, I, 32, 33 (trans. Sewter, pp. 25–6); vii, 8 (trans. Sewter, pp. 212–13)). For the five western *tagmata*, see: Oikonomidès, *Préséance*, pp. 329–33; Ahrweiler, "Recherches", pp. 26ff. Cf. Kühn, *Die byzantinische Armee*, pp. 247ff.

106. See: Attaleiates, *Historia*, pp. 29.2ff.; Cedrenus, *Compendium historiarum*, ii, pp. 562, 625ff.

107. Psellos, *Chronographia*, vii, 7–8 (trans. Sewter, pp. 212–13).
108. Cf. Attaleiates, *Historia*, pp. 114, 126, 160, for example, where the order and discipline of the imperial forces is highlighted; see also: J.-C. Cheynet, "Mantzikert: un désastre militaire?", *B*, 50, 1980, pp. 410–38 – see p. 425f.; "Les effectifs de l'armée byzantine aux Xe–XIIe s.", *Cahiers de civilisation médiévale*, 38, 4, 1995, pp. 319–35, at 332.
109. See the succinct account in Angold, *Byzantium 1025–1204*, pp. 93–8, 109, 127–8. For Manuel's training programme, see Kinnamos, *Epitome*, pp. 125–6; and for the speech of the Byzantine commander in 1167, see Choniates, *Historia*, pp. 155–6.
110. See P. Magdalino, *The Empire of Manuel I Komnenos*, pp. 231–2. For Kekaumenos, see *Strategikon*, 10.27–8.
111. See: Choniates, *Historia*, pp. 153–7; Kinnamos, *Epitome*, pp. 271–3. For other references to tactical subdivisions in the battle line, and the taxiarchies and their commanders, see: Choniates, *Historia*, pp. 23, 102, 125, 152; Kinnamos, *Epitome*, p. 58. For John's arrangement, see Choniates, *Historia*, pp. 29–30.
112. See Anna Comnena, *Alexiad*, xv, 5, 6 (trans. Sewter, pp. 485, 487), one of many examples. For the Cilician campaign, see Choniates, *Historia*, p. 138. For Manuel's advice, see Choniates, *Historia*, pp. 152, 193, for example.
113. See *Alexiad*, xv, 3.
114. McGeer, *Sowing the Dragon's Teeth*, pp. 257–65.
115. Shepard, "The uses of the Franks in eleventh-century Byzantium", pp. 300–2. For the square formation after the tenth century, see: Smail, *Crusading Warfare*, pp. 198–9; McGeer, *Sowing the Dragon's Teeth*, pp. 278–9. In 1159 on his return from Antioch, Manuel permitted the troops to break formation and return independently to their homes. In the event, many were attacked by Turkish raiders, and it was only when the emperor reformed the main body of the army that the stricken forces were rescued. Choniates implies strongly that the usual marching order, in dense formation, would have prevented or considerably reduced the effects of such attacks: see *Historia*, p. 110.
116. See *Const. Porph., Three Treatises*, p. 52 and n. 35; and (C) 453–4, with commentary, pp. 242–4 for further sources and literature.
117. *Theoph.*, p. 359 (trans. Mango and Scott, p. 499); Scylitzes, *Synopsis Historiarum*, pp. 203–5; Attaleiates, *Historia*, p. 161. For the defeat of Damianos Dalassenos in 998, see: H.F. Amedroz and D.S. Margoliouth, *The eclipse of the 'Abbasid Caliphate. Original chronicles of the fourth Islamic century*, 6 vols (Oxford, 1920–1), VI, pp. 240–1; and M. Canard, "Les sources arabes de l'histoire byzantin aux confins des Xe et XIe siècles", *REB*, 19, 1961, pp. 284–314, at 299–300. For the retreat of 1177, see Choniates, *Historia*, pp. 195–6.
118. Leo diac., *Historia*, ix, 9; Anna Comnena, *Alexiad*, x, 4 (trans. Sewter, p. 305); and Niketas Choniates, *Historia*, p. 35. For Moroleon, "stupid Leo", see Scylitzes, *Synopsis historiarum*, p. 218.84–8.
119. *Theoph.*, p. 491 (trans. Mango and Scott, pp. 673–4); I. Dujcev, "La chronique byzantine de l'an 811", *TM*, 1, 1965, p. 214. For 813, see Scylitzes, *Synopsis historiarum*, p. 18.36–50; for 838, see *Th. cont.*, p. 128 (with p. 178, a description of the same events mistakenly ascribed to a later battle).
120. See *Theoph.*, p. 500 (trans. Mango and Scott, p. 684); *Scriptor incertus*, p. 337f.; and *Th. cont.*, pp. 272–3.

121. Analyzed and discussed in Kaegi, *Byzantine Military Unrest*, pp. 186–254.
122. For kin and group solidarities respected in the composition of units on the field, see, for example, Niceph., *Praecepta*, i, 10–17; iii, 73–5; iv, 2–5; *Syll. tact.*, § 44.6; and the comments of McGeer, *Sowing the Dragon's Teeth*, p. 183. See also Attaleiates, *Historia*, pp. 39–43. On the social implications of the relationship between soldiers and their leaders, see Chapter 7 below.
123. Leo, *Tact.*, i, 15; ii, 1–53; xx, 1–5; *Const. Porph., Three Treatises*, (C) 250–66; and cf. 468–73 (the emperor's address to the soldiers, promising them rich rewards if they fight well).
124. *Tact.*, xx, 4, 18, for example. A well-known example of Nikephros Phocas' discipline is as follows. While on the march against the Arabs in North Syria, one of the infantry, becoming weary, discarded his shield. Having been found out by the emperor, he was ordered to be punished by his platoon commander (*lochagos*): he was to be lashed, have his nose cut, and be paraded around the camp as a warning to others. The junior officer failed to carry this out, however, and when this was discovered by the emperor, the latter suffered the same punishment: Leo diac., *Historia*, iv, 57–8.
125. Leo diac., *Historia*, iii, 37. There are many other examples: Alexios Axouch and Andronikos Kontostephanos under Manuel I, for example, figure prominently in the account of Niketas Choniates.
126. Psellos, *Chronographia*, I, 25 (trans. Sewter, p. 22); Scylitzes, *Synopsis historiarum*, p. 406.
127. Attaleiates, *Historia*, pp. 114–16.
128. Attaleiates, *Historia*, pp. 117.22–118.13.
129. Leo diac., *Historia*, i, 9–10.

Chapter 7   Warfare and society

1. For an excellent discussion of this material, see Athena Kolia-Dermitzaki, "Byzantium at war in sermons and letters of the 10th and 11th centuries. An ideological approach", in Oikonomidès (ed.), *Byzantium at War*, pp. 213–38.
2. See W. Wright, *The Chronicle of Joshua the Stylite* (Cambridge, 1882/Amsterdam, 1968), §§ liv (p. 44), lxx (p. 58), lxxvii (pp. 62–3) for baking bread; and §§ lxxxvi (p. 68) and xcv–xcvi (pp. 72–3) for the damage wrought by the *foederati*. For Evagrius, see *The Ecclesiastical History of Evagrius*, eds J. Bidez and L. Parmentier (London, 1898/Amsterdam, 1964), vi, 5 (English trans. E. Walford, *Ecclesiastical History: A History of the Church in Six Books, From A.D. 431 to A.D. 594 by Evagrius* (Bohn's Ecclesiastical Library, London, 1854), pp. 451–2).
3. See especially the novel of Anastasius on the situation in Thrace: *CJ*, X, 27.2/10 (a. 491–505) (*Codex Iustinianus*, ed. P. Krüger (*CJC*, II) (Berlin 1919)); and cf. a novel of Tiberius Constantine remitting taxes for certain eastern provinces, but alluding to the hardship caused by the presence of soldiers and warfare: Just., *Nov.*, clxiii (also in *JGR* (Zepos), I, Coll. 1, nov. XII).
4. See especially P.D. Jonge, "Scarcity of corn and cornprices in Ammianus", *Mnemosyne*, 4th ser., 1, 1948, pp. 238–45; Jones, *LRE*, p. 629 on the effects of the presence of a large expeditionary force at Edessa in 503 and 504 (while an

exception, the example is nevertheless useful in giving some idea of the problem the presence of a large army created), and p. 630 for the evidence for price-fixing. For the *quaestura exercitus*, see Jones, *LRE*, p. 482f., and for Maurice's order and the context, see Kaegi, *Byzantine Military Unrest*, pp. 106–13. Note also Maurice, *Strat.*, I, 9.47–54 on marching through "friendly" territory and avoiding harm to the rural populace.

5.   *Tactica*, ix, 1–3; xvii, 36.
6.   For example, Maurice, *Strat.*, i, 6.19, 13; i, 9 (= Leo, *Tact.*, viii, 10, 14).
7.   For example, Attaleiates, *Historia*, pp. 107.23–108.1, 126.14–15.
8.   Cf. Attaleiates, *Historia*, pp. 116.18–19; and see 146.18–22.
9.   For the rowdy behaviour and damage to property and persons caused by Nikephros' soldiers in the city, see Skylitzes, *Synopsis Historiarum*, p. 274; for Armenian indiscipline, see E. McGeer, "The legal decree of Nikephros II Phocas concerning Armenian stratiotai", in Miller and Nesbitt (eds), *Peace and War in Byzantium*, p. 135; and for the depredations caused by the fleet, see *Actes de Lavra*, I, no. 10, ll. 15–18. The story of the girl who had been robbed is recorded in the *Life* of the eleventh-century wandering monk Lazaros of Galesion (a mountain near Ephesos, where he eventually established himself): the girl is robbed by "the army of Armenians passing through at that time", undoubtedly one of the many *tagmata* recruited by the empire in that period: *Vita S. Lazari monachi in monte Galesio*, in *Acta Sanctorum Novembr.*, iii, 508–88 – see 513E–514B. For Choniates' remark, see *Historia*, p. 209; and cf. Kinnamos, *Epitome*, p. 71.
10.   Psellos, *Chronographia*, vii, 45 (trans. Sewter, p. 230) and vii, 46 (trans. Sewter, p. 231). For later evidence, see M.C. Bartusis, "The cost of late Byzantine warfare and defense", *Byzantinische Forschungen*, 16, 1991, pp. 75–89, esp. pp. 77–80.
11.   The wealthy and powerful were most successful in gaining exemption: see the letter of the general Nikephros Ouranos to the *krites* of the Thrakesion theme appealing for exemption from the billetting of troops which he claimed was crippling his household (in Darrouzès, *Epistoliers*, no. 42.241–2); or the letter of the patriarch Nikolaos Mystikos on behalf of the widow of a *drouggarios* of the *Vigla*: *Epistoliers*, no. 31.120–1. See especially *Nicholas I, Patriarch of Constantinople, Letters*, eds and trans. R.J.H. Jenkins and L.G. Westerink (Dumbarton Oaks Texts, II) (Washington, DC, 1973), nos. 92.10–26, 94.31–40 (extraordinary impositions for the Bulgarian war), 150, 183 (concerning the imposition of military burdens and renewed general imposition of extraordinary levies on Church lands and clerics), and further evidence discussed in Haldon, "Synone". Michael Choniates complains about three extra levies in a single year for the fleet on the district of Athens: Michael Choniates, i, p. 308 (*Michael Akominatou tou Choniatou ta sozomena*, ed. S. Lampros (Athens, 1879–80/Groningen, 1968)), for example. For other examples, see Haldon, "Synone", esp. pp. 127–49. On the public post, see: Jones, *LRE*, pp. 830–4; Hendy, *Studies*, pp. 603–13; Laurent, *Corpus*, II, pp. 195–261; and Oikonomidès, *Préséance*, pp. 311–12.
12.   *CIG*, IV, xl, no. 8690.
13.   See the comments of the editor regarding Constantine's programme of fort-building in Thrace: Niceph., *Short History*, § 73 (p. 219); and for Nikephros I, see *Theoph.*, p. 484 (trans. Mango and Scott, p. 666). For the inscriptions, see CIG, IV, xl, pp. 325–6, no. 8699 (for the year 1006); p. 366, no. 8797 (possibly for the reign of Michael III). The second inscription suggests that the walls in

question may have been constructed through the agency of the domestic of the Scholai and his soldiers.

14. H. Grégoire, "Note sur une inscription gréco-araméenne trouvée à Farasa", *Comptes-rendus des Séances de l'Académie des inscriptions et belles-lettres*, 1908, pp. 434f.

15. For *kastroktisia*, see Sp. Troianos, "Kastroktisia", *Byzantina*, 1, 1969, pp. 41–57, and Ahrweiler, "Recherches", p. 37, with note 2. There are many inscriptions, mostly commemorating rebuilding and repairs to walls and towers. They date from the fifth century on, although their number decreases over time. Many include a reference to the reigning emperor(s) or an indictional year which sometimes helps to date them. But it remains for the most part unclear who actually did the work, although the officer(s) in charge are named. For some examples, see H. Grégoire, *Recueils des inscriptions grecques chretiénnes d'Asie Mineure* (Paris, 1922), nos 302–4 (at Attaleia, for 909–10, 911–12, 915–16); no. 226 (at Hieron/Didymes in Caria, for 988–9); *CIG*, IV, xl, nos 8817, 8689. There are a number of others.

16. Anna Comnena, *Alexiad*, x, 5 (trans. Sewter, p. 308).

17. See: Skylitzes, *Synopsis Historiarum*, p. 274; Attaleiates, *Historia*, p. 151; Kinnamos, *Epitome*, pp. 199, 299, for example.

18. See Chapter 2.

19. See A. Harvey, "The land and taxation in the reign of Alexios I Komnenos: the evidence of Theophylakt of Ochrid", *REB*, 51, 1993, pp. 139–54, at 143–9. For the later twelfth century, see J. Herrin, "Realities of provincial government: Hellas and Peloponnesos, 1180–1205", *DOP*, 29, 1975, pp. 253–84. For demands on timber and related products see A. Dunn, "The exploitation and control of woodland and scrubland in the Byzantine world", *BMGS*, 16, 1992, pp. 235–98, esp. 268ff.

20. See: Haldon, "The organisation and support of an expeditionary force", pp. 141–4; A. Harvey, *Economic Expansion in the Byzantine Empire 900–1200* (Cambridge, 1989), pp. 105–8; Oikonomidès, "L'évolution de l'organisation administrative de l'empire byzantin", pp. 125–52.

21. See Michael Choniates, i, pp. 308–10; ii, pp. 106–7. For the general situation, see: N. Oikonomidès, "La décomposition de l'empire byzantin à la veille de 1204 et les origines de l'empire de Nicée: à propos de la 'Partitio Romaniae' ", in *Actes du XVe congrès int. d'études byzantines*, I (Athens, 1977), pp. 1–28; Angold, *The Byzantine Empire 1025–1204*, pp. 263–82.

22. Choniates, *Historia*, pp. 38–9 (Asia Minor); 73 (the citizens of Kerkyra: "because they were unable to abide the overbearing and insufferable tax collector . . .", decided to hand the city over to the Normans of Sicily) (trans. Brand, p. 43).

23. See: Leo, *Tact.*, viii, 26; Lemerle, *Agrarian history*, p. 122f.; and Dagron's comment in *Le traité sur la Guérilla*, p. 282. For the growth of personal retinues and ties of dependency, see Magdalino, "The Byzantine aristocratic *oikos*", in *The Byzantine Aristocracy, IX–XIII centuries*, ed. M. Angold (*BAR*, S221) (Oxford, 1984), ch. 6. For conflicts over billeting and supplying soldiers in the late Roman period, see in general MacMullen, *Soldier and Civilian*, pp. 86ff.; as well as Jones, *LRE*, p. 631f. For private retinues and soldiers in the sixth century, see the discussion with further literature in D. Feissel and I. Kaygusuz, "Un mandement impérial du VIe siècle dans une inscription d'Hadrianoupolis d'Honoriade", *TM*, 9, 1985, pp. 397–419.

24. Rescript of 527: H. Grégoire, *Recueil des inscriptions grecques chrétiennes*, no. 314; novellae of Justinian: Just, *Nov.*, 28, § 4, pr. (for Hellenopontus, a. 535), 29, § 3 (for paphlagonia, a. 535), 30, § 7.2 (for Cappadocia, a. 536); Justinian, *Edict.*, VIII, §§ 2, 3 (a. 548); for the Egyptian petition, see Feissel and Kaygusuz, "Un mandement impérial du VIe siècle", at p. 413 and n. 65. Note that the term *bucellarii*, originally referring to privately hired and maintained soldiers, was coming by the later part of the sixth century to refer to such soldiers hired under state auspices who could be brigaded together and employed in regular military duties like ordinary soldiers: see Chapter 4 above.
25. See: J.F. Haldon, "Ideology and social change in the seventh century: military discontent as a barometer", *Klio*, 68, 1986, pp. 139–90 (repr. in *State, Army and Society in Byzantium*, II); Kaegi, *Byzantine Military Unrest*.
26. For a valuable account of this process in sixth-century Syria during the period of warfare between the Persian Sassanid state and the Romans, see F. Trombley, "War and society in rural Syria *c.* 502–613 A.D.: observations on the epigraphy", *BMGS*, 21, 1997, pp. 154–209. For Eirene's measures, see Oikonomidès, "Middle Byzantine Provincial Recruits", pp. 135–6.
27. For refugees in the 570s, and their effect on the regions into which they moved, see the *Life* of the patriarch of Constantinople, Eutychius *(Vita Eutychii Archiepiscopi Constantinopolitani*, in: *PG*, 86, 2, 2273–2390) at 2344B–D, where the feeding of people from Nikopolis, Neokaisareia, Zela and Komana and other districts in Armenia and eastern Pontus from the grain stores of a monastery at Amaseia is described. For the seventh century, see esp. H. Ditten, *Ethnische Verschiebungen*, pp. 45–65, who details the evidence for the movement of refugees in the war-torn regions of both the Balkans and Asia Minor, with the most recent literature on the subject. See also Haldon, *Byzantium in the Seventh Century*, pp. 103–12, 144–5 (sources and literature). Good sixth-century comparative material can be found in Trombley, "War and society in rural Syria". For Nikephros I, see *Theoph.*, p. 482 (trans. Mango and Scott, p. 663).
28. The best general survey remains Vryonis, *The Decline of Medieval Hellenism in Asia Minor*, pp. 144ff. For the Byzantine evidence, see the survey of F. Trombley, "War, society and popular religion in Byzantine Anatolia (6th–13th centuries)", in N. Oikonomides (ed.), *Byzantine Asia Minor (6th–12th cents.)* (Athens, 1998), pp. 97–139.
29. See Haldon, *Byzantium in the Seventh Century*, pp. 332–7, 366–9.
30. See the survey of H. Ahrweiler, "L'Asie Mineure et les invasions arabes", *Revue Historique*, 227, 1962, pp. 1–32; Haldon, *Byzantium in the Seventh Century*, pp. 114–17, 143–5; and the texts cited in A. Ilieva, "The Byzantine image of war and peace: the case of the Peloponnese", *Byzantinische Forschungen*, 19, 1993, pp. 183–92. For references to devastation, see, for example, the *Life* of Philaretos, whose home was in Paphlagonia and whose herds had been driven off by raiders: M.-H. Fourmy and M. Leroy, "La vie de S. Philarète", *B*, 9, 1934, pp. 85–170, at pp. 115–17, 137; or the *Life* of the tenth-century magnate Michael Maleinos, whose properties in the devastated regions of Charsianon in east-central Anatolia he improved by careful investment: L. Petit, "Vie de S. Michel Maleinos", *Revue de l'Orient Chrétien*, 7, 1902, pp. 543–603, at pp. 550.20–1. Although many of these *Lives* are full of literary *topoi* and rhetorical artifice and should not always be taken at face value, they had to represent a recognizable reality for their listeners or readers, and there is every reason to believe that the general situations

they describe are more or less accurate. The *Life* of St Peter of Atroa and the collection of posthumous miracles he worked provide classic examples of the normality of warfare, soldiers and military matters in Byzantine life: see *La vie merveilleuse de S. Pierre d'Atroa*, ed. V. Laurent (Subsid. Hag. 29) (Brussels, 1956), §§ 20, 23, 36, 39, etc.; and *La vita retractata et les miracles postumes de saint Pierre d'Atroa*, ed., trans. and commentary V. Laurent (Subsid. Hag. 31) (Brussels, 1958) – see §§ 109, 110, 111, etc. For the eleventh century, cf. the *Life* of Lazaros of Galesion, where soldiers and the background warfare are taken for granted throughout the text (*Vita S. Lazari monachi in monte Galesio*, in *AS Novembr.*, iii, 508–88).

31. See *Vita et Miracula Theodori (tironis)*, in: H. Delehaye, *Les légendes grecques des saints militaires* (Paris, 1909), pp. 183–201, at pp. 198–9 (miracles 7, 9).

32. For the battle, won by the forces of Constantine V over the troops of Teletz, the Bulgar khan, see: *Theoph.*, pp. 432–3 (trans. Mango and Scott, p. 599); Nikephros, *Short History*, § 76 (trans. Mango, p. 149). For the bones still to be seen, see Nicephorus, *Antirrheticus iii adversus Constantinum Copronymum*, in: *PG*, 100, cols 376–533, at 508B. See P. Alexander, *The Patriarch Nicephorus of Constantinople. Ecclesiastical Policy and Image Worship in the Byzantine Empire* (Oxford, 1958), pp. 168–70.

33. They were estabished in the newly founded *polis* of Nea Ioustinianoupolis, near Kyzikos (probably the former harbour suburb of Artake), named after the emperor of the time. See W. Brandes, *Die Städte Kleinasiens im 7. und 8. Jahrhundert* (BbA, 56) (Berlin, 1989), pp. 115–18.

34. The most comprehensive and detailed analysis of these movements is Ditten, *Ethnische Verschiebungen*. But see also the older work of P. Charanis, *Studies on the Demography of the Byzantine Empire* (London, 1972), esp. "The transfer of population as a policy in the Byzantine empire", *Comparative Studies in Society and History*, 3, 2, 1961, pp. 140–54, (repr. in Charanis, *Studies*, III); and "On the ethnic composition of Byzantine Asia Minor in the thirteenth century", *Prosphora eis ton Stilpona P. Kyriakiden* (Thessaloniki, 1953) (repr. in Charanis, *Studies*, VIII).

35. Harvey, *Economic Expansion in the Byzantine Empire*, pp. 207–24; Magdalino, *The Empire of Manuel I Komnenos*, pp. 123–40.

36. For the settlement of the Serbs, see Niketas Choniates, *Historia*, p. 16. For the situation along the west coast, see the comments of Odo de Deuil, *De profectione Ludovici VII in orientem,* trans. V.G. Berry (New York, 1948), p. 107; and for Attaleia, see William of Tyre, *Historia rerum in partibus transmarinis gestarum. A History of Deeds Done Beyond the Sea*, trans. E.A.Babcock and A.C. Krey (New York, 1943), 2, p. 178.

37. See esp. Vryonis, *Decline of Medieval Hellenism*.

38. For plague and disease, see *ODB*, p. 1681, and the discussion in L. Conrad, "Epidemic disease in central Syria in the late sixth century. Some new insights from the verse of Hassān ibn Thābit", *BMGS*, 18, 1994, pp. 12–58, with a good survey of earlier literature and the demographic issues. On population movement, see G. Dagron, "Minorités ethniques et religieuses dans l'Orient byzantin à la fin du Xe et au XIe siècle: l'immigration syrienne", *TM*, 6, 1976, pp. 177–216, and *Le traité sur la Guérilla*, p. 244 and n. 26, as well as Conrad, "Epidemic disease in central Syria in the late sixth century" and Trombley, "War and society in rural Syria, ca. 502–613 A.D."

39. Haldon and Kennedy, "Arab–Byzantine frontier"; Vasiliev, *Byzance et les arabes*, I, p. 87; Dagron and Mihaescu, *Le traité sur la Guérilla*, pp. 239–57.
40. See G. Dagron, "Apprivoiser la guerre. Byzantins et arabes ennemis intimes", in Oikonomidès (ed), *Byzantium at War*, pp. 37–49, at pp. 40–2; *Le traité sur la guérilla*, pp. 239ff., 280ff; and compare the statement in the treatise *Campaign Organisation*, § 28.24–6. On the "chivalric" aspect of Byzantine military culture at this time see McGeer, *Sowing the Dragon's Teeth*, pp. 219–22. For the Frankish mercenaries who fought for the empire, see the remarks of Attaleiates on the reasons for Romanos IV pardoning the rebel Crispin, "because of the man's bravery and glorious deeds . . ." (*Historia*, pp. 124–5, 171); or Nikephros Bryennios on the martial qualities of Roussel de Bailleul (*Nicephori Bryennii Historiarum libri quattuor*, ed. P. Gautier (Brussels, 1975), p. 195). See A. Kazhdan and S. Franklin, *Studies on Byzantine Literature of the Eleventh and Twelfth Centuries* (Cambridge, 1984), esp. pp. 66–7.
41. For further discussion, see four contributions by P. Magdalino: "The Byzantine aristocratic *oikos*" and "Byzantine snobbery" in M. Angold (ed.), *The Byzantine Aristocracy, IX to XIII Centuries* (Oxford, 1984); "Aspects of twelfth-century Byzantine *Kaiserkritik*", *Speculum* 58, 1983, pp. 326–46, and in particular "Honour among Romaioi: the framework of social values in the world of Digenes Akrites and Kekaumenos", *BMGS*, 13, 1989, pp. 183–218.
42. Thus the emperor Maurice earned the hatred of many soldiers and other subjects when he refused to ransom a large number of prisoners from the Avar Khagan, who is reported to have had them massacred. There is probably no truth in the story (which does not appear in the near-contemporary account of Theophylact Simocatta), but it is nevertheless indicative: see Kaegi, *Byzantine Military Unrest*, pp. 108–9.
43. In general on the issue of the treatment of prisoners-of-war, see the detailed analysis of S. Patoura, *Prisoners of War as Agents of Communication and Information* (Athens, 1994) (in Greek); and *ODB*, art. "Prisoners of war", pp. 1722–3. On recruitment of prisoners into imperial forces, see Chapter 3 above; and for the settlement and marriage of prisoners-of-war, see *De Cer.*, p. 695. There is a useful and accessible tabulation of recorded exchanges of prisoners between *c.* 769 and the later tenth century in Toynbee, *Constantine Porphyrogenitus and His World*, pp. 390–3. See the account by the tenth-century writer Mas'udi, translated in Vasiliev, *Byzance et les arabes*, II, 2, pp. 405–8.
44. For Constantine V's execution of Bulgar soldiers, see *Theoph.*, p. 433 (trans. Mango and Scott, p. 599); for Basil's actions, see *Th. cont.*, p. 283 (during his campaign against Germanikeia in 878); for Alexios I, see Anna Comnena, *Alexiad*, viii, 6 (trans. Sewter, pp. 259–60); for prisoners as spies, see R.A. Khouri al-Odetallah, "Unofficial exchanges, purchases and emancipations of Byzantine and Arab war captives", *Graeco-Arabica*, 4, 1991, pp. 109–13, and esp. Patoura, *Prisoners of War as Agents of Communication and Information*, pp. 125–31. See also Toynbee's discussion, *Constantine Porphyrogenitus and His World*, pp. 383–9. The extracts from Arab chronicles of the ninth and tenth centuries in Vasiliev, *Byzance et les arabes*, II, 2, contain many examples both of the massacre or execution of Byzantine prisoners for a variety of reasons, as well as of more humane treatment. For the situation in the tenth century, and the variations in attitudes to Muslim prisoners according to the general political-ideological situation, see L. Simeonova, "In the depths of tenth-century Byzantine ceremonial: the

treatment of Arab prisoners of war at imperial banquets", *BMGS*, 22, 1998, pp. 75–104. For the recommendation to kill or send on prisoners, see *Skirmishing*, § 11.30–1.

45. See, for example, the miraculous release from imprisonment of a soldier through the intercession of his saint: *Miracula S. Georgii*, ed. J.B. Aufhauser (Leipzig, 1913), pp. 22ff. (events of the early tenth century).

46. For Saif's letter, see Yahya ibn Sa'īd, in Vasiliev, *Byzance et les arabes*, II, 2, p. 96. For the sons of Dalassenos, see *Histoire de Yahya ibn Sa'id d'Antioch, continuateur de Sa'id ibn Bitriq*, eds and trans. I. Kratchkovsky and A. Vasiliev (Paris, 1924–32), p. 456. There are several tales, some of which were certainly exaggerated for propagandistic purposes, of captured soldiers in particular who, refusing to surrender their faith, were executed: see *ODB*, pp. 800–1. For the portraits of Byzantine and Arab warriors, see Vasiliev, *Byzance et les arabes*, II, 1, pp. 123.

47. For a brief survey of Roman practice and arrangements, see Dixon and Southern, *The Roman Cavalry*, pp. 98–106.

48. Maurice, *Strat.*, ii, 9 (Leo, *Tact.*, iv, 15. The derivation of *skribon* is debated. *Skribones* were also the officers in charge of the subdivisions – *banda* – in the *tagma* of the *exkoubitoi*: see Haldon, *Byzantine Praetorians*, p. 560, n. 855. It appears to derive from *scribo/scribere*, and relates to the writing down/recording/ registration of names); *Campaign Organisation*, § 31.20–3. For the events of 1165, see Kinnamos, *Epitome*, p. 238.

49. See Paul of Aegina, *Epitome iatrike*, ed. I.L. Heiberg, 2 vols (Leipzig, 1921, 1924), vi, 88: "Peri belon exaireseos" ("On the extraction of arows"). On Byzantine medical science and practice, see O. Temkin, "Byzantine medicine, tradition and empiricism", *DOP*, 16, 1962, pp. 95–115, and the entries "Medicine" and "Disease" in *ODB*, pp. 1327–8 and 638 respectively.

50. See Procopius, *Wars*, VI, ii.14–32; and cf. *Th. Sim.*, *Historia*, ii, 6 (trans. Whitby, p. 51), for an account of the multiple wounds from which a soldier died after a battle with the Persians. Byzantine surgical instruments have been excavated from various contexts and suggest – in combination with what can be gleaned from the medical treatises themselves – that surgical practice was quite advanced relative to much of the medieval world: see entries "Medicine" and "Disease" in *ODB*, pp. 1327–8 and 638. For a twelfth-century example, see Kinnamos, *Epitome*, p. 62.

51. Choniates, *Historia*, p. 191.

52. J. Koder, "The urban character of the early Byzantine empire: some reflections on a settlement geographical approach to the topic", in *Seventeenth International Byzantine Congress. Major Papers* (New York, 1986), pp. 155–87; Brandes, *Städte*, pp. 44–131; for its implications for the state and social relations in general, see Haldon, *Byzantium in the Seventh Century*.

53. See: A.H.M. Jones, *The Greek City from Alexander to Justinian* (Oxford, 1940), pp. 259ff.; E. Kirsten, "Die byzantinische Stadt", in *Berichte zum XI. Internationalen Byzantinisten-Kongress*, V, 3 (Munich, 1958), pp. 1–35, at pp. 10ff.; D. Claude, *Die byzantinische Stadt im 6. Jahrhundert* (Byzantinisches Archiv, 13) (Munich, 1969), pp. 176ff.; E. Patlagean, *Pauvreté économique et pauvreté sociale à Byzance* (Paris, 19), pp. 156–235. Note also A.H.M. Jones, "The economic life of the towns of the Roman empire", *Recueils de la Société Jean Bodin*, 7, 1955, pp. 161–92 (repr. in Jones, *The Roman Economy. Studies in Ancient Economic and Social History*, ed. P.A. Brunt (Oxford, 1974), pp. 35–60). For further literature

see Haldon, 'Some considerations on Byzantine society and economy in the seventh century', pp. 78ff., and most recently, Brandes, *Städte*, for a full analysis of the archaeological and textual evidence for the decline of the late antique city and the development of the situation revealed in the sources for the later seventh and eighth centuries.

54. Jones, *The Later Roman Empire*, pp. 712ff.; Jones, "The cities of the Roman empire: political, administrative and judicial functions", *Recueils de la Société Jean Bodin*, 6, 1954, pp. 135–73; E. Frances, "La ville byzantine et la monnaie aux VIIᵉ–VIIIᵉ siècles", *Byzantinobulgarica*, 2, 1966, pp. 3–14, at pp. 5–10; Kirsten, 'Die byzantinische Stadt', pp. 25ff.

55. See the account, with literature, in J. Russell, "Transformations in early Byzantine urban life: the contribution and limitations of archaeological evidence", in *Seventeenth International Byzantine Congress. Major Papers* (New York, 1986), pp. 137–54.

56. Summarized in Brandes, *Städte*, pp. 81–120, 124–31.

57. See especially J.-M. Spieser, "L'Évolution de la ville byzantine de l'époque paléochrétienne à l'iconoclasme", in *Hommes et richesses dans l'Empire byzantin, IVᵉ–VIIᵉ siècles* (Paris, 1989), pp. 97–106, esp. 103f.

58. See in general Brandes, *Die Städte Kleinasiens*, and Brandes, 'Die byzantinische Stadt Kleinasiens im 7. und 8. Jahrhundert – ein Forschungsbericht', *Klio*, 70, 1988, pp. 176–208.

59. See the discussion in A. Dunn, "The transformation from *polis* to *kastron* in the Balkans (III–VII cc.): general and regional perspectives", *BMGS*, 18, 1994, pp. 60–80, critical also of the otherwise useful survey of W. Müller-Wiener, "Von der Polis zum Kastron", *Gymnasium*, 93, 1986, pp. 435–74.

60. Brandes, *Städte*, pp. 81–131; with Dunn, "The transformation from *polis* to *kastron*", and J.F. Haldon, "The idea of the town in the Byzantine empire", in G.P. Brogiolo (ed.), *The Idea and Ideal of the Town between Late Antiquity and the Early Middle Ages* (Leiden, 1999), pp. 1–23.

61. C. Foss, "Late Antique and Byzantine Ankara", *Dumbarton Oaks Papers*, 31, 1977, pp. 29–87, at pp. 74–8; Brandes, *Städte*, pp. 107–8; Haldon, *Byzantium in the Seventh Century*, pp. 112–13. For Amorion, see: R.M. Harrison, N. Christie et al., "Excavations at Amorium: 1992 interim report", *Anatolian Studies*, 43, 1993, pp. 147–62; C. Lightfoot et al., "Amorium excavations 1993: the sixth preliminary Report", *Anatolian Studies*, 44, 1994, pp. 105–28. For the historical situation of the city in the seventh–ninth centuries, Brandes, *Städte*, pp. 133–5. For comparative plans and figures, see S. Hill and J. Crow, 'Survey at Amasra', in *IX. Arastirma Sonuçlari Toplantasi* (Istanbul, 1992), pp. 87–92. See also the general discussion in C. Foss and D. Winfield, *Byzantine Fortifications. An Introduction* (Pretoria, 1986).

62. It has been argued that this means that the whole ancient city area continued to be occupied: see, for example, F. Trombley, "The decline of the seventh-century town: the exception of Euchaita", in *Byzantine Studies in Honor of Milton V. Anastos*, ed. Sp. Vryonis, Jr (Malibu, 1985), pp. 65–90, and – with a slightly different dating – C. Zuckerman, "The reign of Constantine V in the miracles of St Theodore the Recruit (BHG 1764)", *Revue des Études Byzantines*, 46, 1988, pp. 191–210. Alternatively, it has been suggested that the text(s) in question consists of *topoi* and that only a citadel is actually meant: see A. Kazhdan, in *Erytheia*, 9, 1988, pp. 197–200.

63. C. Lightfoot, in *Anatolian Studies*, 44, 1994, pp. 105ff.
64. Compare the example of Ephesos, which served as a refuge for the local rural population, as a fortress and military administrative centre, but also retained its role as a market town. Survey and excavation suggest that it was divided into three small, distinct and separate occupied areas, including the citadel: see C. Foss, *Ephesus After Antiquity: A Late Antique, Byzantine and Turkish City* (Cambridge, 1979), pp. 106–113. Sardis similarly shrank to a small fortified acropolis and one or more separate occupied areas within the circumference of the original late ancient walls: see C. Foss, *Byzantine and Turkish Sardis* (Cambridge, MA/London, 1976), pp. 55–61; Miletos was reduced to some 25 per cent of its original area and divided into two defended complexes: see W. Müller-Wiener, "Das Theaterkastell von Milet", *Istanbuler Mitteilungen*, 17, 1967, pp. 279–90; C. Foss, "Archaeology and the 'Twenty Cities' of Byzantine Asia", *American Journal of Archaeology*, 81, 1977, pp. 469–86, at p. 477f.; Didyma, close by Miletos, was reduced to a small defended structure based around a converted pagan temple and an associated but unfortified settlement nearby: see Foss, "Archaeology and the 'Twenty Cities' of Byzantine Asia", p. 479 with literature. There are many other examples: see the survey of Brandes, *Städte*, pp. 82–111, 132ff. with further literature and sources.
65. See the survey with examples in Foss and Winfield, *Byzantine Fortifications: An Introduction*.
66. See: Howard-Johnston, "Byzantine Anzitene", in S. Mitchell (ed.), *Armies and Frontiers in Roman and Byzantine Anatolia*, pp. 246–61; W. Saunders, "Qal'at Seman: a frontier fort of the tenth and eleventh centuries", ibid., pp. 291–303; and T. Sinclair, "Byzantine and Islamic fortification in the Middle East – the photographic exhibition", ibid., pp. 305–36.
67. See: M. Angold, "The shaping of the medieval Byzantine 'city'", *Byzantinische Forschungen*, 10, 1985, pp. 1–37; Harvey, *Economic Expansion in the Byzantine Empire*, pp. 198–243.
68. See Haldon, in *Const. Porph., Three Treatises*, pp. 242–3.
69. Haldon, *Const. Porph., Three Treatises*, pp. 243–4; R. Vari, "Zum historischen Exzerptenwerke des Konstantinos Porphyrogennetos", *Byzantinische Zeitschrift*, 17, 1908, pp. 75–85, at p. 83; on commanders' speeches to their troops, see the examples in Haldon, *Const. Porph., Three Treatises*, pp. 243–4. A treatise "On harangues" was compiled in the tenth century, closely associated in the manuscript tradition with other military treatises. For the orators, see Maurice, *Strat.*, ii, 19 (called *kantatores*); Leo, *Tact.*, iv, 6 (called *parakletores*).
70. See especially McCormick, *Eternal Victory*; *ODB*, art. "Enkomion", pp. 700–1; Kolia-Dermitzaki, "Byzantium at war in sermons and letters", esp. pp. 231–4. For John II's entry, see: Choniates, *Historia*, p. 19; Kinnamos, *Epitome*, p. 13.
71. See C. Mango (ed. and trans.), *The Homilies of Photios, Patriarch of* Constantinople (*DOS*, 3) (Cambridge, MA, 1958), pp. 74–110. See, for example, a letter of the tenth-century official Symeon *magistros*, in which the disruptive effects of an Arab raid in the 960s are described: Darrouzes, *Epistoliers*, ii, no. 86.
72. For a useful survey of this material, see Kolia-Dermitzaki, "Byzantium at war in sermons and letters", pp. 220–2. For Lazaros and the former prisoner, see *Vita Lazari*, 529B–D.
73. Anna Comnena, *Alexiad*, xv, 10 (trans. Sewter, p. 505).

74. See, for example, the remarks of Liudprand of Cremona on his visit to Constantinople in 968: "The Greeks and Saracens have books . . . where one finds
written the number of years of each emperor's life . . . and whether he will have
success or failure against the Saracens . . . for this . . . reason, the Greeks, full
of courage, attack, and the Saracens, without hope, offer them no resistance,
awaiting the moment when it will be their turn to attack and that of the Greeks
to make no resistance." See *Liudprand of Cremona, Works*, trans. F.A. Wright
(London, 1930): *Legatio*, § 39 (ed. J. Becker, *Liutprandi episcopi Cremonensis opera*
(Leipzig, 1915), pp. 195–6); and discussion with Byzantine and Arab sources in
Dagron, "Apprivoiser la guerre", pp. 42–7; and *Vita S. Ioannicii* (a Petro mon.),
in: *AS Novembr.*, ii/1, pp. 384–434, at 386C–387A.

75. See *Const. Porph., Three Treatises*, (C) 199–202. The books used by sailors for
"reading the weather" were not simply navigational aids, some were compiled
specifically with naval warfare in mind, and included substantial horoscopic
elements, and determined in addition on what days of the week naval warfare
should be undertaken or avoided. See G. Dagron, "Das Firmament soll christlich
werden. Zu zwei Seefahrtskalendern des 10. Jahrhunderts", in G. Prinzing and
D. Simon (eds), *Fest und Alltag in Byzanz* (Munich, 1990), pp. 145–56, 210–15.
For Constantine VI, see *Theoph.*, pp. 467–8 (trans. Mango and Scott, p. 643).
On astrology in Byzantium, see *ODB*, art. "Astrology", pp. 214–16; art. "Horo-
scope", pp. 947–8. For Alexios I, see Anna Comnena, *Alexiad*, xv, 4 (trans.
Sewter, pp. 481–2); for Manuel I, see Choniates, *Historia*, pp. 95–6.

76. See the discussion in Chapter 1 above.

77. See in general the discussion in Kolia-Dermitzaki, "Byzantium at war in sermons and letters".

78. See P.J. Photiades, "A semi-Greek, semi-Coptic parchment", *Klio*, 41, 1963,
pp. 234–5. For the Syrian material, see Trombley, "War and society in rural
Syria, *c.* 502–613 A.D."

79. See W.M. Ramsay and Gertrude Bell, *The Thousand and One Churches* (London,
1919), pp. 525–6, and inscr. nos 13, 42, 43. The dating of the inscriptions
remains problematic, but the eight–tenth centuries are generally accepted.

80. See the story of the soldier Leo who was forced to send his only son George
on an expedition against the Bulgars in the early tenth century because he was
himself too old to serve actively: *Miracula S. Georgii*, pp. 21.6–13, 22.7–9; in a
slightly different case, a widow in the early tenth century is able to obtain the
help of a high-ranking churchman in pleading for her son to be exempted from
the call-up because of her poverty: see Darrouzès, *Épistoliers*, ii, 50 (130–1).

81. See, for example, Maurice, *Strat.*, i, 6.7; 8.16; vii B, 13; viii, 1.28, 35 (repeated
in Leo, *Tact.*, viii, 7, 20, etc.). For the treatment of those who fail to return
from leave in time for the muster or who deliberately fall behind the expeditionary column, see *Const. Porph., Three Treatises*, (B) 42–5 (and cf. Maurice, *Strat.*,
i, 6.4, 7.14 = Leo, *Tact.*, viii, 4, 15); and for the registers and the campaign
muster, see *Campaign Organisation*, § 29. For Ioannikios, see *Vita S. Ioannici*,
337C–338C, 311B. There are several other examples of soldiers who deserted,
often to hide in monastic communities: see Haldon, *Byzantine Praetorians*, p. 327.
The punishments for desertion under various conditions are specified in the
military codes dating from Roman times but revised in several different versions
during the sixth and ninth centuries: see W. Ashburner (ed.) "The Byzantine

Mutiny Act", *JHS*, 46, 1926, pp. 80–109 (earlier version); and ed. E. Korzensky, "Leges poenales militares e codice Laurentiano LXXV", *Egypetemes Philologiae Közlöny* (Budapest, 1930), pp. 155–63, 215–18 (both repr. in: *Jus Graecoromanum*, eds I. and P. Zepos, 8 vols (Athens, 1931/Aalen, 1962), ii, pp. 75–9, 80–9). For the events of 880, see *Th. cont.*, 303. Further examples of military discipline and punishment for desertion in the field are noted in Chapters 5 and 6 above.

82. See: Leo, *Tact.* xi, 11; N. Svoronos, *Les novelles des empereurs macédoniens concernant la terre et les stratiotes*, ed. P. Gounaridis (Athens, 1994), p. 118.1–2.

83. See, for example, L.S.B. MacCoull, "'When Justinian was upsetting the world': a note on soldiers and religious coercion in sixth-century Egypt", in Miller and Nesbitt (eds), *Peace and War in Byzantium*, pp. 106–13; for the middle Byzantine period, see Haldon, *Byzantine Praetorians*, pp. 125–8, 137–8, 184–9, 232–3, 243–4. The Varangians were particularly disliked as alien "enforcers" of imperial policies or commands: see Blöndal, *The Varangians of Byzantium*, esp. pp. 188–90. For a soldier treated with considerable hospitality (more than necessary – the landlord's daughter at the inn where he was staying attempted to seduce him!). See *Vita Nicolai Studitae*, in: *PG*, 105, cols 863–925, at 893f; and *Relatio Nicolai ex milite monachi*, in: *Synax. CP*, 341–4, at 341. 22ff. – two separate stories, but very similar and both drawing on the same source. Although the story occurs in a hagiographical context, and with a specific motive in mind, the motif itself must have been recognizable enough to the contemporary audience or readership. This seems to have been a popular story of the time concerning the catastrophic defeat at the hands of the Bulgar khan Krum. For discussion, see L. Clugnet, "Histoire de S. Nicolas, soldat et moine", *Revue de l'Orient Chrétien*, 7, 1902, pp. 319–30 (= Bibl. Hagiogr. Or., 3 (Paris, 1902), pp. 27-38); see also E. Follieri and I. Dujcev, "Un acolutia inedita per i martiri di Bulgaria dell'anno 813", *Byzantion*, 33, 1963, pp. 71–106, and cf. p. 90, note 1; see also J. Wortley, "Legends of the Byzantine Disaster of 811", *Byzantion*, 50, 1980, pp. 533–62.

84. See Haldon, "Ideology and social change", pp. 139–42. For the integration of soldiers into local society, see also Haldon, "Military service, military lands, and the status of soldiers", pp. 44–7; for useful comparative examples from late Roman Egypt, see J.G. Keenan, "Evidence for the Byzantine army in the Syene papyri", *Bulletin of the American Society of Papyrologists*, 27, 1996, pp. 139–50, with further literature. See also J. Wortley, "Military elements in psychophelitic tales and sayings", in Miller and Nesbitt (eds), *Peace and War in Byzantium*, pp. 89–105.

85. On the Justinianic monopoly and later developments in the control and production of weapons, see Haldon, *Byzantine Praetorians*, pp. 318–23. For the tenth-century text, see *Synopsis maior Basilicorum*, in: *Jus Graecoromanum*, eds I. and P. Zepos, 8 vols (Athens, 1931/Aalen, 1962), v, pp. 1–598, at pp. 453–4 (0, 7.2). For examples of private citizens defending themselves, see T. Kolias, "Weapons in Byzantine society", in *Daily Life in Byzantium* (Athens, 1989), pp. 463–76 (in Greek) – see pp. 472–3.

86. For the extent of imperial control over "prohibited goods" see H. Antoniadis-Bibicou, *Recherches sur les douanes à Byzance, l' "octava", le "kommerkion" et les commerciaires* (Paris, 1963), esp. pp. 50f. and 78f.; and see J. Koder (ed. and trans.), *Das Eparchenbuch Leons des Weisen* (*CFHB*, XXXIII) (Vienna, 1991), § 4.1; § 4.8; § 6.13; § 8.1. For the Avar emissaries, see Menander Protector, *Fragmenta*, no. 9 (in *FHG*, IV, p. 205).

87. For weapons as gifts, see T. Kolias, *Byzantinische Waffen*, p. 134; for weapons for the pro-Byzantine faction at the Hungarian court, see Kinnamos, *Epitome*, p. 223.

88. See Kolias, "Weapons in Byzantine society", pp. 469ff., with further examples.

89. Cf. the soldiers of the disbanded *tagmata* in 786/7, for example, or in 813, see Haldon, *Byzantine Praetorians*, pp. 318–19. For troops being equipped with weapons, see Chapters 4 and 5 above.

90. See R. Riedinger (ed.), *Concilium universale Constantinopolitanum tertium*, 2 vols (Acta conciliorum oecumenicorum II/2.1–2) (Berlin, 1990, 1992), p. 886.20–5 (= J.D. Mansi (ed.), *Scarorum conciliorum nova et amplissima collectio* (Florence, 1759–1927), xi, p. 737f.). For the context, see Haldon, *Byzantium in the Seventh Century*, p. 441f.

91. See Kazhdan and Epstein, *Change in Byzantine Culture in the Eleventh and Twelfth Centuries*, pp. 62–73, 99–119.

92. This institutional distinctiveness was no different in the earlier Roman world from which it derived, of course. See, for example, Ramsay McMullen, *Soldier and Civilian in the Roman World*; for the later Roman and early Byzantine period, see Haldon, "Ideology and social change in the seventh century", pp. 158–61.

93. For further discussion and literature, see: Haldon, *Byzantine Praetorians*, pp. 113–14, 322–3 with sources; E. Sander, "Die Kleidung des oströmischen Soldaten", *Historia*, 12, 1936, pp. 153ff.; Ramsay McMullen, "Some pictures in Ammianus Marcellinus", *Historia*, 46, 1964, pp. 435–55. For the Varangians, see *ODB*, p. 2152.

94. For some examples of local officer recruitment in the ninth and early tenth centuries, see Haldon, *Byzantine Praetorians*, p. 331 and note 1021; on the settlement and assimilation of foreigners, see Lemerle, *Agrarian History*, p. 133f. for a commentary; for the Banu Habib and the Kurds, see Toynbee, *Constantine Porphyrogenitus and His World*, pp. 82–5.

95. See Haldon, *Recruitment and Conscription*, p. 54, note 94, p. 71, note 126. This military property, *peculium castrense*, was differentiated in classical Roman law from property derived through inheritance or other income not connected with military service. See J.B. Campbell, *The Emperor and the Roman Army, 31 B.C. – A.D. 235* (Oxford, 1984), esp. pp. 231ff.

96. Soldiers were not the only specifically exempted groups, although their privileges seem on the whole to have been wider. In the later tenth and eleventh centuries (and probably before), those owing service in respect of the post (*exkoussatoi tou dromou*), of provisioning military personnel (*prosodiarioi*) and those who worked in imperial armouries were similarly immune from certain state corvées. For discussion of soldiers' privileges and the question of *praescriptio fori*, see: Haldon, *Byzantine Praetorians*, pp. 304–7, with notes 915–26, and *Recruitment and Conscription*, p. 54, note 94, p. 60, note 104; Dagron and Mihaescu, *Le traité sur la Guérilla*, pp. 264–72.

97. See Dagron and Mihaescu, *Le traité sur la Guérilla*, xix, 6f.

98. Several letters from the tenth and eleventh centuries refer to the fiscal oppression suffered by soldiers. One text records how a soldier was chased off his holding which was on church land and eventually murdered. The official in question was brought to justice and compensation was awarded. But the case illustrates the sort of treatment the lowlier soldiers may have received at the hands of more powerful officials. See Haldon, "Military service, military lands, and the status of soldiers", p. 55 and n. 132.

99. See: Jones, *LRE*, pp. 635–6, 668, 675; Haldon, *Byzantine Praetorians*, pp. 103–5, 115–16, with sources and literature.
100. Leo, *Tact.*, iv, 1; Haldon, *Byzantine Praetorians*, p. 602 and n. 999.
101. Leo, *Tact.*, epilogue, lvii; and see Haldon, *Recruitment and Conscription*, pp. 45–8, 57–9 for sources and examples.
102. See Haldon, "The organisation and support of an expeditionary force".
103. See Haldon, *Byzantine Praetorians*, pp. 107, 325, for sources and discussion.
104. Relevant sources and details for all these aspects can be found in Haldon, *Byzantine Praetorians*, pp. 301–7, 326–8, dealing primarily with tagmatic troops of the four imperial *tagmata*, but touching also upon the regular non-tagmatic soldiery. The government intervened at several points to attempt to help impoverished soldiers (although less from philanthropic as from fiscal reasons), especially in the reigns of Eirene, Nikephros I and Basil I, and under the tenth-century emperors Romanos I and Constantine VII. See Haldon, *Recruitment and Conscription*, pp. 41–78.
105. See Ibn Hawkal, in Vasiliev, *Byzance et les aarabes*, II, 2, p. 413, and *ODB*, p. 1801 with further literature.
106. Maurice, *Strategikon*, vi, proem, 1; viii, B 9.
107. Maurice, *Strategikon*, proem. (trans. Dennis, pp. 8–9). For further discussion, see Chapter 5 above.
108. See W. Ashburner, "The Byzantine Mutiny Act", *JHS*, 46, 1926, pp. 80–109. These codes are embodied in whole or in part in Maurice's *Strategikon* (i, 6–8) and the *Tactica* of Leo VI (viii).
109. On the question of leadership, see Chapter 6 above; see Leo, *Tact.*, ii, 1–53 for recommendations on the quality and character of leaders; on largesse before battle, see Haldon, *Const. Porph., Three Treatises*, pp. 225–6 (on (C) 261f.).
110. See the detailed discussions in Kaegi, *Byzantine Military Unrest*, pp. 49–52, 127–31.
111. For tagmatic discipline, see Haldon, *Byzantine Praetorians*, p. 324f.; on the Varangians, see Attaleiates, *Historia*, pp. 294–6; on the *themata*, see Kaegi, *Byzantine Military Unrest*, pp. 293ff.
112. See: Haldon, *Recruitment and Conscription*, pp. 35–6; W.E. Kaegi, Jr, "Some seventh-century sources on Caesarea", *Israel Exploration Journal*, 28, 1978, pp. 177–181; E.L. Wheeler, "The occasion of Arrian's *Tactica*", *Greek, Roman and Byzantine Studies*, 19, 1978, pp. 351–65, at 357–60 (with Leo, *Tact.*, xviii, 6); McGeer, *Sowing the Dragon's Teeth*, pp. 217–19. For Leo VI's advice, see *Tact.*, iv, 39, with iv, 38 and 40.
113. See: Haldon, "The organisation and support of an expeditionary force", p. 138 for examples; McGeer, *Sowing the Dragon's Teeth*, pp. 263–4, 321–2, 326–7.
114. The system of temporarily transferring such soldiers while exempting their properties from supporting them for a fixed period was called *adoreia*: see Haldon, "Military service, military lands, and the status of soldiers", pp. 29–32. On *apelatai*, see Dagron and Mihaescu, *Le traité sur la Guérilla*, pp. 254–7.
115. Haldon, "Military service, military lands, and the status of soldiers", p. 57.
116. See: Lemerle, *Agrarian History*, pp. 115–56; Svoronos (ed.), *Les novelles des empereurs macédoniens*, pp. 162–73 (Zepos (ed.), *JGR*, i, pp. 47–48.
117. Texts and literature discussed by McGeer, *Sowing the Dragon's Teeth*, pp. 200–1, and P. Magdalino, "The Byzantine army and the land: from *stratiotikon ktema* to military *pronoia*", in Oikonomidès (ed.), *Byzantium at War*, pp. 15–36 at 16–26.

118. See: Haldon, *Recruitment and Conscription*, p. 46; Dagron and Mihaescu, *Le traité sur la Guérilla*, pp. 186, 267–72.

119. For the changes in the eleventh century and the evolution of the *strateia* and military lands, see Oikonomidès, "L'évolution de l'organisation administrative de l'empire byzantin au XIe siècle", pp. 125–52; for the development of the institution of *pronoia*, see Bartusis, *The Late Byzantine Army*, pp. 162–185; see also Magdalino, *The Empire of Manuel I Komnenos*, pp. 231–3.

120. And see the remarks on this subject in Chapter 5 above.

121. Kekaumenos, *Logos nouthetetikos*, §§ 242–6 (pp. 95.4–97.27).

122. For some elements in this picture, see J. Shepard, "Aspects of Byzantine attitudes and policy towards the West in the tenth and eleventh centuries", in J.D. Howard-Johnston (ed.), *Byzantium and the West, c. 850–c. 1200* (Amsterdam, 1988), pp. 97–117; R.D. Thomas, "Anna Comnena's account of the first Crusade: history and politics in the reigns of the emperors Alexius I and Manuel I Comnenus", *BMGS*, 15, 1991, pp. 269–312; M.V. Bibikov, "Das 'Ausland' in der byzantiniscehn Literatur des 12. und der ersten Hälfte des 13. Jahrhunderts", in J. Herrmann, H. Köpstein and R. Müller (eds), *Griechenland – Byzanz – Europa. Ein Studienband (BbA, 52)* (Berlin, 1985), pp. 61–72. See also Angold, *The Byzantine Empire, 1025–1204*, pp. 203–9.

123. For Attaleiates' remarks, see *Historia*, p. 146.18–22. On attitudes to foreigners and foreign soldiers, see A. Kazhdan and A.W. Epstein, *Change in Byzantine Culture in the Eleventh and Twelfth Centuries* (Berkeley/Los Angeles/London, 1985), pp. 172–4; and esp. Oikonomidès, "L'évolution de l'organisation administrative de l'empire byzantin", p. 144. For Roussel de Bailleul, see: *Nicephori Bryennii Historiarum libri quattuor*, ed. P. Gautier (Brussels, 1975), p. 187; Vryonis, *Decline of Medieval Hellenism*, pp. 106–8; Shepard, "The uses of the Franks in eleventh-century Byzantium", pp. 300–2.

124. See J. Shepard, "Aspects of Byzantine attitudes and policy towards the West", p. 109f., notes 164, 165. The sources appear to treat all soldiers as more or less equal, although reference to their privileges and legal status is never direct. For the *prooimion* in question, see R. Browning, *Notes on Byzantine prooimia* (Wiener Byzantinistische Studien Bd. 1: Supplement) (Vienna, 1966), p. 29 (x).

125. Jones, *LRE*, pp. 641–3, 676.

126. Thus Constantine V rewarded a ranking soldier, apparently from an Armeniak cavalry detachment based in Thrace, by promoting him to the position of *kentourion* (i.e. centurion), an archaism for kentarch: *La vie d'Etienne le jeune par Etienne le diacre*, ed. and trans. Marie-France Auzépy (Birmingham Byzantine and Ottoman Monographs, 3) (Aldershot, 1997), § 54, trans. p. 252; similarly, a letter of Theodore of Stoudios refers to a man promoted on merit to the rank of *komes*: *Theodori Studitae Epistulae*, ed. G. Fatouros (*CFHB*, 31, 1–2) Berlin/New York, 1992) *Ep.* 160. For the pattern of promotion, see H. Ahrweiler, "Un discours inédit de Constantin VII Porphyrogénète", *TM*, 2, 1967, pp. 393–404.

127. See the section on Kallistos in "De XLII martyribus Amoriensibus Narrationes et carmina sacra", eds B. Wassiliewsky and P. Nikitine, in: *Mémoires de l'Acad. impériale de St. Petersburg*, classe phil.-hist., viii ser., 7 (1905), no. 2, 22–36.

128. De S. Maria iuniore, in: *Acta Sanctorum Nov.*, iv, 688–705.

129. De Eudocimo, in: *Synaxarium Constantinopolitanum*, ed. H. Delehaye (Propylaeum ad Acta Sanctorum Novembris) (Brussels, 1902), 857.

130. *La vita retractata et les miracles postumes de saint pierre d'Atroa*, ed., trans. and commentary V. Laurent (Subsid. Hag. 31) (Brussels, 1958), p. 111. 1ff.; *La vie merveilleuse de S. Pierre d'Atroa*, ed. V. Laurent (Subsid. Hag. 29) (Brussels, 1956), p. 39. 46ff.
131. De Petro Thaumaturgo, in *Synax. CP*, 121f.
132. For further examples see Haldon, *Byzantine Praetorians*, pp. 608–9 and n. 1021.
133. As ably demonstrated in Kaegi, *Byzantine Military Unrest*.
134. For Manuel, see *Th. cont.*, pp. 24.2–4, 110.1ff., 120.21–2; for Andreas, see *Th. cont.*, p. 284.9–15. The same information is given in the parallel chronicles of Symeon Magister, Leo Grammaticus and the Continuation of the Chronicle of George the Monk.
135. *Th. cont.*, p. 89.15–19, and R. Guilland, *Recherches sur les institutions byzantines*, 2 vols (= *BbA*, 35) (Berlin/Amsterdam, 1967), 1, pp. 437–8, 568.
136. See Haldon, *Byzantine Praetorians*, pp. 334–5 and notes for sources and literature.
137. See the prosopographical details for some tagmatic commanders in Haldon, *Byzantine Praetorians*, pp. 354–8, and the analysis of the social elite of the empire in J.-Cl. Cheynet, *Pouvoir et contestations à Byzance (963–1210)* (Paris, 1990), pp. 207–48. For Ibn Hawkal, see Vasiliev, *Byzance et les arabes*, II, 2, p. 413.
138. See above, and n. 89.
139. On the evolution of this elite, and individual careers, see the excellent analysis by Cheynet, *Pouvoir et contestations*, pp. 249–301, 321–425; on their role in the military administration and leadership, see pp. 303–13.

Appendix 1   Weights and loads

1. See R.P. Duncan-Jones, "The size of the modius castrensis", *Zeitschrift für Papyrologie und Epigraphik*, 21, 1976, pp. 53–62. Note that the conclusions and equivalences given in L. Mitteis and U. Wilcken, *Grundzüge und Chrestomathie der Papyruskunde* I, 1, Leipzig 1912, LXVIII, as well as the assumptions made on this basis by a number of other scholars: cf. E. Patlagean, *Pauvreté économique et pauvreté sociale à Byzance, 4ᵉ–7ᵉ siècles*, Paris 1977, p. 51; J. Irmscher, 'Preise und Löhne in frühen Byzanz', in *Studien zum 8. und 9. Jarhundert in Byzanz (BbA, 51)* (Berlin, 1983), pp. 23–33, at 26; both following Schilbach, *Byzantinische Metrologie*, p. 111 (and assuming a rate of *artaba : modioi* of 1 : 2 or even less), have been considerably revised in more recent work. See esp. R.P. Duncan-Jones, "The choenix, the artaba and the modius", *Zeitschrift für Papyrologie und Epigraphik*, 21, 1976, pp. 43–52, at 52; D. Rathbone, "The weight and measurement of Egyptian grains", *Zeitschrift für Papyrologie und Epigraphik*, 53, 1983, pp. 265–75; and also J. Gascou, "La table budgétaire d'Antaeopolis *(P. Freer 08.45 c–d)*", in *Hommes et richesses dans l'Empire byzantin 1: IVᵉ–VIIᵉ siècle* (Paris 1989), pp. 279–313, at 286–7. The *modios xystos* (or "flat" *modios*) seems to have been almost the same as the later *annonikos modios*: Schilbach, *Byzantinische Metrologie*, p. 99.
2. See Schilbach, *Byzantinische Metrologie*, p. 95 and n. 4. A weight ratio of barley : wheat of 5 : 6 can be derived from ancient documents in conjunction with figures taken from the modern weights and volumes for these grains: Schilbach, *Byzantinische Metrologie*, p. 95 n. 3, with further literature.
3. Schilbach, *Byzantinische Metrologie*, pp. 162ff., 174.

4. Schilbach, *Byzantinische Metrologie*, p. 99.
5. See W.C. Schneider, 'Animal laborans. Das Arbeitstier und sein Einsatz im Transport und Verkehr der Spätantike und des frühen Mittelalters', in *L'Uomo di fronte al mondo animale nell'alto Medioevo* (Settimane di Studio del Centro Italiano di Studi sull'alto Medioevo, 31) (Spoleto, 1985), pp. 457–578, at 493–554.
6. W.B. Tegetmeir, *Horses, Asses, Mules and Mule Breeding* (Washington, DC, 1897), p. 129.
7. Cassiodorus, *Variae* (MGH [AA], xii, 1–385); iv, 47.5; v, 5.3; this seems especially light, although compares well with the 6 *modioi* mentioned in the ninth-century *Vita Philareti* (M.-H. Fourmy and M. Leroy, 'La vie de S. Philarète', *B*, 9, 1934, pp. 85–170), 131.2–3 – although the text does not in fact suggest that this is a maximum.
8. *CTh.*, viii, 5.8, 17, 28, 30 etc. For further comparative discussion, see B.S. Bachrach, 'Animals and warfare in early medieval Europe', in *L'Uomo di fronte al mondo animale nell'alto Medioevo*, pp. 707–51, at 716–20.
9. *Const. Porph., Three Treatises*, (C) 549–53. For the middle and later Byzantine *modios* (there were at least four different measures thus named) see Schilbach, *Byzantinische Metrologie*, pp. 95–6, 97–108.
10. *Const. Porph., Three Treatises* (C) 411–4, 549–53. For pack-saddle and harness, see *CTh.*, viii, 5.47 and *CJ*, xii, 50.12.
11. See: Engels, *Alexander the Great and the Logistics of the Macedonian Army*, pp. 126–30; Hyland, *Equus*, pp. 153–6, 255–7.
12. See Hyland, *Equus*, p. 154 and Table 5, with sources.
13. Cf. Maurice, *Strat.*, i, 2.4; *Skirmishing*, § 16.
14. See *CTh.*, viii, 5.47 and *CJ*, xii, 50.12. For the carrying capacity of horses, ponies and mules, see Schneider, "Animal laborans. Das Arbeitstier und sein Einsatz im Transport und Verkehr der Spätantike und des frühen Mittelalters", 457–578, at 493–554.
15. See the points made in this connection by D. Engels, *Alexander the Great and the Logistics of the Macedonian Army*, p. 22 and n. 35.

Appendix 2   Feeding armies: grain

1. For the Roman and later Roman periods, see: R.W. Davies, 'The Roman military diet', *Britannia*, 2, 1971, pp. 122–42, esp. 125f.; G. Webster, *The Roman Imperial Army of the First and Second Centuries A.D.* (London, 1969), p. 254f.; Jones, *LRE*, p. 628f. For the middle Byzantine period, see T. Kolias, 'Eßgewohnheiten und Verpflegung im byzantinischen Heer', in *Byzantios. Festschrift für Herbert Hunger zum 70. Geburtstag*, eds W. Hörandner, J. Koder, O. Kresten and E. Trapp (Vienna, 1984), pp. 193–202, at 197–199; and on types of bread, see Ph. Koukoules, "Onomata kai eide arton kata tous Buzantinous chronous", *EEBS*, 5, 1928, pp. 36–52, at 45–6, 49–50 and, in a revised form, in *BBP*, 5, pp. 12–35; H. and R. Kahane and A. Tietze, *The Lingua Franca in the Levant. Turkish Nautical Terms of Italian and Greek Origin* (Urbana, IL, 1958), p. 555f. For *bucellatum* and its qualities, see esp. Procopius, *Wars*, i, 13.12–20.
2. *Syll. tact.*, § 57.2. On the *klibanon* (or *kribanon*), from Lat. *clibanum*, see Koukoules, "Onomata", 48; *BBP*, 5, pp. 26–7.

3. *P. Oxy.*, 1920 (*The Oxyrynchus Papyri*, eds B.P. Grenfell, A.S. Hunt et al., London, 1898ff.), with the comments of A.C. Johnson and L.C. West, *Byzantine Egypt: Economic Studies* (Princeton, NJ, 1949), p. 183, assuming that the Roman pound of 327.45 g is meant.

4. Using the Roman pound of 327.45 g.

5. On returns on milling and grinding, see D.W. Kent-Jones, 'Processing of major food groups: cereals and other starch products', in *The New Encyclopaedia Britannica*, 19: *Macropaedia*, 15th edn (Chicago, 1995), pp. 346–55, at 347–8; and L. Smith, *Flour Milling Technology*, 3rd edn (London, 1945).

6. See M. Kaplan, *Les hommes et la terre à Byzance du VIᵉ au XIᵉ siècle. Propriété et exploitation du sol* (Paris, 1992), pp. 28–9; Koukoules, "Onomata", pp. 36–41; *BBP*, 5, pp. 12ff.

7. For statistics on baking, see the appropriate chapters in S. Matz (ed.), *The Chemistry and Technology of Cereals as Food and Feed* (London, 1959); and D.W. Kent-Jones, "Processing of major food groups", pp. 350ff.

8. See *De Cer.*, 659.7–12.

Appendix 3   Daily rations

1. *Const. Porph., Three Treatises*, (C) 396–401.

2. Thus Engels, *Alexander the Great and the Logistics of the Macedonian Army*, pp. 14–15, takes 150 lb (68 kg) as the average load.

3. Following Engels, *Alexander the Great and the Logistics of the Macedonian Army*, pp. 17–18, based on Roman arrangements (1 tent per 8 men, each tent weighing about 40 lb/18.2 kg, thus permitting a pack-animal to carry 5 or 6 of them. This would be an extremely heavy load, however, and the proportion of animals to men may well be too low). For Leo, see *Tact.*, vi, 29.

4. *Alexander the Great and the Logistics of the Macedonian Army*, p. 22 and note 35.

5. *Campaign Organisation*, § 21.22–3 (trans. Dennis, p. 302f.).

6. *Skirmishing*, § 16; cf. Maurice, *Strat.*, i, 2.4.

7. *Const. Porph., Three Treatises*, (C) 59–66, 84–5.

8. *Const. Porph., Three Treatises*, (C) 332–45.

9. The horses and mules would require about 8 gal (36.4 l) per day, the personnel a minimum of 4 pints (2.26 l) water. In dry or desert conditions these requirements increase considerably.

10. Engels, *Alexander the Great and the Logistics of the Macedonian Army*, pp. 20–2.

Bibliography

Details of sources and literature occurring only once or twice will be given in full in the notes. English translations are given where they are available.

Primary Sources

Actes de Lavra, première partie, des origines à 1204, eds P. Lemerle, N. Svoronos, A. Guillou and D. Papachryssanthou (Archives de l'Athos, Paris, 1970).

Agathiae Myrinaei Historiarum libri V, ed. R. Keydell (Berlin, 1967); *Agathias, History*, trans. J.D.C. Frendo (Berlin/New York, 1975).

Ammianus Marcellinus, Works, ed. and trans. J.C. Rolfe, 3 vols (London/Cambridge, MA, 1935–7).

Anne Commène, Aléxiade, ed. B. Leib, 3 vols (Paris, 1937, 1943, 1945); index, P. Gautier (Paris, 1976); *The Alexiad of the Princess Anna Comnene*, trans. E.R.A. Sewter (Harmondsworth, 1969); *Alexiad*, trans. E.A. Dawes (London, 1928).

Strategy: Anonymi Peri strategias, The Anonymous Byzantine Treatise on Strategy, ed. and trans. G.T. Dennis, in *Three Byzantine Military Treatises*, text, trans. and notes (*CFHB*, 25 = *DOT*, 9) (Washington, DC, 1985), pp. 1–136.

Anonymus De obsidione toleranda, ed. H. Van Den Berg (Leyden, 1947).

Attaleiates: *Michaelis Attaliotae Historia*, ed. I. Bekker (*CSHB*) (Bonn, 1853).

Bryennios: *Nicephori Bryennii Historiarum libri quattuor*, ed. P. Gautier (*CFHB*, 9) (Brussels, 1975).

Campaign Organisation and Tactics, ed. and trans. G.T. Dennis, in *Three Byzantine Military Treatises*, text, trans. and notes (*CFHB*, 25 = *DOT*, 9) (Washington, DC, 1985), pp. 241–335 (text, pp. 246–326).

Cedrenus, *Compendium historiarum*, ed. I Bekker, 2 vols (*CSHB*) (Bonn, 1838–9).

Chronicon Paschale, ed. L. Dindorf (*CSHB*) (Bonn, 1832). *Chronicon Paschale, 284–628 A.D.*, trans. M. and M. Whitby (Liverpool, 1989).

CIG: *Corpus Inscriptionum Graecarum*, eds A. Böckh (vols 1 and 2), I. Franz (vols 3ff.) (Berlin, 1828ff.).

CJ: Codex Justinianus, ed. P. Krüger, in *CJC*, II, 13th edn (Berlin, 1963).

CJC: Corpus Juris Civilis, I: *Institutiones*, ed. P. Krüger; *Digesta*, ed. Th. Mommsen; II: *Codex Justinianus*, ed. P. Krüger; III: *Novellae*, eds R. Schöll and W. Kroll (Berlin, 1892–5, repr. 1945–63).

Const. Porph., Three Treatises: Constantine Porphyrogenitus, Three Treatises on Imperial Military Expeditions, ed., English trans. and commentary J.F. Haldon (Vienna, 1990).

CTh.: Theodosiani libri xvi cum constitutionibus Sirmondianis, eds Th. Mommsen, P. Meyer et al. (Berlin, 1905).

DAI: Constantine Porphyrogenitus, De Administrando Imperio, I: Greek text ed. Gy. Moravcsik, English trans. R.J.H. Jenkins, new revised edn (*CFHB*, 1 = *DOT*, 1) (Washington, DC, 1967); II: Commentary, ed. R.J.H. Jenkins (London, 1962).

Darrouzès, J., *Épistoliers byzantins du Xe siècle* (Archives de l'Orient chrétien, 6) (Paris, 1960).

De Cer.: Constantini Porphyrogeniti imperatoris, De cerimoniis aulae byzantinae libri duo, ed. J.J. Reiske (*CSHB*) (Bonn, 1829).

De Them.: Costantino Porfirogenito, De Thematibus, ed. A. Pertusi (Studi e Testi 160) (Città del Vaticano, 1952).

De vel. bell.: Nicephori, De velitatione bellica, in *Leonis Diaconi Caloensis Historiae Libri Decem*, ed. C.B. Hase (*CSHB*) (Bonn, 1828), pp. 179–258;

ed. G.T. Dennis, in *Three Byzantine Military Treatises*, text, trans. and notes (*CFHB*, 25 = *DOT*, 9) (Washington, DC, 1985), pp. 137–239 (text, pp. 144–238);

ed. G. Dagron and H. Mihaescu, in *Le traité sur la Guérilla (De velitatione) de l'empereur Nicéphore Phocas (963–969)*, text G. Dagron and H. Mihaescu, trans. and commentary G. Dagron (Paris, 1986), text, pp. 28–135.

Evagrius: *The Ecclesiastical Hitory of Evagrius*, eds J. Bidez and L. Parmentier (London, 1898/Amsterdam, 1964);

trans. E. Walford, *Ecclesiastical History: A History of the Church in Six Books, From A.D. 431 to A.D. 594 by Evagrius* (Bohn's Ecclesiastical Library) (London, 1854).

Genesius: *Iosephi Genesii Regum libri quattuor*, eds I. Lesmuller-Werner and I. Thurn (*CFHB*, 14) (Berlin/New York, 1978).

Ibn al-Fakīh: Ibn al-Fakīh al-Hamadānī, *Description of the Land of the Byzantines*, trans. E.W. Brooks, in "Arabic lists of Byzantine themes", *JHS*, 21, 1901, pp. 67–77 – see pp. 72–7.

Ibn Khurradādhbī: *Abū'l-Kāsim 'Ubayd Allāh b. 'Abd Allāh b. Khurradādhbīh, Kitāb at-Masālik wa'l-Mamālik*, in *BGA*, VI, 76–85.

John of Ephesus: *The Third Part of the Ecclesiastical History of John of Ephesus*, ed. and trans. R. Payne-Smith (Oxford, 1860).

Justinian, *Novellae*: in *CJC*, III.

Kekaumenos: *Soveti i rasskazi Kekavmena: socinenie vizantijskogo polkovodtsa XI veka*, ed., trans. and commentary G.G. Litavrin (Moscow, 1972);

also in older edn: *Cecaumeni Strategicon et incerti scriptoris de officiis regiis libellus*, eds B. Wassiliewsky and V. Jernstedt (St Petersburg, 1896/Amsterdam, 1965).

Kinnamos, *Epitome*, ed. A. Meineke (*CSHB*) (Bonn, 1836);

trans. C.M. Brand, *The Deeds of John and Manuel Comnenus* (New York, 1976).

Kletorologion of Philotheos, in Oikonomidès, *Les listes de préséance*, pp. 81–235.

Kudāma: *Abū'l-Faraj al-Kātib al-Bagdādī Kudāma ibn Ja' far, Kitāb al-Harāj*, in *BGA*, VI, pp. 196–9.

Leo diac.: *Leonis diaconi Caloensis Historiae libri decem*, ed. C.B. Hase (*CSHB*) (Bonn, 1828).

Leo gramm.: *Leonis Grammatici Chronographia*, ed. I. Bekker (*CSHB*) (Bonn, 1842), pp. 1–331.

Leo, *Tact. Leonis imperatoris tactica*, in *PG*, 107, cols 672–1120; also ed. R. Vári, *Leonis imperatoris tactica* I (proem., const. i–xi); II (const. xii–xiii, xiv, 1–38) (*Sylloge Tacticorum Graecorum*, III) (Budapest, 1917–22).

Mansi: *Sacrorum Conciliorum nova et amplissima Collectio*, ed. J.D. Mansi (Florence, 1759ff.).

Maurice, *Strategikon: Das Strategikon des Maurikios*, ed. G.T. Dennis, trans. E. Gamillscheg (*CFHB*, 17) (Vienna, 1981);
G.T.Dennis, *Maurice's Strategikon. Handbook of Byzantine Military Strategy* (Philadelphia, 1984).

Niceph. patr.: C. Mango, *Nikephoros, Patriarch of Constantinople. Short History* (*CFHB*, XIII) (Washington, DC, 1990).
older edn: *Nicephori Archiepiscopi Constantinopolitani Opuscula Historica*, ed. C. de Boor (Leipzig, 1880), pp. 1–77.

Niceph., *Praecepta*: E. McGeer, *Sowing the Dragon's Teeth. Byzantine Warfare in the Tenth Century* (*DOS*, XXXIII) (Washington, DC, 1995), pp. 3–59 (text), pp. 61–78 (notes).

Nicholas I Patriarch of Constantinople. Letters, eds R.J.H. Jenkins and L.G. Westerink (*CFHB*, 6 = *DOT*, 2) (Washington, DC, 1973).

Nikeph. Ouranos, *Tactica* – see McGeer, *Sowing the Dragon's Teeth*, pp. 88–163 (text), pp. 165–7 (notes) (chapters 56–65 only);
J.-A. de Foucault, "Douze chapitres inédits de la *Tactique* de Nicéphore Ouranos", *TM*, 5, 1973, pp. 281–312 (chapters 63–74 only).

Niketas Choniates: *Nicetae Choniatae Historia*, ed. J.A. Van Dieten, 2 vols (*CFHB*, 11, 1–2) Berlin/New York, 1975);
Niketas Choniates, Historia, trans. H.J. Magoulias, *O City of Byzantium* (Detroit, MI, 1984).

Not. Dig.: *Notitia Dignitatum Utriusque Imperii*, ed. O. Seeck (Leipzig, 1876).

Procopius, *Buildings*, ed. and trans. H.B. Dewing (Cambridge, MA/London, 1940).

Procopius, *Secret History*, ed. and trans. H.B. Dewing (Cambridge, MA/London, 1935).

Procopius, *Wars: Procopius, History of the Wars*, ed. and trans. H.B. Dewing (Cambridge, MA/London, 1914–28).

Psellos, *Chron.: Michel Psellos, Chronographie*, ed. P. Renauld, 2 vols (Paris, 1926, 1928);
Michael Psellos, Chronographia, trans. E.R.A. Sewter (New Haven, CT, 1953).

Sébéos, Histore d'Héraclius, trans. F. Macler (Paris, 1904).

Skirmishing – see *De vel. bell.*

Skylitzes, *Synopsis Historiarum*, ed. J. Thurn (*CFHB*, 5) (Berlin/New York, 1973).

Sylloge Tecticorum, quae olim 'inedita Leonis Tactica' dicebatur, ed. A. Dain (Paris, 1938).

Sym. mag.: Symeonis Magistri ac Logothetae Annales a Leone Armenio ad Nicephorum Phocam, in *Th. cont.*, pp. 603–760.

Th. cont.: Theophanes continuatus, Ioannes Caminiata, Symeon Magister, Georgius Monachus continuatus, ed. I. Bekker (*CSHB*) (Bonn, 1825), pp. 1–481.

Theoph.: Theophanis Chronographia, ed. C. de Boor, 2 vols (Leipzig, 1883, 1885);
The Chronicle of Theophanes Confessor, eds and trans. C. Mango and R. Scott (Oxford, 1997).

Th. Sim.: *Theophylacti Simocattae Historia*, ed. C. de Boor (Leipzig, 1887; revised and emended edn p. Wirth, Stuttgart, 1972);
Theophylact Simocatta, History, trans. M. and M. Whitby (Oxford, 1986).
TIB: Tabula imperii Byzantini:
1. J. Koder and F. Hild, *Hellas und Thessalia* (Vienna, 1976);
2. F. Hild and M. Restle, *Kappadokien (Kappadokia, Charsianon, Sebasteia und Lykandos)* (Vienna, 1981);
3. P. Soustal and J. Koder, *Nikopolis und Kephallenia* (Vienna, 1981);
4. K. Belke, *Galatien und Lykaonien* (Vienna, 1984);
5. F. Hild and H. Hellenkamper, *Kilikien und Isaurien* (Vienna, 1990);
6. P. Soustal, *Thrakien (Thrake, Rodope und Haimimontos)* (Vienna, 1991);
7. K. Belke and N. Mersich, *Phrygien und Pisidien* (Vienna, 1990);
9. K. Belke, *Paphlagonien und Honorias* (Vienna, 1996);
10. J. Koder, *Aigaion Pelagos (die nördliche Ägäis) (Vienna, 1998)*.
Vegetius, *Epitome rei militaris*, ed. C. Lang (Leipzig 1885);
Vegetius, *Epitome of Military Science*, trans. N.P. Milner (Liverpool, 1993).
G. Zacos and A. Veglery, *Byzantine Lead Seals* (Basel, 1872), vol. I, parts 1–3.
Zonaras: *Ioannis Zonarae epitomae historiarum libri XIII usque ad XVIII*, ed. Th. Büttner-Wobst (*CSHB*) (Bonn, 1897).

Selected literature

Ahrweiler, H. (1960) "Recherches sur l'administration de l'empire byzantin aux Xe–XIe siècles", *BCH*, 84, pp. 1–109.
Ahrweiler, H. (1962) "L'Asie mineure et les invasions arabes", *Revue Historique*, 227, pp. 1–32.
Ahrweiler, H. (1966) *Byzance et la mer: la marine de guerre, la politique et les institutions maritimes de Byzance aux VIIe–XVe siècles*. Paris: PUF.
Angold, M. (1984) *The Byzantine Empire 1025–1204. A Political History*. London: Longman.
Bartusis, M.C. (1992) *The Late Byzantine Army. Arms and Society, 1204–1453*. Philadelphia: O. Penn. Press.
Bishop, M.C. (ed.) (1985) *The Production and Distribution of Roman Military Equipment. Proceedings of the Second Roman Military Equipment Research Seminar* (British Archaeological Reports, Int. Ser. 275). Oxford: Oxbow.
Bishop, M.C. and Coulston, J.N.C. (1993) *Roman Military Equipment from the Punic Wars to the Fall of Rome*. London: Batsford.
Brandes, W. (1989) *Die Stadte Kleinasiens im 7. und 8. Jahrhundert (BbA, 56)*. Berlin: Akad. Verlag.
Brooks, E.W. (1898) "The Arabs in Asia Minor (641–750) from Arabic sources", *Journal of Hellenic Studies*, 18, pp. 182–208.
Brooks, E.W. (1899) "The campaign of 716–718 from Arabic sources", *Journal of Hellenic Studies*, 19, pp. 19–33.
Brooks, E.W. (1901) "Arabic lists of Byzantine themes", *Journal of Hellenic Studies*, 21, pp. 67–77.
Brown, T.S. (1984) *Gentlemen and Officers. Imperial Administration and Aristocratic Power in Byzantine Italy, A.D. 554–800*. Rome: British School at Rome.

Cameron, Averil (ed.) (1995) *States, Resources and Armies: Papers of the Third Workshop on Late Antiquity and Early Islam*. Princeton, NJ: Darwin.

Delbrück, H. (1990) *History of the Art of War* (4 vols), trans. Walter J. Renfroe, Jr. Lincoln, NE/London: University of Nebraska Press.

Dennis, G.T. (1997) "The Byzantines in battle", in Oikonomidès (ed.), *Byzantium at War*, pp. 165–78.

Ditten, H. (1993) *Ethnische Verschiebungen zwischen der Balkanhalbinsel und Kleinasien vom Ende des 6. bis zur zweiten Hälfte des 9. Jahrhunderts*, eds R.-J. Lilie, Ilse Rochow, Friedhelm Winkelmann and I. Ševčenko (*BbA*, 59). Berlin: Akad. Verlag.

Dixon, K.R. and Southern, P. (1992) *The Roman Cavalry. From the First to the Third Century A.D.* London: Routledge.

Dixon, K.R. and Southern, P. (1996) *The Late Roman Army*. London: Routledge.

Donner, F.M. (1981) *The Early Arabic Conquests*. Princeton, NJ: Princeton University Press.

Dunn, A. (1994) "The transformation from *polis* to *kastron* in the Balkans (III–VII cc.): general and regional perspectives", *BMGS*, 18, pp. 60–80.

Eickhoff, E. (1966) *Seekrieg und Seepolitik zwischen Islam und Abendland*. Berlin: De Gruyter.

Elton, H. (1996) *Warfare in Roman Europe, AD 350–425*. Oxford: Blackwell.

Franklin, S. and Shepard, J. (eds) (1992) *Byzantine Diplomacy*. Aldershot: Variorum.

Grosse, R. (1920) *Römische Militärgeschichte von Gallienus bis zum Beginn der byzantinischen Themenverfassung*. Berlin: Weidmann.

Haldon, J.F. (1975) "Some aspects of Byzantine military technology from the sixth to the tenth centuries", *BMGS*, 1, pp. 11–47.

Haldon, J.F. (1979) *Recruitment and Conscription in the Byzantine Army c. 550–950: A Study on the Origins of the stratiotika ktemata* (Sitzungsber. d. österr. Akad. d. Wiss., phil.-hist. Kl. 357) Vienna: Verlag österr. Akad. d. Wiss.

Haldon, J.F. (1984) *Byzantine Praetorians*, Bonn/Berlin: Habelt.

Haldon, J.F. (1985) "Some considerations on Byzantine society and economy in the seventh century", *Byzantinische Forschungen*, 10, pp. 75–112.

Haldon, J.F. (1986) "Ideology and social change in the seventh century: military discontent as barometer", *Klio*, 68, pp. 139–90.

Haldon, J.F. (1990) *Byzantium in the Seventh Century. The Transformation of a Culture* (2nd revised edn) Cambridge: CUP.

Haldon, J.F. (1993) "Military service, military lands and the status of soldiers: current problems and interpretations", *DOP*, 47, pp. 1–67 (= *State, Army and Society in Byzantium*, no. VII).

Haldon, J.F. (1995) "Administrative continuities and structural transformations in East Roman military organisation c. 580–640", in Haldon (1995) *State, Army and Society in Byzantium*, no. V. Aldershot: Variorum.

Haldon, J.F. (1995) "Seventh-century continuities: the *Ajnad* and the 'Thematic Myth' ", in Cameron (ed.), *States, Resources and Armies*, pp. 379–423.

Haldon, J.F. (1995) *State, Army and Society in Byzantium. Approaches to Military, Social and Adminitrative History*. Aldershot: Variorum.

Haldon, J.F. (1997) "The organisation and support of an expeditionary force: manpower and logistics in the middle Byzantine period", in Oikonomidès (ed.), *To empolemo Byzantio (Byzantium at war)*, pp. 111–151.

Haldon, J.F. (1999) "Chapters II, 44 and 45 of *De Cerimoniis*. Theory and practice in tenth-century military administration", *Travaux et Mémoires*, 13.

Haldon, J.F. and Kennedy, H. (1980) "The Arab–Byzantine frontier in the eighth and ninth centuries: military organisation and society in the borderlands", *ZRVI*, 19, pp. 79–116.

Harvey, A. (1989) *Economic Expansion in the Byzantine Empire 900–1200.* Cambridge: CUP.

Hendy, M.F. (1985) *Studies in the Byzantine Monetary Economy, c. 300–1450.* Cambridge: CUP.

Hoffmann, D. (1969) *Das spätrömische Bewegungsheer und die Notitia Dignitatum* (Epigraphische Studien, 7/1) Dusseldorf: Rheinland-Verlag.

Hohlweg, A. (1965) *Beiträge zur Verwaltungsgeschichte des Oströmischen Reiches unter den Komnenen* (Miscellanea Byzantina Monacensia, 1). Munich: Inst. f. Byz. u. neugr. Philologie.

Howard-Johnston, J.D. (1995) "The two Great Powers in late Antiquity: a comparison", in Cameron (ed.), *States, Resources and Armies*, pp. 157–226.

Hunger, H. (1978) *Die hochsprachliche profane Literatur der Byzantiner*, 2 vols (Handbuch der Altertumswissenschaft, xii, 5.1 and 2 = Byzantinisches Handbuch, 5, 1 and 2). Munich: Beck.

Hussey, J.M. (ed.) (1966) *The Cambridge Medieval History*, IV: *The Byzantine Empire*, 2 parts, revised edn. Cambridge: CUP.

Hyland, Ann (1990) *Equus: The Horse in the Roman World.* London: Batsford.

Jones, A.H.M. (1964) *The Later Roman Empire, 284–602: A Social, Economic and Administrative Survey*, 3 vols and maps. Oxford: Blackwell.

Kaegi, W.E., Jr (1981) *Byzantine Military Unrest 471–843: An Interpretation.* Amsterdam: Hakkert.

Kaegi, W.E., Jr (1992) *Byzantium and the Early Islamic Conquests.* Cambridge: CUP.

Kaplan, M. (1992) *Les hommes et la terre à Byzance du VIᵉ au XIᵉ siècle. Propriété et exploitation du sol.* Paris: Sorbonne.

Kolia-Dermitzaki, A. (1991) *Byzantine "Holy War": The Concept and Evolution of Religious Warfare in Byzantium* (in Greek). Athens: Basilopoulos.

Kolia-Dermitzaki, A. (1997) "Byzantium at war in sermons and letters of the 10th and 11th centuries. An ideological approach", in Oikonomidès (ed.), *Byzantium at War*, pp. 213–38.

Kolias, T. (1988) *Byzantinische Waffen* (Byzantina Vindobonensia, XVII). Vienna: Verlag der österr. Akad. d. Wiss.

Kühn, H.-J. (1991) *Die byzantinische Armee im 10. Jahrhundert.* Vienna: Fassbaender.

Lee, A.D. (1993) *Information and Frontiers. Roman Foreign Relations in Late Antiquity.* Cambridge: CUP.

Lilie, R.-J. (1976) *Die byzantinische Reaktion auf die Ausbreitung der Araber* (Miscellanea Byzantina Monacensia, 22). Munich: Inst. f. Byz. u. Neogräzistik.

Lilie, R.-J. (1977) " 'Thrakien' und 'Thrakesion'. Zur byzantinischen Provinzorganisation am Ende des 7. Jahrhunderts", *JöB*, 26, pp. 7–47.

Lilie, R.-J. (1984) "Die zweihundertjährige Reform: zu den Anfängen der Themenorganisation im 7. und 8. Jahrhundert", *BSl*, 45, pp. 27–39, 190–201.

Magdalino, P. (1993) *The Empire of Manuel I Komnenos, 1143–1180.* Cambridge: CUP.

Mathissen, R.W. and Sivan, H.S. (eds) (1996) *Shifting Frontiers in Late Antiquity.* Aldershot: Variorum.

McCormick, M. (1986) *Eternal Victory. Triumphal Rulership in Late Antiquity, Byzantium, and the Early Medieval West.* Cambridge: CUP.

Miller, T.S. and Nesbitt, J.S. (eds) (1995) *Peace and War in Byzantium.* Washington, DC: CUA.

Mitchell, S. (ed.) (1983) *Armies and Frontiers in Roman and Byzantine Anatolia* (British Archaeological Reports, Int. Ser. 156). Oxford: Oxbow.

Naval Intelligence Division (1941) *Turkey*, vol. 1, Geographical Handbook Series, BR 507. London: Naval Intelligence Division.

Nicolle, D. (1995) *Medieval Warfare Source Book*, 1: *Warfare in Western Christendom*. London: Arms & Armour Press.

Nicolle, D. (1996) *Medieval Warfare Source Book*, 2: *Christian Europe and Its Neighbours*. London: Arms & Armour Press.

Obolensky, D. (1971) *The Byzantine Commonwealth. Eastern Europe 500–1453*. London: Weidenfeld & Nicholson.

Oikonomidès, N. (1972) *Les listes de preseance byzantins des IXe–X^e siecles*. Paris: CNRS.

Oikonomidès, N. (1976) "L'evolution de l'organisation administrative de l'empire byzantin", *TM*, 6, pp. 125–52.

Oikonomidès, N. (1988) "Middle Byzantine provincial recruits: salary and armament", in Duffy, J. and Peradotto, J. (eds), *Gonimos. Neoplatonic and Byzantine Studies Presented to Leendert G. Westerink at 75*. Buffalo, NY: NYUP, pp. 121–36.

Oikonomidès, N. (ed.) (1997) *To empolemo Byzantio (Byzantium at War)*. Athens: National Research Foundation.

Oman, C.W. (1885/1953) *The Art of War in the Middle Ages, A.D. 378–1515*, revised edn J.H. Beeler. Ithaca, NY: Cornell University Press.

Ostrogorsky, G. (1968) *History of the Byzantine State*. Oxford: Blackwell.

Pryor, J. (1992) *Geography, Technology and War. Studies in the Maritime History of the Mediterranean 649–1571* (2nd edn). Cambridge: CUP.

Ramsay, W.M. (1890/1962) *The Historical Geography of Asia Minor* (Royal Geographical Society, Supplementary Papers IV). London: John Murray/Amsterdam: Hakkert.

Shepard, J. (1985) "Information, disinformation and delay in Byzantine diplomacy", *Byzantinische Forschungen*, 10, pp. 233–93.

Shepard, J. (1993) "The uses of the Franks in eleventh-century Byzantium", *Anglo-Norman Studies*, 15, pp. 275–305.

Smail, R.C. (1995) *Crusading Warfare, 1097–1193*, ed. C. Marshall. Cambridge: CUP.

Sullivan, D. (1997) "Tenth-century Byzantine offensive siege warfare: instructional prescriptions and historical practice", in Oikonomidès (ed.), *Byzantium at War*, pp.179–200.

Tomlin, R.S.O. (1987/90), I, pp. 107–33. "The army of the late empire", in J. Wacher (ed.), *The Roman World*. London: RKP.

Toynbee, A. (1973) *Constantine Porphyrogenitus and His World*. London: OUP.

Treadgold, W.T. (1995) *Byzantium and Its Army, 284–1081*. Stanford, CA: Stanford University Press.

Van Berchem, D. (1952) *L'Armée de Dioclétian et la réforme Constantinienne*. Paris: Geuthner.

Vasiliev, A.A. (1950/68) *Byzance et les Arabes* I: *La dynastie d'Amorium (820–867)*; II: *Les relations politiques de Byzance et des Arabes à l'époque de la dynastie macédonienne (Les empereurs Basile I, Léon le Sage et Constantin VII Porphyrogénète) (867–959)*, eds H. Grégoire and M. Canard (Corpus Bruxellense Hist. Byz. I, II). Brussels: éds de l'Institut d'histoire et philol. slaves.

Vryonis, Sp. Jr (1971) *The Decline of Medieval Hellenism in Asia Minor and the Process of Islamization from the Eleventh through the Fifteenth Century*. Berkeley/Los Angeles/London: UCLA Press.

Whitby, L.M. (1988) *The Emperor Maurice and His Historian: Theophylact Simocatta on Persian and Balkan Warfare*. Oxford: Clarendon.

Whittow, M. (1996) *The Making of Orthodox Byzantium, 600–1025*. London: Macmillan.

Winkelmann, F. (1985) *Byzantinische Rang- und Ämterstruktur im 8. und 9. Jahrhundert* (*BbA*, 53). Berlin: Akad. Verlag.

Winkelmann, F. and Brandes, W. (eds) (1990) *Quellen zur Geschichte des frühen Byzanz* (*BbA*, 55). Berlin: Akad. Verlag.

Index

INDEX